ALSO BY ELIZABETH FRANK

JACKSON POLLOCK

LOUISE BOGAN

ELIZABETH FRANK

1 9 8 5

NEW YORK

ALFRED · A · KNOPF

LOUISE BOGAN

A PORTRAIT

This is a Borzoi Book published by Alfred A. Knopf, Inc.

Copyright © 1985 by Elizabeth Frank

All rights reserved under International and Pan-American Copyright Conventions. Published in the United States by Alfred A. Knopf, Inc., New York, and simultaneously in Canada by Random House of Canada Limited, Toronto. Distributed by Random House, Inc., New York.

Throughout this volume, letters, journal entries, and other material written by Louise Bogan are published in whole or in part here for the first time and are copyright © 1984 by Ruth Limmer, Trustee, Estate of Louise Bogan. All rights reserved. Unpublished material by W. H. Auden is copyright © 1984 by the Estate of W. H. Auden; not to be reprinted without written permission. Unpublished material by Edmund Wilson is copyright © 1984 by Helen Miranda Wilson.

Owing to limitations of space, acknowledgments for permission to reprint previously published material can be found on page 461.

Library of Congress Cataloging in Publication Data

Frank, Elizabeth.   Louise Bogan : a portrait.

Bibliography: p.   Includes index.

1. Bogan, Louise, 1897–1970—Biography.

2. Poets, American—20th century—Biography,   I. Title.

PS3503.O195Z66   1984   811'.52 [B]   83-48853

ISBN 0-394-52484-5

Manufactured in the United States of America

FIRST EDITION

To ARF, MGF, ADF, JRF—

   "Now that I have your heart by heart, I see."

And to the memory
of JAMES CLAY HUNT
Professor of English,
Williams College, 1941–1977—

   "Now that I have your voice by heart, I read."

CONTENTS

ILLUSTRATIONS

Following page 174

POSTCARD PHOTOGRAPH
OF LOUISE, CA. *1900*

THE HOTEL MILTON
IN MILTON, MASSACHUSETTS

LOUISE'S MOTHER,
MARY HELEN SHIELDS

LOUISE'S FATHER,
DANIEL JOSEPH BOGAN

MARY SHIELDS BOGAN, *1897*

DANIEL BOGAN, *1900*

LOUISE, AGE SIX MONTHS, *1898*

LOUISE'S ELDER BROTHER, CHARLES

LOUISE ON HER ELEVENTH BIRTHDAY
WITH HER BROTHER, CHARLES, *1908*

LOUISE, IN BALLARDVALE

LOUISE, CA. *1911*

CHARLES AND LOUISE IN BOSTON, *1911*

LOUISE AND MISS CAROLINE GERVISH

LOUISE, *1922*

ILLUSTRATIONS

ACKNOWLEDGMENTS

I AM DEEPLY GRATEFUL to Maidie Alexander Scannell, Louise Bogan's daughter, and to Ruth Limmer, her literary executor, for their unstinting generosity, patience, trust, and encouragement. To Barbara Howes, David and Marianna Mandel, William Maxwell, Robert Phelps, Elizabeth Roget, May Sarton, and William Jay Smith—friends of Louise Bogan who befriended me and aided the preparation of this book through the sharing of memories and letters—I owe, too, a profound debt of gratitude that extends to the late F. W. Dupee, Helen Spencer Humphries, Archibald MacLeish, Margaret Mead, Louis Untermeyer, John Hall Wheelock, and Katharine S. White.

The following people aided my work in innumerable and incalculable ways, and I hereby acknowledge their contributions with the greatest pleasure: Léonie Adams, Ben Belitt, Kay Boyle, Herbert Cahoon, Malcolm Cowley, J. V. Cunningham, Richard Eberhart, Leon Edel, the late Martha Foley, Clement Greenberg, Jap Gude, Curtis Harnack, Rufina McCarthy Helmer, Arthur Cort Holden, Richard Howard, Victor Lange, Katie Louchheim, Mary McCarthy, Margaret M. Mills, Louise Townsend Nicholl, Beata Sauerlander, Nina Schneider, Grace Schulman, Karl Shapiro, Ben Sonnenberg, Robert Penn Warren, Glenway Wescott, Richard Wilbur, Janet Lewis Winters, and Barbara Holden Yeomans.

Special thanks are due to: Donald Allen, LeRoy C. Breunig, Ashley Brown, Margaret C. Carroll, Marshall Clements, Isabelle Eldridge, Jane Freeman, Arline C. Harrington, Elinor Langer, Frank Nutter, Gloria Oden, Ned O'Gorman, Sister Angela V. O'Reilly, Richard Parker, Nancy L. Poland, Gwilym R. Roberts, Ruth Lisa Schechter, Ruth A. Sharpe,

Anne Speakman, David Stivender, Mary E. Stoops, Althea Wallace, Sister M. Daniel Wallace, Lucille Schulberg Warner, and Arthur Frank Wertheim.

Over the past eleven years, my colleagues have offered assistance and encouragement, and I wish particularly to thank Diana O'Hehir of Mills College; Jonathan Aaron, Don Gifford, Lawrence Graver, and Fred Stocking of Williams College; Frank Lentricchia of the University of California, Irvine; Jonathan Goldberg, Barbara Harman, and Artem Lozynsky of Temple University; and Carol Karlsen, William Wilson, and Tom Wolf of Bard College.

I have benefited from the helpful guidance of librarians and curators and wish to thank, in particular, J. Richard Phillips, John Lancaster, and Darlene Holdsworth at the Amherst College Library; Lola Szladits at the Berg Collection of The New York Public Library; Diana Haskell of The Newberry Library; Kenneth Lohf at the Butler Library, Columbia University; Margaret M. Mills and Hortense Zera of the American Academy and Institute of Arts and Letters Library; Howard B. Gotlieb of the Mugar Memorial Library, Boston University; and Mary Leen at The Bostonian Society. I would also like to thank the Beinecke Rare Book and Manuscript Library at Yale University, the University of Washington Libraries, the Princeton University Library, the Holt Library at Miami University, and the University Libraries of Washington University for their help with my requests.

I wish to thank Temple University for a Grant-in-Aid of Research and a Faculty Summer Research Fellowship; the American Council of Learned Societies for a Grant-in-Aid; and The Newberry Library for a Fellowship for Individual Scholars. This work was also generously supported by a Fellowship for Independent Study and Research from the National Endowment for the Humanities.

My thanks to Alice Quinn, my editor at Knopf, for her insight into the problems of biography; and to Howard Buchwald, Susan Crile, and Constance Kheel, my affection and gratitude for their sustaining friendship.

FOR PERMISSION to quote from unpublished materials by Louise Bogan and her correspondents, grateful acknowledgment is hereby made to Ruth Limmer, Executor, Louise Bogan Estate, and to the following:

The Trustees of Amherst College, for materials in The Louise Bogan Papers at The Amherst College Library; Edward Mendelson, Executor, The Estate of W. H. Auden, for letters from W. H. Auden; Barbara Dupee, for letters from F. W. Dupee; Aileen Ward, Executor, Jean

Garrigue Estate, for letters from Jean Garrigue; Mary Jarrell, for letters from Randall Jarrell; Beatrice Roethke Lushington, for letters from Theodore Roethke; Helen Tate, for letters from Allen Tate; Phyllis deKay Wheelock, for letters from John Hall Wheelock; E. B. White, for letters from Katharine S. White; and Malcolm Cowley, William Maxwell, May Sarton, and William Shawn, for their own letters to Louise Bogan.

The Archives of the American Academy and Institute of Arts and Letters, for letters of Louise Bogan and Raymond Holden to Rolfe Humphries; the Henry W. and Albert A. Berg Collection, The New York Public Library, Astor, Lenox, and Tilden Foundations, for letters of Louise Bogan to Kathryn Italia Iff Lanz, Elizabeth Mayer, and May Sarton; the F. W. Dupee Papers, Rare Book and Manuscript Library, Columbia University, for letters of Louise Bogan to F. W. Dupee; Charles Scribner's Sons and the Princeton University Library for letters of Louise Bogan to John Hall Wheelock in the Archives of Charles Scribner's Sons; The Newberry Library, for letters of Louise Bogan to Morton Dauwen Zabel in the Morton Dauwen Zabel Collection; the Theodore H. Roethke Papers, University of Washington Libraries, for letters of Louise Bogan to Theodore Roethke; the Collection of American Literature, the Beinecke Rare Book and Manuscript Library, Yale University, for letters of Louise Bogan to Fred. B. Millet and Edmund Wilson, and Raymond Holden to Edmund Wilson; Curtis Harnack, for letters of Louise Bogan to Elizabeth Ames in the Yaddo Archives; and to Mrs. Barbara Holden Yeomans, for permission to quote from Raymond Holden to Rolfe Humphries and Edmund Wilson.

E . F .

FOREWORD

LOUISE BOGAN seldom talked about her life. From time to time she might offer a listener some fragment of her history, as rich in insight as it was sparse in detail, but more often she spoke so elusively of the past that little in the way of a complete narrative managed to emerge. To those correspondents who committed the blunder of asking for biographical information, Bogan would reply—when she bothered to reply at all—that there were certain details, possessing "tragic interest alone, and these I never describe or explain."

She was a woman whose passion for reticence bordered on obsession. Self-revelation she equated with confession; and since, in her view, to confess was to ask for pardon, an act she considered as useless as it was ignoble, she was incapable of opening the coffers of her experience in any direct way. The art of her poetry is to a very great extent devoted to the task of dissembling confession through symbol and form, so that we are given the texture of feeling and not the naked fact.

In all probability, it was not her natural gift alone, but an early determination to achieve psychic survival that led Louise Bogan toward the path of strict detachment. Some independence from the impossible actuality of life was required, some absolute severance between the living moment and its preservation in words was necessary to her existence. From the time she began to write at the age of fourteen, she veered not only toward the poem in form, with its music and figures, but toward the impression, or *aperçu*, "the perception of a great maxim," Goethe tells us, "which is always a genius-like operation of the mind: We arrive at it by pure intuition, that is, by reflection, neither by learning nor tradition."

For a temperament like Louise Bogan's, autobiography would have been more than an embarrassment: it would have been a self-perpetrated violation of the heart. Yet the private woman and the professional writer within her both realized that in her poems, letters, and journals there was a good story to tell. What then was the obstacle? The truth itself.

We must try to imagine then the courage it took for Louise Bogan to go against the grain of her temperament by keeping close at hand for over thirty years a set of memoirs she hoped to publish one day as fiction. Some of the earlier sections appeared as short stories in *The New Yorker* between 1931 and 1934, but for most of the time between her first conception of the project in the late 1920s and its final entries, written in July 1966, she returned to her "long prose thing" with painful infrequency.

At her death, this work added up to some seventy handwritten pages, published in January 1978 in *The New Yorker* under the title, "From the Journals of a Poet." Ruth Limmer, Louise Bogan's literary executor, reassembled sections of the work, together with previously published stories and other uncollected and unpublished materials, in *Journey Around My Room,* which was published in 1980. Calling her *assemblage* an autobiographical "mosaic," Miss Limmer gives us the ghost of an autobiography, but not, as she herself points out, "the autobiography Louise Bogan would have written had she chosen to." In these pages, however, we see the woman deeply suspicious of confession taking the necessary steps to overcome her resistance. For a short while, Louise Bogan looks backward into time and finds it possible to tell the truth, to understand, and to forgive.

The story remains incomplete. Some final capacity to pursue memory to its source fails her. The obstacle and the fear return; the close narrative texture loses density and momentum. Toward the end of the journals there comes only a record of the struggle, mostly futile, against depression.

Faced with Bogan's own distance from her past, we who would undertake the biographical quest on her behalf should pause for a while in wonder and humility. In an era of abundant and workable psychoanalytic materials, there appear to be few truths of mind and heart beyond our reach. Yet privacy that is violated for the sake of literary and cultural history remains violated, and the innermost secrets of a proud and dignified spirit have a way of retreating when too strenuously pursued.

Nevertheless, something stopped Louise Bogan dead in her tracks, not once, but many times. Until we discover this principle of arrest, even the most copious supply of documentation and the most perceptive psychological guesswork will be of little advantage in our attempt to enter the sanctuaries of either the life or the work. What we must do, instead, is to look at them long and hard, until, as Bogan herself learned from Hopkins and Rilke, they begin to look back at us.

I

1897 ❀ 1929

THE
SUDDEN
MARIGOLDS

1 TARGET FOR THE WIND

LOUISE BOGAN, conceiving of her "long prose thing" as a work of fiction, wanted to give it the title *Laura Daly's* [or *Daley's*] *Story*. It was also to have this epigraph from La Rochefoucauld:

L'accent et le caractère du pays où l'on est né demeure dans l'esprit et dans le coeur comme dans le langage. *

New England was her native region. She was born at eight-thirty in the evening of August 11, 1897, in the small mill town of Livermore Falls, Maine. What she came to know about her ancestry reached back, on her father's side, only as far as her grandfather, James Bogan, who was born in Londonderry, Ireland, in the 1830s. Nothing is known about his mother and father, only that his grandmother, on one side or the other, was Scots. When still a young boy—that is, before the potato famine in the forties—James went to sea and settled in Maine, where, as Bogan liked to let it be known, he was for many years a captain of sailing vessels out of Portland harbor. By all accounts he did very well for himself, building a large house on what was known as Captain's Hill with bricks carried over from England. He and his wife had twelve children. The eldest, Daniel Joseph, one of four sons, was born in Portland in 1861, and accompanied his father as cabin boy on a voyage lasting several years from Portland to South America. The ship, as he told his granddaughter, Maidie Alexander, Louise Bogan's only child, was called *The Golden Sheaf,* and there was a parrot in a cage hanging from a sturdy hook in the saloon. It wasn't until the end of the voyage, during the

---

* "The accent and character of one's native region live in the mind and heart just as in one's speech."

unloading of the ship at Portland, that Daniel Bogan discovered that the saloon floor could be lifted up (Captain Bogan, it turned out, was in the habit of smuggling cigars, rum, and panama hats, and hiding them under the floor). The parrot was imported for the aviary the captain kept in the back yard of his house. Even though his wife hated birds, he would bring an exotic one home after every voyage, and eventually there were twelve birds for the twelve children.

Daniel Bogan never talked about his boyhood until after his wife died. Mary Helen Murphy Shields Bogan wasn't particularly interested in anything he had to say. The Bogans bored her, and she expressed her boredom and disdain without regard for the consequences.

She was the daughter of a woman born an O'Neill, in Dublin, who had married a schoolteacher named Murphy. Almost nothing is known about her parents: neither their first names nor their birth dates, nor when they married, nor why and when they came to America. Murphy either enlisted or was conscripted into the Union Army and was killed in the Civil War shortly before or after his daughter was born in Portland, Maine, on February 22, 1865. What became of Mary Helen's mother, if she was indeed his legal wife, no one knows. Mary never mentioned her own mother; when she said "mother," she meant a woman by the name of Shields, who ran a prosperous saloon in Portland with her husband. The couple had adopted her, and raised her as their beloved and much-fussed-over only child. Mrs. Shields dressed her in exquisitely cut and tailored clothes. Mary was sent away to be educated at what the Shieldses considered one of the finest "select" schools in New England, Mount Saint Mary Academy in Manchester, New Hampshire, run by the Sisters of Mercy. Here she became accomplished in the ways young ladies were accomplished in those days: she learned to sing and play the piano, and to conduct herself becomingly with others.

Mary was a high-spirited girl, who could handle horses well. Upon hearing that the Catholic church in Portland was intending to sell a part of the church cemetery to a company proposing to convert the land, situated next to water, into docks, the indignant Mary—whom everyone called May—went rushing around town with her horse and carriage trying to drum up sentiment against the plan.

Naturally, having educated and dressed the girl at considerable expense, her family expected Mary to marry well. While the union that took place with Daniel Joseph Bogan in 1882, at the same church in Portland where they were both baptized and buried, was entirely respectable, he being the son of a retired sea captain and, owing to his exquisite handwriting, clerk in the D. J. Brown Paper Company, it was hardly the prestigious or profitable alliance which had undoubtedly been envisioned for her. During Louise Bogan's childhood, her mother would often torment herself—especially on holidays—with feelings of guilt toward Mrs. Shields. Just what Mary Shields did to her adoptive mother is unclear, and Bogan herself explained nothing of the matter to her own daughter. Louise seems not to have known the Shieldses, and she never mentioned them in her correspondence or work, except to use their name, once, in a short story called "The Long Walk."

One curious fact exists. At the time of their marriage, both Daniel, who was twenty-one, and May, who was seventeen, were about five feet, four inches tall. Afterward, May kept growing, adding five inches to her height, so that eventually, at a statuesque five-foot-nine, she towered over Daniel, whose height had remained the same. "I don't think my grandmother ever forgave my grandfather for not growing," Maidie Alexander Scannell has said. In a photograph taken the year of the wedding, May Bogan stands perfectly straight, an uncommonly pretty young woman whose pleasure in her own beauty is evident in the way she unresistingly allows the camera to gaze at her crimped brown hair, her clear eyes, her full, impertinent mouth, and her well-formed nose. The tailored jacket with its pinched waist, and the draped shirt with lace jabot are perfectly cut and styled. On her head she wears an Empress Eugénie hat with a bow cascading to the neck. She loved hats. The ones she wore were always large, with veils.

In 1884, when May was only nineteen, a son, Charles Joseph, was born. The years between his birth and Louise's are a blank, except that in between there was a second boy, named Edward, born nobody knows what year, who died at the age of four or five months.

In 1897, Livermore Falls was a busy mill town in Androscoggin County, near Lewiston, with a history typical of other New England mill towns. Elijah Livermore, a large landowner, had built the first mill in Livermore in the early 1780s. Sixty years later, expanding business led to the laying out of Livermore Falls in the northwest corner of East Livermore, where increasing numbers of grist, saw, and shingle mills drew a large population of French-Canadian and Italian laborers. In 1881 a Scot named Hugh Chisholm arrived in Livermore and founded the Umbagog Pulp Company, which he consolidated later with other mills to form the still-flourishing International Paper Company. Daniel Bogan had risen through the ranks to become clerk and then superintendent.

By the turn of the century, New England had begun to register signs of diminished health, though it would take another generation, and World War I, to put an end to its economic well-being. Much of the stony land ceased to be farmed, and forests began to overwhelm once-cultivated fields. Dry walls crumbled and the stench of wood pulp from the local mills hung in the air over village and pasture alike. The climate was brutal, with temperatures often dipping to $-20°$ F. during the interminable winters. People abandoned their farms; sons and daughters grew up and got out, many going west. Despite activity in the towns themselves, the bleakness of lost hopes and pointless futures was beginning to settle over the region. Those staying behind as mill hands faced poverty and alcoholism; those with a desire to rise in the world faced deadened aspirations as company men. Religious and ethnic rivalries festered, and on Saturday nights violence would almost invariably erupt between the Irish and the French-Canadian Catholics.

The Bogans were Irish and Catholic, but owing to Daniel Bogan's white-collar position in the company, Louise was born on Munsey Avenue, in a strictly English-speaking, Protestant section of town. The mill-owned superintendent's house her family occupied was situated on a bank above the mill, and had a cupola and Victorian "gingerbread" eaves Louise was to remember only from photographs.

Her parents were not rich, but they were by no means poor. Housekeeping placed few burdens on her mother, who could always get help from the pool of young hired girls from Nova Scotia who came over "with a sack of apples and a letter to the minister." But having been, as the saying goes, "gently reared," May Bogan thoroughly disliked Livermore Falls. To her, it was a hick town with nothing but mill hands in it, unable to offer a single outlet for her vitality, love of music, and romantic charm.

Louise Bogan later said that she had retained virtually no memories of Livermore Falls. She dated her life as a self-conscious, observing, and impressionable being from 1901, when her family, for reasons that have remained obscure, moved to another mill town, Milton, New Hampshire. Perched on the Salmon Falls River about fifty miles south of the White Mountains, with a local mix of mostly Yankees and some French Canadians, Milton had leather and paper mills which provided work for men who boarded in rooming houses and hotels. Here, in The Hotel Milton, run by Charles Bodwell and his two sons, and familiarly known as Bodwell's—a name that fascinated the four-year-old Louise—the Bogan family spent the next two to three years. Louise shared a room with her mother, while Daniel and Charles presumably shared another. The hotel faced both the Caricade Paper Mill and the old flume, a mile-long stretch of very rapid white water dropping nearly a hundred feet over a rocky series of falls.

The Hotel Milton sent a horse-drawn carriage to meet passengers at the train station, and Louise remembered riding in this carriage the day she and her mother arrived, and seeing the name of the town set out in coleus and begonia beds as they rode into Milton. In the distance she saw a "long high blue mass . . . above the trees." "Is it the sea?" she asked her mother. "No," May replied. "It is the mountains."

The hotel was a many-gabled clapboard structure with a veranda on the second story as well as the first, and many shuttered windows. It must have seemed enormous to Louise, with its endless rooms and stories and stairs, with chambermaids and waitresses and guests coming and going. Her memories begin with Bodwell's and Milton. Here she explored weed-filled lots and pastures, where once she cut her thumb so deeply on a piece of glass that she could later list the scar as an identifying mark on her passport (as well as refer to it in the late poem, "The Sorcerer's Daughter"), and here, too, she used to bury her doll Mag and dig her up again, and poke a little ring inside the crack of a staircase in the hotel. While at first she seems to have spent much of her time playing alone, watching what was going on around her, there were afternoons with rough and sometimes bawdy French-Canadian children who took her into the "long rough pasture" behind the hotel to eat "rhubarb with salt, and an occasional raw potato." Afterward, Louise would come back to the hotel to find her mother talking in low tones with one of her "familiars"—waitresses in the barroom-café or the dining room, or "Mrs. X . . . a dried up, emaciated woman with a sharp nose and ferret eyes: a little horror."

To her daughter, May Bogan was beginning to emerge as a separate and troubling person. Freed from the stifling isolation of Livermore Falls, she seems to have organized an active and very secret social life for herself in Milton. At some point Louise became aware of dim goings-on at the hotel, whisperings and intrigues at whose center her mother occupied some dread-inspiring role: conversations excluded her; secret signals were exchanged in her presence. Gradually, without any actual consciousness of it or any basis in experience with which to compare or understand what was happening, she began to breathe in the atmosphere of the "secret family angers and secret disruptions . . ." Once, she went blind for two days, and only realized that her sight had come back when she could see "the flat forked light of the gas flame, in its etched glass shade, suddenly appearing beside the bureau." What had she seen, she later wondered: "I shall never know."

How much turmoil she actually witnessed is something that we, on our part, shall similarly never know. How much, after all, does a child have to see to reach the conclusion that, in Laforgue's words, *"La vie est vraie et criminelle"*? From a very early age she was present at scenes of violence between her parents. One in particular she never forgot: it takes place in lamplight, with an open trunk, its curved lid thrown back, in the middle of the room. Her mother bends over the trunk, folding things, crying and screaming. Her father is somewhere in the shadows, and he groans as if he has been hurt. The terrified child, swept into her mother's arms and carried out of the room, knows that her mother is running away, but remembers nothing more of this scene until she finds herself inexplicably in another: "It is morning—earliest morning. My mother and I and another woman are in a wooden summerhouse on a lawn. The summerhouse is painted white and green, and it stands on a slight elevation, so that the cool pale light of a summer dawn pours around it on all sides." The scene is not so much indistinct as abbreviated, spelling refuge and peace, however temporary.

Meditating many years later on the reasons leading up to the failure of her second marriage, Bogan looked back at the dismal attachment her parents had endured. The family fights had developed their own pattern. Her mother, again usually on holidays, would explode in rage, shrieking at Daniel Bogan and insulting him so viciously that, in the 1930s, explaining her aversion to the Left, Bogan told a friend that she found Marx "too vituperative for my taste. . . . Calling people foul dogs and short-armed apes always reminds me of some of the things my mother used to call my father when I was a child."

She tried to locate the point where the trouble had all begun, and the question, as pertinent to her own difficulties as to her parents', had no ready answer. The respectable marriage of the high-spirited girl to the unexciting sea captain's son had been wrong from the start, the product of who-knows-what misapprehension and adolescent nonsense. Judging from the anecdote about the cemetery and the church, it seems that Mary Shields had a rebellious streak, and a taste for drama. As she contemplated marriage, possibly the spoiled, impulsive girl believed that it would bring her autonomy of a kind wherein she could say and do whatever she pleased, have a household, and a man who loved her, under her thumb. Daniel Bogan probably found her ways enchanting, and at that time may have struck her, as he later struck his granddaughter, as "feisty and cocky, the way little guys often are." At any rate, he was able to take care of her, and few choices outside marriage were available to a girl who wanted to make something of her life.

"In the youth of a handsome woman," Bogan later wrote, "two currents and two demands run side by side in almost perfect accord: her own vanity's desire for praise and love, and the delight in the praise and love so easily given her." When these begin to run dry, as they inevitably do, "a terrible loneliness and an hysterical dis-ease take their place. For the energy once expended on delight and conquest now has nothing on which it can be dissipated: it is continually meeting small defeats and rebuffs; it is like a river which has made a broad bed for itself, but now has dwindled into a tiny stream that makes hardly any show among the wide sweep of pebbles that show the boundaries of its former strength." Such a woman then might well use whatever is left of her beauty to regain the delight and love, or their illusion, which have managed to disappear and which she still considers her due.

In 1937, Edmund Wilson published a play called *This Room and This Gin and These Sandwiches,* a nostalgic re-creation of life among a group of young Greenwich Village "types" in the early 1920s. The main characters are Arthur, an architect, who has gone to college and writes poetry, and Sally Voight, a young actress whom he loves and sleeps with but who does not love him. Wilson had been in love, in real life, with Edna St. Vincent Millay during the period the play represents, but during the time he was actually writing it he had been enjoying a companionable and confiding friendship with Bogan, and he endows his Sally with a background and disposition that unquestionably derive from a detailed familiarity with Bogan's past.

During a quarrel reminiscent of squabbles between Bogan and Wilson, Sally accuses Arthur of taking a "superior tone" because he has gone to college:

ARTHUR: College isn't so much fun.

SALLY: It's more fun than starting out in life without a cent of your own.

ARTHUR: Now you're in one of those moods when you talk as if you were a proletarian. You're not a proletarian—you've always belonged to the white-collar class. Your father was a foreman—a boss: you belonged to the upper stratum of Braxton Falls, Mass. You had a very good education.

SALLY: There's no real upper stratum in a mill-town.

ARTHUR: That's not true.

SALLY: What do *you* know about it? Do you imagine that when the mills close down, a foreman's any better off than anybody else?

The quarrel continues, with Arthur complaining that four years of college prepare you for nothing but a return to the world it was supposed to help you escape from in the first place:

ARTHUR: . . . you realize . . . that you've just been taken out and polished up, and that now you've been put back on the shelf!

SALLY: You at least had a nice quiet shelf. I never had any quiet at all. My mother used to have love affairs and take me with her and make me wait for her out in the hall, and my father would threaten to kill her, and my brother would fight with my father. *You* never had poverty and fighting at home and no prospect of ever getting away from it!

Bogan's revelations in her journals confirm this testimony. May Bogan had lovers—men she called "admirers"—and assignations with them for which she spent hours bathing and dressing and putting on rice powder and fresh underclothes and earrings. In the journals, Louise remembers: "The door is open, and I see the ringed hand on the pillow; I weep by the hotel window as she goes down the street, with *another....*"

Bogan chose to keep silent about her mother's affairs, and it took nearly a lifetime for her to summon the courage to write down only so much as she put into her journals. The scene was unspeakable, horrifying. So we don't know whether it happened once, or many times, or where, or with whom. The men who were her mother's lovers: who could they have been? Mill workers? Hardly—not for the girl who had been "gently reared." Merchants? Unlikely, considering May Bogan's contempt for shop-owning folk. Men her husband worked with? Again, unlikely, because they too were not quite good enough. Doctors, lawyers, mill-town professional men? In at least one case, yes. In her journals Bogan tells us her mother loved one doctor for years. Whoever he or the others were, they must have been handsomer, brighter, richer, more important, and taller than dull, short, faithful, unromantic Daniel Bogan, capable of drawing her into a snare of infatuation so reckless that she let her husband find out that he could do nothing to change: that he was who he was, and not the man she desired in her bed.

Other questions remain unanswered. Why did May Bogan take her child along to her trysts? Was it folly, or "pure" Victorian ignorance which allowed her to think that whatever sexual goings-on Louise might chance to see or hear would pass over her head or be easily explained away? Or did she, in her own dramatic and unthinking way, require an audience, someone in the family to see and know that beauty and spirit such as hers did not go unappreciated in the world? She was not a woman armed with access to systematically acquired self-esteem and personal fulfillment, so her search for these was clumsy, furtive, and to a very great extent, fruitless. Yet she gave Louise an unformulated but nevertheless urgent endorsement for a life of autonomy and experience, although she was at a loss, as Louise was later, to pursue these without hurting herself and others. She trapped Louise, making her the object of selfish purposes, so truth, for Louise, became charged with danger and doubleness. If Louise had told anyone what she knew about her mother, she too would have been guilty of betrayal, and would have targeted herself for her mother's rage. Yet, by keeping silent, she became an accomplice in the deception of her father.

Bogan never tells us how Daniel dealt with his hurt and humiliation. On one occasion May disappeared for several weeks. When she came back, thinner and shabbily dressed, she spoke tenderly to her husband and children, addressing them almost formally by their full Christian names. She swept and cleaned and changed the paper on the kitchen shelves, and after a few days, opened the piano to play and sing. So he must have forgiven her, over and over again. She was the heart of the family, the perennial problem-child who establishes the emotional tone and weather. Everyone's well-being depended on her doings and dealings. She had a hunger for experience that was never appeased, a jealousy for the prerogatives of independence enjoyed at that time only by men. In later years, when she was well into middle age, there was even a comic aspect to her huge frustration. At some point Daniel went to New York for a meeting at the Waldorf-Astoria of the superintendents of all the New England paper mills. According to Mrs. Scannell, "Nana [Mary Bogan] was so mad that here was Grampie living it up in New York that she took all his clothes out in the back yard and burned them."

But when Bogan was a child at home, there was little enough to laugh about. Her brother Charles and her mother were extremely close. May doted on him, and Charles adored her, taking her side in bitter quarrels with his father. Louise's instinct toward her mother "was to protect—to take care of, to endure . . . the instinct of a little boy." At some point, perhaps when the scenes of rage, the disappearances, and the returns had been repeatedly played out, she stopped fearing what she later called this "terrible, unhappy, lost, spoiled, bad-tempered child. . . ," this "tender contrite woman, with, somewhere in her blood, the rake's recklessness, the baffled artist's despair. . . ." From Louise, May Bogan exacted a passionate love in which fanatical loyalty became indistinguishable from fanatical jealousy, and in which desire would always be accompanied by recrimination. "I never truly feared her," Louise later concluded. "Her tenderness was the other side of her terror." Even so, by the age of eight, or even perhaps as early as five or six, Louise Bogan was an exile from conventional life, and had become, "what I was for half my life: the semblance of a girl, in which some desires and illusions had been early assassinated: shot dead."

THE BOGANS moved again in 1904, just before Louise turned seven. They came to Ballardvale, Massachusetts, a mill and manufacturing town in Essex County—situated on the Shawsheen River east of Lowell and south of Lawrence, regularly served by the Boston and Maine Railroad, and eventually absorbed by the town of Andover. Ballardvale produced brass and bronze goods, rubber, and fine flannels for which it was world-famous. In the 1904 Ballardvale Directory, Daniel J. Bogan and his son Charles were both listed as employees of the so-called Stopple Factory, or Ballard Vale

Natural Lithia Spring Water and Bottling Works, a company started in 1880 by a man named Paul Hannigan, who advertised his bottled spring water as "pure at its source, purer than Poland Springs Water," even though the lithia was pumped in by a hidden pipe. In 1890 men from Lawrence and North Andover bought out the business and started shipping the water all over the world in barrels, carboys, and bottles, though a problem soon arose with the discovery that the water failed to keep over a long period of time, owing to contamination by the cork stopper. The problem was solved when a chemist named Stanley invented a metal cap lined with blocked tin foil, called the "crowned seal." While employed at the Stopple Factory, Daniel J. Bogan invented a milk jar cap machine "for cutting, pointing, mating and separating each cap and color dropping into its own container and counted by the counter on mach [sic]." He filed a patent for the machine on January 25, 1905, and assigned it, "For $1.00 and other considerations," to a man in Andover who soon dropped dead, so that although the cap was adopted and used, Daniel himself never made a cent from it.

In Ballardvale, the spring water was hauled in five-hundred-gallon sprinkling carts drawn by two horses and bottled at two brick buildings near the Lowell Junction Railroad Station. A man by the name of J. Henry Gardner was station agent, and it was with his family that Louise and her mother, arriving in June or July with no house ready for the family to live in, boarded for the next two or three months. The Gardners had two children, a son named H. Joseph, and a daughter, Ethel. They lived on Tewksbury Street, on a hill leading down to the depot.

Having lived in Bodwell's since the age of four, Louise had never known stable household life. It was a revelation:

Order ran through the house. There were no bare spaces, or improvised nooks and corners; the kitchen shone with paint and oilcloth; the parlor, although minuscule, was a parlor through and through. The dining room, with its round table, always ready for a meal (the turning castor-set in the center, the white damask cloth), was used to eat in, three times a day, and the meals were always on time. There was a delightful little sitting room, off the front porch. And beyond the sitting room, in one of the ells (our bedroom was above it), ran Mrs. Gardner's workroom (she sewed) with a long bare table, a dress form, and a cabinet-like bureau where she kept her materials. This was the first workroom I had ever seen. I used to dream about it for years.

Inside the Gardner home, objects of use were also beautiful. The doorstop was a seashell; white net curtains with a lace border hung at the windows; the rug had a small pattern of flowers, and the door of the music cabinet had a marquetry design. Taste combined with economy; the Gardners had "*one of everything* and everything ordered and complete." Sauce boats, berry dishes, castors on the table, napkins in napkin rings, plants in pots, a blanket at the foot of the bed, an afghan on the sofa spoke of needs anticipated, wishes met. The charm of custom and care made a lasting impression on the not-quite-seven-year-old child. Mr. Gardner could not have made much money, but there was no sign of want. To Louise it even seemed that there were certain luxuries. Ethel Gardner, who was a few years older than herself, had a ring tree "made of white china with a tiny green figure of delicate leaves on its saucer-base. The 'tree' part was shaped like a leafless miniature tree, with at least three tiny branches—and a light scattering of gold, like powder, outlined its twig-like arms." In the front yard there was a swing, with heavy rope and a wooden seat:

> The swing that could go high, and from which
> one had no fear of falling.
> No fear, no fear . . .
> No fear at Mrs. Gardner's!

Eventually the Bogan family moved into a house of their own on Chester Street, and then to another on Oak Street, with clapboarding, a mansard roof, an oak tree in front, and a veranda. There were two bands of fancy woodwork—a row of zigzags and a row of scallops—beneath the mansard eaves, giving the slate roof a touch of elegance. On moving day the horse-drawn furniture wagon arrived with the legs of chairs sticking out from under the quilts and draperies, and Louise discovered worn green window shades flapping loudly at the top of the open sash windows that overlooked the thickets, the yard, and the houses two fields away.

This was the house where Louise learned to read during the winter of 1904–05. She had been finding it a difficult task. The previous summer she would stare at the pages of print, furious at her failure to make out their meaning. She had to be taught her letters in school—the Bradlee School in Ballardvale—and she had to have books read to her. But that first (and last) winter on Oak Street, she had come down with scarlet fever and been put to bed in the parlor; then, with the sudden spurt of maturity which so often follows recovery from childhood illnesses, when she returned to school she discovered she could read. Those pupils who worked well in the morning were often given a simple reader in the afternoon, as a reward. The book was called *Heart of Oak,* and for Louise, "its contents were as delicious as food. They *were* food; they were the beginning of a new life."

The following year the family moved back to Tewksbury Street, to a house opposite the Gardners. Here Louise's reading life took shape. The first book she actually owned was *Grimms' Fairy Tales,* with illustrations by

Rackham going around the cloth cover from front to back. She could shut out the shouting between her mother and father, or her father and brother, and believe the stories, believe that Rapunzel let down her hair, and that the twelve princesses wore out their shoes dancing in the castle on the island in the lake. The illustrations were proof that the stories were true, even though she knew at the same time that they could *not* be true: "I had the double vision of the born reader, from the beginning."

In the house on Tewksbury Street there was a stove in the dining room that stood out from the wall. Behind it, on the floor, Louise would arrange herself on an old imitation astrakhan cape that had belonged to her mother, and read everything in the house. First she went through her brother's books: *Cormorant Crag, The Young Carthaginian,* and one called *Cuore: An Italian School Boy's Journal,* which she loved. "There's a young book-collector in it, who arranges his books according to color, and I was determined to do the same, at the age of ten. And then there are wonderful stories about crossing the Andes, and tales of pathos and heroism designed to wring the hardest Mediterranean heart," she later recalled. Some instinct kept her away from the usual *girls'* books, though she read *Salammbô* and *Pilgrim's Progress* without understanding either. But sitting on the rug, feeling its pile against the palms of her hands, the grain of the book covers, and the soft woolen cape on her knees, while the coal burned steadily in the stove, she found freedom and a measure of peace.

IN "DOVE AND SERPENT," a short piece published in *The New Yorker* in November 1933, Bogan recalls Ballardvale in autumn. The wind blew fiercely, scattering leaves against sidewalks, wagons, people, and trains. Sudden changes in light and shade threw half the town into relief. When the children, excited by the wind, would run home from school, old Jack Leonard would come out onto his veranda, cursing and beating a stick against the railing as the children yelled at him in fear and derision. He lived alone in a house where "the curtains hung in rags at the windows and a jumble of old crates and cans cluttered the doorsill." Leonard was a blacksmith, and in the mornings, after she had finished cleaning the lamps, Louise's mother would stand by the window, gazing toward his house:

The window had sash curtains over its lower half. My mother's gaze was directed through the upper, uncurtained panes. Sometimes she would stand there for a long time, perfectly still, one hand on the window jamb, one hand hanging by her side. When she stood like this, she was puzzling to me; I knew nothing whatever about her; she was a stranger; I couldn't understand what she was. "There's old Leonard again," she would say, "kicking the cornstalks."

In winter, life in the Tewksbury Street house narrowed in to the sitting room and kitchen, the rooms with stoves. Mrs. Bogan would receive visitors—if she happened to be on speaking terms with them—Mrs. Parsons or Mrs. Gardner, and sometimes a woman named Dede, who seemed to Louise:

dry and wizened (like Mrs. X in Milton). Her face had the ugly look of the queen of spades in a pack of cards. She wore a cotton wrapper, summer and winter, and a shawl was pulled over her head and shoulders: a mill woman's shawl, the use of which was dying out in the town. She lived in a dead-looking cottage up the hill, with her husband and a cringing hairy dog. She was confidante, and, I suppose, go-between.

Louise's mother would instruct her to stay in the sitting room while she shut the door behind her, entering the kitchen to talk in low voices with her friends. One time, when it was bitterly cold, old Jack Leonard came to the kitchen door, and Louise sat, rigid with fear, listening to the sounds of her mother talking with him. He came again, and every time, Louise was so terrified she thought she could not bear it.

I could not understand why he should want to come, or why my mother should want to open the door to him. I should have slammed the door in his face, put out all the lights when I heard his footsteps on the path, drawn down the blinds, pretending that the house was empty. I could not see how my mother could bear to sit in the same room with such ugliness, such age.

One evening Louise glimpsed through the open door Jack Leonard sitting in the rocking chair beside the kitchen window, peeling an apple with a knife. Her mother had made him a cup of tea and given him a plate of bread and butter. He was a big man, and his face, with its beaked nose and thick, tangled beard, frightened her:

He lifted his head and saw me and grinned down into his beard. If he had put out his hand to touch me, I could not have been more frightened; with half a room between us, I stood transfixed by that smile. "It's Mr. Leonard," my mother said, and lifted the stove lid, shifting the kettle to one side. "It's a cold night, and I'm giving him a nice hot cup of tea to warm him up."

The peel fell to the floor and old Leonard closed his knife with his thumb. Then I heard him speak the first words that were not curses. "We must be wise," he said to my mother. "We must be as wise as the serpent and as gentle as the dove. As the serpent, as the dove," he said, and picked up the cup of tea from its saucer. The peeled apple lay on the table beside him.

As a child, Bogan saw the world as she saw the print on the page before she learned how to read. Her failure to make out its meaning cast a spell over her even as it frustrated her; her bafflement, in a sense, *was* the spell. Things—objects, rooms, weather—even more than people, promised and withheld meaning, while meaning itself remained an elusive compound "of bewilderment and ignorance and fear." So Louise determined to meet and master appearance; she studied the pattern cast by the shadow of leaves on clapboard walls in autumn; the big garlands of the parlor wallpaper; the fissures and geometries of frosted panes; the look and feel of seasons and times of day. Reality for her was a visual field, rich with mysterious accents and correspondences.

When Louise's mother embarked on one of her dreaded excursions to the city, which inevitably meant another chapter in her secret, amatory life, Louise was put in the care of Mrs. Parsons, a sturdy Congregationalist matron. Her son had gone to a military academy, and his sword hung in Mrs. Parsons's living room, on a wall, next to a doll dressed in a paper skirt holding string:

I used to look at these two objects for long unbroken periods; they possessed some significance that I could not pry out of them with my eyes or my mind. The doll and the sword were so pretty and so unexpected. The sword had a tasseled belt twisted around its handle. The doll's little feet under the paper skirt, the string appearing from the middle of a rosette in its sash, its bisque head and real hair and hard small mouth open in a smile—this was a problem I could not solve. As I remember my bewilderment, my judgment even now can do nothing to make things clear. The child has nothing to which it can compare the situation. And everything that then was strange is even stranger in retrospect. The sum has been added up wrong and written down wrong and this faulty conclusion has long ago been accepted and approved. There's nothing to be done about it now.

In her puzzlement, Bogan learned how to see and how to accept a painful inconclusiveness until it became a pleasurable mystery. The doll observed on those sad afternoons while her mother was away with somebody else emerged years later, transformed to symbol in the "dreadful painted bisque" of the doll in "Kept," a poem in which she puts her childhood to rest. The doll is there, retrieved from the stores of memory where it lives alongside the Ballardvale weathervanes, the mothers with their apron strings flying in the strong autumn gusts, the cold plaster and stone in winter, and the lights showing "across the river in the chill dusk in houses and in the mill."

The house on Tewksbury Street Bogan later remembered as the happiest in her life. Every morning she left it with her father, accompanying him to the station platform to say goodbye for the day. Each morning he gave her a cigar-y kiss and a penny whose Indian and wreath and date she would carefully scrutinize. At night the sound of his footsteps reassured her.

Inside the house, in a space between the dining room and the parlor, there were bookshelves actually built into the wall, filled with Charles's books and books her mother had acquired, usually from itinerant book salesmen. In the parlor there was a center table, piled high with volumes by Celia Thaxter and Lord Byron, and underneath it a wicker basket containing a stereopticon. This fascinating instrument, which had a picture of the Vatican Library, "opened up the world of art and grandeur." Its three-dimensionality was altogether mysterious: "You could almost see around corners, and the lamps and the carvings and the chair and table legs came right out at you."

Later in her life Bogan had a recurring dream about this house, in which she returned to it as an adult and put her chairs and pictures and above all her books in it: "Sometimes the entire second floor has become a library, filled with books I have never seen in reality but which I have close knowledge of in the dream. I rearrange the house from top to bottom: new curtains at the windows, new pictures on the walls. But somehow the old rooms are still there—like shadows, seeping through. Indestructible. Fixed."

The life she discovered while learning to read at this house was her own; no person and no event could take it away from her. Unlike appearances, which confounded her, books were generous with their meanings. The child's eye, ravished by illusion, learned also how to scan the world with a saving detachment. Louise closely observed the mill-town inhabitants, in both Milton and Ballardvale, men and women with scarred faces, pitted skins, filthy nails, their bodies thin from lung disease and bloated from drink. The economy and order of the Gardner home did not prevent her from taking in the dingy rooming houses and hotels, with their "dark green and brown interiors," their ugly electric signs, their "varnished furniture, grotesque wicker chairs, and dusty carpets," where, she believed, she too would end up, and "rock away my ancient days . . . if the downward sweep of fortune's wheel caught me off balance."

At the same time she peered with intense sympathetic curiosity at the windows, lighted or shuttered, of houses and stores. Forms of life, rich and meaningful, at present beyond her reach, but inevitably to be entered upon one day, had to be taking place behind them. If a cloud of childhood depression made her imagine an old age in a dreary rooming house, a gust of youthful exhilaration swept her toward the open immensity of her own future:

And what of that feeling of unearthly splendor, of great promise, terrible delight, at some seasons of the year? Or the excitement which came with early darkness, and cold; or with summer heat, letting down torrents of brilliant summer light, that had to be shut out of the houses? This look and sound of promise fled through the town with the trains, and with the ripples on the river. "Some day! Some day!" it said.

This promise could be referred to nothing. The child lives in a region it knows nothing about. So that whatever memory of childhood remains is stable and perfect. It cannot be judged and it can never disappear. Memory has it inexplicably, and will have it forever. These things have been actually "learned by heart."

In addition to sight there was sound, and it too carried promise. The iron-rimmed wheels of carriages mixed with the steady echo of horses' hooves. The Lowell and Boston trains whistled and roared. Roosters and human voices called from neighboring fields, and, as in Milton, water poured over the wide mill dam. Above all, there was music—in the home and outside. May Bogan sang and played the piano, often accompanied by Charles. From the age of six or seven, Louise took piano lessons and played five-finger exercises; she later remembered what it was like to practice at the Gardners' piano, on top of which lay Mr. Gardner's flute, "in a worn black leather case." Music was bred into New England life. "People used to listen to band-concerts," says a tired and cynical woman in one of Bogan's unpublished stories. "In dusty parks, full of dusty walks, dusty children and dusty leaves."

In a different mood she wrote:

Music, in those days, belonged to its own time and place. No one today can remember with the same nostalgia (my generation is the last to remember) the sound of music on the water (voices and mandolin or guitar); of band-concerts in town squares or in Army parade grounds, in the twilight or early evening, with a string of lights in the distance marking the line of the bay; or under trees in what was actually, then, a romantic "gloaming." How poignant the sound of piano music, played however inexpertly, along some city street; or even, in those days, when every child was exposed to piano lessons, and the "upright" in the parlor was a sign of respectability and some slight edge of affluence, along some suburban road, or some half-country lane! Laforgue has caught the effect, at the moment, I suppose, in the 80s, when it was most usual—

"*Pianos, pianos, dans les quartiers aisés.*"

IN JULY 1906, Louise was sent to Mount Saint Mary Academy in Manchester, New Hampshire, the same convent her mother had attended. May Bogan's need for escape seems to have been periodic, and once again a season of abandonment and neglect had come around. With a woman known to Louise as Aunt Anne, a children's nurse who had some money and lived in Newport, May spent a good part of the next twelve months traveling across the country to California. Aunt Anne had instigated the trip, but there was, as the family knew, an "admirer" who accompanied them.

Whatever other effects the absence of her mother may have had, we can be sure that Louise's schoolwork did not suffer. She was now in the fifth grade, a year ahead of her peers, and although she was in a new school, and living away from home for the first time in her life, she got a mark of 100 in her Catechism examination at the end of the year, winning the Honors Award—a book—in the Children's Department. In her other subjects, spelling, geography, grammar, and history—all except arithmetic—she achieved marks in the 90s, which placed her in Rank 1 of the school.

The following year Louise became aware of the complexities of class and background. Later she recalled with bitterness the nuns cosseting their golden-haired favorites and giving them the better portions of food. Dark-haired Louise became so thin she regularly fainted during athletics and had to be kept aside by the nurse, who gave her graham crackers and sherry with an egg in it, a concoction she loved. Many of her schoolmates came from well-to-do families, with mothers who no doubt seemed "normal" and made regular visits. Louise was lonely. She later remembered falling in love with an altar boy and writing him "a passionate letter, which was later found by a nun, and almost resulted in my getting expelled, then and there." Surrounded by strangers, she was on her guard: "I used to lie in confession regularly . . . from the time I first confessed, at the ripe moral age of about nine, through a harp draped with a dust-cover, in the convent parlor. (They must have been varnishing the confessionals.)"

Her immediate anxieties were centered on the school operettas, those lavish end-of-year ceremonies of effort, rivalry, and hysteria. In Bogan's earliest piece of prose, "A Chapter from My Autobiography Concerning Early Aspirations," which appeared in one of the 1912 issues of *The Jabberwock,* her high school literary magazine, she recounts how, at the convent, she determined to become "one of the world's greatest operatic stars." Chosen to play the Fairy Queen (a leading part) in *The Golden Sickle,* a junior-school operetta to be performed by "The Minims" at the annual commencement exercises, she soon found herself the object of envy by her "sworn enemy," one Rosemarie Trainer, who considered herself a superior person "because she was twelve, lived in New York, and had a brother in West Point." Remarking that boarding school was "about the best place in the world to make bitter enemies as well as close friends," Louise went on to say that Rosemarie spread the evil report that her voice cracked on the high notes. This made Louise so angry that she resolved to give up her role as Fairy Queen and devote herself to inflicting assorted miseries on the iniquitous Miss Trainer, although she soon thought better of the plan, and continued "on my operatic way in haughty silence."

On commencement morning, with her Dutch clip grown out and now curled and brushed by the older girls, Louise felt the excitement of the oncoming performance. Sister Amelia, the director of the operetta, kept pinning portions of her costume to her skin as she nervously dressed the show's star. By the time Louise tottered onto the stage, she was shivering with panic. Her debut, she informs us, was by no means a triumph, to the evident satisfaction of Rosemarie Trainer, and though she thereafter took part in many school operettas, all traces of operatic ambition had disappeared by the time she left the convent.

The story is remarkably prophetic both for its matter-of-fact acceptance of envy and persecution and for the humor and detachment which place the incident in perspective. The girl of fourteen looking back at her nine-year-old self tells the tale of a battle fairly typical of those she chose, and that chose her, for the rest of her life. The social world was to her, from its beginnings, composed of malice, gossip, insult, cliques, cruelty, pettiness, and preferment, and from just as early a point she realized that she could buckle under and resign her role or, as she put it, continue "on my operatic way in haughty silence," with a good deal of added humor and good sense. That these saving graces existed at all, and had permitted Louise to forge a remarkably whole and self-forgiving view of the world by the time she reached early adolescence, suggests that her life at home must have contained some leavening principle that nourished her against the family dissensions and her own complicated nature.

She always had a love of common life, its "rough joy and silly pleasure," its "lying and lust and horseplay," and these must have formed part of the texture of living. May Bogan's own mother—the woman born O'Neill—had once "picked up her mother-in-law and was restrained only with some difficulty from dropping her down a stair-well," and May herself appears to have transmitted to her daughter a powerful and sanity-preserving pleasure in laughter and fun. She was likely to burst into song, often sentimental Irish standards like "Danny Boy," and her speech was vigorous and colloquial. "Every old sock has its old shoe," she would say about married couples, or "Enough is enough, and too much is plenty." She used common slang, phrases like "queer as Dick's hatband" and "my eye and Betty Martin," and she adored clothes. Louise remembered the way she would talk about the trim of a cherished dress. " 'Narrow red velvet,' she would say, or 'white Val lace'; and the color and delicacy of the wide circles would be perfectly brought back into being. Or she would describe the buttons on some coat or winter dress: 'cut steel' or 'jet' or 'big pearl.' Suddenly all the elegance of her youth came back." She dressed Louise as well as she dressed herself, and in photographs both mother and daughter appear with striking elegance. To take pains over the details of fittings and materials suggests some degree of companionship, some shared pleasure and indulgence.

As a child, Louise loved cats, and liked to dress them up. Her daughter later found in her papers a picture she had cut out of a cat wearing a mob cap, and on birthdays Louise and Maidie would often exchange cards with old-fashioned pictures of dressed-up cats.

Bogan wrote so little about her father that it is difficult not to conclude that, despite his presence in her life as a source of affectionate reassurance, he hardly existed for her as a strong influence. She once declared that he was " 'weak' and simply didn't matter." Yet she was fond of him, and always kept his calipers hanging on the wall above one of her desks.

Her brother Charles was another matter. As the son of a beautiful mother with an active, illicit erotic life, Charles had a difficult time. Bogan later wrote that he "had suffered his minor death, before I was born; he had been set apart from normal love long ago." From what few accounts there are, it seems that blight settled upon his life at an early stage and took effect in the form of an inability to leave home and make an independent adult life for himself. He appears to have worked as a salesman at the Stopple Factory in Ballardvale, as he is listed as such in the 1908 Ballardvale Directory; what he did for a living when the family later moved to Boston remains a mystery. Like his mother, he had a fierce temper. Writing many years later to twenty-six-year-old Theodore Roethke, Bogan reflected on her brother's paralyzed will, and recalled how, "from the age of 26 to 33 [sic], when death providentially took him . . . he stayed at home and didn't put up a fight, except toward the last, when he used to knock down doors and smash windows with chairs, and be brought home, beaten to a pulp."

On more than one occasion he pawned Louise's trinkets, including her Cross for Excellence, which she had received at the end of her second year at Mount Saint Mary's. Charles himself seems to have gone to school in Portland; Louise later made notes for a section in her memoirs about the "blankets ready for school journey to Portland (cottage, hammock, fishing)."

According to Louise's daughter, her mother called her brother "Charlie," and, like her own mother, "adored him and he adored her. He called her 'Babe,' and when she was very little she swallowed a small medal around her neck and he picked her up by the heels and swung her until it fell out."

In later life she almost never mentioned him. Once, during what she called a "bummel," or excursion into the country, with her friend Rufina McCarthy Helmer, she visited Ballardvale, where, according to Mrs. Helmer, "she pointed out the house they had lived in, and . . . enjoyed seeing the familiar places in the town." When she went into a small store, the women who ran it remembered her brother, "and that seemed to please Louise."

What Charles was doing when World War I began is not known. Perhaps he was jobless and found military service a relief. In October 1918, just a few weeks before the Armistice, while fighting in France, he was killed at Haumont Wood, at the age of thirty-two. From the haunting waste of his life came "To My Brother Killed: Haumont Wood: October, 1918":

> O you so long dead,
> You masked and obscure,
> I can tell you, all things endure:
> The wine and the bread;
>
> The marble quarried for the arch;
> The iron become steel;
> The spoke broken from the wheel;
> The sweat of the long march;
>
> The hay-stacks cut through like loaves
> And the hundred flowers from the seed;
> All things indeed
> Though struck by the hooves
>
> Of disaster, of time due,
> Of fell loss and gain,
> All things remain,
> I can tell you, this is true.
>
> Though burned down to stone
> Though lost from the eye,
> I can tell you, and not lie,—
> Save of peace alone.

The poem says all that Louise Bogan *could* say about her brother, and, except for the "long prose thing," she never again mentioned him in her writings.

LOUISE BOGAN believed that all her talent came from her mother's side of the family, so that the source of psychic hurt in her life seemed to her also the source of the means to triumph over that hurt. Whatever damage

Mary and Daniel Bogan inflicted on Louise's capacity to give and receive "normal" love, they never tried to suppress her gifts, which were brought to birth with the inextinguishable strength of all powers as natural as they are compensatory.

In January 1954 she remembered an event that took place between the time she learned to read and the time she began to write. She could not recall whether it was the year she was kept out of school after leaving the convent, which would have been 1908–09, when she was eleven, or the year before she was sent to the convent, 1905–06, when she was eight; she guessed it was the later date. She had accompanied her brother and father to a private hospital room to visit her mother, who was recuperating from an operation, one that "marked a kind of limit to my mother's youthful middle-age; and brought in the worser hopes and the lessened energy of a distinct later period." There was a Dr. X, whom Louise's mother "had loved for years" and who had arranged for the room in the "Yankee hospital." As Louise later gathered, he "must have faded out from the picture soon thereafter, with consequent tragic reverberations."

It was Sunday, and the room was large, with "dark brown woodwork, a fireplace with colored tiles and a mantelpiece, a sunny window and wicker chairs." Mrs. Bogan was sitting up in bed wearing a pretty nightgown, her hair in two braids. She was "in one of her truly loving moods, when affection rayed out from her like light. Someone had sent her a long box full of pink roses. Who could this have been? Not any of us."

Louise instantly disliked the roses. They struck her as false, off-putting in their suggestion of artificial sentiment. They came, too, from the outside, the world of her mother's "admirers," and, as Louise put it, from

"the other" world . . . the conventional, Yankee world which I was on the verge of entering with real closeness, in which I would always have friends and allies, but also ill-wishers, if not enemies; the world of school and church then alien to me; of accents not quite mine; of genteel manners; of the *right* side of things. —The roses rather struck a chill into me—was I eleven?—and I found myself moving away from my mother's bed toward the fireplace, on the opposite wall.

There she saw a small glass vase into which someone had placed a casual bunch of French marigolds. They had dark yellow petals with brown blotches and speckles, amidst a few "carrot-like leaves." So far Louise had never been especially fond of flowers. She liked the yellow daisies, black-eyed Susans, and cinquefoil growing in the mill towns, and she liked tansy, chicory, jill-over-the-ground, and weeds, but the French marigolds had quite another effect upon her:

The sight of the flowers gave me such a shock that I lost sight of the room for a moment. The dark yellow stood out against the brown woodwork, while the dark brown markings seemed to enrich the sombre background. Suddenly I *recognized* something at once simple and full of the utmost richness of design and contrast that was mine. A whole world, in a moment, opened up: a world of design and simplicity; of a kind of rightness, a kind of taste and knowingness, that shot me forward, as it were, into an existence concerning which, up to that instant of recognition, I had had no knowledge or idea. *This* was the kind of flower, and the kind of arrangement and the sense of arrangement plus background that, I at once realized, came out of impulses to which I could respond. I saw the hands arranging the flowers and leaves, the water poured into the vase, the vase lifted to the shelf on which it stood: they were my hands. A garden from which such flowers came I could not visualize: I had never seen such a garden. But the impulse of pleasure that existed *back* of the arrangement—with its clear, rather severe emotional coloring—I knew. And I knew the flowers—their striped and mottled elegance—forever and for all time, forward and back. They were mine, as though I had invented them. The sudden marigolds. That they were indeed sacred flowers I did not learn until many years later.

These flowers, as she saw them and responded to them, reflected the essence of every line of poetry and prose Louise Bogan was ever to write. It is not merely that in the moment's illumination she discovered taste and found its power jolting. An awakening took place: she became an artist before she could know it and before ambition and knowledge could bring their influence to bear upon her choices. Against her mother's ill-health and infidelity, against the family fighting and lower-middle-class constraints, against the imperious banality of the Yankee world, and against the enmity or indifference of others, she could now carry "the sudden marigolds" as a shield to deflect the cold light of estrangement and dread into warmer illuminations of mystery and form. Collecting shells later in life, keeping flowers in a vase or, when she couldn't afford flowers, lemon or rhododendron leaves, she remained faithful to the marigolds, to what they had brought forth in her. Dreary, ordinary, puzzling life as it simply *was* could never wholly trap her again.

THE CONVENTIONAL YANKEE WORLD Bogan anxiously sensed in her mother's hospital room claimed her soon enough. She later remembered the March morning in 1909 when she heard the Boston train approaching the Ballardvale station: "The steam shrieks out of the engine and smoke trails out, into the clear morning, from the smokestack, blotting out the willows and the mill dam. The conductor lifts me up to the step."

This was her last morning in Ballardvale. Her family was moving to Boston to make a new start after a terrible period of quarrels and a long separation (the details of which are otherwise unknown).

The part of Boston the Bogans moved to was not much older than Louise herself. The family took an apartment in a new red brick apartment house surrounded by empty lots and fields where boys played baseball, in "one of the drearier suburbs, to be reached by trolley car from Dudley Street." This was Harold Street, in Roxbury, and it had been laid out and named in March of 1886, with sections added between 1888 and 1897. It was very near Franklin Park, and its boundaries were Walnut and Seaver streets. The Bogans had a "railroad" apartment: "a center hall ran from the front door to the kitchen, with parlor, parlor alcove, the large bedroom, the dining room opening out from it." There was a smaller bedroom beyond the kitchen, where Louise's father, and sometimes her brother, slept. Louise slept as usual with her mother "in the other bedroom, which had some respectable furniture in it, and a view over the open sunken field."

Lace curtains were hung at the window, the piano was played, and Louise's mother saw to it that supper and Sunday dinner appeared on time. What her father and brother were then doing for a living has been lost to time, as well as the practical reason for the change from small town to city life.

Bogan later remarked upon "the life of the mind, growing up inside the outer life, like a widely branched vine . . . the individual *free* being, forced to begin small, like a sturdy shoot, but humble, which does not make much of a target for the wind." When she left Mount Saint Mary's in June 1908, aged ten years, ten months, with her Cross for Excellence, she had already skipped a year of school and finished the sixth grade. Despite inner and outer turmoil, or perhaps because of it, she had worked beautifully, and although we don't know why her parents kept her out of school in 1908–09, it almost certainly made no difference to the rest of her formal education. This period of freedom from school routine may even have had an extremely salutary effect. The revelation of "the sudden marigolds," coming as it did during that year of unregimented time, may not have been so sudden after all, but the first flowering of a new growth nourished by months of reading and solitude. Already at the convent, as Louise tells us herself, she had experienced a form of high ambition, and although she had given up the immediate goal of being an opera singer, she had clearly imagined a destiny of some magnificence. When in 1909–10 she finally returned to elementary school in Boston, she began to write "at length, in prose," and "acquired the interest of one of those intelligent old maids who so often showed talented children their earliest talents—opened up their earliest efforts by the application of attention and sympathy." It may well have been with the support of this teacher that Louise's mother got the idea of enrolling her in the fall of 1910 in the Girls' Latin School, which was then and still is a public high school for superior students.

From 1910 until 1915, "for five most fruitful years," Bogan received the best classical education then available to girls in this country. Strictly college preparatory, the school saw to it that students were given thorough training in English composition, classical languages, history, mathematics, and science. Louise took Latin, Greek, and French, and by the time of her graduation had read Xenophon, the *Iliad,* and a good deal of Latin poetry and prose. She was a member of a literary and debating society called The Athenian Club, and had the good fortune to come under the influence of Miss Caroline M. Gervish, A.B., who for many years headed the Department of English. Respected and admired by her students, Miss Gervish read George Herbert to her students, as well as A. E. Housman, a poet who, as Bogan later recalled, was considered "very far out" in 1915. By that time she had already been writing poetry for three years. "I began to write verse from about fourteen on. The life-saving process then began."

At the end of the school day, Louise would come home and write a long poem or sonnet sequence, usually in the style of William Morris, Swinburne, or the Rossettis. Hours were spent in the local branch of the Boston Public Library, where she read *Poetry: A Magazine of Verse,* from its very first issue. Her apprenticeship was steady, and by the age of eighteen she had accumulated "a thick pile of manuscript, in a drawer in the dining room—and had learned every essential of my trade."

She found her first readers in the audience of *The Jabberwock,* the Girls' Latin School literary magazine. Between 1911 and 1915 her poems and compositions appeared in nearly every issue. The lurking Yankee prejudice she sensed that day in her mother's hospital room now flourished openly. The late short-story writer and anthologist, Martha Foley, a G.L.S. classmate, recalled that Ernest Hapgood, the headmaster, sent for Mrs. Bogan to tell her to warn Louise not to expect to become editor of *The Jabberwock,* since, as he explained, "*no Irish girl* could be editor of the school magazine." It was this incident in particular that Bogan perhaps had in mind when she later wrote, "It was borne in upon me, all during my adolescence, that I was a 'Mick,' no matter what my other faults or virtues might be." This was the time in Boston when shops sported signs saying "No Irish Need Apply."

The tall, thin girl from Roxbury, despite the headmaster's bigotry, managed to fill issue after issue with her writing, and, like the aspiring writer Ruth in Martha Foley's story, "One with Shakespeare," to be credited with the publication of no less than four poems in *The Boston Evening Transcript*. In the story, Ruth is a class ahead of Elizabeth (Martha Foley herself), and as the two girls and two other friends (one of whom is called Eileen) walk home from school, they exchange deep thoughts about the universe. Ruth—that is, Louise Bogan—says, "I felt the rhythm of the universe last night . . . I was sitting on the roof in the dark and I felt the night all around me." When asked what she means by "the rhythm of the universe," she says, "Oh, you know. The way someone said the stars swing round in their course. And that's why I never, never want to study astronomy. I want only to imagine the stars. That's so much more beautiful than any facts about them can ever be."

Eileen disagrees vehemently, and begins to discourse on the distance light must travel from the stars to the earth, when Ruth impatiently interrupts her: "Stop! Don't give me facts about the stars! You can have those facts about your stars, if you want. But leave me my stars to love as I please."

Later on, of course, Bogan was fascinated by "facts about the stars," and read books about astronomy. Martha Foley's fictionalized memory of her, however, is entirely consistent with the nobility appropriate to a post-Swinburnean high school laureate. All the girls at school knew that Louise had great talent, and she was designated Class Poet. In fact she devoted so much time to her calling that one year she was "conditioned," i.e., received Incompletes, in every subject except English.

Unquestionably Bogan's natural ability was superb. In matters of sound and rhythm her earliest efforts were precise, exacting, and sophisticated. Her first printed poem, "The Lily and the Little Soul," with eight stanzas in iambic octosyllabics, appeared in one of the 1911–12 issues of *The Jabberwock;* here is its first stanza:

> There was a lily in the place
> Where all the other flowers are—
> The blushed hushed evening closed it in;
> And then there came, (O white sweet face!)
> The little soul into that place
> From the strange land that lies afar
> Beyond the scarlet and the sin.
> The little soul came softly in.

From its skill and finish it is obviously not the first poem the fifteen-year-old poet had written. A large repertoire of lyric conventions has been learned, including inverted syntax, apostrophe, and alliteration. Her imitation of the slow full cadences in the Pre-Raphaelite poetry of Morris and Swinburne is flawless. She later remarked that 1911–12, the year she wrote the poem, was the same year she had first read Collins's "Ode to Evening," which she considered the *slowest* poem in English and "which put me entirely off Swinburne, who was insidiously having his way with me, at that time."

Actually, the Swinburnean influence was not so easily outgrown. Bogan's ear never lost the Pre-Raphaelite penchant for the filled-out line, in which every vowel, consonant, and syllable receives its complete, unhurried value, but she learned variation and flexibility through experience, and from an unerring taste for surprise. The plenitude of sound in "A Night in Summer," an even more remarkable poem printed not only in the 1911–12 *Jabberwock* but also in *The Boston Evening Transcript,* and thus Bogan's first poem to appear in "the public prints," creates a dramatic slowness:

> The restless sea before my window breaks
>> All night beneath the stars that bend to see;
>> Full of unrest, and sad and longingly,
> It sings its soft, sad song as day awakes.
> And, oh, the tender lullabies it makes
>> That seem so full of some sad memory,
>> Of cadences that come and swiftly flee,
> And leave a gentle murmur in their wakes.
> I cannot sleep with all its whisperings,
>> I lie wide-eyed and hear the tide's swift rush
> Against the sand and sea-weed of the beach—
>> All through the night until the dawn it sings,
> Each ripple sighing—fading each in each—
>> And always, "Hush"—and always, always "Hush!"

Extravagant in its mellifluous Swinburnean diction, the poem nevertheless has the auditory perfection—the sheer richness of assonance and consonance—and the absolute control of progression that mark it as Louise Bogan's own. In whatever she wrote in either verse or prose, her style is recognizable through this stately, commodious, and flexible pacing. It is her own, too, for another reason. The strong nouns and verbs carrying the memory of a night of listening to the sound of the sea, "the tide's swift rush / Against the sand and sea-weed of the beach—" would be echoed late in life, in "Night," where "what drinks, drinks / The incoming tide" and "Where shell and weed / Wait upon the salt wash of the sea." She had struck her note, and it was the pure lyric note, as she often put it, of "memory and desire."

The intense and unconscious looking she had practiced since earliest childhood now gave her prose an assurance uncharacteristic of a writer so young. The "candid yet fierce intensity of a child's gaze, that knew all the tricks of sight; that could stop on the pane, to examine the flaws, the reflections, the colors in the glass, and could then plunge beyond, to gather up the texture of the opposite walls or the trees in the street; from which hints of weather, times of day, turns of the season could not be hidden" was able, as childhood was ending, to report its findings with an already long-acquired expertise, as in "A Walk in Autumn," an essay in another 1911–12 issue of *The Jabberwock:*

When we reached the heart of the woods, it seemed twilight, although it was still late afternoon. Under the branches still thick with yellowing leaves there was a gloom, pierced only by occasional shafts of pale sunshine, sunshine that seemed almost opal, so thick was it with the smoke of brush fires and with the mists of autumn.

Over the next three years her *Jabberwock* pieces continued to show remarkable advances in both technical and thematic maturity. The authority so characteristic of her adult voice began to make itself felt, and motifs that occupied her for the rest of her working life emerged, as in "Poplar Garden," the earliest poem based upon her response to seeing a work of art:

> Where is the source from whence this glow proceeds?
> Thou, Daphne, set above where grass burns bright,
> Wind-thrilled, arms flung unto the breathing light
> With trees blown dark behind, like shivered reeds?

This marble girl is the first in a series of figures of frozen life. She will appear later in "Statue and Birds," with "hands flung out in alarm / Or remonstrances," and in the horrifying paralysis of the narrator in "Medusa." Life stopped dead in its tracks, young female beauty arrested in the act of moving toward life, or away from it, already compelled the adolescent poet's imagination to visionary formality, just as the work of art as a burning core of mystery and meaning was already capable of eliciting sustained meditation in speech. More specifically, sexual conflict as itself emblematic of a more general conflict over the claims of life became with this poem the central subject of the poems marking the end of Bogan's early adolescent work and the onset of mature concerns. "The Gift," the very last poem she printed in *The Jabberwock,* in November 1914, exemplifies this conflict:

> My love stands mute by the door
> With her empty hands at her side,

She seems too pale, too sombre-lipped,
  Too sorrowful for a bride.

She has put on her lovely array,
  Her form is glowing in white,
And on her brow, between the flowers
  Her hair folds, soft and bright.

She is deaf to the whispering spring
  That has come to the fields of the land;
Only her eyes speak, only her eyes
  And the empty cup of her hand.

I have brought thee a gift for thine hand!
  Clasp your fingers and hold it fast.
Lift up thine eyes and let them speak joy,
  Open thy lips at last!

The hesitant bride, as full of desire as she is of fear, is another Daphne terrified of forces about to overwhelm her. In later poems this girl-woman would embody various aspects of resistance to nature, instinct, and time. Whatever keeps back, doubts, hesitates, and flees from experience in Bogan's poetry had its first expression in her, just as the male speaking voice in the poem reappears later on, transformed into the fire or drumbeat or wish or exhorter who overtakes the resisting heart and restores it to partial, flawed, but still joyous life.

In this simple lyric, Bogan's talents stand forth in their full character: commanding simplicity of diction; powerful manipulation of rhythm; conflicting emotions fully sustained. She had trained herself thoroughly and was ready, by the time she graduated from high school in June 1915, to move on to subjects of greater scope and technical difficulty. Beyond that, she was ready to embark not simply upon a career as a writer, but upon a courageous immersion in what goes by the name of the "literary situation." The one prevailing that year she graduated from high school and entered Boston University offered no clear-cut direction for the young poet. Things were pretty much the way T. S. Eliot, in a statement Bogan later incorporated in her own *Achievement in American Poetry,* had found them when he himself was starting out:

Whatever may have been the literary scene in America between the beginning of the century and the year 1914, it remains in my mind a complete blank. . . . Undergraduates at Harvard in my time read the English poets of the '90s who were dead: that was as near as we could get to any living tradition. Certainly I cannot remember any English poet then alive who contributed to my own education. . . . I do not think it too sweeping to say, that there was no poet in England or America who could have been of use to a beginner in 1908. The only recourse was to poetry of another language. Browning was more of a hindrance than a help, for he had gone some way, but not far enough, in discovering a contemporary idiom. And at that stage, Poe and Whitman had to be seen through French eyes. The question was still: Where do we go from Swinburne? And the answer appeared to be, nowhere.

This same question haunted Louise in 1915, although she was less systematic, perhaps, in her searchings. Eliot, conscious from the outset of his provinciality, appears to have pursued enabling influences; Bogan, stumbling through half-formed tendencies and intuitive leanings, happened upon them. Her own self-appointed (and lifelong) task was to read everything she could get her hands on. In 1914–15, she inscribed her name in a crimson commonplace book embossed with the words *Books That I Love* and in the space provided at the top of every page wrote down the author, title, and date each book was read. Curiously, following unknowingly the same path out of Swinburne that T. S. Eliot had taken, she too turned to "poetry of another language," reading, in December 1914, *The Symbolist Movement in Literature,* by Arthur Symons, the very same book that had led Eliot to Mallarmé and Laforgue. Malcolm Cowley has pointed out that, at Harvard, after the undergraduate years of the "Tragic Generation," whose members included the poets William Vaughn Moody, George Cabot Lodge, and Trumbull Stickney, "there was always an undercurrent of interest . . . in French Symbolist poetry," and it is possible that the teachers of both English and French at the Girls' Latin School, including Miss Gervish, would have known of the prevailing interest and communicated it to their advanced pupils.

Louise's remarks in the commonplace book are brief and simple, with a strong, professional, book-reviewish ring. She had clearly read book reviews in newspapers and magazines, and was determined to emulate their considered crispness. About Symons she wrote: "Symbolism, the movement, is closely defined, and the 'Conclusion' is a notable piece of recapitulation. Of Maeterlinck Symons says: 'There is a sort of religious calm in these deliberate sentences into which the writer has known how to introduce that divine monotony of great style.' " She was able to focus and to generalize, to formulate remarks that captured the essence of the work under inspection, and she responded to style, having an intuitive grasp of its ability to reveal the writer's temperament. At this early point, without exterior prompting, she naturally aligned herself with those currents then coalescing as poetic modernism. Going on to read nearly all the writers Symons discussed and recommended—Rimbaud, Villiers de Lisle-Adam, Mallarmé, Verlaine, and

Maeterlinck—she took his definition of Symbolism as an escape from exteriority, rhetoric, and materialism very much to heart, noting his praise of Huysmans's *The Cathedral* and transcribing the passage in which Huysmans points out "how inert matter, the art of stones, the growth of plants, the unconscious life of beasts, may be brought under the same law of the soul, may obtain, through symbol, a spiritual existence." Her imagination, fed by the intense *looking* of childhood, eagerly adopted Symbolist aesthetics as its own, and would always be engaged in transformations and correspondences, the two essential operations of the Symbolist mind.

Bogan's adolescent readings included Bernard Shaw, Aubrey Beardsley, Nietzsche, Wagner, Max Stirner, and Walter Pater. Pater, in particular, awakened her imagination. After reading his *Miscellaneous Studies* in the fall of 1914, she remarked in her commonplace book: "His style is a slow moving, rapturously cadenced miracle. It is articulateness combined into a hardly felt intricacy." In his prose she sensed, and loved, the seamless labor of "wrought style," with its intimations of "the life and sway of a music beyond speech." She was especially taken with an essay of Pater's called "The Child in the House," transcribing into the "Favourite Passages" section of her commonplace book long passages on the child's love of home, which Pater treats as an accumulation of sensations and associations captured by *things* and *atmospheres* acting as symbols.

She went on to read Pater's *The Renaissance,* marking down both the famous passage on La Gioconda in the chapter on Da Vinci and the exhortation to the reader in the "Conclusion" to burn with a "hard, gem-like flame." With Symons and Pater endorsing a life of sensations rather than thoughts, Bogan went on to find in Alice Meynell's essays the prose instrument she latched onto as her own. It seemed to her that Meynell could transmute "the transient impressions of the spirit, the delicate adventures of the eye, into word and form." The *aperçu,* with its distillation of sensation and fact, and its power to convey essences, struck her as the summit of artistry, and she marked down passages from Meynell's *The Spirit of Place* to train herself in techniques of compressed and evocative description.

She continued to read widely in late nineteenth-century literature, noting down Oscar Wilde's *Salomé,* Gerhart Hauptmann's *The Assumption of Hannele,* and in January 1916, during her year at Boston University, Amy Lowell's *Six French Poets: Studies in Contemporary Literature.* In the list of titles under the "Books to Read" section of the commonplace book she included Balzac's *Père Goriot* and Sir Thomas Browne's *Religio Medici,* while the "Favourite Passages" section thickened with additional long transcriptions from Maeterlinck's *Pelléas and Mélisande, Alladine and Palomides,* and *The Death of Tintagiles;* Symons's translation of Laforgue's *Moralités*

Légendaires; and large blocks of Amy Lowell's descriptions of Verhaeren, Samain, Remy de Goncourt, Henri de Regnier, Francis Jammes, and Paul Fort. She recorded a passage on cats from Jammes's *Pensée des Jardins.* By early 1916, writings in English began to take up more room in the commonplace book, and touchstones appeared from Louise Imogen Guiney's poems, John Donne's sermons, Rabindranath Tagore's *Gitanjali* (which had been appearing in *Poetry: A Magazine of Verse*), and Robert Louis Stevenson's letters.

Many years later she came to view her nascent literary self with a combination of pride and dryness. "I never was a member of a 'lost generation,'" she boasted to her friend Morton Zabel. "... I had no relations whatever with the world about me; I lived in a dream, populated by figures out of Maeterlinck and Pater and Arthur Symons and Compton Mackenzie (*Sinister Street* and *Sylvia Scarlett* made a great impression on me) and H. G. Wells and Francis Thompson and Alice Meynell and Swinburne and John Masefield and other oddly assorted authors." The world of semi-erotic, twilit "decadence," of vaporous yearning, shadowy emotions, and scenes of tragic impossibility mixed with a bohemian code of noble independence was irresistible to her. "I could play the piano scene (imperfectly, it is true!) of *Pelléas and Mélisande* over and over again, without one qualm!" she once remarked to Janet Lewis, the poet and novelist and wife of the poet and critic Yvor Winters. "All was modern beauty in those days. My sense came late."

As if contemporary French and English letters weren't enough, the omnivorous and freshly self-trained poet turned in 1915 to lyric poetry by women for yet another infusion of emotion and technique. In the poems of Christina Rossetti, Alice Meynell, Lizette Woodworth Reese, and Sara Teasdale, she found vigorous syntax in short forms and high, controlled feeling. Nature, mutability, love, and loss were constant motifs, but they were woven through with a tight pattern of irony and restraint that implied passion all the more intense for having been mastered. One of the poets who had a powerful influence on her was Louise Imogen Guiney, from whose *Happy Ending* (1909) she transcribed "A Talisman," a poem she continued to regard as a favorite much later in her life:

> Take temperance to thy breast,
> While yet is the hour of choosing,
> An arbitress exquisite
> Of all that shall thee betide.
> For better than fortune's best
> Is mastery in the using.

> And sweeter than any thing sweet
> The art to lay it aside.

The poem's paradox was precisely the theme Bogan herself would soon explore in her own poetry—the conflict between the heart and the mind. Central as it was to the seventeenth century, it was also the core of the feminine lyric vein Bogan would soon discover in the work of her slightly older contemporaries, Edna St. Vincent Millay and Elinor Wylie.

From Imagism she took what she needed without becoming an orthodox practitioner of the method. Later she claimed that no poet of her generation could escape the influence of Imagist *aims*. While remaining steadfastly Swinburnean in the acoustical handling of her verse, she began to work toward a precision and sensuousness in her imagery that can only have come from a penetrating understanding of the Imagist ideal.

After graduating from Girls' Latin School in 1915, she spent a year at Boston University, where she took courses in English literature, receiving A's in all of them, and published two poems in the 1915 Christmas issue of the *Boston University Beacon*. One of these is a graceful but otherwise uninteresting imitation of a medieval carol, while the other, which elaborates the reluctant-virgin theme of "The Gift," shows her efforts to integrate her well-tuned Pre-Raphaelite voice with a new Imagist exactitude. Called "The Betrothal of King Cophetua," the poem tells the story of "King Cophetua and the Beggar-Maid," which Bogan had probably found in Percy's *Reliques of Ancient English Poetry* and seen illustrated in Edward Burne-Jones's picture of the same name. Bogan's poem dwells upon the girl's bewilderment as she is brought to the king's courtyard:

> "Your name?" he asked.
> "I have not any name."
>   Her round voice held the sound of windless streams
>   Fringed to the bank with grasses—of old dreams
>
>   His youth knew.

The poem continues in a rich pictorial vein, with sun on the girl's feet, evening shadow on her breast, and a casket of jewels "like flame into the dark," which crashes to the ground and spills its treasure, sending the girl to the king's side where, "wild and sweet," she hears him say:

> "I am a king . . .
> . . . But if I give you jewels, land,

And you spurn all, I have no other thing.
Nor more to give, if it be not love you seek."
Leaning, he took her face between his hands;
She turned her eyes to him, and did not speak.

This is the same girl whose "eyes speak" and who brings only "the empty cup of her hand" in "The Gift," the same girl who will stand, mute and hesitant, in poems to come. In "Hugh Selwyn Mauberly," Ezra Pound, seeing Burne-Jones's painting, had been moved to describe the eyes of Elizabeth Siddal, the model for the Beggar-Maid, as "Thin like brook-water, / With a vacant gaze." Bogan, on the other hand, had seen there a being on the verge of experience, fearful of being deceived and ensnared, but unable ← to turn away.

A MEMOIR, called "Letdown," published in *The New Yorker* in 1934, tells of a crucial period in Louise's coming of age. It takes us back to 1910–1912, her thirteenth to fifteenth years, when she was just beginning to write and to take her ambitions seriously. Boston was still new to her. Its architecture, the "copies of palaces in Italy, churches in England, and residences in Munich," fascinated and delighted her. Walking through Copley Square, its center "occupied by a triangular plot of grass, garnished at its three corners by large palms growing in tubs," she would have seen Trinity Church (a French Romanesque building by H. H. Richardson), the New Old South Church, with its Venetian detailing, and along the square's west boundary, on Dartmouth Street, the Boston Public Library. "The sight of imitation true Gothic," she wrote, "imitation true Italian Renaissance, and imitation false Gothic revival often gave me that sensation in the pit of the stomach which heralds both love and an intense aesthetic experience. And to this day I have never been able to extirpate from my taste a thorough affection for potted palms."

The art teacher at the Girls' Latin School, noticing that Louise had a knack for drawing, recommended that she take art lessons from a real artist, and that is how she came to study privately with Miss Cooper: "Miss Cooper lived in the Hotel Oxford, and I lived on Harold Street," she wrote, "and a whole world, a whole civilization, or, if you will, the lack of a whole world, of a whole civilization, lay between." The gap between the two was represented, for Louise, by the big stone Hotel Oxford, whose dark woodwork, bronze and marble statues, plush, gilt, and magenta carpets all betokened a world of sacred rituals and attitudes that threw her into a state of pure awe.

At the top of the building she would go to Miss Cooper's "studio," the likes of which she had never seen before. Though it looked out over the railway yards and lacked a skylight, everything about it had the appearance of having been touched by "the great conflagration of art." There were anatomical casts, death masks, life masks, objects brought back from journeys "abroad," including a little copy of the Leaning Tower of Pisa, and other assorted pieces of evidence for an aesthetic way of life. Every Saturday afternoon, Louise was given a still life to draw and materials to use: "charcoal paper pinned to its board. . . ; sticks of charcoal, beautifully black, slender, and brittle; pastels, running through shade after delicate shade in a shallow wooden box; the fixative; the kneaded rubber." Close by stood Miss Cooper, dressed in Liberty silks and chains of Florentine silver, a woman of sixty or so with white hair and a youthful smile. Although her own watercolors and pastels hung on the walls, she never seemed to be in the process of actually drawing or painting anything. Still, her artistic looks, her artistic atmosphere, and her artistic *objets* were all that Louise needed to believe absolutely in her artistic being: "Personal distinction, in those days, to me meant undoubted nobility of soul. Distinguished physical traits went right through to the back, as it were, indelibly staining mind and spirit." Coming from Harold Street, with its endless construction of dreary, styleless three-family houses, to Miss Cooper and her studio, where on autumn evenings, after the lesson was over, she would be given tea on a tray "on which sat two cups and two saucers of Italian pottery, and a plate of what I called cookies and she called biscuits," Louise became drunk on the atmosphere of art: "Many times, after a cup of this tea, I staggered out into a world in which everything seemed suspended in the twilight, floating in mid-air, as in a mirage. I waited for the trolley car which would take me back to Harold Street in a daze, full of enough romantic nonsense to poison ten lives at their root."

Louise remained under this spell for two years. By the beginning of the third, Miss Cooper, the sum of human perfections, began to change. Sometimes she fixed herself a cup of tea alone, in her tiny kitchen, from which Louise would hear her sigh. She blamed herself for the alteration in Miss Cooper's demeanor, as she later realized young people tend to do, trying to come up with reasons to explain it. Long intoxicated with the idea of Miss Cooper, Louise now took in, with mounting distress, every sign of her diminished attention:

My ears became sharpened to every tired tone in her voice, to every clink of china and spoon, to every long period of her silence. One afternoon she came out of the kitchen and stood behind me. She had something in her hand that crackled like paper, and when she spoke she mumbled as though her mouth were full. I turned and looked at her; she was standing with a greasy paper bag in one hand and a half-eaten doughnut in the other. Her hair was still beautifully arranged; she still wore the silver and fire-opal ring on the little finger of her right hand. But in that moment she died for me. She died and the room died and the still life died a second death. She had betrayed me. She had betrayed the Hotel Oxford and the replica of the Leaning Tower of Pisa and the whole world of romantic notions built around her. She had let me down; she had appeared as she was: a tired old woman who fed herself for comfort. With perfect ruthlessness I rejected her utterly. And for weeks, at night, in the bedroom of the frame house in Harold Street, I shed tears that rose from anger as much as disappointment, from disillusion and from dismay. I can't remember that for one moment I entertained pity for her. It was for myself that I kept that tender and cleansing emotion. Yes, it was for myself and for dignity and gentility soiled and broken that I shed those tears. At fifteen and for a long time thereafter, it is a monstrous thing, the heart.

In the story of Miss Cooper's fall from grace, Bogan tells us everything essential about the person she had become by the age of fifteen. That person was a full-blown romantic, with the romantic's despotic requirement that reality conform to her wish, and the romantic's susceptibility to desolating disappointment. She does not say that Miss Cooper was the first in a line of other infatuations and disillusionments, but she does not need to. It is the idea of "civilization," and not her personal history, that she seeks to define in her memoir, and what she implies is that without a foundation in sympathy and understanding, the joys of style and taste must forever remain hollow. But at fifteen—as she indeed tells us—Bogan was just beginning to learn this, and it was something that would only become clearer to her in time.

2 A LAND OF CHANGE

BOGAN'S FRESHMAN YEAR at Boston University turned out to be her last. To her mother's great pride, she won a scholarship to Radcliffe for the fall of 1916. But she did not go to Radcliffe; instead, she left home and got married.

Just when she met Curt Alexander we do not know. It appears that her mother's friend, "Aunt Anne," who was associated in Louise's mind with her mother's trip west many years earlier, introduced them on one of Louise's visits to Newport. In later years she rarely mentioned Alexander, except to tell her daughter, "I married your father for love, number one, and number two is that you can be sure you're not illegitimate." He was a tall German from a town called Breslau, in Silesia, born in 1888 and trained as an architectural draftsman. Although the circumstances under which he left Germany are not known, he had already completed military service before coming to America in 1912. Leaving behind a mother, named Mathilde, who was an opera singer, and at least one brother, he found the American economy depressed and, unable to find a job in architecture, joined the Army. Owing to his prior military experience, he rose very rapidly from private to corporal to lieutenant, achieving the rank of captain by the time of his death. He was blond, with a proud, serious face and conventionally handsome features.

When it became clear that Louise was determined to marry him, her parents strongly objected. Alexander was not a Catholic and Mary Bogan insisted that he become one before marrying Louise. Not only did Alexander agree to this condition, but he became zealous in his adoption of the faith. This show of goodwill did little to lessen the Bogans' anxieties.

Daniel, too, was unhappy about the forthcoming union. His prospective son-in-law struck him as "very German and 'Achtung'!" Unquestionably both of Louise's parents saw her teetering on the verge of the very same mistake they themselves had made so long ago, and dreaded what would come of her decision.

But having steeped herself in romantic notions of all kinds, what Louise wanted, above all, was passion—consuming, intoxicating, devouring passion. A young woman finding herself desired and cherished, and eager for sexual experience, had only one respectable choice available to her, and that was to marry her lover. To live with him was not yet an acceptable way of life. Over her mother's fierce protestations, which included an actual or threatened heart attack, Louise married Alexander on September 4, 1916, a little less than a month after her nineteenth birthday, and moved with him to New York, where they lived on Bleecker Street.

She had desperately wanted to escape from home, and Alexander was her way out. Going to Radcliffe would have meant staying home with her parents. She was tall, beautiful, and knew that she had talent. Alexander, who was so much older, and European and good-looking, must have seemed to her a providential gift.

As it turned out, they lived only a short time in New York. When war was declared in April 1917, Alexander was sent to Panama to serve with the Coast Artillery in guarding the canal. Whether he specifically requested the assignment, or whether the Army, knowing that he had at least one brother in Germany who might have been a soldier, thought it best to keep him out of combat in Europe, again we don't know. But a month later, in May, Louise sailed on a troop ship, four months pregnant and sick all the way. Alexander was Officer of the Day when she arrived and therefore unable to meet the boat. Louise had broken out in hives, and was no sooner taken off the ship than she was immediately put into quarantine. It was several days before Alexander could come to get her out of the steamy tropical hospital and take her home to the concrete flat in the Junior Officers' Quarters.

She was miserable in Panama. She hated it. She had nothing in common with the other junior officers' wives, and must have found it difficult to observe rank with the spouses of senior officers. And she was a New Englander in a climate so steamy she had to keep an electric lightbulb going in the closet because her clothes were damp all the time, and another in the piano to keep it from going flat. Her shoes were always moldy, and her dresses stuck to her, and she had the additional discomfort of being pregnant throughout the spring and summer months.

She stood it for a while, finding a Chinese woman who made her cool pongee dresses. And she did have a piano. Later she recalled "the veranda in

Panama, with the Barbadians' whetting their sickles on the hill below, the Chinese gardens green, the noise of breakers from beyond the hill, the crochet in your lap, and the cool room shuttered and the sheeted bed. . . ." More than the landscape disturbed her. In "Decoration," a poem published in *Body of This Death* and omitted from later volumes, she describes a macaw which "beats / A flattered tail out against gauzy heats; / He has the frustrate look of cheated kings." The bird's frustration was her own; the reference, to cards, which she played incessantly with Alexander, finding she had little in common with him besides sex.

Eventually the baby was born, on October 19, 1917, at two-thirty in the afternoon, in the hospital in Ancon. The twenty-year-old mother had given birth to a girl she named Mathilde, after Curt's mother and at his insistence.

When the baby was two months old, Louise published two poems in the experimental "little" magazine *Others,* which was edited in New York by Alfred Kreymborg. Perhaps she had managed to meet some of the people associated with the magazine during the few months she and Curt had lived in New York, or perhaps she'd summoned up the courage to submit her work while in Panama. Not surprisingly, the two poems were in free verse, the most "advanced" verse form of the moment, and both dealt with Bogan's recent experiences of marriage and wifehood. The first, "Betrothed," which was included in her later collections, is the culmination of the "Daphne" or "reluctant girl" poems; in it, a girl speaks quietly to her fiancé about her hesitation to marry:

> My mother remembers the agony of her womb
> And long years that seemed to promise more than this.
> She says, "You do not love me,
> You do not want me,
> You will go away."

She thinks of her friend, whose hair, "the color of sunburnt grasses," she will not see "In the country whereto I go," and questions her own expectations and desires. Sexual maturity is an unfamiliar territory, entry into which requires sunderings and renunciations, and the guilt of separation from the reproachful mother.

The hesitation of "Betrothed" becomes disappointment in "The Young Wife," a poem Bogan later thought little of and never reprinted. It is not a good poem, but it looks directly at the disillusionment she had found in marriage and at the desire for a renewing romantic passion. "I do not believe in this first happiness," it begins, and it goes on to question through extravagant images and choked rhetoric the "fruited bough" of marriage. Running parallel to the desire for liberation is a theme of obsessive jealousy of the husband's past lovers, a sense of identification with them as betrayed women, as well as fear of them as rivals.

If Bogan had been longing to go back to New England, the sight of the poems in print must have done a great deal to help make up her mind. Home was where her mother could help her with the baby while she wrote. In May 1918, only a year after her arrival, she left Panama and took the baby back to her parents in Boston. To her daughter she later said that this was only a temporary arrangement until Alexander could rejoin her, although to Ruth Limmer she claimed that it was in fact a true marital separation. It had become clear to her that she and Alexander had nothing in common, a fact that was all the more apparent after the baby's birth, when Alexander inexplicably ceased to desire sexual relations.

On the journey back to Boston, Bogan took the baby with her to visit a Boston University friend named Alison Laing, whose Scots mother exclaimed that Mathilde was too long a name for the "wee bairn," and promptly rechristened the child *Maidie*, the Scots diminutive for "little girl."

Within several months, Alexander had returned to the mainland, and Bogan had moved with him and Maidie to an Army base on an island off Portland, Maine. How this reconciliation came about is not clear, although it isn't difficult to suppose that Bogan found living with her parents as impossible as ever. It was a period of conflict for her, no matter whom she lived with. Her daughter has said, "Someplace it should be recorded that Alexander was, in truth, a demanding person. . . . His wife and his child were *his;* his wants came first." Once, while he was stationed on the island, Louise and Maidie visited her parents during a terrible storm. Louise thought it best to stay the night and telephoned Alexander, who demanded that she come home at once with the baby and make his dinner, regardless of the storm. Visits with him to the Bogans cannot have been comfortable, since Daniel Bogan was finding Alexander's German ways as offensive as ever.

In October 1918, word came that Charles Bogan had been killed in battle at Haumont Wood. His death devastated May Bogan, now in her early fifties, who resigned herself from that time on to the fading of her hopes. Soon diabetes set in, and overweight, and a fanatical renewal of religious faith. Although Charles had never achieved any measurable degree of conventional success, his family had loved him. His death brought an end to the original lonely foursome that had been the Bogan family. Now if anyone was to enter the world and make a mark, it would have to be Louise.

Her decision to leave Alexander was not made hastily, but when she decided to act, she was resolute. In early 1919 he was sent to Fort Dix in New Jersey to take part in the demobilization of soldiers from the Army. Louise and Maidie soon joined him in an apartment on Garden Street in Hoboken, where Louise looked after her child and read H. G. Wells, occasionally taking the ferry across the Hudson to Greenwich Village, where she immediately met people who shared her interests and encouraged her to become part of their world. She had known she was a New Yorker "on first sight," and after six or seven months—by the summer of 1919—she left Alexander. Her parents were now living in Farley, Massachusetts, a small town on the Mohawk Trail near Otter River, where Daniel had secured one of his better posts as superintendent of the local paper mill. With a combination of practical good sense and clear-sighted selfishness, Louise brought Maidie, now two, to live with her parents "in a white house on top of a hill that overlooked a big road," and then returned to New York and rented an apartment at 24 West Ninth Street.

Alexander died sometime the next year, at the age of thirty-two, after developing pneumonia while convalescing from an operation for gastric ulcers. His death made it unnecessary for Bogan to file for divorce, and rendered her eligible for widow's benefits from the Army. So rather than inhibiting her new life, Alexander had made it possible for her to start out alone with some small margin of security. Nevertheless, his death can only have imposed a burden of terrible sorrow on what was by no means an easy separation. Louise had been in love with the man when she married him, and he had given her the chance to leave home she'd so desperately needed at the time. For the disintegration of their love and her inability to stay with him she must have felt some measure of guilt, although not, perhaps, as much as might be supposed. Within a short time of her widowhood, she managed to arrive at a clear and resolved view of her situation, writing in "Survival," a poem published in *The Measure* in 1921:

> I hoped that you would die out from me
> With the year.
> Between you and my heart I thrust
> The glittering seasons.
>
> I denied you with late summer,
> Watching the green-white hydrangea change
> To petalled balls of thin and ashen blue,
> And nasturtiums, hot orange on stems like ice or glass
> Shrivelling by round leaves.

And, in "To a Dead Lover" she wrote:

> I am alone,
> Four years older;
> Like the chairs and the walls
> Which I once watched brighten
> With you beside me. I was to waken
> Never like this, whatever came or was taken.

However much she might realize that she was not to blame for Alexander's death, the transition from marriage to freedom had been fatally touched by tragedy. Had it not been for her talent, now in full flood, Bogan might well have been paralyzed by misgivings and self-reproaches. But her first season was at hand, and it was not only husband and child who must be abandoned, but everyone and everything that held her back from herself and her gift, including the demoralizing kindness of a family "who held out the bait of a nice hot cup of tea and a nice clean bed, and no questions asked, until the mould starts in effacing the last noble lineaments of the soul."

No sooner did she move to Manhattan than she found a center of gravitation in the group of people associated with Alfred Kreymborg and *Others.* And she became, in her own fastidious way, a Greenwich Village bohemian. Kreymborg used to give parties at his place on Fourteenth Street, where William Carlos Williams later recalled meeting Bogan. "Our parties were cheap—" he wrote in his *Autobiography,* "a few drinks, a sandwich or so, coffee—but the yeast of new work in the realm of the poem was tremendously stirring." The poet Lola Ridge had gatherings at her rooms, also on Fourteenth Street, and there were painters' parties at Walter Arensberg's studio. The twenty-two-year-old Army officer's wife was living among people to whom literature, especially poetry, mattered more than anything else. In a very short time she came to know Malcolm Cowley, Paul Rosenfeld, Matthew and Hannah Josephson, Lola Ridge, Mina Loy, Maxwell Bodenheim, John Reed, Louise Bryant, and Conrad Aiken.

In this new life, she very quickly found a lover. From October to December of 1919, she was enmeshed in a love affair with John Coffey, a young Irishman who, as Ruth Limmer describes him, "thought to call attention to the needs of the poor by shoplifting (his specialty was furs) and then, in court, with attendant publicity, testifying to their plight. The plan went awry: having told the police of his long-term, successful thefts, he was sent not to court but to Matteawan, an insane asylum." Coffey was proud of his role as a radical Robin Hood, and liked to hobnob with writers and intellectuals. After his arrest, William Carlos Williams wrote an article on his behalf in *The Freeman,* and Bogan, who had fallen hard for Coffey's Irish outlaw charm, as well as his cause, wrote to Williams, thanking him solemnly for his article and explaining, "My family, immediately authority stamp[ing] John as a maniac, made a concerted effort to back up authority with the result that all communication between John and myself has been cut off. The medical director at Matteawan . . . has assured me that John is decidedly insane and of marked criminal tendencies. . . . Write to John. Tell him . . . that because of the thing he knows endurance can become the long reality. Tell him that there are sources undiscovered and not yet spilled out."

From the high school days when she had read Compton Mackenzie and G. B. Shaw, Bogan had some holdover fantasies of herself as a Fabian Socialist whose sympathies were with the poor and the alienated and rebellious fringes of society. All her life, even when there wasn't a drop of adolescent socialism left in her veins, she cherished the notion that a deep affinity existed between the artist and the criminal. Her liaison with Coffey, although far briefer than her marriage to Alexander, had more lasting emotional consequences. To begin with, it attracted some notoriety when the rumor got started that on one occasion she had stood outside a department store with a fur coat, acting as an accomplice in one of his thefts. Many years later, in 1957, when enmity and gossip in the literary world no longer bothered her very much, she spent an evening in Cambridge, Massachusetts, with some younger friends, regaling them with stories of how she had once been a "gangster's moll" and waited in a car during one of her boyfriend's heists. But it took her a long time to put the affair in perspective. The gossip went around for years, and had a way of coming up again at inconvenient moments. The affair itself lasted only two months. Coffey "betrayed" her, she later wrote to a friend, and broke her heart, and she wanted nothing more than to push the whole embarrassing and humiliating episode aside. Fate, however, managed to leave unquiet traces of the affair. In a letter to Robert N. Linscott written sometime in 1920, Conrad Aiken reported from South Yarmouth, Massachusetts, that "John Coffey and Max Bodenheim and Mrs. Bod., and one Louise Bogan . . . who has her infant (the offspring of a lawful wedlock now in process of dissolution) have all blown in in the last 24 hours, rolling in money, and have hired a house not far away." Aiken later described this household in his novel, *Conversation,* maliciously turning Louise, as he admitted to Malcolm Cowley, "into a pianist (A BAD pianist!) who plays the piano offstage for a whole chapter but never otherwise appears!" Bogan, who considered the unflattering portrait of herself a sign of Aiken's envy and mean-spiritedness, was dismayed, and it is fortunate that she never heard Coffey's own charmless and egotistic comment on the book: "You did a fine job in *Conversation*," he wrote Aiken. "I was glad to have your description of me ... although I felt somewhat chagrined by your repetition of Bodenheim's rationalization that I stole from a desire to support 'genius' like his, as a kind of Robin Hood esthete. My main aim at the time was to make myself more articulate; that is why I consorted with you litterateurs ... I stole to finance my education."

Bogan's memories of Coffey, like those of her brother Charles and Curt Alexander, were sealed in a vault of silence. He had wounded and disillusioned her greatly, and his power over her had been real and disturbing. In "Resolve," a poem published with those on Alexander's death, she wrote of the determination to free herself from an emotional bondage we can be certain applied more to her situation with Coffey than to that with Alexander:

> So that I shall no longer tarnish with my fingers
> The bright steel of your power,
> I shall be hardened against you,
> A shield tightened upon its rim.

Although she was never particularly nostalgic about her early years in New York, to them she owed the first true test of her poetic gifts and spiritual endurance. The city offered refuge from the turmoil of her marriage and allowed her to pursue her destiny unchallenged by provincial morality. By the time she was twenty-two, Bogan had been a wife and mother, had left her husband and given her child to her parents' keeping, had become a widow and a betrayed lover within the same year, and had established a solid and growing reputation as a gifted lyric poet. This was an extraordinary amassing of experience, almost impossible to come to terms with at the time it was all happening. Only later—years later—did the edifice of fortitude and recklessness, energy and bravura, egotism and achievement come crashing down around her. In the meanwhile, her ambition fueled her. It drove and coaxed and comforted and rescued her when she might have become mired in diffidence, guilt, or mindless bohemianism. She had not left her husband, given up her child, and fallen in and out of love with Coffey to be merely a Greenwich Village "type." Neither the doctrinaire feminism then pervasive nor an equally prevalent sentimental libertinage appealed to her. What she had done, she had done out of necessity. It was within her powers, she knew, to become a great poet and woman of letters, and she was determined to make that possibility her life's work and, moreover, to do so without compromise.

WITH MAIDIE SAFELY SETTLED at her parents' home in Farley, Louise took a job as clerk in Brentano's bookstore, traveling home for a visit every few weeks. Maidie, rapidly growing, and doted on by her grandparents, knew that the "lovely lady bringing presents" was her mother. As she grew older, Maidie sensed that although Louise "tried very, very hard to be a mother," and for that matter really "*was* a mother," she didn't think that "instinctively she *wanted* to be a mother. But I think she tried to make it up to me in many ways." Louise was tender and affectionate during her visits, and Maidie never questioned the basis of her mother's absence: "Since there weren't any other children around, I didn't know that this was different. There was Nana and Grampie and Mother, who was this lovely human being who appeared at the time."

In 1921, Daniel and Mary Bogan took Maidie with them to Worcester, Massachusetts, where Daniel was presumably once again working at a paper mill, so Louise began to make her maternal pilgrimages to that city. Back in New York she was immersed in literary life. While working in Brentano's she read Katherine Mansfield's story "Bliss" and suddenly thought to herself, "Here's a woman doing it, at last." Up until then, Viola Meynell, whose novels she had begun to read in 1916, had seemed to her the only woman writer capable of a distinctly feminine kind of insight and perceptiveness. Even Jane Austen, and only toward the end, "was just beginning to look at the landscape, and feel the sorrow in the look of a season, or the light of a time of day." Reading Viola Meynell, Louise discovered, just as she had discovered in Alice Meynell, Viola's mother, the subtle variegations of feeling that give lyrical prose its charm. The feminine mode she was trying to embrace was not so much feminist in any direct way as it was an alternative to the excesses of shapeless, external detail in the naturalism she had grown up on in H. G. Wells, Somerset Maugham, Frank Swinnerton, and Compton Mackenzie. She was also studying Symbolist poetry once again and, according to Malcolm Cowley, she was, along with Hart Crane, Allen Tate, Rolfe Humphries, and Yvor Winters, all of whom became at one time or another her friends, reading Jules Laforgue "with professional interest." Sometime between 1920 and 1923, she developed a friendship with the critic Edmund Wilson, who was at that time writing for *The New Republic* and *Vanity Fair*. In July 1921, Harriet Monroe, founder and editor of *Poetry: A Magazine of Verse,* accepted five poems to be published in the August 1922 issue of the magazine under the title "Beginning and End." This group included "Elders," "To a Dead Lover," and "Resolve," poems in which we can see a clear autobiographical connection to Bogan's ordeals with both Alexander and Coffey. By the end of 1921, at age twenty-four, she was publishing poems in nearly all the advanced and prestigious journals of the day: *The New Republic, Vanity Fair, Voices, The Liberator, Rhythmus, The Literary Review of the New York Evening Post,* and a "little" magazine called *The Measure,* with which she was to have a long association.

The Measure was the offspring of two *New Republic* reviewers, Maxwell Anderson and Padraic Colum, and was founded out of a preference for "the musical and rounded forms" as against Imagism and "the half-said, half-conceived infantilities and whimsicalities of the dominant American school" of such windy Whitmanians as Carl Sandburg and Vachel Lindsay. The revolving board of editors did not reject free verse out of hand; the first issues had poems by Wallace Stevens, Alfred Kreymborg, and other vers librists. But they were latecomers to the 1912 poetic "renaissance," and to strengthen their claims they denied that the movement at its beginning had ever been truly fresh or broken new ground. In his founding editorial Anderson blamed the age, and offered the opinion that *The Measure* would be unlikely ever to publish a great poem:

Poetry, of Chicago, has come out uninterruptedly for ten years without doing it. This is not the fault of the editors of *Poetry.* If there had been masterpieces to print they would have printed them. There have been none. But the ten years of *Poetry*'s history have been useful, fruitful, interesting. Miss Monroe and her band have pioneered well, and if the near future should actually hold a poetic revival in merit as well as in bulk it will be due largely to their efforts.

To the editors of *The Measure,* Edna St. Vincent Millay seemed "just now the most interesting person in American poetry." As yet unaware of new work by T. S. Eliot and Ezra Pound, the magazine, holding neither a rear nor an advance position, endorsed the well-made lyric by Conrad Aiken, Robert Hillyer, Eda Lou Walton, Lola Ridge, Maxwell Bodenheim, Witter Bynner, Babette Deutsch, John Gould Fletcher, Archibald MacLeish, Edgar Lee Masters, Elinor Wylie, and Edwin Arlington Robinson, poets whose work could also be found in *The New Republic.* Though Bogan deplored their poetry, with the emphatic exceptions of Wylie and Robinson, these poets collectively represented a generation now caught up in what David Perkins has identified as the general formal characteristic of modern poetry, "a recurring tendency to retrench deliberately to the minor." Bogan's new and maturing need to move beyond Swinburnean emotion and Imagist precision without going over to the vers-librist camp made her alignment with such retrenchment virtually inevitable. That it occurred when strict, austere, ironic, fire-and-marble poetry by women was beginning to attract attention; when Eliot and Pound were returning to "form" and in doing so setting in motion a widespread repudiation of free verse; when Donne and the "Metaphysicals" and Elizabethan poetry were in the ascendant; and when the poet Ridgely Torrence, Edwin Arlington Robinson's longtime friend, was taking over as literary editor of *The New Republic* on Francis Hackett's departure from that post in March 1922, resulted in overdetermining Louise Bogan's metamorphosis into a poet committed to "form," that is, to stanzas and rhymes and traditional meters, and to the compression and containment associated with minor lyric modes.

Having survived the demise of the "Tragic Generation" at Harvard to write idealistic, meditative poems in rigorous form, Torrence began filling the poetry pages of *The New Republic* with work by Yeats, Hardy, and Graves. He became, as Edmund Wilson did, a mentor to Bogan over the next seven or eight years. Through his interest (she always showed him new poems) she first saw the possibility of merging delicate feminine perceptiveness with the roughness and vitality of Yeats's common speech. She first read *Responsibilities* in 1917 and *The Wild Swans at Coole* in 1921, the same year she read Synge. Early in 1922, Torrence gave her a copy of Kuno Meyer's *Selections from Ancient Irish Poetry*. She was not the only young poet of her time to discover Yeats. Many of those who published in *The Measure* were talking about him and imitating him; Padraic Colum had known him in Ireland and reviewed his books in *The Dial.* For Bogan, however, the general enthusiasm for Yeats was quite beside the point. He not only seemed to her the supreme voice in Irish literature but in all of contemporary poetry; her affinity for him was temperamental, personal, and absolute. From the early 1920s she took him as her standard, measuring everything she wrote against the purity and power of his forms. It was as if in his coarse, straitened post-1914 idioms she heard echoes of her family's speech, and felt the heat of her "mother tongue" at its most incandescent.

DURING THESE EARLY YEARS Bogan worked hard at her writing. In a letter from Worcester written sometime in 1921, she reported to her friend Italia Iff, a fellow sales clerk at Brentano's: "There is a typewriter here, and I write. —O nothing, save the end of a long short story begun in March called 'Egeria' with the appended quotation *'Il y a des femmes muettes.'** It's about a woman who has a genius for expressing herself through others—who has three husbands. It started as a work of art & is

---

* There are silent women.

ending as something I might be able to sell to the Sat. Eve. Post." She could quip all she liked, since she was having some real success. Elinor Wylie chose "Medusa" for inclusion in a group of poems by Joseph Auslander, Maxwell Bodenheim, Genevieve ("Jed") Taggard, and Bernice Lesbia Kenyon in the forthcoming March issue of *The Bookman,* and invited her to tea, and she was an increasingly familiar presence at literary parties and gatherings.

A pocket diary kept from January to September of 1922 helps trace some of her doings. Between January and March she worked at the Hudson Park branch of the New York Public Library, and at the St. Mark's Place branch as well, where she pasted book pockets into books alongside Marianne Moore. "This was the winter before I went to Vienna," she later recalled,

and I was in a dazed state of mind, and Marianne, as well as everyone else, came through to me rather foggily. But I remember very well, working with her in the winter afternoons, upstairs in that library with its general atmosphere of staleness and city dinginess. —Her hair was then a beautiful shade of red; she wore it in a thick braid. She was continually comparing the small objects with which we worked—mucilage brushes and ink and stamping rubbers—to oddly analogous objects; and she smiled often and seemed happy. . . . She had no idea that I wrote poetry, and always treated me kindly, but rather like some assistant more or less invisible to her (as indeed I probably was, being, at that time, more or less invisible to myself, as well). . . .

She could not have been too invisible to herself, and if she was "dazed," she must have been concerned about it, because the diary informs us that she was then in psychiatric treatment with Dr. Samuel A. Tannenbaum, a Freudian who was known for his treatment of other writers in Bogan's sphere of acquaintance. From "Portrait of the Artist as a Young Woman," a poem that remained unpublished until 1980 when Ruth Limmer included it in *Journey Around My Room,* and another, "A Letter," which Bogan published in *Body of This Death* and then considered too personal to include in later volumes, it becomes clear that as she wrote and published and gained technical strength, she was battered by assaults of nihilism and uncertainty. Journeys to the New England countryside were not only fulfillments of her obligation to Maidie, but repeated means of escape from the terror and grief that assailed her. In "A Letter," she wrote:

> This is a countryside of roofless houses,—
> Taverns to rain,—doorsteps of millstones, lintels

> Leaning and delicate, foundations sprung to lilacs,
> Orchards where boughs like roots strike into the sky.
> Here I could well devise the journey to nothing . . .

But then she wonders, "But why the journey to nothing or any desire?" and urges herself to remember "the smell of cold mornings, / The dried beauty of women, the exquisite skin / Under the chins of young girls, young men's rough beards . . ." Every remembrance of desire brings with it an attendant association with pain and betrayal: "The cringing promise of this one, that one's apology / For the knife struck down to the bone. . . ." She knew that she was ill, that growth and time and nature terrified her, but she also knew that retreat and paralysis spelled worse trouble:

> I must get well.
> Walk on strong legs, leap the hurdles of sense,
> Reason again, come back to my old patchwork logic,
> Addition, subtraction, money, clothes, clocks,
> Memories (freesias, smelling slightly of snow and of flesh
> In a room with blue curtains) ambition, despair.
> I must feel again who had given feeling over,
> Challenge laughter, take tears, play the piano,
> Form judgments, blame a crude world for disaster.

She could see herself traduced by her adolescent dreamworld. She was still the sixteen-year-old who played the piano scene from *Pelléas and Mélisande* over and over, intoxicated by a Symbolist vision of impossible beauty and passion, though so far it had failed her utterly in her actual life. But what was there to do with her disillusionment? Should she "play the pavanne / For a dead child or the scene where that girl / Lets fall her hair, and the loud chords descend / As though her hair were metal, clashing along / Over the tower, and a dumb chord receives it?" She had to free herself from her own destroying dreams. Self-mockery was one way, the option within the actual poem. In life, it was work that offered another way out of her emotional impasse. In "Portrait of the Artist as a Young Woman," she sees herself sitting on the edge of her bed, writing

> In terror and panic—but with the moment's courage, summoned up
>   from God knows where.
> Without recourse to saints or angels: a Bohemian, thinking herself free—
> A young thin girl without sense, living (she thought) on passion and air.

Severe psychic pain was a daily fact of life. It had been so from early childhood and it would continue to be so. Early in 1922 it reached an especially acute point. She needed to get away from New York and live alone, where she could write without concern over immediate magazine acceptance. She had a new lover, who had money and later followed her to Europe, but for the time being she wanted to be free of him. Intending to spend six months writing and studying piano in Vienna, she boarded the S.S. *Homeric* on Monday, April 17th, and arrived in Paris by April 24th. There, after a short time spent inspecting the Boulevard Saint Germain, Clichy, and Montmartre, she went on to Zurich, and from there to Vienna, arriving on April 29th.

She has left detailed impressions of her stay in this city, which entered her imagination with a power not unlike the discovery of responsive love. One of her first aesthetic errands was a visit to Schoenbrunn, where she drank in the gardens and fountains, the Baroque architecture and rococo interiors. Just seven doors away from the house where Freud lived she took a room at Number 12 Berggasse with a parquet floor and walls "bearing the images of the Empress Elizabeth and two men climbing a snowy hill." In the salon there stood a big Bechstein, surrounded by "curled and dusty tinsel lace." The landlady, Frau Weinberger, "a widow with a beautiful voice," who "loved an engineer in Baden bei Wien," dusted the chairs every morning, "peering at the woodwork and upholstery through her lorgnette."

Bogan soon arranged a routine of reading and at least trying to write. Mornings she spent in cafés, afternoons she took walks, visited the countryside, and rode the tram to Grinzing for music lessons with a student of Leschetizky's. The acute anguish which her travels had been intended to alleviate did not let up. She still suffered "mindlessly, without reference to events, to reality, to time." Yet she had moments of pleasure and peace:

> The armoire broods and the bed engulfs; the café is warm at ten;
> The lindens give out their scent, the piano its scales; the trams rumble;
>   the shadows in the formal garden take
> The half-attentive gaze of the still-young woman, who will grieve again.

Through the haze of anguish, she noted the light falling against the windows and walls of the Baroque architecture she immediately and passionately loved. She looked at the solidity of buildings and statues, and later remembered the cobblestones, the pensions, the spring leaves and the shadows they cast:

It was a beautiful and a fallen city, smelling of mould, decorated with pediments on which bronze horses, their chariots, and their charioteers, leaped forward, in nineteenth-century arrogance; full of trees touchingly arranged along paths of beaten earth; full of cafés, courtyards, fountains, with broken statues wearing roses and crowns; the stone edge of their basins bore pots of geraniums; full of women's voices singing and the smell of fresh bread in the morning; full of the lumpy and the dead.

She had dreamed of inhabiting such a city, so rich with the forms of civilization, ever since, drunk on the potted palms of the Hotel Oxford, she had taken her drawing lessons and listened to tales of Miss Cooper's travels "abroad." She wrote in her diary, on May 11th: "Beginning to love the walk through the Burg gardens—first the square with the Maria Theresa statue—Then the square where the two horsemen in bronze rear above the lilacs—with the Rathaus spindly in the distance—Then the old Burg . . . and the statues of the labors of Hercules." She was seeking deliverance and renewal, and escape from memories it was easier to confront in a foreign city with its envelope of privacy. Walking through the city, "wrapped in the deadening dream," one night, in the Redoutensale, the large formal reception hall in the Hofburg, she "remembered oil lamps," those fixtures of her mother's morning life, when, with her large hands, she would cut the wicks and fill the bases with oil. One night she dreamed about her brother; on another day she noted in her journal that she felt "remorse concerning Curt." Far from her mother, and from the immediate past, she found joy in music, hearing art-songs for the first time, among them Mahler's *Kindertotenlieder,* which she thereafter always loved, and discovering what became a passion with her, Mozart's music. "He never meant very much to me before," she wrote Italia Iff. "I love his deliciously logical . . . *Sonaten* . . . my music teacher . . . plays them deliciously, so cleanly—like harmony rung on glass."

She read a great deal, including *Anna Karenina* in French and *Portrait of the Artist as a Young Man.* Noting on May 24th that she was "thrilled" to receive the May 10th issue of *The New Republic,* with "Memory" printed beside Elinor Wylie's "Little Sonnet," she remarked that she felt "very confident, and happy" and wrote the first draft of "Girl to Juan," the next day changed to "Girl's Song." The sudden influx of optimism quickly evanesced, and in a short time she began to feel dispirited and homesick. How much the presence of her moneyed lover interfered with her solitude and her writing is, again, open to speculation, but it soon became clear that she was not having a very productive time. Thanking Harriet Monroe for the payment of twenty-two dollars for "Beginning and End," she wrote: "This has been a sort of sabbatical six months, since April, during which I have written nothing. Sometime, when I recover the English language, I want very much to send other things to you. I am coming to the belief that in order to write English, you must, occasionally, hear it spoken!"

Eventually she became exasperated at her continued presence in Vienna. She no longer knew what she was doing there, and complained to her friend Italia that she had experienced nothing, not "grief, passion, heady joy, rage, longing: within the period,—my emotional annals have not been enriched by one jot or tittle." True, she had seen beautiful things, heard beautiful music, and experienced moments of resentment and homesickness. But the poet's everlasting duty to keep watch over her emotions had grown tiresome; as to her "innards," she cried out:

O, let them be! Do you remember how I used to date everything by saying—"When I'm twenty-five"? Life was to become as simple as elementary arithmetic then. But it hain't. I still, to quote Arnold Bennett, feel like a quadratic equation.

Out of this exasperation, however, came "Stanza in Afternoon" ("No longer burn the hands that seized"), later retitled "Stanza," an important poem for Bogan, in which she came to terms with the resolution and termination of her first, and easiest, poetic season. Much of her discontent may have had its root in the recognition that never again would poems simply *come* to her, and it was only years later that she was able to regard these six months as a boon. As she explained it to Theodore Roethke, who had been trying, she felt, to *force* things after a period when poems had similarly just *come,* she too had gone through easy periods and had been obliged to learn how to cope with them. The only thing that had saved her, she said, "after my first lot of acceptances, was the fact that I went to Austria for six months, and couldn't get quick action from editors. Then I stopped writing like magazines, and went back to hard, painfully produced poems that sounded like myself."

So in October she went home for a prolonged stay with her parents and Maidie in Worcester, making plans to go back to New York the following December or January. Meanwhile, she immersed herself in poetry, rereading Yeats's *Responsibilities* and Louise Imogen Guiney, and reading A. E. Housman's *Last Poems,* which made a profound impression upon her. New poems soon came, full of grief and rage, resounding with irony: "My Voice Not Being Proud," "The Romantic," "The Frightened Man," "Men Loved Wholly Beyond Wisdom," "The Changed Woman," "Chanson Un

Peu Naïve," and "Fifteenth Farewell," all of them rich with a piercing knowledge of sexual betrayal and spiritual pride.

She found her way to Robert M. McBride & Company, which brought out *Body of This Death* in the fall of 1923, the same season that saw the publication of a hundred copies of Wallace Stevens's *Harmonium,* one of which Bogan bought in the Old Corner Book-Store in Boston. Her portrait, taken in Vienna, appeared in the October issue of *Vanity Fair,* alongside those of Elinor Wylie, Amy Lowell, Genevieve Taggard, Aline Kilmer, Edna St. Vincent Millay, Sara Teasdale, and Lizette Woodworth Reese, accompanied by the legend, "Distinguished American Women Poets Who Have Made the Lyric Verse Written by Women in America More Interesting Than That of the Men." The photograph shows a young woman with a full, strongly shaped mouth, dark hair waved to frame her oval face, and averted eyes. She holds a carnelian necklace in the long curved fingers of her right hand. Quite without guidance, the provincial girl seeking escape from her parents' domestic misery had become infatuated with Pre-Raphaelite music and Symbolist phantasmagoria, only to find herself, like Yeats, beaten back from her vaporous yearnings by experience and reality. Having learned to suspect whatever came easy, she knew how hard it was to resist the seductions of her own talent and skill. Yet she also understood the necessity of such resistance if she were to forge her already tough and yeasty idiom into a durable material for strong poetic utterance. In that commitment to the process of continuous self-criticism, she became a modernist poet. Her emotional life was by no means resolved. The cycle of depletion and renewal, to be played out in her life again and again, had been established. But whatever else lay in store, the period of beginnings was over.

THE TITLE of Louise Bogan's first book of poems is taken from Romans, 7:24: "O wretched man that I am! Who shall deliver me from the body of this death!" Though Bogan later laughed at its solemnness, the poems in *Body of This Death* echo that cry, presenting existence as a constant struggle between flesh and spirit, desire and will, passion and reason, and time and art.

The title is also possibly an echo from a passage Bogan would have read in Arthur Symons's *The Symbolist Movement in Literature:*

It is the distinction of Mallarmé to have aspired after an impossible liberation of the soul of literature from what is fretting and constraining in "the body of that death," which is the mere literature of words. Words, he has realized, are of value only as a notation of the free breath of the spirit; words, therefore, must be employed with an extreme care, in their choice and adjustment, in setting them to reflect and chime upon one another; yet least of all for their own sake, for what they can never, except by suggestion, express.

As Bogan would have understood the phrase, the "mere literature of words" referred not only to naturalism, but to all literary efforts which fail to convert their materials into a tightly woven fabric of meaning. In the practice of her art, she was not a linguistic mystic who believed, as Symons implies the Symbolists did, that words are inadequate to express, except by indirection, the spirit's essential truths. She was a linguistic pragmatist, who believed that words could mean what they said; the problem was for the writer to have something to say. Bogan was always unfailing in her condemnation of the merely "written" piece of work. Writing built up out of ready-made attitudes, self-delighting and abundant talent, and uncritically applied "technique" was certain to provoke her wrath and ridicule. In her view, the farther the art of language detached itself from the actuality of experience while remaining alive to its ungraspable and anarchic magnitude, the more richly that art justified its claim to approximate and even displace experience.

She later wrote: "The poet represses the outright narrative of his life. He absorbs it, along with life itself. The repressed becomes the poem. Actually, I have written down my experience in the closest detail. But the rough and vulgar facts are not there." For the reader with a copy of *Body of This Death* or any of her other books of poetry in hand, this is a tantalizing statement. To read the poems as autobiography violates their privacy, and their formal presence, yet completes their sense. What Bogan knew, of course, and counted on, was the *aesthetic* irrelevancy of the real-life background to her work. The "code" of reference and allusion, once cracked open by biographical speculation, only reveals so much. Like Emily Dickinson, Bogan searched for the axiomatic and the general in experience rather than the particular.

How, then, does she actually conceal the facts? To begin with, they are tucked away inside a remarkably "objective" presentation. No matter how dramatic her lyrics may be, they exist in a common, public syntax. Bogan compresses and condenses language rather than stretching and fracturing it. She puts this language to work by heightening its character *as* speech. There is little description, but a great deal of *action* in the form of vows, commands, exhortations, reproaches, and warnings which turn the poems into such occasions as farewells, indictments, or commendations. A good many of the poems do not represent an "I," and some that do, such as "The

Frightened Man," are clearly an "other," and not the poet herself. The voice, whether attached to the poet or to an observation or meditation, speaks at a remove from concrete circumstance and context. Furthermore, the formal perfection of Bogan's versification enhances the poetry's distance from the personal. Apart from her free-verse poems, Bogan's meters are those traditional to the shorter English lyric from the Middle Ages through the Renaissance and the Romantic period: quatrains in iambic tetrameter; six- and eight-line stanzas in iambic and trochaic trimeter and pentameter; rhymed couplets; varieties of common meter; sonnets and songs. Her mastery of the art of substituting metrical feet for variety and emphasis is paralleled in American poetry only by Robert Frost; her sense of the texture of sound, through vowels and consonants, magnificent. Perhaps from the study of Latin poetry in high school she attuned her ear to long vowels drawn out as if to an extra beat: *low, whole, find, mind, praise, die, fly;* and rich consonants: *chill, hill, boast, most, axe, lax.* She uses rhyme with overt enjoyment of its resonance and function, situating end-rhymes with maximum effects of contrast and association. The pleasure in language that breathes through her poetry is truly physical.

For metaphorical texture she draws figures from the same tradition on which she relies for her versification, the Elizabethan, "Metaphysical," and later seventeenth-century lyric. Bogan uses words like *rage, tongue, mind, heart,* and *fire* much as her Renaissance forebears did, allowing them to gather metonymic and emblematic senses and mixing their traditional and conventional meanings with private associations.

Bogan organized *Body of This Death* as a sequence of moods. The voice changes from poem to poem, remaining richly itself, yet achieving complete utterance with each fresh mastering of emotion in form. The taste awakened by "the sudden marigolds" expresses itself fully with deliberate effects of contrast and design. Only six of the poems had never been published before: "Sub Contra," "A Letter," "Ad Castitatem (To Chastity)," "Epitaph for a Romantic Woman," "Song," and "Sonnet." The rest had already seen print.

The book was dedicated to Bogan's mother and daughter and on the whole exhibits a strong identification with female experience, not all of it viewed sympathetically. It was the fruit of that period in Bogan's life when she herself had made the transition from being her mother's child to her child's mother, and had the driving clarity of a newly won independence of mind. The poems seek meaning in the life lived passionately and even recklessly; they attempt an understanding of it, and a reconciliation with it. The very first poem ("A Tale"), which has remained at the front of all of Louise Bogan's collected editions, is haunted by this search. Its "source" is the decision to marry Alexander and go to Panama with him—dissembled, of course, in a purely metaphoric fable that contained nearly everything she would ever have to say as a poet:

> This youth too long has heard the break
> Of waters in a land of change.
> He goes to see what suns can make
> From soil more indurate and strange.
>
> He cuts what holds his days together
> And shuts him in, as lock on lock:
> The arrowed vane announcing weather,
> The tripping racket of a clock;
>
> Seeking, I think, a light that waits
> Still as a lamp upon a shelf,—
> A land with hills like rocky gates
> Where no sea leaps upon itself.
>
> But he will find that nothing dares
> To be enduring, save where, south
> Of hidden deserts, torn fire glares
> On beauty with a rusted mouth,—
>
> Where something dreadful and another
> Look quietly upon each other.

First published in *The New Republic* in October 1921, it is one of the earliest poems in the collection, and Bogan was extremely proud of it. Robert Frost remarked, after reading it, "That woman will be able to do anything." Curiously, the "youth" is Bogan herself, transformed into a young man for the sake of a "framing" detachment through which she sees her actions as an escape from turmoil and a quest for transcendence. The contemplative introjection of "I think" in the third stanza not only draws attention to the story *as* a story, but suggests again how separate from the matter, and even skeptical of it, the poet is. The poem's riddling tone belongs to someone who sounds somehow *returned* from a sight too terrible for ordinary human eyes, and there is reproach in the last stanza.

The poem which follows, "Medusa," moves beyond "A Tale" in dramatizing the meeting of "something dreadful and another," but it reverses the prediction of the first poem, since this fatal meeting has led not to endurance but to its horrible inversion, immobilization. Again, as in "A Tale," the poem tells a story. The speaker approaches a house "in a cave of trees," and suddenly:

> . . . the bare eyes were before me
> And the hissing hair,
> Held up at a window, seen through a door.
> The stiff bald eyes, the serpents on the forehead
> Formed in the air.

This Medusa is known and recognized; she has been seen before. The speaker violates some unknown taboo by entering this site of freedom and movement, and in punishment is turned to stone. Afterward, like the voice of Emily Dickinson's "Because I could not stop for Death," she speaks from the "dead scene" which had once been alive with "Sun and reflection." Recounting the experience and thereby reenacting it, the speaker is no longer a living body, but "like a shadow," arrested in the equally deadened landscape. This is the dreadful equilibrium of stasis:

> And I shall stand here like a shadow
> Under the great balanced day,
> My eyes on the yellow dust, that was lifting in the wind,
> And does not drift away.

Bogan was so little given to invention that we do no violence to the poem to regard it as a transcribed dream. Theodore Roethke called it "a breakthrough to great poetry, the whole piece welling up from the unconscious, dictated as it were." Interpreting it in psychoanalytic (chiefly Jungian) terms, he saw it as a struggle with the Anima, according to which the house in the cave is a "womb within a womb," and the Medusa the "man-in-the-womb, mother—*her* mother, possibly." Certainly it makes sense to see this terrifying figure as a much-transformed memory of the desired and destructive mother. From this central meaning flows yet another, in which the poem can be read as an allegory of the fate of the imagination when it goes forward to meet itself unprotected. Art requires the shield of form, of the mature personality's defenses, of experience. The speaker transformed into a statue or *thing,* imprisoned in memory, closes the poem, as Roethke points out, on "the self-revelation, the terrible finality of the ultimate traumatic experience." She is locked inside her own speech.

The next poem—the first one about music in the Bogan canon—offers the utter antithesis to this stony paralysis. The title, "Sub Contra," refers to the resonating, very lowest notes of the "tuned frame of strings" (whether piano, cello, or bass viol), and the poem begins quietly, as if it were actually sounding these notes, only to rise and reverberate "Like the mockery in a shell." This shell figure is important, a symbol Bogan uses again, and one linking her to Yeats, who speaks, in "Adam's Curse," for instance, of the shell, "Washed by time's waters as they rose and fell," and from whom Bogan takes the notion (long established in Romantic poetry) of the shell as a chamber echoing earthly, mortal rhythms, such as the pulse, the breath, and the sea. As the rhythm gathers in "Sub Contra," the sealed-in mind surrenders to an outpouring of remembered feeling:

> Lest the brain forget the thunder
> The roused heart once made it hear,—
> Let there sound from music's root
> One note rage can understand,
> A fine noise of riven things.
> Build there some thick chord of wonder;
> Then, for every passion's sake,
> Beat upon it till it break.

The next poem, "A Letter," again lays bare the central conflict of *Body of This Death*. Its speaker has fled from the "land of change," or the world of unstable human relations, but as she ruminates upon the purgatorial indecisiveness of escape, she becomes increasingly responsive to the human world she has left behind. Conflict mounts, as do despair and disgust, until resolution is attempted through a shifting and equally unsatisfactory nihilism—another reason, apart from the poem's high degree of personal revelation, why Bogan struck it out of later collected editions. Just when she wrote the poem is unknown, but it was one of the few previously unpublished works in the book, and I suspect that the "you" to whom it refers at the end is John Coffey:

> This may be wisdom: abstinence, beauty is nothing,
> That you regret me, that I feign defiance.
> And now I have written you this, it is nothing.

The only overt allusion in the poem to a broken love affair, it supplies a conclusive reason for the mood of spiritual desolation. But ultimately the poem remains unresolved. The letter-writer trapped in her own vacillations is another victim of arrested life.

THE ARRESTED LIFE is the trapped and imprisoned life, the life out of step with natural time. Yet freedom, to the fearful and hesitant heart, is perilous, never more so than when it appears as the possibility of love, as in "The Frightened Man":

In fear of the rich mouth
I kissed the thin,—
Even that was a trap
To snare me in.

Even she, so long
The frail, the scentless,
Is become strong
And proves relentless.

O, forget her praise,
And how I sought her
Through a hazardous maze
By shafted water.

One of the puzzling things about *Body of This Death* is the way Bogan makes herself into a youth in "A Tale" and supplies a male voice for "The Frightened Man." In the first poem she is taking a hard critical look at her rejection of New England; in the second, she is taking, I suspect, a hard cynical look at an ex-lover. Putting the words, "O, forget her praise," in the mouth of the poem's speaker is a way of making him—whoever he might be—commit an act of exquisite pusillanimity.

Many of the poems emphasize their character as speech. The act of speaking, the mouth, and the voice in Louise Bogan's poetry are heavily erotic: words and love and anger are all bound up together. As "A Letter" is an explicit demonstration in words, so "Words for Departure" becomes a ritual of speech, an address to an estranged lover who has taken another lover. It recreates one scene of the last afternoon the lovers had spent together, when, awaking to a world fresh with rain and approaching night, they achieved a moment of perfect union:

Hand clasped hand,
Forehead still bowed to forehead—
Nothing was lost, nothing possessed,
There was no gift nor denial.

This moment of perfect connection is simultaneously a moment of pure estrangement. The terrible *balance* of endings is felt.

In the next section the estrangement has come to pass. But the speaking voice remembers and repossesses the lover in language that shows how beautifully Bogan could bend Imagist practice to feeling all her own:

> I have remembered you.
> You were not the town visited once,
> Nor the road falling behind running feet.
>
> You were as awkward as flesh
> And lighter than frost or ashes.

In the third section her valedictory nostalgia turns into high-handedness as she exhorts the ex-lover to join his new lover (with whom he appears to be already well settled). But after he has enjoyed the affair, he must break it off, she advises, with less finality and more open-endedness than he seems to have displayed toward the speaker herself. Bogan later kept the poem out of her collected editions, feeling its ending was too dependent on a fashionable and utterly insincere "Greenwich Village" attitude of toleration toward sexual rivals. Another reason she may have rejected the poem was that she disliked its form. The free verse of "Betrothed" and "Words for Departure" and the sometimes unwieldy decasyllabics of "A Letter" offered her little enough in the way of resistance, whereas traditional meters gave her plenty of opportunities for the building and breaking of rhythms. Bogan works in free verse in "Ad Castitatem," but she formalizes the speech with a slow, ritualistic idiom: "I invoke you," "I call upon you," "Hear me," which have accompanying gestures: "I make the old sign," "I hold your offerings— / Water, and a stone." She calls upon Chastity, "Who have not known you," as a suppliant:

> In this ravaged country,
> In this season not yours,
> You having no season,
> I call upon you without echo.
> Hear me, infertile,
> Beautiful futility.

In its high diction, and its longing for release from the sexual world to a state beyond desire and change, this poem, like "The Frightened Man," reveals Bogan's alignment with the poetry of Edna St. Vincent Millay, Sara Teasdale, and Elinor Wylie. In "The Singing-Woman from the World's Edge," a poem published in *A Few Figs from Thistles* in 1920, Millay sounded the keynote of contemporary female lyricism when she said she sang in the accents of "a harlot and a nun." This ambivalence about sexual identity shows up as well in Elinor Wylie's and Sara Teasdale's poems, many of which, like Bogan's, rely on a renewal of the traditional poetic battle between the spirit and the flesh. In their poetry the unappeasable search for renewable chastity serves as a female form of quest myth, in which the seeker's goal, as Teasdale puts it, is to become as "self-complete as a flower or a stone." In the poem "Sanctuary," Wylie builds on the figure of the spirit as bricklayer, constructing brick by brick "my marvelous wall so thick / Dead nor living may shake its strength." The cell of dreams, however, turns out to be airtight: "How can I breathe? *You can't, you fool!*"

Yet, knowing what Wylie knew about the futility of solipsism, Bogan went on from the stern invocations of "Ad Castitatem" to the pure acceptance of "Knowledge." This poem was the last in the group called "Beginning and End," which had appeared in the August 1922 issue of *Poetry: A Magazine of Verse*. Of the five poems (the others were "Elders," "Resolve," "Leave-Taking," and "To a Dead Lover"), "Knowledge" was the only one Bogan thought well enough of to include in *Body of This Death*. It is a summing-up after the mostly elegiac labors of the four other poems, moving from a seventeenth-century plainness in its first stanza to a perfect Romantic image in its second:

> Now that I know
> How passion warms little
> Of flesh in the mould,
> And treasure is brittle,—
>
> I'll lie here and learn
> How, over their ground,
> Trees make a long shadow
> And a light sound.

It is one of Bogan's consummate lyrics, its movement supple with unexpected pauses and emphases, its change of tone, from stanza to stanza, dramatic and yet unforced. To learn the sound and shadow of trees is to learn mortality, the poetry of earth, the facts and limits of human existence. Yet Louise Bogan knew that women, who crave "passion" and "treasure," as she uses the words in "Knowledge," have much to fear from time. The woman who is dead in "Portrait" has been delivered from the humiliations of sexual rejection and age: she is, at last, "possessed by time, who once / Was loved by men." The love men bear women, in Bogan's view, imprisons women in a fiction that denies their true nature, as in one of her most ironic poems of this period, "The Romantic":

> Admit the ruse to fix and name her chaste
> With those who sleep the spring through, one and one,
> Cool nights, when laurel builds up, without haste,
> Its precise flower, like a pentagon.

In her obedient breast, all that ran free
You thought to bind, like echoes in a shell.
At the year's end, you promised, it would be
The unstrung leaves, and not her heart, that fell.

So the year broke and vanished on the screen
You cast about her; summer went to haws.
This, by your leave, is what she should have been,—
Another man will tell you what she was.

To the romantic, the woman he cherishes is to be thought of with those who remain unawakened by spring, who are, in other words, unaware of their own erotic natures. But the image of spring as the time when laurel builds up its flower suggests a covert, inexorable sensuality existing independent of any man's fantasy. The use of "Romantic" in the poem's title is pejorative, the epithet for a self-deluding fool who would impose his wish upon reality. But in "Epitaph for a Romantic Woman," a poem Bogan inexplicably left out of later editions, the word has a different, and tragically ironic, sense:

She has attained the permanence
She dreamed of, where old stones lie sunning.
Untended stalks blow over her
Even and swift, like young men running.

Always in the heart she loved
Others had lived,—she heard their laughter.
She lies where none has lain before,
Where certainly none will follow after.

In both "The Romantic" and "Epitaph for a Romantic Woman," Bogan's speech is at once high-minded, rich, pointed, and ambiguous. "Admit the ruse" begins "The Romantic," its cajolery an accusation that develops to a harsh indictment. The peaceful declaratives of "Epitaph for a Romantic Woman" tell a tale of passion and defeat as bitter as two brief stanzas can contain. Such speech, in 1923, was daring, and is still trenchant. Bogan's skill in weaving high sexual irony with speech of utmost simplicity works beautifully in "My Voice Not Being Proud," a poem in which she takes a swipe at what her friend and fellow-poet Léonie Adams used to call the "Oh-God-the-pain-girls," ingenue poets of Bogan's and Adams's generation who plaintively descanted on the self-destructive elements common to their erotic lives as women. It's possible that Bogan had Millay's "The Shroud" in mind, from the 1917 volume *Renascence,* in which the speaker shrilly proclaims her readiness to die in punishment for having acted with undue premarital haste; in reaction to the hysterical tone of that poem, and others like it, she wrote, in the first stanza:

> My voice, not being proud
> Like a strong woman's, that cries
> Imperiously aloud
> That death disarm her, lull her—
> Screams for no mourning color
> Laid menacingly, like fire,
> Over my long desire.

To *cry aloud* and *scream for* are extremes we associate with a child's frustration and rage (and possibly Bogan's mother's fits of temper). By contrast, the speaker's strong, determined avowals have the concentration of utmost will, though she disclaims both pride and strength. Such determination proclaims its integrity:

> It will end, and leave no print.
> As you lie, I shall lie:
> Separate, eased and cured.
> Whatever is wasted or wanted
> In this country of glass and flint
> Some garden will use, once planted.
> As you lie alone, I shall lie,
> O, in singleness assured,
> Deafened by mire and lime.
> - I remember, while there is time.

With the last line, the poem's voice confronts all the temptations— without naming them—that can crumble her determination, and suggests that her quiet, Cordelia-like sanity is achieved only by damming up an enormous pressure of feeling. With "The Alchemist," one of the superb poems of the Bogan canon, she returns to the battle between will and emotion. The "Metaphysical" elements of paradox and conceit, which have often been noted in her poetry, find strong expression here:

> I burned my life, that I might find
> A passion wholly of the mind,
> Thought divorced from eye and bone,
> Ecstasy come to breath alone.
> I broke my life, to seek relief
> From the flawed light of love and grief.

> With mounting beat the utter fire
> Charred existence and desire.
> It died low, ceased its sudden thresh.
> I had found unmysterious flesh—
> Not the mind's avid substance—still
> Passionate beyond the will.

Published in *The New Republic* in February 1922, the poem can only refer to the roiling period of 1919–1921 in Bogan's life, when she left Alexander and struck out on her own. Other poems from that time speak of her restlessness and suffering, but in "The Alchemist" she confronts the spectacle of her life with Yeatsian directness and honesty. Though we cannot know precisely what experiences led to the poem, we don't need to. It is enough to know that it is a lonely and wise poem, written by a woman of no more than twenty-five, who understood the irreducible nature of passion and desire, and the final failure of deliberate schemes to overcome them.

Bogan's insights into her own sex are often uneasy. Crankily sympathetic with women, she was nevertheless aware, through her own mistakes and her acute observations of others, of the ways in which women seem to perpetuate their own patterns of defeat and failure, and with these she was impatient. In "Men Loved Wholly Beyond Wisdom" she finds an exact image to evoke the terrible flaw in the way women love men:

> Like a fire in a dry thicket
> Rising within women's eyes
> Is the love men must return.

She then moves from this general observation to the hard personal lesson she finds in the poem's series of *aperçus:*

> Heart, so subtle now, and trembling,
> What a marvel to be wise,
> To love never in this manner!
> To be quiet in the fern
> Like a thing gone dead and still,
> Listening to the prisoned cricket
> Shake its terrible, dissembling
> Music in the granite hill.

Though it begins as observation, the poem turns into revelation, as the speaker counsels herself to hold back the very passion she disparages, completing the poem with a Yeatsian landscape of mastered emotion. The consuming devouring force of love, the "fire in a dry thicket," with its fierce sexuality, must be resisted. The lack of proportion characterizing the love "beyond wisdom" is what is wrong with women in general. In "Women," one of Bogan's most well-known poems, she complains:

> Women have no wilderness in them,
> They are provident instead,
> Content in the tight hot cell of their hearts
> To eat dusty bread.
>
> They do not see cattle cropping red winter grass,
> They do not hear
> Snow water going down under culverts
> Shallow and clear.
>
> They wait, when they should turn to journeys,
> They stiffen, when they should bend.
> They use against themselves that benevolence
> To which no man is friend.
>
> They cannot think of so many crops to a field
> Or of clean wood cleft by an axe.
> Their love is an eager meaninglessness
> Too tense, or too lax.
>
> They hear in every whisper that speaks to them
> A shout and a cry.
> As like as not, when they take life over their door-sills
> They should let it go by.

Bogan is highly specific about women's shortcomings. Their senses are stunted, their imaginations dull, their claims upon the world meager and modest. They put up with their lot; they miss the pleasures of planning, work, and rest. They are limited, misplaced in their kindness, and out of step with the true nature of feeling. They blunder, misjudge, hold back, and in every way defeat themselves. Bogan may have been thinking about another poem; in "Women," Lizette Woodworth Reese had written:

> Some women herd such little things—a box
> Oval and glossy, in its gilt and red,
> Or squares of satin, or a high, dark bed—
> But when love comes, they drive to it all their flocks;
> Yield up their crooks; take little; gain for fold
> And pasture each a small forgotten grave.
> When they are gone, then lesser women crave

And squander their sad hoards; their shepherds' gold.
Some gather life like faggots in a wood,
And crouch its blaze, without a thought at all
Past warming their pinched selves to the last spark.
And women as a whole are swift and good,
In humor scarce, their measure being small;
They plunge and leap, yet somehow miss the dark.

While it is gentler than Bogan's "Women," Reese's poem also projects women as self-diminishing, and both poems share the notion that women are by nature tinged with defective wills, "their measure being small." The unexpected point of view in Bogan's poem, and not in Reese's, and the unavoidable problem, is its obvious *envy* of maleness. Bogan's poem is full of it. Only men, it implies, are capable of broad, unfettered, unselfconscious action. Behind the invidious comparisons lurks the familiar spectre of paralysis; women, it seems, are given to formlessness, ineffectuality, and, therefore, immobility.

Yet no one should base a complete judgment of Bogan's attitudes toward women on "Women" alone. In "The Crows," for example, she perceives courage in the woman who chooses love in old age:

The woman who has grown old
And knows desire must die,
Yet turns to love again,
Hears the crows' cry.

She is a stem long hardened,
A weed that no scythe mows.
The heart's laughter will be to her
The crying of the crows.

Who slide in the air with the same voice
Over what yields not and what yields,
Alike in spring, and when there is only bitter
Winter-burning in the fields.

Bogan was an astute observer of contemporary sexual mores, and pulled off another ironic turn on the O-God-the-pain motif in "Chanson Un Peu Naïve." First published in 1923 in the appropriately sophisticated *Vanity Fair,* it looks incisively at the compulsive misapplication of erotic energy to be found in the promiscuous ingenue:

What body can be ploughed,
Sown, and broken yearly?

> She would not die, she vowed,
> But she has, nearly.
> > Sing, heart, sing;
> > Call and carol clearly.
>
> And, since she could not die,
> Care would be a feather,
> A film over the eye
> Of two that lie together.
> > Fly, song, fly,
> > Break your little tether.
>
> So from strength concealed
> She makes her pretty boast:
> Pain is a furrow healed
> And she may love you most.
> > Cry, song, cry,
> > And hear your crying lost.

The poem is a product of its time, and takes a critical view of "free love," implying that the woman who journeys along the path of impossible, ravaging love affairs is no true heroine, but a self-deluding victim of willful vanity. Her carelessness and imperviousness stem from dishonesty and weakness, yet the destructive cycle repeats itself in the compound of exhaustion, self-deception, and bravado that is the girl's "strength concealed." When she "makes her pretty boast" of having suffered and of yet having remained indomitable, the new lover is seduced into seeing that newfangled creature, the experienced modern woman. Yet the wistful Opheliesque refrains grieve for the naïve part of the spirit which sees the truth and mourns it. Worst of all, there is the inability to resist or change the pattern. "Fly, song, fly, / Break your little tether" holds out the wish for complete severance from emotional subjection. So, once again, the poem deals with paralysis and entrapment.

With so many poems in *Body of This Death* concerned with the wounded and spiritually "ravaged" woman, it is easy to get the impression that Bogan was mired, as a poet and a woman, in a swampland of erotic anguish. In "The Changed Woman," however, she envisions the wounded woman as she awakens once again to life, healed and restored:

> The cracked glass fuses at a touch,
> The wound heals over, and is set
> In the whole flesh, and is not much
> Quite to remember or forget.

The process of self-healing is dramatized even more rigorously in "Fifteenth Farewell." Louise Bogan was at one of her several bests when bidding farewell to an unworthy lover. (She called it the "to-hell-my-love-with-you" mode, adding, "Perhaps we gals are at our best on that note.") Not that she was always successful at such dismissals; by its very title, the poem wittily tells us how hard they are to carry off. After all, this is the *fifteenth* try. The very anger with which the speaker at first addresses the lover gives us a clue about her difficulties. What has taken place seems to have been nothing less than a full commitment; what is now required is, equally, little short of a full break:

> You may have all things from me, save my breath,
> The slight life in my throat will not give pause
> For your love, nor your loss, nor any cause.

She richly feels the strength of her own bodily life:

> Cooler than stones in wells, sweeter, more kind
> Than hot, perfidious words, my breathing moves
> Close to my plunging blood. Be strong, and hang
> Unriven mist over my breast and mind,
> My breath! We shall forget the heart that loves,
> Though in my body beat its blade, and its fang.

Here, sheer force of will overcomes the heart, a deliberate obscuring and dulling of feeling. Only by such force can the strength of feeling be measured. Yet, in a fine shift of mood, the second sonnet reveals such resolution to be excessively strict. The voice in the poem now speaks to a very different tempo: calm, reflective, all rage spent. Loneliness is not "the wide / Scent of mown grass over forsaken fields, / Or any shadow isolation yields." Loneliness *was* the lover's wounding remoteness:

> Your thought, beyond my touch, was tilted air
> Ringed with as many borders as the wind.
> How could I judge you gentle or unkind
> When all bright flying space was in your care?

Now that she is leaving the lover, she discriminates again between the loneliness felt at his side and the loneliness she is going out to meet:

> Now that I leave you, I shall be made lonely
> By simple empty days,—never that chill

> Resonant heart to strike between my arms
> Again, as though distraught for distance,—only
> Levels of evening, now, behind a hill,
> Or a late cock-crow from the darkening farms.

The sexual dignity of withdrawal from the distant lover is fused with the dignity of solitude and peace as she becomes, once again, as she had in "Knowledge," a woman capable of renouncing passion (and possession of the loved man) for an open acceptance of time, with its augurs, in the ending of day, of finality and death.

The rest of the poems in *Body of This Death* do not form thematic clusters so much as they work as independent pieces, which will expand, in later poems, into Bogan's enduring preoccupations. With "Memory" we get some access to what may well have been her understanding of psychoanalysis. Published in *The New Republic* in May 1922, while she was in Vienna, it's more than likely that the poem was written during the months preceding her departure, when she was in treatment with Dr. Tannenbaum. It may be his urgings which she transmuted into the poem's voice:

> Do not guard this as rich stuff without mark
> Closed in a cedarn dark,
> Nor lay it down with tragic masks and greaves,
> Licked by the tongues of leaves.
>
> Nor let it be as eggs under the wings
> Of helpless, startled things,
> Nor encompassed by song, nor any glory
> Perverse and transitory.
>
> Rather, like shards and straw upon coarse ground,
> Of little worth when found,—
> Rubble in gardens, it and stones alike,
> That any spade may strike.

Although it is difficult to speculate upon the psychoanalytic significance of events in the 1919–1923 period of Bogan's life, one reason for her journey to Vienna in the spring of 1922 may have been her exact but unconscious dread of the psychoanalytic process, from which her departure may be understood as a hasty retreat. Considering her lifelong aversion to direct reminiscence, she may well have reached a point where the work of producing memories had become too painful to bear, and the subsequent disaffection and homesickness she experienced in Vienna may have been part of a desolation following this evasion. The shards, straw, and rubble may have struck the fastidious and frightened young woman as unbearably messy and unclean.

Her sense of paralysis, for the most part implicit in a good many of these early poems, is expressed directly in "Statue and Birds." Published a month before "Memory," in *The New Republic* in April 1922, the month she sailed for Europe, the poem is the culmination of the phase that had begun in late adolescence with "Poplar Garden," with its garden and statue. Now the same scene, looked at more closely, and cleared of Swinburnean vapor, appears again:

> Here, in the withered arbor, like the arrested wind,
> Straight sides, carven knees,
> Stands the statue, with hands flung out in alarm
> Or remonstrances.
>
> Over the lintel sway the woven bracts of the vine
> In a pattern of angles.
> The quill of the fountain falters, woods rake on the sky
> Their brusque tangles.
>
> The birds walk by slowly, circling the marble girl,
> The golden quails,
> The pheasants, closed up in their arrowy wings,
> Dragging their sharp tails.
>
> The inquietudes of the sap and of the blood are spent.
> What is forsaken will rest.
> But her heel is lifted,—she would flee,—the whistle of the birds
> Fails on her breast.

This "marble girl" has been turned to stone, it would appear, by some terrible sight or assailant. She is another version of the speaker in "Medusa," delivered from the "inquietudes of the sap and of the blood" into arrested life. But this time the cause of her immobilization is not necessarily neurosis or depression, but the permanence of art itself, by which the girl, delivered from time, has become perfect, stable, and complete. Her lifted heel, however, turns the poem into a "cold pastoral." Art must be freed from its prison of form to leave "the withered arbor" of artifice.

With "Last Hill in a Vista," a Yeatsian rogue-song, such deliverance is partially achieved. It was published in *The Measure* in November 1922, possibly written soon after Bogan returned from Europe, and it implies a reconciliation with the "dirt" of experience:

> Come, let us tell the weeds in ditches
> How we are poor, who once had riches
> And lie out in the sparse and sodden
> Pastures that the cows have trodden,
> The while an autumn night seals down
> The comforts of the wooden town.

This "Last Hill," whether reached through psychoanalytic insight or general spiritual and practical acceptance, is one of Bogan's most important psychic locations. As the site of maximum exposure and least convention, it marks the "more fragile boundary" where art and instinct meet, where the poem's "we" can merge with straw and rubble and soil, freed of guilt and punishment, and where, rather than shrinking from life, the common passions run to meet it.

When "Statue and Birds" and "Last Hill in a Vista" are read together, they tell us that even at the beginning of her life as a poet, Louise Bogan had discovered that the high art of the formal lyric must serve a passionate anti-formalism in life. During her last few days in Vienna, it struck her that writing poetry was going to become, for her, far more difficult than it had ever been before, for the paradoxical reason that it had become too easy, too much a matter of talent and technical mastery. The poem called "Stanza," originally titled "Stanza in Afternoon," which she wrote on Sunday, September 10, 1922, is an unsparing statement on the subject of burned-out creative precocity. The "Small wreaths from branches scarcely green" are Bogan's first poems, the bulk of which formed *Body of This Death*, and, as the figure implies, she considered them premature and immature. The febrile visions and the hunger for a more-than-human beauty of which they speak have dissipated, leaving only "cloud that men may look upon." With the final two lines, "Leda forgets the wings of the swan; / Danaë has swept the gold away," Bogan makes it clear that even her first exhilarating encounters with inspiration have resolved themselves into the disaffection of experience.

New work lay ahead, and it would have to be cut from the cloth of what she had become, and that was a person whose large natural talent was almost beside the point. The poetry would no longer spring from the gift for poetry, but from its meaning as a source of deliverance and reconciliation. What had been the means of escape would have to become the means of return.

While many of the poems in *Body of This Death* engage in the war between her various embattled inclinations, the book ends neither with exhaustion nor despair. Its last poem, "Sonnet," is a defiant surge of independence:

Since you would claim the sources of my thought
Recall the meshes whence it sprang unlimed,
The reedy traps which other hands have timed
To close upon it. Conjure up the hot
Blaze that it cleared so cleanly, or the snow
Devised to strike it down. It will be free.
Whatever nets draw in to prison me
At length your eyes must turn to watch it go.

My mouth, perhaps, may learn one thing too well,
My body hear no echo but its own,
Yet will the desperate mind, maddened and proud,
Seek out the storm, escape the bitter spell
That we obey, strain to the wind, be thrown
Straight to its freedom in the thunderous cloud.

Whoever the "you" of the poem may be, the poet turns upon that figure with savage resistance. Even at the risk of solipsism, the mind will belong only to itself. As in "Last Hill in a Vista," danger will be chosen, if it means freedom, and the poem's final affirmations suggest that despite Bogan's vigorously expressed dislike of the Romantics, she was a Romantic poet through and through. Although in matters of form she did not hold to the Romantic doctrine that the poem should imitate the shape of the thought processes which brought it into being, but was a classicist who firmly held that a poem must obey laws of form imposed by tradition, there resounds through the poise of her syntax and the tissue of her metaphor the Romantic's hunger for all possible freedom of spirit. Such freedom was not, she had realized in "Sonnet," to be found in "the thunderous cloud," or, in "The Alchemist," in "passion wholly of the mind," but could exist only in the assent to time, earth, and the body, which, as she was forced to learn again and again, are as sordid as they are sublime.

REVIEWERS, ON THE WHOLE, whether they liked *Body of This Death* or not, found the poems too obscure. Mark Van Doren, proclaiming in *The Nation* that the book was "packed as tightly with pure poetry as any thirty pages have been for a generation," sympathetically observed that the poems came from "some ultimate source" too intense for language, and A. Donald Douglas, in *The New Republic,* showed a similar benevolence in noting that the very fierceness and pride of the poems earned them the title of obscurity "in all its dignity. They don't present words like glass beads traded to worshipful savages. They don't seduce the eyes with a metallic brilliance of figurines wrought upon a brazen screen." But Robert

L. Wolf, who was married to Bogan's friend and fellow-poet Genevieve Taggard, was less generous, and complained that "her words too often lockstep upon themselves, like prisoners of some terrible intensity," while other reviewers found the verse fitfully and uncertainly trying to express the inexpressible. "Her words are like the rough marble before the sculptor has applied his chisel . . ." wrote the unsigned reviewer in *The Dial;* "they are crudely hewn, jagged, and often only obscurely significant; the author appears to be grappling with substantial but formless conceptions which she cannot mould either because she has not the power, because she is insufficiently practised, or because she lacks the patience of the skilled artist." John Weaver, the curmudgeonly reviewer of *The Brooklyn Eagle,* simply dismissed the book, and in *The Freeman* John Gould Fletcher charged Bogan with "an emptiness of thought that is positively painful."

While the hostile reviews obviously brought little pleasure to the twenty-six-year-old poet, there was much in the favorable ones to encourage her increasingly fervent ambition. Even before the book's publication she was beginning to push herself beyond the accomplished magazine lyric of disabused female experience, and to attempt more acute speculations about nature, time, and fate. The poems she wrote over the next six years and eventually collected in *Dark Summer* (1929) reflect this metaphysical expansion, and have an exciting uncertainty about them, as if Bogan were continually being surprised by new and unsuspected poetic powers.

The appearance of *Body of This Death* marked yet another achievement, and that was Bogan's full participation in the New York literary world. A good many of her lifelong friendships took root during this period and quickly flourished. The most important of these was with Edmund Wilson. She later said that he was one of the first people she met on coming to New York. She may have met him through his first wife, the actress Mary Blair, whom she knew and liked, and had in turn possibly come to know through one of her lovers at the time, an actor, who otherwise disappeared quickly from her life. By April 1923, only shortly after Bogan had returned to New York from Vienna and her Massachusetts stay with her parents, she and Wilson were good friends, and he had noted in his voluminous journals that he'd heard her complain, "I feel ready to say 'Blaa!' to the whole world." Early in March 1924 she sent him a note explaining that she was too busy to see him. Lest this be taken as evidence of a love affair between them, it should be said that Bogan and Wilson were never lovers, not at this time or any other. She later described their relationship to Ruth Limmer as that of sister and brother, characterized by a shared sense of humor and broad-ranging play of mind. Wilson may have wisely sensed that in any struggle for emotional power, he would have been no match for Bogan. She, in her turn, tended to be attracted to men possessing a good deal of conventional romantic charms, and short, high-voiced Wilson was in that respect an unlikely candidate for her affection.

He was two years older than she, and already had a reputation among his contemporaries as a kind of literary elder statesman. He quickly singled out Bogan as a prize, taking her on as a star pupil, so to speak, and concentrating his erotic aspirations on the poet Léonie Adams, the pursuit of whose favors he abandoned only when he discovered that she was determined to remain a virgin. Bogan knew who Adams was, having read her poem "Death and the Lady" in *The New Republic,* and when Wilson introduced the two women to each other in the fall of 1923, Bogan told Adams that the poem had "struck her between the eyes." Adams was a 1922 Barnard graduate, working as a waitress in a Waverly Place restaurant when one of her college roommates, a young anthropology student named Margaret Mead, who held an assistantship at Columbia University under William Fielding Ogburn, professor of sociology and editor of the *Journal of the American Statistical Association,* managed to get her a cataloguing job in Ogburn's office for fifty cents an hour. Mead, who occasionally published poems in *The Measure* and had many friends who were poets, arranged to bring Adams into the Ogburn office, and urged her to get Bogan and Louise Townsend Nicholl, another *Measure* insider, to work there as well. Ogburn enjoyed having an office full of working poets, and used to arrive in the morning with a ready supply of baseball jingles. "See," he would say, after reciting them, "I can write poetry too!" Through Mead, Bogan soon met two distinguished anthropologists who wrote poetry for *The Measure:* Ruth Benedict, author of the highly influential *Patterns of Culture,* who wrote her poetry under the name Ann Singleton, and became a good friend of Bogan's, and Edward Sapir, author of the linguistics classic, *Language.*

Bogan, Wilson, Mead, Adams, Benedict, and Nicholl, along with their lovers and spouses, formed a circle of friends who published in *The Measure, Vanity Fair, The Nation, The New Republic,* and any number of other "small" and "advanced" magazines. They attracted new members from a group consisting of the New York transplants of a poetry enclave that had been started around 1918–19 in San Francisco by Witter Bynner and Eda Lou Walton and maintained in New York by Genevieve Taggard and Rolfe Humphries.

Although Bogan enjoyed her friendships with women poets, in Humphries she found another of her closest, wittiest, warmest, and most loyal friends. In November 1969, in the "Commemorative Tribute to Rolfe Humphries" that she read at a dinner meeting of the American Academy and Institute of Arts and Letters, Bogan stated that she first met Humphries in the fall of 1924, just after he came to New York to teach Latin at Woodmere Academy in Long Island, but they must have met at an earlier date, since she was corresponding with him as early as March 1924, when he was teaching at the Storm King School in Cornwall-on-Hudson.

Humphries was born in Pennsylvania in 1894 and graduated *cum laude* from his father's college, Amherst, in 1915. He went on to lead a machine-gun unit in France as a first lieutenant of infantry in 1917–18. After the Armistice he taught high school in San Francisco, where he met Genevieve Taggard and attended the poetry workshop of Eda Lou Walton and Witter Bynner, people with whom he naturally found himself associated when he came to New York. Bogan recalled that in the early days of their friendship, Humphries presented "a seemingly uncomplicated attitude toward life and art. He was continually belying what was patently a gentle and cultivated nature by flights of rather tough and fanciful humor. He was interested in baseball, in the race-track, in vaudeville and musical revues; and he used these locales in his work, long before Pop art existed."

A skilled Latinist who shared Bogan's dedication to the exquisitely crafted lyric poem, Humphries had a gift for slang, irreverence, and ribaldry, and was adept in the arts of burlesque, parody, and all other forms of literary travesty. He was a tall, gentle roughneck, and Bogan had more fun with him in the early years of their friendship than she had with anyone else, and that is saying a good deal, since her capacity for pleasure, despite her chronic psychic difficulties, was considerable. Louise's idea of a really good time was a visit from Rolfe when he would drape his long legs over the chair and "indulge in a complete excoriation of the New York School of Poetry." They also liked to go out dancing together, to vaudeville revues, and to parties that had generous provisions of liquor and wit. "Sunday I expect to have a Free Day," she wrote to him on a postcard marked September 25, 1924. "If you aren't tied up then with an all-health program (physicians in attendance) perhaps we could take a ride on a Staten Island Ferry boat and go out and see a few murders." Her crack about physicians was a reference to the fact that Rolfe's girl friend, Helen Spencer, was an obstetrician and gynecologist.

Unlike Bogan's sisterly (and sometimes maternal) affection for Wilson, her feelings for Humphries, at least in the beginning, were focused in a brief erotic attachment that quickly turned into friendship built on a sound appreciation of his gifts and character. Louise and Rolfe fretted, scolded, and traded private jokes as intimate friends who had for one reason or another decided not to act upon their sexual impulses. Their relationship was grounded in the humor they loved in one another and their nearly identical instincts as poets. Each wrote the same kind of poem—short, compact, ironic—and each relied on the other for vigilance over bad habits. They showed new poems to one another with perfect frankness, quickly developing a commonsense, workshop attitude based on tough technical criticism. In her notes and letters to Humphries, Bogan was afire with ambition. "Oh God," she exclaimed, after reading Goethe's lyrics. "Why were women born with ambition! I wish I could sit and tat, instead of wanting to go and write THE poem, or lie and kiss the ground." Over the summer of 1924 she read Keats and about Keats, and felt "*very* minor," and the spectacle of Goethe falling in love at the age of eighty-three with girls of nineteen made the life of the woman poet seem ridiculously cramped and insignificant by comparison. She jibed at Humphries:

O, you great male poets! Think of the life ahead of you, Rolfe! No rest! No hope! I should think you'd shudder at the thought of being 83, with no relief in sight. You'll fall for a girl of 19, at 83 (vide Goethe) whom you'll see one morning chasing the ducks, you will leap out of bed, write an immortal sonnet, clutch the grizzled throat, and breathe your last. Cicero, with all his talk of escaping from the tiger, didn't count on the capacities of octogenarian male poets.

As her twenty-seventh birthday approached, she became haunted by the spectre of scanty production and entrenchment in the minor. "Oh God," she burst out again, "I thought I'd be a great poet by 27 with fat works ranged on shelves. O well." The problem was her chosen medium—verse minor in form, though not in art. Goethe's "Über allen Gipfeln," from *Wandrers Nachtlied,* was so beautiful it made her want to cry, and though Keats and the Romantics were not to be dismissed, she told Humphries that "the stripped, still lyric moves me more, invariably, than any flummery ode ever written—although, of course, Keats and the Romantics were only partly flummery."

Still, her unrepressed envy of male poets and her reflections on Keats suggest that she was wondering whether she could write a long poem. At one point she wrote to Humphries that she wanted "a lot of fat words. Fat words in fat poems. Latinities like *immoderate* and *commensual* and *ceremonious* and *arrogance.* Also I want a lot of remembrance," and he may have urged her to write a longer "odic" poem—big, ambitious, and, though he would not have used the word, Romantic. To both Bogan and Humphries, Romantic poetry meant emotional laxness and technical formlessness. Nevertheless, the idea of sustained feeling and complex structure enticed her, and she did write a long poem, "The Flume," in the summer of 1924, and, four years later, in "Summer Wish," an extended dialogue in the manner of Yeats.

IN A LETTER to John Peale Bishop in January 1924, Edmund Wilson closed a roundup of recent gossip by noting that Raymond Holden had "heroically left his wife and family and is now living in sin with Louise Bogan. . . . Raymond is trying to get a divorce and marry her." Having just remarked upon the recent marriages of Elinor Wylie to William Rose Benet and Edna St. Vincent Millay to Eugen Boissevain, he concluded that if Holden were successful in carrying out his plans, "all the remarkable women of the kind in New York will be married to amiable mediocrities."

Raymond Peckham Holden, the third child and younger son of Edwin Babcock Holden and Alice Cort Holden, was born April 7, 1894, in New York. The Holdens were an old, wealthy family who had lived in New York for generations. Edwin Holden's father had been the head of the coal department of the Lackawanna Railroad, and Edwin himself was in charge of the railroad's retail coal agency in Hoboken and Newark. The Corts, like the Holdens, though originally from Providence, Rhode Island, had been long established in New York, and were "in metal." Alice Cort's father had made a fortune importing tin plate.

There were four Holden children: two boys, Arthur and Raymond, and two girls, Marion and Frances, and they grew up in an atmosphere of comfort and amenity. Around 1890 their father bought a house on Eighty-second Street near Riverside Drive, when there was still some remaining farmland in the area, and in this house all the Holden children were born. But Edwin had aspirations to be an architect (later fulfilled by his son Arthur), and in 1900 moved his family into a house he had designed himself on Riverside Drive between 104th and 105th streets. He had taken special pains to include a large, beautiful library in the house, so that he could have ready access to his extensive collection of rare books, first editions, and engravings of Washington, Franklin, and other figures in American history. He was an equally avid collector of historical china, fine antiques, and rare *objets.*

Until the birth of his sister Frances in 1900, Raymond was the youngest child, and like many a "baby" of the family, he was much loved. He was a "natural" in everything, especially reading and spelling, and, according to his brother, he consequently disliked obstacles. After attending the Collegiate School on Seventy-seventh Street, Raymond went on to Princeton, where, as a member of the class of 1915, he was a year ahead of his friend Edmund Wilson. In *The Twenties,* Wilson recalls that Holden, at Princeton, was "the victim of a form of Puritan-idealistic inhibition which made him think it dreadful to kiss or make love to a girl, but resulted in his evading this in imagination by imagining that doctors came to him and told him that having intercourse with the girl was the only thing which would save her life." Over a half century later, his brother, Arthur C. Holden, reflected that "Raymond could make himself believe anything he wanted to." Considering himself a rebel and a nonconformist, he left Princeton in his fourth year, before graduating, though not before having formed a number of literary friendships that would serve him well in later life.

During World War I both Raymond and Arthur joined a cavalry unit, Squadron A, in the State National Guard. Pancho Villa's raids along the Mexican border were causing alarm, and the outfit, along with other troops under General Pershing, was sent to McAllen, Texas, in the southernmost part of the state. It was 110° or 120° in the shade there, and Holden suffered a sunstroke; after recovering, he was put on a boat and sent back to New York, where he finished out his military service doing Red Cross work.

From at least 1915, if not before, Raymond cherished the ambition of becoming a poet and novelist, and published poems in *Poetry: A Magazine of Verse, The Nation, The Measure,* and *Vanity Fair.* In 1918 or 1919, he married a young woman named Grace Badger, who was the daughter of a leading criminal lawyer in Boston, and accustomed to living well. With a sizable independent income from trusts established for him by his grandfathers, and a publishing job at Macmillan's, Raymond was able to provide comfortably for his wife and their two children, Elizabeth Annsley Holden and Richard Cort Holden, in a house near Washington Square. He also had a house in New Hampshire. As children, Arthur and Marion Holden suffered from hay fever, and in the spring of 1908 the Holdens started taking a cottage every summer at a resort hotel called the Sunset Hill House in Sugar Hill, New Hampshire. The summer of 1915, Robert Frost was invited to give a poetry reading for a group of well-to-do summer visitors at a hotel near Franconia called the Forest Hill House. Only one person in the audience seemed to listen with genuine sympathy and interest, and that person, whom Frost, as Lawrance Thompson recounts it, made "the focal point of that audience," was Raymond Holden. Holden idolized Frost, who found Holden congenial as a fellow rebel against academic convention. Holden was soon "encouraged to become a regular visitor at the farm," and shortly became a fixture of the Frosts' family life, "joining them in their swimming expeditions, their baseball games, their berry-picking, and their mountain-climbing. With the famous poet, he helped clear the brush from paths through the woods on the farm, walked the country roads, made shopping trips to the village, and shared views on versification."

In 1919, Holden decided to live full-time in Franconia in order to be near Frost while continuing to work at making a name for himself as a poet. The friendship became more complicated when Frost offered to sell Holden "the uphill half of Frost's own fifty-acre farm. Delighted with the possibilities thus made available to him, and considering himself richer than he was, the young man did not even realize that Frost was driving a hard bargain." Frost sold the land to Holden for $2,500, on the condition that should Frost be forced at some point to sell the other half of the farm, with its house and barn, Holden would agree to buy it for an additional $2,500. Thompson points out that Frost's ruthlessness "in gouging a worshipper" was entirely justifiable in Frost's eyes, since "in this case, his liking for Holden and for the young man's poetry was apparently counterbalanced by his eagerness to get back at him for being rich, at a time when Frost needed money."

Apparently unaware of Frost's meaner motives, Holden went ahead with plans to build the house, which turned out to be far more expensive than he had anticipated. In a letter to his daughter Lesley in February 1920, Frost wrote that "Raymond has already spent more than his estimated $15,000, and the building not over two thirds done. His road is going to cost him a lot more before he can enjoy it. He has spent nearly a thousand on water and nothing so far to show for it. I'd feel sorry for him if he wasn't in the profession of being sorry for other people. Don't tell him much. Just say I don't want to see him venture any more money on that spring that, maybe, isn't a spring."

Despite its great cost, the house was built and the Holden family established in it. But Grace Badger Holden was soon extremely unhappy with country life, and although Holden said little to Frost about the growing coldness between himself and his wife, Frost became acutely suspicious of Holden's attentions to his daughter Lesley and irritated by his almost uninterrupted participation in the daily round of Frost family life. Raymond, he complained to Lesley, "makes himself almost too much one of the family. He walks in on us when we are eating and is in and out all day. You can imagine the effect on Mama when she is lying around half sick unable to get meals she can invite him to. He coolly waves a box of lunch he has brought down from Pecketts so we won't have to take care of him when I say we can't and propose sending him to Herberts. I tell him all right let him spread his lunch on our table with ours and we will eat together. The darndest mixup! Irma stays in her room while it lasts. Mama swears. She thinks she knows how he regards us that he treats us so informally not to say rudely. I'm only puzzled. I doubt if he means much harm. I think the benefits will about even up if I introduce him to Harcourt."

The following September, Frost issued a blunt warning to his daughter to avoid a romantic entanglement with Holden. Hearing that Holden was planning to visit Lesley in New York, where she was living and working, he counseled her to get rid of him, "so that not a word was said out about what was the matter. Be away, be otherwise engaged, be anything you please to show your self-possession. He is no sort of person for youthful folly to trifle with. He's been talking all the bold bad stuff of the books he derives his poetry from—talking it right and left. I simply tell you and leave the rest to your common sense."

The paternal admonition appears to have been heeded, and a nasty domestic upheaval averted. Holden, who had spent many companionable hours with Frost in the latter's sugar house and woods, had no suspicion that Frost was getting bored with him, nor the slightest inkling that his friend was pursuing a scheme to move to another farm farther south in New England. Lawrance Thompson, again noting that Frost seems to have had a need to hurt Holden because he was rich, explains that Frost decided to finance his move south by forcing Holden to fulfill their real-estate agreement. Just at the point when Holden's own house was finished, Frost, sick and tired of Holden's company, was "stripping his Franconia house and shipping his furniture to South Shaftsbury, Vermont, by freight."

Holden later remarked, in his tape-recorded "Reminiscences of Robert Frost," that in demanding the execution of their agreement, Frost "had used me as a convenience. I even, for a time, believed that his friendship for me was insincere and motivated by what he thought he could get out of me. This feeling did not persist." Apparently not, since it was Holden who actually drove the Frosts and their daughter Marjorie from Franconia to the railway station at Littleton. Although the friendship managed to survive for many years thereafter, the leavetaking was painful, for, as Holden recalled, "It turned out . . . that I had not only contributed to his desire to leave the place he really loved but had also given him the means of doing it." Frost did not exactly leave Holden empty-handed. For all his malicious envy of Holden's wealth, he believed that Holden had a real (if limited) talent, and he was willing to say so, helping him publish *Granite and Alabaster,* a book of lyrics that came out in 1922 to a respectable critical reception. Its seventy-two poems belong to a lush and fluently versified lyric-pastoral mode, and, as might be expected, the best of them, such as "Firewood," are Frostian in sound and theme:

> The glittering crescent of my blade
> Is stuck with juices of the tree:
> There is the wound which I have made,
> There are the dark boughs over me.
> I swing the axe. The cones are shaken

And the shuddering tree begins to come
With rippling shrieks which might awaken
The gorged fox in his hidden home.
My blood is brightened and my eyes
Are blurred with flashes of a fire
That leaps like wind and only dies
When I have cut what I require.

Early in 1923, Holden was living alone in his Washington Square house. He was uncertain where his life was going. His marriage had recently collapsed and his wife and children were living in an apartment, but he had not yet decided to obtain a divorce. One evening, feeling lonely and unhappy, he went to a bookstore where a fund-raising party for *The Measure* was being held, and where a friend told him that as the author of the well-received *Granite and Alabaster,* he should get to know Louise Bogan, a young poet who was not as yet well known. Louise was pointed out to him, and he soon found himself exchanging smiles, and then talking with a tall young woman dressed entirely in black and wearing a carnelian necklace.

Holden was not especially tall, but he was trim and muscular, with brown, tightly curling hair, and boyishly handsome features. Bogan considered him, as she might have put it, "a real male beauty." His glasses gave him a look of intent seriousness, but he could change his aspect to that of seductive and witty charm. He did not hide the fact that he had grown up with money, spending it profligately on rifles, riding clothes, and expensive cars. He had many talents and interests, and liked to display them. He had a quick and often ribald sense of humor; he adored nature and nature poetry; he was fascinated by American history, and he was socially graceful. Yet, according to his brother Arthur, he had had two nervous crises by 1923, both of them occasioned by what to his friends appeared to be extreme sensitivity and to his family an inability to control his personal finances. "Raymond would refuse to see the cloud coming up so when the downpour came he was just drowned," Arthur Holden has remarked.

Louise and Raymond found that they had a number of friends and interests in common, had dinner that night and the next, and again frequently over the next three weeks, at which point things took a serious turn. Louise was reticent about herself, feeding Raymond only scanty morsels of information at unpredictable intervals. He learned, however, that she worked part-time in the bookstore where they had met; that she was widowed; that she lived in Brooklyn with her mother; and that she had recently come through a disastrous love affair. Raymond soon asked her to move into an apartment with him, but she demurred, citing unexplained obligations about which Raymond by now knew better than to press. Nevertheless, their love affair grew with consuming sexual passion and emotional need, and after he gave up his lease on the Washington Square house, they began living together in a basement apartment at 242 Lexington Avenue.

Holden quickly learned that there were at least two Louises: one a tender, passionate, intensely sexual being, and the other a violent, cruel, and deeply suspicious fiend, who couldn't stand being loved and did everything possible to test and invalidate Raymond's feelings for her. When she finally allowed him to see her poetry, he knew at once that she possessed an uncommon gift, and arranged, without her knowledge, to have the manuscript of *Body of This Death* seen by a friend who worked for Robert McBride. It was thus through Raymond that the publishing contract was secured. The night he brought the contract back for her to sign, he took her out to dinner, ordered champagne, and presented her with the contract itself. Visibly delighted, she squeezed his hand, and signed the contract, but later that night, back at the apartment, she lashed out in drunken rage, accusing him of trying to get power over her, and hurled a glass of champagne across the floor. She then burst into sobs and said that her mother, whom she had seen that day in Brooklyn, had accused her of being a whore and of trying to break up another woman's marriage. Raymond tried to console her, but this was not to be the last of her outbursts, and Raymond himself was soon to learn how abrasive Louise's mother could be.

After Louise finished preparing *Body of This Death* for McBride, she let Raymond read the manuscript. It was only when he inquired about the Mathilde Alexander in the dedication that he learned, much to his surprise, that Louise had a five-year-old daughter living in Brooklyn with her mother. Her unexplained disappearances and "obligations" now made sense, and he encouraged her to spend more time on the weekends with Maidie, sometimes driving Louise out to Henry Street himself in his red Buick. One weekend, troubled by something Louise had said, Raymond drove out to Brooklyn, where Louise's mother not only did not know where Louise was (it turned out later that she was with friends), but subjected Raymond to a vicious tirade against Louise, who, she predicted, would come to no good. But it was Louise's own rages, above all, that distressed him. She was jealous of his closeness to his family, and on one occasion, when he went to South Salem, New York, to talk to his mother about getting a divorce, Louise overturned tables, lamps, and chairs in her fury, leaving the apartment a shambles.

Her violent sexual jealousy was yet another problem. She once invited a friend from Massachusetts to stay overnight with them as a houseguest. No sooner did the guest arrive than Louise announced that she had an errand to do, and disappeared for two whole days, returning only to confront Raymond with triumphant accusations of infidelity (which, though sorely tempted, he had not, in his opinion, *technically* committed). He soon realized that her accusations were meant to be both a trial of his fidelity and a challenge to his manhood, under the banner of neither of which would she ever believe anything he might say in his own defense. Yet Louise's storms, rages, and cruelty were inseparable, to Raymond, from her intellectual fire and sexual ardor, and he found himself living in increasing emotional bondage to her.

Raymond later conjured up the beginnings of their relationship in his autobiographical novel, *Chance Has a Whip.* When it came out in 1935, Louise was furious with what she considered to be its travestied portrait of herself, but the book, despite its flaws, accurately describes the early Bogan-Holden alliance for what it was: a mutual rescue mission. Holden's hero, Hendrick Fillmore, a minor steel executive trapped in a loveless marriage, falls desperately in love with the mysterious and beautiful Leda Putnam. This young woman is recklessly generous with her body, and makes Hendrick, who is the youngest child in his family and has never been taken seriously by anyone, feel like an adult for the first time in his life. In loving Leda, he experiences not just physical intoxication, but acute emotional dependency. Her complexity and vulnerability fascinate him. After many disillusioning love affairs, she has come to accept her status in life as an exile from conventional society and wavers "between an occasional twinge of conviction that she was damned, depraved, a lost soul, and a frequent richness of spirit, a positive charity for those who would not understand even if they knew, the quality which animated her."

Despite her perfect feminine appearance, Leda has, "unmistakably, assumed the moral, the social stature of a man," but she is deeply puzzled by the chronic backfiring of her sexual and moral liberality:

For when she had thought that men ought to praise her for being thriftlessly, improvidently, undemandingly generous, she found them accusing her of being cruel. Hendrick knew, though he never told her so, that this was partly because men could not reconcile the apparent impurity of her behavior with the purity and nobility of the nature which motivated it. Men took her, used her, adored her, vaguely thinking of her as a bad girl and a little excited by the thought. They felt cheated and in a way affronted because in some abstract manner she contrived to make them suspect, in the end, that she was no bad girl at all but a pure and beautiful being whose very purity was, to them, an implied reproach.

Several years of such experience had, at the age of twenty-six, when Hendrick found her, soured Leda no little. She had not come to despise men. On the contrary, she retained a wide and contented pity for them. She did, however, feel that they were vessels too small for the great emotion, and too complex for the simple indulgence which she expected of them. Hendrick recalled with pride that it was he who was in the act of proving the exception to the rule. He would have liked to believe that he had saved her, but even his desire to do so could not make him forget that it was she who had saved him and given him life.

Louise, too, saw herself as Holden's savior. Sometime in 1924 she wrote to Humphries, breaking a date with him:

—O, you'll say, she has cold feet again. No. . . . Raymond is in such a bad way. He is half-mad with discouragement. I believe he really needs me. And because of that I must be what he believes. Now. Some other time, perhaps not. . . .

You see, you're not, and never can be, so completely delivered over to any concept of a woman. That's your strength. That's where you're going to have more quarrying of talent than a lot of others. I can't hurt him too much. I've done enough, God knows, and he's had the patience of a saint. It may not be worth it. But it does something to me.

Rolfe, write to me, come to see me soon. I need you.

Have pity and patience.

Yours, the retrograde woman,
Louise

Louise introduced Raymond to her daughter Maidie, who soon came to live with him and her mother; Louise then gave up her bookstore job. From this time on, Raymond supported the newly constituted family, which moved, late in the summer of 1924, from 242 Lexington Avenue to a basement apartment in a brownstone on West Sixteenth Street. Maidie attended the Montessori School as a weekday boarder, and on Saturdays Louise would come to pick her up in a taxi and take her to Ugobuono's, an Italian restaurant on Sixth Avenue, right off Greenwich, for feasts of spaghetti and napoleons before taking her home for the rest of the weekend. Late one Saturday night Maidie heard a great commotion, with raised voices and shouting. She ventured into the living room to see what was the matter, but was immediately ordered back to bed. It was only many years later that she learned that Mrs. Grace Badger Holden had shown up with her lawyer and a private detective to "discover" Raymond and Louise "living in sin," so that the charge of adultery required by New York divorce law could be substantiated. The unsavory scene had its intended effect, and Mr. and Mrs. Raymond Holden were, in due course, divorced.

Only two years before, in Vienna, Louise had felt lost and griefstricken, followed everywhere by an unnameable anguish. Now she was adored by a man so gentle that his very mildness irritated her. She had, after all, forged her own character by resisting her scolding, tempestuous mother, and she was unafraid of anger, even habituated to it. Holden was not a fighter, neither by nature nor upbringing, and he couldn't handle explosive, cathartic rows. Like his hero, Hendrick Fillmore, he was much readier to give over his very being to Louise, who, like Leda Putnam, was "the fulfillment of a desire of which he had not been conscious as it grew in him, a passion for fulfillment which was far more than merely physical. It was composed of the mistakes he had made, the blind alleys he had wandered into, the pleasures, anxieties, feasts and famines of the history of his spirit." Late in the summer of 1924, unhappy because she could not write a poem, Louise wrote Humphries that she was "mad with Raymond, and work and places to live, and limited incomes and my face and my mind and my will," and invited him to come over "any free afternoons next week . . . and beat me to a pulp (I realize that that's Freudian—but I need a good licking and there isn't anyone around big enough to give it to me). Raymond talks to me when he should kick me down stairs, and say: 'If you don't like that come back and I'll break the three other ribs and your medulla oblongata.' " She was uneasy with Raymond's tenderness, caught in a fatal paradox of simultaneously desiring and fearing the emotional violence she had always known. Raymond, in his turn, kept wanting her to be the soft, angelic creature she had never been and would never know how to be. So while each sought and accepted the other's demonstrations of love, neither could believe that they were, at heart, sincere.

3 THE LEAF CAUGHT WORLD

THE PERIOD during which Bogan and Holden established themselves as a couple was also a time of pleasure and fun. There were many evenings with Humphries and Helen Spencer, Léonie Adams, Edmund Wilson, Scudder Middleton, Genevieve Taggard, Robert Wolf, Margaret Mead, Ruth Benedict, and other people connected not only with *The Measure,* but with *The New Republic* and *The Nation.* Parties were livened up with much drinking of bootleg gin and whiskey, singing of songs, and playing of *bouts rimés* (or rhyming ends), a game in which each player supplies a line for a set of preselected and, as likely as not, hilariously incongruous rhymes. Between Humphries and Bogan letters filled with various kinds of verbal horseplay were exchanged: silly imitations of the footnotes T. S. Eliot had appended to *The Waste Land;* cracks about other poets, especially the older, successful ones like Robert Frost and Carl Sandburg, and lots of wordplay with titles and names. Louise always closed her letters with a mock high-style valediction: "Yours for the advancement of the Ideal," "Yours for the life complicated," "Yours for plaids and pleasures" (this was a sly reference to Louise's scheme to fix Rolfe up at one point with her Scots-surnamed friend, Alison Laing), "Yours for cleanliness and safety (as opposed to dirt and danger)." Rolfe's letters, in turn, always lifted her spirits. On an undated postcard, on which she had drawn a cartoon of a "downcast horse," she wrote, "You write the best letters in the western world. Yours this morning heartened me out of feeling like a large mass of soft material, as the c.w. puzzles would say." She went on to accept her appointment as one of *The Measure*'s revolving editors, adding, "I'll accept anything to break me out of all this lares and penates business. Yours from the House of Atreus."

From this it appears that Bogan felt some degree of guilt over her role in breaking up Holden's marriage and family, and some degree of unease over the domestic turn her life had recently taken. She was not used to being a full-time mother, although, as it turned out, Maidie lived only intermittently at first with Raymond and Louise. Sometime in the spring of 1924, Louise's parents took their granddaughter back to Farley, Massachusetts, near Otter River, where Daniel Bogan once again worked as a mill superintendent. Louise visited them in late spring, staying for several weeks, taking in the "paper-pulp atmosphere" of her youth, and hoping "to stitch up a few pages of literature." She was back in New York over the summer, where, alone and with Raymond, she saw a great many of her women friends— Léonie Adams, Ruth Benedict, Louise Townsend Nicholl, Elizabeth Huling, Eda Lou Walton, Margaret Mead, and Genevieve Taggard, amongst whom there was much movie-going, shopping, and talk about current love affairs and emotional entanglements. Margaret Mead later recalled these days, when the group of young poets, all of them familiar with psychoanalytic concepts, kept a close watch on each other's lives. "Many of our poems grew out of our relationships to one another," she noted, "and the intensities of the contemporary human plots were discussed and rediscussed against the background of the childhood and special temperament of each."

Mead, who was particularly sophisticated in psychoanalytic theory, sensed that among all the young women poets Bogan was especially fascinating and fragile. Mead observed her terrible bouts of jealousy, her tendency to be easily hurt, and, despite her majestic beauty, her extreme lack of self-confidence. At the same time, Bogan's commonsensical way of handling bad days made a great impression on Mead. Apparently her desire to say "Blaa!" to the whole world was occasionally acted out, for when stuck in a fit of depression or anger, she would take down the curtains in her apartment, ride the streetcar all day, go home, and put the curtains back up.

Ruth Benedict was another friend who sensed the presence of permanent unhappiness in Bogan's life. After hearing her read one evening in the winter of 1926, Benedict, noting Bogan's attractive "accent of disdain," could not help perceiving that her friend seemed unhappy, and that if she were to be happy, "that would be a miracle." Margaret Mead remained so intrigued by Bogan's nature that she wrote a poem about her, "For a Proud Lady," which was published in the June 1925 issue of *The Measure:*

> Yours is a proud and fearful heart
> That snares the weather in its mood,
> As once you snatched the morning mists
> All veils for your one maidenhood.

The snow is but a banner white
Run up by God for your defeat;
You take cold winter days to read
Fate patterned in indifferent sleet.

And sweeter weathers have no art
To dull this prophecy of harm;
You only watch the hare-bell's tilt
To hear instead its belled alarum.

Mead also remembered Bogan's frequent references to Viola Meynell, her favorite English novelist, whose intuitions about emotion and its relation to the facts of behavior she considered unparalleled in their exactness and delicacy. A Meynell story called "Young Mrs. Cruse" was much on her mind and she talked about it often. It portrays, simply and closely, the course of a day in which a young wife experiences a wild dread of being left alone in her home where, as her gregarious and much-loved mother's visit draws to a close, she must face the tragic fact that she has married a man she does not love instead of the lover with whom she had, in the past, bitterly and passionately quarreled. "Perception itself—the way impressions of the external world and insights into people sink into the mind and become part of its texture," Mead recalled, "was something else we often talked about." Louise tended to see pattern and correspondence everywhere—in the weather, in human relations—and to the psychoanalytically well-informed anthropologist, this was a trait smacking equally of poetic giftedness and an emotional fragility bordering on paranoia.

Like most of Louise's friends, Mead knew very little about her past, and had no notion of Maidie's existence. Then one day she asked, as Raymond had asked, about the name Mathilde Alexander in the dedication of *Body of This Death*. Louise gave her a straight answer, at which Mead immediately exclaimed, "Louise, stop hiding your child!" and it was soon afterward that Maidie joined the Bogan-Holden household and became a visible part of her mother's life. Mead later remembered coming home to her tiny apartment one day to find both Louise and Maidie sitting on the stairs peeling onions.

NOW THAT BOGAN was an established poet, the production of new poems was much more of a job and an obligation than it had been in the days when each magazine acceptance was a step toward recognition. The responsibility of writing new poems weighed heavily upon her. Early in the summer of 1924 she began to struggle with a lyric called "Thunder," which

89

later turned out to be "The Flume," one of her few long poems. Work on it proceeded slowly. "It's pretty awful," she confided to Humphries. At some point the poem began to develop into a long narrative, one that she dryly predicted would "go down the ages in the *Christabel* class." Disciplining herself with the thought of Keats sitting down every day and writing two hundred lines, she tried to keep to a similar routine, but could not will poetry into existence. Poems came by "grace" or they did not come at all.

Yet Louise Bogan loved hard work. When she couldn't write a poem, she was filled with a sense of worthlessness and disaffection. Fortunately, she had other, more tractable literary jobs at hand. Her first book review, of D. H. Lawrence's *Birds, Beasts and Flowers,* appeared in the spring of 1924, in *The New Republic,* after Edmund Wilson insisted that she begin to write criticism. She was equally insistent that she could not do it, but he ordered her to sit down at her desk and begin. "I remember, in the beginning," she later wrote, "sitting at that desk with the tears pouring down my face trying to write a notice. Edmund Wilson would pace behind me and exhort me to go on. He taught me a great deal, at a period when I needed a teacher." Soon her reviews were appearing with some frequency.

In October she prepared herself for her stint as acting editor of *The Measure.* She would have charge of three issues, December 1924, and January and February of 1925. For all three she secured poems from Léonie Adams, whose first book, *Those Not Elect,* was scheduled for publication the following year. Adams, like Humphries, shared Bogan's commitment to lyric poetry in the high formal line, and over the following decades the two poets, who remained firm admirers of each other's talents, were often mentioned in the same breath. They were not alike, as Rolfe Humphries made it his business to declare earlier than anyone else. "Let us be rid of the notion once and for all . . . ," he said, reviewing *Those Not Elect* in 1925, "despite a common darkness, a north-north-westerly madness in the blood, these two girls are no more alike than Ophelia and Cassandra." The visionary suffered little disenchantment in the poetry of Adams, whose constant theme was the transubstantiation of gross materiality to pure spirit, whereas precisely the inverse characterized Bogan's vision, which was always finding bone and blood in the ashes of a burnt-out transcendence. For the December issue of *The Measure,* Bogan chose some of Adams's loveliest and most intricately wrought lyrics: "Spire of Saint Patrick's and the Moon," "The Barouche," "Discourse with the Heart," and "Our Lady of Victory: Bread and Butter Letter from a Heretic." Another poet who was a friend of Wilson's, Scudder Middleton, contributed some light, witty, and elegant verse. There were poems by one of the earliest contributors to *The Measure,* Louise Townsend Nicholl, and by Lindley Williams Hubbell, a young man who later carried on an extensive correspondence with Bogan and then moved to Japan where he joined a Zen monastery and continued to write verse "in form," some of it highly erotic.

As the fruit of Bogan's taste and judgment, the December issue of *The Measure* served up a fine compendium of elegance, variety of tone, and high craftsmanship. Bogan made the principle of this taste explicit in her own contribution to the issue, a review of *The Sleeping Beauty,* by Edith Sitwell. Comparing Sitwell to Stravinsky, she credited both with a drive "toward a loveliness intricate but unlabored." In language characteristic of the images in her poetry, she remarked that Sitwell's stanzas "open and close upon their rhymes like panels of a screen," and that Sitwell's wit was always "very dark or very bright, like the mottle in tortoiseshell."

Among notable contributors to the January issue were Countee Cullen, with three poems and a review, and Edward Sapir, at this time chief of the Division of Anthropology of the Canadian National Museum in Ottawa. Sapir, incidentally, was someone else to whom Louise Bogan's poetry seemed both beautiful and obscure. Writing some years later to Ruth Benedict, he remarked, "And I had thought I was one of the Simple Simon school, and here are you severe and lofty-dictioned Parnassians—you and Léonie and Louise Bogan, whom I for one am certainly not understanding (Louise, I mean)—and where do I come in?"

He might well have asked the question after reading the February 1925 issue of *The Measure,* the third and last that Bogan edited. She decided to include a letter to herself from Rolfe Humphries along with, to borrow Sapir's phrase, a "severe and lofty-dictioned" editorial of her own called "The Darkness of the Contemporaries." The two pieces show how in matters of critical theory Bogan and Humphries stood to each other as poetic fraternal twins. Each attacks current fashion in his and her own way, Humphries deriding the aesthetic pretensions of George Moore's recently published *Anthology of Pure Poetry* in a brash, colloquial style, and Bogan exhorting her juniors in a voice both stern and magisterial, as if lately returned from the Delphic oracle. Young poets, she points out, afraid that no one will listen to them unless they package their work in contemporary modes, look through current magazines and write what they see there, rather than examining their own interiors:

The young Pope served his time by polishing the epigrams of the old Wycherly. Young Goethe paid tithe to *Sturm und Drang*. Old bones are good for young teeth. But when the teeth are cut they should bite into their own food. Youth should be harangued into arrogance: into courage to learn the heft and swing of English poetry in the tradition when everyone is writing free verse, to exact from itself its own medium and that only, when the magazines are lined with neat sonnets and quatrains. If it write poetry at all, it should do it with conviction. A poet, even a young one, does not ask an editor if there should be a comma in line three. He should be willing to battle with the editor because of that comma.

The mystic recognizes his own dark night of the soul, if he feels an emptied heart, cut off from whatever thing he considers grace. Youth, posturing in a stale gallery of mirrors or with one ear to the ground, alert for rumors, often thinks that he stands in the full light of creation. To be cut off and not to know,—that is the triple darkness.

Her language is at once pithy and haughty. Then suddenly the love of common speech breaks through, and she writes of "the heft and swing of English poetry" as though she had held the tradition in her two hands like an axe. Her instinctive reticence keeps her from speaking as if she has actually experienced an "emptied heart," although we know from her letters that she suffered badly while waiting for poems to arrive. But here, as in most of her later criticism, she achieves authority by telling what she knows without giving a corresponding, and unnecessary, account of how she knows it.

IN THE DIVORCE AGREEMENT, Raymond's ex-wife received a settlement plus the proceeds from the sale of the Franconia house, and he was obliged to pay alimony and child support as well. Now that he had responsibilities to Louise and Maidie, he badly needed a job. Though he could no longer afford to live as a wealthy man, he liked to maintain a comfortable standard of living, which meant a nice apartment and domestic help. Yet he had already gone through the greater part of his inheritance. His financial difficulties seemed chronic to Louise, who never knew at this or any other time just how much money he had at his disposal.

In June of 1925, Raymond, Louise, and Maidie all moved to 93 West Cedar Street in Boston, where Raymond had taken a job as editor of *Travel,* a magazine published by Robert McBride & Company, the same firm that had published *Body of This Death.* On July 10th, Louise and Raymond were married in Putnam, Connecticut, by "a young Congregationalist minister, in a parsonage," who looked, as Holden wrote to Humphries, "very frightened, on the strength of a marriage license issued by a fine old gray haired town clerk who kept calico and butterick [sic] patterns in the back of his shop and a straight and dignified old wife in the front. Following the ceremony," he continued, "the bridal party, consisting of 1 Bogan, Louise, 27, fem., 1 Holden, Raymond, 31, mle., 1 bottle red wine, 1 sedan, Essex, hired, 4 eggs, boiled, 8 sandwiches, assorted, repaired to the shade of a linden tree somewhere in the banlieues of Woonsocket and there spread its spread, checking in at the gasoline livery in Boston about twelve (midnight)." Maidie was absent from the wedding, sick in Massachusetts General Hospital with a high temperature and what later proved to be scarlet fever.

Raymond Holden's widow, Mrs. Barbara Holden Yeomans, has pointed out that by the time of Louise and Raymond's marriage, "Raymond was well aware of the dichotomy of Louise's personality, but she had become essential to him, and he realized that much as he deplored the hostility and violence in her nature, there was as much fascination in this evil side as there was in her good and lovable side. He later felt that though it had not occurred to him at the time to search deeply enough to find out if he really wanted to marry her, a part of him had always had deep-seated reservations." These reservations, which Louise, on her side, no doubt harbored as well, went underground, as the couple, with Maidie, settled into a domestic routine. In August, the Holdens moved to 66 Fayette Street, where Louise spent many happy months. During the day, with Maidie away at school and Raymond at his office, she had the apartment to herself. It had been many years since she had first come to Boston, "at the age of the impossible heart, when the mind flew out to inhabit with warmth and compassion the rooms behind shut windows and drawn blinds," and now, after she had gone forth to meet and live the life she had so fervently imagined, she was herself inhabiting such rooms, where, on sunny mornings, in delicious solitude, as she sat on her low couch surrounded by books and papers, "happy and safe and calm," she could hear children crying in unison, "from the public school across the way, 'A prairie is a *grassy* plain.' " She soon wrote to Ruth Benedict that she had written a new poem, "If We Take All Gold," in which she speaks of taking "Sorrow's gold" out of the "clean house" and storing it away "under dark heaped ground," and by December there were two more poems, "Winter Swan" and "Didactic Piece," also concerned with cycles of change, present happiness and past suffering.

Her parents now ceased to play any practical role in her life, apart from their continuing devotion to Maidie. As long as Louise had made visits to their home, and relied on them for childcare, she had been close to the original source of turmoil and conflict. It wasn't that her parents still fought or that her mother still led a secret life. Since Charles's death, May Bogan had become a stout and religious lower-middle-class matron, inconsolable over the loss of her son. But once Louise and Raymond were married, she stopped scolding. The balance of power shifted. Louise was now successful, as a poet and as a woman. She was in charge of her child's upbringing, and her parents, as well as her memories of the past, faded into irrelevance.

Her happiness took various and satisfying forms. She made peach jam, read Chekhov, went to the symphony, and listened to music on the radio. She wrote rich, funny letters to Wilson, Ruth Benedict, and Humphries. At Christmas the household received the addition of two white mice, Ossip and Wossip, who could dance, and for whom Raymond built a little two-story apartment, with a runway between the upstairs and the downstairs; later on they had another pair Raymond named Wurlitzer and Spinoza. Raymond was doing well, and was able to provide a cleaning lady for Louise. Soon he changed jobs, moving to the advertising department of Raymond & Whitcomb Co., Tours and Cruises. There were no fights, no raised voices, no bitter scenes, although Louise adamantly refused to let Raymond take the cruises his employers expected to be part of his job. Maidie, who had never known her own father, was devoted to Raymond, and he returned the devotion, conscious of having defaulted on his obligations to his own two children. Raymond and Louise shared a love of beautiful things, and together they bought, stripped, and refinished antiques, which were then easy to find in the numerous Boston antique shops.

Rolfe Humphries and Helen Spencer also got married the summer of 1925, and now the two couples exchanged riotous and ribald letters about the goings-on of their respective households. Raymond and Rolfe tried to outdo each other in bawdiness, a good deal of it inspired by outright filthyminded contemplation of Helen Spencer Humphries's professional life as an obstetrician-gynecologist. On January 26, 1926, Holden, with Bogan quite possibly acting as an unrecorded collaborator, knocked out the following frolic (parts of which are illegible):

Humphries & Spencer
Glands and Umbrellas
335 E. 17th Street
Gents:

Our receiving dep't acknowledges receipt of parcel containing one (1) aluminum clap-trap of roasting and baking variety. We regret to say that Mr. Austin's remains [?] had long since gone out with the sludge, so that we are not able to test out the cooking qualities of the implement. We especially like the steam-escaper, which will afford much innocent amusement to our Mr. Holden, licensed beef-taster extraordinary. At present we [are] contemplating moving Ossip and Wossip into the roaster and baker as they have a rather bad odor. In consideration of the bad odor which aluminum has at the present time we feel they may feel more at home there.

The letter continued with a startling piece of information: Raymond was in Mass. General, with a spot on his lung:

His liquid intake is being watched carefully; his liquid output is being scrutinized eagerly by crowds of nurses. He sweats fully and wears a white bisque corset with cerise shoulder straps. He somewhat resents being asked to void at a moment's notice for the benefit of laboratory technicians below stairs.

Could you, from your abattoir gland dealer, procure the _____[illeg.]_____ of a Norwegian sea-urchin, to be used in the compounding of an immunizing potion, against reading the New York literary papers?

Signed
(Yours for glass ducks and enemas—
Holden Bogan Ltd.)

Humphries sent back letters in kind, some of them accompanied by wildly farcical pieces such as "The Sex Life of the American Woman" and the "Noun and Verb Rodeo," the latter an imaginary literature-reading contest. Jokes about baseball, genitalia, bodily functions, drinking, and poetry flew between the two couples, who shared a love of leisure, liquor, and verbal horseplay. For the most part, the actual writing was done by Rolfe and Raymond, which meant that Louise's own correspondence with Rolfe went into abeyance. She listened and laughed and approved, no doubt, as Raymond invented pseudonyms and mimicked pedantic and wordy styles, but appears to have contributed little to the actual writing of the letters, although she shared the fun of sending a questionnaire to Humphries from *Who's Who in American Poetry,* which she and Raymond filled out together with mocking and ridiculous answers. Raymond and Rolfe were both crazy about baseball, and when Louise and Raymond had lived in New York, the men had dragged her to numerous ballgames, which she must have found extremely dull. "No one was ever less sports-minded," Ruth Limmer has said. This was the era when the baseball player Grover Cleveland Alexander was known as "The Great Alexander," a nickname soon applied to Maidie, and then by the giddy foursome to each other, who exchanged news about "the great Bogan," "the great Holden," and "the great Humphries." Thus Raymond wrote to Rolfe early in March 1926:

We suppose you would like to have a picture of the home life of such representatives of the Boston Bourgeoisie as we like to think ourselves. . . . The great Bogan is sewing on her spring wardrobe in the fatuous hope that there may be a spring—at the same time asseverating with the other foot that she is no poet and that her spouse lies awake nights trying to keep her from being one. . . .

The letter hinted that Bogan and Holden were experiencing some more or less unfocused problems as writers who were living together. Holden himself had recently finished his first thriller, and was on the verge of completing a long narrative poem, called "Landscape with Figures," which he had been working on for four years. Yet it was at just this point that Bogan found she was once again having writing difficulties. "The great Bogan also snapped to with a lilt all about SPRING which, upon being confronted with the remark that it was a good poem elicited the retort that it couldn't be because she wasn't a poet any more," Holden continued. "Then we began criticising it and finally 'elicited' from her the statement that she liked it herself."

Allies of each other's creative work as they may have tried to be, and colleagues as they may have been in the frenetic production of epistolary capers, Bogan and Holden deeply envied each other. She resented his facility, and occasionally expressed open contempt of it. Some years later the poet and Scribner's editor John Hall Wheelock heard her say, with marked disdain, "I don't much like that," after Holden had recited a new poem to a group of friends, and another friend remembered visiting them, again some years later in New York, and finding Louise sitting on the windowsill with a pair of manicure scissors with which she was cutting a poem of Raymond's into confetti and letting the pieces float out into the air.

Raymond, however, seems secretly to have harbored the suspicion that he was a better poet than Louise. Sending Rolfe one of his sonnets, he wrote,

We think it excellent. —Miss Bogan's one suggestion is that the swell holm-oak figure be kept for the last line, but she is always one to overdo things, and is probably wrong. Enclosed, please find a poem by Miss B., which sounds like all the poems published in Oxford annuals, for the last fifty years, from the days when Yvette Guilbert wore black gloves and rubbed her makeup off on Arthur Symons' knee, or neck, as the case might have been. All of which goes to show that Miss B. is retrogressing and will soon be in the stage where all her buttons are safety pins. And a fine spectacle that will be, you may be sure.

Though Bogan may well have laughed out loud at Holden's description of her poem (which cannot be identified), the deep rivalry ran on undiminished. Holden had always written about nature, but now Bogan was turning to that subject—to shadows, trees, swans, and landscapes. Fundamentally she did not admire or respect his affirmative and philosophical treatment of natural themes. She held back from the rhymed epistles Holden could churn out by the minute. Not long afterward, when she and Holden were living in Santa Fe, she wrote one or two of these to Edmund Wilson, but, as she later explained to Humphries, Raymond "sort of had a sinecure on that, in those days, and he was so fluent and clever at it that I thought I was just a runner up and so stood back and watched. First chop or nothing, that's my unfortunate tendency."

To a certain extent, Bogan's envy of Holden's literary facility was a partial motive for her assiduous labors at self-education. He had had all the "advantages" and had even considered himself a rebel against formal education, whereas she, no less rebellious in her refusal to go to Radcliffe, nevertheless had the auto-didact's insatiable need to close the educational gaps wedged open in the first place by her youthful impatience and arrogance.

Long quiet hours in Boston gave her the chance to read and reflect. The summer of her marriage she took on Henry James, reading him swiftly and critically, and, in a memorable letter to Edmund Wilson, written July 10th—the day of her wedding (she makes no mention of it!)—offering a set of lucid, strongly colored remarks about *The Spoils of Poynton, The Europeans, Washington Square, The Aspern Papers, The Princess Casamassima,* and *The Turn of the Screw.* Her letter included a brilliant parody of what she called the "echolalia" in James's method of rendering dialogue. After concluding that James was "at once a great artist—such a sense of life, of differentiation, of light and movement!—and an old fool," and offering a cascade of witty *aperçus,* she apologized to Wilson, saying, "I bore you, perhaps, dear Edmund, by all this. You have had it figured out for yourself years ago, no doubt." This onrush of diffidence suggests not only that when Wilson was her audience she still felt cowed by his erudition and air of authority, but that there was a powerful inhibition at work against a pleasurable awareness of her own sturdily growing critical acumen. It was safer, perhaps, as Holden's wife and Wilson's friend, to regard herself as not quite up to their Princetonian standard, even though, as a literary conversationalist, Holden appears to have been no match for either Louise or most of their friends. Her need for vigorous, irreverent, probing talk was as strong as her appetite for food, and although the literary horseplay she enjoyed with Holden must have supplied her with some nourishment, she nevertheless wrote to Wilson that she had "no one to talk to, you see, so you will let me steam at you occasionally, won't you?" So great was her desire for intellectual companionship that she even wrote about James to Margaret Mead in Samoa; Mead recalled that she was hard-pressed to explain the letters to the curious natives.

It was Bogan, and not Holden, who was taken seriously by the larger literary world; it was Bogan who received an invitation, in February 1926, from Elizabeth Ames, the director of Yaddo, to join the first roster of visitors at the newly founded artists' and writers' colony in Saratoga Springs the following summer. She accepted, and went there in August for a month of hard work in a studio with views of pine trees on three sides and another through a plate-glass window of an oat field, a Baroque marble pool, and mountains. Four weeks of industry (punctuated by extreme irritation at the intrusive Elizabeth Ames, whom at one point she wished to punch in the nose) resulted in two (unidentified, and probably lost) stories, and two poems, "Feuer-Nacht" and "Dark Summer," which mark the change between earlier and later moods in *Dark Summer* and hint at the forces which, though dormant at present, were later to erupt with real violence of feeling.

That fall of 1926, when Bogan returned from Yaddo, the Holdens moved back to an old brownstone walkup in New York at 320 East Fifty-seventh Street. Holden had been given a three-month leave of absence from Raymond & Whitcomb to do advertising and publicity for the firm in New York, and Bogan, who was delighted with the change, looked forward to seeing her New York friends again. Holden, however, who had been hospitalized for pleurisy the previous winter, suffered a bout of fatigue and physical collapse, for which his doctor now ordered a six-month period of complete rest and absence from worry in order to ward off the spectre of an incipient tubercular condition. Raymond's adoring and fretting mother offered the couple enough money to go anywhere they thought best, and they entertained the notion of a trip to the south of France, deciding that it was too "unmedical," though the cheapest place by far. Eventually they chose the American Southwest, where the air was clear and dry, and where, as Louise explained to Elizabeth Ames, a "scattering of congenial people" existed in the vicinity of Santa Fe. Departure was planned for the end of November: "The apartment is to be sublet, and we are to follow that wisest of precepts, that one must be ready to begin one's life anew at any moment, pack a few books, blankets and pots and pans, and ship to the canyons. Even with all the disruption perhaps it is happiest not to have fixed stars overhead."

After a long train journey to Chicago, where they were hospitably entertained by Harriet Monroe, the Holden-Bogan-Alexander trio arrived in Santa Fe the day before Thanksgiving and went to a hotel at which, instead of getting turkey, stuffing, and cranberry sauce for dinner, they were served Long Island duck and frogs' legs, a detail which Louise found cheering but which was remembered with horror by her daughter, who had recently turned nine. That same day, they heard about a small, cool house with a timbered ceiling and a sleeping porch, and rented it immediately.

Santa Fe actually did possess the "scattering of congenial people" they had hoped to find, among them poets Witter Bynner and Arthur Davison Ficke, who were notorious for having published in 1916, under the respective names Emanuel Morgan and Anne Knish, a poem called *Spectra*. It was a parody of Imagism and received a certain amount of attention as a bona fide contribution to experimental verse before being exposed as a hoax. Bynner gave riotous boozy parties at his house, and among his guests was a woman named Dorothy Dudley Harvey, who hired Raymond to tutor her children and to whom Bogan took an immediate liking. She was born to a rich Chicago family and married to a man named Harry Harvey who owned a ranch outside of Santa Fe. They had two children, and she had once published poems in Harriet Monroe's *Poetry*. Louise was immediately struck by her madcap elegance. At her ranch in Santa Fe she had an old-fashioned dressing table, swathed in black lace. One evening, as she was dressing to go out for dinner, she pulled the lace from the table, wrapped it around herself, attached a large rhinestone pin to one of its folds, and, thus gotten up, serenely went off to her engagement. Natural extravagance, when executed with easy, natural grace, was irresistible to Bogan, who remained particularly fond of her new friend for many years.

Bogan and Holden also became friendly with Yvor Winters and Janet Lewis, who were spending that year in Santa Fe for Winters's health. Bogan used to sit in their living room discussing French poets with Winters or listening as he talked about and read from the works of Rimbaud, Laforgue, Valéry, Mallarmé, Baudelaire, and others who were of interest to them both. Janet Lewis later remembered Bogan as a beautiful young woman, her face masklike in its calm, with eyes set well apart. The two couples went on excursions together, exploring the Santa Fe region, driving to an Indian dance at Cochiti, and sharing a roadside picnic at which Raymond cooked steak over hot coals.

Although Santa Fe offered clear, dry air, a dramatic landscape, and sufficient isolation for uninterrupted work, Bogan and Holden missed their friends in the East, and regularly reported their activities in the rhymed letters that they sent to Edmund Wilson and Rolfe Humphries. Those concocted for the latter carried on the grand tradition of the Boston correspondence. Composed for the most part by Holden, they were titled "The Santa Fecalist," and were brimming with sexual and scatalogical play. Soon after their arrival, Holden informed Humphries that

> You should know that in Santa Fe
> No man may either crap or pee
> Unless within adobe walls
> Nor touch one finger to his balls
> Unless he first has blessed his prong
> With the Pueblo Sun God song.

In one of her own rhymed efforts to Wilson, Bogan reported that Raymond's mother had come for a visit and that

> We saw some Indians dance a wild
> Greek comedy dance, at which you'd have smiled.
> Not a calm rite to grey-eyed Pallas

But a lot of leaping with a phallus.
I told Mrs. Holden succinctly how
These things come out of *The Golden Bough.*
A nice short talk to distract her attention
From a lot of actions I really can't mention.
She took it all in very good part
Although I thought it might break her heart.

Louise and Raymond brewed raisin wine; Louise suffered from a bad tooth and had it taken out; it snowed; there were more visits with Bynner, who once stopped by at five in the morning, rousing Louise and Raymond "to drink whisky and look at the dawn, he being on the way home from a party." Another time he brought over a drunken, hiccoughing Indian who gave both Raymond and Louise Indian names. Raymond wrote a sonnet to John Bannister Tabb, a Catholic poet who published his work in the late nineteenth and early twentieth centuries and had been compared to Emily Dickinson and the seventeenth-century "Metaphysicals," but Louise herself did very little writing. With characteristic double-entendre, Holden remarked in a December letter to Wilson that she had "forced one poem out," but this remains unidentified. In March she complained to Ruth Benedict that "I haven't a poem in me or about me—and feel useless and incompetent, but then summer is my time for poems, or perhaps there aren't any any more." She longed to return to New York, where her friends were, but at the end of April, Raymond wrote to Rolfe that he had been ill for a month with flu and sinus problems, and "the result is that (whisper it not in Barrow St.) we shall not be home before the first of August. This postponement has been the cause of much marital anguish among the Holden-Bogans, both members of which combine having from time to time had qualms about not appearing on 5th Avenue for another three months. God knows the physiographical elements of this place are such that one need not weep at having to remain in it but after all it is out of our world."

Evidently their impatience got the best of their medical prudence, for they left Santa Fe in May, taking thirteen days to drive back to New York in a Ford touring car with Isinglass curtains, and getting stuck in Kansas for five days because of thick rains and mud so deep it went up to the hubcaps. "We stayed at motels too awful even to contemplate," Maidie Alexander Scannell remembers, and her mother was furious for the rest of the trip because someone in Kansas stole her jewelry from the car.

They went back to the apartment at 320 East Fifty-seventh Street. It was the summer of Bogan's thirtieth birthday, and they spent a good part of it in a converted barn in a town called Hillsdale in Columbia County, upstate

New York. There they knew a psychiatrist named Dr. H. W. Frink, whom Louise had met in 1922, when the rich lover who had followed her to Vienna went into treatment with him, while he in turn was studying under Freud. Frink himself suffered from occasional bouts of manic-depressive illness, but at the time that Louise and Raymond knew him, she later recalled, he was living in the country with his children and girl friend, and was "only fitfully peculiar." It was his converted barn the Holdens stayed in while they considered buying a farm themselves and moving to the country. Raymond still cherished the idea of living as a gentleman-farmer-poet, and much as Louise had looked forward in Santa Fe to getting reabsorbed into New York literary life, once she was actually back, she found herself vulnerable to fits of jealousy and to excessive concern about the embroilments of gossip and parties. No immediate decisions were made, however, and for the fall and winter of 1927–28, the Holdens remained in New York.

It was, it appears, a more or less smooth, comfortable time for Louise, although there were periodic eruptions of jealousy and rage. It was almost as if she could not allow things to go too well; clear days had to be followed by storms, although they might be very brief. A reminder of past unpleasantness existed in the fact that Raymond's children attended Friends Seminary, the same school Maidie now went to, and were forbidden by their mother to speak to her. But Louise worked well, at home, writing book reviews for *The New Republic* (as well as two movie reviews for the October 1927 issue), and she read and wrote, keeping, as always, a journal. The group of people radiating from *The Measure* and *The New Republic* now included several younger writers from the South. Robert Penn Warren remembered meeting Louise at Allen Tate and Caroline Gordon's apartment at 27 Bank Street, when excitement before the execution of Sacco and Vanzetti was reaching its peak and was more than likely to be a topic of conversation. "My first image of her," he later recalled, "is of a very good-looking, long-shanked young woman leaning forward and looking about before making an utterance and saying, as she scanned a few strange faces, 'I presume we are all friends here?' "

The private woman whose chronic emotional difficulties could be sensed by intuitive friends like Ruth Benedict and Margaret Mead could nevertheless stand out on social occasions with extraordinary presence. The poet Horace Gregory never forgot the sight of her in the early 1920s at a party in someone's "noisy, ill-swept" Greenwich Village studio, where, "half-reclining on a studio couch, a martini held glittering between the fingers of her right hand . . . it was as if she had been dropped from the skies, as slender, as immaculate as the moon in its last quarter, her oval face in profile, clear and pale." At Petipas's restaurant, where the staff of *The New*

Republic was giving a party for seventeen-year-old John Cheever, who had just been expelled from Thayer Academy for writing a story about the school, labor lawyer David Mandel, who was married to the poet and critic Eda Lou Walton, saw Bogan sitting in Hart Crane's lap. He would later describe her as "a very skinny girl when she was young, but then she fleshed out, later, and she always had that funny aristocratic drawl in the back of the throat, and upright, even portentously aristocratic posture—the long, flat back she got from her mother."

At five feet, eight inches, Bogan was tall, like her mother, whom she further resembled in being able to wear clothes well. In Antibes shirts—the forerunner of the T-shirt—and espadrilles, she looked sportily elegant. She was so attractive and dressed so well that to Maidie, at nine, ten, and eleven, she seemed distinctly unlike other mothers. Once she came to a recital Maidie was to dance in at the Friends Seminary dressed in a very bright blue and red silk dress, with a short pleated skirt. She was wearing high-heeled shoes and her brown hair was pulled back in a bun. Unaware of course of the sometimes peculiar motives adults can have, and the possibility that her mother might have anticipated running into Mrs. Grace Badger Holden among the other parents in the audience, Maidie burst into tears when they later came home. When Louise said, "What's the matter with you, you were marvelous," Maidie (who had had a solo part) cried out, "You don't look like a mother!" Another incident seemed to Maidie to point up her mother's difference from conventional parents. One day Louise announced that a ratty, worn-out doll that Maidie had cherished for many years "was too awful" and would have to be thrown out. While the outraged Maidie had a tantrum in the apartment's small front room, Louise "shut the door, came back very quietly and poured a pitcher of ice cold water over my head. Other mothers would have hit you. I stopped crying, that's for sure. I wanted to kill her."

Maidie, in turn, seems to have inherited her grandmother's Murphy-Shields temper. When Raymond once tried to spank her, she broke his glasses and kicked him in the eye. After that, he never laid a hand on "the great Alexander" again.

THROUGHOUT THE FALL and winter of 1927–28, the Holdens held fast to their dream of owning a farm in the country. The summer of 1928 they went back to Hillsdale, where they found a house, but it needed a lot of work. Rather than travel back and forth between the city and the country, they gave up their New York apartment and moved into the Elmwood Inn in Hillsdale, using it as headquarters while they did the necessary reconstruction and repair work on the house. By October arrangements for buying the house were nearly complete. For their money, Bogan and Holden got about five acres with plum and pear orchards, hollyhocks, and a view of two townships. "Farewell, farewell!" Louise wrote to Ruth Benedict. "We fade into the bucolic!"

The old farmhouse itself needed a good year's solid labor to make it habitable. A heating system had to be put in, the floor scraped, layer after layer of wallpaper removed, and the entire foundation reconstructed. Raymond hired a man to help, and a mason to put in a fireplace and chimney, but the bulk of the actual work he and Louise did themselves.

Louise loved the house, and the hard work. While Raymond put in windows, she planted a bulb garden and contemplated writing a book about common and beautiful flowers. Even though the house was unfinished, and the Elmwood Inn filled with skiers from nearby Catamount, she began to write poetry. "For the first time in a year," she reported to Benedict, "I have heard things in the head while dining under these fabulous trees." She wrote quantities of verse, brought on by a look out the window at the lilacs, roses, and wild vines, a rainy day, the sight of an animal, or an angle of light. "How happy I feel! How easy art really is!" she wrote to Wilson, adding that "almost at once I realize that the thing is just terrible." One of her new poems, "I Saw Eternity," she confided to Ruth Benedict, came from a "mood of katharsis. . . . To think that I should come, at the age of thirty-one, to the stage where I write poems about Eternity!"

In August she asked Edmund Wilson to take a look at her new work and suggest what she should do about getting it published, since Robert McBride, who had brought out *Body of This Death* to no financial gain, considered a new book commercially unprofitable. Wilson suggested that she send a copy of *Body of This Death* to Maxwell Perkins, the chief editor at Charles Scribner's Sons. Within two days Perkins sent a favorable reply, and arranged for her to meet with another Scribner's editor, John Hall Wheelock, who soon proposed a small volume "in distinguished format . . . with better paper, press-work and binding than issued in the ordinary trade edition."

Wheelock, who had been with Scribner's since 1911, was himself a poet bound to a strong, lyrical Romanticism, and he became entirely devoted to Bogan, editing her next three books of poems. From the beginning he was unwaveringly convinced that she possessed gifts of the highest and rarest order, and because he knew from the outset that she was incapable of writing poetry at will, he worried lest there would be an insufficient number of poems to fill out the projected volume. Although in December he and Bogan reached a formal agreement to publish the book, at that time there were too few poems to make up a publishable collection, so Bogan agreed to write more by the following summer. She was surer of her powers at this time than she had ever been before, and apparently trusted that the needed poems would arrive in due course. Delighted with the prospect of a secure and fortifying relationship with Scribner's, she brought up the idea of writing a fictionalized autobiography to be called *Laura Dal[e]y's Story,* in which she would give free rein to the memories of her New England mill-town childhood. She may well have had the idea for this book in mind for a long time, and only been waiting for the right publisher to go forward with it.

BY MID-MAY 1929 the house was ready. It had one large room downstairs, and a kitchen, with a line running to the pump at the well. Upstairs there were two bedrooms, and a big open space, airy and light, which Louise used as her study. Downstairs there was a parlor, and a small room Raymond used as a study and a place to keep his .22 rifle. When he wasn't reading and writing and working on the house, he hunted rabbits, partridges, and woodcocks, cleaning and cooking them himself, since Louise refused to have anything to do with them.

The household soon included a large German shepherd, named Rendell, and a cat, named Velvet, a gift from Edna St. Vincent Millay and her husband, Eugen Boissevain, who lived in nearby Austerlitz and occasionally came to visit.

Over the summer, greens, peas, squash, beets, carrots, kohlrabi, broccoli, and berries came from the garden. Louise, who had finished her long poem, "Summer Wish," shortly before moving into the house, concentrated on finishing up her manuscript; with Edmund Wilson regularly sending Louise books to review for *The New Republic,* she had plenty of work. Raymond, too, was busy, finishing a book on Abraham Lincoln.

In July, Wilson came to visit and, fortunately, left detailed notes in his journal. On or near the Holdens' land there was an old ore pit, forty-seven feet deep, which had been turned into a pond. Wilson took a swim in it and then, impressed by Louise's way of seeing patterns in nature, noted down her remark that the water "looked as if it were braided—and that the ripples were like willow leaves." In the evening, the trees stood out against the darkening blue mountains. A screen of poplars or aspens created a margin for the wood. He could hear the sound of trains, "long, dull, honest daily country trains." At night the fireflies glimmered in the dark, and when Wilson returned through the summer mists after his walk, he could see into the house, with its "lamp-lit interior" and "the tired people buried in their chairs."

Dark Summer, Bogan's second book of poems, came out in September

1929, with a dedication to Raymond Holden. The book was beautifully designed, and Bogan was enchanted with the leaf ornaments and hips and haws on its front page. Reading the book, actually holding it in her hands, "gave me a great sense of elation," she wrote to Wheelock. "A female lyrist of no small ability, I said to myself."

From Yvor Winters she got one of the most intelligent and most favorable reviews she was ever to receive. He praised such poems as "The Mark," "Come, Break with Time," and "Simple Autumnal" for their pure lyricism, which, he asserted, could demand and bear comparison "with the best songs of the sixteenth and seventeenth centuries, whether one select examples from Campion, Jonson, or Dryden."

He chided her for a tendency to drop into "minor, decorative digressions" in the long line, an "incorrect technique for a long poem, whether narrative or philosophical," and remarked that her poems were complex in feeling, though not in idea, but she knew him well enough to understand that when he said she distrusted "certain ranges of experience that either might or might not involve some kind of spiritual looseness" as a cat avoided water, he was bestowing high praise indeed. It would take only "a turn, a flicker," he believed, "to transform her into a major poet; it is conceivable that the flicker may be taking place as I write, that it may even have occurred in her book, *a mon insu!*" The very least that could be said was that she belonged in company with the best English lyricists, and that she was "beyond doubt one of the principal ornaments of contemporary American poetry."

For Bogan and her friends, it was a full season. Léonie Adams had just published her second book, *High Falcon,* and its dedication to Louise Bogan and Raymond Holden pleased them both. The book, Bogan wrote to Wheelock, was "full of extraordinary loveliness—and a sharpness that I, for one, could not put a name to. She has the greatest talent in the really grand manner of anyone writing in America today," she observed, adding, "I wish it were not so near, and dependent on, the dreadful dream in her own heart." She may have meant, by this somewhat mysterious remark, that Adams was a seeker of romantic transcendence in a way that Bogan herself had long understood to be dangerous to psychic survival.

Wilson also published a book of poems that fall. It was called *Poets, Farewell!* and contained a mixture of serious and light verse, about which Louise wrote to him in a vein that nicely captures the tone of this period of their friendship. Her favorite poems, she remarked,

are you to the exclusion of everyone else I ever heard about; they are full of nobility, as music can be,—a real nobility, that is both form given and impressed. In fact, if they were mine, I'd break down and cry about them, and I hope you will do this (again I speak with great seriousness—Paul Elmer More couldn't be more serious) if you have neglected it up to now. I'd do it myself, if I could, but tears have dried up in me, my good fellow, these many years.

Moments are reached, in some lives, where every sense and every faculty is in use. Such moments belong to an endless present and are, in some sense, eternal. One cannot remember when they began, and one is too absorbed to fear or anticipate their end. If the past impinges at all, it is in dreams which are forgotten upon waking. Thus it is all the more bewildering when such times of happiness end. They seem so certain to go on forever, since nothing about them even hints at a built-in flaw in their design. When they go, they go forever, and the balance can never be righted.

In blissful distance from the New York literary world, from the sorrow of her childhood and the struggle of her recent past, Louise Bogan watched peacefully as the fall of 1929 turned to the stark New England winter. The living room, she wrote to Janet Lewis, was polished and clean "like the inside of a nut-shell." On Sunday afternoons, while Raymond noisily shingled the roof and she read and wrote, the Philharmonic concerts played on the radio.

The week of Christmas, 1929, was spent at the home of Raymond's mother in South Salem, New York. The day after Christmas, Raymond telephoned the man who tended the forced-air furnace and instructed him to light a fire, so the house would be warm that night when he, Louise, and Maidie returned. Raymond was careful to tell the man not to open the damper all the way, only enough to heat the house, since it would be, after their week's absence, very cold.

Situated on a hill on Collins Street, the house was high enough so that, as the Holdens' car approached town, Louise, Raymond, and Maidie could see smoke coming out of the chimney, and Louise remarked how nice and warm it would be inside. Stopping in town briefly to pick up the week's mail, they went into the post office. There the postal clerk told them that their house was on fire, and that the firemen, at that very moment, were trying to save it. The man who tended the furnace had opened the damper too wide, and the whole wooden floor had caught fire.

As Mrs. Scannell remembers:

So we got back in the car, drove pell mell, well, as pell mell as you could drive through the snow, and got there to find the local fire department standing there. Raymond and Mother managed to break the front door down. But the whole place, with all its old wood, was going up fast. Mother's small cherrywood table got taken out. Raymond stood in his workroom and started throwing out books. Mother couldn't get up the stairs. All her manuscripts were lost. And finally they pulled Mother and Raymond out. They both got burned. Not badly. Just slightly scorched.

We were all bundled up; it was freezing. I just stood there, with tears going down, and Mother said that I only said to her, "Oh, Mother, all your lovely things." All the things that Mother and Raymond had really slaved over—everything was lost.

Almost everything was gone: most of the poems, notebooks, and stories Louise had written from 1912 on. Letters from friends. Her books. The furniture she and Raymond had stripped and refinished together and jewelry that had belonged to her mother, including the turquoise and diamond-chip earrings May Bogan would fasten on when dressing to meet one of her "admiring gents." Raymond, too, lost all his books and possessions. And Maidie lost her doll collection, her antique maple furniture, the grass skirt Margaret Mead had given her. Her grandparents had recently presented her with a large collection of photographs, including baby pictures of her mother, and these too were lost. Somehow, the commonplace book that Louise had kept from her Girls' Latin School days was saved, along with her 1922 Vienna journal; that, and a pine desk, built by Dr. Frink, a cherrywood table, and the clothes the three of them had on their backs, were all that were saved from the fire.

Mrs. Scannell does not remember where they spent that night. The house was insured, but Raymond, who had recently invested the rest of his inheritance in the stock market, lost most of it in the Crash. So rebuilding was out of the question. In a little over a week's time, they were back in New York, with an apartment rented at 5 Prospect Place in Tudor City.

The title poem in Edmund Wilson's *Poets, Farewell!* and those in Bogan's *Dark Summer,* plus the letters she wrote to others, are all that remain of what was to be the happiest time in Louise Bogan's life:

> Poets, farewell!—farewell, gay pastorals!
>   Clear amber cider-brandy; green-eyed cats;
>   Dim "blues"; blue willow-pattern dinner plates;
> Waking to birds and light from four white walls;
> Green deeps of ponds the sun-burned bather cleaves,
>   Dark water, warm by gusts or loded cold;
>   Blue hills, green valleys like great maps unrolled;
> Weeds in the garden; horners in the eaves.
>
> —We have rhymed under gray skies in the stubble grass
>   Sped plunging motor-rides with drunken song—

> Had Wyatt with breakfast, Yeats with the final glass.
> —Poets, farewell!—O subtle and O strong!—
> Voices, farewell!—the silver and the brass—
> I leave that speech to you who have the tongue.

THE POEMS in *Dark Summer* are arranged in a loosely chronological sequence. The first section contains poems published for the most part between 1924 and 1927, and is followed by a section devoted to "The Flume," the long poem written in the summer of 1924. The third section consists of a selection of poems from *Body of This Death,* and is followed by a group of poems "in a later mood." The final section is again devoted to a single long poem, "Summer Wish," which Bogan finished just before she and Holden moved into the Hillsdale house in May 1929. Between the earlier and later groups it is difficult to single out strong differences. The earlier poems emphasize change, the later ones fulfillment, but both groups have a lowering inquietude.

On the whole, *Dark Summer* is a more difficult, obscure, and satisfying book than *Body of This Death.* Natural observation gives a new freshness and vigor to Bogan's language, and signals a shift away from the earlier book's almost exclusive preoccupation with the psychology of sexual conflict.

In the very title of the book lies its core of meaning. The phrase *dark summer* is an oxymoron, a paradox of the senses, capable, as dreams are capable, of reconciling opposites in a chiaroscuro of suggestion and association. Throughout the volume both *dark* and *darkness* recur with obsessive frequency. There is the dark of the grave in "Sonnet," of forgetfulness in "If We Take All Gold," of renewing rest in "Tears in Sleep," of shadow in "Division," "The Mark," and "The Cupola." While each of these poems gives a particular force to its use of *dark* or *darkness,* in all of them it comes to stand for latency, concealment, and imminence, for whatever lies at a remove from will and control. Above all, it signifies the deepest layer of the unconscious, where hidden instinct gathers force and prepares to obliterate the powers of both reason and resistance by which the "vulgar upper consciousness" makes its claim to mastery.

In the first poem of the book, "Winter Swan," Bogan reveals a new and fresh engagement with observation. Looking at a swan gliding across an icy pond, Bogan's speaker experiences such a moment of acute anxiety that she feels herself estranged from time. The whole poem is about this disjunction and disunity. The romantic imagination can no longer succeed in its attempts to imbue the external world with its own coloring and texture.

Garden and earth, which had formerly been compliant with desire, are "hollow," although "Within the mind" and "Under the breast" the "live" and "willing" blood still burns. In the elegiac questioning of the swan's detached existence and the heart's yearning for a landscape like itself, the poem establishes two orders of time, the first being nature's time, the second being what, in "Didactic Piece," Bogan calls "the heart's wearing time," which is time clocked and charted through the seasons of feeling. Swept up in the anguish of perceiving that the world and itself are not the same entity, the poem's voice cries out:

> But speak, you proud!
> Where lies the leaf-caught world once thought abiding,
> Now but a dry disarray and artifice?
> Here, to the ripple cut by the cold, drifts this
> Bird, the long throat bent back, and the eyes in hiding.

The labor of acknowledging and putting away the past continues in the next poem, "If We Take All Gold," whose fairy-tale tropes of treasure and house give an aphoristic transparency to an otherwise complex sequence of psychological insights:

> If we take all gold
> And put all gold by,
> Lay by the treasure
> In the shelved earth's crevice,
> Under, under the deepest,
> Store sorrow's gold:
> That which we thought precious
> And guarded even in sleep
> Under the miserly pillow,
> If it be hid away
> Lost under dark heaped ground,
> Then shall we have peace,
> Sorrow's gold being taken
> From out the clean house,
> From the rifled coffers put by.

First published in *The Nation* in October 1925, three months after Louise Bogan married Raymond Holden, it represents a truce with the self, enacted after a psychic battle has taken place, the terms of which require nothing less than the dispersal of fiercely hoarded misery. From the "clean house" of the new beginning, Bogan equates "sorrow's gold" with both refuse and stolen treasure which must be "Lost under [the] dark heaped ground" of the unconscious. Only there, leaching into the soil of lost memories, can it serve the cause of "peace."

Having confronted the past in the volume's first two poems, Bogan now goes on, in "The Drum," to crown her labors with triumphal joy, as passionate instinct rises up with full force. A celebration of rhythm, it is one of those poems Bogan wrote with flawless control over diction and meter. As in the earlier "Sub Contra" in *Body of This Death*, she interweaves consonance and assonance to great imitative effect. It is almost possible to hear the suspended silences between beats, as the poem's percussion just averts regularity and offers continual surprise. This formal gaiety and manifest delight in the pulse and sound of language are precisely the poem's point, the "answer" to the "blood refused" of neurotic suffering.

In "Division," "The Mark," and "The Cupola," Bogan returns to the intense *looking* of "Winter Swan." These are difficult poems, concerned with correspondences between perceived natural fact and intuitions about absence, isolation, time, and fate, and each abounds in more or less abstract renderings of emblematic configuration. In the first stanza of "Division," for instance, the poet observes shadow with an increasing pressure of selection and compression:

> Long days and changing weather
> Put the shadow upon the door:
> Up from the ground, the duplicate
> Tree reflected in shadow;
> Out from the whole, the single
> Mirrored against the single.

And just as the speaker in "Winter Swan" had cried out to the silent bird in protest against the dismantled perfection of summer, so here the speaker cries out to the patterned shadow, not to question or protest, but to answer it, as it were, or recount how *seeing* imprints in the memory an image of the fleeting moment:

> Replica, turned to yourself
> Upon thinnest color and air—
> Woven in changeless leaves
> The burden of the seen
> Is clasped against the eye,
> Though assailed and undone is the green
> Upon the wall and the sky:
> Time and the tree stand there.

Had Bogan's journals and notebooks from the 1920s survived the Hillsdale fire, chances are they might have revealed a good deal about her growing interest in perception. We might well have found brief, richly observed descriptions of natural scenes: colors of earth and hills in various seasons, light at different angles and different times of day. These would have made a good deal more evident her affinities with her American Romantic forebears—Emerson, Thoreau, and Dickinson—with whose imaginations hers most certainly establishes continuity. In "The Mark" she writes a "Metaphysical" poem that recalls figures as disparate as Donne and Vaughan and the Surrealist painter Giorgio de Chirico (whose early paintings of piazzas transected by menacing shadow were, curiously, called "Metaphysical"):

> Where should he seek, to go away
> That shadow will not point him down?
> The spear of dark in the strong day
> Beyond the upright body thrown,
> Marking no epoch but its own.
>
> Loosed only when, at noon and night,
> The body is the shadow's prison.
> The pivot swings into the light;
> The center left, the shadow risen
> To range out into time's long treason.
>
> Stand pinned to sight, while now, unbidden,
> The apple loosens, not at call,
> Falls to the field, and lies there hidden,—
> Another and another fall
> And lie there hidden, in spite of all
>
> The diagram of whirling shade,
> The visible, that thinks to spin
> Forever webs that time has made
> Though momently time wears them thin
> And all at length are gathered in.

Throughout the poem, Bogan concentrates on the fateful indivisibility of man and shadow, capturing the dread of mortality implicit in the notion of time as a web and the urgent desire for escape that it breeds. Only at noon—the shadowless moment—is escape possible, when the eye is momentarily deceived into an illusion of timelessness. But time moves inexorably on, as the apples of late summer drop "unbidden" into the lap of mortality.

With "The Cupola," Bogan gives the play of light and shade a more "realistic" treatment, one based, perhaps, on her impressions of an old house in Hillsdale. The mirror hung on the wall of a cupola, with its image of mixed oak and beech leaves, becomes "a handsbreadth of darkest reflection," with *darkest* sustaining the weight of intimation and imminence that anchors the entire book in disquietude. Yet the mystery of the poem is that the whole scene it records is quite accidental and casual: "Someone has hung the mirror here for no reason" and

> Someone has thought alike of the bough and the wind
> And struck their shape to the wall. Each in its season
> Spills negligent death throughout the abandoned chamber.

Thus the "abandoned chamber" becomes a *camera obscura,* projecting the chance episodes of seasonal life with utmost passivity and unintentional art.

Bogan's instinct to compress her meditative and metaphysical impulses into the strict brevity of the formal lyric was sound. In "Didactic Piece," which she placed in the fourth and "later" section of the book, she attempts an extended meditative poem, with largely unsuccessful results. It is impenetrable in places, and fails as a whole, despite some fine passages, particularly the opening evocation of the two orders of time, the human and the nonhuman, and the two orders of reality they command:

> The eye unacquitted by whatever it holds in allegiance;
> The trees' upcurve thought sacred, the flaked air, sacred and alterable,
> The hard bud seen under the lid, not the scorned leaf and the apple—
> As once in a swept space, so now with speech in a house,
> We think to stand spelled forever, chained to the rigid knocking
> Of a heart whose time is its own flesh, momently swung and burning—
> This, in peace, as well, though we know the air a combatant
> And the word of the heart's wearing time, that it will not do without grief.

The poem goes on to develop what might be called the internal monologue of an enraptured visionary, cleansed of sorrow, and perhaps guilt, and newly intoxicated with the hold that the visible, natural world has over his imagination. Like a censer, "momently swung and burning—," he is consumed by joy against which he uninnocently guards himself by the warning that grief and change are also part of the nature of things:

> The limit already traced must be returned to and visited,
> Touched, spanned, proclaimed, else the heart's time be all:
> The small beaten disk, under the bent shell of stars,

> Beside rocks in the road, dust, and the nameless herbs,
> Beside rocks in the water, marked by the heeled-back current,
> Seeing, in all autumns, the felled leaf betray the wind.

This reversion to grief and change as a check upon joy occurs not just in the poems about perceiving the natural world, but in a number of lyrics in *Dark Summer.* "Cassandra" follows "Division," and "Girl's Song" follows "The Cupola." Both of these are dramatic and personal, and both speak of a fatality irreconcilable with any simple acceptance of natural faith. "Cassandra" is the more idiosyncratic poem, an impassioned outburst by the woman who feels the terrible burden of her gift of poetic speech. The mode is emblematic or quasi-allegorical, as it had been in "Stanza" ("No longer burn the hands that seized"), as if the poem were inscribed or engraved as a motto underneath a picture of the doomed Trojan prophetess. Warning those who pursue their own destruction, Cassandra can speak only in the accents of madness, the speech of truth but not of persuasion or belief. She is cursed by clairvoyance, cut off from the ordinary lot of her sex:

> This flesh will never give a child its mother,—
> Song, like a wing, tears through my breast, my side,
> And madness chooses out my voice again,
> Again. . . .

She is the voice of fury itself, "The shrieking heaven lifted over men, / Not the dumb earth, wherein they set their graves." Her knowledge is apocalyptic, her urgency daemonic, the symbol of that part of the psyche which drives the conscious mind to recognize truths it is reluctant to accept. For Cassandra, poetry assaults and afflicts her, setting her off from humankind and rendering her the doomed and solitary witness of "the shambling tricks of lust and pride." Thus the poem serves as evidence for what Harold Bloom was the first to say: that Louise Bogan, while "usually categorized as a poet in the metaphysical tradition or meditative mode . . . is a Romantic in her rhetoric and attitudes." From its hidden source, poetry creates speech which is profoundly *other* and *opposed* to the received notions of men.

A more conventional lyric theme can be found in the strong, simple speech of "Girl's Song." Bogan wrote it in Vienna on May 25, 1922, and its composition gave her some trouble. The first stanza originally read:

> Winter, that is a roofless room,
> Tavern to rain, was our love's home.

But she had already used the phrase, "This is a countryside of roofless houses,— / Taverns to rain,—" in "A Letter." Clearly an image based on a vivid memory of New England landscapes, it was changed to

> Winter, that is a fireless room
> In a locked house, was our love's home.

This eccentric, sad metaphor captures the bitterness and irony that Bogan sustains throughout the entire poem. She worried about its tone, asking Rolfe Humphries, who wanted to publish it in *The Measure* during his acting editorship, if it didn't sound "*too* Housman," too pastoral, melancholy, and ironic. Humphries must have reassured her, since she made no further changes.

It is one of Bogan's consummate "girl's songs," a cross between a traditional lyric on spring's return and a girl's lament for the betrayal of love and her lost innocence. This mix of genres was already familiar in the seventeenth century, where, as in Campion's "The peaceful westerne wind," irony is found in the *contrast* between spring's return and love's death. Bogan's disabused speaker, however, sees an identity, and an inevitability, in the simultaneity of the two events. Addressing her imagined rival, she prophesies the same fate she herself has suffered, speaking no more as a "girl" but as an experienced woman. Here the heart's time and nature's time beat out the same rhythm:

> Now when the scent of plants half-grown
> Is more the season's than their own
> And neither sun nor wind can stanch
> The gold forsythia's dripping branch,—
>
> Another maiden, still not I,
> Looks from some hill upon some sky,
> And, since she loves you, and she must,
> Puts her young cheek against the dust.

THE THREE POEMS which conclude the first section of *Dark Summer*, "Feuer-Nacht," "Late," and "Simple Autumnal," are extraordinary, rich with complex harmonies of sound and meaning. Bogan never mentions "Late" in her letters and papers, and, to my knowledge, it has been overlooked by both reviewers and critics. Yet it is as strong and as bleak a presentation of spiritual desolation as exists in her work. Its images of a broken psyche extend as far back as the brutal desert landscape of "A Tale," as the no-longer ecstatic imagination surveys the "sterile cliff" and "cold pure sky" of its emptied visions. Thus barren, maddening, and mocking, the world stands denuded and hostile. The screaming cormorant, the "Stony wings and bleak glory" that "Battle in your dreams" appear to have walked out of some Yeatsian nightmare. Cryptic as the poem is—for we know nothing about its composition or background—its sense of desolation and derangement is unmistakable. Two poems from the later, second part of the book—"Fiend's Weather" and "I Saw Eternity"—speak of a similar mood of wild embitterment and terrible clairvoyance. In "Fiend's Weather" there is a windstorm of disillusionment, so that the mind now sees the world with a fierce knowledge of reality:

> In this wind to wrench the eye
> And curdle the ear,
> The church steeple rises purely to the heavens;
> The sky is clear.
>
> And even to-morrow
> Stones without disguise
> In true-colored fields
> Will glitter for your eyes,

The same mood of enraptured despair produces the equally driven and ecstatic vision of "I Saw Eternity":

> O beautiful Forever!
> O grandiose Everlasting!
> Now, now, now,
> I break you into pieces,
> I feed you to the ground.
>
> O brilliant, O languishing
> Cycle of weeping light!
> The mice and birds will eat you,
> And you will spoil their stomachs
> As you have spoiled my mind.
>
> Here, mice, rats,
> Porcupines and toads,
> Moles, shrews, squirrels,
> Weasels, turtles, lizards,—
> Here's bright Everlasting!
> Here's a crumb of Forever!
> Here's a crumb of Forever!

The poem inverts the beginning of Henry Vaughan's "The World":

> I Saw Eternity the other night
> Like a great *Ring* of pure and endless light,
>   All calm, as it was bright,
> And round beneath it, Time in hours, days, years
>   Driv'n by the spheres
> Like a vast shadow mov'd.

Vaughan's poem held a deep attraction for Bogan, who was fascinated by the planetary dance. True to her contrast-loving nature, she preferred the pre-Copernican picture of the universe, yet held to her modern sense of man's diminished and dependent position within its law-governed order. It is an act of daemonic despair to break the harmonious unity of Eternity and light, and to feed its fragments to the lowly creatures of the earth.

Bogan composed "Feuer-Nacht" at Yaddo, in August 1926, and like "The Alchemist," it charts the course of relentless passion. Figurative to the point of allegory, but built out of private metaphors, its "shuttered eye," "leaf-shaped flame," rock, sedge, and grass belong to the same rough geography, that inner New England, of Bogan's early poetic world. In German, *feuer* means "passion" as well as "fire," and the title's "night of fire" suggests a wild, dangerous, and forbidden conflagration that burns at night, witnessed from a secret place, devouring everything in its path. Like the "fire in a dry thicket / Rising within women's eyes" of "Men Loved Wholly Beyond Wisdom," this is love at its most savage and violent, strangely enhanced through being contained in the stark formality of the poem's structure.

"Simple Autumnal" follows, and it is one of the great lyrics in American poetry. The poem's long lines steadily bear the burden of unreleased, shored-up emotion in a dirgelike rhythm that moves with all the dignity of a solemn procession:

> The measured blood beats out the year's delay.
> The tearless eyes and heart, forbidden grief,
> Watch the burned, restless, but abiding leaf,
> The brighter branches arming the bright day.
>
> The cone, the curving fruit should fall away,
> The vine stem crumble, ripe grain know its sheaf.
> Bonded to time, fires should have done, be brief,
> But, serfs to sleep, they glitter and they stay.

Because not last nor first, grief in its prime
Wakes in the day, and hears of life's intent.
Sorrow would break the seal stamped over time
And set the baskets where the bough is bent.

Full season's come, yet filled trees keep the sky
And never scent the ground where they must lie.

This sleep, this stupor that arrests life appears as the refusal to mourn, a perverse defiance of that process Freud called "grief-work," whereby painful memories must be reexperienced, and relinquished. The tenacious avoidance of pain engenders a deeper suffering. The exhaustion of the girl in "A Letter," who craves only her food "and sleep," the stone speaker of "Medusa," and the stone girl with lifted heel in "Statue and Birds," have all suffered this paralysis, this inability to surrender to the claims of life. Yet, according to natural law, grief exists for precisely this purpose, to awaken the sufferer to feeling and time. Its course is limited, its role "not last nor first." The delay must end, and life win out. Bogan made this point clear to herself in altering the last line. When first published in *The New Republic* in December 1926, it read: "And never scent the ground where they will lie." This she changed to "And never scent the ground where they must lie," an emendation that precisely defines the poem's conflict, being a statement of necessity, resistance to which is possible only through the narcosis of denial.

The poem is a cry for deliverance not *from* but *to* the body of this death, to the liberation of grief and integration into the seasonal cycles of ripening and decay that are the principal themes of *Dark Summer* as a whole. Behind it lies a terrible fear of sterility and estrangement from natural life. The landscape of "Simple Autumnal" sets forth, as no poem of Louise Bogan's had yet done, the task her poetry as a whole had assumed as early as the adolescent "Poplar Garden"—to seek alliance with life, through art, rather than escape, and to set the wintry, betrayed, stunned, and sleeping heart to beating.

FIRST PUBLISHED in the June 1925 issue of *The Measure,* "The Flume" was included in *Dark Summer,* but then removed from all subsequent collections. It is perhaps Bogan's most openly autobiographical poem, and, considering her belief in the superiority of art detached from its source, obviously unacceptable to her. But it was an extremely useful poem for her to have written. Thinking that she was temperamentally unfit for long narratives in either prose or verse, she found that she could tell a complex story set down in long, untiring writing bouts. More important, the poem also allowed her to cut away an abundance of crystalline nuggets from the matrix of childhood memory. In a letter to John Hall Wheelock from Hillsdale on December 7, 1928, thanking him for his praise of the poem, she wrote that she had spent her childhood in mill towns and "was happy to be able to do something with that remembered noise of water." The flume reached back as far as memory could go, to Milton, where she later remembered that it "cascaded down the rocks, with bright sun sparkling on the clear, foamy water. My mother was afraid of the flume. It had voices for her; it called her and beckoned her. So I, too, began to fear it."

The woman in the poem, like Louise's mother early in the century, is married to a man who leaves every day for work. But there the resemblance between the two ends; the woman in "The Flume" is much closer to Louise herself, who, when she was writing the poem in the summer of 1924, was consolidating her relationship with Raymond Holden and trying hard to overcome the distrust that reached back to Milton and her betraying mother. Modeled on Viola Meynell's short stories, but composed in verse, the poem attempts to exorcise Bogan's fear by giving it distance and a separate shape blended of memory and invention.

The poem did not start out as a long narrative. At first, Bogan had wanted only to write a lyric about thunder. "Did you ever have that kind of mindless, idealess compulsion that you must do a lyric called 'Thunder' (or any other name)?" she wrote to Rolfe Humphries on July 22, 1924. Two days later she informed him that she hoped to finish the passage on lightning (which eventually became Part II) and that in it she planned to concentrate on the thunder more than the lightning, adding that "the lightning startles me merely, the thunder would wring me with fright were I a mole underground." By the end of August, the poem had become a narrative, and an exasperating one at that. She informed Humphries that she had lost all interest in its heroine, "who used to rush around the house hoping she'd be betrayed. I'm sure she's been betrayed by this time and has taken to washing dishes and having babies, like any other milky-breasted female, married to a he-man." By September 6th, the end was in sight. The lightning passage was finished and there was only one more part, out of four altogether, to compose. At what point the poem strayed from its original preoccupation with thunder to the flume itself has not come to light, despite Bogan's occasional progress reports to Humphries.

The poem's story could not be simpler. The heroine, going about her daily tasks in a fury of suspicion, searches the house for clues of her husband's infidelity. In a sudden storm she experiences her inner turmoil and the outer tumult as a single madness, hearing the sound of the flume, in the momentary stillness between roars of thunder, as a symbol of the love she cannot accept. At last, returning to her home after what appears to be an attempt to run away, she undergoes a moment of illumination that restores her to wholeness and enables her to love and accept love in return.

Throughout, the poem is studded with precisely recalled and imagined details which establish the mingled atmosphere of the simple New England house, its rootedness within the seasons, and the woman's wild emotion:

> The fields have gone to young grass, the syringa hung
> Stayed by the weight of flowers in the moving morning.
> The shuttered house held coolness a core against
> The hot steeped shrubs at its doors, and the blazing river.
> She in the house, when he had gone to the mill,
> Tried to brush from her heart the gentlest kiss
> New on her mouth. She leaned her broom to the wall,
> Ran to the stairs, breathless to start the game
> Of finding agony hid in some corner,
> Tamed, perhaps, by months of pity, but still
> Alive enough to bite at her hands and throat,
> To bruise with a blue, unalterable mark
> The shoulder where she had felt his breath in sleep
> Warm her with its slow measure.

She searches the rooms of the house for a letter or a ring, anything "to set her grief, / So long a rusty wheel, revolving in fury," but all she hears is

> . . . the noise of water
> Bold in the house as over the dam's flashboard,
> Water as loud as a pulse pressed into the ears,
> Steady as blood in the veins . . .

Because of the "guilt in her to be betrayed," the "terrible hope" that her husband cannot love her, she cannot sleep in peace beside him:

> At night his calm closed body lay beside her
> Beyond her will established in itself.
> Barely a moment before he had said her name,
> Giving it into sleep, had set the merciful
> Bulwark of spare young body against the darkness.
> Her hair sweeps over his shoulder claiming him hers,

> This fine and narrow strength, although her hands
> Lie, shut untenderly by her own side.
> Her woman's flesh, rocking all echoes deep,
> Strains out again toward ravenous memory.
> He lies in sleep, slender, a broken seal,
> The strong wrists quick no more to the strong hand,
> The intent eyes dulled, the obstinate mouth kissed out.
> Outside the dam roars. He is perhaps a child,
> With a child's breath. He lies flexed like a child,
> The strong ribs and firm neck may count for nothing.
> She will think him a child. He is weak and he will fail her.

In Part II the terror within is matched by the terror without. The thunder comes as she huddles against the dusty wallpaper, sweeping her up into the whirl of her suppressed instincts—the same movement of feeling presented in "Feuer-Nacht." Suddenly she loves her life and its orderly tasks in "the free still air." This stillness deeply present within her is the stillness (as opposed to the terrible "purpose" of her obsession) of nature in its darkest, most primitive, mysterious, and abiding form:

> —Still—still—everything quieter then
> Than the very earth escaping under the plough
> The depth beyond seed of the still and deep-layered ground
> Stiller than rock; than the blackest base of rock,
> Than the central grain crushed tight within the mountain.

Yet she fights this stillness, saying nothing to her husband when he returns except what might be said casually at dinner time about a storm. Still she fights acceptance, wishing to hurl the thunder at the growing earth and the love, the "itching love / So much like sound," pulsing within her like the waters over the flume.

In the final section the woman, who has run away, returns to her house. Her husband is still at work, but there is a good fire in the kitchen that "has turned the stove lids golden-red." As she "pulls the frozen patch of veil from her mouth / And stands, like a stranger, muffled from the cold," her obsession—the "unsated pulse of fury"—returns. But she soon becomes aware of the winter's deep quiet; the flume is frozen solid, its customary roar silenced:

> And here at last the lust for betrayal breaks.
> Her blood beats on, and her love with her blood
> Beats back the staring coldness that would kill her,

Laying a palm over the ebb and return
Of her warm throat, heard now for the first time
Within this room. Soon he will find her,
Still dressed for flight, quiet upon his bed,
When he has hurried from the weighted cold
Toward the faint lamp upstairs. She will lie there
Hearing at last the timbre of love and silence.

ON THE SUBJECT of withdrawing the poem from later collected
editions, Bogan wrote:

I have never been quite sure about "The Flume." It came from the right place, and
I worked hard on it, and it has some nice moments—the hot stove and the no-sound
of water—which were actually observed and lived with, at one period of my life.
Perhaps I have the feeling that one doesn't get out of that kind of obsession so easily—the "facts" are false, at the end. When I'm dead, someone will gather it up and
insert it in the *works*, I suppose. With notes!

The truth was that, in life itself, Bogan had never quite conquered her
own obsession with betrayal, and fate had conspired with her fears. The
ending *is* melodramatic and "easy." Still, the heroine's experience of love as
the onrush of a bodily force, far from being false, was and remained a central
ideal in Bogan's faith, both as an artist and a human being.

NOT SURPRISINGLY, the poems that come after "The Flume,"
those Bogan gathered as the fruits of a "later" mood, are filled with further
intimations of pain and blight. The title poem, "Dark Summer," published a
year after Bogan married Holden, registers a vision of consummation from
which the speaker and her companion are unaccountably excluded:

Under the thunder-dark, the cicadas resound.
The storm in the sky mounts, but is not yet heard.
The shaft and the flash wait, but are not yet found.

The apples that hang and swell for the late comer,
The simple spell, the rite not for our word,
The kisses not for our mouths,—light the dark summer.

Akin to the thunder section in "The Flume," the poem sketches a pastoral ceremony of erotic fulfillment within time. But unlike the late comer,
who will receive the fruit and the kisses, the speaker and her lover seem to

be caught within a premature, unripe, and unripening love, prevented once again by some nameless obstacle from participating in the flow of natural time and love. Another kind of sexual pessimism haunts "Tears in Sleep":

> All night the cocks crew, under a moon like day,
> And I, in the cage of sleep, on a stranger's breast,
> Shed tears, like a task not to be put away—
> In the false light, false grief in my happy bed,
> A labor of tears, set against joy's undoing.
> I would not wake at your word, I had tears to say.
> I clung to the bars of the dream and they were said,
> And pain's derisive hand had given me rest
> From the night giving off flames, and the dark renewing.

Bogan has made this poem the vehicle of an extraordinarily subtle insight into one way in which neurotic grief and suffering ultimately provide a defense against passion. In her "cage of sleep," the speaker of the poem is separated from the "stranger"—the other, the lover—whose presence is true, and real, and as such far more dangerous than the "false grief" that afflicts the dreamer. And "For a Marriage" stops at nothing short of sexual cynicism. Out of a pretty trope of sentimental exchange, which might well have a source in Sidney's "My true love hath my heart and I have his," Bogan constructs an elaborate (and somewhat labored) conceit of marriage as a double-edge sword—the wife's neurotic character—which the husband (suitor-courtier-knight) must "clasp on." In return for girding himself with this weapon, he gets to "keep his life awake," an ever-ready defender of his wife against herself. At the very least, "he will know his part," have a purpose, role, and destiny, and these in turn will shield him against the recognition of his own weaknesses.

In such poems as "Simple Autumnal" and "Tears in Sleep," the mode of contrast, so essential to Bogan's poetic imagination, in which public and private images forge ironic antitheses, resembles Baroque chiaroscuro, in which illuminated masses move in and out of heavy shadow. A description of Renaissance tropes as "both openly resplendent and artificially shadowed" applies equally well to Bogan's figures, with their strongly pictorial contrasts of light and dark. In yet another way her preoccupation with light and dark places her securely within the tradition of the American Renaissance. Critic Clement Greenberg has pointed out that "chiaroscuro, literally and figuratively, was the favorite vehicle of Victorian poetic meaning." Bogan, who apprenticed herself to Victorian poetry, shares the tendency of Hawthorne, Poe, Melville, Dickinson, and, later, James, to work with "oppositions which heave a retreating, inward-directed force like that of contrasts of light and shade within deep space."

Bogan's chiaroscuro took its tone and technique from seventeenth-century lyric poetry, its mixing of private and public symbols from Symbolism, and its precision from her American eye for visual fact. In the brief lyric, "Song for a Slight Voice," a poem in which musical instruments serve as intricate emblems much as they do later in the magnificent "Song for the Last Act," Bogan presents the figure of a heart likened to a viol "Stained with the dark of resinous blood," evoking a cluster of chiaroscuro-like impressions incapable of naturalistic analysis. In "The Crossed Apple," she mixes Yankee and Baroque sensibilities to perfection, blending the traditional fairy tale with a plainly worded yet ecstatic vision of earth, and setting forth the apple as both an archetypal symbol of temptation and fall, and a matter-of-factly observed object in nature, much as Thoreau himself might have discussed it. During the Hillsdale period she was avidly reading Thoreau, and may well have encountered this paragraph in "Wild Apples":

These apples have hung in the wind and frost and rain till they have absorbed the qualities of the weather or season, and thus are highly *seasoned,* and they *pierce* and *sting* and *permeate* us with their spirit. They must be eaten in *season,* accordingly,—that is, out-of-doors.

The speaker in "The Crossed Apple" makes a similar claim:

> Eat it; and you will taste more than the fruit:
> The blossom, too,
> The sun, the air, the darkness at the root,
> The rain, the dew,
>
> The earth we come to, and the time we flee,
> The fire and the breast.

The surprising end—"I claim the white part, maiden, that's for me. / You take the rest"—is gloriously mean-spirited: the speaker well knows that the red half, "Sweet Burning," is full of love's poison. Such a poem comes out of the freedom to mix genres. In "Sonnet," however, with its stately and solemn language, Bogan displays a sense of obedience toward convention, with somewhat uncertain results. She herself was not absolutely sure about the poem. Writing to Ruth Benedict in March 1929, she asked her friend to be "*perfectly* critical about it. Is all this bone business just funny?" The bone business *was* funny. And there was a touch of "fine writing" of the sort Bogan was ordinarily the first to censure. The intricate meditative sonnet on high "Metaphysical" matters was not her forte, despite the recent example of Elinor Wylie's estimable results with the form. Bogan needed a core of drama, common life, and strong speech to give vitality to her work. Yet, in "Come, Break with Time," she writes an extremely meditative, "Metaphysical," and at the same time *simple* lyric. Vaughan's trope of Time "in hours, days, years / Driv'n by the spheres / Like a vast shadow," echoes in it through the antiphonal language of command and defiance that prevails in *Body of This Death* but with the exception of this poem is fairly muted in *Dark Summer*. In this poem, however, Bogan offers two voices, one that exhorts and another that retorts. The exhorting voice, which belongs to the nature-hating will, counsels the defiant heart to cease commerce with change, and its insidious, soothing tones are directed at a heart both wearied and weakened by time. The besieged yet defiant heart can only utter, *"I shall break, if I will."* The exhorting voice, hearing this ambiguity, bypasses it with its own executioner's sophistry in "Break, since you must," an oracle preempting all choice and counseling only compliance with necessity. This severance from time may be death, but it is more likely the sleep of "Simple Autumnal," or the paralysis of "Medusa," where comfort is gained only by becoming virtually insensate.

With "Old Countryside," Bogan completes the group of poems in the "later mood." Bogan later said that she saw the poem as holding to some of the Imagist precepts, primarily direct treatment of the *thing,* whether subjective or objective, and strict avoidance of any word not bearing directly on the presentation of the matter at hand. The poem is filled with such directness: the "slant shutter," "mansard roof," the mirrors in the attic (like those in "The Cupola"), the creaking clapboards, the "You" of the poem "braced against the wall. . . , / A shell against your cheek," the brown oak-leaves, dry trees, the "scrawled vine," the "rose-branch . . . / Red to the thorns," and "The thin hound's body arched against the snow." As the facts which demonstrate that "all has come to proof," these sharply etched images have the edited exactness of memory, the extraordinary clarity of watchful intuition marking a cycle of fulfillment:

> Long since, we pulled brown oak-leaves to the ground
> In a winter of dry trees; we heard the cock
> Shout its unplaceable cry, the axe's sound
> Delay a moment after the axe's stroke.
>
> Far back, we saw, in the stillest of the year,
> The scrawled vine shudder, and the rose-branch show
> Red to the thorns, and, sharp as sight can bear,
> The thin hound's body arched against the snow.

Pain edges this final vision. The rose-branch stands naked, the hound holds its body back from the snow, and the shuddering vine, in being "scrawled," suggests some indecipherable message which can only be understood in retrospect. The poem's imagery, which on one level is as public and precise as an illustration to some book of *très riches heures,* is on another level a hieroglyphics of fate.

Published in the August 1929 issue of *Scribner's Magazine,* "Old Countryside" is Bogan's poem of love and praise to the months she and Holden spent working on the Hillsdale house. It is Holden who braces the wall and holds the shell, the figure of stability and harmony. The two people in the poem have come full circle; they share a past of labor and of lived-out time. Thus the last two stanzas are all the more haunting. The "unplaceable" cry of the cock, the as yet indistinct possibility of betrayal, echoes at the end, and the hound's arched back remains as taut and poised as suspicion.

H A R O L D B L O O M, calling "Summer Wish" Louise Bogan's "most ambitious poem," believes that it marks "the crisis and mid-point of her career," but this was to come in the next decade of her life. "Summer Wish," however, does sum up a period of personal and poetic fulfillment, and it is her one great poem in a major style and major mode, capable of standing alongside Yeats's "The Tower" and Stevens's "Sunday Morning" as a testament of renewal and acceptance.

In a letter to May Sarton in 1954, Bogan remarked, "The last time I lived with the full cycle of the seasons was more than 20 years ago, when Raymond and I had the little house near Hillsdale. 'Summer Wish' came out of that." It came, too, out of her obsession with sexual betrayal, which once again provides the poem with its obsessive structure of *antithesis.* She says, in her prefatory notes to the recorded reading of the poem, that its dialogue form is not strictly an imitation, although "the form of a dialogue between two voices is one often used by Yeats," and adds that the "background of the poem is New England."

The poem's roots reach deep into the history of the English lyric, as far back, in fact, as the medieval lyric, "Sumer is icumen in," which is echoed in the epigraph to "Summer Wish," the opening lines of Yeats's "Shepherd and Goatherd": "That cry's from the first cuckoo of the year. / I wished before it ceased." They are spoken by the Shepherd, the affirmative voice of Yeats's poem, whose wish is objectless, a cry of pure desire simultaneous with the cry of the early cuckoo.

Yet another of Yeats's poems, "Ego Dominus Tuus," provided a model. On May 1, 1929, Bogan wrote to John Hall Wheelock that "Summer Wish" was "really coming to life. For a time I despaired of it; now it has its shape and sound, a climax or two and an ending that really excites me, all in the mind; one or two good intensive spurts will finish it, I trust."

She added that it would take the form of "a colloquy between *This One* and *The Other*," phrases which are translations of *Hic* and *Ille*, the voices of "Ego Dominus Tuus," who act out the Yeatsian division between the known self and its unknown other.

Within this highly formal structure, Bogan presents a meditative eclogue on the problem of despair. The two voices remain voices, not characters, although the subject matter is exactly the same as that in the versified, highly psychological short story of "The Flume." Each voice has its own sound, its own rhythms, diction, and tone through which Bogan shows the power of language to create and sustain a point of view which each speaker assumes to be "objective."

Thus, in "Summer Wish," Bogan's task is not to absorb the negative self within the stronger affirmative self, but simply to get the First Voice to speak the language of the Second. It is no easy goal. The First Voice perversely misinterprets everything the Second says, throwing out embittered, querulous challenges to it, in an attempt to disqualify whatever the Second Voice offers by way of affirmation or assurance. Wisely, the Second Voice quietly outmaneuvers the First by responding with *description* rather than retort. But it must work hard. The First Voice proclaims deception, concealment, and doom with consuming pessimism. Summer is not the season of renewal, but the harbinger of autumn and mortality:

> We call up the green to hide us
> This hardened month, by no means the beginning
> Of the natural year, but of the shortened span
> Of leaves upon the earth. . . .

With the knowledge that such despair devours everything offered to appease it, the Second Voice makes no counterargument, but rather mingles pure praise in a surface of pure description:

> In March the shadow
> Already falls with a look of summer, fuller
> Upon the snow, because the sun at last
> Is almost centered. Later, the sprung moss
> Is the tree's shadow; under the black spruces
> It lies where lately snow lay, bred green from the cold
> Cast down from melting branches.

Through this calm exposition, the Second Voice in effect gives a reasonable explanation for the appearances the First Voice regards with dread. It looks forward rather than back, delighting in the inflections of change. To the Second Voice the vernal equinox cannot lie: it augurs the "look of summer"; but the First Voice finds this "A wish like a hundred others," cracking open the Second's optimistic almanac as if it were a bitter nut of delusion. With fanatic resistance, the First Voice shouts out its denials:

> You cannot, as once, yearn forward. The blood now never
> Stirs hot to memory, or to the fantasy
> Of love, with which both early and late, one lies
> As with a lover.

To the First Voice, desire, volition, the capacity to make wishes are not only pure illusion, but blind egotism:

> Now do you suddenly envy
> Poor praise you told long since to keep its tongue,
> Or pride's acquired accent,—pomposity, arrogance,
> That trip in their latinity? With these at heart
> You could make a wish, crammed with the nobility
> Of error. It would be no use. You cannot
> Take yourself in.

This despairing confession forms the heart of the poem. To wish—to be capable of desire—is, in effect, to write a poetry of praise: of what, to the resentful and cynical will, *looks like* arrogant insincerity and mere literature. Incapable of this simple rite of acceptance and faith, the First Voice bitterly acknowledges its own sense of futility. With its picture of the world stemming from its own broken, paralyzed self, it can only see the world *as* itself.

The Second Voice, evading the First's animadversions as it had at the beginning of the poem, urges it to "Count over" what exists separate from itself.

> . . . lilies
> Returned in little to an earth unready,
> To the sun not accountable;
> The hillside mazed and leafless, but through the ground
> The leaf from the bulb, the unencouraged green
> Heaving the metal earth, presage of thousand
> Shapes of young leaves—lanceolate, trefoil,
> Peach, willow, plum, the lilac like a heart.

To the First Voice, this vision is neither spontaneous nor true, but made up of disguised remnants of memory and dream. Having failed to relinquish the past, the First Voice sees it concealed in every aspect of the present!

> Now must you listen again
> To your own tears, shed as a child, hold the bruise
> With your hand, and weep, fallen against the wall,
> And beg, *Don't, don't,* while the pitiful rage goes on
> That cannot stem itself?

The First Voice now reveals itself distinctly as a *woman's,* as it continues its litany of pain and despair:

> Or, having come into woman's full estate,
> Enter the rich field, walk between the bitter
> Bowed grain, being compelled to serve,
> To heed unchecked in the heart the reckless fury
> That tears fresh day from day, destroys its traces,—
> Now bear the blow too young?

Against this outburst, more a soliloquy than a reply, the Second Voice invokes the pattern and movement of the growing light of early April. It is light "there's no use for," existing purely in itself, independent of memory, desire, dream, or any form of human illusion, and "misplaced" because it affirms a world detached from the human. True to itself, the First Voice senses a snare and rejects this vision of tranquility, conjuring up, in another recapitulation of Bogan's private obsessions, the "betraying bed" and its "embrace that agony dreads but sees / Open as the love of dogs." These are eyes made not to see beauty, but the pornographic horrors of jealousy. For the First Voice, spring's arrival and sexual betrayal are identical, as they are for the speaker of "Girl's Song."

Persistent, assured, and transcendent, the Second Voice offers a visual parable that recalls both "Division" and "The Mark," pointing to the human freedom to make everything, or nothing, from the visible:

> The cloud shadow flies up the bank, but does not
> Blow off like smoke. It stops at the bank's edge.
> In the field by trees two shadows come together.
> The trees and the cloud throw down their shadow upon
> The man who walks there. Dark flows up from his feet
> To his shoulders and throat, then has his face in its mask,
> Then lifts.

In these lines Louise Bogan achieves mature poetic vision, mapping out a place for human life in a universe defined by mortality rather than by man's relation to himself, freeing him from solipsism only to prepare him for death. It is at this point at last that the First Voice hears what the Second has said. Questioning itself, it sees its own madness, its own unintelligibility, and its own brooding narcissism:

> Will you turn to yourself, proud beast,
> Sink to yourself, to an ingrained, pitiless
> Rejection of voice and touch not your own, press sight
> Into a myth no eye can take the gist of;
> Clot up the bone of phrase with the black conflict
> That claws it back from sense?

Admitting that it perverts reality and speaks in an indecipherable private language which shuts off the possibility of shared meaning, the First Voice goes on to acknowledge its division of "the gentle self" into "a yelling fiend and a soft child." Out of this, the confrontation necessary for renewal takes place, and although its tones are still defeatist, the First Voice accepts "a vision too strong / Ever to turn away."

As if sensing that the First Voice has now reached a point of maximum openness, the Second responds with a Blakean vision of evening: "In the bright twilight children call out in the fields. / The evening takes their cry. How late it is!"

The antiphon of children and evening echoes the epigraph, with its cuckoo's cry and Shepherd's wish. Going on to present a vision of ultimate order within time, the Second Voice brings the poem to resolution:

> Fields are ploughed inward
> From edge to center; furrows squaring off
> Make dark lines far out in irregular fields,
> On hills that are builded like great clouds that over them
> Rise, to depart.
> Furrow within furrow, square within a square,
> Draw to the center where the team turns last.
> Horses in half-ploughed fields
> Make earth they walk upon a changing color.

As the Shepherd's wish merges with the cry of the bird, the First Voice fits its voice to the Second's: "The year's begun; the share's again in the earth." No longer a traitor to itself, it pours out its joy, rich with the laughter of "the natural life," as Yeats's Goatherd calls it. Laughter draws the poisons, "aconite, nightshade, / Hellebore, hyssop, rue,—" and leaves freedom for the wish:

> Speak it, as that man said, *as though the earth spoke,*
> By the body of rock, shafts of heaved strata, separate,
> Together.

The man referred to in these lines is Thoreau, who wrote, on March 3, 1841:

I hear a man blowing a horn this still evening, and it sounds like the plaint of nature in these times. In this, which I refer to some man, there is something greater than any man. It is as if the earth spoke.

This human vision now overwhelms the First Voice:

> Speak out the wish.
> The vine we pitied is in leaf; the wild
> Honeysuckle blows by the granite.

At last, when the Second Voice speaks to the First, it can guide it, confident of shared vision:

> See now
> Open above the field, stilled in wing-stiffened flight,
> The stretched hawk fly.

Like the end of Stevens's "Sunday Morning," with its casual flocks of pigeons, and the bird's "sleepy cry" among the "deepening shades" of Yeats's "The Tower," the poem concludes with an earthly moment that makes no claims beyond its own evanescent completeness. Though the poem may well be Louise Bogan's "Resolution and Independence," as Harold Bloom has called it, its assent is not to human endurance, but to nature and time as the something-more-than-human that defines, and gives an unassailable dignity, to the human.

II

1930 ❀ 1935

SOJOURN
IN HELL

4 FEUER∽NACHT

BOGAN AND HOLDEN put the money from the insurance policy on the Hillsdale house into the stock market, where they promptly lost it. Even had the investment prospered, it could not have given back "the things gathered over years, nor the books, never to be exactly replaced, and our work put into walls and rooms," as she explained to Harriet Monroe. Catastrophic though the fire was, it was not, to be sure, a tragedy. Life went forward on the Holdens' return to New York City in much the way it had gone forward before their move to the country. Louise worked at home, writing poems and book reviews, while Raymond soon landed a job as managing editor at *The New Yorker.* Louise's attitude was calm and sensible: "After all, it is more important to be alive without possessions than dead either with or without them."

The three members of the family were soon comfortably settled at 55 Prospect Place in a three-room twelfth-floor apartment, whose only drawback was its proximity to a foul-smelling slaughterhouse. Maidie boarded during the week at Woodmere Academy, the small, good country school on Long Island where Rolfe Humphries taught Latin.

Organized and realistic, Holden and Bogan managed to reestablish themselves on what appeared to be a sound footing in a remarkably short time. In truth, from the beginning, the new life did not go well. The aftershock of the fire marked the exacerbation of emotional difficulties Bogan had succeeded over the years in withstanding, subduing, and, except in her poems, concealing to a large extent from herself. She was writing strong reviews for both *The New Republic* and *Poetry,* and her reputation as a poet was secure. In March, Sara Teasdale, whom she had long admired, wrote to commend her poems and invite her to tea. But Louise was incapable of enjoying either praise or friendship. Little by little, during the winter and spring of 1930, she became the victim of an insidious loss of appetite for work accompanied by an equally insidious loss of appetite for life. This creeping malaise soon took the form of actual paranoia when she began to suspect that she was the butt of revived literary-world gossip about her love affair—over now for some ten years—with the fur-thief John Coffey, and her supposed participation in a number of his department-store thefts. She was miserable, and, upon receiving the John Reed Memorial Prize from *Poetry* in October 1930, in recognition of *Body of This Death, Dark Summer,* and poems published in *Poetry* itself, complained to Harriet Monroe that the hazards of self-exposure seemed to outweigh the rewards.

Before long, she was stranded in what she called "creative despair," a state with sources reaching far back into her childhood and the *sturm und drang* of her first marriage and early years in New York. For a long time she had looked at herself and seen an intoxicating portrait of a precocious, gifted, and beautiful young woman, a reckless bohemian and inspired seeker of art and freedom. Now, at thirty-two, surveying what she saw as her thickening body, and her two slim volumes of poetry, she suffered an overwhelming loss of power and uncertainty of direction. Her early self lay in ruins about her, silenced and played out. During the summer of 1930, a time of superficial calm marked by cheerful letters to Maidie at camp in Pennsylvania, a visit with Raymond to Edna St. Vincent Millay and Eugen Boissevain at Austerlitz, New York, and a thirty-third birthday, celebrated by a party where the guests played poker and Ping-Pong and consumed an angel cake with room for only "two dozen candles," Louise began to keep a notebook, one that was to replace another lost in the fire, in which "five years of life were put down purely and with the insight which I can no longer clearly claim." She recognized that she was in the grip of an emotional and creative crisis, and, despising passivity, felt that the task ahead was nothing less than total artistic and psychic reconstruction.

First and most important, she would teach herself to write all over again:

But, I said, if I could put down part of a year, in proof of work, and in defiance of idleness. Part of this year, when, to my own knowledge, what once was strong and unbroken is now strong and broken. If I could write with the awkwardness of maturity and truth, in a style as hard as a brick (for as I begin I feel how soft the lines run, after a year when the imagination and the will have slept a long sleep, blinded in each other's arms). It is not in the language of a dream I wish to speak. I could learn perhaps, the run and complexity long envied in the styles that do not flag, even when faced by the necessity of long factual exposition. The styles as complex and delicate as tackle made for some job requiring skill, patience and strength: a tackle composed of blocks and rope, combining at once the principles of the lever, the inclined plane and the wheel.

The Symbolist, who as a teenager thought reality a poem by Tennyson, took notes that summer of 1930 on Colette and Tolstoi, and discovered that nothing and no one, least of all Louise Bogan herself, should be exempt from the truth:

It is necessary to remember and to choose. You must say out to the end what you have long managed to suggest. You must give up symbols. You must be able to see well. To feel clearly and to place every phrase in proportion to the rest. The hardness of a rich will must serve you completely; subtle as a diagram, proven and complex, ordered, rearmed, detailed—that is work, the imagination said. The will and I have slept, and we awaken now only to catch you in the symbols of ourselves.

She would track appearances, not their underlying meaning. She would not depend on talent: "You will write out of ambition or out of fear, not out of the incredible force that brought you and left you where you are." She began to note what she saw and felt:

I saw the clear afternoon, casting the shadows of chairs one way in the room, so that the season was as clear within a house as out of doors. The shadows had the time of day written into them, as well as the look of autumn.

It is early October, and a day of great clarity. The river throws up every barge solidly and the light falls on the setbacks of the buildings strong and bright. October light has more time in it than any other. The day says "Late" with its light, as summer mornings say "Early" with theirs.

A style seemingly devoid of effects—the opposite of the "wrought style" she had loved as a girl in Pater and Alice Meynell—now held out the greatest charm to her. She looked at New York with a vision akin to the painter Edward Hopper's in its simplicity and order:

It is a day for everything. The trees in the little park are dry and brown, because they have not been planted deeply; under them women in careful costumes sit and read, or talk to one another. The elevated train reverberates on its rails, and children have built a fire in the lot where they have not yet put up an apartment— the smoke drifts a long way, as clearly defined as the sound. Smoke drifts from the chimneys of the tenements—not much smoke—as from a poor fire, but from the apartment buildings a steady blue stream goes out sideways into the air. Little figures of men on steelwork streets away sometimes come into view; the booms of derricks hold cables at clear angles, slender as threads. Light falls through the windows of empty apartments and lies on the floor marking the empty rooms with rectangles. The light falls against the leaves of plants, upright in the pots, and upon the lemon and tomato in the fruit dish, and upon the faded and dusty chintz of a chair that has worn through a summer.

She could feel the poignant mystery of time and things, but failed to get what she believed to be the whole truth from herself. Her notes struck her as evasive and incomplete. In symbolism she could disguise the truth; in the external treatment of facts she could avoid it. A year later, after months of observing, she wrote: "I cannot yet put down all the truth as I see it: but I shall train myself and sometimes this thing will come out truly, in detail, alive, possessed, understood, first; thereafter written out. My own angers, my own despairs, therefore—and all the matters before which I now fall silent."

Chief among these was her conviction that Holden was continually in search of other women to conquer. Aware as she was of her tendency toward hysterical jealousy, Louise could not help believing that her fears had a foundation in reality. Certain that he had had occasional affairs since the early stages of their relationship, she had, more than once, suffered from hating and fearing a woman she considered her rival. Holden's denials did little to assuage her suspicions; his protestations of adoring love sounded hollow and rhetorical to her ears. Coming home from a long day at *The New Yorker,* he found her testy, accusing, and bitter. On Saturday nights, with Maidie home for the weekend, the three would go out for spaghetti to Joe and Rose's, a Third Avenue delicatessen that dispensed bootleg grappa in teacups from a tiny "restaurant" behind the icebox. After a good many of these, Raymond and Louise and Maidie would walk home, and a fight would invariably erupt in the street, with Louise yelling at Raymond and Raymond yelling back. These shouting matches would continue until they reached home and went to bed, and were never referred to the next morning. Louise became more and more obsessed with what she saw as Raymond's inability to tell the truth about women and money. Nothing in her life came to matter as much as getting a straight answer from him. Like the woman in "The Flume," she was virtually *determined* to be betrayed, lied to, made a fool of.

As her inner life sank in upon itself, however, her literary fortunes improved. Katharine S. White, head of the fiction department of *The New Yorker,* had only recently succeeded in persuading Harold Ross to publish serious poetry. Up until then he had favored light verse only, and in May 1926 the magazine had published a light and witty lyric of Bogan's, "Consolations of Religion." Thinking that serious poetry "would be not only useful but important to the magazine," Mrs. White wrote to all the good poets she knew, asking them for work, and between December 1929 and January 1931, she published three more of Bogan's poems in the magazine: "Old Divinity," "For an Old Dance," and "The Engine." Now that it published serious poetry, the magazine, its editors believed, had an obligation to enhance the taste and knowledge of its intelligent, receptive, but not necessarily poetically informed readers. When Bogan published her first review of poetry for *The New Yorker,* in March 1931, and thus inaugurated the magazine's custom of offering two omnibus surveys, fall and spring, of "The Season's Verse," she little knew that she was to perform this service, faithfully and unstintingly, for the next thirty-eight years.

As fortifying as her association with the magazine may have been, it did not, however, keep her overburdened emotions from finally running down. In the middle of March 1931, when her first *New Yorker* review was about to appear, she wrote to John Hall Wheelock at Scribner's, explaining that she had gone to visit her family in Portland, Maine, to search for some "peace of mind." By April 11th, she had made the decision to seek help, and voluntarily became a patient at The Neurological Institute on Fort Washington Avenue and West 168th Street. There, no more than a block from the apartment house where she would eventually live from 1937 until her death in 1970, having "refused to fall apart," she reported to Wheelock, she was "taken apart, like a watch."

For a year she had been tortured by a state she described in the rough draft of a poem as a "burned and angry solitude" and a "fever in the brain." Her body felt as "empty as the dead." She hated and feared other people and was envious of other women writers. During the day, by herself, she drank too much, and took long streetcar rides through the city, sunk in desperate moods of self-revilement. She harbored grudges, collected injustices, and rehearsed scenes of rage, sneering at the world and believing it sneered at her.

Her hospital routine included hydrotherapy, weaving and knitting, and private conferences with a young doctor by the name of McKinney. Bogan responded to his interest and compassion with something bordering on feelings of love, and Dr. McKinney, in turn, was so taken with his patient that he was once moved almost to tears in her presence. She had the warm support of her friends, who recognized her as a person of very special sensibility. Harriet Monroe confided that she too had once had a nervous breakdown, and Janet Lewis, Katharine S. White, and John Hall Wheelock all made Bogan feel that her sufferings were bound up in important ways with her life as an artist. Edmund Wilson wrote, in a manner at once blunt and tender, that he had "been there myself"—referring to his own nervous breakdown in the spring of 1929, and that she was without question "one of the people that I value most and count most on." He went on to remind her that things in general had become rather difficult:

These are times of pretty severe strain for anybody, to lapse into a vein of editorial generalization. Everything is changing so fast and we are all more or less in a position of having been brought up in one kind of world and having to adjust muscles, socially, sexually, morally, etc., to another which is itself in a state of flux. Still, we have to carry on, and people like you with remarkable abilities, even though they're more highly organized nervously than other people, are under a peculiar obligation not to let this sick society down. We have to take life—society and human relations—more or less as we find them—and there is no doubt that they leave much to be desired. The only thing that we can really make is our work. And deliberate work of the mind, imagination, and hand, done, as Nietzsche said, "notwithstanding," in the long run remakes the world.

What Louise's friends did not know, though they may well have suspected it, was the extent to which her chronic lack of faith in Raymond lay at the very heart of her crisis. In her acute distress she was more convinced than ever that he stood to her in the relation of an enemy, out to undermine and harm her, and she enlisted McKinney as an intermediary in her efforts to protect herself from him. She refused to see Raymond directly, insisting that he talk with McKinney first, and relayed her own messages to Raymond through the doctor. Raymond's asseverations were always the same, that he loved Louise, adored her, needed her, couldn't live without her. But whether she should continue to live with him was precisely the question, for her. At one point during her hospital stay she entertained the notion that the two of them should live separately in their apartment, he in the back and she in the front, a plan that Raymond immediately rejected as unnatural. As she improved, she remained convinced that she was not yet ready to live with him on a full-time basis, and she was jittery about the prospect of spending whole nights with him.

Raymond saw her breakdown almost solely as a response to himself, rather than an eruption of pressures that had been accumulating for a long time. His own role, even as antagonist, was central; her hospitalization, in his eyes, was almost exclusively an action on her part to remove herself from his presence. His letters to her are pleas on his own behalf, reassurances that he was hard at work correcting his own character defects. He was certain that she loved him and was doing violence to them both by trying to punish herself and kill their love with her belief that he had ever been untrue to her.

Nevertheless, in her reply to Wilson's letter, she made no mention of

Raymond's role in her sufferings, though acute anguish colored every word. "Dear Edmund" she wrote:

Your letter came just now. It made me laugh and cry, so you can easily see that I have been separated into my component parts. Rather queer parts they turned out to be, too. They lie all about me as I write—(that sounds like the Psychiatric Institute and Robert Browning in a letter from Lake Como, at one and the same time). Yes, to continue the figure, there they are. There's a broken mainspring, vulgarly known as the capacity to love. There are a few odd cams that we won't go into. And there's the nicest shiniest sprocket, beautifully studded with those little things they call jewels, which turns out to be my affection for you. And that's the truth. I have always vaguely suspected that you were the friend I liked best in the world, and that suspicion is now a certainty. And I did think that I had done something to make you dislike me. In my high sneering and fleering days (now gone forever), I did things to many people with that subconscious end in view. I am glad that you are still my friend. I have often wanted to see and talk to you this winter. But I couldn't impose my own sufferings on anyone else. Too proud. Too sensitive about other people's rights and feelings. It was best to go to an innocent bystander, a disinterested observer, like McKinney. You understand now that you have been a great solace to me many times, don't you? And that I've never really sneered and fleered? I've often shouted that you were a great darling, from the housetops.

I've got to get up and out of here soon; I've got to go on "notwithstanding," but I don't know how the hell how. I have a slight delusion that it was I who broke the "notwithstanding" record for the years 1916–1931 inclusive. Maybe not. Whatever the answer is, it has not yet appeared, written in letters of fire as high as a horse on the walls of this distinctly dreary madhouse cell. McKinney may know. I like him. He thinks I'm smart. But, dear Edmund, I am so tired. I'm so smart and so tired. I'm like the man in Chekhov who goes around saying "cannon off the red!", or that other man who is reduced to making notes of facts in a little book. I'm a great compendium of people out of Chekhov, as a matter of fact, including the pockmarked man called Waffles and the Charlotta woman who produces rabbits out of hats. Life under the Romanovs.

Yes, everyone is a great big old Romanov. Everyone was a horrible old bloated sneering old Romanov this time last week, at least. Today I don't know. Yesterday I fell in love and was happy and looked sixteen. Today I don't know. If I feel love again, it seems that I must take it with me, in full bloom, into a nice commodious steamheated mausoleum, and stay with it there until the solar system breaks down. One with the solar system. That's really quite a comforting thought. . . .

I read *Uncle Vanya* and cry. I cry a good deal. You have now brought Thoreau to mind and I shall have many's the good cry about him, all alone in that cabin eating corn-meal mush and loving the wood chucks.

I wish I were a continuation of a kid and Virginia Woolf. Flying around producing round solid novels and feminine intuition, and thoughts on great writers. I wish I could get the hell up from here and fall in love with an intern. I also wish I were dead, but that's old stuff, once thought up by a big old sneering old sybil in a cage. To hell with it. Who cares?

No, dear Edmund. It will be all all right soon. Armed with second-hand radiance borrowed from the redoubtable McKinney, I shall no doubt bounce from this bed with a whole series of masterpieces, written by hand, and wrung from the bowels and brain. The last person to let society down. The very last.

While she couldn't write poetry yet, she could produce some spirited verse, adding this squib at the end of her letter:

> At seven, hot water, enemy of sleep;
> Coffee and rolls at eight; at nine an hour
> Of therapeutic weaving (though I weep);
> After a sunbath and a needle-shower.
> A round of Russian Bank; the doctor asks
> "How's the depression?" It's a lovely day
> Devoted to most simple-minded tasks.
> Massage. Now sleep the afternoon away.
>
> My God, what was the crime. Did I deserve
> Therapy, out of possible punishments?
> What the betrayal, that the faded nerve
> Must bloom again by means not making sense?
> O, I shall mend! Even now I grow quite well,
> Knitting round wash-cloths on the paths of hell.

She soon moved, under McKinney's supervision, from The Neurological Institute to Cromwell Hall, a sanitarium on a large estate in Cromwell, Connecticut (much frequented by Sara Teasdale, who was also susceptible to nervous disorders), where she was to convalesce by continuing to follow the routine sketched in her verses to Wilson. She faithfully took her steambaths and needlesprays, her massages and sunbaths, and her walks on the landscaped estate of the sanitarium, reading more Chekhov, lyric poetry, and, strikingly, Swift's *Journal to Stella* (a book very possibly recommended to her by Wilson), hoping, in all humility, that she would soon be able to write poetry again.

To her amazement, a poem, "Hypocrite Swift," simply *arrived* on April 26th, in cadences echoing her recent lines to Wilson. Astounded that she had written anything at all, she enclosed it the next day, "hot from the pen," in a letter to Wilson, explaining that she had started out to write an exercise, and that the exercise had "turned out really to be a poem." With almost inhuman detachment, she penetrated to the core of Swift's impaired capacity to love, and saw the yearning and despair inside his bitter wit:

On walls at court, long gilded mirrors gaze.
The parquet shines; outside the snow falls deep.
Venus, the Muses stare above the maze.
Now sleep.

Dream the mixed, fearsome dream. The satiric word
Dies in its horror. Wake, and live by stealth.
The bitter quatrain forms, is here, is heard,
Is wealth.

What care I; what cares saucy Presto? Stir
The bed-clothes; hearten up the perishing fire.
Hypocrite Swift sent Stella a green apron
And dead desire.

Seeing Swift, as she does in the poem, from the calm and stern perspective of Venus and the Muses, she freed him—and herself—from paralyzing blame and guilt, and in the act of writing found the courage to go on. Life with Raymond seemed worth another try. She loved him still, and needed him, although, as she wrote him, she still believed that he was hiding some essential part of himself from her. "I don't know how I can convince you that I'm not," he replied, adding that "subject to the ordinary run of male weaknesses, it's not my concealment of anything but your reading into me things that aren't there which causes you to have misgivings." He said again what he said repeatedly throughout her breakdown, that the cause of her feelings of hate and distrust of him was the hate and distrust she felt for herself. He was happier now than he had been for months, he continued, because in the past few weeks he had come to believe once again that she loved him. He needed to feel that she loved him; his whole life, he confessed, he had been haunted by the thought that no one could really love him, and he wanted her to be the one to cancel his doubts beyond all others.

He too, he continued, had suffered from loneliness and desolation during the bitter time before she had sought treatment, and he too had been searching himself for clues to their difficulties. Louise, after all, had been convalescing in comfort, with a doctor and nurse in attendance, while he had been waiting for her to return to her right mind. If she could only see that her problems were self-imposed, they could begin again, and go about the business of cherishing the genuine love they felt for one another. Persuasive and appealing, Raymond succeeded in getting Louise to agree to come home. After spending the rest of May in Cromwell Hall, she returned to New York in June, with some small measure of restored self-confidence, but with the equally strong awareness that she was by no means "cured." "Several mechanisms have broken down," she explained to Harriet Monroe, "and a strange new period has set in, in my heart and mind. I feel at once renewed and disinherited."

She was eager to work, and there was plenty of it for her to do. *The New Yorker* assigned her a profile of Mrs. Gertrude Vanderbilt Whitney as well as one on Willa Cather. To Maidie, away at camp, she wrote that she worked all day in the New York Public Library at Forty-second Street, "with my whole body dripping wet with moisture," as well as at home, taking time out for sponge baths between paragraphs. She was also managing to have some fun, going to hear Beatrice Lillie sing "Mad Dogs and Englishmen Go Out in the Midday Sun," and "There Are Fairies at the Bottom of My Garden," and attending a *New Republic* deck tennis party with Raymond where she fell down and wrenched her knee. "Mr. Thurber of the N.Y.er was on [sic] that party. He told me that I was damned handsome, and thought we ought to see more of each other!" she reported to thirteen-year-old Maidie. "He has a glass eye, poor dear. Anyone who falls for me is sure to have something missing."

Returning, as if she had never left off, to the new style of observation she had begun in the 1930 notebook, she turned her attention to prose fiction, publishing five stories in *The New Yorker* between June and December 1931, all of them based in one way or another on her own memories, observations, and experiences. Her friends at *The New Yorker* were quick to praise them, and both Harold Ross and Katharine S. White were extremely eager for her to do more. In their enthusiasm over her talents, however, Bogan's *New Yorker* allies overestimated her range. When Mrs. White saw the profile of Gertrude Vanderbilt Whitney, whose new museum of American art would open in the fall, she was forced to turn the article down on the grounds that Louise hadn't presented the facts in any but the most perfunctory way. She tactfully suggested that both the magazine and Louise treat the Whitney piece as something she had had to grind out after her illness, and that as soon as possible she should go back to writing short stories. Not surprisingly, once she was asked for stories, Louise's ability to write them temporarily subsided. She continued to work, nonetheless, writing a profile of Willa Cather, producing a spring omnibus review, and reviewing Allen Tate's *Poems: 1928–1931* so sharply that he wrote her personally to accuse her of having been "venomous" and out to make "as damaging a case as possible." To this she replied with even more detailed criticism of the book. Anyone keeping a close watch on her spirits might have concluded that she was in fine high form—the very last person, as she might have said to Wilson, to let life and literature down.

IN OCTOBER 1931, Raymond, Louise, and Maidie moved to a big apartment on the top floor of a brownstone at 306 Lexington Avenue between Thirty-seventh and Thirty-eighth streets. Louise worked in the large dining room in the back, and there was also a living room, two bathrooms, a master bedroom, and a small hall bedroom for Maidie, who nearly died in November of the following year when the woman living in the apartment immediately below committed suicide by turning on the gas, which leaked into Maidie's room. Waking up, she staggered into the living room and passed out, but was revived by a rescue squad.

With the income from his *New Yorker* job, and a trickle of trust income, Raymond was able to provide Louise with a full-time maid. As insiders at *The New Yorker,* they were a most sought-after couple, attractive, witty, and sophisticated members of an attractive, witty, and sophisticated literary coterie. Everyone knew that the gin Raymond made in a big stoneware jug kept in the bathroom was the best in town, and people dropped in several times a week for cocktails. There were parties, with Edmund Wilson supplying "topical songs . . . written at high speed and sung to a tune that borrows Kern's rhythms and Gershwin's melodic line," *bouts rimés,* and plenty of conversation and conviviality. Rolfe Humphries and Helen Spencer were likely to show up, as well as other old friends like poets Léonie Adams, Scudder Middleton, and Elizabeth Huling, who was on the staff of *The New Republic.* From *The New Yorker* there were cartoonist Peter Arno and his wife Lois Long, Wolcott Gibbs, movie critic John Mosher, book and art critic Robert M. Coates and his wife, and Katharine and Andy (E. B.) White. Wilson, along with his wife, Margaret Canby, was perhaps the most regular guest. After his wife accidentally died in the fall of 1932, he recalled in his diaries the blissful feeling of once having fallen asleep on the floor of the Holdens' apartment with his head against her shoe; and he noted another occasion, in 1933, when Raymond, who had been fired from *The New Yorker* and was researching a freelance article on obstetrics for *Fortune,* lectured Katharine S. White "about it like a venerable old authority," telling her "who had had a Caesarian, about Caesarians—somebody mentioned something and he replied with tremendous gravity: 'Very dangerous! Very dangerous!' "

Louise and Raymond did not always see eye to eye on whom to invite over. Literary agent Jap Gude remembered one evening in the early thirties when Raymond invited the Leftist novelist Mike Gold to the house. The evening wore on, with Gold and Holden talking about various social ills, and Louise finally just disappeared. "She had gotten bored," according to Gude, "and had gone to take a bath!" By themselves, Louise and Raymond began to fight again, and the Saturday night flare-ups after spaghetti and grappa at Joe and Rose's resumed. Louise accused him constantly of wanting other women, and of being the object of other women's designs. On one occasion she got so angry she threw a pot of hot coffee at him; on another, Raymond got so exasperated that he hit her, knocking her down on the stoop of their brownstone and hurting her eye. She found him childish and weak, and couldn't stand his financial dependence on his family. She was irritated by his inability to break through his writing blocks, and was occasionally insulting about his poetry in company. Wilson, who had little respect for Holden, although he found him congenial enough for an evening's drinking, left a telling sketch of the Bogan-Holden household during the winter of 1932–33:

Louise and Maidy [sic] playing piano the night that Raymond (Holden) went out with his mother to Radio City: Raymond's crawled back into the womb tonight. —A little piece of the Kreutzer Sonata, a little fragment of Glück—with a one! and a two! and a three! and a four! —I was touched and delighted by it. . . . She had kept her music and managed to pass it on to Maidy, in spite of Raymond. Raymond came back and said we were drunk.

Raymond was not the only apparent obstacle to Louise's happiness; their life of literary gentility seemed menacing and corrupting to her, and in some of the *New Yorker* stories she was writing at the time, she as much as said so. The young woman who surveys her friend's guests at a cocktail party in "Sunday at Five" grinds her teeth and thinks she must suffocate from the atmosphere of "opaque eyes and pretentious voices." In "Conversation Piece," written in 1932 and published in August 1933, young Mrs. Tracy, a Jamesian character in that she is someone "on whom nothing is lost," notices, when drinks are served at the home of Mr. and Mrs. Williams, an older couple whom she and her husband are visiting, that "Little ships in full sail stood perfectly still in a bulb in the stems of the cocktail glasses." Tired out from the heat, and paired with Mr. Williams, who offers thoughtful banalities on the necessity of form in the arts, Mrs. Tracy carefully observes the way her husband knows how to steer through a perfectly rehearsed—and quietly flirtatious—conversation with Mrs. Williams about antiques. The implication is that Mr. Tracy is born to a false manner that Mrs. Tracy at once envies and detests, even though, as the two couples gossip about people they know, Mrs. Tracy, downing cocktail after cocktail, proves herself as adept as her companions in the art of polite and malicious chatter. Nevertheless, talking at high speed, she becomes detached from the scene, letting her eyes go "all around the room, gathering up details. They followed the graceful curve of the Regency chair legs, of the gilt rococo mirror, of the precious and chaste *fauteuil* upon which she and Mr. Williams sat. They sailed purely and calmly along with the little ships imprisoned in the stem of the cocktail glasses."

Behind Mrs. Tracy's silent and ironic gaze raged Bogan's growing hatred of everything she considered redolent of upper-class and upper-middle-class pretension: "refined" manners, "well-bred" accents, and "nice" people; Ivy League attitudes; New York clubs (Raymond belonged to The Players' Club); Atlantic crossings; children whose doting mothers thought them "talented." The woman who once wrote to Rolfe Humphries that "I do love tables, chairs, libraries, silk underwear, clean sheets, food cooked to order, paper and pencil and music" would visit Raymond's mother, at South Salem, New York, and like Mrs. Tracy, cast an indicting glance over everything she saw:

—The Whistlers, the George Washington clock and plates, the good, solid, perfectly tasteless food, the passion for glass and china (fostered by a Jewish woman with a Spanish shop, who spent her life fostering glass-and-china-and-barber's-basins-(brass)-and-tooled-leather-and-hand-woven-linen passions in members of the bourgeoisie). The fine bindings in the library, the pages uncut. The Garden Club. Marion's [Raymond's sister's] boat-house (fixed up so charmingly with Spanish and Italian and Early American junk, as above). Clock-golf. The tennis court that nobody ever used. The rather dotty butler Mrs. H. was frightened of. —They were all frightened of something, I never could make out what.

She was as attuned to *things* as she was to times and places, and could feel the way furniture absorbed boredom and stuffiness just as she could tell the hour and season in a shaft of sunlight. The material comforts available to her through her marriage to Raymond both attracted and repelled her. Early in 1933 she wrote in her journal:

Last night I woke and remembered the smooth architecture of clubs, good homes, fine shops, across the threshold of which I have never set foot nor shall ever set foot. I realized the sense of security in *place,* almost in life, that these outward symbols must give to those who frequent them. It is simple, at four in [the] morning, to feel an outcast. And is it to the imaginative that such a feeling comes full force? Does the stenographer feel rootless because she has never dined at the Plaza or bought her clothes at Jay-Thorpe's?—a quite different idea than snobbishness. The feeling arises from an imaginative grasp of what *these things must stand for,* the comfort they must give, to those who just miss taking them as a matter of course. Even to anyone bred straight into them they must give some solidity, no matter how matter of course they have become.

Louise Bogan, "the little Irish girl from Roxbury," had not been bred to them. Civilization, culture, and the possibility of an ordered life she had been forced to discover for herself, in Mrs. Gardner's housekeeping, in the potted palms of Copley Square, and in the terrible acknowledgment, so hard won, of Miss Cooper's human imperfections. She had not known what fine bindings were until she visited her friend Alison Laing at Radcliffe in 1916 and saw a paneled room full of books in Italian, all bound in tooled leather; and she had not awakened to architecture, and Mozart's music, until her Vienna journey in 1922. She knew what it was like to live without beauty and custom, and she couldn't help believing that, in their purest form, they could not be consumed or faked. With his riding breeches and boots and appropriate tweed jackets from Abercrombie & Fitch, his knowledge of antiques, and his familiarity with beautiful objects and "nice" people, Raymond, it seemed to an envious Louise, skillfully exploited his birthright of privilege, and it infuriated her to see his frank self-indulgence in the ruses of social egotism. She was even more censorious of her own desire for triumph across the dinner table, and *bons mots* on the living-room sofa. Contemptuous of all merely social success, she was convinced that the literary world revolved around cronyism and collusion, and although she had reviewed friends and been reviewed by them, she lashed out, in her journal, against people who reviewed their friends, exchanged favors in print, and went to P.E.N. dinners. She dismissed her own temptation to go to one such dinner, "looking as regal as possible," as "a childish and ignoble idea":

My life and hopes cannot be in that direction. So I'll turn it down. The world is not for me and can never be—I have not been trained to it and my approach to it is too easy, too false. I can assume too cleverly all the ignoble trappings that others assume with effort, and by the fey lightness and ease of my assumptions I am self-mocked and self-betrayed. No: all that is not mine and is not for me. But I must fear and desire it less. I must hate it less. I must learn to observe and judge, and forget to blame.

Her own dark secret, zealously guarded from the world, was that she was still far from well. "The continuous turmoil in a disastrous childhood," she noted in her journal in August 1932, "makes one so tired that 'Rest' becomes the word forever said by the self to the self. The incidents are so vivid and so terrible that to remember them is inadequate: they must be forgotten."

Since forgetting was the one thing she could not do, the time had come for her to put a shape to her memories. After reading Xavier de Maistre's *Voyage autour de ma chambre,* she commented, on September 29, 1932, that while it was not as interesting as she had expected it to be, "Such a voyage around every room one lives in would be of inestimable value to oneself, one's children; in a journal there's often too little of this kind of thing. The description should be detailed, pointed and brisk. Times of day and the look of sunshine or firelight or early evening should be included." She went on to write her own "Journey Around My Room," and, like de Maistre's piece, hers is an extended rumination upon the things in her bedroom—the mantelpiece, the Japanese print, the shells from a beach in Maine, the wallpaper, varnished floors, and fireplace. Gazing at these with an interested and curious eye, she says, "The initial mystery that attends any journey is: how did the traveller reach his starting point in the first place? How did I reach the window, the walls, the fireplace, the room itself; how do I happen to be beneath this ceiling and above this floor?"

Then, suddenly, as if the objects in the room were a scrim in a theater behind which lies another scene that suddenly brightens, Bogan enters the past and it is March 1909, in Ballardvale, the morning on which, instead of saying goodbye to her father as she has done for nine hundred mornings, she is about to take the train to Boston: "That is the reason for my presence here. I took the Boston train in March, 1909."

At once the traveler is back inside her room, as if the journey from Ballardvale to Lexington Avenue had been direct and uninterrupted. But now, scanning the room for a clue, for some sign of purpose, her eyes come to rest upon a bookshelf holding *La Madone des Sleepings, Apologia Pro Vita Sua,* Whitehead's *Introduction to Mathematics,* the poems of Baudelaire, William Drummond of Hawthornden, and Waller, the plays of Chekhov and Thomas Middleton, *Walden, or Life in the Woods, The Turn of the Screw,* Montaigne's *Essays* and *Taras Bulba.* Under this "truly horrifying array of literature" stands a desk, with pencils, photographs, lamp, ashtray, empty stamp box, postcards, paper knife, "and a large quantity of blank paper." But the traveler does not stop here. Her eyes, still searching the room, move past the north wall, containing "nothing of interest save the bed and the traveller moored therein," and the east wall, whose space is taken up by a large, beautiful, and serviceable armoire. Its size and stability should "hearten the traveller," but, here, just when the end is in sight, the catastrophe of the journey takes place. In the depths of sleep, the traveler has a dream in which she hears the mill dam foaming—what we know must be a compound of the Milton flume and the Ballardvale dam—and sees the rapids which she must swim:

Give over, says this treacherous element, the fear and distress in your breast; and I pretend courage and brave it at last, among rocks along the bank, and plunge into the wave that mounts like glass to the level of my eye. O death, O fear! The universe swings up against my sight, the universe fallen into and bearing with the mill stream. I must in a moment die, but for a moment I breathe, upheld, and see all weight, all force, all water, compacted into the glassy wave, veined, marbled with foam, this moment caught raining over me. And into the wave sinks the armoire, the green bureau, the lamps, the shells from the beach in Maine. All these objects, provisional at best, now equally lost, rock down to translucent depths below fear, an Atlantis in little, under the mill stream (last seen through the steam from the Boston train in March, 1909).

The room was Bogan's bedroom at 306 Lexington Avenue; the books, those she was reading in the fall of 1932, while writing the piece. In her private history, the writing of "Journey Around My Room" signified that she had arrived at the mystic's "dark night of the soul," and now faced a long ordeal of psychic exploration.

The miracle was that she could write at all. The actual daily processes of living and working were becoming so difficult for her as 1932 stretched toward its end that she must often have wondered how she managed to cope. Note after note reached Mrs. White at *The New Yorker* apologizing for delays in finishing pieces. Struggling with "Journey Around My Room," she explained:

A series of minor life crises—and the thing is begun but can't be finished today. *Don't* think me tiresome! I do mean well and you know that I always finally come through. But it hasn't been fun, trying to work, these last few weeks. I don't want to sound like a figure in high tragedy: I'm just giving you the facts.

A new personality was groping its way toward definition, and there were moments when Bogan's puzzlements broke through to a piercing lucidity:

The idea that she is splendid, brave, beautiful, an enchantress, a woman of talent breaks, after a certain age. She no longer wishes to write (as E. Sitwell has said) poetry that flays off her own skin before an imaginary audience petrified with admiration and delight. She walks more slowly in the street and looks around her with a thoughtful and candid eye. "Why, these are my fellow creatures! I am one of them."

At the age of thirty-five, she was awakening to find herself in a world of other people. There were events which did not touch her, lives which ran their whole course without even a moment's grasp of her own important existence. That she could imagine and sympathize with others heartened her. The world was no less terrible, but it was bearable, and full of the rewards to

be gained from a sincere curiosity about its ways. She was still, as she might
have put it, cut off from grace, still angry, cynical, bitter, and despairing, but
she had her blessed, saving detachment. Reviewing a set of notes kept over a
three-month period, she couldn't help being struck by "the rancor and hatred in them, if not the envy and jealousy. When I at last come into myself,
or reach the point that can be reached in that direction short of the philosophic conversions which I fear, perhaps this rancor will disappear." For the
time being, it consumed her, and she filled the 1932 notebook with a full
range of disparaging observations, noting that John Dos Passos, whom she
heartily disliked, "in his attempt to clarify American women careerists gets
exactly nowhere," and that "The M.[abel] Dodges of this world take everything they want, surround themselves with objects, people and *movements*
(analysis, thinking with the stomach or glands, Lawrence, Jeffers & the
like.—)." And once again, she turned her wrath, this time in private, upon
Allen Tate:

Have at you, Allen, and *Poems 1928–1931*! My thorough dislike for this particular
book may sound like an obsession, but I am often confronted by people who cannot
see what I mean when I condemn it as bad writing, bad thinking, bad approach and
completely lacking in intuitive flow.... Allen stands for ideas, for philosophic
bases, for moral values.... I shall never be able to understand how such fakery
goes down with really sensitive people.

She sensed betrayal in the air: by the gifted, of their gifts; by culture, of
its standards; by her husband, of her love. Wishing fervently to have done
with the envying poet and jealous wife she had become, at the same time she
recognized a salutary clarity in her capacity for Swiftian outrage, or *saeva
indignatio*. One benefit in keeping a journal, she thought, was in tracking
her hatreds, year after year:

We shall hate so much, if we live fifteen years longer: at the end we can compare
these hatreds, or someone can mosaic them for us and our "irritable substance" can
be somewhat charted. That sort of chart is important. Let us be truthful—you,
Louise, be truthful. And do not shrink from your hatreds. They may be a cover for
other emotions—let that also stand. If I did not hate, if I had not hated pretense and
falsehood in others, how false, how pretentious I should have been myself! The
germ of it is in me. By hatred of other's faults let me be cured!

Pity assaulted her as much as hatred and contempt. The sight of a
black man on the bus, with a hatbox in his lap, looking at advertisements,
was so painful that life, while she watched him, seemed unbearable. Old
people seen on the streets, or sitting at Woolworth's luncheon counters or in

automats wrung her heart just as the hopeful shopkeepers in Ballardvale and Boston had sent waves of pity through her body many years ago, when she had begun to realize that destiny favored some, and neglected others. The capacity to love, unable to settle itself on persons, moved out to the universe. She looked out upon the late summer light "on leaves in the evening," and noted that it "looked as though it did not come from the sun, but from space itself, or from some element in a universe so distant from our own that it must be felt, never seen, and never named." Under this light, anger and pity dissolved, for a brief moment, in peace.

Beyond her own inner ranklings, beyond her feelings of dismay and abandonment, as her friends Rolfe Humphries, Edmund Wilson, and Léonie Adams appeared to defect from detached aesthetic pursuits to the embroilments of organized politics, she was becoming unsettled by the spectre of fascism. Commenting on the season's new novels, she wrote in the fall of 1932:

Novels will more and more open out into the scene as it exists. That is, they will not only be written realistically, but they will have some sense of economic, political-social forces. Writers can no longer shut their people into drawing rooms or attics and let them pullulate among themselves. But is every novelist who heralds this transition bound to unburden his own little fanaticism in so doing? . . . Thousands of destined individuals with eyes too near their nose, who admire Hitler, are upon us, and thousands of novels riding their author's *idée fixe,* disguised slightly by means of wide views into economics, are about to appear.

The whole thing is fortunately easy to spot. I hereby spot it on Sept. 7, 1932.

But her persisting animosity disturbed her. She wondered whether her tendency to disparage other writers came from an abstract disapproval "of their principles, their (to me) fake principles, ambition, pretensions and hidden arrogance," or was she "merely a disappointed woman and inarticulate artist who must lash out at people from some inner compulsion?"

She did not know the answer, and she wished she did. She suspected that she was afraid of people, and protected herself against them through her hatred, but she was not sure. What she could detect, with some certainty, was a growing need to detach herself from the world:

As the circle of what I can do without widens and the center of things which I must have narrows and becomes more and more concentrated, the quiet in the heart which I prize, but have never achieved, may become more possible. That provincialism of heart which requires *things*—objects—has left me almost completely. Now a room with sun in it, a half day's leisure, a fire, cigarettes, unlimited books, a piano and some music, a clean bed and a garden in the summer seem all the materi-

als necessary for my life. (A little food, as well!) One or two friends, no acquaintances, and even no lover, if a relationship including a lover also includes tiresome incompatibilities and deadened perceptions.

Abhorring the atmosphere of literary, political, and economic fanaticism of both the Left and the Right, which she perceived to be engulfing European and American culture, she was forming a new ideal. Late in the fall of 1932, noting that Lawrence of Arabia had just published his translation of the *Odyssey*, she wrote in her journal:

He may be a spy, a tool of the British government, as some say: his present way of life, in its furious denial of every bourgeois value, excites me as nothing in hagiology. His present life is a kind of sainthood in our time (the explanation that he lives among men because he is a homosexual is easy, perhaps true—does not really matter). Better to live among men if you are a man of genius, than among women or with one woman. The genius with one woman destroys the *woman:* witness Tolstoi with an ordinary wife, Carlyle (a genius, if a warped one) with a potential genius: Jane Welsh, a great wit, a woman of the utmost fire and intelligence. Or witness Chopin and George Sand (whom he could not destroy, but upon whom he brought every nasty spoiled boy trick to bear). —Lawrence has his books, his large collection of recorded music for the phonograph, his speedboat, his racing motor bicycle. He has his power leashed into an inferior position; his tasks, as a Trappist has his tasks,—his freedom to range in the world of the intellect transcending that of a Trappist. He has had power and has repudiated it; he has taken up a life without power and without philosophic pretensions (that is what I most admire in him). He suffers; he wishes to die; all that can be enjoyed he takes: books, the music of Mozart: he wishes "to be forgotten of his friends." He wants £4 a week: no more: "far too much trouble to work for more." A true angry saint: D. H. Lawrence's opposite—for David Herbert ranged the world looking for something he could not find: he tied himself to a woman whom he could not do without: he raged because he could not "touch" men, because the "primitive sense of touch" was lost. (There never was a primitive sense of touch.) Not for the man of genius, the man driven by a fury, shaken by the burning impact of life itself: that impact that strikes us all, to which we harden ourselves gradually, until we need to feel it no more.

As she sat and wrote alone all day, overcome with melancholy "at five o'clock, when taxis outside on Lexington Avenue hollowly sound their horns, and street cars grind by with that hysterical zoom," her desire to live as a secular monastic was intense. She cast back over the past, over the months in Panama, when she had waited for the birth of her child, over mornings in Boston, when she had worked contentedly alone, hearing the children chanting their lessons in the school across the street, and wondered if her destined time had come and gone, squandered in smoking cigarettes, making love with Raymond, eating and quarreling and drinking, devouring thousands of books; in bouts of jealousy, envy, rancor, and grief. Perhaps, she mused, her special, her chosen time was now, a dark October day, on which she found herself writing her journal in her bedroom, "with emptiness in your body and heart; beside the small fire, drying your hair,—older, more tired, desperately silent, unhappily alone, with faith and daydreams (perhaps luckily) broken and disappearing." Perhaps this very instant was her time, "—pretty late—but still your own, your peculiar, your promised and presaged moment, out of all moments forever."

F O R T U N A T E L Y, Bogan had a new friend, a critic and scholar in whom she could confide with far more assurance of being understood than she believed she would find in either Humphries or Wilson. Morton Dauwen Zabel was born August 10, 1901, in Minnesota Lake, Minnesota, and was one day short of being exactly four years younger than Louise, a fact they liked to invest with some importance. Like Bogan, Zabel had been raised in a Catholic family, but he had remained close to it, living with his sister and mother until the latter's death, and afterward with his sister. In February 1929, the young professor of English at Loyola University in Chicago had been appointed associate editor of *Poetry* magazine, and the following December he wrote a review of *Dark Summer*. Of all the book's reviews, his was the most penetrating as well as the most admiring. To him, Bogan's poems were intellectually and emotionally rich, the fruits of "a creative patience rivaled by that of few other living poets."

The friendship between Bogan and Zabel grew directly out of this review. When he came on a visit to New York in September 1930, he had tea with her at 5 Prospect Place, and thereafter they always arranged to see each other when he came to town. In his memoirs, Horace Gregory describes Zabel at that time as "an extremely blond young man, obviously shy. Although no single feature of his face resembled those of Gerard Manley Hopkins (as seen in photographs), his nervous sensibility gave the illusion that he recreated the looks and manner of the Victorian poet: he had the same radical depth of feeling, the same passionate concern for ethical values in poetry, and was contemptuous of shoddy, merely liberal opinions." In Zabel, Bogan found a person who shared her admiration of the secular monastic ideal. Zabel—though well taken care of by his mother and sister— lived a simple, frugal existence dedicated to a fanatical belief in the value of high culture. He was extravagant in one thing only, the accumulation of books and records. An accomplished pianist, he particularly cherished vocal music, as did Bogan. At the same time, behind his rimless spectacles there lurked a giggler and a gossip who found her merciless wit as enchanting as her lyric gift. John Hall Wheelock thought Zabel was in love with Bogan, in a silent, worshipful, unobtrusive sort of way, but there's no evidence that he ever declared his feelings, or that she ever encouraged them. He was devoted to her, however, and although they were to quarrel many times in their long friendship, he elected to be eternally (and therefore irritatingly) responsible to her for as long as he lived, putting himself at her disposal in times of psychic and financial need. When she complained that she could not work, he would goad and chaff her, knowing how destructive her perfectionist's temperament could be. In the winter of 1935, after one of her outbursts of disaffection and paralysis, he coolly wrote:

I noted that you bade farewell—again!—to Memory and Desire. Good, but for God's sake let it be the last time, and now please knuckle down and unleash the pure untrammeled truth. You've done a few things more perfectly than most people ever do any; but it isn't enough, and time is slipping, and you'll have to write your prose achievements pretty soon. Or the new poems. Don't spend too much time blocking out, throwing down outlines, getting the feel, and waiting for the irresistible. Think of James, Conrad, Charlotte, Chopin, and W. S. Landor, who could get down to business in white gloves or during a raging tooth-ache or grief-stricken by four family deaths running or throwing up bits of lung or with hair and fingers all over butter. You're much too finicking, wanting a large space and clear table, outward harmony and inward agreement, and a lot of preliminary blocking out. But take time, only don't let it run away.

In Zabel, the determined auto-didact found yet another tutor, one who was, moreover, thorough, canonical, and scholastic where Wilson was freeranging, selective, and high-handed; reverent and inflexible where Wilson was dismissive and elastic. Zabel stood for the academic degrees Bogan had in youth avoided but whose usefulness she now acknowledged, the life of learning as distinct from the world of letters. As a product of the pre–World War II Ph.D. curriculum, he had received a strong foundation in classical and modern literatures. Although he dogmatically rejected political and social concerns from the domain of literary studies, concentrating primarily on formal and philosophical issues, his belief in the autonomy of art made him a superb reader of poetry. When, in the early years of their friendship, Zabel set Bogan to reading James's short stories, saying, "Now give me careful reports of those you read; I'll grade them conscientiously," she knew she had found an infinitely patient instructor, to whom she needn't apologize for gaps in her knowledge, one she needn't fear boring on the grounds that he had figured it all out for himself years ago. He demanded much from her, and she was a most willing pupil: "Your determination to get more out of me sets all manner of notions stampeding through my thoughts," she wrote. At the same time, from the beginning of their friendship, much as she valued his guidance, she trusted her own taste and intuition more, finding him frequently sanctimonious and narrow-minded. Sending him Colette's *Ces Plaisirs,* a study in varieties of human sensuality, she wrote that she would "never forget the venom with which you pronounced Madame Colette's name over that third glass of wine." Furthermore, he had a blind spot, as far as she was concerned, about Thomas Mann, whom she could never consider more than an overstuffed bourgeois bird.

These differences in taste and temperament only nourished their friendship. As the decade advanced, Bogan began to feel isolated in her love of what she called "beautiful letters," and knowing that Morton would be delighted to hear about what she was reading and writing gave her the courage to pursue her love of aesthetic purity for its own sake. Early in May 1932 she wrote somewhat acerbically that "Edmund's mien has lightened considerably. He expects the 'poignant bourgeois note' to fade from poetry fairly soon now. The poignant bourgeois cry. Brought on, according to Edmund, by colliers and the industrial revolution. This remark was fostered by Trotsky's *Literature & Revolution,* I believe." Zabel, she assumed, was likely to find this as fatuous as she did. And in August 1932, after apologizing for not writing for some time, she noted that she had read Chekhov's *Letters, The Lady with the Little Dog, The House on the Mezzanine,* Koteliansky on Chekhov, Empson's *Seven Types of Ambiguity,* Kay Boyle's *Year Before Last,* and August Conat's *Alexandrian Poetry Under the First Three Ptolemies,* sensing that the list, on its own—the taste it spoke for, the appetite it served—would elicit Zabel's recognition and approval. He was one of the few, she believed, who really stood for high standards and would speak out for them. So she began to rely on him more and more as her periods of depression returned, along with "ideas of lost joy, impossible happiness, an insufferable past and a doubtful future."

TOWARD THE END of the long and painful self-scrutinizing of her 1932 journal, the thirty-five-year-old Bogan now wrote:

To live my life, at last delivered from ambition, from envy, from hatred, from frightened love, to live it until the end *without the need of philosophy,* that is all I ask. I fear the philosopher as I fear the ambitious, the seeker for God; the self-satisfied proud. In them lies evil, amen.

She desperately wanted to step outside her marriage and see if she could stand on her own, supporting, and supported by, her intellect, common sense, and work. Zabel, who was worried about her, urged her late in the summer to apply to the John Simon Guggenheim Memorial Foundation for a year's fellowship abroad.

It was a move she would never have made without his prodding. Maidie, at fifteen, still appeared to be in need of consistent attention, and Raymond, who had recently lost his job at *The New Yorker,* and had few prospects for employment outside of occasional freelance articles, resented the thought of being left to struggle alone for a year. He remembered, too, that she had refused to let him go on the cruises required of his travel-agency advertising job. Eventually he relented, realizing, as he must have, that the alternative to Louise's going to Europe was sure to be another breakdown. (*The purpose being that___!*)

In her application to the Foundation, she explained that she wanted to spend a year in Europe

because for ten years I have lived in America, without any opportunity for travel abroad. If it is true, as someone has said, that the poet of today should live at the crest of contemporary feeling, and must thoroughly derive from the contemporary situation, then it is important that he, in maturity, should spend some time outside his own country; be given the opportunity of estimating the life and work of his time, as well as his own group in his own land.

I want to travel as widely as possible in the period granted by the Foundation; meet my contemporaries, my seniors and the newest generation of writers in Ireland, England, France, the Scandinavian countries, Germany, and if possible, Russia; live as much as possible outside the bounds of any particular literary coteries; keep a close journal, and write poetry.

In Bogan's current state of fear and isolation, deciding whom to ask for recommendations was a terrible problem. With Zabel's advice, she considered Zabel himself, Robert Hillyer, S. Foster Damon, Mark Van Doren, Ridgely Torrence, John Hall Wheelock, Edna St. Vincent Millay, Harriet Monroe, and Robert Frost. Her lack of official education worried her. "Bear, bear on the mind," she urged Zabel, "on the capacity of the brain, on the long scholar's head, on the know-without-having-learned intuition, on the bred-in-the-bone aptitude, on the up-from-Livermore-Falls-Maine coming-through, on the seeking-out-as-her-own-nicety of choice, on the made-a-life-for-herself-through-choice-in-spite-of-evil-chance stamina." She was pleasantly surprised by some of the replies, particularly the one from Robert Frost, who crustily explained:

If I decide against you you won't be supposed to know it and so can't openly bear me any grudge. But I shan't decide against you. I think you one of the best of us and should like nothing better than to help you get a Guggenheim. What I should like, however, doesn't necessarily get you one, as it might if I had gone on the committee of awards when I was asked a year or two ago. I don't know all the people they have there now and there may be someone with whom any boost you had from me might easily be as bad as a knock. If there is, it is upon your head for not looking into the matter through your detective agency beforehand. The politics of poetry is a game that has to be very carefully played.

When word came, early in March 1933, that she had been awarded a fellowship for a year abroad, to begin April 1st, she was overwhelmed. Writing to Harriet Monroe, she said that she was feeling "a little abnormal, because I fear so much and expect so little: help from outside has come so infrequently to me that I have taught myself never to expect it, and never, if possible to ask for it." Aware that she had come out of her breakdown with a patchwork self, she felt she was being given a period of what Edmund Wilson was fond of calling *recueillement,* a period of rest and solitude and revaluation. For at least a year she had been thinking and feeling, if not living, as an independent woman, suspicious of Holden and estranged from him, although still dependent on his worshipful attention and his sexual ardor. A year's separation would do them both good, she believed, clearing their minds and encouraging them once again to strengthen and renew their love. Maidie was a self-reliant, sensible girl, who could take care of herself, and, after all, Raymond was a devoted stepfather who would be available for weekends and crises until Maidie joined Louise in Europe for the summer.

Planning to sail early in April for Genoa, and to visit Sicily before going on to Venice, Florence, Rome, Siena, and Padua, Bogan hoped to travel light, read books, absorb the spirit of place, write her journal and, if they were "given" to her, poems. The prospect of the year ahead was exhilarating, and a little daunting. It had been a long time since she had arrived in Paris, en route to Vienna in 1922, "with ten dollars in my pocket and two dresses, one coat, one hat, one pair of shoes, and a dreadfully small store of stockings and underwear, to my back." Would she be able to face arriving in Rimini, alone, hot and tired, or finding herself stranded in "some hostelry of the wind-grieved Appenine during a particularly hard blow. . . "?

Apparently she would. Loneliness and fatigue would challenge her spiritual discipline. Forced back upon her own resources, she would exercise new powers of observation, and satisfy the intense appetite for *looking* which had grown steadily over the years. Having recently read Osbert Sitwell's *Winters of Content* and *Discursions on Travel, Art and Life,* with their rich descriptions of Italian churches, she was eager to refresh her eyes with examples of her beloved Baroque art and architecture, "a style to be preferred, in my opinion," she remarked to Zabel, "(and I held this opinion long before

I had ever read a word of the Sitwell brothers,—after I had seen the work of Fischer von Erlach in Wien), in many ways, to the Gothic, and certainly far surpassing Romanesque." Like the statue of Daphne in Bogan's early "Poplar Garden," warm Italy beckoned to her wintry heart. If she gave herself over to it, with her whole being, it was possible that she would once again find joy and contentment in being alive.

5 ITALIAN MORNING

EDMUND WILSON left this account of Bogan's departure on Saturday, April 1st, on the Italian liner S.S. *Rex:*

—In her new brown traveling suit and round brown hat tilted on one side (Do I look like a Lesbian? I don't look like a Lesbian, do I?) she looked like a Steichen or German photograph, standing behind the glass of a window half slid to the side—shy, self-consciously good-looking and proud, making occasionally gestures and expressions in answer to our signals. —The ship slipped so easily out of the dock—elegantly pinched-up white stern, new modish low-cut funnels with the colors of Italy about them—stood still a few moments in the river, then turned out toward the sea, flying the Italian flag.

Maidie was crying, as was Betty Huling; and Raymond, who had never wept in public before, broke out in sobs. "There you were going away—a part of me, not just of my flesh, but of everything I am, all my breaths and moments," he wrote to her the next day, enclosing two sonnets he had written immediately upon returning to the empty apartment. In one of these he described himself crying out

> . . . your name against my pillow.
> All the space in the world cannot take away
> From the eyes of my heart, from my fingers,
> The shape of the burning ripeness of you that lingers
> Over my flesh that saw you vanish to-day.
>
> Saw you diminish, and wanted you! Now in the night
> Wanting you still, all of your length at my side,

All of your slenderness here in the curve of my arm,
The dark of your hair on my face, drowning the light
Of these tears that are bitter because my heart is denied
The warmth of the only mouth in the world that is warm.

The letters that Louise wrote to Raymond between April and August of 1933 have been lost. His letters to her, and the notes and journals she kept while she was away, have survived, and they make it clear that as soon as she sailed, a terrible uneasiness overwhelmed them both. From the beginning Raymond referred to their separation as a test, a time for each to live and grow through individual inner strivings which would cancel out the doubts that had eroded their love in recent years. But his reiterations of this theme were rarely couched in purely optimistic terms. Two days after she left he referred to her "hysteria" and his "anxiety," adding that at supper the night before his mother had talked at great length about Louise and said "how proud and pleased you should be—with the Guggenheim, not me."

On the boat, Louise began a new notebook, filling it with information and quotations from guidebooks to Italy, preparing herself for a saturation in time and place, art and history, at the same level of passionate engagement as the Italian journeys of Goethe, Henry James, and D. H. Lawrence. She assiduously listed the contents of Santa Maria del Popolo, in Rome, took notes on Bernini's *Daphne,* Coreggio's *Danaë,* and the treasures she should expect to find in the Ludovisi collection of antiquities at the Museo Nazionale delle Terme. She wrote down directions for walking tours in Florence, as well as recommendations concerning the qualities to be observed in Fra Angelico ("his skill in composition; his mastery of light; and the pleasure he must have had in painting") and the pictures in the Uffizi.

Arriving at Genoa on April 8th, that night she sailed to Naples in order to take the mailboat to Palermo the following evening. From the first moment, she found Italy entrancing. Genoa, she wrote Maidie,

although it is supposed to be quite an ordinary town, seemed very beautiful to me. The houses are square, of lovely pale stucco and stone; they go up steep hills and face the harbor row after row. In the clear sun you can almost count the windows. The Mediterranean really *is* deep aquamarine color. The Italians really *are* charming people. And the coast from Genoa on, this evening, was exquisite. Bare gray stone hills coming right down to the sea, dotted with little towers, little houses! O darling, it is like heaven. I can't believe how beautiful it is.

Nevertheless, she added, she wasn't happy: "But I mustn't be too sad, because I have some work to do, and why be too miserable the first time one is in Italy? A little sad, but not too much!" The homesickness that had dogged her in Vienna in 1922 threatened her once again, but she had a purpose to hold fast to, and writing letters could be a part of it. The business of serious *looking* began as soon as she reached Naples, and she wrote Maidie about the officers in blue caps, the Fascists in uniform, the nuns, monks, priests, and seminarians—"these last wear red stockings, black gowns and purple socks"—and she reported that she had sat all afternoon in her hotel with a Sicilian woman who had lived in New Orleans for ten years and spoke "broken English with a pronounced southern accent. 'I gotta four chillun,' she said."

The morning of April 10th, Louise arrived at Palermo and was immediately enchanted by the sight of donkey carts, with the donkeys, as she wrote Maidie, "all dressed up in an elaborate harness covered with red pompoms and *bells.*" Everywhere she saw flowers in garlands festooning windows and balconies, bookstores packed with old books and prints, gardens and more gardens with cacti, nasturtiums, verbenas, and palms. The cathedral in Palermo, she reported to Zabel, was "the most exquisite building I have ever seen or ever hope to see. The facade is so subtle and so pure, the tower so springing and intricate. Its color is deep gold, against the sky." To Maidie she wrote, "There's not a fake note anywhere. On one side of the town there are steep volcanic hills; at the other end is the sea. You can see the sea at the end of the streets, high up in the sky, and very blue." Reporting that she had successfully carried out the purchase of a notebook, pencil, and cake of soap, she quipped, "So you see, I *do* manage pretty well, by myself!"

With that notebook in hand, Bogan began her Italian journal. It is composed, to a large extent, of brief notes which she presumably intended to expand later into fuller passages of prose, and their very hastiness and brisk inconclusiveness suggest a private bedazzlement and profusion of response that made her months in Italy a thorough adventure in seeing that would have to wait till later to be recollected in tranquility. Her letters to Wilson and Zabel are more leisurely, rich with the assurance that her impressions would be greeted with enthusiasm and shared delight.

She found Sicily's color and light ravishing. Of San Giovanni degli Eremiti in Palermo, she noted:

Beautiful courtyard garden: lemon, oranges, mimosa, fig, flowering fruit trees. Pale gray bare interior: cupolas resting on rectangular pillar. Square at bottom, round at top. Outside, the domes a delicate red against the pure light sky.

Her reawakened love of *form* marveled, again and again, at the infinite transformations of inanimate stone and marble into living works of the hand.

In Monreale it was marble Baroque angels "climbing up a pile of stones," and the cathedral's extravagances of inlaid brass and marble, its cloister pillars ornamented in "stripes, both curved and straight, lozenges, zigzags." Along the Via Maqueda in Palermo it was the stone figures, both male and female, "all of the most delicate and sly voluptuousness, depravity. The females slyly lift their breasts or cover their pudenda with their hands." In the Norman church near the Piazza Bellini it was the "Byzantine figures, full of grave movement" which stayed with her. She was discovering, as if for the first time, the actual physical concreteness of civilization: the miracle, to her, of handiwork and artifice, of *making*, in all its subtle ingenuity and imaginative joy.

The human scene, so fresh and new, charmed her equally. She made notes about chance encounters on boats and trains and in hotel restaurants, always attentive to the moment's unconscious revelation of destiny or character. In the streets of Palermo she watched the way "women and children carry babies in their arms. The baby sits bolt upright and looks as though fixed to the arm by some mechanism. This attitude of mother and child, so touching, never seen in America, even in the home."

Everywhere she noted the Fascist symbol: on flowerpots, railway engines, the lapel buttons of two white-haired gentlemen. Details of dress fascinated her: the "broad, strapped sandals" worn by a monk, a priest with a hat "broad from side to side" and "a long soutane."

On April 13th she wrote to Maidie from the Grand Hotel des Temples in Agrigento, where she had gone for one night only to see the remnants of Greek temples by the sea. It was the height of summer when she arrived. Fields and gardens bloomed with flowers:

I walked out toward the temples when I arrived and smelled the mimosa—like my perfume, only a million times more delicate. The birds are singing at the top of their lungs and the sun is so clear, so pure. The Mediterranean, out beyond, is a color I have never seen before, so delicately blue, with sails high up in it, as though in the sky.

But she was also, as she confessed in her notebook, "terribly lonely and depressed," already beginning to rely on a bottle of cognac bought in Palermo to get to sleep at night. On the one hand, she could write that she was beginning to feel so separate from her life in New York that she could not remember the people she knew there or the fact that she had ever read Chekhov; on the other, contemplating two women she had met on the S.S. *Rex,* she wrote sourly, in the third person:

She couldn't make out whether her lack of enthusiasm for life was a result of slackening energies, or whether it was that her experience had turned out fundamentally uninteresting, and perhaps through her own fault cut to a banal pattern, so that she met humorless and pushing Jewesses in a period that surely deserved something better.

It is interesting that in the midst of perceiving and deploring the Fascist threat, she was prone to her own eruptions of anti-Semitism. She was often weepy, and often inconvenienced, to the point of weariness and tears, by her traveling arrangements. The long train ride from Siracusa to Messina was made bearable only when a pistol-toting Fascist train guard was kind enough to make her compartment comfortable for the night. (This incident prompted Bogan's observation that fascism was "rather like a boy scout movement. My care was perhaps the guard's good deed for today.") Reaching Naples again after her Sicilian tour, she wrote to Maidie that she was eager to get to Rome, "where I can settle down and read and write for a time! My poor mind has been so full of bag-keys and did-I-leave-the-soap? and how-much-is-twenty-lire? that I haven't had a moment's real intellectual exercise since I left the ship." Perhaps when she got more settled she would feel less lonely and homesick. She missed Maidie and worried about her, and she missed and worried about Raymond. His first batch of letters had been waiting in Naples when she arrived, and along with their sonnets and outpourings of passion had brought the news that he had come down with a terrible cold.

Having tasted summer in Sicily, she arrived to spring in Rome, immediately falling in love with the city's light and air. She longed with a ready heart to embrace Rome as journal-keeping travelers before her had done, yet even as she surveyed its fallen stones and lusty fountains, she found herself "utterly empty of that emotion of *joy*" she had felt in Sicily. Her heavy-heartedness returned, especially when she read Raymond's next sheaf of letters, written at the rate of at least one, and sometimes two, a day. He had sent three more sonnets, picturing himself in one as a felon "hanged from the gibbet of Orion's arm," "punished for a love that was too warm," condemned to "A bitter term, with hope and help denied" while his lover knew nothing of "this death that I who love you die." He repeatedly emphasized that whereas *she* was at the start of a period of unlimited freedom and adventure, *he,* on the other hand, was stuck in the empty apartment, balked in his attempts to write a play, faced with a hot New York summer and a difficult search for work in various advertising agencies. Curiously, what she was doing and seeing aroused almost no response from him. He passed over without comment everything she presumably had written to him about her travels and observations.

There was one subject, though, about which both Raymond and

Louise had much to say. From the moment their correspondence began, she could not seem to resist the temptation to taunt him about the ample sexual possibilities available to him as a free man in New York. She was as obsessed as ever by the thought that he would betray her, and she could not keep her tormenting fears to herself. This gave him, in addition to the recital of his difficulties with work and loneliness, unlimited opportunities to reply with loving expressions meant as reassurances but actually sounding much more like reproaches. "But, darling, please no recrimination!" he wrote early in April. "When you passed Gibraltar, Villefranche and Genoa, I was lying in bed with a temperature of 103°, beyond any feeling that a cablegram, or anything but your face against mine would help." He wanted her to come home—now. Robert Coates had just given up *The New Yorker* book department; why didn't she come home in June and take it over, for sixty dollars a week? He missed her, he told her over and over, "from bed and heart! You don't know, oh, you don't know! Or perhaps distance has taught you," he scolded her. "Do you think now of this house as a place to get out of, and of my evening homecomings as merely an opportunity to be testy and mean?"

Although we can't know what she wrote in reply, we do know that she had no intention of going home this early. Writing to Zabel from the Pensione Francini near the Aurelian wall, she said that she loved Rome immediately,

from the moment when the bold, bad fountain in the Piazza d'Esedea burst upon my sight. I loved the boldness, the vigor, the light, the sweep of the city. . . . S. Andrea della Fratte has the most beautiful Baroque belfry I ever laid my eyes on. . . And how beautiful are all the stairs, pouring up and down hill, and the gardens and the fountains, so alive with light and water at its fullest artificial display.

She went often to the Borghese Gardens, sitting and looking out at the flowering trees. Visiting the Roman forum, she noticed the rubble of stones and wrote:

The pathos of man's great striving with stone, for pomp, for grandeur, stones that fall into rubbish, palaces that stand like heaps of rubble. But the words, laws, arrangements of reason, discoveries in form, remain. (So many inscriptions, in the city! The emperors, the popes, all carved out their names on marble that had split, or shall one day split in two. The popes did not learn the lesson that stone is not everlasting.)

At Saint Peter's she loved the sight of the fountains churned into white foam by the wind, and at the Vatican Library she saw the Great Hall of the

Reading Room, which she "used to gaze at through the stereopticon when I was ten. The most terribly decorated room in the world, without doubt. More frightful vases, lumps of malachite mounted in gold etc. Then rooms with ugly albumish books displayed behind glass and a small exhibit of frightful modern paintings." As a lapsed Catholic with vivid memories of her two years in a convent school, she felt a profound aversion to the Vatican, and did not go back a second time to the Sistine Chapel.

The long journey from her provincial youth to her present life struck her forcibly one night when she heard Rachmaninoff play in a concert at the Augusteo: "Rachmaninoff, who was to me, in Boston, 1918, the symbol of the cosmopolitan artist." She was both suffering from and enjoying the mental restlessness which may mean creative and emotional vitality—or may not. She would be depressed one day, in better spirits the next. She tried to write a poem, and failed, and got depressed again. She felt she was neglecting her diary, but took the time to note the singular emotion of "turning in desperate antipathy against love, worry, the ties that chafe the heart and mind." Such a mood soon yielded to detachment, and to a sense of the value of her present difficulty: "It is interesting," she observed, "even in the midst of loneliness, to possess oneself enough so that one can feel that whatever will happen will be different enough, will be in some way bearable enough. One thing's ending bears another's beginning. And nothing, even desolation, lasts too long."

Fortunately, she managed to find some companionship. She knew an American woman whom she referred to in her notes as Edith, who appears to have been studying voice in Rome, and two other Americans, a Mrs. Grant and her teenage daughter. She disliked the daughter, describing her in the journal as pretty, pretentious, and ill at ease, but Mrs. Grant was "splendid, with a fine sense of humor," "a fine wreck of a woman, doing her best not to die," who "loves life: a kitchen, beer—but . . . doesn't want anything." The woman named Edith took her one evening to an area beyond the Piazza del Popolo to a gathering at the home of her singing teacher and his wife. Unexpectedly introduced into an "artistic" Italian home, Bogan recorded the evening in vivid detail:

A large room, brightly lighted. Whitewashed walls, low seats and tables. A palm or two. The people completely without life or *chic* or intelligence. Bad even featured glaucous eyed look on painter. The wife young pretty, mascara'd eyes, fine skin, blonde hair. An Englishwoman whose portrait stands against the wall. Horse-faced, a stutterer, a peerer, with a soft shriveled mouth. The pictures technically in the class of slick commercial art in America. Full of texture and girls playing lutes and soft fleshed nudes badly composed. The man sells these to young women who own "the biggest department store in Rome"—white hat, husband in "clear" suit.

Awkward badly dressed young girls. The young women look vicious and petulant: the older ones have some dignity, dress rather well, good eyes and teeth. Sit with arms folded *high* on bosom, the body a soft fattish shape below. Dressed in open work black with purple hat.

A cup of tea and the inevitable small bun concealing a slice of ham.

O God, what vulgarity, what death! This is the class that Fascism no doubt feeds on—the middle class, without ideas—trying for *chic* and artistic life. Not a book, and not a drink.

A tide of homesickness and heartache again flooded her when she left Rome for Florence, on Tuesday, May 2nd. She arrived sad and remained sad for virtually the entire eighteen days of her stay. Her hatred of Florence was intense. The houses were the wrong color, the shops ordinary. Catching her first sight of the Duomo and the Campanile, she hated them too, particularly the Duomo: "faded bad marble patterns weatherbeaten into bad color, set down in a square too small."

Writing, May 3rd, that she was "Almost out of my head with grief," she began a cable to Raymond, but thought better of sending it. His letters, reaching her in Florence, tortured her with slipperiness. Raymond was beginning to enjoy a varied and active social life on his own. Reporting that he had gone to a farewell party for Malcolm Cowley (who was going to Tennessee for ten weeks to write a book), he added, "The nights are terrible, and I can't make myself believe that going to bed with any one else would make them anything but more so." It was just this seemingly innocuous introduction of the hypothetical possibility of extra-marital sex, brought up only to be ruled out, that drove Louise wild with anxiety. Casually referring in the same letter to another upcoming party whose hostess had asked him to bring "*extra* girls," he joked, "Do you realize how close I've been to you? That I don't know any extra girls well enough to ask them? Is that shameful? I don't know." Louise was incapable of accepting this as a declaration of love; she immediately wrote in her journal that Raymond was being exploited by the hostess and bedeviling Louise herself with half-truths. In one letter he said that the very thought of her started a flow of tears, enclosing a copy of Hopkins's sonnet, "No worst, there is none. Pitched past pitch of grief," and exclaiming, "I'm a man, and this is the world, but I love you, I cry out to you—don't, don't be so far away!" Then, in another, dated Easter Sunday, April 16th, acknowledging her "sweet cables" (sent from Palermo and Naples), he wrote that he could not help "regretting bitterly—and a little resentfully—the hours we have spent together and which you (or you and I together perhaps) have so savagely spoiled." She could feel his resentment, and knew that he included himself in the blame only for courtesy's sake: their troubles, he believed, had always been *her* fault. On Tuesday, April 18th, having received two letters from Gibraltar (in which it appears that she once again brought up the topic of infidelity), he wrote:

It seems to me that, hard as it is, if this absence enables you to look straight at my life and my love for you, instead of around corners and through prisms of half-truth and faulted memory, you will see what it is, and why it is what it is, and be proud and happy in it, rather than miserably apprehensive for it. I know so well what you have done for me that I can, easily, if you will let me, forget the times when you have tried to undo it all. But what's the use of talking. I love you, you are my wife, my mistress, my love, my dream and my reality. The defects of my character nor the pettinesses of yours can't change that. I love you and I always shall.

You say tell you the truth. I'm telling you the truth (I've been too sick to muster or have any confessions to make) and that is that against my hope that your protestation of love is genuine and fundamental, is the fear that it was wrung from you by the durance of wrenching departure, and that what made you suffer so was the fact, not that you were confronted with a world in which I should not share your bed and spirit, but that I was being left to the she-wolves of New York and that it would be they, not you henceforth who would be given the chance to destroy me. This is the truth. And I love you so much that it matters a great deal what the answer to that question is. It is as important to me that you love me, not merely my ability to hurt you, as it is that I love you more than the bonds which that love imposes on me. Oh, I do love you so much, and miss you so dreadfully! You *can't*, can't have any idea.

She had written to him that she was going about with tears in her eyes, and he admitted that he was too, adding:

Other women have no terrors for me. No one could be like you. I could never *love* anyone else. I could probably relieve myself in someone if sufficiently drunk and sufficiently pressed, but I don't get drunk (and I have drunk very little since you left) and so far I am not seriously pressed and the thought of women (as you put it) *as* women, is horrible to me. For I really love *you*. And it's worth being delicate and pure for, love like that.

She simply did not know *what* to think. Every time she sought reassurance from him—and there can be no question that she sought it not just repeatedly but hysterically, fanatically, maddeningly—his words of solace managed to have a small, haunting qualification in their tone. His persistent incantation of if-I-ever-do's and I-would-only-if's struck a chill right down to the bone. When he mentioned, as an afterthought ("I was almost forgetting to tell you . . ."), a party he had gone to for which he had made up his mind "that it wouldn't be very creditable if I didn't produce a girl, so I did, in a rather sketchy and ill-considered manner," she must have felt something very close to frenzy.

The young woman "produced" for the occasion, Miss X, was someone Raymond was to mention frequently over the following months. She was an acquaintance met while he was still at *The New Yorker,* where she hoped to find work. She had not made a great impression at the party, Raymond remarked; Edmund Wilson had escorted her home. Oh, and had he ever mentioned her before, or said that she was pretty? If so, he couldn't imagine why. Miss X had frightfully unattractive teeth, and was altogether not so very prepossessing. Louise needn't have any worries on *her* account.

But Louise worried terribly, and wept. All she could do was to fight her sadness, and make efforts to absorb as much of Florence as she could stand. She visited the Bargello and saw portrait busts by Donatello and Verrocchio, Michelangelo's Leda, "Cellini borzoi, Della Robbia upstairs. A beautiful building in the afternoon sun." The Medici chapel depressed her, so she looked at people instead, noting down "types" she saw: old women, young men. She made a note about the "round rosy wreaths" on the wallpaper in her pension room (this later showing up in "Italian Morning") and observed that "The olive leaves, on young trees, seen against green grass, are *blue.*" Her journal, in its present phase, was getting dull. She knew this and bore down on herself, expanding her notes on the Medici chapel and rapidly setting down impressions of the Giottos in Santa Croce. On May 10th she remarked that she planned to write a piece called "Short Guide to Italy," and wrote down the words, "Laura Dailey's [sic] Story." She was, possibly, feeling ready to go on with her childhood memories. The next day she wrote, "Today I felt as though some power—the Florentine air, my solitude, my refusal to yield to the old obsession of anxiety and fear—had, for a little while at least, given me the mitre and crown." On May 16th she went to Siena for the day, and found the interior of the cathedral "lovelier than any I have seen thus far." Soon she reported that she had shut herself up in her room and done some writing. Her friends Mrs. and Miss Grant were now in Florence, and, fascinated as she was by them, she decided one night, "when kept awake by a howling cat, that the thing to do was move on. Too much struggle against the faint impulse to pay the Grants' bill, or the carozza fare, or the cigarettes or the matches. The general atmosphere of drifting bad. And no real full life or feeling of joy. Much more contented, when alone."

The point of coming to Europe was to be free of attachments, no matter how enjoyable. To drink dark Trieste beer with Mrs. Grant at four in the afternoon, at a table in an outdoor café, under an umbrella, was a pleasure and a comfort, but Mrs. Grant, despite her perfect lack of desire for people and things, was no artist and no secular monastic. Like some character out of a Hemingway story, she lived for that four o'clock drink, and the conversation and dinner and after-dinner drinks that inevitably followed. Bogan, with real work to do, knew that such moments were all too seductive in her present sadness. She was already too fond of her evening cognac.

So on Saturday, May 20th, she took the train for Venice. At first it promised to be another Florence, "ugly and spoiled." But her first reactions, especially after a day of traveling, were not always to be trusted. Disappointed as she was with her first view of the Piazza San Marco, she was just as immediately taken with the Basilica. Walking around a corner to the water, she saw "the bridge beside the Bridge of Sighs" and wondered "what was the poem of Hood's about the girl who *jumped off* the Bridge of Sighs, that I read as a child? But no one could *jump off* it," and felt better. Her spirits were much improved the next day, when she wrote to Edmund Wilson, as she said, "from the city of Casanova, Goldini, Lord Byron, Percy Bysshe Shelley (known to his intimates as 'The Snake'), Tiepolo, John Ruskin, a few assorted Byzantines and the most beautiful courtesans in the world." She went on to say that she was living in a room in a pension that just happened to be in

John Ruskin's house, in case you care to know. It faces a wide but rather ugly canal, behind the Accademia. Venice thrills me right down to my marrow. The air, the light, the marble houses (some of them listing rather dangerously), the casual air of the ugly people (all dressed alike, all acting alike, with not a real look of zip or personality in one of them), the masts and gardens seen from my window. I adore it all.

Her energy, which she hadn't experienced in full flood since Sicily, now burned with a high flame. Her room was dark and unpleasant, but it had a view of a little canal and a garden wall with a statue, and she reported in her diary that she was feeling "perfectly happy." Her surroundings once again seemed full of interest. At dinner she found herself conversing with an attractive American man, traveling with his daughter. She was struck by the girl's saying that "I've been in Europe practically all my life." The next day the "handsome American father gives me *keen look.* He and daughter leave in afternoon. . . . Why does he leave her in Europe?" she wondered. "Probably involved with divorce. He has the look." Exploring the Basilica, she encountered a strange sight: a thousand Fascist children, in uniforms, all of them small, about the age of six, and "pretty scrubby," being shown around and genuflecting.

On May 24th she sat down at a table and wrote the first part of a story, sending it off as soon as she had finished it to *The New Yorker,* where it was published the following July. It was called "The Last Tear," and it is a brief, ironic, and compassionate portrait of the Grants—here called the Reads—Americans living in Europe, the mother asking little more of life than some peace, a good drink, and a charming café in which to enjoy it, the daughter raised to no useful profession, continually in search of "nice" people from whom she can inveigle a week here or ten days there in some fashionable place or other. Bogan gave her own impressions of Florence to Mrs. Read, who, loving Rome, "the light, the air, the rude Romans, the bronze, the marble, the orange stucco, the fountains, and the gardens," also loathed Florence: "She thought the Duomo a fright; she could not bear the wide stretches of unrelieved gravel edged by small trees that the Florentines called *piazze,* or tolerate the tooled leather and silver knick-knacks in the shops and the weatherbeaten English in the streets."

Completing a piece of work made Bogan feel that, after seven weeks in Europe, nearly every single one of which had been marred by homesickness and heartsickness, she had hit her stride at last, able to master her loneliness and to meet each day as an adventure. She now turned her attention to painting, taking in Carpaccio's cycle of the *Legend of St. Ursula* in the Accademia in Venice, and traveling to Padua for the day, where the Mantegnas in the Ovetari Chapel of the Eremitani Church—seen, luckily, before they were destroyed in 1944—struck her as

Superb. Thrilling. Unbelievably lovely design, color. Figures that look *in* and out of the picture, regardless of the spectator, thoroughly caught up in the matter in hand (which happens to be the martyrdom of S. Christopher). One set of frescoes divided in the middle by a pillar, part of the composition. Garlands divide others. The youth who leans against the *side* of the picture [*The Martyrdom of St. James*] is [one] of the most extraordinarily subtle effects in painting. A trick taken out of its class, transposed into an intellectual effect.

Going up the Sospiri canal, she looked at patterns of ironwork on balconies, carved wooden garlands on doors facing the canal, and flowers in windows; she smelled the stench of refuse floating in the tides.

Her good spirits continued when, on Thursday, June 2nd, she took the Trieste train to Milan, changing there for Como. From Como she wrote to Maidie that she had hated to leave Venice: "It is *the* loveliest city in the world." Como itself failed to impress her, but nearby Bellagio, which she visited the day after her arrival, struck her as "marvelous. . . . Green hills come down straight into the lake and in the distance rise the Alps with snow on their summits." She added that she herself was feeling "marvelous" and looking healthy and brown from the sun. Her journal was free of sorrow, for the time being. She had found her footing as a woman who knew how to travel alone, detached from home ties, though not mindless of them. The prospect of imminent companionship may have cheered her. Her stay in Como was brief, and on June 3rd she took the train back to Milan, changing for Genoa, then changing again at San Remo to a French train, which took her along the Côte d'Azur to (as she duly noted) Mentone and Monte Carlo, Eze and Beaulieu, stopping finally at Villefranche, where she disembarked to a warm greeting by her friends, Harry and Dorothy Dudley Harvey.

THE WEALTHY HARVEYS were living in Villefranche in a house called La Réserve. Formerly a hotel with a restaurant, it stood at the edge of the sea, with a terrace full of cacti and flowers. The rooms, Bogan wrote to Harriet Monroe, were "papered with kindergarten colors. Books, paintings, lithographs, Chinese hangings and bowls of carnations and geraniums and bougainvillea and cherries and squashes and oranges hang on the wall, crowd the tables, and desks and very often the chairs. Outside the bay is aquamarine, when seen from a height, and Prussian blue, when seen in the distance." She was given a room on the top floor that looked down over the water; she made a drawing of the fireplace, lamp (with torn lampshade), and glassed-in bookcase. The Harveys enjoyed life on a grand and carefree scale, furnishing Louise with plenty of wine, brandy, good meals, and conversation. She was taken to Nice and St. Jean, and to a fiesta one evening in Villefranche, where she and Dorothy and another friend drank Pernod and *fine* in a café, while Louise noted how the "umbrellas turn round to the tune of the carrousel."

One day John Dos Passos came to lunch. Louise had never liked him or his writing, and now, despite his friendship with Edmund Wilson, and even in her relaxed mood, she found that she still disliked him. "Dos P. a great slider-away from conversational difficulties," she remarked in her journal. On another afternoon Henri Matisse, "A grand old man," dropped in for tea, and was later reported to have had a long talk with another Harvey houseguest on "the secret communication between the artist and nature: 'Too much is bad.' "

Rested, received into the bosom of a sophisticated couple who considered her a fine acquisition as well as an entertaining companion, Louise began what she called a *cahier,* or notebook, as distinct from a journal, although she wrote no more than a single day's entry before going back to her travel diary. On this single day, however—June 15th—she described the delicate orange-pink color of the cactus flowers on the Harvey terrace, and then the terrace itself:

The pilasters of the terrace are painted a pale turquoise blue, that exists only in paint and not in nature.

The palms by the station cast down a patterned shade. Across the bay a pink house stares at me with pale green blinds, disposed like too many eyes in a face.

O God what beauty in the sun! A white gull and a black swallow dip into the water.

There was, as well, an unusual note of erotic revery:

In the dream of great passion, that moves the sleeping body upon the bed in a kind of catalepsy, the landscape runs by in a [*illeg.*], sketched in carelessly by the sleeping mind. But how lovely, how extraordinary, that it should be there at all, and that the passionate organs seeking release and satiety, should bother with any semblance of a scene. How we create within ourselves.

Returning to her travel diary, she wrote a spirited portrait of her friend Dorothy Dudley Harvey. The woman whose style had seemed so enchanting in Santa Fe in 1925–26 now appeared to have a number of irritating pretensions. Louise quarreled with her "(or rather, she with me) ... I *sneered* at her, I did *nothing* but *sneer* at all she said," and, with the atmosphere somewhat strained the next day, Louise spent a diplomatic cooling-off morning in Nice, returning for lunch to find relations between Dorothy and herself apparently restored. Over the next two days, while working hard on a *New Yorker* poetry piece, she thought about what had passed between them, and wagered that she would never "get Dorothy's philosophy and general attitude down. Spoiled Chicago girl who thinks herself profound thinker and feeler.... Terrific vanity: regard for *nice* people appears. 'I don't know how you *came* to have such beautiful hands.'" Yet dressed in a "blue lisle shirt, slightly lighter blue pants with silver buttons on hips, white satin scarf, white hat," Dorothy looked charming. Louise really was fond of her friend, and the days of reading and writing by the sea, with people she knew, and good meals, were wonderful for her.

On June 23rd, Louise went to Cap Brun (Toulon-Var) to have lunch with Ford Madox Ford and found herself invited to stay on not just for a few days, but for the rest of the summer and all winter, if she chose. Her actual stay lasted a week, and she was a great success with the Ford household, which included Ford's young wife, the painter Janice Biala, and her brother, the painter Jack Tworkov. "I have been fed, housed, given to drink, cosseted and posseted all round," she gaily wrote to Zabel. She noted in her diary that the Ford house had a terrace of beaten earth and trees planted in a circle of stones.

The first afternoon, she walked with Ford along a pine-strewn path to the sea, sleeping that night in a room which had, in addition to tormenting mosquitoes, a painting on the wall of people moving through trees, and a set of "graveyard hue frescoes," which she contemplated from her hard bed. Ford used to get up very early and write before breakfast. By 10 A.M. he was finished for the day, and ready for company. The Fords took her everywhere, and there was a long evening when Ford read aloud from one of his manuscripts, fortified by "many glasses of *marc* (the most potent liquor in the world)." At sixty, he was not only one of the foremost modern English novelists, but a living witness to the generation that had included Hardy, James, Conrad, and Wells, and reached back to the high Victorian era of his grandfather Ford Madox Brown and his father Ford Madox Hueffer. Louise wondered what he thought about, "all alone with Janice's kind heart and rough manners, after his years in the world," and wrote down something he said about himself: "You don't want people to get their hooks into you, but you like to get your hooks into other people."

For the time being, her solitary travels were at an end. Louise returned to the Harveys only to prepare to meet Maidie, who disembarked on July 2nd from the S.S. *Rex* on the pier at Cannes, in curls, white hat, and gloves. Louise was delighted to have her daughter with her. She was sixteen, a good traveling companion, interested in the art and architecture so dear to her mother, and at the same time able to amuse herself during the hours Louise spent reading and writing. Together, on July 5th, they left for Milan where, happy as they were to be in Italy, they learned that on account of the fall in the dollar Louise's fellowship funds might be used up before the year was out. Depressed by this sudden turn of events, she and Maidie moved on to Venice, which Maidie immediately hated, bursting into tears and complaining about the dirt and the beggars. It was a mood that would soon pass, Louise realized, writing in her diary that she was trying "to bear up patiently!" but the truth was that she herself was "pretty dejected all around."

Because her days in Villefranche had been filled with conversation and outings, she'd had very little time to brood about Raymond, although the tone of their correspondence changed drastically during her first week there. The letters she had received during her May sojourn in Venice had been loving, on the whole. He still wept at the thought of her absence, and felt useless and talentless without her. And just before she left for Villefranche, he'd written that they were "learning something" about the value of their love. But then, in his next letter, he reported that he had seen Miss X and her friend, "both of whom I think you would like," and Louise was furious. She sent accusing letters from Venice, to which Raymond quickly responded with a letter whose good-natured cajolery barely concealed his resentment:

What a letter that was! The one from Venice in which you said so hoity-toity, "But *I* don't drink gin!" *Sweet!* You make me wonder. I've been building so much on the hope that you really have gotten over those self-centered notions that have been (with the help of a little resentful stubbornness on my part) so disastrous in the past, and then you, who are vacationing abroad amidst the things you have wanted to see and who ought to be having at least an interesting experience, write to me who remains at home in the same narrow environment, for whom no benevolent foundations or governments are lifting a finger, as if I and the silly, empty-headed people I see were drinking champagne out of silk-hats and slippers while you fried in hell!

Curiously enough, the same day that Raymond was writing this letter—June 7th—Louise remarked coolly in her journal that he appeared to be entering a new phase, since the people he mentioned in his letters were not members of their regular group of friends. It was her last journal remark about him for many weeks, although in their letters the game of accusation and reproach was now being played in deadly earnest. In the letters she received at Villefranche, he threatened that if she didn't stop accusing him of sleeping with someone else, he would stop writing to her. Defending himself, he again reminded her that she was having a vacation and enjoying herself, and since this was so, the only possible explanation for her hysterical fits must be physiological, that is, pure premenstrual lunacy. Just because he saw people whom he liked didn't mean that he wasn't miserable without her, although he had had a tolerably good time at a beach party with Andy and Katharine White and Miss X, who was "rather attractive and reasonably intelligent—intelligent in the sense that she knows things rather than that she forms opinions of her own." Louise, of course, was a woman who did form opinions of her own, and one of them was that Raymond was almost certainly cheating. Referring to the relatively more cheerful letters she had sent him from Venice and Como, with their nonetheless plaintive repetition of the phrases, "if you are still mine" and "if you want it"—meaning her love—Raymond wrote, in the second week of June (so she received the letter no earlier than eight to ten days afterward):

Darling, why should you feel that way? It seems to me that I have been the one for several years to say that—not you. Why should you speak that way unless you are beginning to feel that you can do without me and suppose, in consequence, that I could do without you?

Once again, he added that, admittedly, he had considered "whether or not it would be possible to find someone to go to bed with who could be completely and thoroughly forgotten the next morning, but so far the thought has not seemed very attractive. . . . I warn you though, you silly Darling, that if there's any more talk about 'not troubling to trust me' I'll go and do something and have a flashlight picture taken to send you."

II 1 9 3 0 ~ 1 9 3 5

The letters she received on arriving back in Italy continued to reproach her for her conjectures. No, she was absolutely wrong about Miss X: "I'm not trying to *make* anyone and have met no rebuffs from anyone." Miss X was an unpretentious and kind young woman of thirty who was causing him no trouble whatsoever and, moreover, he wasn't defending her, but rather himself from Louise's charge of deception. They were both growing up, he said, and he was beginning to do some real work of his own. "Please help me by being Louise—my Louise (as I am your Raymond), and not an anxious, hysterical little girl who someone has left alone in an empty house." He had spoken in his June 18th letter about her "old, mean-spirited, self-destroying hysteria" and said, "I think that sometimes when you are having a good time you may feel guilty (which you shouldn't) and that then you will try to make yourself believe that *I* am indulging in some romance bringing with it complete forgetfulness of you." But Raymond was beginning to lose patience, and sent off a cable demanding "no more nasty letters." Responding to her most recent accusation that he was sleeping with Miss X, and to her reference to another alleged affair "as something which you didn't 'find out about' for seven years," he exclaimed, "For Christ's sake, Darling, do we have to have the pain of separation all this time and *with* it the return to that old horror of insanity that made life so difficult when you were here sometimes?"

On July 10th, Louise and Maidie traveled by train from Venice to Salzburg, where they remained through August. Louise intended to go on to Germany, where she wanted to visit Munich, Nuremberg, Würtzburg, and Bremen, and she hoped, too, to see Ireland, either with Maidie or alone. But having been alerted again by the Guggenheim Foundation that her fellowship was likely to be "telescoped," or prematurely concluded, owing to the drop in the dollar, and that she might well have to return to America as early as November, she made Salzburg her headquarters until her plans became clearer.

It was there, in Salzburg, that Raymond's early July letters reached her on July 15th. Reading them over a bottle of beer, she believed they were insincere. The next day she wrote in her journal that she had tried to write a letter, but had finally torn it up. Another letter from Raymond arrived July 20th, and marked a turning point in their difficulties that summer. He was not happy without her, Raymond said, and was not learning to do without her (as he had said a couple of times), "but I'm learning to realize that there is more to your presence in my life than any continual hysterical ideological reference. (Having written that it doesn't sound as if it made sense but I think you know what I mean.)"

On reading this letter she wrote in her journal:

Postcard
photograph
of Louise,
Christmas,
ca. 1900.

The Hotel Milton in Milton,
New Hampshire, in 1902, when
the Bogan family was living there.

Louise's mother,
Mary Helen Shields.
Taken in Portland,
Maine, in 1881, when
she was sixteen.

Louise's father,
Daniel Joseph Bogan.
Taken in 1882,
when he was twenty-one,
the year he married
Mary Shields.

Mary Shields Bogan.
Taken in Portland, Maine,
in 1897, the year of
Louise's birth. After
her marriage, Mrs. Bogan
grew five inches, so
that, eventually, at
five feet, nine inches,
she towered over her
husband, who remained
about five feet, four inches.

Daniel Bogan.
Portland, Maine, 1900.

Louise, age six months.
Livermore Falls, Maine, 1898.

Louise's elder brother,
Charles. Ballardvale,
Massachusetts, ca. 1908–09.

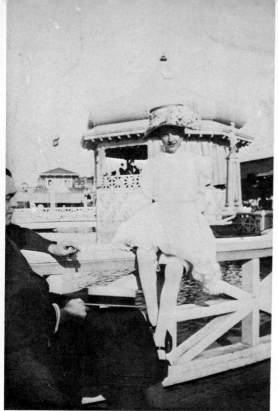

Louise on her eleventh birthday with her
brother, Charles (partially obscured), 1908.

Louise, in Ballardvale,
age eleven.

Louise, ca. 1911.

Charles and Louise in Boston, 1911.

Louise, shortly to leave
for Vienna. March 21, 1922,
in New York City.

Louise and Miss Caroline Gervish,
her English teacher at Girl's Latin School
in Boston, ca. 1915.

Corporal Curt Alexander,
Louise's first husband,
about the time they
married, 1916.

Two photographs from
her first trip abroad.
Both taken in August, 1922,
in Gargellen, Voralberg, Austria.

Louise and
her daughter,
Maidie Alexander.
Otter River,
Massachusetts,
1922.

Louise at Yaddo in the summer
of 1926. The figure of her
companion is mysteriously excised.

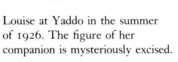

Raymond Holden, her second husband, whom
she married in 1925, and Louise. Santa Fe, New Mexico, 1926–27.

Raymond and Maidie (above) and Louise in the doorway (above right). The Hillsdale house, August, 1928.

Louise in the south of France.
Taken by Ford Madox Ford in 1933.

Louise in Provincetown, Massachusetts, in 1936—most certainly on a visit to Edmund Wilson. Taken at the home of John Dos Passos.

Louise in 1937 at 709 West 169th Street. Taken by the lover whom none of her friends ever met.

John Hall Wheelock,
Louise's editor
at Scribner's.

Morton Dauwen Zabel.

Louise and Elizabeth Mayer, with whom she translated
Goethe's *Elective Affinities,* ca. 1948.

Edmund Wilson.

Rolfe Humphries.

W. H. Auden.

Theodore Roethke.

William Maxwell.

May Sarton.

Louise, photographed by Rollie McKenna
in November, 1951, when she was fifty-three.

Louise at Stone-Blossom, the home of Glenway Wescott,
Hampton, New Jersey, late 1950s.

Louise at MacDowell in 1963.

Two photographs of Louise taken just a few days before she died.

The realization that there's no real place for me in 306 Lex. Work out my own peculiar nature as hardly ever before: the combination of intense reserve and intense abandon, or desire for abandon. R's phrase, no doubt picked up from MacMaster "continual hysterical ideological reference." That more or less tears it.

MacMaster was Phil McMaster, about whom Edmund Wilson has left a brief sketch in *The Thirties:* an old Princetonian who drank heavily, worked in cancer research at the Rockefeller Institute, and "had gone in for psychoanalysis but couldn't stomach Jews, human lice, in Psychoanalytic Association." What Raymond meant by the fancy piece of psychological jargon was, of course, Louise's obsessive jealousy, bracketed now as pathological. She hated the phrase itself, and was probably furious that he had been discussing their private troubles with someone else.

In his next letter Raymond complained that her letters were "very different from the early (April and May ones). Can't you write to me as if I were a person, not a letter box?" Her tone seemed impersonal to him, the letters

so well-written that it's like reading a good travel book but listen, they never have anything of your thoughts and feelings in them! You say such pompous, silly things about "learning to be alone," "taking lovers" etc., that I don't know whether you must write to me as you would do a hack piece for the *Evening Journal* or really like it. And you have the nerve to say that *I* never comment on what *your* letters contain! And furthermore I generally first hear of your movements from others than you. Betty [Huling], for instance, told me when you arrived in Villefranche and reported that you said you were happier than you had ever been in your life.

Then there was a tender letter, saying that he might be able to join her in Europe if a writing job for a drug and cosmetic trade quarterly came through. He felt unwanted, and sensed that she was becoming indifferent to him, yet he still longed, he said, for "one touch of rich intellectual and physical reality—a touch which only you have ever provided for me and which I think I deserve to have of you." But by July 28th the drug and cosmetic trade journal job had fallen through, and there were no new prospects, even with the various advertising agencies that had used Raymond for freelance work, for at least two or three weeks. Without work and income, he would be unable to join Louise and Maidie in Europe. There was the possibility of getting back at least a part-time job at *The New Yorker,* but it depended on Ross's approval, and apparently Holden and Ross were not on the best of terms. In the meantime, he owed half the rent, the apartment was "filthy and decaying and shows your absence," and Inez, the maid, hardly came at all anymore, since Raymond could not pay her, and when she did come she did very little work, because it was too hot. He was staying away from his family and refraining from asking them for financial help "because I feel as if I had promised you I wouldn't (and because I don't want to)." His friends were taking off for other parts—Betty Huling to Bennington, Edmund Wilson to Provincetown, Miss X to California. "So I shall be without company."

His plight touched her, and she wrote lovingly to him to bear up and be patient. But while Raymond was waiting for her letters, and writing his sad, lonesome bulletins about his job difficulties, Louise had been brooding over his July 6th letter—received July 20th—and had written to him that same day—July 20th—a letter, she noted in her journal, saying that "for the present I shall write no more." Raymond was hurt, shocked, and furious. He returned the letter to her, convinced that she could only have composed such a tirade in what he again referred to as a premenstrual "brainstorm." On no account must she write such letters ever again, "Because I'm only human and not divine. I can't stand them." One thing must remain clear between them, he insisted—"Namely: I love you, adore you, need you, hunger for you, trust you, but I will not stand being made the tool of your inner disturbances." Furthermore, if she returned to him

with that same fiendish, spoiled-child belief that there ever was anything between me and [Miss X] (or anyone else for that matter) and are unwilling to admit the facts and the truth to yourself for the sake of preserving that emotional instability which sometimes seems to delight you so, I shall certainly not live with you. You have never had to take the consequences of your cruelty to other people, but if you keep that up, you will.

As threatening as this letter sounded, it may actually have reassured her. Louise knew better than anyone else how daemoniacal she could be, particularly when enraged by jealousy, and how cruel, too—as Raymond said. She may have regretted sending her July 20th letter, for after mailing it she wrote yet another letter, hesitated to send it, and remarked in her diary, "This is foolish and proves nothing. Best to wait and let things work out of themselves. Refuse to fling myself about in silly agony any longer. Must break that habit as I must break the soaking in strong drink." And so, with the exception of Raymond's angry return of her July 20th letter, matters quieted down for the time being.

LOUISE AND MAIDIE loved Salzburg. The streets were full of people wearing Austrian costumes and riding bicycles, and there were plenty of beer gardens where they could rest from their walking. Louise began to write with keen enjoyment and acuity of observation, returning to the Villefranche notebook on the rainy Wednesday of July 12th:

On old women's fingers the diamonds and emeralds and rubies surrounded by chip diamonds, the diamonds standing by themselves lifted by gold prongs, testify to the powers once existing in the old flesh, the fallen chops, the neck wrinkled upon itself, the eyes lifeless behind the lids like lizard skin. These gems continue to praise, to attest to, a beauty long since passed. They are the signs of victories, the bright unfading testimony to beauty,—hard stones, capriccios in the light, everlasting. This flesh once deserved such a tribute, but it has fallen and the diamonds alone embody the secret conquering lustful power of young flesh—

She received a long letter from Edmund Wilson which he jokingly called a "refined *Atlantic Monthly* essay," but it contained a detailed description of his old family home in Talcotville, where the side of the house had a "gray, dappled effect . . . which resembles the light and shade in shallow rivers and recalls certain effects in your poetry." Knowing how much the cosmopolitan and description-loving Wilson would enjoy what Raymond disparagingly called her "guide-booky" letters, she wrote to him about Salzburg, sketching in the late-Renaissance and Baroque houses, the medieval streets, and the Italian squares:

Mozart was born here, as you know, in the middle of the 18th century, when everything had begun to blossom out into rock-work and artificial waters and parks and little toys that worked by hydraulic pressure. There's a *schloss* called Heilbrunn about 20 minutes from town that's a marvelous specimen of rococo in its hey-day. There's a grotto wherein a gilt crown shoots up on a shaft of water and another wherein artificial birds produce liquid notes, by some liquid feat or other, and another wherein a whole shower of rain falls, at the touch of a button, on the heads of unsuspecting tourists. The rococo bishop used to take his guests out here for a bit of fun. A long stone table sits in the garden, in front of a semi-circular wall imitated from the Villa d'Este. On either side of the table are ranged stone seats, each with an innocent-looking hole in the middle. The guests sat on these seats, and wham!— a squirt of water rose from the hole, inundating their hinder-parts in no uncertain way. If this isn't pretty rococo, I don't know what is. To have played this joke once, with wooden seats, should have been enough. But no. The seats are of stone, and there they still stand, and the guide turns the nozzle.

All of which explains Mozart's music better than volumes on the subject. Tunes written for plays was what the old boys wanted. Mozart fooled them by introducing the heart, mind and highly-organized nervous system into his productions. —Last night I heard the first concert of the Festspiel. It was given in the courtyard of the Residenz, the bishops' townhouse, exactly as it was given when Mozart wrote it: candles in gloves attached to the music-stands and all the rest, with the exception of perukes and small-clothes on the musicians. It thundered and lightened a little and the church bells struck the hour and the quarters and the ex-quisite-delicate intricate music went on undismayed, displaying its wit and contin-ual slight surprises and whimper of strings and accents of oboe and horn and dou-ble-bass. I really think it the purest and loveliest music in the world. Here was the seed from which Beethoven sprang,—so exquisite, so amusing, so amorous and melancholy, so clear that not a moment of fakery could creep in, so mathematically constructed that it could stand beside Euclid unashamed.

With a sudden purity of attention, and liberty of feeling, she wrote without fatigue or obscurity or reliance on symbol. This was prose with the same authority of voice as her poetry, but differing from it not just in rhythm and progression but in the way in which the mind's pleasure in find-ing itself in *this* place at *this* moment became instantly transformed into a set of facts about that pleasure.

She was troubled that she had not written any poetry since leaving America in April. In June, while staying with the Harveys, she had written John Hall Wheelock that "the nameless goings-on that mean poetry beat out rhythms in my head from morning to night, so that something of that sort will happen soon," but nothing of the sort did happen. Finding herself in Salzburg on her thirty-sixth birthday—and birthdays were always stock-taking occasions for Bogan—she observed in her journal that her inability to write poetry

comes to this: that I can write now only when in a rage (of anger or of hatred), or in a state which I can only describe as malicious pity. And the emotion that writes tender and delicate poetry is so much akin to the emotion of love that it *is* love, to all intents and purposes.

And how long it had been since she had felt *that* emotion: "The letting go, the swoon, the suffused eyes, the loose hand, the constriction in the throat: *the abasement, the feeling of release.*"

These were exactly the emotions she was unable or reluctant to feel now, and there was little prospect for their recovery. She had been reading over her attempts on the "Milton Ballardvale narrative," which she had evi-dently brought with her to Europe, and finding "the earlier attempt, written when in a state of high tension during Dr. McK.[inney] period 2 years ago, the best. Determined to get down to day by day narration, although the tension at present is lamentably lacking."

The mood in which she now found herself—despite the Salzburg letter to Wilson—was once again that of spiritual dryness:

Everything seems *closed* to me. The light no longer falls with the look of mystery and desolation, as once. I do not any longer care or *feel* about what goes on behind strange walls and strange windows.

I no longer feel, nor care to feel. The long rhythms once set up in my consciousness by passionate concern over things or people have died down. I see how dully middle aged men and women—especially men—pace about. From a little youth they fall so grimly into creatures without flavor—no carriage, no spring, no share in life. I, too, must have this look of being stranded, this *commonplace* aspect that cannot wring my own heart or others.

But one thing has happened: I no longer remain for long outside myself, so that agony induced by the actions of other people can tear at me not so much and not so long. No longer *given over,* or *impressed into service,* or a point determined by others' sines and cosines. (Not so much. A little still, but not so much!)

This was what she wanted to be, but was not—at least not yet. Thoughts about Raymond destroyed all her attempts at self-protective detachment. Though he wrote that "something in you won't give up, no matter what the facts are, the idea of being betrayed," and swore his innocence, he could not convince her that he was telling the truth. She heard *Der Rosenkavalier* at the Mozarteum the evening of August 1st, and, later in her room, noted that the "presentation of the Rose music brought back Hillsdale, where we used to play it on [the] phonograph." The difference between her happiness before the Hillsdale fire and the present sorry, angry chaos of their marriage made her steel herself to face what was rapidly turning into defeat and failure. Writing, again about *Der Rosenkavalier*— "Really a mature idea in the libretto. The Marschallin had worked out what must happen and met the situation as though she had long rehearsed the part she must play"—Louise was rehearsing what her own part must be on her return to New York. With her fellowship reduced, and with a growing desire not to postpone the inevitable, she was seriously considering going home at the end of August. Her decision was neither sudden nor rash. She continued to walk through Salzburg, seeing the sights and hearing the Festspiel concerts. She began to teach herself Italian, and this stirred up memories of her Boston girlhood, her youthful yearnings for art and culture, the long distance from the Boston of 1910-1915 to the Europe she had absorbed in the past four months, and the woman she had become in the interim. Repeatedly meeting the word *destino* in her Italian book, she was struck by how often hers had changed, and set down, in her journal, every address she had ever lived at—and could remember—since her first marriage:

—From Greene Avenue, Brooklyn, Fort Sherman, Canal Zone, Barrow Street, Farley (and the strangest change there, purely due to chance)—or did it begin in Garden St., Hoboken, or the day in Boston when I walked [went?] to [*illeg.*]'s office? Or 12th Street, Varick House, Farley again, 94 Fifth Avenue (chance once more), the cottage by the lake in Worcester, the farm at Charlton Depot, 15th

Street, Vienna, the lodging with Italia in 48th Street. Worcester again (that strange crowded room, with the piano on the landing outside, was *after* Vienna—how incredible!), the apartment on Sullivan Street (chance again) with the furniture made out of raw wood; D. Brown's studio on 14th St.; the apartment with Marion; the house at 99 Henry St.; and then the long series of dwellings with R: the 1st 11th St., the 2nd 11th Street (how we used to speak of these, and now speak of them no more!). The basement on Lexington Avenue (and a whole lump of mixed destiny there!); the apartment on 16th Street, that clinched that destiny for good; the room near Columbia, with Léonie & M. Mead & Ruth getting mixed up in affairs; Boston again: the furnished room on Marlborough Street, the apartment on the hill, the apartment on ———— Street (I have forgotten its name and the house is torn down)—sunny rooms, real happiness for a time, although I let down. Yaddo; 57th Street (also razed to the ground), Santa Fe. 57th Street again, and the Léonie disorder. Hillsdale—Mrs. Mallory's and our house.
Tudor City—God, god.
Lexington Avenue.
Palermo, Rome, Florence, Venice.
Toulon.—Salzburg. And now?

This list stands as proof of Bogan's many references, few of them detailed, about the turmoil and anguish of her early adult life. Following the constant stress of her childhood there came an equally constant flow of changes leading up to and continuing beyond her attachment to Raymond. What pattern did she find in this itinerant catalogue? A quest, perhaps, as well as an exile and an escape? Musing on the trip to Dublin she still hoped to make before going back to America, she remarked that it would be "closing a circle begun when my grandmother left it."

As she contemplated her destiny, detaching her fortunes, and her identity, from the life she shared with Raymond, he was writing his last letters from New York. Things were still going badly for him. He was down to his last few dollars. His writing (a detective novel, and a "play-novel") was going nowhere. Two *New Yorker* "casuals" had been rejected as uninteresting. On August 10th, she decided "absolutely to go back to America on August 31st," then, in the same moment, wavered, hoping to salvage at least the chance to go to Ireland. She saw her life in "306 Lex. very clearly, starting in its usual round the day after my arrival. Surely even loneliness in Ireland would be better than that." So she postponed her decision once again, and refrained from writing the Guggenheim Foundation. She read and wrote and noted in her journal, "a sudden flash of the joy of *writing*. H. James gave me this, in *The American*. His meticulous and neat and careful and *crisis-less* way."

The days in Salzburg were by now proceeding with a semblance of routine. German planes circling overhead dropped Nazi leaflets, urging the Austrians to join the Third Reich. During the day, Maidie took singing lessons at the Mozarteum; late afternoons came to a rest with *café mit schlag* and a leisurely read of the *Herald-Tribune.* In the evenings there were concerts. Louise was very unhappy. At the very least, trouble, and quite possibly catastrophe, awaited her in New York. Preparing herself for suffering, she rehearsed attitudes, bitter, ironic, energy-consuming attitudes that she hoped would protect her from loss and devastation. In the Villefranche notebook she wrote "Lesson 00," which began with a brief sketch of the room she and Maidie shared in their Salzburg pension and concluded:

All places are more or less everywhere. Tea instead of gin will warm the heart. Special knowledge isn't as much as it would seem. The soprano studies for seven years in order to be able to open her mouth and make loud sounds for three hours on end.

Everyone is in the same boat and a hard look from anyone in the world means just about 100 times less than nothing. The calm and unperturbed front is the one weapon against everything.

Never confide. Never worry out loud. Never suspect out loud. Never do anything out loud but exchange a few general opinions on general topics with as much ease and wit as possible.

On August 18th she booked passage to America on the *Europa,* sailing September 21st from Bremen. "Great heartsickness at thought of going home," she wrote in her journal. "But realize that things cannot be allowed to drift any longer."

In the days remaining to her in Europe she did a good deal of writing, keeping her journal through August 26th. Raymond wrote that he might have a job with the research department of the Bank of the Manhattan Company, reporting on various industries. He was determined to get a job and provide a good home for Louise the following winter:

You see I'm not being licked, I keep looking and trying—chiefly because I want to be able to make this winter a comfortable and happy one for both of us. I couldn't bear the thought of you coming back to a welter of bailiffs. The summer has been a terrible strain. I've been so hot, tired, and discouraged this month that I have hardly been able to stand it. Now things look as if they had a chance to be brighter.

In another letter he chattily told her that she would be coming home to a completely rearranged apartment. He and Inez, the maid, had been

doing some fixing. I repaired the broken-legged bedroom chair and we moved the whole bedroom around—chiefly with the idea of shifting the wear and tear on the bad spots on the floor. I moved the hanging shelf nearer the window, put the bed under that (the same tables on either side), shifted the desk to the bed's former location only nearer the entrance door and you can't imagine the difference. Inez is delighted with it and I think you'll be.

In his last letter, Raymond swore again, as he had all summer, that he had never kept secrets from her, and that her belief that he was conducting a secret life apart from her was "nothing but gratification of the pleasure you take in trying to hurt yourself and those you love as a child pulls the wings from flies." And he offered this peroration:

Oh darling you know I know how much you've suffered, and that I love you and want to help you. Don't waste life and love like that. Stop posing and be simple. If you've had bumps and troubles come back where bumps and troubles are the law of the day. Come back to a good solid four-square hell from that nasty sticky heaven of yours. You'll find me waiting for Louise—not for that other silly one.

She gave up the plan to go to Ireland, and tried to sum up the past five months for herself.

It is like this: You have had a fine, interesting, absorbing time.
    You have done a good deal of absorbing.
    That's all anyone needs to know. That's the valuation of the time that they will take in, if given to them with enough vigor in the voice and pleasure in the smile.
    You need some place to work in. That's the door half open.

Late August in Salzburg had the atmosphere of early fall, and it summoned up a mood of elegy. She wrote in her journal:

SALZBURG

The first September days, overcast, half light, half darkness, saturated through and through with a strange, chill, almost intolerable air of grief that produces, in the mind and in the heart, not the agony that it seems to foreshadow and presage, but a strange and piercing joy. For everything stands still and is silent; the leaves lie upon the ground in two colors, withered brown and fresh green; everything has produced out of itself its own look, as under no other light, and, as well, a look of silence and farewell. These are the days when the light seems to fall downward from the whole universe, and not merely from the sunless sky, when the time we know betrays us appears visible in every shadow and sounds like an echo is every step and every voice.
    These are the days when truth is spoken to us concerning our existence. From childhood on, on days such as this, I have heard the unmistakable farewell. As a young girl, as a child, I heard it among scenes now forever vanished and not the

same. Farewell, everything said,—this is here, and passes,—this is the moment between change; this is the hinge on which the future wheels.

The truth spoken, for to all those Septembers it was indeed farewell, a final and dissolving parting, as they passed. And today, between the light and darkness, that close and open irregularly, over the still-green land, under the intense radiance without sunlight of the chill sky, it is also farewell. With great intensity, with grief, with great joy, I still hear the word and smell the change, with a terrible happiness, a heart braced fiercely for this that changes, then as now.

On Saturday morning, August 26th, she and Maidie walked up the Kapuzinerberg, moving through the light and shade of the trees in the sunny, cool day, past stations of the cross leading up to a crucifixion shrine. There were two views, one extending over the railroad side of Salzburg and another beyond the trees. They went into "Mozart's garden house as rough as a piano box. Old prints of early costumes and settings of *Zauberflöte* on walls." She signed the register, "and there was Louise Bogan, New York City, as near the Mozart ghost as she will ever come."

By September 3rd she and Maidie were aboard ship at Southampton harbor. On the 5th, in the middle of the Atlantic, she wrote, "O superb days, when your writing warms you to the marrow!"

With these words she brought her journey to an end, and turned to meet what awaited her at home.

6 THE FLAWED LIGHT OF LOVE AND GRIEF

WHILE IT IS TRUE that Louise Bogan suffered from pathological jealousy, and tortured both Raymond Holden and herself with the suspicion that he was chronically unfaithful, it is also true that within hours or even moments of her return to New York, she had substantial reason to believe that he had indeed been having an affair with the Miss X he'd repeatedly mentioned in his letters over the spring and summer; apparently he had even been living with her at 306 Lexington Avenue ever since Maidie had sailed in June to meet Louise in the south of France. Arriving September 7th, Louise was met at the dock by a pale and nervous Raymond, who not only did not deny the affair, but was, as Louise reported in her journal, immediately "ready to defend his mistress: 'There's no one I know that you cannot know. Certainly I'll bring her to the house.' "

Louise had been waiting for this moment. She had accepted her Guggenheim knowing that a prolonged absence from Raymond would almost certainly lead to such a catastrophe, and in that sense her acceptance of the fellowship, and her constant accusations once she was actually in Europe, had even set it in motion. But she was devastated nonetheless. All her studied attitudes, cultivated indifference, and stoic coolness disappeared "when I saw the house rearranged, evidently with her help and reference to her taste. All the logical, realistic approaches to the problem that I had built up, in the early mornings in Salzburg, with agony and tears, were swept away when I saw the well-bred and collegiate details of the rearrangement." Miss X, and not, as Raymond had reported, Inez, the housekeeper, had helped him rearrange the furniture, or so Louise unshakably believed, and his clumsy lie sickened her. Everything she feared and distrusted about Raymond—his inability to tell the truth—now seemed confirmed, and she bitterly reviled him in scenes of fury and recrimination paralleling in their emotional violence those she had witnessed as a child between her mother and father. With malicious artistry, fate had made her once again the dupe of an irresponsible and beloved person, and she suffered doubly, as a woman who had been sexually wounded and as a child whose already damaged trust had been damaged once again.

What she could not do as a seven- or eight-year-old child she could do as a woman of thirty-six. Five days after her homecoming, with her marital crisis in full bloom, Bogan opened her journal to think and reflect. She examined her 1931–32 journal first, and then, comparing it with her European journal, remarked:

My notes taken in the last six months, with few exceptions, have *been* notes, and little else: notations of things seen, of trains taken, of people, of times of day. This journal, written in the dark months before my departure, when my life had reached a dead end, now impresses me as honest and important. My European diary can—and will—be expanded, but I shall be able to learn a great deal from myself of last year,—from that broken, desperate self, full of rancor, bitterness, despair, from that mind in a body over-fat with alcohol, from those emotions that did not yet know themselves, from those ideas salvaged out of the despair and the distrust of myself and the universe at large.

How strange suddenly to realize that she whom I thought a dead woman was really a growing personality!

Her detachment during this time of grief and disappointment is astonishing. She was able to describe and analyze her most painful feelings, if not to act on them, with acute objectivity. She described Raymond's current situation, and how it had come about in a tone of summary recapitulation, rather than accusation, as if she had been gathering instances, and evidence—as in fact she had—over a long period of time and could now at last present her conclusions:

When I am *newly, freshly* present, I can for a short time represent to him a full and romantic emotion. This, of course, will soon disappear, and he will more frequently and more openly show the resentment, the jealousy, the hatred that he really bears for me in his heart. For a few weeks he will make a great show of devotion and thereafter he will live more and more apart from me, and again take up his dependence on the other.

Louise had always loved Raymond's charm and wit; he took life more easily than she, was more at home in the world. But since the fire she had come to despise (and acquiesce in) what she considered his gravest weakness, a tendency toward what she called "Shelleyism" and he, in one of his letters, "passionate renewing delight." By whatever name, this was an addiction to romantic love. Raymond had grown up reading *The Idylls of the King,* and conceived of romantic love as the only source of emotional drama and significance in life. His hunger to do and risk all for love, to be perpetually scaling its heights and plunging into its depths, was insatiable. Louise, who had also grown up reading Tennyson (and the Pre-Raphaelites), struggled against her own romantic yearnings, and in her fury at Raymond outlined his romantic pattern with scathing clarity. She claimed that he had

no intellectual interests. He cannot read, he cannot judge, he cannot analyze or plan. So he waits for the newest wind of romantic love to blow over him, and again and again writes a new series of sonnets, in which the stars bend from heaven and enter into his beloved's eye. His life is again rescued, blessed and refreshed by a new woman. Nothing, in his actions, seems to him strange or disloyal, because he cannot detach himself from the adolescent image he has of himself: the passionate lover, the poet drowned in his lover's arms.

What appalled Louise was her persisting need for him, as chaotic and contradictory as he was. He apparently considered himself enough of a man-of-the-world to shrug off his own minor sexual indiscretions while at the same time believing in the renewing powers of passion no matter who their source might be. It horrified Louise that she could not break out of her terrible dependence upon the devotion "of a confused and mindless bundle of unresolved emotions like Raymond. I am not yet able to stand by myself, so I share his bed, revile his character and endeavor to build my work on this unsteady basis."

They fought constantly. She fulminated against his deceptions and lashed out at his weaknesses. She ridiculed his romantic rhetoric. He reproached her for not trusting him, for being pathologically jealous, and for refusing to admit that he needed "a change of focus." But just as she needed his declarations of love, he seemed to need, and even enjoy, her angry outbursts, since they supplied him with the moral perspective he could not discover for himself. She felt she had become "a kind of walking conscience, to whom he can refer a *part* of his difficulties and find therein a ready, definite and furious *blame.*"

The dream of living as a secular monastic, surrounded by essential possessions only, now attracted her more than ever. How to leave Raymond and find the courage to stand alone were the obstacles:

Today—on Sept. 12, 1933—I have the perhaps mistaken illusion that somehow the necessary change will come about by my own deed. But I may die with a gallery of R.'s romances all about me, with his latest sonnets to his latest star-lit love singing in my ears. It may be like that—perhaps my fundamental weaknesses, or the profound fatigue of will that struck me eight or nine years ago (the result of turmoil— unspeakable turmoil—suffered in childhood, youth and early maturity) will make me stay through it all and suffer it all and endure it all.

She who had always praised or blamed herself, and regarded every development in life as a performance to be judged, could not expose her humiliation to others, fearing their sympathy, and fearing that secretly they would judge her as she judged herself—a woman who had loved a fool, and been fooled by him. She did not discuss her situation with either Humphries or Wilson, and it was only some months later that she was able to confide in Katharine S. White. But to Morton Zabel she opened her heart, writing in October that she was

all shot to pieces nervously because of some extra-marital goings on of Raymond's, which will, I believe culminate in a separation or a divorce. *Please* do not mention this development to a soul, as the steps I am taking demand the utmost secrecy at the present time. *Do not say a word* to anyone connected with the literary world as my whole chance for a new life depends on my keeping my own counsel (and you keeping it for me!) for a month or so.

What I shall do and where I shall go I can't say. The Guggenheims,—did I tell you!—still consider me a potential fellow and have told me that I could reapply for the unspent portion of my funds sometime—anytime—in the future. I should like to get out of New York, away from all the tie ups here, into some kind of job that would keep Maidie and myself going. I must have regular work, a definite task or I fear I shall break down and I cannot afford to do that. —You are one of the few people in the world to whom I could give my confidence. Where I shall go, or what I shall do, I cannot say, but I certainly will soon leave 306 Lexington Avenue and the role of the deceived wife forever.

Yet she was far from certain that she could leave. She and Raymond circled the possibility of breaking up: it seemed inevitable, it seemed impossible. Raymond's job as a researcher for the Bank of the Manhattan Company involved frequent travel to major industrial cities to gather material about blast furnaces, pipe mills, and electric welding processes for financial reports. Writing to Louise from Cleveland early in the autumn, he acknowledged receiving a wire from her, "though I don't know just what it meant. It seemed to mean that you wanted to make a go of it. I do."

It was her pride that she could not circumvent. While she admitted to herself that it was obsessive and neurotic, her pride made it impossible to forgive Raymond's breach of faith. She was still in many respects the adolescent girl who played *Pelléas and Mélisande* on the piano, and who quested, like the youth in "A Tale," for a changeless world. And she was still, like her own "Hypocrite Swift," savagely intolerant of common failings, so intolerant, in fact, that she even pitied Raymond for being the target of her wrath:

One emotion I now feel, which I felt yesterday, through all my hatred and dislocated resolves and despair, was pity: I pitied R. from the depths of my heart as he stood before me with his carefully chosen shirt frayed a little at the side. I saw him, weak, mixed, fighting against my obsessions as he best knew how, trying to keep his own personality intact against my blows, and I pitied and even respected him. For at my worst, I [am] certainly a fiend, a woman driven by all the assorted forces of a personal hell. And that is another admission that I have never been able to make before, let alone write down on paper.

Her inability to come to a decision about whether to stay with Raymond or leave brought back her 1931 depression. It had never truly disappeared, and its return was vicious. She felt dead to the world, cut off from it, and filled with loathing for what remained of her need for it. At the movies she sneered at the audiences as they watched newsreels, which to her mind were parades of every kind of human disaster and cruelty reported in the fake-genteel tones of a trained announcer. For a period of three days in September she felt

that there was no hope; no peace to which I could turn. The things I want to write must be written in a dead language; the things important to my eyes, the delicate solitude of hearing and sight, what can they mean, to me or to anyone else, in this civilization that whirrs and bangs and grinds like the inside of a carrousel?

Still, if life appeared strange to her now, it was because she was growing and changing. It was a "late growth, at 36. A long slow growth, up through fantasies and childish pride and childish play and childish dreams." If these childish things were truly to be given up, they would have to be mourned, as all true losses must be mourned, and, aware that the conflict between holding on to them and giving them up was plunging her more deeply into darkness and paralysis, Bogan fought back, as always, by placing even greater demands upon herself. Late in September she wrote "Dove and Serpent," which *The New Yorker* published in November, and she met with Wheelock and Maxwell Perkins at Scribner's late in October to discuss how she might continue with *Laura Dal[e]y's Story*.

Another piece, "Coming Out," appeared in the October 14th issue of *The New Yorker*. It was written while she was still in Europe, and is a witty prose caprice, a masterly dissimulation of emotional suffering. As the piece defines it, "coming out" is the more or less logical and practical decision to cast off neurotic suffering and neurotic pride, and emerge into the calm light of ordinary existence. Bogan pokes fun at the grumblings and grousings of the chronically miserable person, and then surveys the options available to him once he decides to crawl out of his isolation: he can love mankind in general or one person in particular; he can hate; or he can feel "very noble or very powerful. Feeling noble or powerful also defies analysis; when one feels noble or powerful in any degree, one feels noble or powerful, and there's nothing more to say." The important point is that no matter what choice he makes, he is certain to see his former obsessions, for at least a moment, with the sharpest clarity: "For one split second you are upheld in a dead calm. You are no longer the world's lost child or the universe's changeling. You are a normal person, ready to join your fellows."

This state of "normality"—of frank, unregretting disabusedness—she was unable to reach merely by willing it. She was brooding now a good part of every day, crying often, unable to sleep. Finally her ability to work deserted her, and early in November she signed herself into the New York Hospital, Westchester Division, on Bloomingdale Road in White Plains. "I've had a bad nervous crack-up, Morton," she wrote Zabel on November 9th, "that has been coming on for some time, so I've really gone away for some months in an earnest effort to clear the whole thing finally. Months or years, I really do not care, as long as I can, after whatever period it is, feel and live humanly again." She was not "puzzled or confused or suffering from any of the major delusions," she explained to Wheelock, "merely prostrated because of certain crises that occurred after my return from Europe." To Katharine S. White she wrote, "I am so sorry. I tried hard and thought I could put things through, but evidently not."

LOUISE BOGAN'S FAITH in psychiatric medicine was unquestioning. As she had trusted her doctor in 1931, she once again trusted the whole apparatus of hospitalization and convalescence. "This time," she vowed to Wheelock, "I shall stay in medical hands until I know where I'm at." A stay of about six months was prescribed. Raymond could afford to pay her medical bills, now that he had a job, and Inez, the maid, was able to help Maidie with meals and chores when he was out of town. Soon after arriving in White Plains, Louise wrote to Maidie: "I shall be very well very soon—better than I have been in years, and able to cope with any difficulty.

So don't you feel peculiar or gloomy for a moment: I'll be able to be happy and make you happy and serene. Just remember what fun we had in Salzburg: we'll have that same kind of happy time again, and this time it will last." Maidie was old enough to realize that her mother was suffering from emotional pain, and she was reassuring, warm, and affectionate in her own letters, writing often, and asking for news of her mother's progress. Louise wrote back in detail:

It is really rather pleasant here, in a way. Everything is done to make the "patients" comfortable; the food is quite good, now and again; the air is delicious and some of the females are really very charming. One woman, a Mrs. [H] from Scarsdale, is perhaps the wittiest and most attractive person I have met in years. She has three daughters and an unlimited fund of wit, humor and anecdote. She has been very kind to me and made the first few days not only bearable but very amusing. The nurses are personable and kindly and the doctors really seem to have some sense, although none of them are *beauties*. . . .

My metabolism, my teeth, my bony structure, my eyes, ears, nose and throat have all been gone over carefully. My tonsils will have to come out, I fear, but the teeth are fairly safe. My eyes and hearing are super-normal and I am pituitary rather than thyroid, if that means anything to you. I weigh *129* pounds, stripped, or did when I came, so you can see what a diet of beer and light wines did for me. . . .

I'm making a whole bevy of baskets for your buttons, needles, thread, waste and trinkets. They tried to get me interested in book binding but I said no. I don't believe in binding books. I'm knitting a grand sweater, dark green on one side and light green on the other: one dark and one light sleeve!

Her tone was equally witty, though not quite so optimistic, in her letter to Wilson, who by this time had learned of her predicament:

I now feel as though I had been thoroughly prepared for taxidermy and then set aside in a de-stuffed condition. My progress toward "normal" thinking and feeling will be slow, I hear. Perhaps when the dogwood blooms in the spring I shall be able to "take an objective view" and make "clear-cut decisions." I *have* graduated from the observation ward (no belts, no scarves, stockings locked up at night) to a hall where slightly more freedom prevails.

To see, close at hand, day after day, walking examples of those mental states usually safely kept from one behind a veil of print opens up Pascal's abyss in no uncertain way.

Later in December she was telling Maidie that she was feeling better, and in her report to Wilson she noted that though she was still suffering from "psychic pains," she was sure that she would get some literary material out of them: "Really nothing like a thorough psychic pain to speed the profound thought and the singing line!"

In general, Louise tried to be scrupulous about keeping Maidie outside the field of her conflicts with Raymond. She remembered the terrible family fights she had witnessed as a child, and refused to enmesh Maidie in situations she could neither understand nor control. Raymond was the only father Maidie had ever known, and she adored him, blaming Louise for the trouble between them, the full details of which she was not to know for several years. There had been harsh words between Louise and Raymond just prior to her entry into the hospital, and communication between them had come to a standstill. Soon after Louise began treatment, she asked Maidie to deliver a message:

Tell Raymond that I didn't mean to be too nasty, and make it clear that all that should be taken as part of my illness. Intimate to him that I should like nothing better than to get back to the point where I could write him full and pleasant letters: letters that resemble someone running to someone else with an apronful of apples and saying "See what I've got!" (Image borrowed from E. St. V. M.)

I haven't many apples in the apron to show anyone at the moment. Life goes on in a nice quiet protected curative way. I knit and read and eat and sleep and tomorrow I may weave. There's a woman here who says, "In weavink there is healink!"

Louise worked hard at confronting her depression. Her December journal entries, made as Christmas approached, reflect a mood of searing bitterness. "It was not God, as in the accepted myth," she wrote, "who gave his only son to be crucified. It was agonized and exacerbated human beings who saw the gentlest, the most tender and compassionate side of life subjected to torture and ignominy, and in retaliation against the dreadful agonies that they themselves must endure, imagined a tortured exemplar of such a life divine." That she saw her own sufferings in this light, that it was her own spirit whose fragility moved her, and that she was herself a victim of torture and shame gave her private ordeal a mythic dimension. It was not so much that she identified with Christ, but that her own experience of pain and betrayal seemed so inexorably a part of human existence.

She was never suicidal, neither in this depression nor in any other she ever went through, but there was a pull away from life that she recognized and battled against by letting the waves of pain, reaching back into childhood, wash over her. Would she ever reach the bottom of it? She observed in her journal that the

bouts of tears prove that grief must lessen, as they lessen. But what of the deep depressions, tearless, that do not lift, the will for death growing and continuing? O, I shall cure myself of this sorrow and go back to a kind of life with a small (but safe) fund of joy; but I shall get older and the deep death-wish may be the thing that waits for me; it may be the crown, the answer, the pinnacle of my life.

To recover joy and outsmart the death-wish were the primary goals of her therapy. She needed a schedule, a plan for her days, and a way of working more easily. Over the past three years—since the fire—she had spent more hours than she cared to count in "barren brooding," she wrote to Mrs. White, adding, "The real tragedy occurs when the drive that should go into creation becomes unhinged and spills over into personal relationships which are unsatisfactory and bear within them the seeds of disaster, at best."

Getting back to work would be a sign that recovery was under way, and she promised Mrs. White that she would soon be sending her a piece "about sanitarium patients taking a walk," which "may be good, if rather grisly." Unpublished during Bogan's lifetime, the piece, called "The Long Walk," describes an afternoon walk taken every day, under the supervision of a nurse, by the women patients at the hospital. These women are of all ages, and come from mostly middle-class backgrounds, with husbands and fathers and lovers and children who, along with life and time, and their own expectations, have failed them. Bogan describes the well-kept hospital grounds, the attending nurse's militant cheerfulness, and the course of the walk itself, which includes a stretch past the hospital director's house, where some of the patients always "laughed at his wife's choice of window curtains, and some who made as if to peer into the dining room window, where decanters and cruets were visible on the sideboard." The women continue their walk until they arrive at a dirt road which ends in a wall. Beyond it they can see the streets of White Plains, and a row of apartment houses whose lights, in the dusk, make them acutely aware that it is the time of day when husbands and children come home for supper, and the evening lies ahead. Each woman now remembers her own "painful inner story" of neglect and rejection:

At this moment Miss Andrews heard again inside her heart her father's voice; he admonished her; he looked at her with love. Little Mrs. Harburg felt the fear that nothing could happen again; that everything was over; that life had closed up against her. Mrs. Shields saw again the face of her husband, that denied her, and felt his shoulder, turning strongly, unhurriedly away from her arms. The young girls felt a flood of wildness and fear go over them; the older women saw the monotonous afternoon light recede away from them, like a tide going out that reveals the ugliness of the beach. At this point Miss Gill heard the voice that told her she must run away, and Miss Shaw felt the need to get rid, for ever, of her sagging and unused body. Some heard or saw nothing, but felt again that pang, nameless and centered below the throat, of sorrow which had become part of them, like an organ in their flesh. Some began to listen to the old story of suspicion and thwarted love, always told in the same words, always ending in a question and an answer they could not bring themselves to acknowledge. Over and over, in the groove worn into their minds, the terrible certainty loosened and moved. That which could not happen, but had happened; that which could not be borne, but which they were bearing.

Louise saw herself among them, saw that they suffered as she suffered, and through this sympathetic clairvoyance, she once again became connected to the world outside herself. Some of her memories were now joyous, and included "those wooden houses behind which I first saw the full depth of the infinite and profound universe and felt the impact of the beauty of the world." She was reading again, finding Yeats's *The Winding Stair* and *Words for Music Perhaps* magnificent. Katharine S. White had written in November that everyone at *The New Yorker* "greatly admires 'Serpent and Dove' in this week's issue—I can't wait for the whole book," and Wheelock pressed her for more details about her plans for its completion. Although Edmund Wilson appears not to have known about these fictional memoirs, he had limitless faith in the therapeutic value of work, and in December suggested that she write "a confession d'un enfant du siècle—maybe Auden's orators would give you a cue. What you really ought to do, I should think is to give literary expression to your internal conflicts and ranklings. You haven't really done this for a long time, have you? Once you get experience out of your system in a satisfactory literary form, you can thumb your nose at the world. —In any case, get out of there as soon as you can— the world needs you and you, it." He also pointed out that he and Rolfe Humphries both missed her terribly and had discussed her abilities at great length one recent evening, with Humphries ranking Bogan far above Millay, and Wilson at first demurring: "but when he challenged me to go through her books poem by poem and then consider yours, I was almost convinced. You are always a first-rate artist and it is a calamity for you to be languishing like this (if you are languishing)." There was every incentive for her to get well. But the healing process itself could not be rushed.

DR. JAMES WALL, the physician who treated Louise Bogan while she remained at "Bloomingdale's," was, at thirty-one, five years her junior. He was a gentle, courteous Southerner, who immediately understood that his patient had more than ordinary gifts, and was reluctant to tamper in any way with their sources. Essentially a Freudian eclectic in his approach to treatment, he did not recommend the arduous and lengthy process of psychoanalysis, preferring to leave the basic psychic structure alone. He did urge Bogan, however, toward a profound and extremely painful revision of her unrealistic expectations of people and of life itself. Who was *she,* he essentially got her to ask, that out of the whole human race she should be exempt from the failings of others? Who was she to demand that Raymond Holden live up to her rigorous standards of honor? And who was she to condescend to the common limits and possibilities of existence? His humor and sympathy provided her with a sheath for the destructive "knife of the perfectionist attitude." Her illness had happened because she needed rest. "Writing," he told her, "is a way of *keeping well.* But when one is sick, everything must be dropped and left and nature must be given a chance to build up the worn mind and body." *Let the will rest,* he counseled her. Action was not always required in a crisis. Life had a way of regulating itself; things worked themselves out without the interference or control of conscious decisions. Louise had often forced situations into premature and faulty resolutions.

In weaving, she found, there really *was* healing. The simple, absorbing tasks of occupational therapy had the desired effect of allowing the unconscious to unravel both ancient and current fixations. Louise was learning how to free herself, as she had never done before, from the demand that her own well-being depend upon the perfect love she had desired from both her mother and Raymond, two people constitutionally incapable of giving it. Beyond this lesson, she was learning that her failure to obtain, or rather, to keep such love was neither a sin nor a crime, but a common, even universal disappointment, and that there was likely to be no one who could have sustained her impossibly high standards of loyalty. She too, she came to realize, was as much a victim of "Shelleyism" as Raymond, in centering her life upon passionate romantic love. She too had sought an unquenchable flame, partly to make up for the erratic and perilous fire struck and then extinguished by her mother. Mary Bogan and Raymond Holden had loved her, but it had been irresponsible, reckless, and ignorant love. Illness meant clinging to that love, and, since she no longer wished to be ill, or needed to be ill, she faced the necessity of letting go, slowly and painfully, of both her mother and her husband.

The basis for this renunciation, and for the whole working relationship between Louise Bogan and Dr. Wall can be found in *The Dynamics of Therapy in a Controlled Relationship,* a book by a Rankian analyst named Jessie Taft. "A controlled relationship, or environment is what one gets in Bloomingdale," Louise pointed out some years later to Morton Zabel (to whom she was recommending the book in particular from a list of psychoanalytic texts sent to him in an attempt to save him "from the state of absolute illiteracy, as far as literature on the modern psychology goes"). This therapeutic setup was beautifully tailored to her needs. It held that it was not the instincts—not envy, competition, and aggression—that had to be overcome, and it was not so much other people, or even the self, but the meaning of *time* that had to be faced:

Time in itself is a purely arbitrary category of man's invention, but since it is a projection of his innermost being, it represents so truly his inherent psychological conflict, that to be able to accept it, to learn to admit its likeness to one's very self, its perfect adaptation to one's deepest and most contradictory impulses, is already to be healed, as far as healing is possible or applicable, since in accepting time, one accepts the self and life with their inevitable defects and limitations. This does not mean a passive resignation but a willingness to live, work and create as mortals within the confines of the finite.

As a poet, Louise had known this all along. Her poetry had always wrestled with time. The conflict between acknowledging time and escaping from it lives in her earliest "betrothal" poems, in the passionate will both to conquer existence and submit to it in *Body of This Death,* and reaches its highest point in "Summer Wish," which in all respects is an imaginative, mythic correlative to the state Taft sets forth with brisk clinical efficiency:

The neurotic is caught in life as in a trap. Fear will not permit him to recognize his own creative power or to admit the destructiveness which he shares with the rest of life. He must be everything or nothing, all powerful or consumed with fear of a reality which is stronger than he, perfect or condemned to an intolerable imperfection. What he needs is to learn to flow with life, not against it; to submit willingly, to let himself be carried by its strength without giving up responsibility for being that particular part of the current which is uniquely himself, yet like enough to the rest to take the same direction, to be moved by similar forces.

Or, as Louise herself wrote to Morton Zabel, in 1936, "that when one lets go, and *recognizes* the stream on which we move as the same stream which moves us within—that it is time and the earth floating our blood and flesh, floating its own child—and stops fighting against the kinship, the light flows in; peace arrives."

One by one, she gave up the remnants of her early hurting self: the provincial girl; the noble, reckless, romantic; the jealous wife, with a touch of paranoia. By mid-January she could feel the suspiciousness lessening:

The monomania which built up a logical devised system of torture from such details as the sound of a person's voice over the telephone or the time and place of a postmark begins to lose its edge of blame and fury, and turns, as the path of a loom changes, subtly, thread newly grouped by thread, into another pattern. The knife becomes dulled, as it were, and is put aside in the drawer, again a tool and not a weapon.

"And supposing it is (or he does)?" *is the first phrase* learned under the new dispensation.

Early in the new year she was moved into the convalescent residence at the hospital. "Well, I've made the Villa, and very pretty it is too!" she wrote to Maidie in January. "I have ruffled curtains and a fireplace (which doesn't work) in my room, and I share a bath with another girl. All in all, it's swell, and soon I'll be back in the great world functioning as per usual, only better." Maidie would be visiting in a few days, and Louise asked her to "bring up some duets and we'll play them on the Villa piano—there's a Steinway grand here." One afternoon Louise visited a friend in Hall 5, where she had spent her first weeks in the hospital, and "what a dismal hole that is, in retrospect!" she exclaimed to Maidie. "I sincerely hope that all my brooding and weeping are over, as I should never care to catch up on my brooding in those surroundings, again." Late in January she wrote Mrs. White that she was ready to resume her reviewing job and gave a guardedly optimistic prognosis. She was better, "but not entirely so. I should be able to issue forth, as cured as can be, sometime in the late spring. I've been such a damned fool about myself and other people for so long (going on 37 years) that it takes a little time." Early in February, however, she was "very busy throwing my random thoughts on poetry into shape."

Dr. Wall was soon permitting her to spend weekends in town—one at a time, rather than two in a row—and these she managed without apparent strain. Returning one evening, she reported to Maidie, she encountered Dr. Wall, who "burst out with loud guffaws when he saw my hat. He thought the cure was complete, then. 'It certainly looks come-hitherish,' said he. 'It's meant to look that way,' said I."

About Raymond she wrote nothing, at this time, in her journal. The previous October, as her illness was worsening, she had moved with him and Maidie to 100 West Fifty-fifth Street, just off Sixth Avenue. It appears that during these weekend visits home she and Raymond lived as a married couple, but one whose future together was still completely uncertain. Each knew that a decision to stay together or separate for good would be made once Louise left the hospital late in April.

WHEN SHE WAS NOT WEAVING and knitting, or walking, or being showered with needlespray, or massaged; when she was not at meals or in session with Dr. Wall, or working on her *New Yorker* reviews, Louise worked on her journal. More memories returned, illuminated with distance, disclosing scenes "with terrific clarity." In "Dove and Serpent" she had already described the weather of a Ballardvale fall, when smoke "blew wildly from chimneys and torrents of leaves were pulled from the trees," and she again recalled the town, drafting a sketch she intended to expand into the background of *Laura Dal[e]y's Story:*

The month, the time of day: children are coming indoors from roads bordered by orchards heavy with apples, into rooms with looped back curtains, and old mirrors. Among the dahlias and asters of the late gardens their mothers pull the dried clothes from the line, reaching their arms above their heads so that their cotton dresses under the shawl thrown about the shoulders are pulled tightly upward from the thin apron string binding their waists. The wind rattles the lattice over the well-head; the house smells of freshly baked bread. It is already dark; the month goes on; the apples will be gathered tomorrow.

She then began to fill her scene—changed to March—with people (including Dan and May, her parents):

At eleven o'clock, in the early March day, the train went by Dan's office, and the bills of lading in the desk, the calendar on the wall, the dust on the floor all rustled and flew one way. Buck's wife shook her duster out of the window. Dede stood in a class room on the second floor of the school and pointed to the division mark, the plus, the minus, the figures of a sum, while above her head, around the four blackboard walls of the room, a garland of perfect lettering in chalk spelled out a long copy-book maxim. The blue bush outside May's window was half bud and half last year's winter-worn bush of seed. James walked down the road, and heard diminishing behind him, as he left it, the sound of his mother's piano. Carrie's dog barked in the hard trodden front yard; the water flew over the mill dam; Queenie turned on her soft warm arm and slept again; Gurney whipped his horse up the hill. Window blinds flapped outward through open upper sashes, and the ovens were hot enough for baking. The old red and green woodwork in parlors repeated the colors of the coleus in the windows.

But with these passages yet another attempt to give form to her childhood memories came, as others had before, to an abrupt halt. The very deepest renunciation which writing the book would entail—the final letting go of the earliest scenes of pain—was still too difficult. Nevertheless, Bogan did not abandon the journal. Blocked as she was in those memoirs, she found that her capacity to see into reality and formulate her findings had grown. In line with her therapy's emphasis upon both the possibilities and limits of time, she suddenly arrived at a new understanding of tragedy. Referring to herself in the third person, she wrote:

She had read Dante, Sophocles, Dostoevsky, Swift—the great ironists and thinkers who put down the universe as essentially tragic. But she never really believed it true. The part of her nature which lived in a poem by Tennyson never really took in the facts or their dreadful implications.

By the "facts" and their "implications" she meant the irreversible and unalterable nature of time and fate. The past was a landscape of unchangeable reality, with the errors and distortions of personal choice and passion equally beyond the grasp, if not the view, of present clarity. Bogan believed that literary treatment was more likely to misrepresent this tragic basis of existence than to acknowledge it. In the journal she ruminated on the nature of the "solution of thoughts" which floats in every human mind upon waking and throughout the day, "our conscious life, in which our heart and pain lie islanded," and which "literature has falsified for centuries."

She had come to understand the tragic dimension of things because she had experienced it. Her depression had taken her on a journey to the outer reaches of human endurance. It had brought her physical pain—a terrible oppression in the breast—and almost inexpressible heaviness and anguish of spirit. But she was becoming able to see it as a crucial transitional phase. Late in February 1934, just when Dr. Wall was permitting her to go home for weekends, she wrote to Janice Biala in France that perhaps,

in the main, the process of partial disintegration is salutary, and even necessary, when sensitive people reach their middle thirties. A good look into that abyss described by so many—Pascal, Dante, Sophocles, Dostoevsky, to name a few—but never really grasped by the mind until experienced by the emotions with some expenditure of blood and tears—such a glance is all to the good, I am sure. It's just as well to know that the ninth circle has an icy floor by experience: by having laid the living hand upon it.

It was time to return to the ordinary world, and leave pain behind. On March 30, 1934, she wrote in the journal, which she had begun in 1930, after the Hillsdale fire:

This book closes four years after it began. A sick and terrible four years. So terrible that I cannot bear to write to the end of the pages. A broken time.

She had cooperated fully in her treatment. Her energy had returned and, in good measure, her high spirits. Some months later she was to hear, from another physician—not Dr. Wall—and to record in her journal, the verdict, "She will never be entirely better—she has too many things to contend with—but she'll be able to do her work." Perhaps, when she left the hospital, she already knew this, and accepted it. To have her work was to have almost everything, and she no longer required perfection from other people. Her *New Yorker* job and her friendships were intact, and a fresh supply of notebooks lay ready to receive new passages for keeping. At the end of April, then, Louise Bogan went back to New York, and the apartment at Fifty-fifth Street, not a consoled woman, but a woman who was as cured as she was ever likely to be.

THE DECISION Louise was incapable of making in October she was fully capable of making in May. The time had come to separate herself, by some recognizable external act, from Raymond. Soon after her return to Fifty-fifth Street he moved out; in July she obtained a legal separation. Shortly thereafter, he and Miss X became openly acknowledged lovers.

The distinction between coming back to an old life and starting a new one, so clear in the hospital, was less easy to maintain once she resumed her daily existence in the city. In order to avoid the idleness which led to futile, debilitating brooding, Louise made staying busy her major concern. During the time that she was sequestered in White Plains, Edmund Wilson had managed to lay his hands on a "fine set of Heine" at a bargain sale at Brentano's, in anticipation of passing a certain number of evenings a week studying German with her. This, he thought, would be a very good thing for Louise, and for himself as well, since he was preparing to read Marx and other German writers for the huge labor that would eventually result in *To the Finland Station.*

When the German evenings finally began in earnest, late in the spring, Bogan and Wilson, meeting twice a week, simply read the Heine straight through, paying no attention to verb forms or case endings, and keeping two dictionaries and plenty of whiskey close at hand. After a half hour's philological concentration, Bogan would look up, smile innocently at Wilson, and ask him if he would like a piece of cake. A piece of cake, she thought, would be a very nice thing at the moment. So forth he would sally to a nearby delicatessen to fetch the cake, and it was only after he had come back with it, and it had been duly consumed, that the two students once again took up their labors.

Having fun was as important to her as keeping occupied. She decided to spend as much of the summer as possible away from New York, and in June, after Maidie left for camp, she traveled to Boston, where she hoped to stimulate her memory with return visits to Harold Street and Ballardvale, and to do some work on her memoirs. She took a room at the Hotel Victoria in Copley Square, but when she found it too hot and humid to work, her friend Mary Prim, who worked at *The Boston Evening Transcript,* persuaded her to take a room for a week or two at The Willey House, just twelve miles north of Boston in Swampscott. It was a good suggestion, for Louise immediately took a liking to the place. As she described it to Maidie, Swampscott was "a nice old-fashioned sea-side resort, with a good though rather dull beach, trees, clams, lobsters and funny stuffed looking people." The Willey House itself was an enormous, many-gabled Victorian structure, with railed porches and shuttered windows looking out over the ocean; it had

everything but a stuffed owl, however. I really love it. The rooms are charming, even mine, which is fifth floor back; the food is delicious . . . and the other guests are priceless. There's an old lady . . . who's as cuckoo as a bat and goes around fulminating against the nakedness of the modern girl in the best old-maid's insanity fashion. There are several gentlemen who have been the victims of unfortunate marriages and are now living with their mothers; there's an English accountant who looks like Charles Laughton and is always endeavoring to get the gals all wined up (so he can wreak his will upon them, probably—I'd like to see him try to wreak his will on me!). There's several "office-girls" on two weeks vacation, and *do* they get themselves up, in several shades of pink at once, usually. Their faces are cream rouge from cheek bone to chin; they wear shoes all punched with fancy little holes; their hats match their gloves and they breathe Azurea from every pore. All this wasted on the ageing mamma's boys and the vinous accountant!

She discovered the Swampscott Public Library, and sank, with a feeling of complete relaxation, into the books she read there, glancing out the windows from time to time into streets filled with trees and frame houses. "The long flood of time from two to five o'clock are the best hours for me, I find," she wrote in her journal. "The early morning is filled with those remnants of wishes and regrets that still float abruptly, without warning, into that portion of my mind that must always wear their indelible imprint." By afternoon the half-conscious mist of memory, desire, fear, and dream had burned off to solid, clear consciousness, and she felt able to work—to read and write—with pleasure and self-possession. This rhythm of the overcast morning and the clear afternoon now struck her as her own rhythm, one she must trust and consent to, rather than fight against, and she found, during these days at Swampscott, that she could work with joy and relax without guilt.

She made friends with a woman named Rufina McCarthy, who was staying at The Willey House and taught English in a Boston high school. Together they took a long automobile drive throughout Boston, Wellesley, Lincoln, and Lexington, no doubt talking and reminiscing about the Boston both had known as girls. Louise's gift for choosing remarkable friends this time brought her an educated, tough-minded, and witty companion, who, while aware of Louise's own talent and achievement, was in no direct way connected to the literary world (although Miss McCarthy's father wrote poetry). There was a shared Irish Catholic background, but also a shared opposition to the Church. For many years to come, both Rufina McCarthy and Mary Prim remained Louise's special Boston friends. With them she went hunting for antiques, enjoyed wonderful lobster and clam dinners, and shared sharp and funny insights into things in general.

Further diversion greeted her in Provincetown, where, late in July, she visited Edmund Wilson and his daughter Rosalind. Wilson was living in a house next door to a drama school, from which Louise could hear the sounds of boys and girls rehearsing all day. Wilson himself was currently interested in writing plays, and three years later brought out a trilogy with the title *This Room and This Gin and These Sandwiches* (the title play centered upon the character Sally Voight, who is partially based on Louise). Wilson's fearless assumption of the role of playwright led her to compare herself and her artistic scruples with him and his. "It is quite true that the perfectionist attitude stems from the fear of appearing ridiculous," she observed in her journal. "Edmund has none of that fear. Other people have written plays; he is a man of letters and he will write a play." Such expectations and such tolerance were qualities she admitted she lacked. Struck with something else Wilson said, she continued her literary self-appraisal:

Edmund spoke of Emerson's lack of real intellectual power. The essays are flashes, held together by no structure of "fundamental brainwork." And the thought struck me that I should take notes happily all my life, not even troubling to put them into form. I am a woman, and "fundamental brainwork," the building of logical structures, the abstractions, the condensations, the comparisons, the reasonings, *are not expected of me*. But it is only when I am making at least an imitation of such a structure that I am really happy. It is only when the notes fall into form, when the sentences make *at least the sound of styles*, that my interest really holds.

Bogan was competitive with Wilson, and in an intensely self-critical and rivalrous mood her prohibition-and-inhibition-laden gifts, so exacting and so censoring, did not stand up well against his polymorphous curiosity, acrobatic intellect, and ebullient self-confidence. She could see, in more detached as well as more self-approving moods, how solid and dense her own mind was, how swiftly apperceptive, how penetrating and acute, but during this midsummer meeting, when she knew she should have been working on *Laura Dal[e]y's Story* and could not do it, the spectacle of his blithe experimentation in dramaturgy was hard for her to bear. She was in general experiencing a certain contrariness over her work. She had written three poems since leaving "Bloomingdale's": "Short Summary," "Man Alone," and "Italian Morning," the last a poetic distillation of her time in Italy, which so moved Wheelock that he wrote to her saying it made his "editorial heart ache to think how restricted your output has been thus far." She half-thought these poems might be her last, and predicted to Morton Zabel, in the middle of her visit to Wilson, that at best she had perhaps two or three poems left in her. She even thought it might be best, for her emotional well-being in general, simply to give up poetry altogether. But in August she informed Wilson that she had written and sold yet another poem, "Poem in Prose," and that she had brought forth "a lot of subliminal mewings, roarings, and retchings, on odd scraps of paper." She was filling her notebooks with observations, memories, and drafts of poems, as well as countless notes from her reading.

Some of her new vitality appears to have been released by a love affair she was having with a man who lived in Boston. She did not discuss him directly with anyone, but from her notebook we learn that he was a librarian, a friend of Edmund Wilson's, European, and fascinating to her, with his thick hair, his Jewishness, which she equated with his exuberance and warmth, and his voluble and affectionate candor. She wrote, in "Poem in Prose," of the difficulty of describing him: "I turned from side to side, from image to image, to put you down, / All to no purpose; for you the rhymes would not ring—" and it is true that she made many prose notes about him over the summer. She also wrote, in her poem, that "It is you that must sound in me secretly for the little time before my mind, schooled in desperate esteem, forgets you—," knowing that the affair, which was a matter of only some months, had built-in limits it was crucial for her to acknowledge. It was wonderful, however, for her to have some love, particularly of the nonsuffering kind. She and her friend talked together about their lives, and he appreciated her in all her complexity. The affection and fun they shared did not end when the affair did, and they remained friends for many years after.

Bogan was in every way a richer, more substantial person than she had been before her illness. Irony of the bitter variety was losing its attraction, striking her fundamentally as an expression of an inadequate supply of responsibility and courage, while irony based on gentle and tolerant amusement at human fallibility was becoming essential to her perception and judgment, in particular as applied to herself. She wrote out a draft of a poem, "Lines Written in a Moment of Such Clarity as Verges on Megalomania," in which she observed:

It now appears that I am to learn by experience
Every last peculiar dodge and mendacity of the mind;

And emotion's every nuance will not come to me by hearsay—
It is necessary and possible for me to examine them at first hand,
    and not as museum specimens, I find.

She was no longer neurotically at a remove from life, but plumped down fully within the traffic of things as they are. Common life entered her field of vision with a transparency she had never granted it before, but at the same time with a surprisingly untranslatable complacency which made it, to her mind, tantalizingly resistant to literary treatment. Looking out over the Swampscott beach she observed:

At times the distillation, through art, of reality into the phrase and the form, seems completely futile: these groups of men and women on the beach, eating their lunch, shouting at their children, are the beings for whom life and time exist: they do not question what they do or what they have: any quality read into them or drawn out of them is false. They are real and their limited awareness is perhaps all that life demands. And the scene in which they move: the thin bright air, the sky lined with cirrus clouds, the narrow breakers moving to shore, the shadows they cast in the sun, the indefinite quality of the sunlight itself upon the sea and the sand—these elements of the scene are so ordinary, so real, so *acceptable,* to the ordinary mind, the normal acceptance, that I wonder how the impulse ever rose to heighten them into literature. Words cannot describe—that is useless. Reality stands and shines or moves and is opaque: the orderly and timid flow of hours, the flat acquiescent look of things. These will never be rendered or distilled because rendition and distillation immediately ruin the level tone and heighten out of proportion the thick, flat scene so perfectly fitted to itself in all its parts.

It is this reality—unstretched and undistorted by the nervous agility of my mind and my sensations that keeps in me the will to stay alive. It is so little, yet when I look at whatever scene it is that lies within the frame of whatever window I face, I say: "I should lose this if this moment were to die." Why should I still cling to a world from which the marrow has been removed, in which I can no longer struggle or beat about or cry, a world reduced to its elements of time, weather and appearance? Why should I desire continuance in a landscape so pierced by my insight that it is incapable of throwing back to me metaphoric reflections of any kind? A world which has become like an opening in the wall, which we take for a mirror and peer at, expecting to see ourselves, and we are not there, and what we took for the reflection of the room in which we stand is in reality a room beyond us, peopled with quite different people than ourselves, and it is air within that frame, not glass and quicksilver.

Such an examination of the world served as an examination of herself and her new relation to reality. She could see how much she differed from the disdainful, idealizing woman she had once been. If the "marrow" had been removed from life, at least life itself remained, with its pulse and flow, its mysterious and even seductive capacity to just *be*. It was now clear that life and death had been the issue all along. "Doomed," she wrote late in the summer, "kept by the strength of my bones from the death early allotted to the Romantics to whom I am blood-sister." Her depression, she realized, had saved her life.

WHEN LOUISE WENT BACK to New York at the end of July, she immediately moved forward with plans for her divorce. She and Raymond had "a nice amicable lunch," as she described it to Maidie, and Louise hired a lawyer after Labor Day. Her thirty-seventh birthday passed uneventfully. She bought herself a loose-powder compact, treated herself to a good lunch and to "one or two other minor ameliorations." A dozen roses arrived from John Hall Wheelock with the note, "To a unique and beautiful person, from her publisher and friend, Jack."

At the end of summer Maidie came home from camp, Louise handed in three poetry pieces to *The New Yorker,* and mother and daughter moved to an apartment at 82 Washington Place. It was the first time they had shared a life in which Raymond Holden did not figure, the first time they had lived together on their own.

Louise was unfamiliar with the new region—the present—in which she found herself. She described it in the draft of a short story as a "strange, almost unvisited region, as lonely as a frontier," strongly divided from the past:

When we are young, as you know, our life in the present is indicated only by the sense of dramatic importance which wraps us round: how splendid we are, how more than ordinarily endowed with meritorious attributes such as courage, desperation and honor, how fit for love! We decorate the future with little vignettes of ourselves in maturing attitudes. In our expectations, we live only through crises and dénouements; boredom and tag-end emotions do not occur to us as possible. We breathe an atmosphere, in our hopes, akin to the atmosphere of print in which figures of literature move; the climate of the future is the dry, perfected climate of the sentence and the paragraph.

Yet life in the present, with the heart secure from the past's torments, lacked dimension. Flatness, literalness, the unthreatening quiddity of things as they are had a way of tipping serenity over to a new kind of paralysis—not that of neurotic suffering, which Bogan had always known—but its opposite (and possibly its double), that of not being able to feel, or suffer at all. The sophisticated woman who meets her lover for a drink in "Not Love, but Ardor," an unpublished story Bogan wrote at Fifty-fifth Street, replies with jaded wit when her lover compliments her on her looks, "The configuration of my arms and breast is like a gentle landscape that should be further enhanced by groups of little sheep," and provokes his irritation with her "captious philosophic calm." Asked why she talks so much about "passion and grief," when she claims to be no longer susceptible to them, she answers:

"Like the immortal gods," she said. "We sit here and feel nothing. Above the battle. In a hollow calm, without suffering. It is thus that the Olympian gods loved and moved, without suffering. To love without love, to suffer without suffering, like the immortal gods."

"You sound more than tired," he said.

"With divine ichor, and not blood, in the veins," she answered.

Cured, calmed, sanded down, Louise wondered whether in renouncing the tendency to cling to people she had given up all large emotions in general. Suffering had exacted too much from her, but "normality" was turning out to have unexpected liabilities. She who had always felt everything felt little now, or controlled her feelings beyond reasonableness. Not surprisingly, she was hardly as safeguarded against emotion as she thought, and late in the summer, anticipating a tryst with her Boston lover still a week away, she wrote:

A day in which nothing moves in you, *since to feel anything would be to feel tears*— The end of a long loneliness, too far prolonged, with the hope of passion a week away deadened and far off. In such days the sense of the body thickening with time beyond love, strikes at the heart, but it is time that must be hurried through and it is disaster that lies beyond it—the disaster of a long burden of life cast upon this strong animal of a body that refuses to die at the right time.

—It is yourself whom you love—and it is a love given where it should be given, after years of having chosen the wrong object. Everything else must be chosen & cherished because it gives toward life, not death. As for *wanting* someone— no. There can be no new love at 37, in a woman. So let there be no pretense of there being any—

Yet she had been "bred to love," as she wrote in "Italian Morning," and had always had some form of sexual love, from a man, however flawed both the man and the love. She still needed such love, and the need was unlikely, despite her "cure," to go away. In a long notebook entry shaped as a questionnaire, she asked herself what it was she had always sought. The answer? "I sought love." The prospect, or rather, what seemed to her the certainty of having to live without it, was a new source of pain. "Made idiot with loneliness, imbecile with grief," she wrote in her journal early in September. She believed that in maturity there could be, for her, no reconciliation between loving herself and loving a man. One loved *either* oneself *or* another—not both. Physical pleasure, and a certain degree of companionship—these were to be had in short affairs, conducted with shrewd self-protectiveness, and cut off with wit and dignity when the ship of dalliance threatened to founder on the rocks of jealousy. But that was all she would allow.

Yet however much her realism and common sense pretended to acquiesce in the renunciation of love, something in her nature beyond health or illness insisted upon it, craved it, and protested bitterly when deprived of it. And once again she was caught in the struggle of her divided nature. The tears shed out of the longing for passion and the chastening axiom forbidding love to the woman of thirty-seven gave proof that Bogan had both cracked and healed along psychic fissures which had always existed in her nature, and were as unalterably splendid as they were unceasingly perilous.

I T I S U N L I K E L Y that we will ever know how much fiction Louise Bogan actually wrote. Taking stories and prose pieces together, we arrive at a total of twenty-six works, all but four of them dated in the 1930s. The stories she wrote but did not publish in the twenties perished in the 1929 Hillsdale fire.

Bogan had mixed feelings about fiction. In her 1935–36 notebook she remarked that she could never be happy writing fiction, because fiction, "unless it is half poetry, is always a put up job on reality." She considered herself lacking in the gift of invention; storytelling based on truth and bathed in reminiscence and feeling was her natural and chosen genre. From an early age she preferred fiction which maintained a high fidelity to sense experience—to sight and hearing—rather than to elaborate plot or philosophical purpose. After a brief and initial enthusiasm for Compton Mackenzie and H. G. Wells, she discovered the novels of Viola Meynell, reading *Columbine* in 1915, and thereafter considering her the single contemporary writer whose style expressed her own tastes and preferences.

It is at first difficult to understand Bogan's high opinion of Meynell, whose ordinary, middle-class characters are immersed in utterly quotidian lives. The novels are singularly free of melodrama, plottiness, and contrived effects. Not even the faintest trace of social criticism or political awareness invests the page. Yet it is just this fidelity to the domestic and insular scale of her characters' lives that allows her to render them with great psychological keenness and extraordinary warmth and intuition.

Still, Meynell was only a starting point; other writers provided examples and fueled her courage. Turgenev's lyrical realism, combining brilliantly observed detail with a strict integration of mood and episode, seemed as much "hers" as Meynell's, and Chekhov's spare mixture of pathos and irony struck her as the most masterly of all. From both of these nineteenth-century Russians she learned to favor the essential detail. She had a scenic imagination, and saw places and moments as ineffable wholes, full of contrasting patterns to be glimpsed and sketched, rather than as detailed surfaces to be lingeringly and lushly portrayed. She admired Colette, but had little of Colette's sensual reach. For Bogan, it was the eye that limned the erotic implications of things. And for this reason it was Henry James who, next to Chekhov, aroused her most passionate sympathy. It took a full ten years, for she hadn't been much impressed when she first read him in 1925, but in 1935, after writing stories of her own, she remarked to Theodore Roethke that she had just finished reading *The Bostonians,* and had found it "magnificent," copying down the following passage for Roethke's consideration:

". . . the bald bareness of Tarrant's lair, a wooden cottage, with a rough front yard, *a little naked piazza* which seemed rather to expose than to protect, facing upon an unpaved road, in which the footway was overlaid with a strip of planks. These planks were embedded in ice or in liquid thaw, according to the momentary mood of the weather . . ." [L.B.'s emphasis]

This, she added, was "the sort of thing I want to put down someday, about how Milton, New Hampshire, looked, in my childhood." It was, to use Katherine Mansfield's phrase, "rooted in life," exactly the quality Bogan herself wanted to achieve.

THE EARLIEST SURVIVING STORY by Louise Bogan is "Keramik," written in 1926 and published in *The American Caravan* of 1927, the literary yearbook edited by Van Wyck Brooks, Alfred Kreymborg, Lewis Mumford, and Paul Rosenfeld. It is a strange story; Bogan never wrote another like it. She twists its heavy atmospheric detail and muted eroticism together like coils in a thick braid. The scene is Vienna, in the early twenties (although it is only the mention of "Bellaria Street" and a pronounced though unspecific European ambiance that indicates this), and an elegant old man dines alone at a French restaurant, having ignored his regular dinner engagement with his young mistress, who has angrily gone out to dine by herself and quite possibly pick up a younger man.

It is the end of summer, the first cool night of approaching autumn. When the old gentleman returns to his impeccably furnished rooms, it becomes clear that in breaking his engagement with his mistress, he is breaking with his last woman, and with a lifetime avocation of collecting beautiful young women. He now remembers them all, these young women who have been his mistresses: "He had taught them all something and had learned nothing in return. There was always more to teach."

As the young woman whom he has just abandoned takes her coffee in a nearby garden, the old man drinks a cherry brandy in a room filled with ceramic figurines, and recalls one young woman who remains, beyond the others, special to him. Sounds of someone playing a Schubert song on a piano drift through the open window; the one "wise, quiet girl" he dreamily remembers is at that very moment being taken home by a young man somewhere who entreats her to allow him to see her again. Half in pity, half in cruelty, she tells him, "I had an old lover. That is over now. 'I kiss your heart!' he said once to me." The memory yields to the moment, and the old man listens to the music.

And this is all that happens in the way of events. The story is a strange mixture of aesthetic preciosity and bold execution. The style and the story are about the decay and the solipsism of the pure aesthete, whose life reaches its end with one perfect "keramik," the memory of that one perfect girl:

She leaned against the gently curved cover of the inlaid chest. Her ivory shawl swept the reddish wood that was the color of a violin. Flowers, fruit, urns, and naked children were abruptly hidden by the ivory skirt that swept down to the thin, pure feet and ankles. Her hair was as pale as wheat over the square forehead, warmer with yellow in the heavy coil at her neck. Her amber beads, strung on red silk, hung down along her slight bosom and waist and thighs,—bright, weightless, almost to her knees.

The cigarette in her fingers went to ash. Not once did she raise it to her lips. She was inlaid against the blue window, intagliated into the dusk. Weeks would pass: the last leaves would skip over the paved courtyard, and snow would go by in white currents. She sat there leaning forward, bending forward from the curved wood, her body secure and desireless, her cigarette in spark and ashes.

Chords struck at random in some room out beyond beat against his hollow old heart. The brandy seemed to lie there, still holding its red funnel shape, in the block of his breast as in the liquor glass.

She leaned forward, curved like a plume. His ears at once heard and said the music.

Bogan's earliest preoccupations resonate in the story. The silent girl, with her yellow hair and "secure, desireless body," recalls the girl in "The

Betrothal of King Cophetua" in being an object of pure erotic and aesthetic contemplation, while the rebuffed mistress, who hungrily and vulgarly hopes to meet someone new, seemingly relieved to be out of the old man's grasp at last, is reminiscent of the stone girl, with her lifted heel, in "Statue and Birds."

The style verged on sibylline obscurity, and in the short pieces of "heightened" prose she composed after writing "Keramik," she began to move away from this heavily perfumed and hermetic mode toward the freshness of direct statement. Two of the pieces in the new style, both published in *The New Republic* in March 1928, are adventures in *seeing*. The first of them, "Winter Morning," is a single expanded sentence made up of a chain of prepositional phrases (or *visions*) locked into place by the main clause: "it is winter morning." The scene is New York, viewed with a panoramic eye that takes in all the variety and energy it meets, from lingerie stores "hung with cheap crisp chemises all cut from the same pattern" to "sleekly packed apartments, whose doormen must soon come back to be seen behind the grilled doors like captured admirals" and its museums and newsstands, and prison and subway entrances. Like Charles Sheeler, John Marin, and Edward Hopper, Bogan notices "the fenestrated towers that shoot upward from the eye, bent backward from the vision, balanced on narrow steel, but firm as though buttressed by the very earth's iron kernel, springing upward as though never to fall, and littered, throughout their shelved floors by desk, chair, telephone, watercooler, typewriter in interminable, incredible number."

A week later *The New Republic* published her "Art Embroidery," a pointedly ironic picture of another feature of modern city life, the needlework section of a large department store, with its cottons, wools, silks, needles, thread, pillows, patches, and patterns. Bogan had been doing a good deal of sewing in 1927, after she, Maidie, and Raymond came back from Santa Fe. She made curtains for the apartment, and clothes for Maidie, and she frequently visited such places. There she observed other women buying patterns and materials, having no art but "art" embroidery, staving off the emptiness and grief of their lives with their sewing. She initially situates herself among them as the elevators open and they surge forward:

To push through this female crowd is difficult. These backs and arms and sides have a terrific solidity. They have clean gloves, obstinately bright glances (a veil pulled over the sagging lines that have been creased by animal pain, and by grief more deep than the flesh can remember; over the dull eyes so used to door and window, table, bed and chair, the curtain raised in the morning, the lamp lit at night, the known faces pressed again and again into the eyes, slightly perfumed bosoms, neat shoes.

Personal revelation plays no part in either "Winter Morning" or "Art Embroidery," although "Soliloquy," which appeared in the 1928 edition of *The American Caravan,* was Bogan's most personal piece of prose to date. It is a meditation that unfolds as she walks through the city, frustrated and angry over her fear of telling the truth about her own life in writing, and it suggests that as early as 1928, before she had conceived the idea of writing *Laura Dal[e]y's Story,* before the Hillsdale fire, and before the months of self-critical brooding leading up to the first collapse and the urgent notebook exhortations to turn away from image to fact, Bogan felt the necessity of outgrowing her early symbol-based style. "Soliloquy" captures some of the struggle to do so. In the midst of a Baudelairean cityscape, it asks how to grasp "the penny of poetry in the pocket, though it cannot be spent for mature ends, or even minted out of the grown-up nature, in the brilliance of its piteous copper." The piece's internal monologue oscillates between the impulse to reveal and the impulse to conceal:

That's a sizeable fur collar that you wear—walk in it up and down, and play that long game of forgetting, as though there were not enough lumber in the heavy mind, struck out of remembrance. Forget everything the moment that it happens: that's an excellent method of getting down a street, or up a stair, or into a house. Forget Bodwell's: the bar-room downstairs, and the bloody collar that made such an impression upon your young eye when you saw it lying in the gutter, one Sunday morning. Forget those faces stuck to the heart like leeches, that you would wish to multiply into many, but which remain so few. Go in more for metaphor, that cloak, that subterfuge, and less for wincing. "It is like—" "It is like—" that's the way to get out from behind that proud visage, that hearty, indelible sneer.

As the piece continues, Bogan relaxes her customary tight grip on both privacy and logic, as fragments of imagery and speech well up, loosened into a stream of self-mocking confession and self-conscious modernist literary experiment.

At heart I am not a moralist. At heart I am a dropped smock fit for any quatrain of Swift's. But when I am tired I like to shop for clothes, and when I am hungry, I approve of patting on the head the defenceless, the docile deer. I also like to pretend that I am living in everywhere I have ever lived, at the same time. Do have some tea out of these cups of Florentine leather bought in that charming shop run by the gentlewoman with the blue teeth. Upstairs I have love enclosed in a parenthesis. The feudal idea really sprang from the merchandising of sprockets and cams. Keep your relatives out of my way. They were brought up under a bureau. I don't approve.

Come home; come home. To the white iron bed and the scolding mother, the white dish of meat and potatoes on the table under the gas. There's a fire in the stove.

At this point it was only in the veiled and elliptical gestures of "automatic" writing that Bogan could touch upon the past and the near-past: Bodwell's, her angry mother, her irony and despair brought with her, like suitcases, to all the places in which she had lived. Yet the loosely associative quasi-Joycean idiom grated against her temperament. Ultimately, for her, it didn't *fit*. The only way to tell the truth was to disguise it through invented fictions, for which she was equally unsuited, or to try to find a pattern in which she could imply, and even state a great deal, without having to show the facts she found too horrible for direct viewing. The five stories she published in *The New Yorker,* between June and December of 1931, following her incomplete recovery from her first "nervous collapse," demonstrate just how successfully she managed the transition between the indirect style of her Symbolist youth and the new direct style of mature observation, and the eight stories she published in the magazine between January 1933 and January 1935 show how far her lyrical realism could serve the ends of an enduring vision of time and place.

Thus the thirteen *New Yorker* stories, which separate themselves into sketches, prose caprices, and actual fully rendered tales, tend to fall roughly into two groups: those that reflect Bogan's observations of herself, and those that grow out of her observations of others. There is no exact way of knowing where the disguises of fiction are at play, though intuition, like a dowser, guides us toward those stories where Bogan writes about herself, and those where facts appear to have been changed but not invented.

The form of her stories is almost always Chekhovian. Detachment, brevity, and objectivity keep the matter at hand both at a remove from sentimentality and under close inspection. For Bogan, as for Chekhov, all truth about human beings is ironic, often pathetic, and tragi-comic. Bogan is severe with fools, herself included, although beyond her wit and severity her stories are marked by the delicacy of her sensibility and the belief that in its inexplicable mystery, life is likely to suffer catastrophe at just those points where it seems most fortified.

Bogan demonstrated considerable virtuosity in the sophisticated subgenre commonly known as the "typical *New Yorker* story." This is the light, satiric sketch of contemporary life in which, while little in the way of incident occurs, meaning impinges from viewpoint, nuance, and tone. "Sunday at Five," published in December 1931, is a good example of the form. It takes up only a page, and with extreme economy presents a young woman seething with rancor as she silently observes the guests at a Sunday afternoon cocktail party at her friend Amy's apartment. The insipid, rehearsed conversation and the studied "modernistic" decor enrage her to a point of almost adolescent misery and vituperation:

She hated Amy. She must have hated her for years. She hated Amy's room. She hated her own and Amy's friends. She hated herself. She wanted to go over at once, in order to get the whole thing straight, and say: "You have the bleakest, the most opaque eyes it has ever been my misfortune to see. And, to make it worse, they are set practically on the side of your face." She wanted to shout down, in a fishwife voice, the well-bred laugh of Alison, on her right. She wanted to yell, to the group on her left: "Shut up about morals. Morals are an intellectual pastime and you've never had a reasonable thought in your life."

Speech tears through this woman like song through Bogan's Cassandra, speech which seems rather outsized for the occasion. A better fit between occasion and response exists in "Conversation Piece," in which a woman having cocktails with her excessively socially adept husband at the home of another couple keeps her increasingly dissociated and irreverent thoughts again moving parallel to the conversational banalities. Here, too, Bogan creates the impression that the wife's mocking estrangement and sardonic irony cover a deeper layer of suffering. It is not difficult to infer that both the woman in "Sunday at Five" and the woman in "Conversation Piece" are Louise Bogan, watching herself, seeing her own fury and sadness, able to order her impressions into "literature" and thus to free herself, if only temporarily, from seething inner conflicts.

She saw others with even greater perspicuity. In "The Short Life of Emily," she presents a faultless prose sonata, trailing Emily Hough, who is forty, poor, and "moderately mixed and sad," out of the elevated train which she has taken to the wrong side of town. Why is Emily being followed? Because, the narrator announces, "in a moment or two, she is to undergo a rare experience, an intense vision usually afforded only to those who are young and in love, to those who are rich and powerful and gay, or to those who, by some not quite normal mechanism, can imagine that they are all of these things and more."

Emily has no idea that in a short time she is to have this rare experience. She merely continues to walk to the office of Mr. Doherty, the man who manages the money left to her by her dead Aunt Clara, her attention aroused by the enormous and delightful variety of *things* in the world. Then, just as she passes a crowd in front of the philatelist's shop, she begins to have this odd, this extraordinary, this critical experience, the "idea for the sake of which we have followed her thus far."

Because it is sunny, because it is brisk, and mild, because of her almost neighborly feeling for this street.which, if she always kept her wits about her, she never might have seen at all, because of the quiet groups of people in front of the interesting windows, because she has a vivid sense of Aunt Clara's recent and untimely demise, suddenly, as she hesitates to cross Nassau Street, she says to herself, half aloud and with a shy burst of conviction: "I am alive." She not only says it, but she feels it. She is extant; she is quick; she breathes; she is in motion; she lives.

"The fact of her solid existence in the only life she will ever have has never struck her before. . . .": it is hardly a common experience, and it takes some time to sink in. For another wonderful instant, everything is lit up by the radiant inference that if she is alive, then everyone else is too. At the next moment, however, as she steps out of the elevator car at the fifth floor of Mr. Doherty's building, her conviction of existence disappears as suddenly as it had arrived:

The car door slams, and she is alone. Almost instantly, she forgets that she lives, that she breathes, that she has being—as is only natural, as we, too, in her place would forget. This is the fifth floor: that is all, suddenly, that she can really take in, or remember.

When "The Short Life of Emily" was published, Katharine S. White wrote to Bogan that E. B. White had called it "the best short story *The New Yorker* ever published." Its sophistication and lightness never break, yet at heart the story carries a subtle insight about how unbearable it is to feel intensely alive, since such emotion is invariably enmeshed with intimations of mortality.

Bogan's wit had the particular virtue of enhancing the texture of scenes without dominating it. She always knew how to integrate her barbs and stings with the matter at hand; she was as witty as any *New Yorker* writer of her generation without in any sense being a humorist. Her first *New Yorker* story, "Hydrotherapy," published in June 1931, is a brief sketch of an unnamed "she" (who is Bogan herself), taking her second treatment in a sanitarium like Cromwell Hall for people with nervous disorders. Attended by a fat nurse who makes bright, casual remarks, the woman, like the woman in "Conversation Piece," is someone whose powers of observation rise in proportion to the sinking of her spirits. Preparing for a steambath, she looks around her and absorbs the details: "The excessively pretty girl who was almost well of sleeping sickness buttoned the strap of her bathing suit and stepped into the keyhole tub. How odd that sleeping sickness should attack excessively pretty girls, and that a tired psyche should be her own lot."

For a moment, her detachment falters, and then, as she steps into the steam cabinet, it returns, only to yield instantaneously to fear, as the cold flaps of the cabinet enclose her:

Her hands were cold on her knees. She was terrified again. The pretty girl slowly raised a pretty right leg. That was ridiculous, of course, and she should laugh or cry. What would they do if she began to cry: large, hot tears, from the eyes in her protruding head? Let her out and slap her on the back? Keep her in till she melted? My God, the liberties people took with you when your heart broke!

Stuck inside her cabinet, the woman begins to feel better. She relaxes, and her mind wanders gaily and freely. She is taken from the cabinet, planted on a stool, and sprayed with a needlespray shower, first hot then cold, that hits her square in the diaphragm, making her squeal with sudden loss of breath. For a moment as brief as Emily Hough's epiphany, she feels "very strange. Just for a split second, as she caught the eye of the fat nurse who winked, she stopped suffering."

Bogan turned her wit to the lessons of her second breakdown as well, leavening the melancholia of "To Take Leave" with a brisk personification of the "horrid twain"—Sorrow and Romantic Attachment—to whom she announces that she has had *enough*:

I have dragged you far south and quartered you in houses triply sealed against the sun, in a country of cracked church bells, oranges, lemons, mimosa, and cinerarias, where the honey has a bitter taste and the coffee smells of chloroform. Together we have taken refuge from the blinding streets in museums, where we were bored by small funerary objects, astounded by great sprays of coral rooted in bronze helmets, and pleased by various forms of painting and sculpture. We have listened to fountains in gardens. We have sat, long Sunday afternoons, in the parlors of third-class hotels, among the stopped clocks and the cracked ormolu. With breast-high furniture all about us, we have heard the punctual after-dinner clatter of thick dishes echo against the steep, stained courts of *pensions;* in the morning we have stumbled over the slattern mop and pail; at night we have turned to sleep in rooms soaked through and through with the pattern of bad wallpaper. Together we have experienced the misery of things and the grandeur of nature (for volcanoes, oceans, and mountain passes have not been unknown to us).

She has grown tired of waiting upon the whims of her abstract companions, and has finally come to a firm decision:

Plans for your liquidation occupy me more and more. This is a short speech to take leave. So goodbye, grief. Goodbye, love.

This piece, which appeared in *The New Yorker* in January 1935, was the last story or prose *capriccio* she ever published. Speaking on March 11, 1970, at the Memorial Service for Louise Bogan held at the American Academy and Institute of Arts and Letters, William Maxwell, the novelist and former fiction editor at *The New Yorker,* recalled that although Bogan's friends at the magazine implored her to write more stories, she did not. She could no sooner will her stories into existence than she could will her poems. Still, despite her inhibitions and her high standards, she published three autobiographical pieces in the magazine between January 1933 and October 1934, and they are, as Maxwell pointed out, superb, far superior to her other pieces of fiction. She wrote them in the period after the Hillsdale fire which led up to and through her two breakdowns and they are the only completed sections of *Laura Dal[e]y's Story.* Here, Bogan delved into the past with the pure, disciplined attitude she later described to a young friend who was writing his own autobiography, and to whom she recommended, as a perfect example of the genre, Rilke's *Journal of My Other Self:* "For, as in all good art, the thing that is important isn't 'O, this all happened to me! how wonderful I and it were!' but 'Why did this happen at all? What is the mystery, that It happened, and I was there in the first place for it to happen to?' " This mystery of time and place can be felt in each of the three pieces. In them, the past is an untouchable picture. Unable to change what is seen, Bogan can only look at it and reflect upon it, leaving it intact, yet by this very process intangibly becoming a part of it once more.

The first story, "Journey Around My Room," which, as we have noted before, is based on "Voyage Autour de ma Chambre," published in 1796 by the Comte Xavier de Maistre, "presents the narrator—Bogan herself—anchored to her bed, addressing the reader with civilized distance, yet conjuring up the chiaroscuro of memory and association:

The most advantageous point from which to start this journey is the bed itself, wherein, at midnight, or early in the morning, the adventurous traveller lies moored, the terrain spread out before him. The most fortunate weather is warm to cool, engendered by a westerly breeze, borne from the open window toward the ashes in the grate. At midnight, moonlight lies upon the floor, to guide the traveller's eye; in the early morning, the bleak opacity that serves the traveller in this region as sun brightens the brick wall of the house across the yard, and sheds a feeble reflected glow upon all the objects which I shall presently name.

The room is "largish," and "almost square in shape." With Thoreauvian exactness she marks the eastern, western, and northern boundaries of the room, its nearness to the Empire State Building and the Lexington Avenue elevated trains, and describes the wallpaper, varnished floors, and fireplace, above which

a plain deal mantelpiece of ordinary design supports a row of books, a photograph of the News Building taken from the Chanin Building, four shells from a Maine beach, and a tin of Famous Cake Box Mixture. Above these objects hangs a Japanese print, depicting Russian sailors afflicted by an angry ocean, searchlights, a burning ship, and a boatload of raging Japanese.

How is it, the narrator asks, that she has come to this place? Why is it that her journey starts here: "Some step started me toward this point, as opposed to all other points on the habitable globe."

Suddenly, that point dissolves to another scene. It is a bare, windy March morning, and the narrator's father walks with her down the hill toward the train station, as he does every morning:

Old Jack Leonard had backed his horse up in front of Shattuck's store. A bag of potatoes, a ten-gallon kerosene can, and a black hound sat in the wagon, and a yellow cigar ribbon, tied to the whipstock, fluttered in the cold air. Across the tracks, the willows by the bridge let fall into the foaming water a mist of reddening boughs. The mill dam roared. The windows of the mill sparkled in the March sunlight falling without warmth.

It is March 1909, in Ballardvale, Massachusetts, and instead of saying goodbye to her father for the day, as she usually does, the narrator realizes that this morning is different, for it is the morning she took the train to Boston. Then, suddenly, she again finds herself inside her room, secure in her bed, not letting go of the mystery of her presence in just this place and just this moment. Again her eyes move slowly around the room, tracking objects and memories, until, in the process, the atmosphere of security and of known and familiar landmarks increases, until suddenly the traveler's glance alights on the armoire and the "catastrophe of the journey inevitably occurs." Here, as we have already seen, the piece reaches its climax, as Bogan enters a recurring dream. She hears the mill dam foaming and roaring with water and sees the rapids which she must swim, and into which the room and the objects in it now sink to depths "below fear" as her memory returns full circle to the March 1909 Boston train.

Suddenly, in this final illumination, Bogan's autobiography and her lyric art meet. The "journey" recounted here is a descent into psychic depths, past memory and past fear, into the most primitive sources of serenity and acceptance: acceptance of fate, of time, of the isolation and loneliness of individual destiny. It shares in the substance of myth, displaced in the guise of a *New Yorker* "casual" essay.

The second piece in the autobiographical trilogy, "Dove and Serpent," while more explicitly narrative than "Journey Around My Room," undertakes another journey into the past, and therefore another quest for the sources of psychic survival. Bogan goes back to the Ballardvale of autumn afternoons, when

everything in the town went wild . . . and blew about the streets. Smoke blew wildly from chimneys and torrents of leaves were pulled from the trees; they rushed across the sidewalks and blew against wagons and people and trains; they blew uphill and fell from great heights and small ones; they fell to the ground and into the river. Clouds rode high in the sky; the sun shone brilliantly everywhere. Or else half the town would lie in the shadow of a long cloud and half the town would stand shining bright, the weathervanes almost as still in a strong blast coming from one quarter as in no wind at all, the paint sparkling on the clapboards. Sometimes in the late afternoon the full sun came from two directions at once, from the west and reflected in a full blaze from the windows of houses looking westward.

These are the days when children come home to kitchens that smell of freshly baked bread and ironed clothes, and days when old Jack Leonard comes out on his veranda and curses and beats a stick against the railing as the children, running home from school, call out "Crazy old Jack" in mocking fear. This is the scene of Bogan's memory of Mrs. Parsons, in whose sitting room the young and observant Louise was fascinated by the woman's son's sword and a doll in a paper skirt. Childhood's central mystery, as Bogan sees it, has its baffling mathematics: things don't add up; they have too many reasons, or none at all. From her contemplation of the sword and the doll, Bogan moves forward with the only description of her mother ever to reach print in Louise's own lifetime:

My mother's quick temper often estranged her from her neighbors. She was then a woman of forty, beginning to be stout. She carried herself well and could be extremely handsome when she troubled about her appearance. She went about her life with an air of great secrecy and she was very much alone. She would stand, early in the morning, when the kitchen was floating in sunlight, beside the sink, cleaning the lamps. She had large, beautiful, but clumsy hands; when she was tired or nervous she could not hold anything in them—everything she touched tumbled to the floor. She took up the scissors and cut the lamp wicks; she washed the lamp chimneys that were so prettily beaded around the top; she filled the base of the lamps with oil. After she had finished, she would stand by the window that looked toward old

Leonard's house. The window had sash curtains over its lower half. My mother's gaze was directed through the upper, uncurtained panes. Sometimes she would stand there for a long time, perfectly still, one hand on the window jamb, one hand hanging by her side. When she stood like this, she was puzzling to me; I knew nothing whatever about her; she was a stranger; I couldn't understand what she was. "There's old Leonard again," she would say, "kicking the cornstalks."

Without spelling out the facts of her mother's secret life, Bogan adumbrates them simply by lightly picturing her mother looking through the uncurtained panes into old Jack Leonard's back yard, and remarking her own puzzlement. How little the child actually *knows*, yet how purely does it *sense* things.

Plunged into the textures of recollection, Bogan plays upon the memory of winter cold:

After the blaze of summer that had parched paint and shingle, winter was closing in to freeze wood and stone to the core. The whole house, in winter, turned as cold as a tomb. The upper rooms smelled of cold plaster and cold wood. The parlor was shut; the piano stood shut and freezing against the wall; the lace curtains fell in starched frigid folds down to the cold grain of the carpet. The little padded books on the table, the lace doilies under them, the painted china vases, and the big pictures hanging against the big pattern of the wallpaper all looked distant, desolate, and to no purpose when the door was opened into the room's icy air.

On such days, late in the afternoon, Bogan's mother would make tea for her neighbors, Mrs. Parsons and Mrs. Gardiner (elsewhere, *Gardner*), with whom she would speak "in low secret voices" while Louise, sitting alone in the sitting room, and listening to the women, could see the lamp lit in old Leonard's back room. She had been sent away from the adults, banished from the warm kitchen and the women's talk, and now, as an adult, remembering this, she reflects that secrecy, for her mother,

was bound up in her nature. She could not go from one room to another without the intense purpose that must cover itself with stealth. She closed the door as though she had said goodbye to me and to truth and to the lamp she had cleaned that morning and to the table soon to be laid for supper, as though she faced some romantic subterfuge, some pleasant deceit.

On the fateful evening Louise glimpsed her mother with old Leonard and heard him speak the words, "We must be as wise as the serpent and as gentle as the dove. As the serpent, as the dove," she felt, "if he had put out his hand to touch me, I could not have been more frightened; with half a room between us, I stood transfixed by that smile."

The words remained in her memory as an unsolved equation:

I did not know what they meant then, and I do not know what they mean now. It is such memories, compounded of bewilderment and ignorance and fear, that we must always keep in our hearts. We can never forget them because we cannot understand them, and because they are of no use.

If there was one lesson to be drawn, though perhaps not stated, it was that her mother had an artist's instinctive ability to sit side by side with ugliness and age, with strangeness and loneliness, to look at it, know it, and find the common humanity between herself and the other. It is this that the child had yet to learn.

This, too, is the lesson of "Letdown," Bogan's last excursion into the past, and the story of her art lessons with Miss Cooper in the Hotel Oxford in Boston. The memoir, like "Journey Around My Room" and "Dove and Serpent," travels toward catastrophe, illumination, and some understanding of the subtle growth of experience. In the end, the adult Bogan's verdict against the unforgiving and idealistic girl she had once been is as severe as it should be. Indeed, the three *New Yorker* memoirs comprise a sentimental education, and it is on account of Bogan's moral imagination that her failure to complete her book of memoirs is genuinely to be regretted. She understood the stages of moral growth, from savage innocence to compassionate and wise magnanimity, and might well have given us, in the finished work, a unique and compelling American autobiography. But after writing these stories, she stayed away from her memoirs, only returning to them many years later, when it seemed to her that, as an artist, she had nothing left to lose.

III

1936 ❀ 1941

SEVERAL VOICES OUT OF A CLOUD

7 AFTER THE AIR OF SUMMER

AMONG THE MANY NOTES on psychoanalytic theory Bogan put down in her 1934–35 notebook, one stands out from a volume Dr. Wall had recommended, Jung's *Psychology of the Unconscious:*

In psychoanalysis the infantile personality is deprived of its libido fixations in a rational manner; the libido which is thus set free serves for the building up of a personality matured and adapted to reality, *who does willingly and without complaint everything required by necessity.* [Bogan's emphasis] It is . . . the chief endeavor of the infantile personality to struggle against all necessities and to create coercions for itself where none exists in reality.

For Louise Bogan, acquiescence with necessity had come to mean accepting daily work-filled life as a gift, as well as a curb on her desires. It meant consciously searching for ways to find attainable, tangible pleasures rather than those dependent upon the idiosyncrasies of other people. Work leavened loneliness and eased the remnants of depression; it reminded her that life was there to be enjoyed. The elusive quality of "zest" could be recovered. Now, living with Maidie and separated from Holden, freed of destructive attachments and committed to plenty of absorbing review work, she provided herself with opportunities for enjoyment. She went to movies, plays, and concerts in the fall of 1934, wrote short pieces and, as she told Zabel, many "abortive poems." At least twice a week Edmund Wilson showed up for their German evenings, and there were other nights when he came for dinner and talk about Shakespeare's *Histories,* which Bogan was reading along with "all the mental collapse period . . . *Timon* and *Troilus* and straight through the big dramas to the heath in *Lear,* full of real and simulated madmen. Rather rewarding!" she exclaimed to Zabel, adding, "(Do you remember Eliot's phrase: 'The less rewarding Waller'? E. W. and I have a joke about it. Everything, to our minds, is now more or less 'rewarding.')"

It was the happiest season of Bogan's friendship with Wilson. They knew each other so well that he had become almost a member of the family. Maidie called him "Uncle Bunny," and got him to help her with her English homework. At seventeen she had become such an attractive and worldly teenager that he liked to make jokes about wanting to "buy" her, and spoke to both her and Louise with considerable freedom about his own romances. Raymond Holden had once asked him, on the subject of his innumerable girl friends and wives, "Bunny, how do you get those dames into bed?" and Wilson had said, "I talk them into it, of course," an answer that always amused Bogan and Maidie on account of Wilson's "funny squeaky voice." During long evening conversations, that voice could often manage very respectable degrees of projection. Maidie was more than once kept awake at night by the sound of her mother and Wilson "yakking away" to all hours, and there were occasional complaints from irate neighbors awakened by Wilson's reading aloud or arguing with Bogan. The warmth of her kitchen and the rich liveliness of her talk held a special place in his affections. Writing on board the Cunard White Star *Berengaria,* in May 1935, on his way to Russia, Wilson fondly called her "you old pretty pigeon" and told her how much she had come to mean to him during the past year, adding that he wanted her to know

how appreciative of you and how fond of you, my dear, I really am: I have never had this kind of companionship with a woman for any length of time ever before in my life, and I became so addicted to it this winter that maybe it's just as well that I'm going away: you and I really have too much fun together. I'm afraid that if I had a little more money, I'd decide to spend all the rest of my life drinking beer and stout with you.

He was, in a gentle and wistful way, not quite in love with Bogan, and perfectly certain that she was in no danger of falling in love with him. What occasional spats they had were nearly always over literary or political matters, not personal feelings. She was becoming increasingly impatient with Wilson's sympathy toward the Left; he, in turn, still tended to treat her as a star pupil. Their differences rarely lasted long, however, because each missed the other's sense of humor too much to go on without it.

Matters in general were going so well that early that same May, Bogan told John Hall Wheelock, her editor at Scribner's, that she was ready to assemble a new book of poems, to be called *Sleeping Fury*. Delighted with the news, Wheelock immediately ordered her to send him every new poem she wrote, a mandate that for once she was in no mood to resist. She wanted to be in print again, and she had poems to write. As the summer approached, the joy of being alive filled her as never before. Eating, sleeping, breathing, looking out the window, actually allowing herself to feel attractive and to enjoy the admiring glances of men as she walked down the street were newly discovered pleasures fast rooted in the surprising and delightful fact of her own existence. When two new poets entered her life—Theodore Roethke and Rainer Maria Rilke—she went forward to meet them as openly and fearlessly as she had ever greeted any new experience.

RETICENT ABOUT HER PRIVATE LIFE as Bogan may have been, she was no prude. A frank, though never a vulgar sensualist, she considered physical love one of the great gifts of being alive. From Russia, Wilson sent her, early in June, a set of reproductions of Persian miniatures showing lightly clad women drinking wine and playing dulcimers. After twitting about the amorous adventures she supposed *he* was having, she went on to report that

I, myself, have been made to bloom like a Persian rose-bush, by the enormous love-making of a cross between a Brandenburger and a Pomeranian, one Theodore Roethke by name. He is very, very large (6 ft. 2 and weighing 218 lbs.) and he writes very, very small lyrics. 26 years old, and a frightful tank. We have poured rivers of liquor down our throats, these last three days, and, in between, have indulged in such bearish and St. Bernardish antics as I have never before experienced. . . . Well! Such goings on! A woman of my age! He is amusing, when not too far gone in liquor; he once won a φBK and he has just been kicked out of Lafayette, from his position of instructor in English. He is just a ripple on time's stream, really, because he is soon going to Michigan to write a text-book on electrical fields. (How is the Dnieperstroi, by the way? I expect pictures of the Dnieperstroi, and get depraved Persians instead! What would Marx and Engels say?)—I hope that one or two immortal lyrics will come out of all this tumbling about.

The affair appears to have set her pen to flowing right away. Telling Wheelock about it, she reported "writing the most extraordinary Ella Wheeler Wilcoxism, as a consequence. This last will never be seen by human eye, I trust. Never shall I give the feminine sonneteers any competition. O, I'm a strange one, amen't I?" One lyric that did emerge with a justifiable claim to immortality was "Roman Fountain," a testament, among its other meanings, to the renewal of sexual vitality at a time when it seemed to have vanished forever. At least three more good poems also arrived: "Baroque Comment," "Single Sonnet," and "Evening-Star," as well as several others which remained unpublished. Bogan, who was used to the mean-spiritedness of fate, was utterly taken aback at its generosity. A love affair was the last thing she had expected, particularly a love affair with a gifted, young, and lusty poet.

Roethke and Bogan had met before, at a party Rolfe Humphries had given the previous fall at his house in the New Jersey countryside. There, during a "memorable" evening, the fanatically ambitious and obsessively self-doubting Roethke, overcome with hero worship at finding himself in the actual presence of Louise Bogan, whose poetry he had admired for years, later confessed to Humphries that he had felt "like a country boy at his first party,—such an oaf, such a boob, such a blockhead. I don't think I was ever much worse." Roethke ranked Bogan with two other women poets he held in high esteem, Elinor Wylie and Léonie Adams, and when she asked him whether he had figured out all by himself that Genevieve Taggard was "no good" as a poet, he was nonplussed. "Damn her, anyway," he grumbled to Humphries. "She and her Irish digs." He believed that Humphries and Bogan, among their contemporaries, were the only poets who had turned their "full powers to poetry," and, feeling that he had lost his sense of dedication, he hoped that by getting to know Bogan he might be able to recover it. He wanted to write to her, he told Humphries, and one day "to gain her respect."

They met in New York again the following June, and quickly struck up a love affair. At twenty-six, Roethke was physically overwhelming and emotionally gargantuan, a floating continent of exquisite sensitivity, towering despair, insatiable appetite, and howling self-ignorance. Bogan, at thirty-eight, was established as a poet, adept in the mysteries of poetic form which Roethke was determined to master, and ready to be appreciated as an attractive and desirable woman. They had a wonderful time together, drinking and laughing and talking and making love. Roethke was smart and witty, warm and demonstrative, and given to saying such things as "Louise, you're a great minor poet and I'm a bastard, but kiss me."

Delighted with this strange turn of events to the point of telling all her close male friends about it—something she would *never* have done ordinarily—Bogan nevertheless had no illusions about permanence. She calmly sent Roethke on his way back to Michigan with one of her treasures in hand, Gerald Bullett's anthology of lyrics, *The English Galaxy*, and no real conviction that she would ever see him again. A correspondence soon began, with Roethke sending poems to Bogan, anxious to know what she thought of them, and Bogan returning them with the frank criticism she would have given even if he had not requested it. The love affair had no formal ending, but evolved, instead, through distance, tact, and a recognition of the circumstances of each other's lives, into one of those bonds that closely resemble a love affair, namely, an intense attachment between teacher and student.

Sometime in May, only weeks before Roethke appeared on the scene, Bogan began to read Rilke seriously. In the same letter to Wheelock in which she first mentioned Roethke, she burst out, "Why did you never tell me about Rilke? My God, the man's wonderful." Bogan's Rilke was the poet of the *Neue Gedichte* (*New Poems*), the solitary observer of *things*. With the same inner direction that had brought Bogan to the life-saving marigolds in her mother's hospital room, to Yeats's poetry, Mozart's music, the stone flowers of Baroque architecture, Chekhov's "pity and wisdom," and the flexible, natural syntax of Swift and Thoreau, she made Rilke *hers*. He was "right down my alley," she wrote to Wilson, then in Moscow, "as far as feeling into situations is concerned." In the past, without knowing much about him, she had always considered Rilke a rather "mooney individual who waved his fins in the air and mouthed . . ." But now, quite to the contrary, she was discovering that he knew "all there was to know about the sources, agonies, triumphs, needs of the poetic function," being especially good "on the subject of inner stillness, and he has a good, fierce realistic eye as well. I don't know how in hell he lived," she went on; "he ended up by frequenting the castle of the Princess of Taxis and Thurn, or someone of similar name; he never turned his hand to day labor, and he seems to have abandoned a wife and child, at an early stage of the game. But he had what it takes (if you will pardon the vulgarism, Mr. W.)."

She began a Rilke notebook, reading everything she could get her hands on and underlining biographical passages and lines from the poetry. "My God," she wrote Humphries later that summer, "that was the man of the nineteenth and twentieth centuries. He *looked* at things. He looked and looked and looked, and the poems are absolute and true. . . . My merciful God. I'm going to spend the rest of my life humbly looking." She responded passionately to Rilke's visual sense, finding that it corresponded to her own delight in shape and color. In the introduction to his translation of *Requiem and Other Poems*, J. B. Leishman remarks that Rilke noted in his journal "how a Corot in a Hamburg gallery suggested to him that he was beginning to see pictures for the first time," and Bogan, underlining the word *see* in this passage, scribbled in the margin, "I did not *see* them until I was 35." Rilke's inexhaustible patience, which made him able to bear intense solitude and to avoid both distraction and willed labor, as well as his seemingly bottomless depths of insight, struck her, the more she read him, as the epitome of what the lyric poet must both be and do, and renewed her own poetic task with compelling simplicity. Henceforth she would seek "the pure lyric feeling backed up by the best prosody."

She spread the word about Rilke to her friends, setting Humphries to translating the "Lied Vom Meer"; to Wheelock, who knew German, she turned for help with comprehension and translations; from Zabel, who also knew German, she requested prose translations. But her freshest discoveries went into the letters she wrote to Roethke over the summer and fall of 1935, when their mutual ardor was still intense, and she was writing poetry, and knew that Roethke was listening to every word.

Unhampered by the platitudes one might expect to find in an amorous friendship between an "older" woman and a "younger" man, the correspondence between Bogan and Roethke, from its beginnings, served the purpose of drawing out Roethke's undisciplined talent and detaching it from the self-destructive as well as voraciously ambitious tendencies which plagued him. Roethke craved praise, but needed guidance, and when he complained, as he often did, that he was feeling depressed, or drinking too much whiskey and beer, or eating too much sauerbraten and pie, or not writing enough, or writing badly, or suffering from paralysis of the will, or not getting enough attention from magazine editors, Bogan responded, kindly and generously, but with a tacit refusal to prop up his self-pity. With good-humored and often witty patience, she set about teaching him what she knew with virtually complete detachment from the erotic intimacy they had shared. While their affair had created a ground of mutual affection, Bogan was determined never again to torture herself over a man, and held a part of her being in reserve—the part that might allow Roethke to fancy that she was in love with him, or needed him, or nurtured any unfulfilled wishes about him. With a firm grasp of the large facts of Roethke's complex talent, restless intelligence, and befuddled heart, she fed him strong spoonfuls of the exacting technical criticism she and Rolfe Humphries had been exchanging for years.

This meant overhauling poems word by word and phrase by phrase, pausing momentarily to mock her own high standards ("Girls' Latin School for you!"), but never letting those standards down, not even for a moment. She tested every poem he sent with her mind and ear, and her comments, crackling with experience and authority, must have occasionally stung. She steered him away from clichés, advising him to take out the phrase "lyric cry" in a draft of "Open House" and to avoid repeated imperatives, which, she pointed out, had been worked to death in the 1920s (as she ought to have known, since *Body of This Death* was full of them). Repeated adjective-noun combinations had to go; so did words like *effulgence* and *transcen-*

dent. Plateau and *Plato* could not be used in the same stanza; poems should be kept to one or two images only, and Roethke should be on guard against echoing himself. When necessary, she referred to her own poems for examples. "I'd work like hell for texture," she suggested, "sets of sounds running through an entire poem. (For example, if you examine *Italian Morning* you will see that it is built on *l* sounds, and that *circle* in the first line is completed by *marble* in the last.)"

Aware that Roethke might be just as inclined to ignore her remarks as to be hurt or annoyed by them, she urged him to "Really take some of my cracks to heart, on the technical side, my poppet. I'm a great technical expert. 25 years in the technic mines. Don't get mad at any of the cracks. And for God's sake, do some work, funny or otherwise."

What he needed, she thought, was to let himself go, let himself and the poems drift away from each other. He was so terribly attached to his work that he suffocated it. Later on, he could come back, "slyly, as though you *didn't* care and then let the storm begin and the wind (the Roethke, the Brandenburger wind) arise." If she thought he had written a good poem, she praised it, and gave reasons for her praise. "To My Sister" was good, she said, "because it is felt first, outside of literature." He was right *in* the poem, "mad as hell and agonized as hell, and proud as hell." Nothing less would do than complete submission to the poem's emotion, so that, discussing another poem, she remarked, "Not exactly punk, but not created by the entire Roethke." Harsh as she could be, Bogan never thought him lacking in respect for his calling. He might take her cracks amiss; he might "ascribe bitchhood" to her, if he liked. But if she was certain of one thing, it was that he knew that "poetry is an art, and not a dumping ground for the emotions."

We can be sure that Roethke listened well. He wanted to write short, compact, powerful poems like those of Emily Dickinson, Louise Bogan, and Léonie Adams. For a young male poet anxious to write in the tradition of "Metaphysical" verse, Yeats and Eliot, he was profoundly affected by formal poetry written by women; and when he took Bogan's advice, it was likely to be reflected in imitation. In a number of the poems Roethke wrote during this period, echoes can be heard from both *Body of This Death* and *Dark Summer:* "Sub Contra" resounds in "Silence"; "Dark Summer" and "Old Countryside" in "Interlude"; and, as Rosemary Sullivan has pointed out, "The Alchemist" in "Epidermal Macabre." At the same time, it was not in technical matters alone that Roethke's problems as an artist were centered. Being able to tolerate himself was a more acute problem, and facing the ordeal of growing up was more frightening than learning to limit his poems to only one or two images. In one way Bogan wanted to spare him the pain of having to learn from experience alone; in another she wanted him to stop shielding himself from his emotions. She sent him Rilke's *Letters to a Young Poet,* and enclosed German copies of two of Rilke's early poems, which she praised as examples of absolute purity of feeling and penetration of reality, and then admonished Roethke, as a poet, for being afraid to suffer or to feel as he must, if he were ever to write anything genuine. He had a long training in emotional honesty ahead of him, and he would have to learn how to "look at things until you don't know whether you are they or they are you,"—the most important lesson she herself was learning from Rilke.

Of the two enclosed poems, one called "Blaue Hortensie" ("Blue Hydrangeas") had great private significance for her. She sent another copy of it to Rolfe Humphries, and confided that it had struck her "for reasons important only to myself: I have seen the same colors, and was never artist enough to put them down." In the poem, which she considered one of the greatest lyrics ever written, Rilke compares fading hydrangeas to old blue letter-paper

> . . . which the years
> have touched with yellow, violet and gray;
>
> washed-out like a child's apron, no more used—
> nothing else can happen to it now:
> one feels how short the little life has been.

Bogan often used blue stationery, particularly featherweight air-mail paper, extremely light and thin, which faded over the years to the shade she recognized in Rilke's poem. As she went through it, she explained to Roethke how Rilke had plumbed blue hydrangeas to their depths:

Here all sorts of comparisons are brought in, to aid the plumbing process. The color of the flowers is the color of old writing paper, faded into yellow and violet and gray, it is like a child's many-times-washed apron—and by the time the reader gets to that, he is in a state of collapse, for Rilke has re-created the color in such a moving way that it's as though something new had been created in the universe. You see all that, I'm sure. Now, my duck, go look at some of the flora, or even fauna of the electrical area, and do likewise.

That he would actually go and take her advice Bogan very much doubted. Privately she believed Roethke to be a victim of arrested development. "If he could shake off that neurotic seeking for bottle-made oblivion," she wrote to Humphries, "and grow up out of the peacocking town-bullishness bred in him, no doubt, by the fine normal womanhood of Ann Arbor, Mich., he'd be quite a person." Ultimately, she warned Roethke, he would have to fight: against his depressions, his self-indulgences, his temperament, his family, his ambition. She reminded him that she too had been imprisoned

by a family, who held out the bait of a nice hot cup of tea and a nice clean bed, and no questions asked, until the mould starts in effacing the last noble lineaments of the soul. (That's wonderful, isn't it?) And let me tell you right now, the only way to get away is to get away: pack up and go. Anywhere. I had a child, from the age of 20, remember that, to hold me back, but I got up and went just the same, and I was, God help us, a woman. I took the first job that came along. And there was a depression on, as there is now, not quite so bad, but still pretty poor, and I lived on 18 bucks a week and spent a winter in a thin suit and a muffler. But I was free. And when, this last time, I couldn't free myself by my own will, because my will was suffering from a disease peculiar to it, I went to the mad-house for six months, under my own steam, mind you, for no one sent me there, and I got free. —When one isn't free, one is a *thing,* the *thing* of others, and the only point, in this rotten world, is to be your own, to hold the scepter and mitre over yourself, in the immortal words of Dante.

When he complained that he could never be really good, not when the world already had its Shakespeare and its Auden, she wrote back that if one was a minor poet, one was a minor poet, and nothing could be done about it: "being good AND minor is something."

All of Bogan's sensible and witty advice notwithstanding, Roethke rarely let up his grumbling and grousing. He wrote, for example, on May 25, 1936:

Just twenty-eight years ago today little Theodore came into the world. Touching, isn't it? I've never thought much about the passage of time over my flesh, but this time it really gets me down. Twenty-eight, and what have I done? No volume out and I can't seem to write anything. You can say what you want, but *place* does have a lot to do with productivity. Hell, I don't care what happens to me,—whether I go nuts or my entrails hang out; but I can't stand being so mindless and barren as I've been . . .

He was then living with his mother and sister in Saginaw, Michigan, having been discharged from the hospital where he had been treated the previous November for a nervous collapse. To a certain extent he reminded Bogan of her brother Charles, who, before his death in World War I, had been unable to break free from home, and whose frustrations had exploded from time to time in drunken rages in which he would come home in a frenzy and smash up the furniture. Roethke did not strike Bogan as fundamentally doomed or limited, however; he was too talented for that, and her attitude toward his mental distress was compassionate but dry. Her own two breakdowns, she told him, had come about because she had failed to take possession of her own life, and hadn't yet given up clinging to people and whining and crying when they inevitably disappointed her: "I swore I wouldn't get better until Raymond told me the truth, and as he was congenitally unable to tell the truth to anyone, I stayed sick, for three years after that." Normality wasn't such a bad thing, if only he would stop fighting against it. There was just one genuine fight, anyway—the battle against one's own childishness, and work was the best weapon against that. Even better was simply to "let the world go on, bearing you and being borne by you: that's the trick. As old Rilke said:

> Und wenn dich das Irdische vergass,
> Zu dem stillen Erde sag: ich rinne.
> Zu dem raschen Wasser sprich: Ich bin."*

BOGAN'S OWN LIFE was running up against hard reviewing assignments which required endless reading and note-taking at the New York Public Library, and her ever-present incapacity (and unwillingness) to write poetry out of deliberate composition. Moreover, she was beginning to feel the burden of her commitment to put together a new book of poems for Scribner's. Although she published a poem in *Scribner's Magazine* in March 1936, she told Roethke that it had been months since she had actually written one, and that she was going to "start writing an imitation one, right away, a sort of finger exercise, to see if I can get started again." Nothing came from this good intention, nor from a further vow to write a poem a day in time to have a fat selection ready for Wheelock in September. "Yeats said it was harder than break-stones on the road, and it is," she wrote to Roethke, "but there must be some way of starting it, when it doesn't come." In June, writing from The Willey House Hotel in Swampscott, Massachusetts, where she had gone to rest and hear the ocean, she reported that she had not written a poem in six months, but that she would soon be sending him drafts of poems she had written the previous summer, among them one called "Putting to Sea." Later in the summer she sent word that she was working on "The Sleeping Fury," the "scenario" of which had been written the previous fall. It too had been giving her trouble. "I have been trying so

---

* And if the earthly has forgotten you, / say to the still earth: I flow. / To the rapid water speak: I am.

hard to write non-occasional poems for the book, but, unlike Dante and Milton," she remarked, ruefully, "I'm not good at them."

When Bogan made Roethke privy to her own writing difficulties, it was partly for an instructive purpose. She had the good teacher's desire not to appear to be too exemplary. He wasn't the only one who had to endure "those states of waiting for something to turn up"; she had gone through that ordeal not once, but many times already, and had learned that "something always happens." All she could suggest was that Roethke, when blocked, read and write and wait and think until the unconscious passed through its necessary secret preparations and transitions.

By the spring of 1936—about a year after their affair had begun—the shape of their friendship was set. Roethke continued to send dispirited outbursts mingled with slangy ebullience, and poems. Bogan continued to answer, but in milder tones than those she had registered at the onset of their correspondence. All remained quiet between them throughout the fall and winter of 1936. Thereafter, they exchanged letters only after large gaps of time, although each received news of the other through friends, and Roethke made sure to visit Bogan whenever he came to New York. By the fall of 1937, she had little further to teach him. She disliked repeating herself, found his ambitiousness unattractive, and was bored by the role of wetnurse. Roethke was "a big boy now, and should absorb the world, and not be absorbed by it." By the time Roethke discovered Rilke for himself, Bogan's own enthusiasm had long been settled into a calm familiarity with the work, and she was again having trouble writing her own poems. Her remarks began to have a peremptory and disaffected ring. "It really is much better to write about objects and people and things," she declared, "unless a great convulsion takes place within, and tears you apart willy-nilly." But those convulsions do "not occur very often, as time goes on, I find, and when they do occur, they soon pass off." In the fall of 1937, she wrote, "You know, my pet, for a long time I don't think of you at all, but when I do, I miss you." A year later she wrote Humphries that Roethke was writing badly, killing off "his gift at its source" with his drive to succeed, and she took it upon herself to monitor echoes in his work, the presence of which she had made light of in the early stages of their friendship, when Roethke had once written in panic over another poet's charge that he had lifted a line. Now she informed him that there was too much Yeats and Auden in his work. In this she was bringing up an extremely delicate subject, since Auden-imitating among young (and not so young) poets was becoming increasingly widespread. Bogan, who was herself being influenced by Auden, was nevertheless among the most vocal in detecting it in others.

Early in 1940 she pointedly admonished Roethke for having too much

Hopkins in a poem titled "Praise" ("A praise to the resilient: to bones in barred wings"), which had come out in *The New Republic* in December 1939. She had warned him about it before he published the poem, but now, she claimed, several other people had detected it and were wondering why he had allowed himself to let it through. "It is really dangerous to let down the Standard in any such way," she scolded. "For watchful eyes are always upon you, remember; and I'm afraid you've alienated the P. R. boys, with this one."

For Bogan to hold up her own alliance with the *Partisan Review* editors at a time when, to the approval-hungry Roethke, their acceptance of him would have meant something like grace, was downright nasty. Roethke wrote back that he at least hoped that "you told them that I was conscious of what I was doing, at least to the extent of bringing up the matter when I showed you the piece. I may be self-deceived, but I still think that piece is good enough to have an independent existence. And what is an ancestor for anyway? (Ans. To assimilate, not to imitate. . . . Thought I had assimilated, etc.)" He also wanted to know exactly "who were the people and how caustic were they? Hell, that's a tiresome request, but I always seem to learn faster from my enemies & detractors. And I don't hold grudges—just am more careful." He added that it was "sweet of you to bother thus far, since it's always so much easier to say nothing and let people blunder on," and, just before closing, came out with, "Jesus, knowing me is very trying a good bit of the time, I begin to realize. But do bear with me just once more." As Bogan's admonitions and reproaches became testier in her now infrequent letters, Roethke, who was gaining ground as a poet, took them with equanimity. After a meeting with Auden, he reported Auden's belief that Bogan was one of the best poets writing in America, and that her criticism was also of a very high order; two years later, when Bogan herself met Auden and wrote to tell Roethke that Auden thoroughly liked and respected him, she couldn't help adding that Auden had agreed with her that Roethke "should *grow up,* and stop pretending that your childish side is melancholy, WHICH IT ISN'T," virtually saying that she still considered him immature as both a person and an artist.

Inevitably, Roethke did grow up and away. After he sent Bogan the manuscript of *The Lost Son,* she wrote that he would have to do something about the echoes of Joyce: critics would notice them, and if the book came her way to review, she would have to mention them (although at the moment she didn't have time to dig up specific passages).

On a postcard Roethke replied:

Thanks for the solicitude about "The Lost Son." But for once, pet, you're wrong, really you are. I wrote that poem out of real suffering: cut myself off from people;

went into my interior. The only "influenced" line is an exact quote from the bible: "Hath the rain a father:" 1/3 of a line, honey. Eliot has 1/3 of a poem [in] quotation. It's Job and Isaiah, not Joyce, and the reference is there, deliberately, to point to the passage. I have always shied away from J. J. The record I heard twice in 1930. The book I never held in my hand; nor would I read Wilson on him. Brood about this.

Bogan, who had often closed her advisory letters to Roethke with the phrase, "Brood on this," said no more on the subject, and, in her *New Yorker* review, praised *The Lost Son* for its control and purity of feeling, writing, "The poet rises, at the end, to the surface of his obsessive dream to see the world in the light of day," and commending Roethke for "virtues that are instinctive, or that can be acquired only with great difficulty." There was no mention of influences or echoes.

Roethke was astonished, particularly since, as he told Kenneth Burke, "I hadn't gone near her during my last trip." Not entirely willing to let go of her former student, Bogan, having granted him the status of master, urged him the following year to "change away from what you are a master of!" It was the last time she told him how to write. Thenceforth they were content to be old friends who stayed in touch, but they no longer exerted a strong influence on each other's lives. Bogan served as matron of honor at Roethke's wedding to Beatrice O'Connell in January 1953, and was happy to see him enjoying more emotional prosperity than ever before. Her letters throughout the fifties were newsy and chatty, but lacking in literary or personal ardor, as though even in the present she were addressing a person who had become merely a souvenir of a lost intensity. Roethke still cherished Bogan. In the fall of 1958, convalescing from a difficult bout with manic-depressive illness, and seeing a psychiatrist five times a week, he wrote to say that during one of his sessions he had talked about her and wept. "It's obvious that you meant (and still mean) much more to me than I had realized, consciously, though God knows the conscious regard, I always felt, had to be *guarded against:* it was so school-boyish, and heroine worshipping, and no doubt boring to you after a point."

If Roethke's sudden confession was an invitation to revive feelings long ago played out, Bogan was unwilling to take it up. She wrote back only that she was sorry to hear that he had been having a hard time of it, mentioning nothing about what he had unearthed in treatment. Two years later, she was delighted and moved when Roethke made her the subject of a Hopwood Lecture delivered at the University of Michigan. Published in the *Michigan Quarterly Review*, "The Poetry of Louise Bogan" remains the best article ever written about her work. "Her poems create their own reality," Roethke wrote, "and demand not just attention, but the emotional and spiritual response of the whole man. Such a poet will never be popular, but can and should be a true model for the young. And the best work will stay in the language as long as the language survives."

Roethke's death from a coronary occlusion in 1963 came as a shock. She grieved to think of his vanished energy. It was the first of other losses and difficulties to come, and presaged the fading of her own vitality. As she reflected back over the summer of 1935, the young man she had known then must have seemed impossible to recapture, and her fresh, renewed, courageous self almost a stranger to memory.

FROM THE AFFAIR with Roethke there came several poems, as we know: "Roman Fountain" and "Baroque Comment," in particular. But from an odd circumstance there came another, "The Lie," which remained unpublished during Bogan's lifetime. Having learned that Raymond Holden had recently been identified in *Scribner's Magazine* as the author of a book of poems, *Landscape with Figures,* published in 1930, she wrote to John Hall Wheelock that, though he might not be aware of it, "no such book" existed, and added, in parentheses, "(I particularly loved the date, to give the whole thing some authority.)" The matter so incensed her, and struck her as so contemptibly consistent with Holden's mendacity in general, that she offered Wheelock a list of fifteen of her own "non-existent volumes," among them *The Werewolf of Amalfi* (1905), *Moles and Marmots: Their Life and Art* (1921), *My Life in a Mustache Cup* (1926), *Five Bedpillows and a Breeze* (1933), and *My Ornaments Are Arms* (1935). The more she thought about it, the angrier she got. "I hate a lie, O Christ, how I hate a lie," she wrote to Rolfe Humphries, enclosing a poem—called "The Lie"—written in a fine high rage:

> First met when I was young:
> Within the sliding eye,
> Upon the sidling tongue
> I knew the lie.
>
> Innocent, saw the look,
> Dupe, heard the dreadful beat
> When beautiful eye and mouth
> Gave forth deceit.

To make matters worse, toward the middle of the summer, Bogan and Holden reached an impasse. She wanted to leave 82 Washington Place and find a larger apartment for herself and Maidie, but Holden did not send her the money he owed her under the terms of their separation agreement. He pleaded lack of funds, but Bogan believed simply that he was holding back on her and, once again, lying. Their letters, through which they conducted their financial warfare, were a mixture of distance, courtesy, and bitterness. Holden blamed *her* for bringing the marriage to an end, and still maintained that his relationship with Miss X had had nothing to do with his defection from Louise herself. Marriage, he concluded, for people like Louise and himself, was an impossible state of affairs, although he said that he wished to be friends. There was an exchange of remarks about music, and book reviews, but Bogan remained furious, since the money either came late or not at all. Late in the summer of 1935, Raymond began a new campaign to get Louise's maintenance payment reduced. In the long run he was unsuccessful in this, and the sum—forty dollars a week—-was later written into their divorce agreement and paid to Louise until her death. But for the time being, the money was not sent and Louise was under extreme financial duress. Then, early in September, Raymond sent her a copy of his new novel, *Chance Has a Whip,* in which it seemed to Louise that he had given a character based on Miss X her own looks and dramatic temperament, and made her the object of the hero's weak and childish adoration. She sent the book back to Raymond, "and then," she wrote Roethke, "we began a row through the mails. My letters were masterpieces of invective, I will admit, and I hope they find a place in my collected works. (Two volumes of poems and eighteen volumes of invective.)"

Meanwhile, Louise did not have the money to pay her September rent. In the middle of the month she was astonished to find herself served with an eviction notice, followed within a few days by the eviction itself. Though the statuesque and sharp-tongued poet told the sheriff and his men "to get the hell out," she was unable to stop the removal of her furniture, piece by piece, out of the apartment and onto the sidewalk. She had the presence of mind to telephone for a van, put her things in storage, and move herself and Maidie into the nearby Hotel Albert at Tenth Street and University Place, where they had a dark room with a view of a factory building that had one floor devoted to shoemaking and another to the folding and packing of children's sewing sets.

Bogan took the eviction in serene and humorous stride. It was as if the worst that could happen—getting thrown out into the street—had happened, leaving nothing else to fear. At least the room at the Hotel Albert had long windows reaching down to the floor, so that despite the depressing view, there was a touch of elegance to enjoy and be thankful for. Any lingering delusions that Holden would come to her rescue now completely vanished. The fact of her responsibility for her own life, and not just the idea of it, had been forcibly, even brutally impressed upon her, as well as her capacity to meet that responsibility with good sense and a high appreciation of the comic absurdity of its immediate occasion. To Morton Zabel she wrote that she was actually happy—

happy for the first time in my life. At peace for the first time. I thought you gathered that when you were here. I'm just going to try to keep that way, that is all. I know it takes work. I worked and fought for thirty-seven years, to gain serenity at thirty-eight. Now I have it. And it's not dependent upon the whim of any fallible human creature, or upon economic security or upon the weather. I don't know where it comes from. Jung states that such serenity is always a miracle, and I think the saints said that, too. Though there were certain ways, and a certain road that may bring it about, when it comes, it is always a miracle. I am so glad that the therapists of my maturity and the saints of my childhood agree on one score.

In her journal, she confided that the years of confusion and bafflement had perhaps even been good for her. She had written "only what I *had* to write, and escaped writing a lot of lamentable tripe," including "the paeans to married love" and "the unformed and unenlightened critical balderdash." What she couldn't forgive herself

was all that sobbing over damp restaurant tables, and all that morbid thrashing about, and all that tendency toward hospitals, doctors, and sentimental rest-cures. And all that bath of non-identity, that day-to-day manufacture of the self-murderous tools of love-love-love. That endless clinging to the non-self: endless torture, endless *self*-betrayal.

Her residence at the Hotel Albert was short. She changed lawyers once again, began divorce proceedings, and moved at the end of March 1936 to 70 Morningside Drive, a building that housed young academics and their families. She had a room of her own, with a wonderful view that looked out over "bridges, churches, hospitals, elevated trains, gas tanks, apartment houses, chimneys and trees (*but not the streets themselves*)." The sun filled the room in the mornings, and she worked, reading and taking notes for her reviews, spending an occasional day walled up in the New York Public Library, but for the most part contented to be by herself with her books and papers, looking out the window, and overhearing snatches of telephone conversations between the young professors and their wives.

She was making discoveries in her reading, particularly what she called "Freudian discoveries." Dr. Wall had suggested books on psychoanalytic theory, and she was forging ahead with these, searching for explanations to her own difficulties, and curious to learn more about the patterns of neurotic weakness in general. She took down notes on compulsion neurosis from Otto Fenichel's *Outline of Clinical Psychoanalysis,* underlining Fenichel's description of neurotic isolation, wherein patients "suspend all decisions and defer execution until 'later on,' and *never get to anything because of endless preparation for it*" (Louise Bogan's emphasis) and his discussion of depression struck her so sharply that she transcribed it:

A grief-stricken person who has lost an object must loosen the libidinal attachment that binds him to it. This tie is not a matter of a single situation; the libido is attached to thousands of individual memories; and on each of the memories the dissolution of the tie must be carried through, *which takes time.* This process Freud designated the "grief-work" (*Trauerarbeit*). It is comparable to the "working through" (*Durcharbeiten*) that takes place in a therapeutic analysis, wherein a certain interpretation is brought to bear successively on all the individual manifestations of a given idea. The carrying out of the grief work is a difficult and unpleasant task, which many persons try to evade for a time by employing repression, so that the apparent lack of emotion may be due in part to an identification with the dead person.

The writing down of such a passage as this was in itself a species of "grief-work" and "working through" for Louise. It consolidated her therapeutic gains, won with such hard effort at the hospital, and gave her a framework for an understanding of the labor which had been and still was necessary to free herself from her mother and her husband. As she advanced across more territory, she found more energy and optimism available for her work. But she still had bad, dry days, on one of which she wrote in her journal, "Today it seemed as though nothing would ever happen again. Saw my real, half-withered, silly face in a shop mirror on the street, under the bald light of an evening shower, and shuddered. The woman who died without producing an *oeuvre.* The woman who ran away."

At the same time the healing and renewing process moved with an assuring rhythm. The distance between Louise and Raymond increased, and, as in any lengthening perspective, diminished the scale of his importance in her life. She was beginning to look at him with detachment. "But how beautiful he would have been, if he had had a 'good heart'! How life would have flowered, with him! But he *was* the bad heart. The disguised bad heart was the blood in his veins," she wrote in her journal, without great sadness, and with very little bitterness. With detachment and perspective came the complete view, the proportioned view, and this was, as if governed by a law she welcomed but did not seek to analyze, a sign of benevolence in her destiny. It was becoming possible to affirm her existence, with all its losses and trials. Coming across a critical study of Chekhov published in 1923 by William Gerhardi, she found a passage from one of Chekhov's own notebooks that she cherished for the rest of her life:

Essentially all this is crude and meaningless, and romantic love appears as meaningless as an avalanche which involuntarily rolls down a mountain and overwhelms people. But when one listens to music, all this is—that some people lie in their graves and sleep, and that one woman is alive and, grey-haired, is now sitting in a box in the theatre, seems quiet and majestic, and the avalanche no longer meaningless, since in nature everything has a meaning. And everything is forgiven, and it would be strange not to forgive.

She was also, at last, rediscovering Henry James, finding pleasure and greatness in him as never before. "He is such a mixture of sensitive artist and crass *arriviste*," she remarked to Zabel. Another fresh discovery was the French writer Jules Renard, about whose *Journal* she read a review in the *New Statesman* "and knew it was mine. It's really wonderful," she reported to Zabel, "the full and rewarding cahier such as we all should keep, such as I have tried so hard to keep, year after year, with varying results."

Wilson came back from Russia, full of stories about his hospital stay in Odessa, where he had come down with scarlatina, and they resumed their long evenings together. When some anthologies of Victorian verse by women fell into his hands, he suggested that Bogan do a *New Yorker* piece on them, "the point being," as she explained to Katharine S. White, who "handled" her at the magazine, "that when the girls had a restricted life, they were far more ardent, lauding the virtues of husband and connubial bliss in general in far from uncertain terms; while modern female verse tends to vilify and belittle the masculine charms, much of it being written just after or just before some disillusion handed to the woman by the man." Mrs. White was interested; Bogan wrote the piece, calling it "Poetesses in the Parlor," and the magazine published it the following December. The winter of 1936, Bogan broke her customary public silence and gave a reading at Boston University, which considered her a distinguished alumna despite her failure to return after her freshman year, and in the spring another reading followed at Bennington, "a bad, fancy, three-times-removed-from-reality kind of place, and I pity the girls and fear for their futures." Since the last spring she had been thinking and worrying about her book, and in June wrote to Wheelock from Swampscott that it would consist of two long poems, "Goodbye at Sea" (soon changed to "Putting to Sea"), "which will sum up the Holden suffering, endured so long, but now, at last, completely over," and "The Sleeping Fury." In addition she hoped to include some renderings of Lucretius, whom she had been reading and discussing with

Humphries, and of Rilke, as well as a brief selection of "short sharp epigrammatic things." This would hardly reach ten poems, the number she had determined would fill out the book satisfactorily, but she gathered most of what she had managed to write and publish since 1930, and was able to deliver a manuscript of twenty-five poems to Wheelock in the fall.

In what seemed by now a life of perpetual nomadism, Bogan moved again in the fall of 1936, this time to 302 West Seventy-seventh Street. "The room is really very pleasant indeed," she wrote to Maidie, away at a summer music camp; "windows north and south, almost on the corner of West End, so that a little eastern morning light comes in, even. It's really a furnished rooming house, of rather a high order, and if I get neighbors on either side, my privacy will be more or less *nil,* but it's better than 70 Morningside, where you couldn't shut your door at all." It was not the room of her dreams, which, if she were ever to find it, would resemble Edward Hopper's "A Room in Brooklyn"—"uncurtained, hardly furnished, with a view over roofs. A clean bed, a bookcase, a kitchen, a calm mind, one or two half-empty rooms,"—but, with its fireplace, kitchenette, and shower, it would have to do.

With *The Sleeping Fury* divided into sections, Bogan's photograph taken, and the publication day set, a mood of elation swept over her. "O Morton," she wrote to Zabel, in a rare outburst of joy, "so much difficulty has been written and composed! How good life is! How complicated! When I sat behind the stove, in Ballardvale, so complicated and hungry, surrounded by simple, peasant, repetitive hungers and rages, little did I know that all this had been done! What have we to complain of? Nothing! If we love and suffer 8,888 times in our lifetimes, there's always a hero or heroine who has done it 9,999 times!"

This period of happiness was fleeting. On December 21st, not two weeks after she had delivered her manuscript, her mother came down with pneumonia. Soon it became clear that she was dying. For the last few years May and Daniel Bogan had been living in Manhattan at Convent Avenue and 142nd Street. Daniel was working as clerk to a stockbroker. May's romantic hopes—and adventures—had all but died with her son. There were no more violent battles; no more scenes; no more disappearances; no more "admirers"—only the search for atonement and peace of mind, which had led her back to the Catholic Church and frequent social calls on the parish priests. In the summer of 1930, she had traveled with a group of mothers of American soldiers to visit their sons' graves in France. Stopping for a few days in Paris, she gave in to her love of elegance and finery, and bought a beautiful hat. From France and later, after her return to Portland, Maine, where she and Daniel were living before their move to New York, she wrote often to Maidie, urging her to pray to the Blessed Virgin to find a job for "Grampie," Louise's father (then in his early seventies and out of work), because she needed the money to erect a new gravestone, with Perpetual Care, at the cemetery where her foster mother was buried—the woman over whom she had endured so many assaults of guilt, with such terrible consequences for her own children.

She was proud, as Louise saw, to the end. For two days after the pneumonia set in, she refused to go to the hospital. Finally, at Louise's repeated urgings, she consented to go to St. Luke's. "If you could have seen the fight she put up, right to the last," Louise wrote to Morton Zabel. "But now she is a poor dying woman. I wish I could stop remembering her in her pride and beauty—in her arrogance, that I had to fight so—and now I feel it would have been better if I hadn't fought at all. Because under it all was so much love, and I had to fight that too."

Mary Bogan died December 26, 1936, at the age of seventy-one. Not long afterward, Mary Bogan's best friend, "whom my mother had run ragged ever since they were children together in the convent," Bogan later wrote to a friend, said to Louise, " 'Mary's faults were always big faults. Big faults you can forgive.' "

Louise Bogan was not left, on her mother's death, with a bundle of unresolved emotions. In *The Sleeping Fury,* and over the seven arduous years of pain, grief, and gradual letting go, she had faced, over and over, the links both soluble and indissoluble that bound her to her mother. The most important and the most lasting was the legacy of vivid, common, beautiful speech. Her mother had used the expression "As ignorant as dirt," and coming across it again in *Othello,* Bogan had recognized the weedlike durability and vitality of what was literally her "mother tongue." This speech and her mother's musical voice and passionate heart were alive in Bogan's poetry. As for the rest—the innocence and violence of feeling—these Louise had "by heart," and could release her mother into the arms of time.

W H E N *The Sleeping Fury* was published in the spring of 1937, it bore three marks of its origins. The line drawing on the dust jacket reproduced the image of a relief sculpture Bogan had seen in Rome at the Museo Nazionale delle Terme, "L'Erinni Addormentata," or "The Sleeping Fury." The figure, also noted in the museum catalogue as the "Medusa Ludovisi," is from the late Hellenistic period and portrays a female head of remarkable beauty, its eyes closed and lips half-open in sleep. Surrounded by serpentine locks of hair, the face lies in a repose of serenity, innocence, and peace.

When Bogan first saw the sculpture in 1933, she had scarcely emerged from one collapse and was still to face another. She was ignorant of what lay ahead but nevertheless recognized something in the face which became even then a symbol of all she had gone through and still had to endure.

The epigraph from Rilke on the title page of the book acknowledges her understanding of the hidden forces at work during the years between 1930 and 1936, and the lines appeared on the title page of every book of poems she later published:

> *Wie ist das klein, womit wir ringen;*
> *was mit uns ringt, wie ist das gross.* *

This maxim, taken from Rilke's poem "Der Schauende" ("He Who Visions"), in *Das Buch der Bilder* (*The Book of Pictures*), sums up much of what Bogan had come to understand during the years following the Hillsdale fire. It signaled her recognition of her innate romanticism, with its demand that life exceed its limits, but also encompassed a submission, both ironic and tragic, to forces beyond human will and desire.

The third trace of the book's origins is the dedication to Edmund Wilson, who had heartened and revived her during the months of her illness and her separation from Holden, and loyally maintained his faith in her gifts. He was a man to whom participation in reality was essential, and he encouraged her to believe that she had a part to play in a world that would be impoverished by her silence or inactivity. Through him she once again found it possible to speak and to hear her own voice among the other voices of her generation, at a time when to say anything at all, in either verse or prose, often struck her as futile.

The drawing of the Fury, the epigraph from Rilke, and the dedication to Wilson stood for experience which Bogan now thoroughly understood. It could not be translated into "philosophy." In her two earlier books of poetry she had been too anxious to do what she had so acutely diagnosed in Roethke, namely, to disburden herself of tension by putting her emotions too quickly into "literature." Her most important earlier poem, "Summer Wish," was, in comparison with the poems in *The Sleeping Fury,* almost a literary exercise, a ready-made Yeatsian colloquy *before* it was a colloquy between the doubting heart and the trusting imagination. When she wrote "Summer Wish," Bogan wanted desperately to believe in the benevolence of desire as it had expressed itself in her marriage to Holden, and in the poem she gave the Second Voice power to quell the First Voice's reproaches

---

* "How small is that with which we struggle; / How great is that which struggles with us."

and doubts concerning the essential kindness of instinct. But these doubts persisted in the intimations of absence, unfulfillment, and imminent change, in the uneasy sense, in "Old Countryside" and "Dark Summer," of a beautiful scene's sudden transition to the wrong time and the wrong place. These two poems, read in conjunction with "Summer Wish," throw a stark light on the discrepancy between wish and actuality. When the fire destroyed the Hillsdale house, it must have seemed an omen, a sign of the deep *wrongness* of the marriage. But it took seven years for Bogan to catch up with what her poetry had already assimilated. The poems in *The Sleeping Fury* find fresh speech to enact the struggle between the wish, its betrayal, and the aftermath of desolation and renewal which Bogan's two earlier books of poetry stave off.

Arranged in roughly chronological order, with poems written between 1930 and 1934 placed toward the front, and poems written between 1935 and 1936 placed toward the back, the book, as usual, conceals its direct biographical sources. Yet, the poems fall into their own narrative of sorts, although it was only after she had settled on the final disposition of the book's sections that Bogan herself recognized this pattern. But there it stood, the story of her spirit's trial, death, and rebirth, the "dark night of the soul" which she had traversed like any seeker for salvation. As she described the book to Zabel:

The 1930–1933 period—despair, neurosis and alcoholism—is set off by itself, ending with "Hypocrite Swift." Then there is the period of further despair, edged in upon by the period of Beautiful Males (ending with "Man Alone"). Then the spiritual side begins, with a few rumbles from the sensual bassoons and the mystic fiddles. All ends on a note of calm: me and the landscape clasped in each other's arms.

T H E   B O O K   O P E N S with "Song," a bitterly sad and ironic poem declaring the theme of loss at the same time that it establishes a continuity with the pastoral tone of many of the *Dark Summer* poems. The nameless thing which has replaced the heart—"the stock, / The stone,—the deaf, the blind—" and sees birds "Steer narrowed to the wind" in cold conformation to the reality of change is the mind now steeled to the necessity of loss. Stoic indifference and stoic endurance are thus compounded in this slender lyric on the nature of fate. A similar mood of spiritual retrenchment is cause for a quiet form of rejoicing in "Henceforth, from the Mind," a poem coming well in the wake of the fire and one in which the power of summary and suggestion through symbol is taken to a bold limit, as Bogan's voice, moving to its own rhythm, creates speech at once classic in syntax and Romantic in its emotional sweep. Responding many years later to a student's query about the poem, Bogan remarked that both "Henceforth, from the Mind" and "Exhortation" were written in her early thirties, "in the midst of a state which bordered on despair." Filled with affirmations, "Henceforth, from the Mind" is nevertheless shot through with elegy:

> Henceforth, from the mind,
> For your whole joy, must spring
> Such joy as you may find
> In any earthly thing,
> And every time and place
> Will take your thought for grace.
>
> Henceforth, from the tongue,
> From shallow speech alone,
> Comes joy you thought, when young,
> Would wring you to the bone,
> Would pierce you to the heart
> And spoil its stop and start.
>
> Henceforward, from the shell,
> Wherein you heard, and wondered
> At oceans like a bell
> So far from ocean sundered—
> A smothered sound that sleeps
> Long lost within lost deeps,
>
> Will chime you change and hours,
> The shadow of increase,
> Will sound you flowers
> Born under troubled peace—
> Henceforth, henceforth
> Will echo sea and earth.

The poem shows how fruitfully Bogan was still able to rely on the influence of Yeats, both in terms of language and poetic device as well as in its larger preoccupation with diminished possibilities. Speech is "shallow" because it is made of air, not flesh, while the shell gathers sound from memory and not the living present. Those gifts that stay—the "change and hours" of "troubled peace"—bear with them the "shadow" of mutability and mortality, the stamp, that is, of *time*, of brokenness, of partial happiness and flawed satisfactions, and draw the poem within the meditative compass of Wordsworth's "Tintern Abbey," Yeats's "The Tower," and Stevens's "Sunday Morning," great poems of loss and compensation.

What happens when art breaks faith with time, and thus with reality in order to serve the dream of outwitting time, is recounted in "Homunculus," perhaps Bogan's oddest poem. No information apart from its *New Yorker* publication date of May 8, 1930, exists. When it was written, or in relation to what inner or outer stimulus, is unknown; Bogan herself seems never to have mentioned it. It is a highly "literary" poem, having a direct though unexpressed source in Goethe's *Faust, Part II,* where, in the "Laboratory" scene of Act II, Mephistopheles attends the test-tube creation by Faust and Wagner of the "little chemical man," Homunculus. Unlike the equally allusive "Hypocrite Swift," "Homunculus" proclaims no obvious marks of its source beyond its title, although the text incorporates a great many details from Goethe. Early in the scene, Mephistopheles asks Wagner how a human couple could have been imprisoned in the chemical apparatus in such a way as to permit conception of the little man, and Wagner replies (in Walter Arndt's translation):

> O, God forbid! Begetting in the former fashion
> We laugh to scorn beside the new.

This Bogan changes to:

> What man, though lusty-loined,
> What woman from woman born,
>
> Shaped a slight thing, so strong,
> Or a wise thing, so young?

In rapture at the "dainty little mannikin," Wagner exclaims:

> What more do we desire, what more the world?
> For now the secret is in reach.
> Let this vibration but be heard,
> And it will turn to voice, to speech.

Bogan echoes this as:

> This mouth will yet know song
> And words move on this tongue.

With its knowledge of all time and place, Homunculus is, for both Goethe and Bogan, the supreme human creation, the foil against death and the instrument for putting all history to use. So wonderful seems the strange little man that, at his departure, Wagner cries out in distress and Mephistopheles contemptuously leers to the audience: "At last we after all depend / Upon dependents we created."

Bogan's lyric at once glosses Wagner's cry and in effect rewrites Mephistopheles' wisecrack. The speaker of her poem, who sees the little man as a "ruse" to defeat death, adores his consummate perfection, which goes beyond anything possible in nature. Its perfection as art makes mere life, with its lusts and inadequacies, contemptible. Yet it is just this inviolable, superior, arrogant perfection that Bogan punctures:

> It lacks but life: some scent,
> Some kernel of hot endeavor,
> Some dust of dead content
> Will make it live forever.

Homunculus is a toy of art. Possessing the exquisite charm of the miniature, it is nevertheless synthetic and false. Genuine art, Bogan implies, must be born from a copulative impulse, which would transform life into life.

By almost providential contrast, "Single Sonnet" presents the work of art as a living vessel of form, speaking for what Roethke, in "The Poetry of Louise Bogan," called "the sense of a civilization" so often found in her work. The "heroic mould" of the Petrarchan sonnet shapes feeling that would otherwise crush the poet with its "dreadful mass." Bogan did not believe that art existed to "express" feeling, but rather to grace it with form, and by doing so to make emotion bearable:

> Staunch meter, great song, it is yours, at length,
> To prove how stronger you are than my strength.

In "Exhortation," written nearly a year and a half after she wrote "Single Sonnet," Bogan repudiates the benevolence and optimism of that poem as well as the acceptance of "Henceforth, from the Mind." Published in *Scribner's Magazine* in March 1933, the poem "arrived" suddenly on October 31, 1932, and the same day, "two hours after it saw paper," Bogan sent it to Wheelock with this comment:

—Bitter though it be, do try to like it. I think it good, because, on a second reading, it sounded like something I had never seen before, and I always value that as a sign that the vulgar upper consciousness had nothing to do with it. So I feel safe about it, since it seems to have passed through, with authority, like a wave or light or whatever it is.

These remarks place the "fine, frightfully angry, terrifically compressed" poem in a context of conclusion and breakthrough, although, as her journal tells us, she continued to suffer for many months to come. Years later, she told Sister Angela O'Reilly, who was writing a Master's thesis on Bogan's poetry, that "Exhortation" had been written "on the verge of a psychic and physical breakdown (which had roots in reality and partook v. little of fantasy)." What she later understood was that the breakthrough and the breakdown were much the same thing.

Once again, in "Exhortation," a *lesson* must be learned. Bitter knowledge must replace false feeling. With a violence directed as much against the self as against the world, the poem commands the rejection of any form of emotional vulnerability:

> Indifference can be your toy:
> The bitter heart can be your book.
> (Its lesson torment never shook.)

The heart holds a text, the poem implies, printed with the rules and conditions of the dead—both those who belong to the past, and those who are dead in life:

> Know once for all: their snare is set
> Even now; be sure their trap is laid;
> And you will see your lifetime yet
> Come to their terms, your plans unmade,—
> And be belied, and be betrayed.

The anger, so convinced of its claims, so exact in its indictments, fuses a "lyric cry" with a savage moral indictment. But in "Hypocrite Swift," Bogan achieves compassionate irony by granting all the despair to Swift and all the insight to herself (through her co-functionaries, Venus and the Muses). Here too she returns to the "Homunculus" mode, absorbing quotation and allusion into a lyric fabric, though this time giving the borrowings explicit form:

> Hypocrite Swift now takes an eldest daughter.
> He lifts Vanessa's hand. Cudsho, my dove!
> Drink Wexford ale and quaff down Wexford water
> But never love.
>
> He buys new caps; he and Lord Stanley ban
> Hedge-fellows who have neither wit nor swords.

He turns his coat; Tories are in; Queen Anne
Makes twelve new lords.

The town mows hay in hell; he swims in the river;
His giddiness returns; his head is hot.
Berries are clean, while peaches damn the giver
(Though grapes do not).

Mrs. Vanhomrigh keeps him safe from the weather.
Preferment pulls his periwig askew.
Pox takes belittlers; do the willows feather?
God keep you.

Stella spells ill; Lords Peterborough and Fountain
Talk politics; the Florence wine went sour.
Midnight: two different clocks, here and in Dublin,
Give out the hour.

On walls at court, long gilded mirrors gaze.
The parquet shines; outside the snow falls deep.
Venus, the Muses stare above the maze.
Now sleep.

Dream the mixed, fearsome dream. The satiric word
Dies in its horror. Wake, and live by stealth.
The bitter quatrain forms, is here, is heard,
Is wealth.

What care I; what cares saucy Presto? Stir
The bed-clothes; hearten up the perishing fire.
Hypocrite Swift sent Stella a green apron
And dead desire.

Bogan was delighted with having been able to write a poem at all, and left a good deal of information about the composition of "Hypocrite Swift." It was first published in *Poetry* in October 1931, and bore the subtitle "After Reading Swift's Journal to Stella," which she had done while at Cromwell Hall in Connecticut, convalescing from her first breakdown the previous spring. She wrote the poem on April 26, 1931, and sent it to Wheelock the next day, hoping that he would take it for *Scribner's Magazine*. "It's damned literary and allusive," she remarked to him, "but well-turned, I think." It had started out as a "literary exercise" but had suddenly turned into a poem with the lines beginning, "On walls at court, long gilded mirrors gaze," and to the discovery that what she had written was, in fact, a poem, she attributed her "rapid recovery, from then on." *Scribner's* didn't want the poem and neither did *The New Yorker*. Mrs. White wrote that

Ross had rejected it on the grounds that it presumed "a literary knowledge and background that most of our readers would not have and that it would not be understandable to many people." Allen Tate, to whom Bogan had sent a copy of the poem, also remarked upon its eccentricity, although he admired it very much. "I never suspected that you could write such a poem," he wrote, "but seeing is believing, and I think it is very fine. It is the only poem you've done in which a high degree of technical virtuosity is interesting for its own sake and yet just right for what you're saying." When *The Sleeping Fury* was published, Bogan withdrew the subtitle, making the poem less occasional and more "read into and subjective." The *Journal to Stella* had been heartbreaking to read, she told Edmund Wilson. "The passion is so real, so imperfectly dissembled, and the wit is such a strange mixture of roughness and elegance." Bogan's Swift suffers from a despair that barely conceals itself, and from a love too paralyzed by that despair to express itself directly. The *Journal to Stella,* filled with oaths, worldly events, reports of ailments, and the "little language" of Swift's love, yielded "terms," as Bogan uses the word in "Exhortation," of love sabotaged by itself, one of her earliest and principal themes. The blighted ability to love which formed the crux of Bogan's 1931 collapse found an echo of its withered voice in the *Journal,* and, by merging her own pain with Swift's, or rather detaching it and seeing it *as* Swift's, she was able to achieve forgiveness of herself, and understanding. Edmund Wilson was especially taken with the poem. "You ought to send it as credentials to Yeats," he wrote, when Bogan sent him his copy of *The Sleeping Fury.*

Bogan also included two occasional poems in the volume, "At a Party" and "To Wine." The division between the secular world and the timeless world of the constellations, first presented in "Fiend's Weather," with "the broken Pleiades" and "the iron of the Plough," and in the quiet staring of Venus and the Muses in "Hypocrite Swift," returns in "At a Party," where Bogan uses the ancient trope of spirit against flesh to distill a pure drop of misanthropic irony. The spirit says:

> Over our heads, if we but knew,
> Over our senses, as they reel,
> The planets tread, great seven, great two
> Venus, Uranus, in a wheel.

But the spirit is rudely interrupted, when flesh interposes its own design of ironic malice—"wisdom's guide"—and "enmity, that may save us all." As Bogan had implied in the glittering clarity of "Fiend's Weather," and the dead-ended absoluteness of "Exhortation," knowledge of human malice comes as a clear and whole culmination, while the world such knowledge reveals is always broken and obscure. In "At a Party," the triumphant grasp of this knowledge, terrible though it may be, is even a source of elation.

Feeling, perhaps, the stopgap quality of hatred and rage, and understanding how they block access to unbearable emotions of grief and loss, Bogan ended the first section of *The Sleeping Fury* with a picture of secular corruption in "At a Party" and opened the second section with the restorative "To Wine." In this poem, love is "the mandate" of existence and has phases, including tides of betrayal and reunion, which wine magically brings into play: it erases memory and therefore grief, yet arouses desire, and so sets in motion the inevitable cycle of pain. The supremacy of unlocked feeling in "To Wine" appears again in "Poem in Prose," a remarkable, and, for Louise Bogan, experimental piece of work. Using the long free-verse line for the first time since the only marginally successful "Didactic Piece," she struggled with the separation, up till now fairly rigid in her mind, between poetry and prose. Like Yeats, Bogan found it helpful to write out prose versions of poems she had difficulty putting into "form." Neither strictly prose nor strictly verse, "Poem in Prose" reads as a transitional work, something more than prose and less than fully poetry, for reasons the text itself supplies:

> I turned from side to side, from image to image, to put you down,
> All to no purpose; for you the rhymes would not ring—
> Not for you, beautiful and ridiculous, as are always the true
>   inheritors of love,
> The bearers; their strong hair moulded to their foreheads as though
>   by the pressure of hands.
> It is you that must sound in me secretly for the little time before my mind,
>   schooled in desperate esteem, forgets you—
> And it is my virtue that I cannot give you out,
> That you are absorbed into my strength, my mettle,
> That in me you are matched, and that it is silence which comes from us.

The *prose* of "Poem in Prose," then, is not just Bogan's slight term of disparagement for the free-verse line, but, gently and ironically, the speaker's inability and reluctance to "put you down" and "give you out" into time, form, and the past. Prose is thus the medium of the present, of selves "absorbed" and "matched" in their strength of feeling. It is equated with the speaker's "virtue" in resisting the inevitable, so that her weakness is her strength, and her inability to write the poem the proof of the sincerity of her love.

It was as open a love poem as Bogan had ever written, and she was a little embarrassed by it. "I'd send you the new poem I wrote," she said to Edmund Wilson, ". . . but it really is so woodwind and cello that perhaps you couldn't bear it. I'll send it later." As if to clarify for herself the difference between the tenderly "defective" "Poem in Prose" and the acceptable and adequate poem in "form," she moved on to the blunt finality of "Short Summary," a poem that provides an example of almost everything Bogan meant by a poem. It not only has stanzas and rhymes, but a commanding voice, speaking with finality and authority despite extreme pressure of feeling:

> Listen but once to the words written out by my hand
> In the long line fit only for giving ease
> To the tiresome heart. I say: Not again shall we stand
> Under green trees.
>
> How we stood, in the early season, but at the end of day,
> In the yes of new light, but at the twice-lit hour,
> Seeing at one time the shade deepened all one way
> And the breaking flower;
>
> Hearing at one time the sound of the night-fall's reach
> And that checked breath bound to the mouth and caught
> Back to the mouth, closing its mocking speech:
> Remind me not.
>
> Soon to dark's mid-most pitch the divided light
> Ran. The balance fell, and we were not there.
> It was early season; it was the verge of night;
> It was our land;
> It was evening air.

This is speech which fuses the deepest memory of lost tenderness with the firmest resolution to accept the loss. Even more, it is evanescence, the law governing the disappearance of things, which the poem's mystery calls forth. Read with "Poem in Prose," the strict form of "Short Summary" makes clear that formal poetry, among other things, was for Bogan a medium for separating and differentiating herself from persons and situations, and for concluding attachments and times of life. Perhaps, then, Bogan's obsession with betrayal had another source, one deep within herself, in that poetry in form must always have required from her a severing, a repudiation of union with the object, or the person, who had driven her to utterance. To form attachments was thus hazardous, for the very feelings they produced would lead, as it were, to the need to write poetry, and poetry, if it was to be what Bogan took for poetry, inevitably exacted some form of emotional violence toward the attachment.

To break the guilt and the grief of these laws, Bogan attempted, in many of the poems in *The Sleeping Fury,* to loosen the hold of form. In "Italian Morning," which she called "the mutability poem," she used form more liberally than usual. This was the distillation of all the poems she had wanted to write but was unable to write during the 1933 Guggenheim journey in Italy. When she'd submitted it to Wheelock in May 1935, she had asked him to send it back to her in July, saying that she wanted to send it next to *The New Republic* (*Scribner's* finally did publish it in August) and calling it "the best poem I have done in years." It is not without obscurity, having some of the extreme compression which forced Edmund Wilson to say in a 1938 letter to Bogan, on the subject of Laurence Housman's memoir, *My Brother A. E. Housman,* "I thought his excellent criticism of his brother's poetry the sort of thing I ought to have given you the benefit of before *Sleeping Fury* was published—about remembering that the reader knows only what you tell him, etc."

The penetration of place has the steady and comprehensive glance which Bogan was soon to discover in Rilke. The "we" of the poem is the traveler's guidebook pronoun of intense, courteous attention, while the eye conducts a tour around the sleeping-chamber, repeating, in condensed form, the movement of "Journey Around My Room," with the traveler moored to the bed and surveying all she wakes to with an acute sense of mutability:

> The big magnolia, like a hand,
> Repeats our flesh. (O bred to love,
> Gathered to silence!) In a land
> Thus garnished, there is time enough
>
> To pace the rooms where painted swags
> Of fruit and flower in pride depend,
> Stayed as we are not. The hour wags
> Deliberate, and great arches bend
>
> In long perspective past our eye.
>
> Mutable body, and brief name,
> Confront, against an early sky,
> This marble herb, and this stone flame.

The poet surveys the art and architecture of the high-ceilinged room in which she finds herself as if her position in the bed marked out a timeless refuge from a life otherwise relentlessly moving forward. From her horizontal haven, her eye moves through the wealth of painted and architected illusions whose space she is part of, and whose capacity to stave off the mortality they proclaim gives her a temporary release from the burden of belonging to time.

Behind the poem lies Bogan's love of Baroque art and architecture, and specifically, in the final emblems of "marble herb" and "stone flame," her memories of Sant' Andrew della Fratte in Rome, with its tower by Borromini "topped by an iron crown and some stone flames," which, she told Rolfe Humphries some years after she wrote the poem, "I think of . . . a lot . . . it is so lovely in the spring, with all the levels rising, and the marble, and the light in the gardens." The whole poem is steeped in such memories of space, light, ornament, and stone. And from the moment the speaker's heel strikes the earth "with a lonely blow," the poem moves in accordance with Baroque physicality, celebrated in so much painting from Caravaggio through Rembrandt and Poussin. Here the body is the source of the poem's meaning: the body, fixed to the bed (where life begins and ends), meeting its fate and rejoicing in it through the transformation of mutability into art.

The Baroque tendency to anchor itself in a heightened naturalism without sacrificing emblematic or allegorical meaning implies a relaxation of formal strictness and an extension of formal boundaries. Much of the strength and originality of the poems in *The Sleeping Fury* comes from a corresponding flexibility. Bogan mingled and stretched genres with greater freedom than she had ever exercised before. In her 1935–36 notebook, she wrote, "Whatever I do, apart from the short cry (lyric poetry) and the short remark (journalism), must be in the form of notes. Mine is the talent of the cry or the *cahier*." She had always separated the two in the past, but in "Hypocrite Swift" she'd incorporated Swift's own *cahier* phrases into what was essentially a lyric cry, and had poised "Poem in Prose" on the ambiguity between verse form and note form.

In "Baroque Comment," she gave free play to her feeling for the Baroque as both a principle of form and an inner direction, making a lyric out of a single extended proselike remark, stretching the implicit limits of both forms to forge a powerful new synthesis. The poem was written sometime in the late spring or early summer of 1935, shortly after Bogan sent off "Italian Morning" to Wheelock. "I have a poem on hand," she wrote to him, "which I'm not quite sure of, yet, called 'Baroque Comment,' which I'll send you . . . after it is writ out fair. It has some really beautiful lines in it, but it isn't a lyric." By a "lyric" she meant a metrically identifiable, stanzaic, richly patterned fabric of sound, meaning, and feeling, on the order of "Henceforth, from the Mind," "Exhortation," "Short Summary," or "Single Sonnet." Yet the Bogan who loved Baroque form was learning to work with a new plasticity, suggested by an image in "Poem in Prose"—the description of the lover as one of "the true inheritors of love, / The bearers; their strong hair moulded to their foreheads as though by the pressure of hands." The structure of "Baroque Comment" grows directly out of this new plasticity; it is a "swag" of dependent clauses celebrating Bogan's sense of civilization as the sum of the transforming powers of intellect and love. The actual movement of these powers is worked out as the poem holds back its gathering energy in the first section and then spills out from the catalogue of destructive energies the corresponding catalogue of noble sublimations:

> From loud sound and still chance;
> From mindless earth, wet with a dead million leaves;
> From the forest, the empty desert, the tearing beasts,
> The kelp-disordered beaches;
> Coincident with the lie, anger, lust, oppression and death in many forms:
>
> Ornamental structures, continents apart, separated by seas:
> Fitted marble, swung bells; fruit in garlands as well as on the branch;
> The flower at last in bronze, stretched backward, or curled within;
> Stone in various shapes: beyond the pyramid, the contrived arch and the
>   buttress;
> The named constellations;
> Crown and vesture; palm and laurel chosen as noble and enduring;
> Speech proud in sound; death considered sacrifice; . . .

Thus the list continues, culminating its praise with "The turned eyes and the opened mouth of love," an allusion to the expression of mystical-erotic transport on the face of Bernini's St. Theresa, which Bogan had seen in Rome in 1933 and of which she had sent an art postcard to Raymond Holden.

Between "Italian Morning" and "Baroque Comment," Bogan interposed the ironic contrast of "Man Alone," a poem about male narcissism. The man who loves only himself, and who seeks echoes and reflections of himself in his erotic encounters remains incapable of the creative transformations Bogan celebrates in the two flanking poems:

> The glass does not dissolve;
> Like walls the mirrors stand;
> The printed page gives back
> Words by another hand.

And your infatuate eye
Meets not itself below:
Strangers lie in your arms
As I lie now.

As much as Bogan allowed herself adventures into unfamiliar formal territory in *The Sleeping Fury,* she also brought her command of traditional metrical-stanzaic verse to new standards of perfection. In the formal elegy, "To My Brother Killed: Haumont Wood: October, 1918," she bends a shorter variation on the *In Memoriam* stanza to austere, direct, and oracular utterance. The slow inevitable beats culminate in what is in effect a reversal of "Baroque Comment," the revelation of an eternal destroying principle:

O you so long dead,
You masked and obscure,
I can tell you, all things endure:
The wine and the bread;

The marble quarried for the arch;
The iron become steel;
The spoke broken from the wheel;
The sweat of the long march;

The hay-stacks cut through like loaves
And the hundred flowers from the seed;
All things indeed
Though struck by the hooves

Of disaster, of time due,
Of fell loss and gain,
All things remain,
I can tell you, this is true.

Though burned down to stone
Though lost from the eye,
I can tell you, and not lie,—
Save of peace alone.

The poem was an old one, written sometime in the twenties and sent to Rolfe Humphries. In the fall of 1935, when Bogan asked him to send back letters with poems in them, she could not even remember when she had written it. It is a true occasional poem, a communal poem, well suited to be read aloud. In its sense of the impermanence of peace it is not a consoling or an encouraging poem; as an attempt to tell the truth, in meter, it is formidable.

With "The Sleeping Fury," Bogan arrives at the book's centerpiece. A dramatic change from high tension to calm insight runs its course in the poem, in which the speaker addresses a "you" to whom nothing less than the whole truth can be told. Within itself, the poem recapitulates the movement, repeated throughout the volume, from the despair of "Song" and "Exhortation" to the timeless peace of "Henceforth, from the Mind," the calm gaze of Venus and the Muses in "Hypocrite Swift," and the gentle love in "Poem in Prose." The poem consists of prose stanzas, neither "free" in the sense of being unpredictably variable, nor bound to any discernible metrical pattern. Merging the "cry" of feeling with the reflective *"cahier"* remark, Bogan fills the long lines "fit only for giving ease," as she writes in "Short Summary," with vividly pictorial images from an inner myth.

It was in the spring of 1935 that Bogan decided to base the title of her next book of poems, as well as the title poem itself, on the image of the "Erinni Addormentata" she had seen in the Museo Nazionale della Terme in Rome, and when the poem appeared in the December 1936 issue of *Poetry* magazine, it was subtitled "Rome, Museo delle Terme"; but this was removed for the book's publication. "The title poem," Bogan informed the ever-anxious Wheelock in the fall of 1935, "should be rather long for me, and it will be in carefully written quatrains, with, I trust, a good strong ring to them, and that will pull the book together at the center." She managed to write only one quatrain, however, which, though undated, should probably be considered evidence of the poem's earliest version:

> Now it is time to tell of the fury sleeping:
> Having seen so much of both the living and the dead;
> Having turned so much between the heard and the said;
> Having suffered so much between the heart and its keeping.

But this was as far as the scheme of quatrains went. That same fall, Bogan began to work on prose renderings of the poem, taking her cue from Yeats, and these she intermittently took up and put aside throughout the following winter and spring months. It was only in late July 1936 that she could confidently tell Wheelock, "The scenario of The Sleeping Fury, the book's title poem is now finished; nothing to do but find its form." By "scenario" she meant just the prose rendering, and she wrote Humphries that it "was floating around my unconscious for so long that it had become extremely amorphous; I didn't know exactly what I wanted to say. So I wrote down the argument in prose, and it sounds so nice that I hate to work it over, but I must, of course."

Finding the poem's final form took nearly two more months, and the manuscript which Bogan sent to Wheelock in the second week of October was a fascinating palimpsest, rich with remnants of each stage at which the poem had lingered in Bogan's unhurrying and ripening imagination. The scenario is written out on worksheets. On the first, adjacent to the title "The Sleeping Fury," Bogan wrote, "megaera." Megaera was the jealous Fury, particularly bent on punishing sexual crimes. Bogan had found out other details about the Furies in the *Encyclopaedia Britannica,* and, mixing them with her own private associations, set forth the "scenario" thus:

It was so loved, so feared, but now it lies in a symbol before us, fixed and asleep. The hair, wet with grief, lies upon its cheek, no longer in the semblance of serpents lifted in the gale of its movement. It, too, slumbers like a mortal: it can be approached, gazed upon, even touched. It can draw pity from our hearts, and tenderness, as it lies in its solitude. It has scourged us, with its vituperation, hounded us with its cries, dropped us from the ignoble dream, whipped us through a thousand cities, and made horrible a thousand resting places. But now it is alone, and asleep, beautiful as a child whose hair, wet with rage and tears, now clings to its face. It has peace, and we look upon it with mercy, although it has never been merciful to us, and with love.

> It lies, forgetting us.
> I look lonely in my peace
> O beautiful, alone in yours.

As Bogan may well have hoped it would, the prose scenario turned spontaneously into poetry toward the end, finding its own simple rhythm. Later, when she removed the subtitle, she said that she did not want the piece of sculpture to lead to a confusion of the Fury with the Gorgon. But the real reason for removing the subtitle had less to do with external references than with the slow transformation of the text, in the writing process, from an explicit to an implicit *ding-gedicht,* or "poem-about-a-thing." Such a poem starts with a response to an object in the world and becomes, through absorption by the imagination, part of the poet's marrow. In the prose scenario the Fury is first an "it," an intensely dwelled-upon object seen quite literally in a museum in Rome. But in the last lines of the prose sketch, when the prose itself becomes abbreviated and hypnotic, poetry takes over and the observed "it" becomes an imagined "you."

It helps to remember that only a few weeks after she announced the title and plans for the long poem to Wheelock, Bogan discovered the Rilke of the *Neue Gedichte,* and its poems about *things:* flowers, animals, and most particularly, works of art, which Rilke could gaze upon with a seemingly infinite capacity for imaginative penetration and empathy. Just after finishing the final draft of "The Sleeping Fury," Bogan remarked in a letter to Humphries that Rilke had said "that the poem is farther away from men than from things, and I think that is true." While she gazed at the sculptured head in Rome, and then at the postcard with its image, and then at the image which her memory preserved, the figure became detached from all the occasions of viewing, turning from an object into a symbol that she consciously placed within a geography familiar from her earlier work. In her 1935–36 journal she wrote, "To trace the dream-landscape that has grown inside me every night, all my life, along with daylight reality, and which has mountains, ruins, islands, shores, cities, and even *suburbs* and summer 'resorts' *of its own,* related to one another and, many times, recurrent (almost in the sense of revisited)." The setting of "The Sleeping Fury" is this region fused with details picked up from the *Encyclopaedia Britannica* entry about the Furies. Thus the New England of Bogan's childhood becomes transposed to a land in which the most primitive cruelty and the most serene tenderness co-exist:

> You are here now,
> Who were so loud and feared, in a symbol before me,
> Alone and asleep, and I at last look long upon you.
>
> Your hair fallen on your cheek, no longer in the semblance of serpents,
> Lifted in the gale; your mouth, that shrieked so, silent.
> You, my scourge, my sister, lie asleep, like a child,
> Who, after rage, for an hour quiet, sleeps out its tears.
>
> The days close to winter
> Rough with strong sound. We hear the sea and the forest,
> And the flames of your torches fly, lit by others,
> Ripped by the wind, in the night. The black sheep for sacrifice
> Huddle together. The milk is cold in the jars.
>
> All to no purpose, as before, the knife whetted and plunged,
> The shout raised, to match the clamor you have given them.
> You alone turn away, not appeased; unaltered, avenger.
>
> Hands full of scourges, wreathed with your flames and adders,
> You alone turned away, but did not move from my side,
> Under the broken light, when the soft nights took the torches.
>
> At thin morning you showed, thick and wrong in that calm,
> The ignoble dream and the mask, sly, with slits at the eyes,
> Pretence and half-sorrow, beneath which a coward's hope trembled.

You uncovered at night, in the locked stillness of houses,
False love due the child's heart, the kissed-out lie, the embraces,
Made by the two who for peace tenderly turned to each other.

You who know what we love, but drive us to know it;
You with your whips and shrieks, bearer of truth and of solitude;
You who give, unlike men, to expiation your mercy.

Dropping the scourge when at last the scourged advances to meet it,
You, when the hunted turns, no longer remain the hunter
But stand silent and wait, at last returning his gaze.

Beautiful now as a child whose hair, wet with rage and tears
Clings to its face. And now I may look upon you,
Having once met your eyes. You lie in sleep and forget me.
Alone and strong in my peace, I look upon you in yours.

With the poem's statement, "and I at last look long upon you," Bogan achieves the vision she valued so highly in Baudelaire, Rimbaud, Rilke, and Yeats, poets who create the possibility of reconciling the warring elements in themselves without self-loathing or self-protecting distortion. The figure of the Sleeping Fury the poet recognizes as both her "scourge" and her "sister," both of whom are parts of an incorruptible child who rages against her false and cowardly adult double; and, in the crisis of confrontation, at the very moment "when the hunted turns," it is the child-Fury who drops the whip and meets the gaze of the hunted, giving to the task of "expiation" the "mercy" of quiescence. The Fury's sleep, in which she is revealed as the exhausted, beautiful child who has done with her weeping, is her final gift. As she forgets the speaker, the latter feels love's loneliness and strength, as well as the Fury's own loneliness and separateness. In the words of "Poem in Prose," the speaker is now able to "put down" and "give out" the loved and hated symbol, by whom she is content to be forgotten.

In the poem Bogan achieved psychic reconciliation with her mother. The Fury as Megaera is Bogan's own punishing rage against her mother's and Holden's betraying sexuality, and against herself, perhaps, for wishes and acts confusedly and obscurely entangled with the people she loved. But the honesty of the Fury's rage is also Mary Bogan's cry for freedom, and Louise's, and an indictment of "False love due the child's heart, the kissed-out lie, the embraces, / Made by the two who for peace tenderly turned to each other." Through its wholly figurative texture, the poem was as autobiographical as any Bogan ever wrote, and, it should be said, as strong an act of mastery over the facts of the poet's existence as she was ever to put into poetry. She understood this, making it the heart of the book, even before she knew what the poem's form would be.

It is perhaps because she came to understand how permanently the healing and reconciling depths of "The Sleeping Fury" spoke for her changed life that she later transferred "Roman Fountain," which preceded the poem in both *The Sleeping Fury* and *Poems and New Poems,* to its position just after that poem in *Collected Poems, 1923–1953* and *The Blue Estuaries.* The occasion of the writing of "Roman Fountain" was Bogan's affair with Theodore Roethke, and its metaphoric pattern can easily be grasped as a celebration of the rediscovery and renewal of erotic life, extended to creative power as well. It is this equivalence, as a sequel to the reconciliation with the Fury, that the poem embodies. Along with "Baroque Comment" and "Italian Morning," "Roman Fountain" has a further source in Bogan's 1933 Italian journey, where the big bronze fountains in Rome delighted her with their upsurging sun-shot waters. The "texture" of the poem, as Bogan liked to call it, is intricate, rich with alliteration, consonance, and assonance, the one- and two-syllable words striking the ear with authority and moving toward the exalted consummation of the last stanza. The pattern of rhythm and syntax supports a sustained act of *looking;* this poem, as much as "The Sleeping Fury," is an impassioned response to an object become magical through being truly seen. In the first stanza Bogan magnificently captures the swift and subtle movement of the water:

> Up from the bronze, I saw
> Water without a flaw
> Rush to its rest in air,
> Reach to its rest, and fall.
>
> Bronze of the blackest shade,
> An element man-made,
> Shaping upright the bare
> Clear gouts of water in air.
>
> Oh, as with arm and hammer,
> Still it is good to strive
> To beat out the image whole,
> To echo the shout and stammer
> When full-gushed waters, alive,
> Strike on the fountain's bowl
> After the air of summer.

During the summer of 1935, when she was working on the poem, she sent a draft of it to Rolfe Humphries, who made a number of sound suggestions about improving it. She had written "bare/Thick gouts," and he wondered whether the phrase was "too adjectival & is thick too suggestive of opacity—or do you want to suggest opacity?—would *bare clear* spoil it?" He also cogently observed that "The punctuation makes clear the meaning but it is too much burden on the punctuation, for the expectancy is [that] as it is good, with arm & hammer, still to strike & beat out the images, etc., *so* something else which never appears. Then you read it over & find your mistake but that is not a convincing experience," and said that he thought that "the rhythm bumps too much especially for a fountain poem," and offered this variant:

> Still it is good to strive
> O as with arm & hammer
> Beat out the image whole
> Echo the shout & stammer

To these suggestions she gave this answer:

I don't know what to do about "Roman Fountain." It's so sort of footless, as it is. *Clear* would be better before *gouts;* I'll change it. I wanted to get *thick* in, because the point about the fountains of Rome is, that there's so much water in them. None of your piddling little streams. Big gushes as thick as your arm, simply leaping up and scattering around; making a lovely big strong noise; rushing up like whole rivers. Great big bronze gents with great big bronze cornucopias or shells, or something, on their shoulders, and from that, great, enormous thick jumping water. To hell with that poem. It's minor, all save the first stanza. It doesn't do it. It should be all fountain, and no Louise looking at it.

However much self-reference there may have been in the draft she sent to Humphries, the finished poem is virtually all Rilkean penetration of the fountain and hardly any "Louise looking at it." She fused her looking at the fountain with the fountain itself, which became, as it were, a fountain-being-seen, and she let the grammatical awkwardness of the last section stand, trusting the poem's rhythm to make its meaning clear, just as she let the rhythm "bump" as vulgarly and joyously as it could.

WHEN BOGAN SENT WHEELOCK the fair copies of "Roman Fountain" and "Baroque Comment" in August 1935, she mentioned that she thought them the best of a group of about seven poems she had written over the summer. The spirited and witty "Rhyme," however ("What laid, I said, / My being waste? / 'Twas your sweet flesh / With its sweet taste,—"), having been published that June in *The New Yorker,* came too early for this "second blooming." Yet its play of sensuality and gentle regret shares the benevolence of the poems written during the summer of 1935, and the erotic generosity which had come with a new and self-forgiving point of view:

> It's at springs we drink;
> It's bread we eat,
> And no fine body,
> Head to feet,
>
> Should force all bread
> And drink together,
> Nor be both sun
> And hidden weather.
>
> Ah no, it should not;
> Let it be.
> But once heart's feast
> You were to me.

Another short and spectacular lyric is "M., Singing." The M. of the poem is Mathilde (Maidie) Alexander, who was studying voice at Juilliard in 1935 36, and often practiced at home, while her mother accompanied her on the piano. The poem "arrived" on October 14, 1936, after Bogan had heard Maidie singing Fauré's *Après un Rêve,* "which has a rather punk lyric," she remarked to Humphries, "ending on the word *mysterieuse—se,* but by the time that final non-mute *e* has sounded in the air, one is positively cold with excitement. —Or maybe it's only me." From this intense listening she wrote:

> Now, innocent, within the deep
> Night of all things you turn the key,
> Unloosing what we know in sleep.
> In your fresh voice they cry aloud
> Those beings without heart or name.
>
> Those creatures both corrupt and proud,
> Upon the melancholy words
> And in the music's subtlety,
> Leave the long harvest which they reap
> In the sunk land of dust and flame
> And move to space beneath our sky.

The singer is the innocent instrument of the crafty, malign daemons of the spirit who release, while we sleep, the secret that love and hate, anger and tenderness, are in truth the same at their point of origin, which is nothing less than the "sunk land of dust and flame," the region of life and death—again first presented in "A Tale." Together with "The Sleeping Fury," the poem marks another breakthrough into acceptance of Bogan's Romantic inheritance. Much of her life she had fought against it; the last thing on earth she wanted to be was a Romantic poet. But here she understood that what she had been contending with all along, or what—to follow her book's epigraph from Rilke to its conclusion—had been contending with her was not so much destructive rage but daemonic energy, a rich supply of creative, imaginative energy, misapplied, to be sure, in the quest for perfect passionate love, but fundamentally pure. Through the years of despair following the 1929 fire and the miraculous "cure" of the spring and summer of 1934, she recognized that it was possible to turn her "death-loving temperament" to life-affirming uses, and was able, like Wordsworth, to imagine a human—that is, partial, limited, mortal—sublimity. Commenting on "M., Singing," to Rolfe Humphries, she observed, "I don't think the beings should be exactly *corrupt,* but they (the impulses dignified by the personification) are so inhuman, according to waking standards, that perhaps corrupt is right, after all."

By "inhuman" she meant detached, timeless, more-than-human, as in her beautiful elegy, "Evening-Star," a poem whose emotion comes close to the awe and reverence of religious lyrics. To Roethke she remarked, "I thought it a little album piece, and was keeping it in my bureau drawer, for my literary executors to find, after my death. But I must say that it looks extraordinarily pure and defined as compared to the over-stuffed effusions of Bernice Lesbia Kenyon ... and even old False Face Jeffers." When Roethke expressed worry over cribbing lines from Stanley Kunitz, Bogan told him she had been far guiltier in "Evening-Star," which echoed a chorus from T. S. Eliot's "The Rock" in what she called "a perfectly open way. The chorus about light. The word *praise* and the invocation, repeated invocation to light, are identical. If I put it in the book I'm going to have a note acknowledging the source. As long as you know what you're doing you can do anything." She evidently came to feel that her misdemeanor was perhaps no crime at all, for in the text of *The Sleeping Fury,* no note of attribution appears. As Ruth Limmer has pointed out, Eliot's "O Light Invisible, we praise Thee! ... we worship Thee! ... we glorify Thee!" was "neither the verbal nor the emotional equivalent of her own lines." It is rather in those lines of Eliot's coming just slightly later, and beginning with "In our rhythm of earthly life we tire of light ..." that Bogan may have found a starting-point for her third and fourth stanzas. Eliot speaks quietly and compassionately of human weariness, and Bogan captures a similar range of feeling in:

Light, pure and round, without heat or shadow,
Held in the cirrus sky, at evening:
Accompany what we do.

Be with us;
Know our partial strength.
Serve us in your own way,
Brief planet, shining without burning.

This afflicting, intimate, beneficent light flows from Venus, the goddess to whom Lucretius dedicates the opening invocation in *De Rerum Naturae,* parts of which Bogan had been reading and trying to render into English over the winter and spring of 1934–35. Venus also watches over Swift's tormented sleep in "Hypocrite Swift," and treads above the petty malice of men in "At a Party." The calm, eternal planetary order was becoming Bogan's cosmology, and, as the foundation of her poetic vision, replacing the human spirit at war with itself. In later editions of her work, Bogan placed "Spirit's Song" after "Putting to Sea," a poem in which she found herself weltering in a Symbolist tide, with very questionable results. As an attempt to put all the suffering based on Raymond Holden behind her, once and for all, it presents a departure from land toward new and unexplored seas. The scenic and pictorial details are derived from both Baudelaire and Bogan's earlier poems, but they fail to connect with some emerging and ordered experience they are meant to serve. They are also obscure; the text is littered with phrases that don't make sense, not even when the reader forbearingly grants them a Symbolist latitude of meaning. At one point the speaker hears of a land, a new region of "flamy blooms" that recalls, to a certain extent, the beauty and rust, and the dust and flame of both "A Tale" and "M., Singing," but it is difficult to know from the context whether it is a region of sterility or renewal. Rolfe Humphries, to whom Bogan sent the poem in preliminary form, pointed out the contradictions and vaguenesses, and Bogan herself had her own doubts. She was worried, she told him, that "the second-hand Baudelaire touch may vitiate the poem entirely," and that "the land" might sound "a little like something out of H. G. Wells or Aldous Huxley, and maybe should be changed a little not to sound too what-will-it-be-like-in-the-futurish, since all this is a symbol of something or other my uncs., as the later Freud puts it, hates." But she trusted the impulses that had brought the poem into being. "I know what it's about, with my upper reason, just a little; it came from pretty far down. Thank God," she remarked to Wheelock. Writing the final draft at The Willey House in Swampscott, where she could see and smell the ocean as she worked, she may have persuaded herself that the poem was more resolved than it actually was, or even that clarity didn't finally matter.

Whatever the failure of "Putting to Sea," the poem that follows it, "Kept" (placed after "Spirit's Song" in later collected editions), more than makes up for it. She sticks close to her taste for "the natural words in the natural order," and grafts the deepest insight onto the rhythm and speech of nursery rhyme, exploring what Rilke, in the fourth Duino elegy, called the "Zwischenraume Zwischen Welt und Spielzeug," or "the gap left between world and toy." This is not to say that the poem has a source in Rilke. It is far more likely that the poem (whose date of composition is unknown) may echo the nursery rhyme "London Bridge," which she would have come upon again in the Auden-Garrett anthology, *The Poet's Tongue,* a copy of which she obtained in the fall of 1935 and simply devoured, finding it "marvelous: alphabetically arranged . . . so that 'Casey Jones' comes right before 'Song for St. Cecilia's Day' practically, and it has nursery rhymes, and the wonderful nightmare song from *Iolanthe,* and God knows what else." The stanza in "London Bridge" which "Kept" might be thought to echo goes:

> Build it up with wood and clay,
> Dance o'er my Lady Lee,
> Build it up with wood and clay
> With a gay lady.

Although "Kept" keeps time to a slower beat, it begins with words and a stanza form similar to "London Bridge":

> Time for the wood, the clay,
> The trumpery dolls, the toys
> Now to be put away:
> We are not girls and boys.
>
> What are these rags we twist
> Our hearts upon, or clutch
> Hard in the sweating fist?
> They are not worth so much.
>
> But we must keep such things
> Till we at length begin
> To feel our nerves their strings,
> Their dust, our blood within.
>
> The dreadful painted bisque
> Becomes our very cheek.

A doll's heart, faint at risk,
Within our breast grows weak.

Our hand the doll's, our tongue.

Time for the pretty clay,
Time for the straw, the wood.
The playthings of the young
Get broken in the play,
Get broken, as they should.

The poem begins with the voice of the adult world, which calls for an end to make-believe. Intruding with commands that echo the very tick-tock of the clock, the poem's speaker uses the "we" of adult coercion—the nurse's or nanny's "we"—to enforce its inexorable rules. In the second stanza, however, that "we" begins to turn into the Rilkean universal pronoun which includes all mankind in the same community of the heart. This "we" tells us that we must become our pasts, become what we have loved (our mothers, fathers, brothers, lovers), understand that our child's need required them to be perfect, forever faithful and forever kind, and we must, before we let them go, become as indistinguishable from them as the speaker and lover are in "Poem in Prose." Magic, at its moment of fulfillment, becomes logic, as the process of identification culminates in a painful consciousness that the doll, the toy, the childish love object, is simply an outworn symbol of the past. We must experience the deadness that separates the living present from the past, just at the instant when the unity between them seems assured, when our dolls and ourselves are one. Thus, we have absorbed the doll into ourselves, and it remains a part of us forever, while we no longer need the actual object, now "not worth so much."

Curiously, Rilke had written a piece very similar in meaning, though not in form, his essay on dolls ("Puppen"). Since it appeared in an English translation only in 1954, it is unlikely that Bogan knew it, though she could certainly read German. In any case, it stands as a useful coincidental commentary on her poem, a confirmation of her belief in the process of identification and separation necessary to the ordeal of growing up. Clutched till it becomes a rag, eventually thrown into a corner with other broken and discarded toys, the doll, according to Rilke, has been

dragged about through the changing emotions of the day, remaining where they lie; made a confidant, a confederate, like a dog . . . initiated into the first, nameless experiences of their owners, lying about in their earliest uncanny loneliness, as in the midst of empty rooms, as if all they had to do was to exploit unfeelingly the new spaciousness with all their limbs—taken into cots, dragged into the heavy folds of illnesses, present in dreams, involved in the fatalities of nights of fever: such were these dolls. For they themselves never made any effort in all this; they lay there on the border of the children's sleep, filled, at most, with the rudimentary idea of falling down, allowing themselves *to be dreamed;* as it was their habit, during the day, to be lived unwearyingly with energies not their own.

But when we start to live the life we had allowed our doll to live for us, the doll is suddenly "the horrible foreign body on which we had wasted our purest ardour," whereas before it had been the instrument by which we "split our gradually enlarging personality into part and counterpart . . . through it to keep the world, which was entering into us on all sides, at a distance."

The crucial change comes, as it does in "Kept," when we finally separate ourselves from the doll, and *face* it:

It was facing the doll, as it stared at us, that we experienced for the first time . . . that emptiness of feeling, that heart-pause, in which we should perish did not the whole, gently persisting Nature then lift us across abysses like some lifeless thing. *Are we not strange creatures to let ourselves go and to be induced to place our earliest affections where they remain hopeless?*

With the dolls and toys broken "in the play," the poetry of *The Sleeping Fury* suggests another aspect of the changes Bogan had undergone. Yeats had all along provided her with a language for rage and indignation, for savage irony and bitter disappointment, emotions which no longer dominated her or provided her poetry with fuel. While she never let go of the vigorous common idiom she shared with him, she released herself from his influence, finding in Rilke the same infinite range of intuition and perception of which she had come into possession now that she was open to serenity. In "Heard by a Girl," "Spirit's Song," and "Packet of Letters," she puts the Yeatsian influence to rest, sharply commenting upon destructive eras in her life and putting each one firmly into the past (like worn-out dolls): the period of sensual excess in "Spirit's Song," of self-loving and self-deluding vanity in "Heard by a Girl," of murderous passion in "Packet of Letters," whose title refers to the Bogan-Holden correspondence of the spring and summer of 1933, as well as the letters following their separation in 1934.

With "Song for a Lyre" Bogan's freedom to write a Rilkean lyric makes its purest appearance. She managed to leave a complete record of this poem's genesis. Late in October 1935 she visited Edmund Wilson at Trees, his house in Stamford, Connecticut. For four days, she wrote to Roethke, she did nothing but sit in one spot on a couch in the living room, "and all the leaves in the world, or at least all those in Stamford, Connecticut, were falling outside the French windows. . . . They fell and fell, and a brook murmured, and I sat on, thinking, from time to time, 'What a hell of a lot of leaves!' but feeling exactly nothing." Later she wandered through "the really undistinguished countryside. (I like things big, in the countrysides I really love: big trees and hills and enormous vistas, embracing counties.)"

Then, three weeks later, at home in New York, what she had seen and felt was recollected in an exceedingly tranquil poem. To Wheelock she described it as "the only real love song I ever wrote in my life, perhaps. All my black side tried to stop it from coming, but it would come, and it came just the way it is: all of a piece. . . . I thought it would be perhaps touching to have it stand on the last page of the book, clearly and simply ringing out against (certainly) winter, and (maybe) silence."

"Song for a Lyre" does stand at the end of the book, as a pure song with a rich and complex texture. The poem's varied meter continually renews the freshness of its phrasing, as though the speaking voice had become music. The imagery seems to awaken to the soft sound of time itself passing, dispersing in leaves and the flowing stream. In the figure of the "pictured night"—the night seen in dreamlike trance— the lyric elements of "memory and desire" meet in a landscape belonging both to nature and to the inner world, and rise in a crescendo of reconciliation:

> Soon fly the leaves in throngs;
> O love, though once I lay
> Far from its sound, to weep,
> When night divides my sleep,
> When stars, the autumn stream,
> Stillness, divide my dream,
> Night to your voice belongs.

Body of This Death had ended with an act of defiant self-assertion, a Yeatsian proclamation of individual imaginative liberty, wherein the poet's freedom would be found "in the thunderous cloud" of transcendence and moral grandeur. *Dark Summer* had ended on a still-Yeatsian note of ambiguity, with the "stretched hawk" in the "wing-stiffened flight" of uncertain peace. With "Song for a Lyre," Bogan ends *The Sleeping Fury* on a note of serene acceptance, writing a poem fully in form, with a meaning fully matching her hard-won belief that "when one lets go, and *recognizes* the stream on which we move as the same stream which moves us within—that it is time and the earth floating our blood and flesh, floating its own child— and stops fighting against the kinship, the light flows in; peace arrives."

It remained to be seen whether this openness to the flow of existence would liberate or cut off Bogan's access to poetry. In the past, much of her poetry had been bred from conflict. But now, writing to Morton Zabel in December 1935, she remarked that she felt as if she had now achieved almost too much "normality," and

in becoming so full of calm and fortitude, that I have lost something: that I have been cured *too* much, that I have been subjected to a spiritual surgery too inclusive in its effects. I don't recommend to you, this calm I have reached. It may be spiritual death or spiritual narcosis, for all I know. I do know that I have forgotten *how* to hope romantically, to suffer through slights and pride.

The possibility, often said to be feared by people who are both creative and neurotic, that psychiatric treatment would cure their neurosis but in the process kill their creativity, may well have been, for Louise Bogan, uncannily close to the truth. With the publication of *The Sleeping Fury,* her most productive days as a poet were over. She did not immediately stop writing poetry, and the high standard of her work did not lapse, but her career as a critic began increasingly to feed on the energies that had hitherto gone into waiting for poems and nurturing them when they arrived.

Her psychic triumphs were real. "It is as though I had, after thirty years, really come into my whole being," she continued to Zabel, "as though I filled myself, down to the last cranny and interstice, at last." The world could not wound her or terrify her anymore:

I am more indurate than it is, now. The stuff I am made of can withstand objects and times of day and night and presage and change and Rockefeller City, and other people's grandeur, and the oppressor's wrong and the proud man's contumely. All can be met, and all slides off me, like water off a duck's back. Not that I am not frequently enraged. I nearly killed a woman in Macy's the other day, because she pushed me in the side; I spoke and I looked, and she fell back, with vituperations, as though I had scorched her all over. I can feel rage, but I am never humiliated, any more, and I am never lonely.

In *The Sleeping Fury* she had written her richest collection of poems, and she had recovered power and joy. But it was a joy of essentials rather than luxuries, and it was among the latter that she counted love. The only love she had ever known was the destructive kind; once freed from it, she believed that she would never again write poetry as abundantly and dramatically as she had in her youth.

8 THE WAY OF THE LAUREL

A CC O R D I N G to Malcolm Cowley, "Almost the only writers of standing who completely resisted the social impulse of the 1930's were a few professional cynics such as H. L. Mencken and a few gifted poets."

Among the latter he includes Robert Frost, Robinson Jeffers, and E. E. Cummings, but, unquestionably, Louise Bogan also belongs on the list. Although she was an acute observer of the disturbing changes in the world, noting as early as September 1932 what she called the triple developments of Hitlerism, economic *idées fixes,* and collective thinking, her resistance to the social movements of the period was impassioned. She was temperamentally incapable of looking upon any group effort without suspicion. Civilization, for her, was bound up with the purposes of individual imagination and liberty, and she smelled entrapment in the noblest causes, coercion in the appeal to "men of good will."

In his review of *The Sleeping Fury*—one of the most favorable and most discerning—Morton Zabel put Bogan in the company of Yeats and Rilke, and spoke of her lyricism as the antithesis of the "art of public and proletarian purposes," the fruit of strict self-accounting and formal rigor: "Here there is nothing to disguise, prop or confuse the thing said," he observed, "no front of 'beliefs,' no leaning on borrowed arguments or literary and political allusion, and none of that fretting preciosity which has become recent lyric fashion."

Bogan loved the review, especially for Zabel's striking out at the fashion for political engagement. She was unlikely to get support for her views from anyone else, and she knew, besides, that Zabel, who had grown up in the Church, understood intuitively that the roots of her political antipathy lay in her Catholic girlhood. She had never forgotten how at Mount St. Mary's in New Hampshire the nuns had saved the choicest bits of food for their yellow-haired favorites—the girls with "nice" parents and summer homes—and from that time she despised authority and preferment whenever she met it, whether in institutional setups or literary circles. She was nonpolitical to her core, suspicious of the getting, having, and using of power, and during the 1930s, when virtually everyone had some form of political allegiance, she actively refused to align herself politically. She despised socialism, finding it drab and unimaginative, hated communism, was contemptuous of any form of "Social Realism" in either art or literature, and thought those who believed that the world had been born anew in the Soviet Union were fools. This is not to say that she took a complacent view of what was going on in America. She hated with equal fervor the indignity and demoralization visible everywhere in the Depression, and about these she did not keep silent. Having no apparatus of beliefs, she did nevertheless have profound convictions about the value of culture and civilization, and realized that every humane Western tradition was being jeopardized by the international epidemic of hate. As early as 1933 she wrote to *The New Republic* to protest against Granville Hicks's review of her friend Dorothy Dudley (Harvey's) book on Theodore Dreiser, *Forgotten Frontiers: Dreiser and the Land of the Free.* Charging Hicks with a willful and malicious distortion of Miss Dudley's thesis that Dreiser was acutely modern in his perception of the dryness and despair in American society, Bogan set out to demonstrate that Dudley did not "lament the exclusion of the American writer from 'high society,' " as Hicks had alleged, but rather "the exclusion of everyone in the United States from life itself: from the purpose, color and vitality that is the birthright of persons born into a mature and civilized environment." The status of culture as a complete organism, rather than simply its political health, was Bogan's concern, and it seemed to her that the whole era was going mad with name-calling, or the mania of if-you're-not-one-thing-you're-another. Another intellectual fad which infuriated her was the repudiation of the 1920s for its supposedly art-for-art's-sake blindness to social and economic decadence. When Eda Lou Walton, an old friend from *The Measure* who had swung over to the Left and now wrote criticism for *The New Republic,* identified her with the twenties and called her "a dead leaf on a dead branch" (using one of the poetic clichés of the twenties, by the way), and when a young poet professing concern and friendship urged Bogan to remove herself from the "decaying stench" of Edna St. Vincent Millay, she was again furious at the malice, fickleness, and myopia of her contemporaries.

Rolfe Humphries's new political enthusiasms were especially grating. In February 1935, she complained to Zabel that Humphries was "experiencing a violent Marxist conversion, and that troubles and annoys me, and I am not so charitable as I should be. The reconciliation of the warring elements in my own nature was effected in such an unconscious and unknowable Jungian manner that I have become rather impatient with surrogates for religion, and life-lines and rocks of ages and snug harbors and other dogmatic frameworks."

Differences between Bogan and Humphries widened, and by the end of the year, their quarrel had wrought a fissure in their long-standing, affectionate friendship. One night she turned him away from the door, bored with his Marxist gloom and complacency. To her it seemed that he loved being under authority. "I hate authority," she wrote Roethke. "I hate being told what to do and feeling noble and religious about a cause." The whole point of her emotional difficulties had been to free herself from being the *thing* of others, and it infuriated her to watch Humphries worshipfully allowing himself to become a pawn of ideology. His faith in the imminence of a new world order based on Marxism struck her as naïve, and despite his protestations that he could serve both art and humanity, Bogan believed that he was being driven to serve the Communist party for the same neurotic reason that he was driven to submit to his strong-willed wife: namely, that he was a weak and insecure artist who could not take responsibility for his talent or his work.

In general, she viewed the ailments of civilization with a Freudian-Jungian eye. Since 1931 she had come to believe in the unconscious as the source of human achievement and destruction, a power that could wreak havoc if left unacknowledged or, worse, bullied by the superego, but one that was, when properly channeled and integrated, fundamentally on the side of life. It was not that Bogan simply reduced all cultural development to the unconscious; she acknowledged the complex interdependence of historical and economic forces. But intellectual responsibility, she believed, began with self-knowledge; and self-knowledge began with understanding and wrestling with the inner life. Privately she held Marxism to be incompatible with psychoanalytic insight, but in public she treated them as distinct, rather than necessarily opposing, intellectual systems. Her most considered exposition of this distinction can be seen in another letter she wrote to *The New Republic*, this time in April 1936, in response to Malcolm Cowley's review, a month earlier, of Stephen Spender's *The Destructive Element*. Spender had proposed a "change of heart," rather than a change of economic system and had further advocated, as Cowley pointed out, a reconciliation between Marx and Freud, the point at which, in Cowley's view, he went astray. Charging Spender with "an intuitive rather than a logical mind," Cowley argued that psychoanalysis as a social theory—something it often becomes—is fundamentally opposed to Marxism, and no poet or prose writer has ever succeeded in making a synthesis of the two. Auden, for example, is vaguely psychoanalytical at one moment and harshly revolutionary at another; in neither mood does he make himself quite convincing, in spite of his talent. Moreover, we are all of us getting tired of English critical essays that accurately describe the errors of the past and end with a flourish by pulling a white-haired Auden out of a black silk hat. He is a good poet, yes, he has something close to genius, but he is no more a guide to the future than he is a magician's rabbit.

Bogan could not let this pass unchallenged. Agreeing that the current Auden-worship was indeed getting to be a bore, she said that Spender's exegesis of Auden's ideas was nevertheless worth taking seriously. Spender and Auden were not calling for a *synthesis* of Marx and Freud for the simple reason that in their view (and in Bogan's own) the two systems of thought were not opposed, but offered two radically different views of society, as Spender himself had pointed out. Communism's emphasis on the will was quite different from psychoanalytic theory's distrust of the will. The will, Bogan explained, had not yet been analyzed in Marx's time, "and it would be a tragedy if Freud's great discoveries were allowed to be buried under, or disregarded with a sneer or a wave of the hand, in the economic struggle for a new world." Freud had discovered nothing less than the irrational itself, the concealed motives and layers of our being; insight, Bogan claimed, derived from knowledge of the irrational, was the greatest weapon any human being could use in the struggle to change himself so that he might be fit for a new world:

The revolution within should go on coincidentally with the fight against outer evils. For if the outer evils be conquered, and the inner conflicts persist, what then? A new world should have more in it than the production and consumption of commodities. What of the sympathy born of understanding oneself and others, humility before the things that are of us and yet beyond us, grace, humor and pathos? If we are to lift the material world to the level of the ideal, it would be just as well to clear up the ideal, and to know the human springs that feed it. So, when I come upon a Leftist poem that speaks of a nervous breakdown, not as a sign of struggling health, but as a sort of disgrace, or as a dreadful spiritual disease, comparable to a touch of leprosy, perhaps; and when I hear the young speak of Freud as though he were a horrid species of charlatan that the twenties (that dreadful decade!) went in for, as it might have gone in for a professor of palmistry; and when I see, now and again, pert references to the Soul (which, I suppose, we must understand to mean the region where the intellect fades off into man's need for something that transcends himself—the region from which primitive incantation, rhythm and human creativeness in general appear, and into which these things recede)—when these matters are brought to my notice, I shudder. Marx (or was it Engels) stated that he wished to turn Hegelian philosophy upside down. Well, whatever position the nutritious spiritual side of man's nature now occupies, it would be just as well to realize that it is still there. And that psychoanalytic theory has done, and will do, much to make it more accessible, and to disengage it from the fugginess of the merely philosophic ideal.

Cowley had little to say in reply, except to note the existence of a school in Germany, before 1933, of Freudo-Marxists, who had failed to come up with a satisfactory way of adapting society to the needs of the individual. The whole matter, he evasively hoped, would "lead to serious discussion."

For Bogan, such discussion was becoming habitual, and she found herself in constant embattled conversation. Even as she yearned for a life of privacy, the ferment in the New York literary world forced her to take up arms. On the whole, this was a fortunate thing. Just when she was finding certain later poems of Rilke's to have gone so much farther than any previous lyric poetry into the realms of looking and feeling, so that she declared to Zabel that "Yeats seems a spoiled child beside him," the Yeatsian mantle of obstinate outspokenness descended on her shoulders. From the middle of the decade her critical prose, letters, and a good deal of her poetry became rife with opinion and opposition.

Among the ideas popular on the Left, that which upheld the proletariat as both more noble and purer than the bourgeoisie particularly disgusted her. As far as she was concerned, she had no illusions about "the masses." "I came from them," she reminded Humphries, who thought her social ideas little short of depraved, "and I know what they're like." It wasn't that she had any love for the middle class; her view of it was no kinder than that of her Marxist friends. But she found the apotheosis of the proletariat naïve and sentimental, and the Marxist vilification of the bourgeoisie deadly in its solemnity and earnestness. What was needed, in her view, was humor—not hatred—something along the lines of Auden's satiric sharpness in the choruses to *The Dog Beneath the Skin: or, Where Is Francis?* Flaubertian ridicule could puncture bourgeois pride and pretension far better than Marxist preaching. As she wrote to Roethke:

—If only this sort of thing could supersede the disguised Presbyterianism of the Communist Party of America. What they want is a Holy War, and the time for Holy Wars is over. The Revolution should not be a Holy War. It should be a grim, earnest and high-spirited getting together and drawing-out-the-table-cloth-out-from-under-the-fancy-dinner-services-decorating-bourgeois-tables. More of a joke. More of a laugh on the God forsaken fools who thought usury on a large scale could go on, for any length of time. To hell with the sour mugs of Mike Gold and Granville Hicks! O darling, aren't there intelligent and sensitive people enough! I don't mean sops; you know what I mean. Like ourselves.

The answer, which she appended to the letter, was *No*. Her sense of isolation grew stronger the more she saw her ideals of disinterestedness and detachment betrayed. It wasn't just Humphries who had joined the "Comrades": Léonie Adams and Edna St. Vincent Millay were sympathizers with the Communist cause, and Wilson was spending the summer of 1935 traveling in Russia and gleefully reporting back to her skeptical self that the Russians were "celebrating the 74th anniversary of Chekhov's birth." Her own sneering and belittling of their political conversions might not have been as bitter had she not felt herself to be under attack. Not only had Eda Lou Walton and Marya Zaturenska relegated her to the obsolete twenties, but Genevieve Taggard, another friend from the days of *The Measure* who had ceded herself to the Left, included a poem, "I Sigh If She Were Dying," in her new book, *Not Mine to Finish,* that Bogan believed alluded to herself:

> If she were dying in wild leisurely fashion
> Enjoying death with the great bitterness of her nature
> I would be envious of her crowning and eloquent passion
> And write her a message saying, This is your face your
>
> Last accomplishment; make the most of it.
> She is still frittering and mocking and is still withheld
> From the larger matter of her better wit;
> And I who love her neither killed nor quelled,
>
> Think; we are odd women, the two of us. She is
> The wild nature I mirror but do not have; And I
> Am so the hater of waste that I hunger to kiss
> The horrible face of her life and the clothes of her grave.
> I sigh.

After reading Taggard's "opus," Bogan sat down and fired this off to Edmund Wilson:

> *Lines Written After Detecting in Myself a Yearning Toward the Large,*
> *Wise, Calm, Richly Resigned, Benignant Act Put On by a Great Many People*
> *After Having Passed the Age of Thirty-Five.*

> For every great soul who died in his house and his wisdom
> Several did otherwise.

God, keep me from the fat heart that looks vaingloriously
    toward peace and maturity;
Protect me not from lies.
In Thy infinite certitude, tenderness and mercy
Allow me to be sick and well,
So that I may never tread with swollen foot the calm
    and obscene intentions
That pave hell.
Shakespeare, Milton, Matthew Arnold died in their beds,
Dante above the stranger's stair.
They were not absolved from either the courage or the
    cowardice
With which they bore what they had to bear.
Swift died blind, deaf and mad;
Socrates died in his cell;
Baudelaire died in his drool;
Proving no rule.

As Ruth Limmer has noted, these lines were condensed to form the epigram, "To an Artist, to Take Heart," and published in *The New Yorker* in July 1937, and they stand as Bogan's pledge to fight her way through the thirties. She was unimpressed when Humphries assured her that post-revolutionary society would find a place for art, or when Wilson wrote that the fact that the Soviets were reading Pushkin and Chekhov meant that art had a secure place within a revolutionary society. The Revolution, in her view, should take no special credit for it, since it had nothing to do with it. Something constant in the human spirit required its due, though it was just this constant spiritual capacity toward which the Revolution made condescending and eroding gestures. "God keep me from a world," she wrote to Humphries in a burst of irritation, "in which there were no delicate sensibilities that could produce a remark like *Margaret, are you grieving;* or *An expense of spirit in a waste of shame;* that couldn't feel horror over mutability and an excess of joy over the facts of perfectly physical passion, or pity for the maladjusted or horror over the senseless cruel."

While Bogan and Humphries continued to argue with each other throughout the rest of the decade, they both knew that politics was an explosive subject for them, likely to arouse bitter feelings. With Bogan generally on the offensive and Humphries on the defensive, she frequently tempered her attacks with humor. Whatever their political differences, she never forgot that poetry was the basis of their friendship, praising him for having one of the few "true ears now operating in English" and thanking him for his "non-union" help on "Baroque Comment." She and Humphries had been friends for so long that they had precise knowledge of each other's psychic anatomy, and knew just where to hurt each other most. Humphries was aware that Bogan not only disliked his wife but believed that Dr. Spencer and Holden had had a secret affair, and Bogan knew that Dr. Spencer hated Humphries's incessant attendance at party meetings so much that she had issued an ultimatum that he would have to choose between party politics or life with her in their house in Belvidere, New Jersey. So she often rather cruelly baited Humphries for being uxorious; and during one quarrel Humphries, in turn, addressed her honesty with herself, and the problem of her mental instability: "If you know that I am not a nincompoop you also know that a lot of your communistic antipathies proceed from springs that have nothing to do with critical and aesthetic logic but from what might be termed a nice disorder of the private economy."

Like all family quarrels, those between Bogan and Humphries threatened to go too far and reach the point where lasting damage could take place. Eventually the two decided to conclude a "non-aggression pact on political argument," in September 1935. Although this did not last, it reduced their hostilities to border skirmishes rather than knock-down, drag-out war. She still needed his help in preparing the poems for *The Sleeping Fury* and found his technical assistance invaluable. "For Heaven's sake," she wrote sometime in 1935, as she was making headway with the new poems, "let me send the poems to you (and Edmund) as they come. You are better than Edmund, because you get down to brass tacks; he is good about general smells of influence."

One good result of their decision to call a truce was that Humphries turned his quarrel with Bogan into a poem. Called "Words in Your Mouth (Or, Address presumed to be delivered by a centripetal friend)," it was written and sent to Bogan in the spring of 1936. A Yeatsian "mask" lyric, the poem makes Bogan herself its voice:

> So, I have all I need
> Excepting money and love;
> What am I fashioned of
> To pay these any heed?
>
> Unprofitable heart
> And unreplenished purse
> Impoverish no part
> Of one who lives by verse.
>
> Who, safe abed, need never
> Say to the Self, *Move over!*

Nor hear the shared remark
Postpone eventual dark.

Whom, covetous, not itch
Nor dispossession drives
To traffic with the lives
Of those who bait the rich.

O irreducible,
Impregnable, aloof,
What matter whether spell
Precede or follow proof?

Sure, in my own belief,
Past gratitude and grief,
I come to final terms
Only with Time and worms.

L'Envoi
Hence, vain centrifugal fool!
No more approach my state,
Permit me leave to hate
You and the mucker school.

Humphries was in effect accusing Bogan of all the hermetic self-protectiveness she claimed to have given up in her miraculous cure, and cruelly drawing attention to her unmarried and unloved state as well. Yet the poem was in its way more admiring than it may have started out to be. Bogan's response was rather mild. "I don't think it was really written 'to' or 'about' me, the way Jed's [Genevieve Taggard's] masterpiece was," she wrote. "I shouldn't be surprised if in it you were excoriating a piece (projected) of yourself. I think that's the way you and I work." Moreover, no matter how closed to the world he may have thought her to be, since the beginning of the year she had felt her "spiritual side becoming at once more firm and more porous, every day."

As the eventual fate of Humphries's "Words" shows, Bogan's reaction to it was clairvoyant. When he published it in 1942 in *Out of the Jewel* (a volume he dedicated to Bogan, taking her statement that "A minor art needs to be hard, condensed, and durable" as epigraph), he inserted it in Section IV of the book, just after a series of poems written during his involvement with the League of American Writers. "Words in Your Mouth" is in turn followed by the painful lyric "With a Resignation, Untendered," in which Humphries confesses the yearning "to develop the terrible strength I need, / And have not yet known," the longing for the courage to endure solitude and separateness from party. His widow, the late Dr. Spencer, later recalled that by 1940, Humphries had become deeply disappointed in the Communist party, and had gradually withdrawn from it back into poetry.

DESPITE BOGAN'S FEISTY OPPOSITION to leftward literary activities, she was often depressed rather than angered by the cultural situation, particularly by the fate of her contemporaries. At one point in 1936, she wrote to Humphries that she was in the dumps and couldn't seem to get started on a *New Yorker* piece:

I sit down and write, and it sounds like lead or cotton-wool. And I think of the terrible end that overcame everybody of our generation—I saw Cummings the other day and he looked like an old, thin cross-eyed lapdog—and I think "Well, Josephine Herbst keeps turning them out, and so does Evelyn Scott," and then I think of all the boys who worked in steel mills and now are writing like C. Day Lewis, and I think of Dos Passos, who now thinks himself top-dog, it would seem, and I think of Eda Lou Walton, who says that everyone before the present bunch of boys chirped like sparrows, and I think of New Verse, which has now descended to cheap personal witticisms, on the critical side—they call E. Sitwell a fat old woman and speak of "that bird that won the King's Medal" (this is the imitation tough guy touch, I suppose, learned from Hemingway and Faulkner, two birds they are ashamed not to resemble) and I think of too many things, and too many stupid people, and then I wish that I had learned to be a good dressmaker, in my youth, so that I would need to have none of it. But I *must* be able to write something! I always have been able to, in any circumstance, before this.

She was too proud and too reticent to share her private difficulties with the world, but they oppressed her, again, in 1936, when her mother's last illness brought her up against the indignity of poverty. Having little money, she was unable to provide her mother with private care, and she was outraged, as she wrote to Humphries, at the "lousy system that keeps the poor, indigent old from dying as they should." At the same time she attacked the delusion that such suffering could be lessened by a world reborn into collective bliss:

What we suffer, what we endure, what we muff, what we kill, what we miss, what we are guilty of, is done by us, as individuals, in private. . . . I still hate your way of doing things. To hell with the crowd. To hell with the meetings, and the public speeches. Life and death occur, as they must, but they are all bound up with love and hatred, in the individual bosom, and it is a sin and a shame to try to organize or dictate them.

The artist, she believed, must either face the conflicts within himself or give up claiming that he was an artist. Others could try to change the world, but the artist's business was with his own inner microcosm. In Italy she had seen the Fascist threat; in Salzburg, the Nazi: she knew that there was a depression going on. Still, she was convinced that organization meant dictatorship, and while that might be useful for those whose purposes were exclusively social, for the artist it could mean only creative death.

As hard as she was on others, she was even harder on herself. Writing poetry was more difficult than ever. At some point during the summer of 1936 she wrote:

> You labor long to fit the pearl
> Woman, within your learned art,
> That long ago an ignorant girl,
> Weeping, found in her heart.

Curiously, reviews of *The Sleeping Fury*, with the exception of Morton Zabel, who spoke of the book's maturity as hard-won, saw only the serenity it had attained, rather than the struggle to attain it. To Kenneth Rexroth it seemed that the old conflict in Bogan's poetry between the flesh and the spirit had dissolved, leaving nothing but an almost too pure "wisdom" in its place. Allen Tate praised "The Sleeping Fury" as a "philosophical and divinatory" poem, rather than an embodied emotion, and commended Bogan for being "a craftsman in the masculine mode," that is, for effacing her personality and following an Elizabethan lyric technique. Even Ford Madox Ford, in his impressionistic review in *Poetry*, was drawn to the book's formal perfection rather than to its variegated emotions, and cited "passages of thought as static and as tranquil as a solitary candle-shaped flame of the black yew tree that you see against Italian heavens."

She had labored so long and so hard, in fact, that long before the reviews came in, Bogan anticipated a let-down and wisely planned a change of scene. She had spent much of 1936 battling Raymond Holden for her weekly payments. She had moved twice, published a book, and lost her mother. Now it was Ireland, the country of her heritage, that she wanted to see, and she applied for and was regranted the sum remaining from her 1933 Guggenheim Fellowship, cut short when the dollar fell.

Sailing in early April on the S.S. *Washington*, Louise was no sooner out of port than she was afflicted with certain "ideas of reference," which plagued her throughout the trip. As she later reported to Morton Zabel, "Two old battleaxes (female) who had heard me read at the Brooklyn Inst. last winter, and had, evidently, picked up the John Coffey scandal . . . were on the boat going over. They spread the rumor that I was a thief, and I had to endure untold jabberings from the yahoos, for six days." Although she prudently refrained from saying anything about her suspicions in her letters to Maidie, she firmly believed, as she later wrote to Zabel, that during her travels in both Ireland and England, and again on the boat home to New York, she was under constant police surveillance for being the accomplice of a known criminal.

As far as I have been able to discover, there was no basis in fact for her fears. She was never arrested or questioned during this episode (or at any other time) for her association with Coffey. She had always presumed that she had enemies or, at least, ill-wishers in the literary world, and although it is possible that the two women who had heard her read had also caught wind of the Coffey affair (which had happened nearly twenty years before), it is equally possible and highly likely that Louise fabricated the entire situation. In the meanwhile, she traveled in agonizing fear, although she fought hard to stay calm and absorb as much as possible. But everywhere she went—and from mid-April through mid-May she managed to see Cobh, Cork, Dublin, Belfast, Londonderry, Galway, Limerick, Mallow, Killarney, and Cork once again before returning to Dublin—she was tortured by the feeling that she was being watched.

At first, despite her fears, she embraced all she saw. "Ireland is even more beautiful than I thought it could be," she wrote Maidie; "all sorts of racial memories came to life in me as soon as I set foot on shore, and I felt at home immediately." She loved the quayside houses in Cobh, and the "bow-windows, chimney pots and cool, gray stone" of Cork. Describing her journey to Dublin she wrote:

I rode in a *jaunting car* to the station, and the driver made me sit back "so's you'll *look* more comfortable," said he. Then into a sad-looking first-class carriage and the long journey up through the lovely misty spring air. Yes: it is just what everyone says, and more. There *are* ruins on the top of hills, and in pastures, and all over (not *too* many: just enough!). The old walls are lovely, with dandelions and English daisies growing out of them, and there are *jonquils* growing wild in the fields, and yellow gorse, and all kinds of flowering trees (rather small). The people *do* talk literature: the boy who carried my bags in Cobh told me a story about a woman on the *Britannic* whose dog went into 6 months quarantine, fit to break your heart. "And there she was, screamin' and yellin' and jabberin'," said he. Yes, it's all true. They're courteous, and they talk literature. . . .

Dublin is far less close and grubby than I thought it would be. It looks like a cross between Portland and Boston, only nicer than either. . . . The one park (St. Stephen's Green) I've seen, looked like a dream: I never saw a *misty* park in a city before. I bought a map, and the woman in the little shop tried to sell me about eight other things, acting like a Jewish lady and a duchess combined. The maid who brought up my dinner acts like a duchess. They all have great pride and look you right in the eye, and don't kow-tow in the least. I'm proud to have this city's blood in me, I must say. Now I know where my straight back and my chin-in-the-air come from.

Her tone changed over the next few days, as her open-hearted curiosity turned to horror. Suddenly Dublin terrified her. She had never seen such ugly people, with faces that looked full of *conspiracy*. She was soon writing Maidie that "the Irish are seldom really beautiful. The Dublin types are the oddest in the world: rather frightening, in fact. Everyone in Dublin talks like a conspirator: they had to for so long, during the 'troubles,' I suppose. Frankly, they scare me to death." She saw a woman in Dublin, she wrote to Zabel, "so ugly that it was painful. But her face never moved. The complete mask: it might have been stone. And because it never moved it was almost beautiful. —No wonder Yeats celebrated the mask, after living in Dublin. They all live under, behind one." It was a city of fanatics, she thought, remembering what Yeats had said of it, a town breeding great courage and great literature, but frightening in its blindness. "There's a great exhibition and collection in the National Museum, of objects connected with the Easter Week Rebellion (1916)," she reported to Maidie. "It's terrific. The last letters, written the night before they were executed by the English, of all the leaders. Uniforms. Guns. Death masks, including one of Terence MacSwiney, Lord Mayor of Cork, who starved himself to death for 80 days, when the English imprisoned him. —Scared: I was petrified. For you feel the same sort of thing still going on, underneath. A lot of people are still 'agin the government' and it's enough to give one the creeps."

Surveying the terrifying faces of the Dubliners, she remembered the woman evoked in Yeats's "Quarrel in Old Age" ("What fanatics invent / In this blind bitter town, / Fantasy or incident / Not worth thinking of, / Put her in a rage"), forgetting that she had sent the poem's second stanza to Zabel the day after her mother died, and utterly ignoring the fact that she was making a solitary and sentimental journey through a country she had not only visited often in imagination but had identified from her earliest years with all that was both best and worst in the mother whom she was still acutely mourning. It never occurred to her that those conspiratorial faces in Dublin were her own projections, ghosts from the past, in which her mother's hideously ugly women friends, her "familiars," acted as go-betweens at Bodwell's, literally *whispering together* with her mother in the service of her clandestine adventures. Only in the last year had her emotional subjection to her mother finally loosened, and so, when her mother died, a terrible psychic irony was brought into play. For the mourning process required the revival of all those memories that had only just been allayed, after years of interference in Bogan's adult life. Under the circumstances, her journey to Ireland—to the motherland—could not have been more ill-timed. Though she bravely noted effects of light and details of landscape and architecture, conscientiously describing meals, trains, buses, and hotel rooms in her letters home, the heart soon went out of her travels. When the jitters and terrors became unbearable, she decided to go home to America as fast as possible. She was not experiencing, as she later told Morton Zabel, "the old 'psychic pains': the contraction in the breast that once drove me mad; the frightful half-physical 'suffering,'" but something else; a panic had so overwhelmed her that she feared for her sanity. In London, when she arrived to take the boat-train to Southampton, it became so great that

I *did* get down on my knees, in the Carlton Mansions, in Bedford Place, W.C. 1, and I *did* ask the Author of the Universe *please,* if the disaster was going to happen, to make it happen right away: a week of Gethsemane is bad enough: a month is perhaps equal to three or four *Viae Crucis.* "Go ahead!" said I, "break me to pieces; but please God, wait for the final blow until I get back to America! Don't let me go mad in a country where the streets are damp, the population either silly or degraded, the streets draped in bunting for the Coronation. Let me go back to the high, clear, mild skies of my own land, to the "sad, lonely, melancholy American beauty." And there must be a God, Morton, for on the Southampton boat-train, there appeared a tall thin man who proceeded to take care of me like a baby. (No, Morton: it's not another of those things. This was probably, is,—the Angel Gabriel in disguise!). . . . He says *Nuttin* when he means *Nothing;* his parents came from Sligo.—He took care of me like a baby, day after day, while the continued exterior rumors and my own obsessions rumbled and grew. I told him the whole story the second day out, and he nursed me along even more tenderly, thereafter. He laughed me out of it; he tricked me into deck-chairs; he brought me lots of rye, when the panic became too bad. But for that touch of human understanding, I should certainly have started gibbering.

Once she landed on American shores, Louise realized that she had been going through a "mild nervous exhaustion—a sort of psychic infection . . . brought on by prolonged strain." She saw Dr. Wall, who advised a week of complete rest that did in fact manage to soothe and calm her. There was, however, a surprising piece of news to greet her on her return: her divorce from Raymond Holden had become final on May 4th, and on May 8th he had married Sara Henderson Hay. "So you will get some more sonnets, I suppose, soon!" she quipped to Zabel, who, as editor of *Poetry,* was likely to be the first recipient of Holden's latest efforts.

Louise soon regained her customary detachment, and looked back over her Irish ordeal, and the memories of John Coffey it had spawned, with a good measure of compassion toward herself. To Morton Zabel, who lacked the gift of psychological insight and could offer no explanation for what had happened apart from Louise's belonging to the "lost generation" of the twenties, she replied:

But Morton, I never was a member of a "lost generation." I was the highly-charged and neurotically inclined product of an extraordinary childhood and an unfortunate early marriage, into which last state I had rushed to escape the first. And if, at twenty-two, I fell in love, for three months with a boy (of twenty-six) with a criminal record and a Messianic, paranoid set of delusions, I did it quite on my own: I had no relations whatever with the world about me; I lived in a dream, populated by figures out of Maeterlinck and Pater and Arthur Symons and Compton Mackenzie ("Sinister Street" and "Sylvia Scarlett" made a great impression on me) and H. G. Wells and Francis Thompson and Alice Meynell and Swinburne and John Masefield and other oddly assorted authors. What I did and what I felt was, I assure you, *sui generis.* For three months I was in love and believed in what J.C. was doing. From October to December, when he gave himself up to the law. Thereafter, in my terrible suffering, after I had done all I could to help him (including raising $1,000 bail!), I found him out. He had betrayed me again and again and used me shamelessly. So I worked (in Brentano's) and suffered, and dropped him. There are limits to what one can bear, even at twenty-two.

I made one mistake: I have permitted myself to accept the impingement (what a word!) of bourgeois society; I have kept my head up, and I have done a little work. Were I in the ditch, clutching a bottle of gin in one hand, and five bastard children in the other, everything would be splendid. Retribution, indeed! If retribution is dealt out, by God's hand, for sins against the existing order which we commit *out of the warmth of our hearts,* then I agree with the mad priest in Shaw, who decided that the world is Hell, and that we are here to atone!

She had determined, after recovering from her breakdowns, never again to suffer for love, and declared in the 1934 notebook that "There can be no new love at 37, in a woman." And she was now almost forty. But she soon found herself in a love affair with the man who had come to her rescue on the Southampton boat-train—a love affair that was to last for the next eight years, and that she was to call "successful." It took a few months to establish itself. In the middle of July, out of an absurd impulse of self-abnegation, she decided to break the affair off, and wrote him a postcard announcing her decision, and he called up, she wrote Roethke, "yelling 'What in hell *is* this!' and we finally decided to take it easy, and keep it on a casual basis. O, why didn't I know about the trades, years ago? I wasted a lot of time on the professions."

The arrangement between Louise and her lover was private. Her friends did not meet him, and her daughter, now living on her own, rarely spent time with them. Occasionally Louise mentioned him. He was an electrician who lived north of Dyckman Street in Inwood, a section of upper Manhattan near the Bronx, and at the time a heavily Irish neighborhood, and while she never said so, those few people who knew about him presumed that he was unmarried. He wired Louise's lamps and wore an old straw hat when he fixed his car; he took her sailing on his boat, and she liked to cook for him. He amused her and made her laugh, and Louise fell in love.

Finding a place to live, which had plagued her for so many nomadic years, was the next problem to be solved. On June 22nd, she wrote Maidie ("Muvver's ittle *cantatrice*") that she had found an apartment, and "with a minimum of street-pounding!" For forty dollars a month she was now to inhabit two rooms at 709 West 169th Street, "with glass doors between, a kitchenette, a frigidaire, and a bath! One window holds a view (very small) of the river and the back terrace of the Psychiatric Institute. The rooms are rather dull in shape, but *I'll* fix them, never fear." She signed the lease, moved right in, and determined never to wander again. It was "the first apartment I ever had all to myself, and I feel like a newly-wed," she reported to Maidie. When she moved to another, larger apartment in the same building in October 1938, she had finally found the home where she would live for the rest of her life.

Situated between Fort Washington Avenue and Haven Avenue, 709 West 169th Street is an unimposing brick building at the end of the street, the entrance set well back in a narrow courtyard. On 168th Street stands The Neurological Institute, from which Bogan had looked out, during the three weeks she spent there in the spring of 1931, "from the windows of hydrotherapy, over what must have been the very roof under which I now live," and now remembered "seeing a woman hanging out clothes, and wishing that I, too, could be a normal resident of Washington Heights, and hang out clothes in a happy, normal way." The second and final apartment in the building was more spacious than the first, and had, in addition to an entrance area, bedroom, and kitchen, a "middle room" with a large table where Bogan worked and kept her piano. There was also a living room, with books and shelves and bibelots arranged in scrupulous order. With its narrow view of the Hudson, where she could watch the sun fading every day and see boats and barges moving on the waters, the apartment was a place of freedom and solitude, near succor, or at least its symbol, in the form of the hospital, and near both nature and art in the form of the Fort Tryon Park gardens and the Cloisters, which she visited often in spring and fall. With little or no fear of isolation, Louise more than ever felt like working on her memoirs, which she began to think of along the lines of Rilke's *Journal of My Other Self* (*The Notebooks of Malte Laurids Brigge*), a work of intense yet detached interior observation that she had lately been recommending to Roethke and Léonie Adams. What she planned to do, she wrote Zabel, was to write "just anything that happens to come into the mind, and no snobbery about ancestral castles, either."

On August 11, 1937, Louise turned forty. Poised, in control of her destiny (or so it seemed), even blessed with some contentment and joy, she was nevertheless unprepared to run into Raymond Holden in Macy's during the last week in August, and passed him without a word. On August 25th, when he sent her weekly alimony check of forty dollars, he enclosed a note saying, "I see we no longer have a speaking acquaintance. Are you just being 'interesting' or what?" She made flippant mention of the incident in a letter to Maidie, but many years later confessed to a friend that she had gone home and broken down in sobs. Although Louise was to fight Raymond again, through her lawyer, for the alimony which he from time to time unsuccessfully pleaded with her to reduce, and although she praised his next book of poems, *Natural History,* noting in *The New Yorker* that it bore the mark "of the craftsman but not of the mere polisher of words," she never saw him again; and apart from keeping his last name in private life, so that the word *Holden* lay next to the buzzer at the entrance to her apartment building, he disappeared from her life.

By all accounts Raymond Holden's later life was both peaceful and fruitful. He divorced his third wife, married again, wrote and published poetry, became a successful author of nature and scientific books for the young, served in the New Hampshire legislature, worked for the Book-of-the-Month Club, and was active in conservation and library affairs. He passed his last years in Newport, New Hampshire, and died of leukemia in June 1972. His widow, Mrs. Barbara Holden Yeomans, to whom he was married for twenty-three happy years, remembers him as "an almost completely mature person, and the easiest person in the world to live with—unselfish, thoughtful, remarkably even-tempered and unruffled, basically calmly philosophical." Those closest to Louise believed that she never stopped loving him.

THE FALL of 1937 was the freest Louise had ever known. She had her own apartment, plenty of privacy, a lover, friends, and a mind now fully ripened and independent. Maidie was studying at Juilliard and living on her own; during the summers of 1937 and 1938 she was a member of the Chautauqua Opera Company chorus in Lake Chautauqua, New York. No longer needing Edmund Wilson's or anyone else's approval, Louise and her former mentor now entered a period—brief as these things go—of mutual irritation. Though each had occasionally considered the other somewhat *trying,* their disagreements had never been as eruptive as they were at present. "He is getting pretty pontifical," Bogan complained to Zabel, "and I could never work on any of his theories. He'd just say, 'O, you're ignorant!' " Up until then, Wilson knew, saying as much would have hurt her to the quick. He was well aware of her sensitivity about her lack of formal education, as well as her tendency to be impressed by a show of great learning. But now that she had a firm sense of her own worth, she was no longer so easily squelched. It was better, perhaps, "to be an ignorant one with insight than a wise, obtuse-to-delicate-veins-of-value one," she remarked to Zabel. Since the early days of their friendship Wilson had guided much of Bogan's reading, encouraging her to explore various byways of curiosity and interest while he looked approvingly on, and it irked him, she thought, to find her "out of the open-mouthed pupil stage." He had learned a good deal from *her,* she knew, over the years, "as words of mine incorporated into his works tell me," but they had reached the point, whenever they met or talked on the telephone, when they squabbled, and in Bogan's opinion "that's at least a stopping place, if not an end, in either love or friendship."

Wilson, on his side, was finding Bogan unusually hard to take. In November, she visited him for a weekend in Stamford and wrote about it to Roethke, unaware that Wilson too was writing, while she was actually there, to Morton Zabel, in rhymed and very wicked couplets. Mr. and Mrs. John Dos Passos were present, and Bogan hated them both: "He is such a Harvard fake. Bunny loves him," she wrote to Roethke. But Wilson, who had not liked "Putting to Sea," informed her, as he recounted to Zabel, that

> . . . her poetry does not make sense—
> Which arouses a fury of fraud and pretense.

Furthermore, he said, she couldn't stand his

> . . . pet Russian disks
> Wherein the most volatile melody frisks,
> But *would* play the radio—things by Sibelius
> Which I sharply declared to be Finland's worst failures.

When she took it upon herself to proclaim that his friends, including the Dos Passoses, were spies, he reported to Zabel, again without her knowledge:

> Then I read rather stutteringly extracts from Dante,
> While the flaming old Fury drank like a Bacchante.

Luckily, Bogan never learned about this letter, and their minor scrappings rumbled on without catastrophe. Wilson disliked Auden's *Letters from Ireland*; Bogan did not. Wilson remained patronizing toward her criticism, remarking about a piece she had written on Max Eastman, "When you really say something, your reviews are excellent—and you seem to be getting over your inhibitions about saying things," to which she replied, breezily, "I thought I had been saying a few things, now and again, for some years—I certainly have been blowing down stuffed owls like A. MacLeish, for example." Then, relenting a little, she added, more graciously, "But perhaps I am beginning to take more in, and, as you say, give it out better. I hope so." She continued to value his opinion more highly than anyone else's, and was anxious to show him her *Partisan Review* piece, "The Poetry of Paul Eluard," in the fall of 1939—one of the most lucid, packed, and subtle analyses of a poet in his time that she ever wrote. Yet it was as a critic of poetry that she believed Wilson was most deficient. He knew, she wrote Zabel, everything about poetry "but the *essential* thing":

I have often taken Bunny up on his meanness to people like Thibaudet, who, as you know, does the exact thing which Bunny cannot do. —And I chaffed him for writing that Taggard review, just recently. "But I still think she *writes well*," said he. That a woman should write at all, etc. But I have heard Bunny read poetry aloud by the hour, and he has even written some moving stanzas. —Don't ask me to explain what he lacks, or why (although I know, as you know). Thank God, he never reviewed me, that's all I can say.

She knew, too, that despite his quibbles and his occasionally condescending approvals, he deeply respected her critical intelligence and believed in her poetic talent. Her piece on *The Princess Casamassima* in *The Nation*, April 1938, he told her, would probably remain the definitive essay on the book, and he wanted her to keep writing poetry, going so far as to think up poetic subjects for her, preferably ones on which she could exercise her wit. Early in 1941, after an evening spent watching a magician perform tricks, he urged her to write a poem on magic, a subject he thought had great possibilities, and get it published right away in *The New Republic*. She began to turn the poem over in her mind and to work on a few lines, and even wrote a first draft, but she came down with a cold and could not finish it. Wilson kept on prodding her, sending her bits of lore about magic in recent times and a catalogue of magic tricks. Then, just as she was about to go back to work on the poem, Maidie came down with a strep throat, and the poem had to be postponed until the end of the month and possibly even longer. She wrote to Wilson that she was not being merely " 'fastidious' " about the poem, but that he knew, "as few others do, that I am a housewife, as well as a writer; I have no one to sweep floors or get meals, or get out the laundry, or, in the case of sickness, make egg-nogs and squeeze orange juice. All these tasks are very good for me, but they are tasks I never can allow to slip; and in the crisis of illness, I have no free time." She did not mean to reproach Wilson directly, but no doubt could not help remembering the countless times he had written from his house in the country, where, though not a rich man, he was free to read and write because a cook or a wife was making his meals and tending the house. On other occasions she was less indirect and charged him with hidden pockets of middle-classness, including the very serious problem, in her mind, of a defective Sense of Awe. In some way she intuited but could never quite define to her own satisfaction, and despite her great affection for him, she thought Wilson spiritually incomplete.

But it was not simply from Wilson that Bogan became detached in the summer of 1937; it was from her fellow critics as well, who now came in for a good deal of private denunciation. She was particularly suspicious of Marya Zaturenska, who habitually made minute distinctions between the twenties and the thirties, a practice Bogan deplored. "Hasn't anyone ever read any history, for God's sake?" she wrote to Zabel. "I will admit, that even modernly inclined and well-informed Thibaudet, speaks of 'the generation of 1789,' and 'the generation of 1820,' but he thinks in thirty year periods, at least. This silly speeding up of the decades, among New York intellectuals, makes me sick. Of course, very few people of 'the 20s' had the guts to mature, live, fight, or be, over into the 30s. Just mayflies."

Since 1936, Bogan had been assiduously reading French literary and cultural history, and had become persuaded that literary modernism in all its manifestations could be traced from the social, spiritual, and aesthetic crises of the Second Empire. She too adopted the French critic Albert Thibaudet's method of analyzing cultural and literary developments according to broad generational groups. Thus informed and anchored in an historical as well as contemporary outlook, she found herself, as the thirties drew to a close, in ever-intensifying opposition to the current literary-political situation. Eager to sever her ties with *The New Republic,* whose Stalinist line infuriated her, she happily accepted the poet and then contributing-editor Ben Belitt's invitation, in August 1937, to become a contributor to *The Nation*, immediately sending him this reproach to the literary Left:

NEW MOON

Cruel time-servers, here is the crescent moon,
Curved right to left in the sky, facing planets attendant.

Over the houses, leaned in the silent air,
Purest along the edge of darkness infinite.

Under it, men return from the office and factory,
From the little store at the corner of Eighty-eighth Street.

On the gnawed snow, or under the breezes of autumn,
With hope and fear in their hearts, and their arms full of groceries.

Above the trim suit, above the flesh starved or satiate,
Above the set hair, above the machines in the beauty-shops;

Above the young men, thinking the popular song;
Above the children, who now in the dusk go wild.

Crescent, horn, cusp, above the clinics, the lodgings,
Sweet curve, sweet light, new thin moon, now purely at ease,
Above the old, going home to their deafness, their madness,
Their cancer, age, ugliness, pain, diabetes.

On the whole, her actual outbursts of public indignation were few. Among all the "time-servers," the man she singled out for greatest scorn was Archibald MacLeish. Morton Zabel and Edmund Wilson shared her sentiments; among the three, the speechifying poet was privately dubbed "MacSlush." It was not his poetry which irritated her, quick though she was to detect its frequent echoes of Pound and Eliot, but his oratory, his readiness to defend social causes at the expense of the very artistic standards he had until very recently championed. Goaded by Bogan, in the winter and spring of 1941, Morton Zabel published a two-part attack on MacLeish in *Partisan Review*. It was called "The Poet on Capitol Hill," and was occasioned by MacLeish's appointment as Librarian of Congress and the publication of his *America Was Promises*. In it, Zabel charged MacLeish with failure to question the causes of fascism, and with sanctimoniousness, and reprehensible egotism in his pose as a contemporary Milton, Renaissance man, and literary-political-social jack-of-all-trades. In his second installment, Zabel again attacked MacLeish's literary pretensions, noting his failure to grow beyond imitations of Eliot and Pound, and concluding that his terror of the solitude necessary for artistic growth was the motive behind his humanitarian crusades.

Zabel was merely venting in public what he and Bogan had been saying privately for years. She had become especially indignant over a speech of MacLeish's called "In Challenge, Not Defense," which she read on July 8, 1938, and angrily attacked in a letter to Rolfe Humphries, who was at the time still deeply committed to the Left. MacLeish's speech was composed in the then-fashionable tough-guy style and was aimed at people who believed that poetry served ends of its own:

Those who tell us poetry is a parlor game and has no truck with the living of live men or the misery of hungry men or the indignation of believing men. Those who tell us the eternal poetry is the poetry written about the feeling of being dreadfully alone. Those with High Standards. (The impotent have the High Standards: the begetters beget.) Those with the Love of Posterity. (Posterity is the offspring of the childless.) Those who escape into mirrors—into the gentleman-farms and the upstairs rooms with the view of the river and the seminars at five P.M. The loudmouthed disrespectful challenge to all such to come out of their words and their paragraphs into the open air of the art and say their say in the sun with the wind blowing. The loud-mouthed disrespectful challenge to look at the actual world and say what poetry is native to the actual world: to read the poetry of Dante and say what poetry is native to the actual world; to read the poetry of Shakespeare and say what poetry is native to the actual world; to lay their High Standards down alongside the poetry of Dante and Shakespeare and see how small an inch their yardstick measures in the actual world.

Bogan thought this "the most awful tripe I ever read in my life," sophomoric and insulting, not only to her standards but even possibly to herself, who happened to live " 'in rooms upstairs with a view of the river.' (Is that me: and if so, how did he get it?)" She had only one way to oppose MacLeish, Humphries, the Communist party, and the murderous hate-jargon of the day, and that was to make a statement of her own: "I STILL THINK THAT POETRY HAS SOMETHING TO DO WITH THE IMAGINATION: I STILL THINK IT OUGHT TO BE WELL-WRITTEN. I STILL THINK IT IS PRIVATE FEELING, NOT PUBLIC SPEECH," she wrote to Humphries.

In public, she leveled her own potent charges of sarcasm and irony at her target. Reviewing *America Was Promises* late in 1939 in *The New Yorker,* she wrote:

Last year Archibald MacLeish resorted to scaring people, over the radio, with airraid noises and human screams in order to waken the population to "Fascist" dangers. Now he has published a small book of twenty pages with a similar end in view.

After noting the poetry's resemblance to "the now public poet's early 'private' writing," she observed:

The difficulty is that he is writing political poetry, even a kind of official poetry, and therefore the strict checks and disciplines of poetry written for itself (as a result of reality making a direct emotional impact upon the temperament of a trained and exacting writer) do not hold.

She then went on to say, "Bury his gifts though he may, Mr. MacLeish is a private, a lyric poet through and through; it is somewhat of a loss that he did not allow himself to remain one."

MacLeish was not the only contemporary she singled out for betraying the ideals of pure, apolitical art. Malcolm Cowley, Horace Gregory, and Granville Hicks all struck her as prepared and even willing to stifle themselves creatively for the sake of cause-mongering. The nastier, gossipy side of her enmity went into her letters, while more restrained and balanced judgments found their way into her reviews. She spared no one, however, if she thought them subservient to literary fashion. Writing of the young Muriel Rukeyser, whose poetry expressed her interest in social ills, Bogan remarked:

She is earnest, and she has language. After a single reading of her new book, *A Turning Wind,* one is uncertain what ingredients of life and poetry are lacking. After one has reread it, the suspicion arises that Miss Rukeyser is deficient in a sense of human life. A certain amount of rough joy and silly pleasure, of lying and lust and horseplay, existing in humanity, however ill it may be, is overlooked. Miss Rukeyser has rubbed off the soiled and silly edges which mean nothing, and everything.

Bogan's tendency to react with high indignation to what she considered ideological idiocy occasionally led her into unusual outspokenness, as it did in a *New Republic* exchange in 1940, when, in a letter to the editor, she announced that she had suffered "a severe shock" on reading "Cafeteria Afternoon," a poem by Oscar Williams, in the March 11th issue of the journal. Spurred by what she considered Williams's heartless descriptions of the poor and down-and-out, she accused him of "fear, nausea and trembling," emotions which puzzled her, she said, "coming from a poet, one of whose roles, I have always believed, is to love and understand phenomena, and all God's creatures (including his fellow human beings), instead of being frightened by them." As for cafeterias, Bogan could state from experience that they were extremely heartening expressions of modern life. I have a fairly extensive knowledge of them, and can testify that they are far less full of people "with frightened eyes" (except for an occasional demented person), than more bourgeois restaurants. Nor have I "smelled" the unemployed in cafeterias. They are usually full of the destitute, but there is a great deal of decency, courage and strength in this destitution, and I do not wish to sentimentalize "the proletariat" by this remark. Whatever "smell" is given off is a humanly encouraging one.

Williams fired off a reply in which he stated that he considered the letter a "personal attack," and added, "It is becoming well known that Miss Bogan has gotten into the habit of fulminating against her fellow poets." She had misread his poem, he insisted, if she thought that his line "This air smells of unemployment" was an attack on the unemployed. It was, he averred, a protest against the system which permitted unemployment:

Miss Bogan mistakes plain English when she says that I "smell" the "unemployed." I believe it's the duty of the poet to present "grisly" pictures of depressing social conditions, cafeterias included, since such pictures help to rectify such evils. I have not lately seen any of Miss Bogan's poems, but those of hers I noted in the public prints several years ago carefully avoided presenting the hardships of the "destitute."

No direct record of Bogan's reaction to this letter exists. She was not a person who hammered away at her points; having had her say, she kept quiet. By happy coincidence, a sonnet composed by Zabel and Wilson, each writing alternate lines (who wrote which lines is unknown), has survived with its amusing portrait of Bogan at her formidable critical best. It is undated, although it lightly refers to the "ideas of reference" from which she suffered during her 1937 trip to Ireland, as well as to her fondness for cafeterias, and it seems to have been sent as a get-well greeting (possibly in 1944, when she had a minor foot operation):

To L————— B————

Defiant siren of the Sibyl's lair,
Queen of the Spectral Spies and Followed Feeling,
Earth has not anything to show more fair,
So that we seem to stand upon the ceiling.
The very thought of thee gets in our hair.
Dissecting thee can smart like onion-peeling.
A subtle glamor of remote despair,
Blown hitherward, has set our blood congealing.
The rose-twined cottage greets the cafeteria,
Where high and noble spirits slide their trays

And Prone on a Stretcher reigns our fair Egeria.
Oh, call not this the parting of the ways!
We need thee for our standards and criteria,
Thou chiefest of our crutches, props and stays!

The priestess of standards and criteria found a new god in W. H. Auden, and her response to his work forms the clearest picture of her literary and social experience of the 1930s. Though she recognized his technical virtuosity from the beginning, and was ready to call him Eliot's technical equal in *The Dog Beneath the Skin,* she distrusted and disliked him in his pose as spokesman for his generation, especially in the aspect of the youthful railer against elders and higher-ups. She rightly judged that this attitude couldn't last forever, and wanted to reserve judgment until he proved himself further. Nevertheless, almost immediately, echoes of his style could be heard in her poems. "New Moon" wasn't just a protest against the timeservers, but a poem in Auden's witty-compassionate-ironical-colloquial style. During the summer of 1938, Wilson persuaded her to collaborate with him on a group of parodies of contemporary writers. Out of this effort came Wilson's "The Omelet of A. MacLeish" and Bogan's "Evening in the Sanitarium," a poem that started out as a parody of Auden only to turn into a superb observation of modern spiritual desolation. She had come under the influence of Auden's youth and virtuosity almost in spite of herself, just as she had been forced into angry public speech in spite of her will to remain private.

For a considerable length of time she resisted her impulse to admire Auden. When he arrived with Christopher Isherwood in New York in the spring of 1939, she refused Edmund Wilson's offer to arrange an introduction: "I have no interest in seeing them, in their present phase, and I certainly don't want to be displayed to them as a curiosity: a female criminal-poet. Being a poet, I am of course automatically a criminal; but I can't say that I want to spend an evening being examined by two visiting Englishmen, as a queer specimen." What she refrained from telling Wilson was that she had just "laid out"—that is, attacked—*On the Frontier* in the March 18th *New Yorker,* and believed that there was very little chance that Auden and Isherwood would actually want to meet her. Yet Auden's phrasing had been haunting her for a long time. One night in 1936, she told Humphries, just before going to sleep, she thought up an Audenesque poem,

a whole beautiful witty satire . . . all about someone showing someone else over a museum, in the New World, wherein all the bourgeois (and human) foibles were embalmed. The last two lines of it were:

> And do not fail to note, as we pass by
> The Stuffed Adultery, Old-fashioned Lie.

And the next morning, she reported, she had been surprised by the following:

> Not being young, nor a whilom haunter of parks,
> I feel I must love you, love, without literary remarks.
> As one who listens, at least once a week, to five hours of discs,
> It is not me, any longer, who exposes the bony structure to risks.

This, she confessed, had been inspired by Auden's new book, *Look, Stranger!* (*On This Island,* 1937). He seemed to her to be writing wonderfully witty poems, Shakespearean in their condensation of epithet, and she was sure that he was, or was about to be, "the works," especially when "he gets a few bones to gnaw, and reaches forty-five or fifty." His influence over her own work continued, and she used the device of the museum tour guide's voice in "Animal, Vegetable and Mineral." At her most admiring, she still saw plenty to criticize in Auden, finding fault particularly with his politics. In June 1940, she wrote Morton Zabel:

Another rather Shocking Thing, was the review of Yeats by Auden, in the Sat. Rev. of Lit. Old Wystan denied that Yeats even fell into, or knew "the rag and bone shop of the heart," and adds that Y. was a great poet, because he used great diction, and seemed to enjoy writing!! —Poor Wystan! He has a long way to go, and it is a pity that he has been kept swaddled so long in Party Politics. He'll have to go through an enormous crash, to get wisdom, and I think it's improbable that crash will now occur: he is thirty-three. I still insist, however, that he's a man of genius.

When Bogan finally did meet Auden, in January 1941, she discovered that she liked the brilliant young Englishman very much. They were actually introduced one afternoon at Cyril Connolly's mother's apartment (decorated in late Empire style, Bogan did not fail to note) on the corner of Lexington Avenue and Seventy-second Street. Bogan was talking with F. W. Dupee, a *Partisan Review* editor she had met at Edmund Wilson's in 1939, waiting for Mrs. Connolly to return from "doing 'exercises' " somewhere, when suddenly the lady showed up in her hockey suit, accompanied by Auden and his friends. Auden told Bogan that he liked "Animal, Vegetable and Mineral," which had just been published in *The New Republic* in December, that he would very much like to visit her sometime at 169th Street, and that she was "the best critic of poetry in America." The following October, Auden mentioned that he had given her name as a reference to the Guggenheim Foundation, and in November wrote to ask if he could review her new book, *Poems and New Poems,* in *The New Yorker.* In his view there were only four important American poets: T. S. Eliot, Marianne Moore, Laura Riding, and Louise Bogan herself, and he added:

My own impression is that, unless you lose your head, your poetic career is only just beginning. "Occasional" poetry is as good a name, I suppose, as any other for what you have it in you to write, though one could equally well say that now you have turned and looked on your particular Eumenides, you are freed from being the tie of one particular personal occasion ("lyric" verse is apt to be so tied, I think):

What I myself find so remarkable is that you have been able to be profitably influenced by Yeats, without succumbing to that old Cagliostro's rhetoric. Rhetoric is dangerous enough for anyone, but fatal for women, because since all men are children, they can get away with cheek and Irish charm, but while since all women are really grown-up, their work is either "serious," or else acutely embarrassing like Edna's. (For which reason, I don't much care for *Several Voices Out of a Cloud* or *Hypocrite Swift,* clever though the latter is.) My own little cock and bull story about sex in art is this. When it comes to the really important (Religious?) experiences, it does make a lot of difference which sex one is. But there are less important realms of experience where man's irresponsibility makes it easier for him than by a woman* to be artistically successful. If there are fewer women-writers, it is largely because in order to get to the first realm, where everything is so difficult that all human beings are at an equal disadvantage, she has to cross the second realm where she has a special disadvantage *qua* her sex.

It seems to me, that you have successfully crossed it, and what you do now depends on nothing except your talent.

It would be difficult to exaggerate the effect that Auden's letter had upon Bogan. Even more than Eliot, she considered him the only living inheritor of the great tradition of English poetry. He had understood the spiritual labors of *The Sleeping Fury* and *Poems and New Poems,* and recognized how successfully she had avoided the diffidence and preciosity afflicting so much poetry by women. He saw the fruitful connection with Yeats, and heralded the major achievement for which she was now thoroughly prepared. Above all, without knowing the details of her private life, he had completely grasped the significance of the struggle and change she had undergone since 1934. There could be no fuller recognition than that which he now gave.

HAVING FOUND her new personality both resilient and durable, in the fall of 1939 Bogan permitted herself to do something she would never

---

* The phrase "than by [i.e. for] a woman" is at this point inserted above the line.

have allowed herself in the past, and that was to participate in a *Partisan Review* symposium. The seven questions included under the title "The Situation in American Writing," to which she and other American writers were asked to respond, demanded little in the way of truly personal revelation; yet, as she answered them one by one, she managed to disclose more private information about her life than she had ever done publicly before. Addressing herself to such matters as the degree to which she was conscious, in her writing, of a "usable past," her relationship with her audience, the value she placed on the criticism her work had received, her ability to make a living by writing, and the question of allegiances to political or other special interests, the woman who permitted only the briefest biographical facts to appear on the dust jackets of her books and who scorned the invasions of professional literary research replied with inexplicable candor.

To begin with, she wrote that she approved of her "classical" New England education, with its readings in Greek and Latin literature, and she carefully acknowledged the influence on her earliest work of Arthur Symons's *The Symbolist Movement in Literature* and the French poets it had led her to read. She added the English "Metaphysicals," Yeats, who "influenced my writing from 1916, when I first read 'Responsibilities,'" in addition to Poe, Thoreau, Emily Dickinson, and Henry James, whom, she remarked, she had discovered late, and at first with the usual prejudices absorbed from the generally inadequate criticism he had received.

She thought that American culture, as it was dominated by doctrines of success and morality, was still inhospitable to serious writing: "The truly serious piece of work, where a situation is explored at all levels, disinterestedly, for its own sake, is outlawed." She said that she had never been able to make a living by writing poetry, but that it had never occurred to her that she could do so; she simply assumed that American society, in its present state, made little room for the "honest and detached professional writer." But then, she added, the situation differed very little from that which Flaubert had been forced to deal with, again making it clear that she firmly believed modern American society and France of the Second Empire had much in common.

In response to the question concerning allegiances, she gave an extremely full answer, stating for the first (and only) time anywhere that the "real liturgy" of the Catholic Church, rather than the "dreary services" and "dreadful hymnody of the Protestant churches" had made its mark upon her work. Her talent and energy, she said, came from her mother's Celtic ancestry. As to awareness of class, she wrote:

I did not know I was a member of a class until I was twenty-one; but I knew I was a member of a racial and religious minority, from an early age. One of the great shocks of my life came when I discovered that bigotry existed not only among the Catholics, but among the Protestants, whom I had thought would be tolerant and civilized (since their pretensions were always in that direction). It was borne in upon me, all during my adolescence, that I was a "Mick," no matter what my other faults or virtues might be. It took me a long time to take this fact easily, and to understand the situation which gave rise to the minor persecutions I endured at the hands of supposedly educated and humane people. —I came from the white-collar class and it was difficult to erase the dangerous tendencies—the impulse to "rise" and respect "nice people"—of this class.

In the 1930–1933 notebooks, Bogan had uneasily and bitterly confessed what she stated here with apparently effortless detachment. The journey between private anguish and public, unashamed statement had been unimaginably arduous. No one reading these calm and thoughtful replies could have guessed what courage it had taken to write them. But for Louise Bogan, they constituted what she called her *coeur mis à nu.*

Next she addressed herself to the question concerning the political tendency of American writing since 1930. To this she brought to bear both her generational point of view and her psychological insight into the problems of artistic and intellectual growth:

Granted that the economic crisis became grave; it is nevertheless peculiar and highly symptomatic that intellectuals having discovered that "freedom" is not enough, and does not automatically lead to depth of insight and peace of mind, threw over *every scrap of their former enthusiasms,* as though there were something sinful in them. The economic crisis occurred when that generation of young people was entering the thirties; and, instead of fighting out the personal ills attendant upon the transition from youth to middle age, they took refuge in closed systems of belief, and automatically (many of them) committed creative suicide.

She was thinking not only of Hart Crane's real suicide, but of Edna St. Vincent Millay, Léonie Adams, Genevieve Taggard, Eda Lou Walton, Malcolm Cowley, Archibald MacLeish, Rolfe Humphries, and Edmund Wilson; Auden, too, must have come to her mind. All had been swept up in the intoxication of political conversion, and each one, in her view, had become insulated from all but "fashionable" versions of reality, "fashionable" here meaning the tendency to "examine the situation of the sharecropper, for example," rather than "the situation of slum-dwellers in Chelsea, Massachusetts, or Newark, New Jersey." A writer could only pass judgment on the ills of his time through the sincerity and compassion which were inherent in the attitude of detachment. Party must be opposed, no matter how noble the tenets:

For all tenets tend to harden into dogma, and all dogma breeds hatred and bigotry, and is therefore stultifying. And the condescension of the political party toward the artist is always clear, however well disguised. The artist will be "given" his freedom; as though it were not the artist who "gives" freedom to the world, and not only "gives" it, but is the only person capable of enduring it, or of understanding what it costs.

Earlier that summer she had remarked to Zabel that the *Partisan Review* editors were courting her rather zealously: "The Trotskyites gave me quite a rush for a while, but discovered I was 'nice' but 'stubborn.' (Philip Rahv opened up on me one evening, with the same old Marxist line. I *can't* see any difference between *them,* fundamentally, and the old-line Stalinists.)" They too believed the same nonsense about "giving" the artist his freedom, and she scoffed, " 'Give' freedom indeed!"

What the *Partisan Review* questionnaire, the letters to editors, the angry exchanges with Zabel, Humphries, and Wilson over the political situation, and the careful championing of purity and detachment all suggest is that by the end of the thirties, the public and the private Louise Bogan were at peace with one another and not even overly protective of each other's domain. She no longer truly feared gossip or imagined herself the target of undying legend; she no longer cared whether she had enemies or ill-wishers. She felt confident about speaking out on the general cultural situation, knowledgeable about contemporary writing, and aware of her responsibility as a bearer of humane values. Yet, strangely, as the country drew closer to war, a less attractive side of this self-confidence insinuated itself into her thinking. When the Moscow Trials and the Hitler-Stalin nonaggression pact stunned the politically committed, she took a malicious and self-righteous pleasure in the disappointments and defections of those who now found themselves forced to break with the Communist party, the League of American Writers, and any "line" which the new developments now made untenable. "It's because these people never saw anyone but themselves," she wrote to Morton Zabel with heartless oversimplification; "they are Intellectuals; they learn nothing and they practise nothing in the way of life. So, everytime a war comes along they are always wrong. They were wrong last time, and they are wrong this time."

She had spent so much time defending the pure artist from ideological contamination that she now failed to imagine the pain of those who were not necessarily artists, but intellectuals, people who needed ideas to live, and were suffering from the betrayal of their intelligence, ethics, and faith. In her lack of sympathy for them she was guilty of a good deal of arrogance. Despising ex-Communists and Marxists caught up in the struggle to change focus, she regarded their new enthusiasm for Roosevelt as simply another form of self-deception. To her mind, Roosevelt represented a "disguised State Socialism, that is being put over on people without their full knowledge or consent." Her certitude of judgment—what, in a review of poetry would be praiseworthy as her *authority*—became colored by ignorance and bigotry; it was as if she had lost sight of the suffering she herself had undergone in the course of giving up one mode of thinking and feeling for another. Discussing with Zabel the possibility of a new world war, she remarked that the sentiment of patriotism wasn't as strong as it had been in 1917–18, certainly not strong enough to catapult the United States into another war. And World War I, she added, had been useful in its way, a means of liberating people from a dull, absurd, bourgeois Dark Age:

But now, even if a standing army of 2,000,000 men is formed (and that is a terrible thought, is it not?) the whole thing is going to sag because the "trend" is in another direction, in spite of all that Roosevelt says. It is toward Fun and Petty bourgeois laissez-fairism. In spite of the hysteria, I believe that a truly big Hate War cannot be put over. People don't care, any more. . . . The only people who care (and I know that this is a treasonable statement, but it is true, none the less) are the Jews and a few real power-type nuts. . . . The Jews care, terribly. . . . There's a Bogan lying this minute in France; and there's another Bogan who will go to her grave without having one drop of human blood on her hands.

It is almost pointless to say that she was mistaken in her prognostications. But to the extent that she regarded herself as the bearer of the standard of humane detachment, sincerity, and compassion, she was guilty, in her remarks about the Jews, of a certain trivializing nastiness. There can be no doubt that her hatred of war came from a passionate belief in the sacredness of life. Yet the possibility that fascism and Nazism were evils too enormous to be changed by any attitude bred from detached or aesthetic considerations simply eluded her, and she was too ready to ascribe hatred and inadequacy to many persons who felt that they had no choice except to fight.

Once again, fate gave her little margin for charity. The poems written between 1936 and 1941 which went into *Poems and New Poems* speak of Bogan's desire to treasure existence at all costs. As a whole, the book was earthbound and peaceable, but the fall and winter of 1941 were, to say the least, hardly auspicious for its arrival.

III 1936 ~ 1941

IF JOHN HALL WHEELOCK had not been so persistent, Louise Bogan might never have published *Poems and New Poems,* her fourth volume and essentially her first "collected" edition. By June of 1937, *The Sleeping Fury* had sold only 208 copies; in contrast, *Dark Summer* had sold 600 in its first season. Although *The Sleeping Fury* was received well and won Bogan *Poetry* magazine's prestigious Helen Haire Levinson Prize, it did not win—as Bogan and her friends had frankly expected it to—the 1937 Pulitzer Prize for poetry. When that went instead to Marya Zaturenska for *Cold Morning Sky,* Bogan began to feel, perhaps not unreasonably, that the time for wide public recognition was passing her by. Fortunately, she did write poetry over the summer of 1937, and John Hall Wheelock, rejoicing in her continuing productivity, thought to encourage her by bringing up the subject of a new book; Scribner's, he told her, was prepared to go ahead if Bogan would supply enough new work. She was enthusiastic about the project, and promised to have a fresh new manuscript ready for the printers by the fall of 1939. But the poems she hoped to write were not "given" to her, and when fall 1939 arrived, Wheelock felt that there were still too few to fill out a new book. A year and a half later, he was still asking for new poems, but also suggesting that if she would include a cluster of already published light pieces, the slender sheaf could be considerably fattened. Bogan thought this a good idea, and by July 1941, plans for printing the book, which Wheelock christened *Poems and New Poems* (a very Rilkean title), were under way.

Just at this point, however, Morton Zabel got wind of the plan to include light verse, and he immediately launched a vehement campaign against including any but Bogan's most rigorous, austere, and impassioned poems. Even some of her earlier serious work came in for his animadversions; she should cut out "The Flume," "A Letter," and a brief lyric called "Love me because I am lost," in addition to anything written purely for fun. "In all seriousness," he admonished her, "DON'T put your squibs and light poems into the collection. You can make a little book of these some years later if you're bound to. Let this first collection be all and only of your best. You know you're not the kind of poet that can or wants to mix matters up."

His tone was insufferable. He lectured her as if she'd had a sudden fit of unaccountable waywardness. "I know you've subscribed to this comic notion going around that poets and their readers shouldn't be 'snobs'; but this momentary form of fear (and supreme example of snobbishness) will duly pass away, and the high, beautiful, and deliberate knowledge of What Art Really Is will remain; and you'll want your book to be an example of it."

Over the years, Bogan had often questioned and resisted Zabel's more canonical pronouncements. Instinct had led her occasionally to hold back certain opinions and pieces of personal information from him, because, as she complained to Humphries, "What I do tell him is often held over me like a sword when he sees signs of my spiritual discipline, God save the mark, slipping." But because he was more loyal to her work than anyone else, and had such a high and noble attitude toward her talent, it was difficult in this case to ignore his objections. Even though her new friend at *The New Yorker,* the young novelist William Maxwell, was completely in favor of the light verse, and Wheelock, whose ardent Romantic temperament did not interfere with his hearty enjoyment of wit, had no reservations whatsoever about including it, Bogan was worried about risking the charge of fashionableness and triviality. When she failed to send Zabel a copy of the contents of the forthcoming volume, he assumed right away that she intended a tacit rebuke and scolded her once again in a letter whose reproachful parts she copied out and sent to Wheelock:

Now for goodness' sake, don't take this awful stuff about the need for "casualness" in poetry seriously and put in a section of "light" verse that will invite comparison with G. Taggard, D. Parker, and others of that ilk. That argument about the "casual" is villainous and all irrelevant to your purposes. You *know* you were at your best when tight and screwed up to the severest pitch of your job. You may *feel* better somewhat unscrewed, but that isn't necessarily an augury that the unscrewed verses are better; so *please* omit all essays on midnight tears flowing into the ears and diabetes in the starlight. There's no object in publishing this book unless it contains only the best. Keep "The Flume" rather than insert the squibs. Now if you don't do as I say I'll have to write a long excoriational review simply burning you up. I don't want to do this.

Morton wasn't joking about his threat to flay her in print, and Louise, who had regaled him for years with her wit, must have felt furious at this about-face. Nevertheless, she sent a calm reply, reminding him that she was "a many faceted creature," and noting that if Yeats could include "To a Squirrel at Kyle-na-no" ("Come play with me; / Why should you run . . .") in *The Wild Swans at Coole,* "in cold soberness, at the age of *fifty-four,* and print it without setting it off in any way . . . why shouldn't I be allowed to break my tone, occasionally?" The question of whether to include the light verse, which the volume badly needed if it was to be sufficiently full, was finally settled only when Wheelock cleverly remarked that he hoped that Zabel's admonitions did not extend to *satiric* verse, an adjective beside which Zabel's contemptuous use of "casual" simply shriveled up. This put an end to Bogan's difficulties, and the production of the book went ahead. In all likelihood, however, she was still angry at Zabel's treatment of her light verse (and of her) when, the following September, she broke off relations with him altogether over an entirely different matter. Years before, she had made him promise to give her back all the letters she had written him when she should someday reach the point of wanting to reread them. That fall, she went to Chicago for a visit, deciding that the time to get the letters back was now at hand and fully expecting him to honor the promise. Zabel, however, not only refused to give her the letters, but revealed that he was carefully hoarding them for posterity in a special "Bogan Box." Outraged, she attacked him for treating her like a literary figure whom he was putting "in cold storage while still alive." He admired Wallace Stevens and Marianne Moore because, she pointed out, "THEY ARE FIXED AND FINISHED. They will never *surprise* anyone again." But Auden, whom Zabel didn't like, might do *anything*. He was on the side of life and so, for that matter, was she: "I can't become a corpse; not yet, God willing. I love and revere life; and intend to keep on being vulgarly alive, just as long as possible. I'll never fit into a seminar, while above ground."

Zabel and Bogan had had their tiffs before, but this time Louise was truly angry. Morton no doubt defended himself with vigor, for he was never without reasons, but a two-year standoff resulted from the quarrel. It was a true failing in him not to see that in protesting against her light verse he was giving support to her inhibitions, and thereby rendering a great disservice to her continuing vitality as a poet. In lightness and play lived the possibility that she might once again come to enjoy writing poetry, and recover ambition from the simple pleasure of composing. Her talent needed turning and airing, picnics and somersaults, holidays and nights out on the town, so to speak.

The section of "New Poems" in the book opens with "Several Voices Out of a Cloud," a poem that seems to reach out toward the same literate, urbane audience Auden's poems might have attracted. Nothing quite like it had appeared in any of Bogan's earlier books, and in it, she simply took an elegant, powerful swing at the contemporary cultural situation:

> Come, drunks and drug-takers; come, perverts unnerved!
> Receive the laurel, given, though late, on merit;
>   to whom and wherever deserved.
> Parochial punks, trimmers, nice people, joiners true-blue,
> Get the hell out of the way of the laurel. It is deathless. And it isn't for you.

The poem had been "torn off" one evening in the early fall of 1938, sent first to Edmund Wilson, who liked it, and then on to *Partisan Review,* "which won't take it, of course," she predicted to Rolfe Humphries. The magazine did take it, although Bogan included some of its editors, among them F. W. Dupee (who was not yet a friend) and Dwight Macdonald (who later became a respected acquaintance), on her list of time-servers, which happened to extend as well to Malcolm Cowley, Granville Hicks, Kenneth Burke, William Troy (Léonie Adams's husband), Horace Gregory, Marya Zaturenska, and Archibald MacLeish. It was Bogan's final, exasperated riposte to the squabbling and mean-spiritedness of the thirties, and had "arrived" in a rush after she'd read Wilson's parody, "The Omelet of A. MacLeish," and Enid Starkie's biography, *Arthur Rimbaud*. Wilson's brilliant travesty only confirmed her belief in MacLeish's hypocrisy and mediocrity, while Starkie's account of Rimbaud's complex nature both moved her and affirmed her own deepest intuitions about the true, natural artist. Dwelling upon Rimbaud's quest for fulfillment through sensual derangement, his rejection of natural time, his wit and passion-dampening coldness, as well as his troubled relation to his continually betraying mother, the book "was another proof," Bogan declared to Zabel, "that the artist is a madman and a criminal. Starkie doesn't pull her punches, and Rimbaud rises out of his crimes like an angel." Everything Louise had been forced to learn painfully, and by herself, she found summed up when Starkie wrote:

There is no freedom to be fully ourselves unless we have first bought it with submission and many painful concessions, unless we have wearily struggled to the higher regions where alone there is room for development. Too late Rimbaud decided to purchase freedom and the price was by then higher than it would have been earlier. Then, during the best years of his maturity, when he might have enjoyed a certain measure of liberty, feverishly—as he did all things—he was buying it at the high price of the most painful servitude and bitter suffering.

Bogan knew the truth of Starkie's words to the letter, and her poem struck back at the "nice people" who had swarmed across her own private vista of freedom, as well as the "trimmers" and "joiners true-blue" of the political life around her. Rimbaud's season in hell had returned in the calendar of her own life, but she had survived it as he had not, and her poem was a deliberate, triumphant revenge against the inner and outer "enemies of promise."

The next poem, "Animal, Vegetable and Mineral," is similarly rooted in a text. In the fall of 1940, Edmund Wilson wrote to Morton Zabel that he had recently been "haunted" by "a little book on glass flowers. I took it up to show Louise," he continued, "with the result that she, too, became obsessed by it and is now composing a poem on the subject." The little book which so captured the imaginations of the three friends was an illustrated catalogue and essay, *Glass Flowers from the Ware Collection in the Botanical Museum of Harvard University, Insect Pollination Series,* with Sixteen Color Plates, by Fritz Kredel (New York: Harcourt, Brace and Company. 58 pages. $1.50). Taking the ironic *aperçu, "Dieu ne croit pas à notre Dieu,"* from Jules Renard's *Journal inedit,* Bogan revived the technique she had used in "Hypocrite Swift" of integrating prose passages within a lyric structure. The tone, however, was new. Some years before, she had written Zabel that she had a strong desire to write a poem about "things naturally elegant, like pineapples and shells and feathers, but M. Moore has rather a lien on objects characterized by natural elegance, hasn't she? I'd have to be very, very lyrical about them, in order to get out of her class; the class that presents and imaginatively constructs and describes. Shells and feathers and campanulas and acorns and pine-cones and lemons and magnolias . . ."

She found her solution by ever-so-slightly exaggerating, and thus gently parodying, the tone of museum-guide exposition—that civilized, leisurely, unirritatingly pedantic voice of curiosity both aroused and gratified—in which an Enlightenment delight in mechanics weaves itself in and out of a romantic sense of mystery, celebrating the ordered universe of making, and paying homage to the unfathomable Great Artist through His works. As an avid reader of Thoreau's *Journal,* and Hopkins's *Notebooks,* Bogan must have been struck by the catalogue's description of Leopold and Rudolph Blaschka as "two artist-naturalists"; her transformation of the prose text into verse stanzas is based on this theme. The seventh stanza of the poem is a masterly recapitulation and transcription of a long section called "The Pollination of Flowers by Insects." The sober, conscientious sentences describing Darwin's fascination with "the various contrivances by which self-pollination is rendered difficult or impossible," and the ways in which the job of attracting insects is accomplished by the unusual fitting-out of such a flower, for example, as the "species of *Primula,* the cowslip, whose flowers have the stigmas or receptive part of the pistil and the anthers of the stamens borne at different levels in the tubular corolla of different flowers (see Plate XIII)," becomes:

> Self-fertile flowers are feeble and need priming.
> Nature is for this priming, it appears.
> Some flowers, like water-clocks, have perfect timing:
> Pistils and anthers rise, as though on gears;
> One's up when t'other's down; one falls; one's climbing.

Similarly, the catalogue's discussion of Darwin's observations concerning bees and orchids, the patronage of Mrs. Elizabeth C. Ware and her daughter, Miss Mary Lee Ware, the studio of the Blaschkas, and the evidence of prehistoric pollination presented by bees and flowers encased in Baltic amber forty million years old bring the poem's civilized voice to the wonder which lies at the other side of wit:

> Cynics who think all this *bijouterie*
> Certainly lack a Deepening Sense of Awe.
> Here Darwin, Flora, Blaschkas and the bee
> Fight something out that ends in a close draw
> Above the cases howls loud mystery.
>
> What is the chain, then ask, and what the links?
> Are these acts sad or droll? From what derived?
> Within the floret's disk the insect drinks.
> Next summer there's more honey to be hived.
>
> What Artist laughs? What clever Daemon thinks?

Since her "cure," Bogan had come to view the natural world with a mystic's awe, and a conscious delight in her own rapprochement with religious emotion, though not religious dogma. Urbane and aphoristic as it is, the poem's praise of intricate natural mechanics and its almost amorously witty repudiation of "man's Abstracts and Concretes, Wrong and Rightness" correspond to a line Bogan had underscored in pencil in the introduction to her copy of Yeats's *The King of the Great Clock Tower:* "We know the world through abstractions, statistics, time tables . . . such knowledge thins the blood."

The same pure delight likewise informs the charming "Variation on a Sentence," which comes, again, from a prose text, this time a passage from her beloved Thoreau's *Journal:*

Feb. 21, 1855 . . . How plain, wholesome, and earthy are the colors of quadrupeds generally! The commonest I should say is the tawny or various shades of brown, answering to the russet which is the prevailing color of the earth's surface, perhaps, and to the yellow of sands beneath. The darker brown mingled with this answers to the darker-colored soil of the surface. The white of the polar bear, ermine weasel, etc., answers to the snow; the spots of the pards, perchance, to the earth spotted with flowers or tinted leaves of autumn; the black, perhaps, to night, and muddy bottoms and dark waters. There are few or no bluish animals.

She probably composed the poem in May 1936, during or after a brief vacation beside the sea at Swampscott, during which she read Thoreau and was profoundly taken with his powers of seeing and describing. Playing upon the last sentence of the passage, she wrote, out of delight and fancy:

> Of white and tawny, black as ink,
> Yellow, and undefined, and pink,
> And piebald, there are droves, I think.
>
> (Buff kine in herd, gray whales in pod,
> Brown woodchucks, colored like the sod,
> All creatures from the hand of God.)
>
> And many of a hellish hue;
> But, for some reason hard to view,
> Earth's bluish animals are few.

It is a poem that gives us an almost palpable sense of the pleasure Bogan must have felt in writing it. For years she had found pleasure and solace in Thoreau's prose and observations. Passages in which Thoreau charted heat and cold, shadows and tints, patterns and configurations, sounds and rhythms found their way into her notebooks. The infinite variation of his firm, flexible sentences, his rich, yet common English vocabulary, all seemed endlessly inventive and alive to her. And the man's life—his loneliness and ecstasies—moved her, sometimes, to tears. She found joy in simply copying his words down, writing once next to a cluster of transcriptions: "spent a whole Sunday afternoon transcribing these extracts. The sound of the sea: alternate cloud & light. Peace. Happiness."

Yet tranquility and delight were not the only moods that found their way into the "New Poems." Lightness did not exclude sharpness, and Bogan managed to convey acute ironic anguish in "Solitary Observation Brought Back from a Sojourn in Hell" as well as bitter sarcasm in "Question in a Field." She could write powerfully in the most condensed forms: a single sentence with an inner rhyme and an end-rhyme; a question as simple as a nursery rhyme. She could also take almost any kind of material and find the poetry in it. In "The Dream," the lyric which follows the four squibs and "Animal, Vegetable and Mineral," transcription is once again the source of the poem's form, but it is transcription of a psychic event—a dream—into a controlled and finely shaped text. She sent a copy of the poem to Edmund Wilson on February 10, 1937, and wrote that it was "just hot from the Muse," adding, "I really did have this dream." Responding to questions from Sister Angela V. O'Reilly in August 1966, Bogan explained that the poem, written in her late thirties, followed "a complete change in my way of living, and in my general point of view about life (and the universe at large!). It is the actual transcript of 'a nightmare,' but there is reconciliation involved with the fright and horror. It is through the possibility of such reconciliations that we, I believe, manage to live." The horse in the dream—the *night-mare*—that rears up and advances threateningly was

"Fear kept for thirty-five years": the accumulated power of terror and rage Bogan had only recently confronted during her breakdowns. But it is also an archetypal symbol, and the poem's drama presents an allegory of the unconscious in a final and mutually triumphant struggle with the self:

> Coward complete, I lay and wept on the ground
> When some strong creature appeared, and leapt for the rein.
> Another woman, as I lay half in a swound,
> Leapt in the air, and clutched at the leather and chain.

This other woman is Bogan's new self, the "cured" woman, the emergent adult and artist, who tells the frightened, cowering "I" of the poem to throw something to the horse: "Throw him, she said, some poor thing you alone claim." Terrified and despairing, this "I" becomes paralyzed, unable to act out of fear of the horse's hate. Then:

> But, like a lion in a legend, when I flung the glove
> Pulled from my sweating, my cold right hand,
> The terrible beast, that no one may understand,
> Came to my side, and put down his head in love.

The glove becomes a symbol of challenge and submission, a token of the poet's strong feminine sexuality—and perhaps many other things as well. Put at the mercy of the beast, who is not only appeased, but in turn enchanted, the glove in the end represents the poet's whole self, triumphant over the lovingly submissive beast.

WITH "TO AN ARTIST, TO TAKE HEART," Bogan settles the score inaugurated with her response to Genevieve Taggard's poem, "I Sigh If She Were Dying." The long, shapeless tirade she had sent to Wilson in October 1934 was shelved, only to be aged and smoked with the fumes from Yeats's great poem "Lapis Lazuli," so that three years later it appeared, greatly condensed, in *The New Yorker* for July 3, 1937:

> Slipping in blood, by his own hand, through pride,
> Hamlet, Othello, Coriolanus fall.
> Upon his bed, however, Shakespeare died,
> Having endured them all.

No matter how far Bogan had gone in the direction of Rilkean flow, she was still at heart the tough, witty, Yeatsian apostle of endurance.

III 1936 ~ 1941

THEN THERE WAS her new love poetry. She had considered "Song for a Lyre," the closing lyric of *The Sleeping Fury,* as perhaps the only love poem she had ever written. But "To Be Sung on the Water," written in the first acknowledgment that she was able to love again, appeared in July 1937. It was in every way a fusion of memory and desire. Many years later, returning again to her long prose work, she recalled an impression that had lingered since childhood: "Music, in those days, belonged to its own time and place. No one today can remember with the same nostalgia (my generation is the last to remember) the sound of music on the water (voices and a mandolin or guitar)," and this memory had fed her poem. She had also been reminded in writing it of the delicate lyrics of Joyce's *Chamber Music,* and of a Schubert song, "Auf dem Wasser zu Singen." But the poem came out of her love for the man who had helped her through her emotional distress on the boat back from England to America. Just three days before the poem arrived on Wheelock's desk, she had tried to break off the affair, but her lover would not hear of it. The poem must have been written during or just after she had said goodbye, for its mood is elegiac as well as exquisitely tender, its movement all toward renunciation. In its texture the poem is the very epitome of Louise Bogan's art. She believed that the basis of all poetry is rhythm, and that rhythm as we first experience it lives within the heartbeat, pulse, and breath. She made "To Be Sung on the Water" a kind of rowing song:

> Beautiful, my delight,
> Pass, as we pass the wave.
> Pass, as the mottled night
> Leaves what it cannot save,
> Scattering dark and bright.

The words have an incantatory flow, yearning toward an absolute purity of feeling. Similarly, "Musician," which was written about a month earlier, celebrates a renewed and intense eroticism, but in bolder metaphors which equate the body with a musical instrument:

> Now with great ease, and slow,
> The thumb, the finger, the strong
> Delicate hand plucks the long
> String it was born to know.

"Musician" is also a poem about the goodness of fate, the mystery of return and renewal, of awakening amidst desolation and emptiness.

"Cartography" is another deeply intimate erotic poem, its language traveling the length of the lover's physical body, finding therein a map of love and fate:

> As you lay in sleep
> I saw the chart
> Of artery and vein
> Running from your heart . . .

The poem introduces the enduring symbol of Bogan's later poetry—rivers—where life begins and where death is absorbed by a constant rhythm of tides and currents. The poet's *seeing* the loved one's body in sleep, vulnerable beyond his own knowledge or will, is an act of love, but not of possession, for the body viewed as a mirror of earthly life can belong to earth alone. Bogan has come so far from her early poetry that the body of this death is now the body of this life, and humility before this law, rather than deliverance from it, is all her poem seeks.

The sleeping lover, mortal, strong, and beautiful, is another aspect of the sleeping Fury, and sleep itself is profoundly telling in Bogan's work. Peace and self-reckoning take place while the Fury (the mother, the lover) sleeps; night belongs to love when sleep divides the span of darkness into cycles of dreaming; the singer unlooses through music "what we know in sleep." The nightmare terminus in "Journey Around My Room" and the rearing horse in "The Dream" again testify to the power of sleep in Bogan's imagination. Like darkness in her poetry, sleep holds the mystic secrets of being, unifies what is broken, speaks forth, and gives a place to love. Dreams are oracular, permitting the reconciliation of the spirit's warring sides; but they are also fierce and make us suffer, transporting us to the more than-human land of our wishes and fears. For just this reason, "Come, Sleep . . ." is an ironic foil to "Cartography," in that it questions sleep's consoling role.

The poem is another variation on a text, this time a lyric attributed to John Fletcher, which Bogan copied out from her beloved anthology, *The English Galaxy,* on a postcard and sent, without comment, to Morton Zabel in April 1938:

> Come, Sleep, and with thy sweet deceiving
>   Lock me in delight awhile!
>   Let some passing dreams beguile
>   All my fancies; that from thence
>   I may feel an influence,
> All my powers of care bereaving!
>
> Though but a shadow, but a sliding,
>   Let me know some little joy!
>   We that suffer long annoy

> Are contented with a thought
> Through an idle fancy wrought:
> Oh, let my joys have some abiding!

Nine months later, Bogan wrote her own verse "comment" on the poem, sending it to Zabel with the note that it had come "after an afternoon of spiritual exhaustion." The natural world in the poem is sadly *other* from the human:

> The bee's fixed hexagon;
> The ant's downward tower;
> The whale's effortless eating;
> The palm's love; the flower
>
> Burnished like brass, clean like wax
> Under the pollen;
> The rough grass-blade upright;
> The smooth swathe fallen: . . .

This catalogue, like those in "Baroque Comment" and "To My Brother. . . ," establishes a world that is the handiwork of a God Hopkins might worship and Thoreau revere: moreover, its creatures do not have bad dreams in which "the dark turreted house reflects itself / In the depthless stream." Like Hamlet, who cries out, "O God, I could be bounded in a nutshell, and count myself a king of infinite space, were it not that I have bad dreams," Bogan (who begins "The Dream" with the cry "O God") knows the inescapable prison of sleep ("the bars of the dream" in "Tears in Sleep"), and in "Come, Sleep. . . ," the turreted house takes her back to the Victorian Gothic world of "The Cupola" and her own New England childhood.

In "Zone," a poem written in March 1940, she speaks of a psychic realm that is equally troubled:

> We have struck the regions wherein we are keel or reef.
> The wind breaks over us,
> And against high sharp angles almost splits into words,
> And these are of fear or grief.

This is the "zone" of the vernal equinox, an interval partly idyll and partly ordeal for Bogan, to whom the season's light and color seemed unbearably poignant. In the equinoctial moment, wish and regret mingle against the swift sharp turning of the year:

... Now we hear
What we heard last year,
And bear the wind's rude touch
And its ugly sound
Equally with so much
We have learned how to bear.

THROUGHOUT THE THIRTIES, Bogan filled several notebooks with copious extracts from and comments about modern French writers. She may well have come across the French poet Pierre-Jean Jouve through his articles on music, Mozart, and the Salzburg Festivals, published between 1935 and 1939 in the *Nouvelle Revue Française*. Early in November 1939, she sent Zabel her rough-draft translation of the poem "Kapuzinerberg" from his *Voyage Sentimental,* following it a week later with a translation of Jouve's "Mozart," a poem serving as the epigraph of "In Memoriam Salzbourg," an elegiac essay published in the August 1938 issue of the *N.R.F.* Thus "Kapuzinerberg" and "Mozart" (which was never published) are companion translations, and, like "Several Voices Out of a Cloud" and "To an Artist, to Take Heart," belong to the unsystematic but passionate assortment of Bogan's responses to the contemporary panorama of fascism and cultural decay.

Her rendering of "Kapuzinerberg" is clean and condensed. The two poets' sensibilities were so kindred that she had little difficulty with her translations, and was able to match Jouve's tone almost effortlessly:

From the low eighteenth-century window—its thicknesses of pane and blind shut against the sun, its silence, the odor of summer through it—from the low window which reminds one so deliciously of Goethe retired, working, inspiring all Germany—from there—the cascades of hot trees in a morning already sick with future heat.

But she was less successful with the translation from Heine of *"Der Tod, das ist die kühle Nacht . . ."* The poem is too scrupulously accurate and sounds translated. The cadences of Brahms's setting of the song, which she knew well, were too present to her imagination, and she heard her own version more as an "art-song" than a piece of natural speech.

Mixed in quality though her translations were, Bogan discovered in the actual labor of writing them a way of remaining open to creative impulses when they otherwise chose to retreat or even disappear. At about this time, she complained to Wheelock that she had been going through a bout of unparalleled "spiritual dryness." Her human associations continued undisturbed, she explained, "And I feel light and free and do not suffer. But I do not *care,* either. Not a whit. Not a jot. About anything." Such dryness had to be endured, as she now knew, if she was to outsmart the mischief-making whims of the unconscious. And no matter how often she was assaulted by blocks, she refused to submit to compositional routine, bolstering her resolution by reading Rilke's recently published *Later Poems,* in which she was struck, in "To Hölderlin," by his criticism of other poets:

O changingly changing spirit! Look how they all live at home in their cosy poems and make long stays in narrow comparisons. Participators. You only move like the moon. And below there brightens and darkens your own nocturnal, sacredly startled landscape, the one you feel in partings.

Another way of staying afloat came through the parodies Bogan and Wilson conspired to produce over the summer of 1938, their squabbles having long subsided. Wilson believed that *The New Yorker* or *Partisan Review* would be sure to want them, and he urged her to travesty Auden and Muriel Rukeyser. "We will call them specimens of Contemporary Writing for Use in College Courses," he proposed gleefully. On his side of this devil's bargain Wilson produced, as we know, the delicious cruelty of "The Omelet of A. MacLeish," which he published in *The New Yorker,* while Bogan managed to write five parodies, which she published in the December 10, 1938, issue of *The Nation.* One was a brilliant and hilarious imitation of Kay Boyle, whose early fiction she had loved, one of Frederic Prokosch's poetry, two were simply imitations of prevailing mannerisms in lyric verse, and the last, called "Evening in the Sanitarium," was supposedly a parody of Auden. It was one of a pair of poems, the first of which (now lost) she explained to Wilson, "is an Auden parody only because of the fact that I took two words from a poem of his: Scorched and Concocted. —It really isn't very much in his range, and is certainly not informed with his power, but it's vamping, and I may do better. —The second ["Evening in the Sanitarium"] Just Came To Me. And it isn't so hot either." But her doubt about the poem was unjustified, for it remains one of her strongest. In its language it echoes the Baudelaire of "Le Crépuscule du Soir," both the poem in *Les Fleurs du Mal* ("C'est l'heure où les douleurs des malades s'aigrissent!"), and of the *Petits Poèmes en Prose* ("Le crépuscule excite les fous . . ."), as much as it does the Auden who was, as Richard Wilbur later recalled Bogan's characterization, "the poet of sickness especially when given a metaphysical value." But beyond these echoes the poem was a direct reflection of Bogan's own experiences, as once again she drew upon the impressions she had put into the 1934–35 draft of "The Long Walk." Realizing how much the poem owed to actual memory, she dropped the subtitle, "Imitated from Auden," from its original position as epigraph to that of a footnote in subsequent book publications. She herself had witnessed the heartlessness of a world from which rejected wives, mothers, and daughters turn to the banal opiates of knitting and gardening; she had herself suffered from the spiritual malnutrition whose cure lies beyond the unimaginative and cruel middle class:

> O fortunate bride, who never again will become elated after childbirth!
> O lucky older wife, who has been cured of feeling unwanted!
> To the suburban railway station you will return, return,
> To meet forever Jim home on the 5:35.
> You will be again as normal and selfish and heartless as anybody else.
>
> There is life left: the piano says it with its octave smile.
> The soft carpets pad the thump and splinter of the suicide to be.
> Everything will be splendid: the grandmother will not drink habitually.
> The fruit salad will bloom on the plate like a bouquet
> And the garden produce the blue-ribbon aquilegia.
> The cats will be glad; the fathers feel justified; the mothers relieved.
> The sons and husbands will no longer need to pay the bills.
> Childhoods will be put away, the obscene nightmare abated.

She had seen all of these women at "Bloomingdale's," and entered with imaginative sympathy into their feelings. The suburban world spoke for the modern situation, in which the heart is removed from its center, and suffers, not only metaphorically, but bodily, from lovelessness and emptiness, age and neglect.

The last poem in the book, "The Daemon," was, as Bogan later told May Sarton, *"given"* to her "one afternoon almost between one curb of a street and another." It may well have been an echo or a variation of a sentence she had underlined in the essay "Anima Hominis" in Yeats's *Per Amica Silentia Lunae:* "When I think of life as a struggle with the Daemon who would ever set us to the hardest work among those not impossible, I understand why there is a deep enmity between a man and his destiny, and why a man loves nothing but his destiny." It was written in late October or early November 1937 and came at a time when at least some part of Louise Bogan desperately wanted to put poetry behind her for good:

> Must I tell again
> In the words I know
> For the ears of men
> The flesh, the blow?

Her theme, the war between the spirit and the body, still required telling; her gift, exacting, ironic, and relentless, gave her no choice:

> Must I speak to the lot
> Who little bore?
> It said *Why not?*
> It said *Once more.*

The poem's petitioner seeks and is given reassurance. Though this "Daemon" is another version of the Fury ("You who know what we love, but drive us to know it"), its brief speech promises freedom from the rage and passion which had always made writing poetry an ordeal. Here, however, the gentle lyric affirms the poet's vocation without cruelty, banishing self-pity and self-dramatization. Ever-so-lightly self-mocked, Bogan thus meets her destiny, and finds it possible to return its lightness with lightness of her own.

IV
1942 ✿ 1954

CHANGE

AND HOURS

9 THE EIGHT-SIDED HEART

THE REVIEWS of *Poems and New Poems* were, with one or two exceptions, the strongest and most serious Bogan had yet received. Marianne Moore, in *The Nation,* wrote that Bogan's art "is compactness compacted. She uses a kind of forged rhetoric that nevertheless seems inevitable." In *The New Republic* Malcolm Cowley proclaimed, "Miss Bogan has done something that has been achieved by very few of her contemporaries; she has added a dozen or more to our small stock of memorable lyrics. She has added nothing whatever to our inexhaustible store of trash." Stanley Kunitz, in *Poetry,* praised her craftsmanship, her rejection of sentimentality, and her disciplined insights, seeing in her new poems (the ones Zabel had urged her not to publish) "an effort to release her poetic energies more fully and to extend her range." He went on to conclude that "the true world of Miss Bogan's imagination, of which she has up to now given us only fragmentary impressions, is 'the sunk land of dust and flame,' where an unknown terror is king, presiding over the fable of a life, in the deep night swarming with images of reproach and desire."

Mary Colum, writing in *The New York Times Book Review,* was decidedly unimpressed, however. She charged Bogan with writing under the shadow of Yeats, particularly in such poems as "Henceforth, from the Mind," and of indulging in "the poetry of self-absorption, as is the case with many other women poets." It was a grumpy and diminishing review, which probably distressed Bogan, despite the other good ones, but it assumes its appropriately trivial place in contrast to W. H. Auden's, in *Partisan Review,* which remains one of the best statements ever made about her work. He took as his starting point Kierkegaard's definition of genius, according to which, Auden says, genius unfolds from within, developing itself for itself, and he points to the modern problem of the artist's relation to the public:

A public is a disintegrated community. A community is a society of rational beings united by a common tie in virtue of the things that they all love; a public is a crowd of lost beings united only negatively in virtue of the things that they severally fear, among which one of the greatest is the fear of being responsible as a rational being for one's individual self-development.

When the genius yields himself to a public, he becomes a journalist; when his development receives no help from the public, his inner life and his poetry find themselves "at the mercy of personal accidents, love-affairs, illnesses, bereavements, and so forth." Louise Bogan's victory in *Poems and New Poems,* he goes on, is thus over both "the Collective Self" and the "Private Self," her poems the fruit of the axiom "that Self-development is a process of Self-surrender, for it is the Self that demands the exclusive attention of all experiences, but offers none in return." Knowing presumably nothing or at best very little about Bogan's private experience, Auden nevertheless acutely understood the stages of spiritual growth through which she had passed, the temptations faced, the consolations of personal mythology and self-dramatization ultimately rejected. She had now reached the point at which every strong artist must arrive, where "one must go on or under, live dangerously or not at all." Although he could not predict her future reputation, she was nevertheless a poet in whom "one has complete faith as to her instinct for direction and her endurance, and that, anyway, what she has already written is of permanent value." A time would come when she would "be paid the respect she deserves when many, including myself, I fear, of those who now have a certain news value, are going to catch it."

Since Auden destroyed letters sent to him, we will never know whether Bogan wrote to him about the review (it is likely she did), or what exactly she thought of it. We can be certain, however, that it must have meant a great deal to her, just as his November 17, 1941, letter had. Yet the review raised the troubling question of where to go next. If Bogan were to move forward to write major poetry, the equilibrium she had achieved would have to be disrupted. To F. W. Dupee, her friend at *Partisan Review,* she had recently written:

Someone said to me the other day that he didn't see any point in going on with psychiatric help, because THE CENTER was probably a horrible vortex of some kind, full of howls and shrieks and brimstone. I reminded him, in my motherly way, that lots of people have found a center: "the still point of the turning world," where the dove's foot rests at noon; and whether it is grace, as the Christians call it, or reconciliation, as the Jungians call it, it is possible to reach.

But to write poetry—strong, ambitious, fresh poetry—she would have to take new risks and seek out new ranges of experience. And at least the possibility of what to her might mean psychic catastrophe would inevitably accompany any renewed adventures into the creative unconscious. Nevertheless, from the perspective of worldly interests alone (much as she disavowed them), it was clearly time to advance her career. She had four books of poetry to her name, a substantial and growing reputation as a critic, and was only in her early forties. Surely she could afford to pursue fame more aggressively; surely the time had finally come for her stories and memoirs; surely her friends and the world in general were readier than ever to rejoice in her achievements.

What happened is this: after Bogan published *Poems and New Poems* in 1941, she did not write another poem until 1948. It was the longest she had ever gone without writing a poem; and, after it was over, she would never again have such a long dry spell. But for seven years she endured an unparalleled poetic emptiness.

The war did not help matters much. Everywhere she looked she saw hatred. Replying to a letter from twenty-eight-year-old May Sarton, who would later become a friend, but whom Bogan had not yet met, she spoke of a "general distrust and even hatred shown toward lyric poetry" at the time. The distrust of form and emotion was a problem in any era, she noted, but especially in the present, and there was little to do about the current situation except wait it out. Her letter revealed that she was disheartened and stoic, although real discouragement did not set in until just after *Poems and New Poems* came out. "The whole thing will fall down a deep well of indifference, now that we are at war with Japan," she wrote to Roethke shortly before the book appeared, "but one mustn't mind indifference. Did *I* cry when T. S. Matthews whooped up Laura Riding? Or when Dudley Fitts, in this current FURIOSO, stands up for M. Zaturenska as the greatest female poet alive?—NO." As much as she made a point of decrying general public recognition, she could no longer ignore the fact that she wanted it badly, and was beginning to take it as certain that she would never receive it.

The real problem, as she of course knew, was that she was once again finding it difficult to write. When Auden wrote to her about his *Partisan Review* piece, he asked what she was currently working on. Perhaps they had talked recently by phone; at any rate, his remarks imply some prior awareness of her difficulties. "It's unfortunate that finding it more and more difficult and less and less exciting to write is only a negative proof," he said.

IV 1 9 4 2 ~ 1 9 5 4

"One is not getting on unless one feels it, but one also feels it of course when one is simply drying up." Wheelock, who was encouraged (and with good reason) by the reception given to *Poems and New Poems,* thought it high time to start thinking about publishing a volume of collected poems. After all, it was the natural next step in the normal career of a poet. Edmund Wilson also favored a collected poems. But Louise balked:

In the set-up of the literary world, I sometimes think that the best thing to do is to do nothing; and to let the wave pass over the head. The American cultural situation is now lower than it has ever been before, so far as conscious art is concerned. There is a great deal of vigorous folk-art, and I am all for this; and people are excited about painting. . . .—All this means that there will be a poetry "revival" in about fifty years: maybe twenty-five. But I am so out of the general line, now; and I really have been so battered about that I don't care any more. What good does it do?

Wheelock pointed out that the cultural situation didn't make the slightest difference, "nor does the question, 'what good will it do?' seem to me to have any bearing on the matter." But Louise was profoundly gloomy, and her growing reputation as a critic didn't alter her feelings. Malcolm Cowley wrote to say that she had been producing "about the best general criticism of poetry that we have"; Jean Garrigue had written late in 1939 to praise and thank her for speaking up, in her reviews, against "soapbox poetry and conversion of Marxism to metaphor, the lament for a tired reliefer, and all that"; and a young poet and critic, Randall Jarrell, wrote to her in March 1941, from Austin, Texas, to say how much he admired her and was grateful for her treatment of Auden: "to accept him with ungrudging admiration is exactly what nobody (no good critic, that is—you'll know all the ones I'm talking about: Empson, even Blackmur, Tate, Eliot, Winters, etc.) of the generation before him has done."

Yet she was determined to see herself as shadowed in obscurity, slighted by the academic world and the literary world alike. One evening early in the summer of 1941, Auden came up to Washington Heights for a visit, "and we had a grand evening," she reported to Zabel, "just *crammed* with Insights and Autopsies, and Great Simple Thoughts, and Deep Intimations," during which Auden said that "he couldn't get over my obscurity; and I told him that it was because I wasn't respectable. 'But that wouldn't count among members of the academic world,' SAID HE, INNOCENTLY." Odd as it may seem, she still believed that she had a "reputation" as a "gangster's moll"—i.e., as John Coffey's accomplice-lover, and that it still influenced people who had some say over prize-giving. Unfortunately, her conviction that she would never live the episode down was hardly softened by the appearance in the winter of 1941 of Conrad Aiken's verbose autobiographical novel, *Conversation,* in which Bogan recognized a cruel caricature of herself around the time of her affair with Coffey.

But the truth is that it was not lingering gossip but her own perverse will that was to blame for her obscurity. Literary lives being as riddled with common human foibles as they are, it's hardly likely that an affair she'd had in the fall of 1919 ever had any influence over matters of recognition. High formal poetry, as she herself was ready to point out many times, rarely enjoyed wide support; and yet she refused to court not only potential readers but those who already knew and admired her work. In March 1940, for example, she was made consulting editor in poetry at *Partisan Review,* but refused to let her name appear on the masthead or accept money for the job. And early in December 1941, just after *Poems and New Poems* came out and was still available in bookstores, she turned down an offer to give a reading and an interview over the New York radio station WQXR, explaining to Roethke that she lacked the sales instinct. Arrogance and vanity played a large role in these decisions. It was as if she resented the thought of having to do anything or take any responsibility whatsoever for the effort of becoming better known.

Thus, as 1941 drew to a close, she found herself in the grip, once again, of "encircling glooms." Although these oppressive moments were not as severe as her former depressions, they nevertheless colored her life with a dull sadness. Her financial situation, never secure, was still precarious. Raymond Holden was erratic about sending alimony payments, and although she had been receiving a salary from *The New Yorker* since the spring of 1936, she did not make enough money to feel confident about handling emergencies. Daniel Bogan turned eighty in 1941, and had health problems which needed special care. Much against the grain, Louise forced herself to ask William Shawn, who was then managing editor of *The New Yorker,* not exactly for a raise, but for some form of supplement:

Since 1936 I feel that I have made the Verse department, step by step, into a real influence. I have had many letters from people whose opinions I respect, telling me that they have respected my criticism, and have always read it with both interest and profit. I feel that I did something toward keeping the flag flying (not to speak of the torch burning!) during the darkest days of political pressures upon writing. And I was touched last winter, to hear that W. H. Auden had spoken his mind freely, saying to many people that I was the best critic of poetry in America.

She received the necessary financial help, but her low spirits did not let up. With the war on, *Poems and New Poems,* which would even in the best of circumstances have hardly become a best-seller, sold poorly. Poetry was on its way out, she announced dourly to Wheelock, and whatever was to come next in literature was being formed, that instant, on the battlefields. When it came into its own, as it inevitably would, it wouldn't bear the slightest resemblance to post–World War I poetry.

Her feelings of being slighted, her pessimism about the state of poetry, and her desire to free herself from depression before it got out of hand led her to break one of her cherished post-"cure" rules: that in difficult times, often the best thing was to do exactly nothing. This piece of wisdom she owed to Dr. Wall, who said that it would at least prevent one from making a mistake, and she had relied on it more than once in recent years. Often dissatisfied with the way she had been treated at Scribner's, she was now outraged that the firm had not taken out even a small advertisement for *Poems and New Poems* in *The New Yorker* when the book came out. In April 1942, by which time the book had sold only four hundred copies, Scribner's turned down a proposal Louise had recently submitted for an anthology of lyric poems, and she felt disappointed, humiliated, and betrayed. It was one thing to be bypassed for the Pulitzer, but it was a shocking thing, she felt, to be so undermined in her projects by her own publisher.

For a year she did nothing, but her grievances rankled. Over the years, Louise had from time to time telephoned Wheelock and asked him to meet her for a talk at Child's at Seventy-seventh Street and Broadway. Once again she telephoned, arranging to meet him there on February 16, 1943. When he arrived, she announced, right away, "I have a bone to pick with you." She refused to go into detail, and would only say that he could have done more for her. She then charged him with always bringing her into his office "by the back door." When she accused him of never having introduced her to Charles Scribner, the founder's grandson, Wheelock replied, "Charlie doesn't meet many authors, he's a foxhunting man." He wasn't sure what had brought on her attack, and tried good-humored forbearance, saying, "I'm not in the mood to quarrel with you, Louise; if I were to quarrel, I'd quarrel with William Carlos Williams or Wallace Stevens, but not with you." His efforts to be gentle and placating were unavailing; the meeting did, in fact, mark her break with Scribner's.

A week later Louise wrote to Wheelock to say that despite the value she had always placed upon their friendship, she felt "immeasurably relieved" by her decision to go her own way:

I don't know what it was, and shall never know; but I am certain that I am not wrong in thinking that there was some obstacle there, which I could never overcome, and which blocked me, in spite of all the flattering things you always said to me. I felt it, and it depressed me. Now all that is over. I can think of my plans without the knowledge that any book I interested myself in doing would be a burden to its publisher: a problem. I should rather never be published again if I had to feel this fog around my projects. And I shall never be published again, unless I find a publisher who will work with me, to the extent at least, of an openly expressed mind, and a good deal of friendly and openhearted enthusiasm.

It's strange when the iron enters into one's soul; but it's v. bracing.

In the past, Wheelock had always known when to coax and cajole, but for once he could give her no answer, at least no answer that would satisfy her. There was a war on; high lyric poetry was unlikely at any time to have a wide market; and critical reception, as distinct from advertising, was more often than not the major source of sales for a book like hers. He pointed out that one project rejected didn't mean that he was unwilling to examine further projects; to the contrary, he was delighted to know of any plans for future work. If she would not listen to this explanation, she would listen to nothing. Finally, her charge that he had always brought her into his office "by the back door" was completely groundless.

So he resigned himself, gracefully and sadly, to a loss that hurt him for the rest of his life. He loved and admired Bogan, and she could never know how much he believed in her and had tried to help her. When Mary Colum's review of *Poems and New Poems* had come out in *The New York Times Book Review* in November 1941, Wheelock had written, without Bogan's knowledge, to John Peale Bishop, Allen Tate, Morton Zabel, Rolfe Humphries, and Edmund Wilson, drawing their attention to the malicious absurdities in the review, and suggesting that they might want to *do* something about it. As Bogan's publisher, he explained, he was not in a position to write to *The Times* himself, owing to the charge of prejudice such a letter would immediately bring down. It is interesting to see how Bogan's old friends responded to Wheelock's act of loyalty. Tate answered that he "should hesitate to get in between two high-spirited Celtic ladies." Wilson replied that since Louise had dedicated *The Sleeping Fury* to him, he was not in a good position to respond either, although he was forwarding Wheelock's letter to Humphries. Zabel and Bogan were still not on speaking terms (a fact that Wheelock probably didn't know). Bishop did not answer. Of all those to whom Wheelock had written, Humphries alone came through with a thoughtful defense of Bogan's merit.

Had Wheelock himself written to *The Times,* he would have called her a poet of genius, the best lyric poet of her generation. Even now, on losing her, he did not allow himself bitterness, and he had every reason to feel bitter, having been wounded to the quick in 1936 when, with her never-to-beswayed-by-friendship integrity, she had declared in a *New Yorker* review that his *Poems Old and New* were weakened by an old-fashioned romanticism. He had neither questioned nor rebuked her for the review, and now he blamed himself for her decision to leave Scribner's, convinced that he had failed her as an editor.

After a short period of estrangement, they managed to remain good friends. In 1951 it was Wheelock who nominated Louise for membership in the National Institute of Arts and Letters, writing Auden to request that he second the nomination, and in 1954 it was Wheelock again who nominated her for membership in the Academy of American Poets. She found her own respect and affection for Wheelock growing through the years. His gallantry, loyalty, and faith in her gifts touched her, as well as his fidelity to the tender and melancholy romanticism he had nurtured in his own poetry, however out of keeping with modernism it may have been.

In breaking with Scribner's, however, there can be no doubt that Bogan cast herself adrift, with very destructive results. She did not find a new publisher for her poetry until 1954, when Cecil Hemley, the poet and founder of the Noonday Press, brought out *Collected Poems, 1923–1953*. By 1948, all her books were out of print and she had no new poems with which to fight the old spectre of "creative despair." The break with Scribner's, moreover, was almost followed by a break with *The New Yorker*. She was sick to death of grinding out two yearly omnibus *Verse* departments and countless brief notices, and the constant reading and note-taking necessary to prepare the pieces exhausted her. Fortunately, this time she did nothing. "Wait awhile, something says. Take it easy. Don't do anything. Let the break come; but don't make it," she told herself; "it is such a bad time that someone must tell the truth, in whatever small quantity. Take the contumely, and keep on reviewing poetry."

Much of her current frustration came from her perfect awareness that she was blocked as a poet. Waiting patiently for poems (with the example of Rilke's patience always before her), she was conscious of the ways in which she evaded deliberate composition. She was falling, she knew, into what she called a "double-boiler existence." This was a phrase she coined to describe her mother's tendency to keep from cooking a special dish for lack of *the right kind* of double-boiler, when she could have gone right out and bought one for fifty cents. Writers who refused to get to work without the perfect setup, with table and chair and pen and ink and *the right kind* of paper, were guilty of the "double-boiler" attitude, and Louise, who quipped to her friends that she couldn't get to work without the right kind of *table*, saw herself giving in to it. She considered giving up working at her beautiful cherrywood table (one of two pieces of furniture that had survived the

Hillsdale fire), and suddenly bought herself a new Swedish-modern table, with two leaves, in obedience to yet another post-"cure" rule: that in order not to be dominated by objects, you must get the thing you need, or not get it, and end the matter there. So she bought herself the table, but still no poems came.

The inner drought had been affecting her in other ways. For some years now she had ceased to keep a close journal. After 1937 she filled her notebooks with recipes, names and addresses, and literally dozens of book lists and passages useful for her reviews. But the sharp, felt *aperçus* she had produced so abundantly in the thirties came to a standstill, and by 1943 it had been six years since she had written down her impressions of people, or marked the stages in her interior life, or even noted down the details of weather and season. Then, in a notebook, on a page dated June 8, 1943, she wrote:

Ft. Tryon Park
A cool day morning: overcast. The peonies just over.
The iris out. Also oriental poppies.

Cf. 1944, same time.
Out? Freer? Firmer?
. . . . . .
Rather stale, restless.

There was no elaboration, nor did writing this passage initiate a renewed enthusiasm for keeping a journal. It was as if she had made a note that day merely to commemorate the fact that the era of inner turmoil had passed. She no longer watched her moods to see what literary material they would reveal. Seismic tremors and volcanic rumblings no longer threatened her equilibrium. How often she saw her lover, or with what feelings, we can have no idea. He is never mentioned in letters or notebooks of this period. Maidie was now twenty-six, living with Louise again and working as a medical secretary at Columbia-Presbyterian Hospital. She and her mother cared deeply for one another, but each lived her own life in complete independence. Late in 1943, Daniel Bogan, who had been living once again in Portland and was now in his late eighties, underwent a minor operation, after which Louise and Maidie managed to get "the old gentleman" into a boarding house, with good food, in White Plains. But he missed his friends, and before long went back to Portland for good, and there he seems to have developed a special fondness for a woman who joined him every afternoon for a drink.

Louise thus lived a life of responsible, acknowledged solitude. A certain yearly rhythm had by now become established. She had her fall and spring *New Yorker* verse essays, and in August her two weeks of reading and rest at Swampscott, which she also occasionally visited in March to see and hear the equinoctial ocean. In many ways the woman who had written Bogan's first three books of poetry was difficult to find in the wise, disciplined, and intensely private literary worker. She had once said to John Hall Wheelock, "A woman writes poetry with her ovaries," and had quipped to Roethke that women poets dried up at forty. Certainly there was some serious equation in her mind between menopause (which, according to Wheelock, occurred relatively early in her life) and her inability to write poetry. Reticent about emotional matters, she was almost lockjawed about physical ones, and apart from this remark to Wheelock, made when she was about forty-three, we do not and cannot know what physical and emotional effects she may have experienced during the change of life. But she had once been a slender, passionate young woman, beautiful, gifted, and profoundly responsive to sexual love. Was she reminded of that woman when she wrote to Rolfe Humphries from Swampscott, in August 1943, that she had spent her first two days there fuming over and analyzing

the piano practice of some girl or other. I sat there *sneering:* when all that was required of me was to *listen* and understand just why she was playing as she was: all the notes, in tempo, but badly out of time, and with the twists and *rubatos* of the amateur *expressing* herself. Now, I am a little cured of that. Perfect love casteth out fear; that is true. One has to stop being nasty and hateful, both concerning oneself and others, if one is to stop suffering and stop getting panicky. It is not enough, to get rid of oneself; one must really feel at least *kindly* toward others. Not superior. All right; I know that she was hurrying those triplets in the *Moonlight Sonata.* But I shouldn't have *hated* her and felt fine myself, in a horrid way, because she was.

The young woman playing so badly and so romantically was an image of the young woman Louise herself had once been. To forgive this memory of herself was still harder than to accept it with tolerant humor. Hatred and resentment, and the desire not to have been who she once was, still rose too easily to the surface. The "grief-work" was still unfinished, and what she called her "wisdom" had still a thing or two to learn.

Not being able to write poetry did not prevent Louise from serving as midwife at the birth of someone else's work. Such generosity took place, as it often does at its best, within a friendship with a younger person. In June 1938, St. Clair McKelway at *The New Yorker* wrote to Bogan, asking for new poems on behalf of the new person in charge of poetry, who, he added, was most anxious to meet her, being one of her admirers. This turned out to be William Maxwell, the thirty-year-old Illinois-born author of two novels,

Bright Center of Heaven (1934) and *They Came Like Swallows* (1937). Louise knew who he was, having been so moved the previous December by his short story "Never to Hear Silence" that she had written to Katharine S. White to congratulate the magazine for publishing it and to say that it "made me believe, for a while, again, in the tenderness and strength of the human heart."

After Maxwell and Bogan met, she invited him up to the "isolated regions" of Washington Heights for a walk and hamburgers to be picked up along the way. Another invitation soon followed for a walk in Fort Tryon Park, when spring should have reached a fuller bloom. "The food there is Cracker Jack and Coca-Cola, both of which I like very much.—If war arrives," she added, "I shan't be able to do it, as I'll be in jail, as an alcoholic Quaker." She brought up the subject of her memoirs, explaining that they would be written as a series of disconnected *aperçus,* more or less on the model of Rilke's *Journal of My Other Self,* which had a lot of " 'Here I am in the empty room, within the ring of lamplight, while outside the rain falls on the taxi-cabs and the cripples. It is night, and I have a pencil in my hand' . . . That sort of thing."

Maxwell, as *The New Yorker*'s poetry editor, very much wanted her to contribute new poems, but he understood her reluctance to force them, and didn't press her. Early in 1940 he went on leave from the magazine to work on a new novel, *The Folded Leaf,* but he and Bogan remained in touch. In July he invited her to lunch at the Claremont, and she agreed, saying she was getting over her fear of public places (a fear she had not admitted openly to other correspondents) and explaining, "What bothers me most are *cultured voices,* raised in graceful badinage. I always want to become completely rough; because what I love most in the world is true grace. And the only antidote to affectation is obscenity." They did not as yet know each other very well: she began her letters with "Dear Mr. Maxwell" and "Dear Maxwell," and signed them with her full name, but almost immediately there was an ease of disclosure between them, a frankness and simplicity that had the effect of charm without the vulgar motive of seduction. Their friendship was still in its beginning stages when, during the winter of 1941, he came up to her apartment to listen to records, and had her down for tea at his Patchin Place apartment. She had asked him if he were "tone-deaf or not," adding that if he weren't, he should come to hear some of her Duparc and Mahler songs. He had never heard these songs before, and his reactions to the music thrilled her. He was, she reported to Zabel, "the most wonderful record-listener I have ever met. He really breaks right up, and is shattered, and is frank, and is disapproving, and is delighted, so that it seems another *you* is involved: another expression of one's own taste." The plants on his windowsills, the fireplace, books, and beautiful furniture in his apartment delighted her as well; here was a person whose spirit was in full harmony with her own. "Maxwell is really an exquisite human being," she continued to Zabel, "and I wish there was something between love and friendship that I could tender him; and some gesture, not quite a caress, I could give him. A sort of smoothing. I may be able to work something along those lines later! Seriously, I simply love him like a brother."

Her love for him was by no means that simple. The possibility of danger existed, although she recognized it immediately and cut it short with her sense of humor. She felt, as she said two days later, in her next letter to Zabel, "like the Marschallin, if you must know. . . ," but she quickly termed the matter "absurd" and vowed that there would be no *Rosenkavalier*-like goings on:

No foamings of lace out from the big Baroque (rococo, rather) bed; no scampering of slender young male legs around the boudoir; no large-bosomed breathings and swellings and flutterings and burnings. I haven't any of the appurtenances pertaining to such a situation, from the rococo bed through the bosom; and my whole emotional set is also away from all these things: the cold stern light of the-response-with-insight having burned under the ribs for seven years. Howbeit, I *should* feel like the Marschallin if I could!

The question of a love affair resolved itself with the greatest delicacy and tact. Bogan sent Maxwell an inscribed copy of *Dark Summer,* whose design still seemed to her the most beautiful of all her books (". . . I swear to you it was the book I had dreamed about since I was a child"), saying that it was "the least I could do for a person to whom one can say everything; and to a friend made in the non-friend-making-years (even if you did not happen to be the one who listened to me for four hours on the boat deck, the second night out, and has stuck to me ever since!)." Soon they were calling each other by their first names (although she had gotten used to writing him as "Maxwell"). Then, in August, shortly after she had been to tea in Patchin Place, and left behind a glove and a small turban, she sent him this note:

Something may have been garbled; in some way I have hurt you. That bothers me. Yes. In any acquaintanceship, even the most casual, one sooner or later comes up against the submerged part of the other person; the two thirds of the ice-berg, existing under water. I did not think that this would happen, in the case of our friendship; but since it seems to, there's nothing I can do, because I don't know what the obstacle is. Anyhow, dear young Maxwell, remember that you owe me nothing, not even that hat, which you may toss into the nearest ash-can. You will manage your own talent, and do your own work; and the decade from thirty to forty is a wonderful one, believe me. Everything becomes, in it, what it is born to be.

Louise

Maxwell had no idea what she was talking about, and called her in distress to convince her that there was nothing wrong between them. What he was seeing for the first time was the inexorable pattern in Louise Bogan's life, according to which wherever she truly loved, she also expected rejection. The friendship weathered this sudden assault from the ghosts of Louise's childhood, and entered a new stage. Sometime in 1940, Maxwell had showed her the short story which later became *The Folded Leaf,* and she'd been immediately convinced that the tale of a stormy friendship between two adolescent boys was a rare and valuable subject. Insisting that he go on with it, she now intensified her encouragement, and between 1940 and 1944 saw the manuscript through every stage, including second, third, and fourth drafts, and "never once," as Maxwell later recalled, "said couldn't you manage this by yourself now?"

Throughout the composition of the book, Louise made solid technical suggestions. Maxwell had begun his story in the first person, but she urged a shift into the third, explaining that, in general, the first-person delicate observer tends to take up too much room and consequently to get more than a fair share of irony. Since the sensitive narrator tends to know so much more than anyone else in the novel, "one has to play him down a little, merely for proportion's sake, and that is difficult, working with 'I.' " In the third person, she knew, Maxwell would be able to tell the story of his young protagonist's agonizing passage into maturity with the freedom to discover innumerable effects of pathos, humor, and insight.

Still, he found the novel difficult going. When his rough draft had reached four hundred pages, with no end in sight, he wrote: "The problem of form in a long novel is frightening, and once you admit of length you also admit of a kind of insane inclusiveness. I find it hard to believe that I really know what I'm doing or that anyone else will know. New characters keep turning up and telling their life history, just the way they do actually in real life and I'm almost at the end of my patience." He worried, too, about his style, and asked her to mark "anything that seems like cheap satire, or too easy writing, or just false; and sometime we'll go over it together, God willing." But Louise never accused him of doing anything wrong, saying only, at certain points, that he hadn't got "the swiftest kind of rightness." She made practical suggestions for working through writing blocks: do needlepoint (like the King of Sweden); read Flaubert, Chekhov, James, Rilke, and Viola Meynell; and be on good terms with yourself: "You'll have to be at least pleased with your life, or the Blocks will get you. I do want this book to get written. Let me help if I can." She was interested in his time of life, fascinated by the unfolding evidences of human and creative growth she saw in his work, and for his thirty-fifth birthday in 1943 sent him this quotation (itself a quotation) from Marianne Moore's "In Distrust of Merits":

> When a man is prey to anger,
> he is moved by outside things; when he holds
> his ground in patience patience
> patience, that is action or
> beauty . . .

and noted, "You're getting old enough to understand it." He did understand it and, what's more, was deeply grateful for all that she was doing for him. "Thank you for realizing, in the midst of your own difficulties, that I would be waiting for your approval and unable to go on very far without it," he wrote her. She was too lenient, he thought, and yet her lenience was itself an effective form of criticism: "From the criticisms that you do make I manage to construct greater severity for my own attitude toward what I am doing." Her intuitions were of great service to him because, fundamentally, she and Maxwell lived in the same creative universe. Like Louise, Maxwell had a wonderful eye for things and places, especially as these were altered by time. He wrote from his home town during a return visit:

My destination was the street I grew up on, and when I turned into it I began to weep uncontrollably. The houses and lawns and trees were so *small*. The strange thing about it is that I have been up that street many times since I have been grown and it never looked small before, so I must always have gone back to it as a child, until now. I came to our house, stripped by time of its shrubs and flower beds and vines and even of its grape arbor, looking bleak and shoddy, and with a sign on the porch: TOURIST HOME, and I thought my heart was going to break.

Pieces of furniture and the weather seemed to live in his imagination as vigorously and sadly as his characters. What Bogan later called "the bizarre, disordered, ungainly, furtive, mixed elements of one's life" were equally Maxwell's special domain, in which the extraordinary-ordinary disasters of family and friendship occurred, in which characters—often children—were at a loss and often baffled by things, and in which the heart had to construct its own makeshift wisdom by simply going through whatever it had to. His form was the novel, hers was the poem; but in sensibility they were both lyric poets. Once, during one of their walks in Fort Tryon Park, during the period when Maxwell was working on the novel, Bogan turned to him and, quoting Yeats, said, "The innocent and the beautiful have no enemy but time."

At last, in September 1944, Maxwell sent her the completed manuscript of *The Folded Leaf*. After reading it through, Louise asked him this question about the last paragraph:

... is it true that the boy actually gets rid of all his childhood, then? —Couldn't there be a loophole remark, in which it could be hinted that getting rid of one's childhood is almost a lifetime job; unless real steps are taken? Of course, Lymie has taken what would seem to be the ultimate step—attempted oblivion—but he has come back to life where everything is so partial that one has to renew the fight almost day by day. —I came upon a remark of Goethe's, famous to everyone but me, no doubt, from the last part of *Faust II*, in which he says that one must fight for one's spiritual freedom *every single day*.

We do not know what Maxwell had written before Louise suggested a "loophole sentence," but the last two paragraphs of *The Folded Leaf*, as published, read:

When he emerged from the sheltering trees and came out on the golf course, there was a peculiar lightness in his step. Although he didn't realise it, he had left his childhood (or if not all, then the greater part of it) behind in the clearing. Watched over by tree spirits, guarded by Diana the huntress and the King of the Woods, it would be as safe as anything in this world.

It would never rise and defeat him again.

The phrase in parentheses was the "loophole," quietly inserted, leaving to implication all that Bogan had counseled about the battle for spiritual freedom. Only one problem remained—the title—and soon she sent Maxwell the third strophe in the Choric Song of "The Lotus-Eaters" ("Lo! in the middle of the wood, / The folded leaf is woo'd from out the bud"). She had first seen the quotation in a book about Shakespeare by J. W. Mackail, she said, and it had "the adolescent sorrow about *growth;* which always seems tragic to the young," and was one of "the moving themes of your novel." He took his title from the passage, and the whole passage itself as an epigraph to which he carefully appended Tennyson's age, twenty-four, when it was written. And he dedicated the novel "For Louise Bogan."

BOGAN'S GENEROSITY toward Maxwell, and the pleasure of standing so close to his work seemed to have a quickening effect upon her. In June 1941, F. W. Dupee wrote to say that he saw in her a great deal of literary energy which is now getting quietly poised for a real leap. You must get to work on those Gothic memories: with your sense of Period and of People, you'd do them wonderfully. And you have the kind of quarrel with the world which makes a perfect generating principle of reminiscences, as with Rousseau.

Clearly she had spoken to Dupee as well as Maxwell about her prose memoirs. She now felt that she could produce five or six more stories, as well as some occasional poems, over a ten-year period—not, to be sure, a crushing agenda. In May 1945 she wrote Maxwell that she had taken out the manuscript and placed it on her writing table, and that the thick pile of disconnected pieces had both disheartened and reassured her: "I don't want to confess; I want to create; and the hatred of confessing has been one thing that has held me up all these years," she confided to him. This time it was his turn to coax and encourage a resistant gift:

What is this reluctance to confess? Freud says somewhere that all people betray themselves through the very pores of their skin. And my own experience has been that confession leads straight lickety split to creation, if you are of a certain temperament, and creation, as you have pointed out . . . is inevitably confession. I commit murder now night after night in my dreams, and am coming to take pride in it. And in the victims. Only the confessions of small people are embarrassing, and God knows you're not SMALL!

But Maxwell's warm and affectionate remonstrance notwithstanding, the stories and memoirs remained untouched. This was disheartening for Louise, and might have led to the kind of self-recrimination which made returning to the work even harder, except that her literary and social isolation was beginning to lessen through purely external developments. To begin with, there was a reconciliation, early in the summer of 1943, with Morton Zabel. He appears to have come to New York, called her and seen her, and to have left a wild and exhilarated record of this event in a letter written soon thereafter:

Dear Sweet Puss:

You won't give in. Oh, no. So I guess I'll have to give in. But then you *did* give in, didn't you?—so I guess further that it's my turn now.

And how have you been feeling since our Great Convergence, our Celebrated Reunion, our Beautiful Love-Hate-and-Reparation Performance of three weeks ago? Didn't it make you feel *much* better? Didn't it give the old spring a good crank? Doesn't the heart beat lighter, the spirit flit more gaily, and time move with a lighter wing? Now don't be afraid to say "Yes." I'm not. We certainly gave dat ol' dabbil, GUILT, a swift kick in the pants that time—and see how easily it was done! . . . Of course I suppose I was an awful pushover; a Crawler on all Fours; an Abject Meliorist; an example of anything but moral and intellectual rigor. But then I *liked* it that way: it was *My* Louise all over again as in the olden, golden Time Long Ago, and made me feel as warm around the heart as My Antonia: there we sat, the *aperçus,* recognitions, and insights flying like fireworks—I basking, buoyed, ensorcelled, et Louise, toute entière, à sa proie attachée!

> And lo, how the flow'rs of Philosophy sprang,
> The violets of Virtue shot up with a bang,
> The lilies of Love and the roses of Rue,
> And Agony's asphodels. Boop-boop-a-doo!
> She told me how anger ennobles the spirit,
> And how lovely is rue, if you know how to wear it,
> And how fury enlarges the Character's riches
> (Provided it's spent on the right kind of bitches),
> And how to take blows on the chin and breadbasket,
> And sing while you take 'em "A tisket, a tasket!"
> And to brag while they fall and to boast while they rain
> "IT'S HELL—but I don't feel a pang or a pain."
> When she had me all weaving and gasping for air
> She announced, "*I'm* an Artist, like Charles Baudelaire."

They were back to their gossiping and teasing, their squabbling and eye-to-eyeing. Letters between New York and Chicago once again flew through the mails, with much relief and satisfaction to these two often isolated and solitary people.

Yet another sign of change came when Henry Allen Moe, the director of the Guggenheim Foundation, asked Bogan to give her opinion of twenty-five grant applicants currently under consideration. This boosted her morale enormously, since, as she told Zabel, she had believed for the last ten years that Moe never listened to her opinions whether she was for or against anyone. She was invited onto the jury for the Harriet Monroe Poetry Award at the University of Chicago and asked to give the Hopwood Lecture at the University of Michigan, in the spring of 1944. On June 8th of that year, exactly twelve months after she had sat in Fort Tryon Park and written a brief journal passage, she again took stock in her notebook:

A cool morning. Sun. Neither "stale" nor "restless"!

Ft. Tryon Park

Out? Freer? Firmer?
These were the questions I asked of the future, last year on this date. —The answer to all of them is: *Yes:* to a great extent: *Yes.*

Not v. *far out*. But I have a little more money ($40 a month). I have had some recognition: Moe & the H. Monroe prize judging; and the Michigan lecture.

Also, I have begun to write a little more easily. I have penned down *two major ideas:* folk art & the importance of the detective story. I have continued to do good N.Yr. reviews.

I have many more projects "working" for the future. A long rambling piece of prose (autobiography in the form of a "thriller"). A further elaboration—dissection of the "crime" story. Poems ("The 19th Century")

I have got my father settled.

I know my enemies.

I think I can outwit them.

So: ? June 8/ 1945. Out? Freer? Firmer?

The additional money came from *The New Yorker*. The "folk art" piece, "Some Notes on Popular and Unpopular Art," published in the September–October 1943 issue of *Partisan Review,* served her once again as her Hopwood Lecture; and the "detective story" piece, "The Time of the Assassins," appeared in the April 22, 1944, issue of *The Nation*. Both pieces were superb. Neither the autobiographical thriller nor her plans to write poems went on to further development at this time. Yet she was "out," "freer," and "firmer." Since she was attached to the idea that she had enemies (both inner and outer), her conviction that she could "outwit them" was a sign of robust and confident emotional health, and the entry was basically an affirmation of strength and wholeness.

ONCE THE WORLD began to rediscover Louise Bogan, it seemed unable to get enough of her. Early in November 1944 she received a letter from Archibald MacLeish, who was then Librarian of Congress, inviting her to meet with him about the prospect of becoming a Fellow in American Letters at the Library of Congress. A little nonplussed at receiving so courteous a summons from a poet whom she had so relentlessly excoriated during the previous decade, Louise drafted a reply in which she noted that in the past she had always considered her value as a writer to depend in part on maintaining her separation "from most of the activities of the literary scene." In recent years, however, her attitude toward working with groups of people had become more flexible "in what I was glad to find a natural way; a part of the process of growth." She closed on a conciliatory note: "I don't want to sound sententious; but I do want you to know that I was touched to receive your invitation at this particular time." She knew she would join distinguished company, and that her associates at the Library would include Willard Thorp, Katherine Anne Porter, Allen Tate, Carl Sandburg, Mark Van Doren, and Theodore Spencer; and she also believed that since the isolation of her life over the past six or seven years may well have strengthened her writing block, it was possible that she might be aided creatively by returning to an external routine that included contact with her fellow writers.

Not long after she accepted her appointment as Fellow, she turned down an offer from Russell Noyes to teach creative writing at the University of Indiana at Bloomington, giving as the reason her heavy critical commitments and the desire to return to creative work "that recent material difficulties have rather blocked." But in private she resolved "to come off it, or come out of it, and accept all invitations to speak, read, teach or turn handsprings, in public," and she actually read her poetry one evening at the YMHA, sharing the platform with Dorothy Parker, who "took it all quite nicely, too, and I rapidly worked out of my dismay at facing a totally Parker audience (Maidie sat there sweating with sheer terror, after seeing what I had been gotten into)." Parker showed up wearing a magenta turban and a mink-lined coat, but Bogan, who was wearing a tweed suit and a little close-fitting hat, remained unruffled. "O yes," she wrote proudly to Zabel, "I have learned a great deal since I saw you last. I am now an expert at judging the saturation point of any given audience to my works. I can now rise, as cool as a cucumber, and look them over, and shape the thing up. I can even cut and edit my own prose, *on my feet,* when I feel things are running overtime. The Michigan lecture taught me something."

She was expanding her social life too, attending a big *Partisan Review* party in May 1944 at the home of Philip Rahv and his wife, the architect Nathalie Swan, where she saw Marianne Moore for the first time since they had worked next to one another in the St. Mark's Place Branch Library, the winter of 1922, before Louise went to Vienna. Moore greeted Bogan "with great pleasantness," Louise wrote to Morton, "and kept remarking that I had done her a great service in writing that poem to my brother. (I never quite understood this.)" Apparently she did not know that Marianne Moore's brother had served in World War II as fleet chaplain on Admiral Nimitz's flagship in the Pacific. The party moreover served as the occasion for a reunion between Bogan and Allen Tate, who, shielding her against an onslaught of "small groups of very small Young (usually female) writers of verse" and "admirers," eventually escorted her away from the party and into a taxi which drove through the rain up to Washington Heights, "and many were the anecdotes and memories—of those far away days when we all lived in tenement houses, were young and thin and beautiful, loved our husbands and wives, worked hard at everything, including shovelling coal and cooking large dinners for ten people." Tate remarked that Louise, in those days, had looked "emaciated"; and it was true that at present, just on the verge of forty-eight, she was, like her mother before her, tall and solidly filled-out to the point of stoutness.

Young people had begun to write, asking her to read their poems and write articles for their heroically edited "little" magazines. A young man, J. D. Salinger, "has been bombarding me with poems for a week or so," she wrote to Maxwell in November 1944, and a group of women who taught at Yale but had been educated at Bryn Mawr wrote to her as one of the Harriet Monroe poetry award judges to ask her to vouch, as she put it to Allen Tate, for "Marianne Moore's transcendent worth."

Her first meeting with the Fellows in American Letters of the Library of Congress, which took place in November 1944, went beautifully. She had drinks, went to dinners, and, to her own surprise, discovered that she enjoyed every minute of it. To Zabel she wrote that it was all "v. good for me, because I had for so long indulged in tail-lashings about the good seed being passed by, etc. etc. I was becoming a little peculiar on the subject, and it did me good to face reality that was somewhat rosier in hue than usual." She hinted to Zabel that yet another development was about to be set in motion out of her Washington connection, but that she would have to wait a little longer to announce it. This was her appointment, in June, as Consultant in Poetry to the Library of Congress for the year 1945–46. She held back from accepting for two or three weeks, and then, as she wrote Maxwell, "found that all my thought-up *refusals* were actuated by pure fear. So then I had to embrace a non-fearing acceptance." *The New Yorker* agreed to hold her reviewing job for her, and, with her New York affairs in good order, off she went to Washington just after Labor Day. There she was lent an apartment by the poet Selden Rodman, which she described as a "combination of something out of Joseph Conrad's earlier period ('Almayer's Folly' or 'The Outcast of the Isles') and those Joseph von Sternberg chicken-coops in which Marlene Dietrich used to find herself, ten or twelve years ago."

The work at the Library she found delightful. She had a suite of offices, with a view of the Capitol, "an intelligent young assistant who treats me like a Mandarin," and a worthy project in the compilation of a "checklist" of books published in the humanities in Great Britain between 1939 and 1946, as a record of achievement in *belles-lettrist* publishing during the impossibly difficult period of the war. She was homesick for New York, managing to get back to the city every other weekend, but at the same time made a new and lasting friendship with Katie Louchheim, an aspiring poet who later became Deputy Assistant Secretary of State under Presidents Kennedy and Johnson. Mrs. Louchheim later wrote a memoir of Louise Bogan for *The American Pen* (Spring 1975), in which we may find a vivid portrait of her friend during the late 1940s. She recalled a taxi ride from the

Capitol to Mrs. Louchheim's house in Georgetown on a dark, rainy day in 1948, when Louise had come to Washington for a meeting of the Fellows in American Literature:

As I sat beside her, I tried to memorize her face. She had a crisp commanding presence, bright eyes and a small mouth. Some intuitive reaction told me she had mastered terror, climbed over difficulties, and come out with her laughter intact. She laughed a lot, her laughter was deep in her throat and mocking. There was something diabolic about her; this was a woman one could both admire and fear. And yet she encouraged one to talk, she dug at one, insisting on knowing who one was and what one was about.

Mrs. Louchheim was especially struck by Bogan's dislike of pretension:

She was particularly hard on aristocrats and I once watched her make fun of a Washington VIP, who had been name- and place-dropping at a party. Amused and mocking, she and Wystan Auden took turns telling each other where they had been and whom they had met. Auden's list included Balliol, London, and Tyrol, hers included Worcester, Ballardville [sic], Boston, Mass. . . . They also let drop that they had eaten "crumpets with Coleridge, partridge with Proust." I watched the snob limp away, having overheard them. After putting the dignitary down, she laughed shamelessly at her own wit.

For Louise, going to Washington to take up the appointment as Consultant had taken courage, not only to enter a public role, but also to enjoy her success. To Zabel, who she thought would insist that as a pure artist she should remain unsullied by peripheral activity and refuse to accept the appointment, she wrote that she had become "a chastened person who does not go all stiff and bug-eyed at a little success." Good fortune worked in surprising ways. "During those eight long years in Washington Heights," she wrote to Rolfe Humphries, "I thought the magic influence which wafted me in 1917 into a concrete Government flat in the wilds of Panama had tapered off. But O no! Once the Subject of Queer Events and Places, always such a subject. I shouldn't surprise myself if I spent my old age in (1.) The Kremlin or (2.) a grass hut in Malaya."

She had discovered before that a period of beginnings was often one of endings as well. The affair which had begun early in the summer of 1937 was now over, the lovers having drifted apart soon after the war. She seems to have accepted its end without regret or great sadness. On June 6, 1945, in the middle of deciding whether or not to accept her appointment in Washington, she once again took inventory of her general situation, and did not mention her love affair. Much had happened during the year, including a brief hospital stay for a foot operation in June 1944, her annual vacation at Swampscott in August, a visit in October to Auden at Swarthmore, and William Maxwell's marriage. She had read at the Library of Congress, lectured at Bard College, and given a reading over the radio; on June 20th, she was scheduled to read at Bennington. On all of these she now reflected:

Ft. Tryon

The day for my yearly check up on destiny! (2 days earlier than last year.)

Cool & sunny, after one of the coldest springs on record. Black gabardine suit, aqua blouse, no hat.

Quite tired, after finishing Benet [*The Dust Which Is God*] and *Tahl* [by Jeremy Ingalls] but happy to be free for a time. . . . Active, interested, full of plans.

The year has been quite extraordinary. My "public" life increased by leaps & bounds. It will be interesting to see, next year, if this was a *false alarm,* or what!

The "enemy" business [she had spoken the year before of knowing who her enemies were] seems to be in abeyance (in reality). In my consciousness: much less apparent.

The things I wish for now are:

1) semi-permanence in city-country set up.
2) Some grace really to write my long prose.
3) Some physical freedom to match my gaining spiritual freedom.

My *"ambition"* is finished. Now I only ask continued vigor, and the ability to see, interpret, and *move around.*

People less & less important. Little M.'s [Maxwell's] marriage passed unwept.

Washington? I do not think it could work out.—Something analogous? Perhaps.

A really amazing year. Now, we shall see!!

—— June 1946

Out? Freer? Firmer?

This was to be the last of these annual check-ups. When her year in Washington was over, she returned to New York and her *New Yorker* job, as well as a new job as consultant in *belles-lettres* at Doubleday & Company (which she held until 1947, when the firm cut back its expenses). Even if ambition had vanished, she still hoped to do some creative work, although a new restlessness overtook her and made any writing, including her critical tasks, seem unrewarding. Something about the Indian summer of 1946 filled her with longing. As she described it to Rolfe Humphries:

It condenses and reflects too many sultry (and sullen) feelings in my own breast! O dangerous age of 49! O thoughts like dahlias and all late, coarse summer flowers, that linger on till frost! "Emotionally mature," indeed! If I could only write poetry, all would be well, and all manner of things would be well. Or fall in love with gusto, in a coarse, dahlia-like way!

And she added:

Well, the discipline of the writing table will probably save me in spite of myself. —I have to do a piece on the surrealists, this week. And I think I'll begin my memoir-in-the-form-of-a-horror-story—behind my consciousness' back, as it were: by writing a journal, and hiding it away from myself—under the linen in the middle-drawer of the chest. —No creative work in five years! "No wonder you are calm," as you said to me once, ". . . the daemon has been silenced, and whatever silenced it is sitting pretty."

In June 1947 she was entering, she wrote Humphries, the *seventh* year "of being uninvited by the Muse," and when George Dillon, the editor of *Poetry,* sent her a telegram asking her to contribute poems for the magazine's thirty-fifth anniversary issue, Bogan scrawled a reply, in pencil, on the telegram: "Regret having no finished work on hand at present. Thank you. Regards."

It was her old enemy—paralyzing guilt—which had silenced her daemon, but in addition to this latest influence of the Fury an insidious change had taken place over the last six or seven years and that was, as her remarks to Humphries indicate, the virtually complete cessation of her libidinal life. I do not mean sexual activity as such, but rather her capacity to have and to yield herself up to compelling desires, whether attached to people or to poems. In some deeply recessed part of her being she was well along in the process of renouncing desire, or "the wish," as she had used the word in "Summer Wish." She no longer cherished a vision of future achievement or reward; she no longer hoped for fame. Sources of pleasure were reduced to the available and the solitary: having a good meal, reading a good book, sitting by the sea at Swampscott—all of them worthy, all of them essential to any civilized life, yet none of them able to replace some larger investment of vitality and emotion, such as that to be found in love and ambition. Ambition, which had seemed more of a curse than a blessing, she was relieved to have foregone, and a love affair seemed no longer within the range of possibility, although it certainly would have been possible had she *chosen* to search for rich and fruitful emotional attachments.

There is evidence that she was once again disturbed by this state of being emotionally becalmed. Some days were so bad that she found herself teary and restless and yet unable to crack through her own impermeable psychic fortress. She had been who she was, after all, since 1934 or 1935, and had been distressed by the reduction in her ability to feel or suffer since at least 1937. But what had then been a reborn personality was now a familiar self, a piece of clothing so beautifully made it could never wear out, much to its owner's secret dismay.

Yet the surge of metaphors pouring out of her in the fall of 1946 with the phrase "late, coarse summer flowers, that linger on till frost" was a sign that a still-warm poetic (and thus erotic) core continued to burn within. She would soon turn fifty, and because she was a woman to whom a strong grip on reality was essential, thoughts of death set in. Yet she could not allow herself to feel fully the regret and longing which would free her to write poetry, to face the eventuality of death with poetic courage. The situation of "Simple Autumnal" had returned. She watched the elegiac autumn mood wax and wane, writing again to Humphries:

The weather has changed, thank God; and I no longer wish to be an Old Languorous Tiger-Lily, yearning by the Pond; or an Old Blowsy Dahlia by the Fence ("peering through the railing, In a manner unavailing . . ."); or even a Left-over Ragged Rose banging against a Trellis. —Far better to be a Nice Old Cool Cucumber, tendrilling circuitously in a curcurbitous way; or a Fine Old Melon, coyly resting on a nest of Straw; or, best of all, a Monstrous Old Huge Pumpkin, swelling with sun and memories, and not afraid even of frost; and with a certain secret kinship to the Witch and the Warlock, who, in November, keep the last of their Summer Covens, under the Hill.

Bogan understood these autumnal stirrings. But her new public life kept her from brooding about them, and for the time being they ceased to trouble her. *Mademoiselle* magazine asked her for an article, and she obliged with "The Heart and the Lyre" for their May 1947 issue. Here she remarked, ironically enough, that

The fear of some regression into typical romantic attitudes is, at present, operating from feminine talent; and this is not a wholly healthy impulse, for it negates too strongly a living and valuable side of woman's character. . . . Certainly it is not a regression to romanticism to remember that women are capable of perfect and poignant song; and that when this song comes through in its high and rare form, the result has always been regarded not only with delight but with a kind of awe.

Wilson came up to Washington Heights for a fine evening of drink and talk. (" 'I can only drink the v. *finest* brandy,' he said, 'now that I am so rich and have the gout,' " Louise recounted to Zabel.) Wilson's *Memoirs of Hecate County,* which she had admired, was about to undergo an obscenity trial, and he was soon to marry his fourth wife, Elena Thornton.

Louise worked herself into a high rage over *A History of American Poetry, 1900–1940*, by Horace Gregory and Marya Zaturenska, two poets she had loathed for years and whose book she thought dreadful, filled with "paranoid hatred, fears, malice, misinformation, fake erudition, quotations from Sam Johnson, etc., etc." And there was plenty of activity in her own life: in January 1948 a Fellows meeting in Washington; in February a poetry conference, with R. P. Blackmur, Norman Pearson, Joseph Campbell, Robert Fitzgerald, Marianne Moore, and Mary McCarthy at Sarah Lawrence College, after which Bogan shared a train back to New York with Moore and McCarthy. "I must see Marianne in the spring," she wrote Zabel. "She keeps making rather awe-struck remarks about my nature, the sources of which I can't make out. She thinks I live in some sort of danger. . . . I don't understand where she got that idea." In May she joined Robert Lowell, Marianne Moore, and Allen Tate in a reading at the New School, with lots of old friends in the audience, including Ruth Benedict and Margaret Mead in the front row. Her resistance to teaching finally broke down when Theodore Roethke engineered an invitation, which she accepted, to teach a summer session at the University of Washington, and this too she found she enjoyed. Upon returning to New York in the fall, there were more events to look forward to: another talk to be given at Bard College, "On the Pleasures of Formal Verse," and a new meeting, in November, of the Fellows in American Letters.

When she heard that T. S. Eliot was to be present at the latter, she was delighted. "So I shall at last behold Him in the flesh: yellow eyes and all!" she wrote Zabel. At the meeting itself, Bogan found Eliot enchanting. She sat beside him at lunch, and carefully observed him during various conferences. "How beautiful is the combination of physical beauty (even in slight decay), high qualities of mind and heart, and *perfect humility*," she wrote to Zabel. She and Eliot talked about form, the novelist's talent, little magazines, modern architecture, and Eliot's cat poems. She noted how he sat quietly throughout the meetings, smoking incessantly and sharpening a pencil with a pen-knife. His charm lay for her in his frailty, his perfect manners, his physical beauty. "Well, it is all too late and too sad—but I must love him, in a mild distant, sisterly way," she wrote Zabel, appending the last stanza of Marvell's "The Definition of Love."

As it turned out, the meeting had historic consequences in the literary world. The Fellows, who included—in addition to Bogan and Eliot—Léonie Adams, Conrad Aiken, W. H. Auden, Katherine Garrison Chapin, Paul Green, Robert Lowell, Katherine Anne Porter, Karl Shapiro, Theodore Spencer, Allen Tate, Willard Thorp, and Robert Penn Warren—voted to bestow the first Bollingen Prize for poetry on Ezra Pound, for *The Pisan*

Cantos, a decision that outraged both the general public and many of the Fellows' peers. Among the Fellows themselves, Karl Shapiro had voted against Pound in the belief that the poet's anti-Semitic beliefs ultimately detracted from the aesthetic quality of his literary work. Many years later Bogan told Ruth Limmer that "she regretted the prize, and if she had to vote again, she'd not have chosen Pound; Karl Shapiro had been right."

When the meeting was over, Eliot went on to Stockholm to receive the Nobel Prize and Bogan went back to New York and to her thoughts, suddenly reawakened, of late summer flowers. She took out a set of lyric notes long ago put aside in a file and wrote the first draft of "Song for the Last Act," in which she broke through to memory and desire even as she faced the inevitable end of life. And with this poem, suddenly sprung to life by Bogan's meeting Eliot, the long barren spell came to an end.

S H E   W E N T   O N to enjoy her stint at the University of Washington, and in the spring of 1949 gladly accepted another semester's position (this time through Zabel's efforts) at the University of Chicago, from which she had recently received the Harriet Monroe Award for her achievement in poetry. Over the next sixteen years she taught poetry at a variety of colleges and universities, including New York University, the University of Arkansas, the University of Washington again, Brandeis University, and at the Ninety-second Street YMHA in New York. As a teacher, she remained distant from her students. She had a real fear of becoming enmeshed in their emotional needs, but she gave herself wholly to the responsibilities of managing the class and the materials. Every class was a fresh experiment. *"There's no going back to notes,* in any absolute sense," she wrote a friend after she had been teaching for three or four years, ". . . the stream of life deposits so much sediment in the spirit, even during two years, that new freshness has to be brought forth, and presented to waiting student ears!—Wystan told me that he always *tears up* his notes, after he has given a course; this is drastic, but I can see that it is also wise."

She always organized her classes along the lines she worked out during her first presentations at the University of Washington, where she wanted above all to justify the ways of form to her students. Thus she always began by asking the students to list the ways in which rhythm was a part of human life. She herself would name the rhythm of the blood and its counterpoint in breathing, and from there the students would go on to list walking and rowing, hammering, ironing, picking cotton, and other activities in which rhythm played a necessary role. From these she led them to the simple beats of nursery rhymes and brief lyrics, onto complex metrical-stanzaic forms such as the sonnet and the great ode. Her approach to teaching poetry corresponded to her practice as a poet in being physical and intuitive before it was conceptual and analytic; she wanted her students to read with the ear as well as the eye. She spoke frequently of favorite poems, and these provide us with a personal anthology: Housman's "Tell me not here, it needs not saying" and Pound's "The River Merchant's Wife" for examples of the shift from nineteenth- to twentieth-century poetics; "the silver cord, golden bowl passage from Ecclesiastes, really analyzed down to its last vowel and consonant (I get this out of a book by a learned Oxonian). . . ," for texture (assonance and consonance); and fragments from the "Ode to Autumn" for special effects (m, z, l, and s sounds). As much as she disliked New Criticism for its theoretical posturings, she was a skillful practical critic along New Critical lines, good at close textual analysis, and able to unearth tension and ambiguity with the best of them. Nearly forty years of intimate knowledge of the tools of her trade also came in handy. When she dealt with speed and tempo, she would read Collins's "Ode to Evening" aloud to her students, considering it the slowest poem in the language. Other poems she referred to often included Hopkins's "Spring," Robinson's "The Sheaves," Roethke's "The Waking," Rossetti's "The Woodspurge," Eliot's "Marina" and "Sweeney Agonistes," Stevens's "The Curtains in the House of the Metaphysician," Richard Eberhart's "The Fury of Aerial Bombardment," Ridgely Torrence's "The Son," Trumbull Stickney's "Mnemosyne," Abbie Huston Evans's "To a Forgotten Dutch Painter," Edna St. Vincent Millay's "Little Elegy," and Janet Lewis's "In the Egyptian Museum," as well as selections from Donne, Davies, Meredith, Basho, Lorca, Edith Sitwell, Auden, Ransom, and Coleridge. These were all used as demonstrations in her argument that the lyric poem came from, indeed embodied, an intense concentration of feeling, occurring "when the moment of experience the poet has to express is especially rich and complex in its content, saturated, perhaps, with reflection and imaginative association, to express which requires a v. full and extensive use of his art."

Under this definition she could thus include the complex architecture of Milton's "On the Morning of Christ's Nativity" and Keats's "Ode to a Nightingale," as well as the shorter lyrics she loved. It was crucial, she told her students, to keep trivial emotions out of poetry; form was not enough, art must derive from life. Students were instructed to go *outside* themselves. One assignment she often gave her students was to go look at a natural object and write down a poetic notation of it in prose. Expression should remain direct and uncomplicated, and emotion should be simple, issuing from the heart, not the "ego." A former student in Bogan's 1956 YW-YMHA class, the poet Gloria Oden, remembered Bogan's counsel to put the whole personality into a poem, although not necessarily in confessional or autobiographical form. She also recalled that even though Bogan disliked holding conferences with students, she would occasionally invite one to her home for wine, cheese, and a session of intense, thorough criticism, given with courtesy and detachment and a tacit understanding of youthful vanity and ambition. (Did she remember, at these times, her intoxicating hours with Miss Cooper, in the Hotel Oxford, when she was thirteen and fourteen?) She was generous with *written* criticism, writing to Oden that "my advice to you is (sounds!) banal, I fear: write, rewrite; read, re-read. Read *anything* which you feel as *yours.* I recommend Yeats' *Autobiography* and his essays; they are full of creative wisdom." And she added, "Keep your *abstract* thought for the prose, your *emotions* for the poetry."

One of her former New York University students, the poet Ruth Lisa Schechter, recalls Bogan in the fall of 1960. She was always punctual, arriving promptly in class at 6 P.M. with her "brown hair . . . always drawn back under a headband, a velvet ribbon with what looked like a small cameo around her throat." She was "allergic to the cliché and thought of it as a form of laziness, always insisting on freshness, honesty and clarity. . . . We all resisted it; we all needed it." She did not encourage writing in free verse or the idea that poetry existed to express emotion; it was art, and "something to work hard at." Her Wednesday evening classes became "intense, two-hour, word-by-word surgical sessions of literary dissection." Bogan compared a good poem to a clock, and if one word, line, or stanza were wrong, "the poem could never tell the right time." She struck her students as a perfectionist, difficult to satisfy: "Integrity of language was her mandate." She was austere, reserved, and rarely used superlatives with her students. When she said, upon occasion, "The poem is working now," or "The magic is there," the student knew that it was "a true compliment." And she had, Schechter adds, the "funny habit of wanting to feed us, not only with poetry. She would dig into her purse and hand out candy lifesavers as if to pacify us, or lubricate our tongues."

Bogan also found herself receiving letters from young poets who sent her their manuscripts and asked for advice. In April of 1955, Ben Sonnenberg, Jr., who is now the founder and co-editor of the magazine *Grand Street,* wrote to Bogan and sent her some poems, and her reply tells us a great deal about her attitude toward ambition in the young as well as about her early experiences as a writer:

Dear Mr. Sonnenberg:

I am sorry to have been so tardy in answering your letter, and acknowledging your poems. This is a v. busy season for me; but a short break is now appearing. Meanwhile, I have given your work a good deal of thought, for I think that you could use some hard professional advice. And I think that you will take it in the way I shall try to give it: realistically.

I feel that you realize the difference between "self-expression" and art—how closely the two are linked and yet how useless the first is, without the second. I am not talking about "form" or lack of form, but about the necessity in writing, of a tough artisan side. Ideally, one gets through this side, partially at least, quite young; it is the technical side that young performers, for example, have to get perfect around the age of twelve or so. With young writers the same kind of apprenticeship should occur. The writers you admire—the names Joyce and Rimbaud turn up— were tremendous technicians, from youth on; Rimbaud even had a trace of Victor Hugo, at one time. Eliot went through two or three apprenticeships—in Harvard to people like Dowson and others of the end-of-the-century school; later to Jules Laforgue; and even later to Gautier and the Jacobean dramatists. You have a real feeling for language and you express yourself naturally through the senses (the main way any writer who is not primarily an abstract thinker must), but you do not seem to be excited by the *forms* of poetry. I may be wrong, but I feel that what you will end up writing will be prose. That is my first point.

The second point will seem, perhaps, as stiff and as unfeeling as the first! But I want to make it, in any case. It is concerned with [the] general problem of youth versus education. You are, it is perfectly apparent, well ahead of your "age-group" in certain natural gifts; and you are perhaps irritated by the idea of protracted university training. But you must remember that there is always a *group* of brilliant young people in every generation; and if you do not find your young equals now, it will be v. difficult to make true liaison with them later. For the talented young, adults are important, it seems to me, only as teachers; it is terribly difficult to attach oneself, from the age of say nineteen, through twenty-five or so, to the true adult world, in any feasible sense. If a young person does this, mistakes are so many and so various (mistakes of judgment, of misplaced trust and affection etc.) that a great deal of time is wasted; and the whole business has to be gone through again at a later date. I know this from experience, for I married at nineteen, after one year of college, and I have been forced to educate myself, the hard way, ever since. The mere fact of learning several languages young, is so important; of striking against different minds and different points of view and of learning that art is invariably *long.* —Nowadays there is so much choice: you may be a nascent archeologist, for all you know; or a born Egyptologist, or psychologist, or a novelist, or a critical intelligence of one kind or another. You can study anywhere—in Europe, America, Asia; you can shift from one thing to another until the *compelling* subject comes into view. It is what *compels* us, that we are born to express and to become part of. And, except in v. rare cases, this compulsion does not show up (even in the case of poets) until twenty-three or twenty-four. I didn't write a line that was really mine until about the latter age.

With your gift for writing, you can work through and find out. But remember, you must let some of it *happen to you:* you must try to remain "open," as Rilke says,

347

to existence, and not use the will too much. The will is a great deal, but I prefer to think that destiny has a hand in the business, too.

I hope I haven't sounded too stuffy! Good luck, and let us meet, sometime after my various jobs quiet down, in May.

Sincerely yours,
Louise Bogan

She often mentioned the work of her contemporaries while teaching, reading from, and commenting on the poems of Léonie Adams, Rolfe Humphries, Theodore Roethke, and Marianne Moore, the two versions of whose poem, "The Steeplejack," she often referred to when analyzing syllabic verse. It must have been disconcerting for her, in the fall of 1956, to discover Marianne Moore sitting in her class at the YMHA. Elizabeth Bishop later recalled meeting Louise at a party and asking her about the workshop and Moore's presence in it: "Poor Miss Bogan! I am sure Marianne never dreamed what suffering she was causing her. It seemed that Marianne took notes constantly, asked many questions, and entered into discussions with enthusiasm. But the other students were timid and often nonplussed, and so was Miss Bogan, besides feeling that she was sailing under false colors and never knowing what technical questions she might be expected to answer next."

With her own production of poems greatly diminished, Bogan's life as a teacher did her "a world of good," as she might have put it. She was so consummately adult, so obdurately mature in her manners and attitudes, and yet so responsive to the vitality and optimism of young people that teaching kept her emotionally supple. She never allowed a student to forget that poetry was allied with mystery and sacredness, and thus kept alive her own need for replenishment from these sources. The students could not give back as much, but their very existence was a reminder of different, past stages in her life, stages with which she had to maintain at least minimal connection if she were ever to write poetry again in any quantity.

Still another direction opened up with the development of a new friendship. In the fall of 1948, just after returning to New York from a teaching stint in Seattle, Bogan threw herself into a piece of translation with Elizabeth Mayer, a German woman who, with her husband, the psychiatrist William Mayer, and her children, had left Germany in 1936. Dr. Mayer, a Jew who practiced in Munich, thought that the Nazi regime would soon blow over, but Elizabeth Mayer was less sanguine and insisted that the family go to America. Settling in New York, the Mayers opened their doors to distinguished European exiles who had taken up residence in that city or were on their way to other places of refuge.

Elizabeth Mayer had studied art history as a young woman and was a fine musician; in Munich she gave German lessons to British and American students, among them Norman Holmes Pearson and Peter Pears. When, in 1939, Pears and his friend Benjamin Britten toured the United States and Canada, the young singer introduced Britten to Mrs. Mayer, and, owing to their status in England as conscientious objectors, the two young men remained in America with the Mayer family. Soon, another young friend, this one a poet, arrived from England, and from 1939, the name W. H. Auden began to appear with increasing frequency in the Mayer guest-book. Auden dedicated his *New Year Letter* (1940) to Elizabeth Mayer, and gave her a photograph of his mother, whom he greatly resembled, holding him as a very young child. Auden considered Mayer and Bogan the two most cultivated women in New York so he naturally introduced them to each other, in 1948, with the quite intentional hope that they'd become friends, and each obligingly found the other admirable. When Victor Lange, professor of German at Cornell University, commissioned them to do a translation of Goethe's *Werther,* they embarked upon a long and fruitful collaboration.

With Bogan writing out the manuscript in longhand to keep a natural, flowing tone, they finished the initial labor of translation in less than a month. Mrs. Mayer put the German into a more or less literal English version, which Bogan purified into as idiomatic and smooth an equivalent of Goethe's prose as she could. As they worked, Bogan felt intense pleasure at seeing the manuscript pages piling up. Something should be said, however, about Bogan's imperfect qualifications as a translator. She had, of course, attempted translations before, with a good deal of success, rendering Pierre-Jean Jouve's "Kapuzinerberg" with skill, and capturing the tone and movement of the originals in translations of poems by Paul Eluard and Ivan Goll which she published in *Partisan Review.* But she was on far less certain ground in German than in French, as the awkwardness of her translation of Heine's *"Der Tod, das ist die kühle Nacht..."* suggests. She claimed to have learned some German at the Girls' Latin School, although there is no record of her having studied it there, and her stay in Vienna in 1922 gave her hardly enough time to become fluent in the language. She could read German lyric poetry with the aid of a dictionary, but, as she confessed to Humphries, she really couldn't read the language *properly.* While she appears to have had an excellent "passive" sense of the language, her grasp of grammatical nuances, as well as her knowledge of vocabulary and idiom, were limited.

The reader looking for exactitude in her German translations is unlikely to be satisfied. What he will find instead are renderings "after" the original. Bogan compensated for her lexical and syntactic deficiencies in

German with her perfect ear in English. She could go straight from Mrs. Mayer's literal version to her own graceful approximation. Where Goethe, for example, wrote *"wenig enblattert,"* Mrs. Mayer put "only slightly stripped of their leaves," which Bogan turned into "sparsely leaved," preserving Goethe's brevity and euphony, although sacrificing, to be sure, the exact shade of meaning.

Bogan's collaboration with Mayer went so successfully that Auden, who had approval of the final text, urged them to include Goethe's *Novella* in the volume. This they did, and went on to collaborate yet again on Goethe's *Elective Affinities,* publishing this translation in 1963, fourteen years after they had finished it. Their first Goethe translations, of *Werther* and *Novella,* were not published until 1971, when both women were dead. In fact, the first of their translations to be published was also the last they did together: Ernst Juenger's *The Glass Bees* (1961).

Working with Elizabeth Mayer gave Bogan some of the most satisfying hours of her later life. Mrs. Mayer was thirteen years older than she, and a woman whose strong character and warmth Louise found positively nourishing. Her personal history, moreover, was rich. She had known D. H. Lawrence and Rainer Maria Rilke, and had many anecdotes about life in Europe, both literary and artistic, during the first quarter of the century. Louise loved to visit Elizabeth at her home at 1 Gramercy Place. There the large black Bechstein, which had been brought over from Germany and "come through all her difficulties in splendid shape," and the square silver sugar box, always present for coffee and tea, struck her as simple and elegant affirmations of a spirit perpetually open to art or friendship. As the daughter of a Lutheran pastor at the court of a German prince, Elizabeth was blessed, as Louise observed in her journal, with "faith in her bones." "We must always be a little in love," she had once said to Louise, who had always found being a little in love more a trial than a blessing. Between the two mature, cultivated women, with their ripened intuitions about the world, there grew a strong bond of affection, a companionship as well as a collaboration. Each valued Goethe for the view he expressed in his autobiography, that our virtues and our faults stem from the same source, and we cannot root out the latter without damage to the former. They shared the enrichment of breathing in the atmosphere of a single great mind. "What a work we have accomplished," Louise wrote Elizabeth at the completion of their translation of *Elective Affinities.* "Truly, we are remarkable women, and *Charlotte* (*this* Charlotte) would approve of us."

THE TIME HAD COME when Louise's friends were beginning to die. Harry Harvey, the husband of her old friend Dorothy Dudley Harvey, died late in 1948, the same year in which Genevieve Taggard died. Bogan had not spoken to Taggard since the latter had written "I Sigh If She Were Dying," but as young women in the early twenties, both had worked on *The Measure,* and Taggard's exit was a reminder that their generation was advancing in years. A greater loss came with Ruth Benedict's death, also in 1948; Louise, again, had not had an active friendship with Benedict for many years, but she had cared for her nonetheless.

In December 1951, fifteen years after Louise's mother died, her father, Daniel Bogan, suffered a fatal heart attack in Portland, at the age of ninety. He had enjoyed his newspaper and cigar almost up to the end, and in death, "The poor old gentleman looked v. noble, and very much at peace," Louise wrote Zabel. The funeral took place at St. Dominic's, in Portland, the church where Daniel had been christened, served as altar boy, and married Mary Helen Shields. Bogan was moved by the ceremony: "The meeting of the coffin at the door of the church by the priest and acolyte is particularly impressive, is it not?" she noted, then added, "I am still *lapsed,* however."

The life to which she returned from Portland had become even richer in public recognition and activity. She had received, earlier in the year, a thousand-dollar grant from the National Institute of Arts and Letters, to which she was elected early in 1952. And early in '51 she had been commissioned, by Henry Regnery Company, to write a short history of poetry since 1900, which was published later in the year as *Achievement in American Poetry: 1900–1950.* She was asked for essays: the Introduction to the Harper's Modern Classics edition of W. H. Hudson's *Green Mansions,* in 1951, and, in 1954, "The Situation in American Poetry" for the *Times Literary Supplement.* She had stood by the Fellows in American Literature, refusing to review Robert Hillyer's *The Death of Captain Nemo* in the fall of 1949 after he attacked them in *The Saturday Review of Literature* for endorsing Pound for the Bollingen Prize. "After the workout he gave to our characters and aims," she wrote William Shawn, "I feel that I should be fighting *prejudice in myself*—and that would never do!" Then the original group disbanded, and without old friends like Allen Tate and Willard Thorp, Bogan did not feel like returning. "So that phase of things is over," she wrote to Zabel. She was still considered very much a public voice, however. In Part III of the *Partisan Review* symposium, "Our Country and Our Culture," published in the fall of 1952, she was asked to give her views concerning changes in the contemporary intellectual situation in America, in particular the relationship of American intellectuals to mass culture and the possible sources of cultural nourishment in an America no longer dependent upon Europe. Bogan's answers, as might have been expected, were undogmatic and concentrated upon spiritual issues. She sees the need for a rejection of sophistication and of modernism as an *official* culture; she warns of the depletion of the older generation of intellectuals. She is not against mass culture, considering its vitality essential for new cultural growth, but she is worried about mechanization and the close dependence of popular art on advertising: "It is the loss of the tragic sense of life which weakens the tensions of the human spirit; it is the mechanical laugh following the mechanical 'gag' which deadens sensibility and helps to solidify tameness and conformity."

She was once again a publishing poet. In 1952, in contrast to her situation in 1947, she could send "After the Persian" to Karl Shapiro for *Poetry*'s fortieth anniversary issue. Soon a new publisher for her poetry appeared: Cecil Hemley, of the Noonday Press, and plans went forward to publish *Collected Poems, 1923–1953,* with *Selected Criticism: Poetry and Prose* following in 1955, the same year that Bogan shared the Bollingen Prize with Léonie Adams.

And a new friendship was prospering. May Sarton had first written to Louise Bogan in the spring of 1940 to ask her what she thought about the perilous situation of lyric poetry. Sarton was twenty-eight years old at the time, and the author of two books of lyric verse, *Encounter in April* (1937) and *Inner Landscape* (1939). They almost met in 1944, when Sarton invited Bogan to read at the New York Public Library, but at that time Bogan still distrusted public performance, and declined the invitation. Again, in 1947, Sarton wrote to say that since she had first read *The Sleeping Fury* in 1937, she had considered Bogan's poetry the epitome of lyric art: "I have few masters and they are mostly French. But you in America have been always a source of humility and joy, a pure standard to me." Several more years passed, and then Bogan finally agreed to meet her admirer. In the fall of 1953 she invited Sarton to her apartment on 169th Street.

Sarton has written a detailed record of that visit in her memoir of Louise Bogan, published in *A World of Light: Portraits and Celebrations:*

Then I remember vividly the sense I had of coming into rooms as intimate and revealing as a self-portrait. It was "Louise's place" from the big dining room table, strewn with papers, where she worked, to the living room it opened into. Here here were shelves and shelves and shelves of books, a sofa, chairs and small tables, the colors peacock blue and gray, I believe. There was nothing that looked interior-decorated, fashionable, or anything but simply beautiful and appropriate.

From the windows one caught a glimpse of the Hudson from beyond the tall Presbyterian hospital and it was quite clear at once by the way she showed it to me that this "piece of the river" was a kind of barometer of Louise's moods and at the same time a kind of release from them. Then or later she often reminded me that

Manhattan is an island. She liked to think of herself as not connected with the mainland, but an inhabitant of that special province, the city of New York.

The woman who greeted Sarton was tall, with large bones and hands, and "strange aqueous eyes, changing and transparent like the sea, sometimes green, sometimes gray, always lucid." With this meeting, another association began in the course of which Bogan patiently bestowed what creative wisdom she herself had won through long practice and hard experience upon a younger writer eager for technical and emotional guidance. Like Theodore Roethke and William Maxwell, Sarton was an avid student, hungry for criticism, but more volatile than the others in her reactions to it. Bogan's frank acknowledgment of her own difficulties softened the otherwise extremely direct comments she made on her young friend's work. She wrote to Sarton about her new book, *The Land of Silence,* saying that she had been impressed with the way some poems showed "that you have come into yourself and are able to render your mature findings in your own way." But other poems, she felt, seemed to come from *"an impulse toward literature"* rather than as "direct impulsions from life."

In Sarton's growing affection for Bogan, a complication developed that Bogan had never faced so directly before. Sarton was in love with her, and desired an *amitié amoureuse,* of which Bogan knew herself, for many reasons, to be incapable. The love Sarton offered was immediate and unconditional, "the integrating force which joins all my worlds." For Bogan, the memories of her mother barred the way to any exchange of erotic emotion between herself and another woman. She had experienced "successful," unrecriminating love only once in her life, with the 1937–1945 lover; and, for her, the knowledge and experience of such "successful" love was enough. Yet she was not, she assured Sarton, like Rilke, "who wanted love and yet was an adept at rejecting it." What Louise could and did accept was the knowledge of, and to a great extent the responsibility for, receiving May Sarton's love as an expression of an artistic and emotional period of growth Sarton was just then undergoing. That she could not return the feeling in the way it was offered was no proof of its invalidity. "I *do* give back," Louise pointed out, "but I cannot repeat a pattern. That is the truth I learned when I was *ill:* break out of the pattern in some fashion, in order to grow and be free. I feel that you must find a pattern in which the possibility of *immediate joy* is present."

That the love at issue would be that between two women was secondary in Bogan's mind to the primary question of keeping her psychic fortress—built at great cost—secure from invasion. Out of tact she did not say what she later once remarked to Ruth Limmer, that homosexual affairs had to be *dull,* since partners of the same sex, who were necessarily "on" to each other's ways, could experience little of the mystery of psychic exploration. To Sarton herself, it was the past and its legacy that she emphasized, observing that she had suffered so horribly from pathological fidelity and pathological jealousy that she had been *forced,* during her depressions, to renounce her old personality: "A new personality emerged; and it is this person that you now know." This person's heart, like the pool in the second part of "After the Persian," was "eight-sided," and when Sarton asked her to explain what this expression meant, Bogan replied that the octagon

is somehow symbolic of freedom. Love of things, I suppose, understood, more than love of human beings. . . . The delight in objects, both natural and artifacts, which has grown in me ever since the *obsessive* person was left behind (or buried, if you like, in the lowest layer of the dream). The delight of the collector, which you sensed in my room; the delight of the naturalist (which I never had, when young, except in flashes, but which makes me scrutinize everything, from flowers to rocks on the shore, in these later years); the delight of the amateur in the arts (the piano and embroidery); the delight of the cook and the housewife. . . . All these are substitutes, I know; but they keep me alive and not only happy but occasionally full of joy. I do not speak of the delight of the maker, for writing has never been anything (except v. rarely) but tough and artisan to me.

This same person now proffered Sarton "all that I can proffer any human being. Which isn't, I suppose, v. much; but all of it is fresh and real and non-*patterned.*" If *desire* should ever return accompanied by *benevolence,* she would be there to accept it. In the meanwhile, the best she could do was wait, in the Rilkean spirit of inspired, receptive patience, and offer the younger artist help in her work, for "the work is really, for us, the important thing. The channels must be kept open so that it may live and grow."

One of the benefits of Sarton's discipleship was that Bogan was often made to define her statements more closely. Eager to capture every nuance of Bogan's wisdom, and at the same time often not sure exactly what Bogan had meant, she questioned the maxims so often included in her mentor's letters. On one occasion Bogan closed a letter with the exhortation, "Be good," and when Sarton wrote back to ask what it meant, Bogan answered:

What do I mean when I say "be good"? Certainly I say it without moral connotation. Spiritual, rather. Let the heart and will rest, for a short period, every day. Let life take over! How pompous that sounds! But how necessary such recession is.

For Sarton, who was inclined to drive herself to daily exhaustion, this was particularly sound advice. From time to time Bogan detected a certain impatience and irritability in Sarton's struggles with her work and temperament, and for these she had no ready answers. "Dear May, how I wish that I could set you *carolling*," she replied to one anguished outburst. "But I am not the Muse; and one must wait and pray for grace." Sarton was to feel in retrospect that she was never quite sure what Bogan thought of her work, and this doubt remained to the end. She later recalled that Bogan once said to her, "You keep the Hell out of your work," the truth of which she later acknowledged. Anger, grief, despair—all these emotions were crucial to lyric poetry, the very heart of form, according to Bogan, and to skirt them was to evade the truth of creative experience. Sarton listened carefully to Bogan's advice, and worked harder at loading her poems with more difficult emotions. New poems came, poems which Bogan praised for their "troubled turn toward those frightening figures (symbols) of the subconscious, that are so difficult to touch, and to use." At the same time Sarton was never quite certain that Bogan believed she had taken these difficult emotions as far as they could go.

Sarton also had her own misgivings about Bogan's creative situation, astutely sensing a discrepancy between the sententious aspect of Bogan's "wisdom" and the actual difficulties of her current life. As a profound admirer of Bogan's earlier poetry, she could not help feeling that Bogan was hiding behind her criticism, using it "as a legitimate screen between you and what takes more of us, is more painful, more disturbing etc." But Bogan pointed out that there was a basic difference in their temperaments:

I have been *forced* to learn to wait, to be patient, to wait for the wheel to turn. You are by *nature* impatient and drastic. I have *been forced* to find a way of loving my destiny; of not opposing it too much with my will. (You remember Yeats on the Body of Fate, etc.) I have *been forced* "to forgive life" in order to get through existence at all. If all these pressures have been put upon me, it must be for some reason; and my "peace" and "calm" are, as I have said again and again, too hard won to be lightly tossed aside. —You understand this. Believe me, I am *not* "afraid." Lazy, perhaps, but fearful, no.

At the same time Bogan was her working self more openly with Sarton than she was with other friends, knowing that Sarton cherished the special solitude and discipline of the woman who lived for her work. In one letter, after praising Sarton's recent *New Yorker* piece on her mother's childhood in Wales, Bogan wrote that the heat had just broken, and

the Hudson is at its most lovely deep blue, and the sunlight has begun to shift over into that sad, poignant *September* angle: pre-equinox. These are the kind of days I like best in the *world*—almost worth the agony of August heaviness that precedes them. —Perhaps Florence shares the same poignance of light; I remember that

Vienna did, years ago, early in September. —Now I can fill my pen and start working!

By work, however, Bogan meant, as Sarton well knew, knuckling down to *The New Yorker*'s verse department, not poetry; and for Sarton— as Bogan well knew—work meant the deliberate composition of poems. Discussing Brewster Ghiselin's anthology, *The Creative Process,* with Sarton, Bogan brought up Henri Poincaré's emphasis on the preliminary conscious work that must precede the intuitive flash, and the second period of conscious work which follows the flash: "I guess it's the *preliminary conscious task* that I side-step, at present," she said. Feeling the creative injustice of what seemed to be the permanent impasse at which Bogan had arrived, Sarton urged her to write poems "not in form," saying,

This might be one of the blocks you are making, and a very small one, easy to get rid of! Surely the "Persian" sequence is proof that all this is nonsense. It might even be that what you have to say now demands a wholly different sort of expression, distilled in a different way, *relaxed* in some way—and that you are stopping its flow by trying to go back to another time and another kind of expression (where tension was part of the necessity, where form was the discipline against self-pity etc.).

Behind the extraordinary balance Bogan had achieved in living, Sarton believed that Bogan had

erected all too successfully barriers against the whole elemental part of your nature and that within this stockade your living self is a prisoner, a prisoner who is beginning to be afraid of ever going out again, who is becoming in fact "adjusted." . . . Some of your theories are simply justifications and concealed fears, aren't they? . . . I well understand, for instance, your theory that at a certain point of maturity relying on personal emotion, on relationships for motor power would mean going backward rather than forward, or—a better image—not going down one level deeper, which is what you want of course. On the other hand life *is* relationship and the going deeper, it sometimes occurs to me, may be simply in the wisdom one can bring to them, not on avoiding them, not feeling less, but feeling more and differently.

This letter, which Sarton wrote on Bogan's fifty-seventh birthday, beautifully distinguishes the younger woman, with her faith in possibilities, from the older, with her acceptance of limits and her understanding that some things could not be changed. Happily, they were able to work on a project together, and put aside their mutual dissection in the absorption of an actual job. Sarton was running into "knots" in her current novel, and

Bogan suggested that she try to disentangle them by translating French poetry. Sarton then sent drafts of some Valéry translations through the mail, and these Bogan liked so much that she suggested a collaboration on more of Valéry's work.

Like the novelist Elizabeth Roget, who collaborated with Bogan several years later on translating *The Journal of Jules Renard,* Sarton found Bogan's French dismayingly inadequate to the task of translation, most of which she was forced to do herself, with Bogan "scrutinizing," as she called it, the results. At the same time, the poetic intuition Bogan brought to bear upon the final versions of the texts gave Sarton an invaluable sense of Bogan's taste and judgment. Originally commissioned by the Bollingen Foundation for inclusion in a complete edition of Valéry in translation, the work was rejected when the Bollingen editors decided to publish the French text alongside a literal translation, but the results of several months of companionable collaboration eventually found their way to *Poetry, Metamorphosis,* and *The Hudson Review.*

A few months before Sarton's first visit to 169th Street, Bogan had taken out her "long prose thing," and begun making a set of entirely new notes. This time she stayed with it, writing faithfully, if not regularly, until July 1966. If she was ever going to go back to her memoirs, and put her gift once again to use, it would have to be now. She was "out," "firmer," and "freer," a complete human being, or as complete as she would ever be, and she knew that if she did not face her memories now, she never would.

On June 26, 1953, she wrote, "For people like myself to look back is a task. It is like reentering a trap, or a labyrinth, from which one has only too lately, and too narrowly, escaped." Thus, to return to these notes took courage, for there was much at risk in conjuring up the world of Milton and Ballardvale, with the "terrible rooming houses with a milk bottle and a brown paper bag on nearly every windowsill" and the "Terre Vague—uncultivated land, filled with 'chance vegetation.'" Yet it was necessary to go back, and Bogan once again obeyed the mandate, again seeking deliverance through the "final antidote" of love and forgiveness:

This attitude comes hard and must be reached with anguish. For if one is to deal with the people in the past—of one's past—at all, one must feel neither anger nor bitterness. We are not here to expose each other, like journalists writing gossip, or children blaming others for their own bad behavior.

Entries came between June 1953 and August 1954, and touched upon both the present and the past. It was as if Bogan were actually measuring the distances between years. She recalled her childhood fears of eventual poverty and squalor, the fantasy so detailed and dreary that her escape from it seems almost miraculous. She remembered the poignant sound of piano music in the town streets, and she told the story of seeing the "sudden marigolds" in her mother's hospital room. She wrote about rereading Raymond Holden's letters and cables from the summer of 1933, as well as some of her own letters to him:

The extraordinary thing about the revived experience was its power to bring back the moments in time, in place—the vignettes of pain, placed in a series of settings. Also the same sense of being *trapped*—of being used, of being made an *object*. This nightmare effect stayed with me for about a day and a night—in which I relived the whole set of emotions, felt from that April through that September. But on the second morning I came out of it all with a perfectly cool and contemporary reaction: it was all too *boring* to review any longer, in memory; or to re-feel, in life.

She saw, too, how much her powers of observation had grown since her 1933 European journal, and she hoped that this return to the long memoir would help her get back to "pure writing *as such:* to 'creative' writing, as the phrase goes." A number of brief passages followed, one of them a set of acerbic remarks on Virginia Woolf's egotism and both *Mrs. Dalloway* and *Orlando,* the others crisp and subtle *aperçus* on the equinox, and the sound of rain, and winter days spent working alone. But the notes, it would appear, were going too well, which meant that the inner prohibitions against successfully completing them must have returned. Once again, Bogan put them aside and did not return to them until January 1958, a hiatus of three and a half years. There was, however, the gratification of being in print again, when the Noonday Press published *Collected Poems, 1923–1953* early in 1954.

IN THE PROCESS of dividing *Collected Poems* into five sections, as though each one formed part of a five-act drama, Bogan discovered that she had only three new poems to add to the whole: "After the Persian," a poem in five parts, first published in *The New Yorker* on November 3, 1951, and again in the fortieth anniversary issue of *Poetry* magazine in October 1952; "Train Tune," written in August 1950; and "Song for the Last Act," which, as we recall, Bogan wrote in December 1948, in the wake of meeting T. S. Eliot in Washington. Another poem, "The Catalpa Tree," published in *Voices: A Journal of Verse* (Fall 1951), she decided to keep out; it was not up to standard, having a stiffly nostalgic tone.

In "After the Persian," Bogan resolves to embrace all that she has done, including that which has resulted in failure and incompletion, from a paradisal—that is, regenerated and remorse-free—footing. It was not a completely new poem, having been recomposed, Bogan informed Rolfe Humphries, from a set of notes. How long these had been lying in their folder she did not say. She originally planned to call the poem "From the Persian," but changed the preposition to "After" at the insistence of the "checkers" at *The New Yorker,* lest the first title imply that the poem was a translation, which it wasn't. The emended title is still misleading, since it suggests a "rendering," if not a close translation, from an original in another language. What the title in fact refers to is the whole accumulation of impressions and associations which Bogan slowly absorbed over many years of looking at Persian art at the Metropolitan Museum of Art in New York and the Boston Museum of Fine Art. She loved to send "art postcards" to her friends, many of whom received reproductions of exquisite Persian miniatures, rich in details of clothing, eating, drinking, hunting, and love-making. Often there would be a figure in a garden, a poet or maiden in repose, alone or attended, sheltered by a border of flowers and birds. The details of "After the Persian" are thus distillations of visual memory. The vines and moths, the hunt and fountain and pool, have been gazed at and entered into.

Perhaps to offset the possibility of an overwrought verbal enameling, Bogan gave each section of the poem its own free-verse movement, throughout which a stately balance is maintained by phrasing at once deliberate and intimate in address. Bogan wanted the poem to sound "v. ordinary, in spots," she told Humphries, and this she achieved by the firmness and assurance of the speaking voice, which sounds utterly *planted* in the beautiful landscape. From the beginning, there is a silent "other" present, to whom the poem's speech flows as an address:

> I do not wish to know
> The depths of your terrible jungle:
> From what nest your leopard leaps
> Or what sterile lianas are at once your serpents' disguise
>   and home.

These lines recall images and symbols from Bogan's earlier poems: the Medusa's serpentine head; the Fury; the desert of "A Tale"; and the land of "flamy blooms" in "Putting to Sea." All are summarily rejected; there will be no more seasons in hell. In one of the most beautiful passages Louise Bogan ever wrote, she describes a new kind of existence:

> I am the dweller on the temperate threshold,
> The strip of corn and vine,

> Where all is translucence (the light!)
> Liquidity, and the sound of water.
> Here the days pass under shade
> And the nights have the waxing and the waning moon.
> Here the moths take flight at evening;
> Here at morning the dove whistles and the pigeons coo.
> Here, as night comes on, the fireflies wink and snap
> Close to the cool ground,
> Shining in a profusion
> Celestial or marine.

The pacing echoes Old Testament psalms, not only in rhythm, but in the celebration of peace and plenty, and the freedom, or respite, from violence. The dweller on the temperate threshold knows what lies outside: the region of the hunt, which is equally the site of the quest. Within her sanctuary the speaker knows death and suffering as facts which have to be acknowledged when the "trophies" are brought home

> To bleed and perish
> Beside the trellis and the lattices,
> Beside the fountain, still flinging diamond water,
> Beside the pool
> (Which is eight-sided, like my heart).

Trellis and lattice, fountain, diamond water, and octagonal pool become for Bogan what Byzantium's gold-hammered singing-birds are for Yeats, symbols of enduring artifice in a natural world of death and aggression. They speak of the merging of form and feeling, of intricate, delicate structure, of an art of limits and the limits of art, of solid perfections in making and harvesting.

In the third section, Bogan returns to another of her enduring motifs: "All has been translated into treasure." The notion of *translation* is equivalent, in her mind and the practice of her art, to metamorphosis. But then, having her treasure, the poet divests herself of it in Section IV:

> Ignorant, I took up my burden in the wilderness.
> Wise with great wisdom, I shall lay it down upon flowers.

She has turned the wilderness she knows into a garden, and, like Prospero throwing away his book, resolves to free herself even from wisdom at the end.

In the final lines of the poem, the implicit dialogue renews itself, as the speaker bids her visitor farewell in language reminiscent of certain phrases of the Bethge text on which Mahler based "Das Lied Von Der Erde":

> Goodbye, goodbye!
> There was so much to love, I could not love it all;
> I could not love it enough.
>
> Some things I overlooked, and some I could not find.
> Let the crystal clasp them
> When you drink your wine, in autumn.

With "After the Persian," the art of "translation" in Bogan's poetry reaches its highest point. The symbols expropriated from Persian painting provide highly sophisticated, sensuous emblems for a private yet archetypal myth of serenity and sublimation. As if by deliberate and dramatic contrast, "Train Tune" goes back to the roots of lyric poetry in onomatopoeic chant. Like many so-called primitive poems, the crucial repeated word occurs at the *beginning* of each line, rather than at the end, so that there is a percussive heaping-up of associations that always returns to the same starting point. The "tune" heard by the traveler takes him on a journey which simplifies but shares the nature of "Journey Around My Room," in which *things* and *places* carry the traveler through a geography of loss and recovery, all the while keeping the train's actual beat to make the kind of poem Bogan loved so much, in which a true rhythm in the actual world directs the whole.

Her greatest demonstration of rhythmic instinct is "Song for the Last Act." "The Recovered Poem," as she called it when she rewrote it on December 21, 1948, had her very oldest and most persistent symbols: the garden with statues; flowers; the late summer about to become autumn; the text which must be painfully spelled out; the quest or voyage. She places them, in the poem, in a single broad landscape, illuminated by a fading sun sinking in a deepening perspective. Central to the poem is the refrain of having the loved one "by heart," a phrase she used again in 1959, when writing new passages in her memoirs. Having something by heart is possessing it, knowing it so completely, so utterly in memory that its presence is no longer necessary.

In "Song for the Last Act," the memory and the heart are one and the same. Thus they can give back the loved one, in performance or recitation, fusing "subject" and "object," or "self" and "other," without making a muddle out of the chiaroscuro of fusion. The body of the text—the printed page, the musical score, the lover's body—is no longer necessary. What exists instead is the "real" text or person, lodged in the possessor/giver's heart, absorbed into his very being. Only in this way does Freud's "grief-work" complete itself in separation. Real mourning and real love are thus the same, for both require the renunciation of the object. To go through the process of loss and emerge intact, capable of acceptance and even of joy, we must displace the dead body (of love, of time) with its living memory; melancholy must become song; fact must become symbol; experience must be translated—literally *carried over*—into myth. This displacement serves as the central act of imagination in Bogan's poetry from its earliest to its latest stages, and "Song for the Last Act" enacts this process in consummate speech:

> Now that I have your face by heart, I look
> Less at its features than its darkening frame
> Where quince and melon, yellow as young flame,
> Lie with quilled dahlias and the shepherd's crook.
> Beyond, a garden. There, in insolent ease
> The lead and marble figures watch the show
> Of yet another summer loath to go
> Although the scythes hang in the apple trees.
>
> Now that I have your face by heart, I look.
>
> Now that I have your voice by heart, I read
> In the black chords upon a dulling page
> Music that is not meant for music's cage,
> Whose emblems mix with words that shake and bleed.
> The staves are shuttled over with a stark
> Unprinted silence. In a double dream
> I must spell out the storm, the running stream.
> The beat's too swift. The notes shift in the dark.
>
> Now that I have your voice by heart, I read.
>
> Now that I have your heart by heart, I see
> The wharves with their great ships and architraves;
> The rigging and the cargo and the slaves
> On a strange beach under a broken sky.
> O not departure, but a voyage done!
> The bales stand on the stone; the anchor weeps
> Its red rust downward, and the long vine creeps
> Beside the salt herb, in the lengthening sun.
>
> Now that I have your heart by heart, I see.

The vision of quince and melon, dahlias and the shepherd's crook summons up Bogan's very early "Poplar Garden" and "Statue and Birds," with their vision of classical statuary, but also Bogan's love, nurtured in the intervening years, of Baroque emblems and pastoral imagery. The language of the second stanza, swelling with an almost unutterable burden of pain and betrayal, goes far back into Bogan's childhood memory of being unable to read and staring at the printed page in bafflement and frustration. The voice of the loved person (and that voice stands for what the lover says—his very words) is another such indecipherable page, a musical score which must be "read" and "spelled out." Similarly, Bogan's memories of her mother return in this stanza. She too had to be "read," and it was in connection with her that the "storm" and "running stream" of both "The Flume" and "Journey Around My Room" first emerged as symbols of terror. Again there is an echo of catastrophe just as the stanza reaches its end; again, just as in the two earlier works, the crucial act of *giving over* takes place, and Bogan's Romantic heritage, suppressed and resisted for so much of her life, rises to complete this three-act drama of renunciation and acceptance as the "red rust" which recalls the rusted mouth of beauty in "A Tale" and the quest now fulfilled in the "voyage done" meet the wharves and architraves of a life's work.

William Jay Smith has pointed out that Bogan began with

the sense of the stanza itself and the refrain. In her words, she had hit upon the form right off. What she did not know was how the form was going to change in the course of composition. She had originally set down four stanzas, inspired by the etchings of Claude Lorrain, the seventeenth-century French classical painter, whose landscapes are usually painted against the light and yet are always fully luminous, bathed with mysterious and subtle indirections. . . . It is interesting that, although Miss Bogan calls her poem a song, it is not the *sound* that predominates. It is the *vision* that is all important, for even in the second stanza where she is speaking of music and the sound of music, it is music as depicted, as scored, on the page—music that must be *spelled out* and *read.* The simple, external vision of the garden at the beginning, the thing that is *looked* at, as one looks at the thing *seen,* seen truly, finally, and inevitably: "O not departure, but a voyage done!" What has been looked at has been read and seen, and the poet's journey has been completed.

"Song for the Last Act" is the great poem of Bogan's poetic decline, the last of the era which had encompassed her tumultuous youth and arduous arrival at maturity. For the last time, the rhythms move with Yeatsian force, and the symbols spill over in cornucopic richness. This is not to say that she wrote no further poems. There were more to come; and more life to be lived too.

10 ON THE TEMPERATE THRESHOLD

IN HIS 1960 HOPWOOD LECTURE at the University of Michigan, Theodore Roethke observed that, unlike much American poetry, Louise Bogan's best lyrics had "the sense of a civilization behind them—and this without the deliberate piling up of exotic details, or the taking over of a special, say, Grecian vocabulary." The same thing could just as aptly be said of Bogan's criticism. It is always informed by experience and values measured against the idea that literature functions as a complex institution with crucial ties to social, historical, and spiritual continuities. For Bogan, the autonomy of literature's formal aspects is axiomatic, but she also takes it as given that literature bears a rich and at times unchartable relationship to the life of the times.

The single view and the shifting perspective are both at her disposal. She writes in a leisurely fashion, her prose vigorous, compact, open to every nuance of taste and discrimination. Generally speaking, her chief preoccupation is maturity: maturity in the artist, the art, the period, and the civilization at hand. Her end, as Marianne Moore has remarked, is to unite "instinctiveness" and "coming to terms with one's self" with "laboratory detachment."

Bogan wrote book reviews for a living. Her criticism was a species of journalism. Space was limited, and she had therefore to foster a style of generalization specific enough to tell the reader exactly what he was likely to find in the book being reviewed, yet broad enough to situate the book in a cultural and literary context. Each piece was necessarily about a separate literary occasion, and for this reason it is difficult to find systematic theses or principles in her criticism. What she actually arrived at, as a critic, was a style of pure exposition, relatively free from any form of advocacy except that concerned with assessing the ultimate value of the work under consideration. Her two collected volumes of essays, *Selected Criticism: Poetry and Prose* (1955) and *A Poet's Alphabet* (which was published posthumously in 1970 and includes the former in addition to a number of uncollected pieces published after 1955), form a miscellany that is remarkable for its consistent tone and sustained preoccupations.

Her first piece of critical prose was a contribution in the December 5, 1923, issue of *The New Republic* to a symposium called "Views of American Poetry." There, she joined Amy Lowell, Vachel Lindsay, Elinor Wylie, Alfred Kreymborg, and Joseph Auslander, each of whom offered an assessment of current poetic trends. Bogan herself presented a meditation called "The Springs of Poetry," as compressed and complete a summary of her view of the sources of inspiration as she was ever to make. In it she observes that because poetry comes from the irrational, the poet, in setting out to write his poem, must resolve the "tight irrational knot of his emotion." Unless he attempts to divert himself, or rather, the emotion, with some less taxing activity, the endeavor to resolve the emotion becomes a task laden with terror, desperation, and doubt. She agrees with Aristotle that strong emotions such as grief and anger "are most faithfully portrayed by one who is feeling them at the moment," and that poetry demands that its maker have the gift of utterance at such times; yet, she continues, "Few poems are written in that special authentic rage because even a poet has a great many uses for grief and anger, beyond putting them into a poem. The poem is always a last resort." Thus, when the poet finally writes his poem, the text is the proof of his desperation—the authentic sign of the finality and the exigence of his feeling. In the poem, the poet "makes a world in little, and finds peace, even though, under complete focussed emotion, the evocation be far more bitter than reality, or far more lovely."

Even at this very early point, the basis of Bogan's poetics is the actual confrontation between the poet and his emotion. Writing a poem is thus an act of courage and integrity, replete with un-pleasure as well as relief, and so difficult that the poet, seeking to escape the pressure of relentless feeling, often writes a poem at third, fourth, or fifth hand,

bred out of some delicate fantastic ruse of the brain. Even at its best a poem cannot come straight out of the heart, but must break away in some oblique fashion from the body of sorrow or joy,—be the mask, not the incredible face,—yet the synthetic poem can never be more than a veil dropped before a void. It may sound, to change the images, in ears uninitiate to the festival, but never to those, who, having once heard, can recognize again the maenad cry.

The "synthetic" or "imitation" poem is not just the poem written out of the poet's deliberately sitting down and forcing a poem into existence, but it is also what results when the poet fails to detach his emotion from its source. The poet must discover in himself that poetic countryside which "could claim him completely, identify him rigidly as its own under the color of every season." It must be a landscape of essential emotions and essential utterances, "most completely blessed by that reticence celebrated by the old prophetic voice: 'I kept silent, even from good words . . . the fire kindled, and at the last I spoke with my tongue.' " Only in this way could passion find its own form in poems which, like Yeats's later works, are "terribly beautiful, in which the hazy adverbial quality has no place, built of sentences reduced to the bones of noun, verb, and preposition."

The language of "The Springs of Poetry" is cut from the same cloth as the poems in *Body of This Death.* It is compressed and high-minded in tone, its constructions somewhat stiff. But just as Bogan's poetic style developed greater naturalness over the next ten years, so did her prose style. She later pointed out to Morton Zabel that, whereas she changed as a *writer* over the years, thanks to her training in journalism, she changed very little as a *critic.* As a critic, she had "undergone no conversions, changes of *standpunkt,* color, creed, skin, faith or place. I write my criticism, what there is of it, out of my innate feeling for form, sincerity, music, truth, beauty, etc. etc., and my innate distaste for nincompoopery, dopishness, chaos, murk and balder-dash." Her greatest talent as a critic was her ability to place herself at the center of another's work. While she would not do this unless some inner sympathy or likeness existed between herself and the writer at hand, she never made the writer or the work appear to be extensions of her own per-sonality. To a very great extent she was high-minded but not high-handed, and was as unegotistical as a critic can be while still coloring her opinions with her own preferences and prejudices.

Bogan's first full book review was of D. H. Lawrence's *Birds, Beasts and Flowers,* which she published in July 1924, in *The New Republic.* Ed-mund Wilson had been managing editor of the magazine since 1921, and had recently come back to it after taking leaves of absence to work at *Vanity Fair* and *The Dial;* at his urging, she began to write reviews. In fact, he in-sisted on it, and when she cried out in fear, "I can't, I can't," he arranged for her to lock herself up in a room and write while he paced behind. His instinct that she would make a superb book-reviewer was readily confirmed. Her piece on Lawrence was a finely shaped mixture of sympathy and cen-sure, marked throughout with acute psychological insight. Unable to stom-ach the dogmatism which she felt to be the book's central weakness, she aptly characterized the conflict at its heart:

They are poems that cry, implicitly, for existence to have done. They ask an isolation absolute, man's spirit to be a naked stalk, standing trembling and alone in a lush physical world. Mr. Lawrence has turned his back on humanity that strains for illusion, not identity, and gives his allegiance to beasts (if they be strong, single beasts) and to fruits of the earth.

She might have been reviewing parts of *Body of This Death*. It too had been fired with a passion for escape from time and existence. Yet she remained detached, and few could know that she understood Lawrence from her own depths. This capacity for poetic sympathy, however, made her particularly skillful in unearthing the essential conflicts within a poet's work. She was fascinated by *origins,* and the sources of a poet's manias, infatuations, intensities, and prejudices, nearly always making it her business to inform the reader about the poet's early development, and fixing his relation to himself before situating him within his culture. She asks what promises the poet has made, kept, and broken to his art, and presents his life as a landscape over which his gifts must somehow make their own way. Thus, reviewing Edith Sitwell's *Troy Park* in December 1925, she notes the poet's use of nursery rhythms, and observes that "She at once stands within the clever clockwork kingdom she has made, and contemplates her own dead childhood." The authenticity of *Troy Park* lies in its break with the fantasy world, "because a human voice has cried within it out of mature horror and despair." Here, for the first time, Bogan equates maturity with the facing of the terrible emotions which dance attendance upon the unresolved obsessions of childhood.

Interestingly enough, most of Bogan's reviews in *The New Republic* in the late 1920s dealt exclusively with books by women. In addition to Edith Sitwell, she reviewed Sylvia Townsend Warner, Louise Imogen Guiney, Viola Meynell, Hildegarde Flanner, Lizette Woodworth Reese, Ellen Glasgow, Elizabeth Shepley Sargent (Katharine S. White's sister), Virginia Woolf, Rebecca West, Djuna Barnes, Sofie Andreyevna Behrs Tolstoy, Colette, and Katherine Anne Porter. There was no particular plan to this; Edmund Wilson just kept sending books by women, and Bogan evidently found nothing to complain about in the arrangement. She never draws attention to herself in these reviews, as a woman writing about women, and rarely favors the cause of female sensibility as a thing apart from human feeling in general. But clearly she believes that at least the possibility of feminine sensibility exists, and can be brought to successful or unsuccessful expression, and she is fearless in gauging its weaknesses and strengths according to the criterion of maturity. Thus she takes Louise Imogen Guiney to task for hiding her talent "behind the mask of the girl wearing laurels," and praises her old favorite, Viola Meynell, for the adult sympathy with which she creates "childish women struck by a passion that troubles and unnerves them, conventional girls startled by a single emotion as relentless in their hearts as the drive of purpose in the will, or by two conflicting desires that go on at the same time, like two voices in music, not defeating each other, but rather aiding and enriching the nature that bears them up to the moment when they must break apart for one to live at all."

Like good lyric poetry, Bogan points out, the novel written by a talented woman novelist is faithful to the psychological realities of domestic life, and this fidelity consists above all in the imaginative grasp of fact. As she explains in a review of Katherine Anne Porter's *Flowering Judas:*

The fact, and the intuition or logic about the fact, are severe coordinates in fiction. In the short story they must cross with hair-line precision. However far the story may range, the fact and its essence must direct its course and stand as proof to the whole. The Truth alone secures form and tone; other means distort the story to no good end and leave within the reader's mind an impression far worse than mere banality.

As often as not, Bogan's objections to the work of women writers as childish, girlish, adolescent, theatrical, and illogical were actually accusations of emotional dishonesty. Reluctant to review *Time's Profile,* a book of poems by Hildegarde Flanner, because the poet had been associated with *The Measure* and because, to Bogan, it seemed "a breach of etiquette . . . to review a book of poetry by a woman contemporary," she went ahead with the review, apparently "after much urging on the part of Edmund Wilson," to say that Flanner had substituted a "vanishing personal deity . . . for nebulous adolescent mysticism," and chided Rebecca West in her review of *Harriet Hume* for rendering characters "made of less awkward material than flesh and blood. They are automata, produced by joinery of a high order." In one of her best reviews of this period she finds the honesty and fidelity she cherished in *Chéri* and *Mitsou, or How Girls Grow Wise,* by Colette, of whom she writes:

Her pages are singularly free from allusion and echoes of literature. She can be compared to little but herself because she has written her discoveries down just as she herself made them. She has lived her life—as a provincial girl, the wife of a Parisian man-about-town, a dancer in a music hall, a woman of letters—and written of it concurrently. She has not checked the development of her talents by regrets for the past or yearnings into the future. The steps of her life, the ripening of her perceptions, appear as clearly in her novels as in the facts and dates of her biography.

In the same review she compares Katherine Mansfield to Colette, and complains that Mansfield's talent "leaves off where Colette's begins." Mansfield seeks out easy emotions—nostalgia, pity, and regret—and cannot discover "the difficult human relationship, grasp it in essentials, reduce it to form," as Colette has done in the complex and moving scene at the end of *Chéri,* when Chéri, returning at last to Leah, finds catastrophe in his revulsion from her aging body.

Bogan was not uniformly sympathetic to women writers. Two pieces from this period are notable failures of both perception and sympathy. In her review of *The Diary of Tolstoy's Wife, 1860–1861* and of *The Countess Tolstoy's Later Diary, 1891–1897,* she finds Sofie Andreyevna's shock at reading the details of her husband's premarital debaucheries a symptom of bourgeois failure to realize that "Tolstoy had a real passion to be understood and loved in spite of the brutality and sensuality which he knew to be part of himself." She exempts him from the obligation, which she believed to be every artist's, to come to terms with his obsessions and compulsions, and she overlooked brutalities which a later generation of women would be less inclined to ignore. The other inferior review was of Virginia Woolf's *A Room of One's Own.* Aside from a tart description of Woolf's earlier style ("the point-to-point method which she has perfected—like the technique of a moving camera, that projects the argument through space and time, as it develops, by means of such phrases as 'I thought, opening the door,' or 'I repeated, standing under the colonnade among the pigeons and the prehistoric canoes' "), the review is as dull and pointless as a high-school book report. For Bogan to withhold judgment was so odd that it seems unlikely to have been merely an instance of her not-quite-coming-up-to-standard. Bogan's later reviews of Woolf suggest the partial explanation that even this early Virginia Woolf was her *bête noire,* of whom she was deeply envious. Like another English novelist, Elizabeth Bowen, whose *The Death of the Heart* Bogan greatly admired, but the unchecked brilliance of whose style she thought affected and self-indulgent, Woolf had advantages of education, class, and personal relations which, in Bogan's view, got translated into arrogance and artistic complacency. The tendency to rely upon the oblique or partial view struck her as the alibi for an inability to grasp human relations in their intricacy of motive and extremes of feeling—exactly, she thought, those areas in which Colette excelled, and excelled *instinctively,* too. Woolf's nonfiction, she thought, was "frequently intellectually pretentious and always emotionally immature." Yet Bogan's rancor is excessive; there is something begrudging in her tone.

She was in general aware of her literary envy. While it amused her at times to see herself as the target of jealousy from the wives of male poets, she found the envy between women poets, herself included, an unpleasant thing. Her slightly older contemporary, Babette Deutsch, reviewing *Body of This Death* unfavorably in the *New York Sun,* called Bogan—as Bogan described the review to John Hall Wheelock—a " 'cold, old rood-screen maker,' " and for this Bogan wanted to "smash her face" (the two women later became friends). "*What* an invidious comparison," she commented further, "and how women poets love one another!"

BETWEEN JANUARY 1931 and October 1937, Bogan published a number of reviews in *Poetry: A Magazine of Verse,* which she had first read in 1912, at the age of fifteen, in the Roxbury branch of the Boston Public Library.

In her *Poetry* reviews, Bogan was free to address an audience that regarded poetry with the highest seriousness, and she accordingly permitted herself, within the limits of brief coverage, the utmost concentration and insight. In her review of Edwin Arlington Robinson's *Collected Poems* and *The Glory of the Nightingales,* she inspects the plight of the New England poet without explicit reference to her own New England background, but there is bred-in-the-bone intuition in her situating Robinson against a region where generations had endured "a difficult life wrung from hard fields and precarious seafaring, and a climate that bred seven months of snow and a summer that passed in a flash." Robinson's New England of miscast and misspent lives was very much Bogan's own; her mother might well have been one of *The Children of the Night.* Reviewing Edna St. Vincent Millay's *Wine from These Grapes* in February 1935, she approaches the discussion of Millay's crisis of maturity by stating, "The poet, particularly, as he matures, is faced with the antagonisms of complexity and loss: if he is capable of any growth he has more intimations to synthesize and more disorganization to bear, while comforting delusion softens the brutality of each new crisis, as it arises, with lessened power." She is capable of aphoristic point, yet her voice, arranging the considered insights phrase by phrase, does not have a cold or analytic relationship to the matter at hand.

Each year, between March 1931 and December 1968, Bogan wrote on an average of two "omnibus" reviews and innumerable short notices, or what she called "blurbs" for *The New Yorker.* These were often extended reviews of one or two poets, or fully developed essays on general poetic topics. She worked constantly for the magazine, and the development of her critical powers is traceable in its pages over the years. At first she tried to inject as much humor as she could into her pieces, never allowing serious considerations to dominate her tone. Her shifts into droll acerbity and verbal high spirits were fearless, as in her review of Robinson Jeffers's *Solstice:*

"Whoever," warns the jacket blurb, "is irritated by poetry will be irritated anew." And whoever, let us add, is irritated by adverbs will be driven to a point of frenzy, stage directions for ballets requiring, as they do, only too many of those horrid parts of speech. "Writheswoonfully" and "vanitously," even "pirouettingly," may be withstood; before "withfully" and "atishly," the badgered spirit quails.

But she soon became more comfortable with her serious and sincere side, and ceased to give in to the feeling that she must amuse her urbane audience. Thus she wrote with complete straightforwardness of the *Poems of Gerard Manley Hopkins* that it was the stuff of "genius and agony, put down in secret. There is nothing to say about it. It exists in this book, and anyone who thinks that poetry has something to do with the terrible, unaccountable processes of the human spirit can buy the book and thank Heaven for his luck."

The New Yorker staff wisely left her very much alone. She worked at home, visiting the magazine's offices at Forty-third Street very infrequently. For many years, the person who "handled" Bogan—arranging with her which books she would review, discussing the poems and stories she submitted to the magazine—was Katharine S. White, the wife of E. B. White. Mrs. White became a steadfast friend, sympathetic to Louise during the 1931 and 1933 breakdowns, and always candid and kind when she had to inform her of an unfavorable editorial judgment.

Although Bogan's association with the magazine was for the most part peaceful, over the years there were a number of tense moments. She was outraged when her poem "To My Brother . . . " appeared on October 26, 1935, with a misprint, so the line that should have read "All things remain," went "All things indeed." There was also a cartoon on the same page that struck her as vulgar and inappropriate.

From time to time, she was annoyed by the magazine's taste for extreme particularization of fact. In a letter to Wolcott Gibbs written in response to Harold Ross's criticism that the description in "Conversation Piece" was not exact enough, she wrote that "if Mr. Ross wants the house in 'Conversation Piece' placed on the north side of 37th Street, and described in detail as a 'large old-fashioned brownstone mansion, with a stoop,' I'm afraid someone will have to write that in for me, because I certainly don't see any sense in writing it in, as myself. I've placed the house in New York (as opposed to Jersey City) and even the most bewildered person in the world, in the sense of the person most prone to bewilderment, ought to be able to read the rest in." Another time she was full of admiration for Ross, when he cut "a longish and rather pompous piece on Auden" so that "the points positively bristled, and the style had been stepped up no end."

Those who worked with her at the magazine—Mrs. White, William

Maxwell, and William Shawn—knew that Bogan was inordinately sensitive. According to Mr. Shawn, she was so finely tuned that she "could hardly walk into a room without vibrating." Although she was entirely free to choose the books she wanted to review, she regarded each piece as an enormous project requiring months of reading and note-taking, and to Mr. Shawn it seemed that she was afflicted with a "burdensome conscience"; her occasional inability to turn a piece in on time oppressed her with guilt. Fortunately, she found in her friendship with William Maxwell a devoted advocate who was always happy to act as her "liaison" with the editorial staff, and in this way a number of unhappy moments were smoothed over.

Apart from the sheer labor that went into producing the reviews, what further troubled Bogan at *The New Yorker* was the occasional rejection of a piece or a proposed idea as too specialized and "highbrow." In one essay on Rilke and Stefan George, she went into a good deal of detail concerning the differences of opinion between the two men, and was asked to cut out the piece for the reason that the magazine could not afford to print such specialized discussion. Her poem "The Dream" was rejected because, as Mrs. White put it, "it isn't for a magazine like *The New Yorker,* really," and "The Sorcerer's Daughter" was sent back as too difficult for *New Yorker* readers. Bogan was distressed by this attitude, which played a role in her deliberations, in 1943, about whether to leave the magazine. A change came, however, in 1952, after Ross's death, when William Shawn became the magazine's editor. Mr. Shawn not only wanted the best serious poetry available; he also wanted a greater variety of poetic styles. Early in 1952, Mrs. White asked Bogan to recommend poets for the magazine, saying she hoped it could publish more poetry by Auden and Marianne Moore as well as by younger, unknown poets. Bogan quickly responded, and one of the younger poets she recommended without qualification was Adrienne Cecile Rich, whose work delighted Mrs. White.

When Bogan resumed writing for *The New Republic* in 1932 and began to write for *The Nation* in 1938, it was in part to make ends meet. The work was sometimes tedious, and she often disliked the books she reviewed. "O pray that I can go through another couple of years of hackwork without giving out and becoming completely stale and repeating myself," she once wrote wearily to Rolfe Humphries. "After Maidie gets out into the world, I want an anonymous job, that will not demand signed opinions in the public prints."

Presenting signed public opinions naturally embroiled Bogan in an occasional controversy. She was not intentionally malicious in her criticism, but being unsparingly honest, she often hurt and angered friends and strangers alike. When she reviewed Allen Tate's *Poems: 1928–1931* in *The New*

Republic in March 1932, she condemned the book for failing to deal with the truth of poetic feeling, and declared that despite the strong talent evident in "Ode to the Confederate Dead," "Mr. Pope," "Obituary," and "Epistle," Tate was bent on sabotaging his gift. Moreover, she disparaged the Fugitive alliance: "A vaguely philosophic and disturbed tone disguised much expression that was Romantic, much that derived straight from Eliot, or from the Symbolists through Eliot, and very little pure form or formal feelings."

Tate, who had known Bogan since 1927, when he had written to her about the interesting possibility that they shared Irish ancestors on the Bogan side, now wrote again, calling the review "venomous" and complaining that "nearly every sentence is a slight mis-statement, almost a quibble." Bogan replied that she had not been judging Tate as a person or a friend: "I was reviewing a book of poetry which aroused in me respect and irritation in about equal measure. If you objected to the tone of my review, I objected, straight down to a core beyond detachment, to the tone of some of the poems." Tate was outraged, she believed, because he considered himself the possessor of a superior background in philosophy. "You ask me how a poem can have authority," she continued. "I cannot answer, except to say that some poems do. And finally you turn away with an ill-dissembled 'Faugh' from what you consider my presumptuous infringement on a specialized nomenclature."

As much as Bogan cherished the virtues, in criticism, of detachment and disinterestedness, she was frequently naïve about the consequences of their actual expression in public. On the question of separating truth-telling from friendship, she ran into some skeptical resistance from Morton Zabel, who knew that she could be tactless and cruel. She, of course, considered him naïve in most personal and literary affairs, prone to hero worship and literary pretension. But he considered it part of a critic's responsibility to take into account what sort of human effect his reviews might have. After writing an unfavorable review of a book of poems by Ben Belitt, and remarking to Louise how decent and forgiving Belitt had been, he exclaimed, "But don't ask me foolish questions such as 'What has the telling of truth to do with friendship?' You know damn well that even after we're certain that what we consider the truth IS the truth (no easy job), the telling of it has everything in the world to do with friendship—and with love too—and if you think either of these latter institutions are bulwarks against 'truth-telling,' you have only to recall your own experience and that of the rest of mankind to be reminded that THEY ARE NOT. Life isn't so simple, you silly girl."

Bogan's quarrel with Tate is complex in that it is also characteristic of her quarrel with the criticism of her time. She was, above all, an auto-didact, and her abandonment of a college education after her freshman year remained an unresolved matter in her mind. Like many auto-didacts, she had been thrown back so absolutely upon her own intuitions and experiences that she had come to trust these almost unquestioningly and to base her criticism on felt, personal, and unsystematic perceptions; she was impatient with the ways by which ideas are turned on the wheel of argumentation and critical exchange. She could not see herself as a member in a community of critics; she could not work from a central critical paradigm, shared by or even questioned by mutually contending equals. With those she considered better educated than herself, she was fiercely, furiously competitive, simultaneously defensive and aggressive, blindly judging the use of philosophical discourse in criticism as intellectual fakery and exhibitionism, and greatly oversimplifying the virtues of criticism which instead incorporated "images." As much as she esteemed Eliot's essays and I. A. Richards's practical approach to reading, she loathed New Criticism, and in a 1941 review in *The Nation* of John Crowe Ransom's *The New Criticism,* charged him with the "new snobbery" of abstraction: "To think, and to express oneself in images, is becoming rather vulgar. 'Behind every percept lies a concept,' and how tiresome and amateur to have percepts at all!" She jabbed at Ransom's notions of "objective cognitions," "structures," and "textures," even though the concept of *texture* later became central to her teaching. She sarcastically quoted Ransom against himself in the statement, "I do not know why *dusty death;* it is an odd but winning detail," and held against him his praise of Yvor Winters's "structural analysis" and his opinion that William Empson's *Seven Types of Ambiguity* was "the most imaginative account of reading ever printed." She disliked Ransom's method of "close reading," and accused him of failure to approach literature for "its unique power of expressing with every degree of directness absolute differences in men, and the subtle processes by which these differences are achieved," concluding her attack with a quotation from Richards's *Coleridge on Imagination:*

Our Neo-Classic Age is repeating those feats of its predecessor which we least applaud. It is showing a fascinating versatility in travesty. And the poets of the "Romantic" period provide for it what Shakespeare, Milton, and Donne were to the early eighteenth-century grammarians and emendators—effigies to be shot at because what they represent is no longer understood. So the Chinese student today bicycles gaily and ribaldly around on the Altar of Heaven.

As might be guessed, Ransom leaped to a reply as quickly as Tate. In a Letter to the Editor dated September 20, 1941, he accepted Bogan's criticism of his book as "tense" and "abstract," but scolded her with T. S. Eliot's dictum that "it behooves the critic to write about poetry in prose language rather than poetical language." He was surprised, he said, that his book had not fallen into the hands of a reviewer who "would examine its arguments," instead of the hands of "a lady looking for literature and 'images.'" Noting how she had gone to her "beloved library of the writings of I. A. Richards," and therein been supplied "with the image of the Chinese riding bicycles around the parapets of heaven," he offered to defend Richards against Bogan, and proceeded to do so by implying that she had not read that "abstract and possibly tense book" *The Meaning of Meaning* and Richards's *Interpretation in Teaching*. If she hadn't read the first, she was a four-flusher; and if she hadn't read the second, "she will have to go down as a three-flusher."

Bogan's spunky reply to Ransom serves as her reply to the critics of her time. Agreeing with Eliot that the critic should write about poetry in prose language, she pointed out, following I. A. Richards, that different kinds of prose vocabularies exist, and "if one is to be a true critic of literature, beneath any vocabulary must exist a state of sensibility, an intuitive grasp, an open mind, and a generous and humble heart." She decried the textbook approach to literary studies, with its reduction of experience to method and mechanics, and quoting Richards from *Interpretation in Teaching,* she added—("'interpretation,' mind you!")—that "it is perhaps important to insist that abstract thinking is not a highly specialized, sophisticated intellectual feat," then concluded: "And may I say that, having reviewed books for eighteen years, and lived for forty-four, without ever having been called a lady, a four-flusher, a three-flusher . . . or (implicitly) a fool, Mr. Ransom's pure truculence in calling me all these things made me laugh very much? P.S. And it is the 'altar' of heaven, not the 'parapets'!"

Bogan was to carry on this quarrel for her entire critical life, not through polemics, as she did here, but through the medium of her critical style and stance. While the critics of her generation—Cleanth Brooks, Kenneth Burke, R. P. Blackmur, in addition to Ransom and Tate—were, as she well knew, strongly gifted men of letters, she nevertheless thought of them, perversely, defiantly, even desperately, as an encroaching phalanx of abstract, overingenious, and deliberately obscure mandarins, out to safeguard their academic and social prestige by demonstrating the need for a priestly class of explicators and interpreters. Nothing could have enraged Bogan— "the little Irish girl from Roxbury," who had left Boston University after her freshman year—more than what seemed to her their complacent assumption of intellectual superiority. She refused to treat criticism as the province of specialists. She was at heart an Arnoldian and Flaubertian belles-lettrist, who thought literature, or art, through its purity and autonomy, a criticism of life; and she agreed with George Saintsbury that "the critic does his best work, not in elaborating theories which will constantly break down or lead him wrong when they come into contact with the myriad-sided elusiveness of Art and Humanity, but in examining individual works or groups of work, and in letting his critical steel strike the fire of mediate axioms and *aperçus* from the flint of these."

Bogan wrote the kind of criticism she liked to read: peppery, down-to-earth, elegant, freely ranging through both wit and profundity. Once, after rereading Saintsbury on nineteenth-century literature, she wrote to Zabel that Edmund Wilson frequently chided her "for my belles-lettristic ways, and I do love the thought running uniform and true throughout the balanced sentence: Saintsbury had the best Gibbon-formed style I know, with so much lightness and wit in it, so much gaiety and taste (albeit Tory in general tone)."

This love of shaped thought, controlled and free, informal and complex, had everything to do with her fresh enthusiasm for Henry James in the mid-1930s. His perceptions, embedded in the rich intelligence of a semicolloquial and semiperiodic style, had found the perfect idiom for direct yet modulated expression. What he saw—his actual building-up of motive and character—struck her as wonderfully compassionate and knowing. She read *The Bostonians* and found it a brilliant portrayal of homosexual passion; she read the *Notes on Novelists* and admired James's understanding of George Sand; she read *The Princess Casamassima* and saw in it the whole spectre (and spectrum) of modernist politics and literature. By the summer of 1936 she had built up her own armature of insights about James, from which she shaped two fine critical pieces, one of them on *The Princess Casamassima*. After reading it, she had sent Zabel a flood of impressions:

. . . I think it a remarkable book. Why the comrades haven't done something with it before this, I don't know, for they could twist its meaning, distort its pathos, to their own ends, if they really tried. Of course, James's wisdom, working so freely over human beings at that particular period of his career, is making a point that cannot be *twisted* to any uses; it merely exists as statements about the human situation should, in art. Hyacinth is the Artist complete and entire: and even his origins (a murderess and an aristocrat) could be taken symbolically, I suppose. And all classes fail him; when he allows himself to be caught by their dreary purposes (the Princess's neurotic enthusiasm, Muniment's unimaginative purposes, rather crass and heartless,—or even Millicent's magnificent vitality) he is lost. He falls between them all, and dies. His tools, his art, and his responses (to Paris, Venice, etc.) were his job, his life, and he came to know that he had betrayed that: he had not taken the magnificent old Germanwoman's advice; he had let the center of his life, his real reason, go. . . . I really think that "the figure in the carpet" was James's horror of the world as it is made, and possessed by the monsters both above and below, and that the lonely figure of the artist, the gentle, the spiritually endowed but materially disinherited, is the warp that makes the design. —I am so glad I came back to this novel. I read it ten years ago, in my high-flown, really sensuous, blind, unsympathetic, stupidly romantic days, and I hated it: I had no idea what it was about.

In her *Nation* piece on the book, Bogan turns this into a more reflective series of observations. She dismisses the view, held by Brooks and Spender, that the low-bred but sensitive Hyacinth is a yearner after the upper classes, noting that if Hyacinth has a fault, "it is that James has distilled too purely into his creature the sharp insight, the capacity for selfless devotion, the sense of proportion, the talent for self-mockery and gentle irony which seldom exist in genius without an admixture of cruder ingredients." Despite this reservation, she found in Hyacinth's destiny a parable for the fate of the artist in the 1930s, and her essay is as much a warning as it is an unearthing of a little-known treasure.

Bogan also cherished James for his renderings of New England. In her piece on *The Bostonians,* she did a most uncharacteristic thing, and inserted some of her own memories and impressions into the essay. It was as if the only way she could register her response to James's presentation of the book's New England setting was to affirm his apperceptions with her own:

Here is the top layer shot through and through with the humanitarian feeling which must, rather guiltily, accompany utilitarian push and compromise—seeking for "roots" and reality. Here is the entire middle class yearning upward, toward "the fragrance of Beacon Street." James bares the many thin layers of provincial snobbery with scalpel nicety. Turns of both vulgar and affected speech; wrong entrances regretted; all sorts of little affronts taken as "liberties"; shabby genteel uneasiness; upper-class *idées fixes* and brutalities of placement. . . ; the beginning of newspaper curiosity into private lives; the pushing tactics of the vigorous outsider—the whole brittle, energetic, shifting scene, filled with cruelty, uncertainty, nervousness, and "nerve"; here it stands in James as in our memory.

She then permits herself to explore one particular place the novel brings to mind, the little "Square," Union Park, which she remembers from her youth:

Set between two busy and now run-down avenues, it takes the form of a flattened oval—that shape dear to the nineteenth century. Great trees shade it, around a grass plot running its length, decorated by two small cast-iron fountains. The red brick houses, with their "salient" bulging fronts running from top to bottom of the façades, exemplify the first Boston architecture purely American-nineteenth-century in character. . . . It was in such a house that Miss Birdseye lived, and that Ransom saw Verena. But things change. Today—and for the last forty years or so—these houses have been shabby boardinghouses or "light-housekeeping" rooms. The roomers, armed with their paper bags of food and their milk bottles, return to them at night under the shadow of the gracious trees, mount the steps beside the flourish of scrolled iron railings, and enter the big doors under obsolete, elaborate "gasoliers." The materialist spirit that thought to build enduring mansions built, instead, the most solid and dismal furnished lodgings.

It is in such lodgings that Bogan, as a child, had dreaded the thought of ending up in old age. And it was a fear that still haunted her. The civilization which nourished James had died; the civilization supporting her would fail her, she believed, in her difficult hours. But this equation, of course, was in no way evident in her essay.

IN HER CRITICISM of Yeats, Rilke, and Auden, the three major poets who influenced her own work so greatly, and who stood as exemplars of the modernist poetic situation, her capacity to enter into the imaginative life of the age is at its fullest. She took modernism to be a complex and as yet unfinished phenomenon, with very discernible roots in the literature and art of nineteenth-century France, but she was, again as an auto-didact, a practitioner of "comparative literature," drawing on the literature of England, Ireland, Germany, and the United States, as well as France, to buttress her perspectives with detailed insights and associations. She had developed a method of writing about literary change in terms of generations, and from Freud, Jung, and her own experience she came to believe in the crucial importance of the discovery of the Unconscious. Yeats, Rilke, and Auden are measured against their periods and against themselves; they are never seen in isolation. The modernist journey, for her, is the interior journey to the innermost depths of psychic terror and desolation, although she finds compelling external reasons—social, political, and historical—that initiate the quest. It is also a search for new life—for refreshment from popular forms and discoveries—and to this she is equally attuned.

The Yeats she revered was reaching the end of his reign when she reviewed his *Collected Poems* in *The New Yorker* in April 1934, but it is his presence and example she keeps in mind when, in the same review, she takes note of a new voice: "For the benefit of those serious students of poetry who must exist somewhere in a collapsing society, I here mention the name of W. H. Auden, an extremely gifted young English disciple of discontinuity, who does not spurn the current spectacle as poetic material. He has set the

Isis and the Cam on fire; there is always the chance that the conflagration may extend to the Hudson and the Thames." Yeats was, for her at that time, the poet whose struggles to achieve maturity were exemplary; while Auden was the poet with that struggle still before him and with gifts of an order high enough to make the scrutiny of his progress worthwhile. But by the time she reviewed *For the Time Being,* in 1944, he had even surpassed Eliot in her estimation. Although she saw in *The Family Reunion* exactly the same process of reconciliation with the private Furies that she had undergone in *The Sleeping Fury,* she found evidence of arrogance in Eliot's religious conversion, and believed she discerned "all the marks of deep depression" in "Burnt Norton." But Auden's conversion, she noted:

occurred on a non-Romantic level, in a region where the beliefs of Christianity and the proofs of modern psychological knowledge meet. Auden has taken less time than Eliot, indulged in fewer gestures, put less emphasis on ritual, in his search for a religious attitude. A streak of Yorkshire common sense, underneath his complexity, has kept the younger man on the side of simple feeling and away from elaborate orthodoxy.

A year later, she reviewed Auden's *Collected Poetry,* and announced that he had "succeeded Eliot as the strongest influence in American and British poetry." How had this come about? Reflecting on the process of artistic maturation, she wrote:

A moment occurs (or should occur) when the growing artist is able to bequeath his tricks to his imitators. The mature writer rejects the treasured "originality" and the darling virtuosities of his apprenticeship in art, as well as the showy sorrows and joys of his apprenticeship to life, often just in time. "How they live at home in their cozy poems and make long stays in narrow comparison!" Rilke once said, speaking of the run of versifiers who never change or grow. Once youth's embroidered coat is cast aside, what is left? Only imagination, ripened insight, experience, and the trained sense of language, which are usually enough.

She continued, in the most crucial review she ever wrote of a contemporary poet, with a further assessment of Auden that reveals the extent to which she had renounced ambition and was all the more ready to discern it in him. It was during her long period of poetic barrenness; she had not written a poem in three years when she published the review; she doubted that she would ever write another. What she said was that in addition to possessing *perfected* virtues—"imagination, ripened insight, experience, and the trained sense of language"—Auden had an extra fund of vitality which made it possible for him to move beyond the sufficiency of his gifts toward the surplus of greatness. It was this margin of abundant and unperfected virtues which she believed she lacked and which empowered Auden to outstrip Eliot. Though the younger poet shared a sense of period and civilization with the older, Auden was "much more exuberant, restless, sanguine, and unself-conscious than the older poet." The great poet, like Yeats, and now Auden, needed an *eternal immaturity* to renew and disrupt the maturity to which he may only have just arrived. As Bogan said later in a review of Caitlin Thomas's *Leftover Life to Kill,* civilization requires the suppression of innocence of heart and violence of feeling: and yet, "it is true, and always has been that innocence of heart and violence of feeling are necessary in any kind of superior achievement; the arts cannot exist without them." Auden successfully sublimated the two in the form of playfulness, experimentation, satiric irony, exuberance, curiosity, and courage, the inexhaustible stores of which set him apart from his contemporaries. In this view of him she did not change. He was still, in her 1960 review of *Homage to Clio,* the undisputed strongest poet of the age, and his new work "shows no corruption of subject, distortion of aim, or souring of emotion."

But what about Bogan's allegiance to Yeats, her first and most important literary influence? When she began to write about him, he had only five years to live. She had been reading and following him closely since 1916, and had lived with an idealized portrait of him constructed out of her need not so much for poetic authority as for a living embodiment of the highest possible poetic achievement. In her 1938 essay, "The Greatest Poet Writing in English Today," keeping her obsession with the roots of poetic failure ever before her, she presented a Yeats in whom she traced "the continually enriched and undeviating course of an inspired man, from earliest youth to age." It was difficult for her to see him in a human light, although to Zabel she had once written about the Yeats who "was all shot to pieces when he first met Lady Gregory," and who underwent "a tragic break, which he lived through and got over, and mended from." In her review of *Last Poems and Plays,* in 1940, he is the monolithic spirit who, although able to write about "lust, betrayal, wildness, and rage" in old age, has rejected "all middle grounds." Her tone is defensive and righteous as she presents the poet as a bulwark against everything she deplores about the literary impurities of the thirties. To the charge that he has written "Fascist marching songs," she replies that "it is impossible to read this last book of poems and not know that to be a slander, even if Yeats's own answer to this lie did not already exist in print."

It was Yeats the *fighter* Bogan upheld to Zabel, but Yeats the *victor* she presented to the public. The reasons for this single instance of stark idealization are complex. During the years of her own uninterrupted battles—with her memory of her mother, her fight to be free of Curt Alexander, her struggle to make her way as a poet, her ordeal with Raymond Holden—Yeats had stood as the epitome of savage, naked, high, and noble truth-telling. He was the consummate poet of confrontation rather than escape. As the fight went out of her, and she achieved a reconciliation with her divided self, her mettle changed. It was no longer the fiery substance of her youth, but now something more formal and more playful—as we can see in "Several Voices Out of a Cloud." The taste for open combat gave way, particularly as she came to admire Auden, to a taste for inventiveness, virtuoso wit, and satiric lightness as superior forms of aggression. As late as the spring of 1948—the year of "Song for the Last Act," which was, among other things, a valediction to Yeats—she remarked to Zabel, with mild reflectiveness and humor, "I think that Yeats tends to bore us, now that we are ripe and mature, because Yeats, unlike all the other poets of his stature, refused *to give in, to flow.* Yeats and [Stefan] George remained transfixed in power and will. Lawrence and Rilke and Mallarmé flowed." In 1951, reviewing Yeats's *Collected Poems,* she revised her earlier opinion and admitted that Yeats "came perilously near adopting ideas of undemocratic coercion and force." Her final view shows a poet whose development has been mixed, a hero who is also a man, and someone too complex to be exemplary:

Even in the midst of his die-hard show—which at moments verged on the theatrical—he slipped in passages of self-mockery bred of self-knowledge; and beneath his praise of crude human vitality a new note of pathos can be detected. Something stiff, divided, and hieratic drops away from the personality. The wiles of the old magician are transcended; and the final impression is one of a self-fulfilled artist using, up to the end, for selfless purposes, the unbroken spirit of an indomitable man.

BOGAN'S FIRST PIECE on Rilke appeared in *Poetry: A Magazine of Verse,* in April 1937, two years after she had begun to read him. By then he had become for her the figure of the artist most completely attuned to the inner nature, the inner self, and the whole universe of inner life which she saw as the real source of poetry. He served her new, reconciled personality the way Yeats had served the young woman so beset by inner and outer conflicts. "Rilke was often exhausted, often afraid, often in flight, but he was capable of growth and solitude, a process and a state denied to the coward's or the delinquent's existence," she wrote in response to the charge that he was excessively detached from other people, fearful of being loved, and irresponsible in his personal relationships. Like Yeats, Rilke had a religious sensibility, and "spent his life creating a religion for himself. But beyond Yeats, who came to believe in man's pride and intellect as guides and symbols, Rilke stubbornly confronting the real world with his sensibilities, continually testing one by the other, came at last to explain the one by the other, and made a connection between them." This was the crucial virtue, for Bogan, to whom the theory of poetry was the theory of the poet, and for whom Rilke stood as the apotheosis of the human spiritual possibilities which were the material of poetry's existence and meaning:

His belief that "one must praise, in spite of all"; that one must renounce, let go, die and be reborn, endure; "that egoism and childish revolt must be silenced"; that the things which rouse the most terrible grief in us (such as the death of the young) must hold for us the deepest meaning; that it is our force which must use the mechanisms of a changing world for its own ends, not the mechanisms which must weaken our force; that we exist (as the rose, "that inexhaustible thing," exists), the fruit of powers beyond us, within us, which we must in some manner trust: such belief, such openness, such adulthood give back to us the healing of which cynicism, hatred, and an insistence on the complete sufficiency of material systems deprive us.

Even Auden never quite called forth praise of equal intensity from her. Rilke the artist—and not the imperfect man—had put into his work those findings of her own which had made it possible for her to continue to live. For Bogan, who wanted wisdom but loathed "philosophy," he was the consummation of poetic identity: anarchic, submissive, patient, and finally, ecstatic in the face of pleasure or pain.

B O G A N's *Achievement in American Poetry, 1900–1950,* which she published in 1951, is an elegant introduction to the place of poetry in modern American literature. Her purpose was "to connect literature with some large pattern of art and life; and to give students definite and workable insight into tone and taste, as well as into formal structure." The book presents a broad survey of crucial moments and poets and does not argue, defend, or uphold a point of view, although Bogan's love of formal poetry comes through unmistakably in the attention given to formal poets, both major and minor. She emphasizes throughout the importance of the culture's ability to tolerate diversity, and she stresses the role of women in bringing new vitality to poetry. There are many felicities of expression, and on the whole the book is workmanlike, professional, and modest in its considered and thoroughly civilized appraisals.

Bogan was fifty-four when the book was published, and the history it presented was largely that of the poetic world she had herself been part of (although she never mentions her own work). The anthology of poems she appended to the book begins with Louise Imogen Guiney and Stephen Crane, and ends with her juniors—Karl Shapiro, Elizabeth Bishop, Robert Lowell, Peter Viereck, Richard Wilbur, and W. H. Auden. She continued to write poetry reviews until 1968, and in the intervening years found it increasingly difficult to find anything sympathetic to say about the very newest and youngest poets as they emerged during the late fifties and sixties. She found merit in the work of Barbara Howes, W. S. Merwin, and May Swenson; she was considerate, curious, and fair-minded in assessing the "Beat" poets with whom she was so temperamentally out of step. But John Berryman, Karl Shapiro, Robert Lowell, and Anne Sexton disappointed her with what she saw as their relentless and theatrical exploitation of personal trauma. Conscious of her own limitations, and worried about becoming an old fogy, she made an effort to respect what she could not enjoy, and, at least toward Sexton, made an attempt at generosity: "To outline personal relationships . . . always at a high pitch of emotion requires courage; to describe fully the dark conflicts of the self without slipping over into the shrill voice of confession or the sobbing note of self-pity requires high control at every conscious and unconscious level."

Bogan's essays on single figures, collected in *Selected Criticism: Poetry and Prose* (1955) and *A Poet's Alphabet: Reflections on the Literary Art and Vocation* (1970), constitute her most enduring achievement as a critic. Whether she writes about Yeats, Rilke, Auden, Dickinson, Frost, Gide, Hopkins, or James, she begins with and always returns to the irreducible mystery of spirit, temperament, and character. When she charts the ways in which Gide "escapes most of the enticements of self-deception"; or observes how Dickinson "mastered that Nature concerning which she had such ambivalent feeling by adding herself to the sum of all things, in a Rilkean habit of praise"; or remarks that Frost "has failed to achieve that last extension and renovation of thought and emotion—that masterful ordering of experience—which we constantly find in the later poems of Yeats," she never falters in her surveillance of the risks, difficulties, and ultimate values of poetry. Her essays on more general topics, among them "Poetesses in the Parlor," "The Heart and the Lyre" (both on poetry by women), "The Time of the Assassins" (on detective fiction), "Some Notes on Popular and Unpopular Art" (on folk art), "The Secular Hell" (on myth), and "The Pleasures of Formal Poetry," as well as her introductions to new editions of Flaubert's *A Sentimental Education* and Hawthorne's *The Scarlet Letter,* testify to her belief in the imagination and the unconscious as the sources of all that is nutritive in human life. As her poetry enacted a spiritual reckoning, so her criticism enacted a cultural reckoning in its insistence that greatness in art could stem only from forces essentially irrational.

IV 1 9 4 2 ～ 1 9 5 4

In spite of her rigorous critical detachment, Louise Bogan wrote about the issues of psychological crisis and reparation as a participant. The struggle to mature, remain open, and surpass the self was immediate and practical, for her; it lay at the center of her creative and personal survival. Once again, the woman who found it so difficult to write her autobiography was able, when she *translated* her knowledge of herself into her appreciative knowledge of others, to put her life to account, and moreover to keep faith with art in the process.

V

1955 ❀ 1970

SONG

FOR THE

LAST ACT

11 NARROWING, DARK HOURS

BOGAN'S LATER YEARS envelop her in full chiaroscuro. In the foreground, bright shafts of light reveal a busy, productive woman, with a full and varied schedule that includes occasional teaching jobs, poetry readings, commissioned essays, *New Yorker* reviews, and social activities. She writes and receives letters from friends, keeps in close touch with her daughter, travels to England and various parts of America, reads for pleasure, embroiders, listens to music, and now and then even writes a poem. Her wit enlivens her letters and conversations with innumerable trenchant observations. Her serenity maintains its equilibrium; she is solid and sane. Then, in the middle ground and deepening into the background, the atmosphere darkens, and the complete and balanced woman appears very nearly becalmed, expecting no further emotional enrichment out of life, certainly finding none, and ignoring, as much as she can, the terrible cost of this resignation. Dark and light shift; then the darkness slowly takes over.

In June 1956, Bogan traveled to Oxford, Ohio, to receive an honorary doctorate in letters from The Western College for Women. It was her first such honor, and it pleased her immensely. While she was there, a new and lasting friendship took root when she met a young English professor, Ruth Limmer, who had grown up in Washington Heights and regularly returned there during college vacations. Bogan urged Miss Limmer to keep in touch, and eventually, whenever Miss Limmer found herself in New York, she would visit. A strong companionship developed. "I think part of my 'charm' for Louise was my born and bred nativism," Miss Limmer has said. "I had played in her haunts when a child; I knew the shops, the libraries, scenes of her daily life; we shared—when we bought food at Sloans (the *original*

Sloans, I do believe, on Broadway and 170th)—sharp memories of its previous existence as a movie house: we had each seen beneath the proscenium, where now the meat counters sat, Gary Cooper and Clark Gable, and all the rest of those American cultural heroes (and heroines)." Bogan and Miss Limmer would have dinner together, go to the movies, and talk. There were few references to Louise's past. She was becoming increasingly withdrawn from her other friends. It was not that she had ceased to care for them, but the effort of traveling downtown, by bus or cab, seemed extreme, and she often canceled dinner invitations, pleading upcoming or just-past visits to the dentist. When she did go out—to an Institute dinner, for instance—it was a grand occasion, and it gave her enormous pleasure to be able to come home from one of these and write to Ruth Limmer right away about who was there and what had been worn, said, implied, or observed. She knew, too, that whatever she had to say about new books and movies would be received with the keenest appreciation.

Neither *Collected Poems, 1923–1953* nor *Selected Criticism: Poetry and Prose* had made much of a splash, although the reviews were generally favorable. Kenneth Rexroth, in the *New York Herald-Tribune Book Review,* called the former the "carefully considered life work of one of America's very best poets," and the anonymous reviewer in the English *Times Literary Supplement* praised Bogan's "flawless lyrics." About her criticism Rexroth was equally laudatory: "There is no trace in these essays of that fraudulent blight on American letters, the Higher Criticism. Miss Bogan has never been so foolish or so vulgar as to give the impression, even for an instant, that she believed poetry was a sack full of gimmicks which could be spoon-fed to provincial freshmen." But Bogan had become convinced that her time for influence and recognition had come and gone, and in the early sixties gave much thought to the matter of a literary executor. She first chose Morton Zabel as her executor and then, after his death in 1964, William Jay Smith. But Smith had an active career as a poet, and she felt that by assuming the executorship he would be depriving himself of time spent in his own behalf. For a brief time she wanted Smith and Miss Limmer to serve as co-executors, then shifted the entire executorship over to Miss Limmer. The change reveals a good deal of ambivalence about her hopes for immortality, for she gave Miss Limmer no instructions whatsoever, except that her papers were to constitute a bequest to her daughter. "She didn't renounce ambition," Miss Limmer has remarked, "but, as it were, gambled it: maybe I'd do something, maybe I wouldn't." As it turned out, Miss Limmer, who co-edited, with Robert Phelps, *A Poet's Alphabet* (published in 1970, only a few months after Bogan's death), has edited *What the Woman Lived: Selected Letters of Louise Bogan, 1920–1970,* published in 1973, and *Journey Around My Room,* published in 1980.

I N 1 9 5 7, just after she turned sixty, Louise decided to break her long-standing rule against going to artists' colonies (she had not been to one since her 1926 stay at Yaddo), and went to the MacDowell Colony, in Peterborough, New Hampshire, for the first of what was to be a series of annual visits through 1964. She was delighted and surprised to find herself serenely productive at the place. The first two weeks of silence and country solitude were slightly disorienting, but soon her resistance to creative work lowered, and she was able to write. In "Revisiting the MacDowell Colony," the poet Maxine Kumin describes an afternoon there, when she and some friends, all of them young poets, came to pay their respects:

> The same cabin, the same stone fireplace,
> red oak blazing in its sooty bin,
> and just outside, October trees on fire
> in the same slant of the five o'clock sun.
> In the rocking chair, Louise Bogan,
> girlish with company back then. . . .
> In the straight chair, theatrically puffing,
> our mentor, John Holmes, with pipe.
> We three novices lined up on the lumpy cot
> while water was coaxed to boil over the hot
> plate and jasmine tea was served in the club
> they would never, o never invite us to join
> who signed the plaque above the hearth
> as evidence of tenancy and worth.

Louise Bogan, her daughter has said, "hated flattery, but loved adulation," and no doubt was in her element when surrounded by a group of young admirers. She could indeed be "girlish," flirtatious, actually, when she knew that every word and gesture was being eyed with affection and respect.

From her first visit to MacDowell came her remarkable and powerful *New Yorker* review of Caitlin Thomas's *Leftover Life to Kill*. ("It is *wonderful*; it is *Beautifully Done!!*" exclaimed William Shawn on the telephone to her, after receiving the piece.) She had in general been working well for the past two years. Teaching had begun to bore her a little, opening the way to renewed promptings about her memoirs and reminding her that "the thing between oneself and oneself is best." There were hints of subterranean activity. Stanzas (unidentified) came to her on a train back to New York from a teaching stint in Bloomington, Indiana, in July 1955, and early the next October she sent May Sarton a card of an etching of the North Portal of Chartres Cathedral with the remark, "The great hunger for utter form, immediately returned. . . . Together with the notion that I should spend several years looking at *old stones*." Sarton wrote after reading *Selected Criticism* to say that she had been moved by its "whole deep inward spring and movement . . . toward the fruits of maturity and about what stops people or what they manage to use and transmute *as they mature*." Surely, she went on to say, a whole new period of "mastery and arrival" was imminent?

But Louise was still blocked about the memoirs, and she knew why. Reading Erich Neumann's *Origins and History of Consciousness*, she found herself especially interested in the Victory of the Ego over the Unconscious. The Fight with the Dragon, she explained to Sarton, "is the fight I seem to be in the midst of, and I know you hope that the unconscious will win. . . ." She then proceeded to read Neumann's *The Great Mother*, after which she remarked, again to Sarton, that it was "the *Horrible* Great Mother that we must conquer, in order to reach the symbolic *Isis*. The symbolism [was] relevant in my case; I don't know about anyone else's."

She had been writing poetry again. In February 1957 she sent "The Meeting" to John Hall Wheelock, explaining that she had been haunted by the story the poem tells for a long time, and had thought to do it first in prose. Then, one morning in the spring of 1956, she'd simply put down the first lines, and the rest followed. On July 17, 1955, she had written "July Dawn," rewriting it in November 1956, when she also managed to rewrite "March Twilight," a poem first written March 1, 1940, and kept in a folder for some sixteen years. Late in 1956 she wrote another poem, "St. Christopher," and rewrote "a rather sappy (I fear) thing called 'Portrait of the Artist as a Young Woman'" which, like "March Twilight," had first been sketched in 1940:

> Sitting on the bed's edge, in the cold lodgings,
>   she wrote it out on her knee
> In terror and panic—but with the moment's courage,
>   summoned up from God knows where.
> Without recourse to saints or angels: a Bohemian, thinking herself free—
> A young thin girl without sense, living (she thought) on passion and air.

Bogan never published the poem, for the reason, no doubt, that Ruth Limmer has suggested: "The poem tells too much, too openly." In it are memories of Vienna in 1922—the cafés and lindens, the sound of pianos, the shadows in formal gardens—and of the cramped, uneasy Massachusetts home of her parents to which she returned, and from which she fled again to New York:

And here once more is the cold room, between thin walls of sadist and lout.
But at last, asking to serve, seeking to earn its keep, about and about,
At the hour between the dog and the wolf, is it her heart that speaks?
She sits on the bed with the pad on her knees, and writes it out.

The poem suggests that Bogan was getting readier to "surround and examine an early phase of the self by means of a later one," as she had characterized Eliot's achievement in her review of *The Family Reunion.* It helped that she had a new or rather revived set of imaginative symbols with which to gird herself for a fresh look into the past. In the early thirties, in "Hypocrite Swift," "To Wine," and "At a Party," she had invoked the planets as beacons of an eternal, suprahuman wisdom. Now, with Robert Phelps, a young novelist whom she met in 1956, shortly after he wrote to her on behalf of a poet in financial straits, she indulged her curiosity about astrology. Phelps was an avid, skilled astrologist, who shared his abundant zodiacal lore with her. Astrology had intrigued her ever since she'd read Yeats's *A Vision* many years before, and, as she remarked to another young friend, the poet Herbert Cahoon, if astrology was good enough for Yeats, it was good enough for her. Elements of delight and awe were equally present in it, she believed, and without imposing religious dogma, it had the sense of an ordered universe essential to religious emotion. At Christmastime, 1960, Bogan sent William Maxwell and his wife a card with a reproduction of a Michael Wolgemut woodcut in Fridolin's Treasury of the True Riches of Salvation (Nuremberg, 1491), showing "The Position of the Planets at the Birth of Christ." In the woodcut, a hand holds a set of concentric circles divided into the signs of the zodiac. The Madonna and Christ Child are placed at the center in a medieval landscape with castle and tree. Bogan wrote on the card: "Dr. Wall says we are in God's hands. (He doesn't know what that means, he adds, but he believes it.) I believe it too."

IN 1957, Maidie Alexander married Austin Scannell. Louise lectured at the Salzburg Seminar in American Studies during the summer of 1958, and then traveled to Switzerland, Paris, and London, eager to explore new and old places whose points of interest she dutifully and elegantly reported in her letters home.

A good deal of incidental writing was on its way: in October 1959, a paper on Emily Dickinson, delivered at the Amherst bicentennial celebration where she joined Richard Wilbur and Archibald MacLeish in honoring the poet; next her foreword to Hawthorne's *The Scarlet Letter,* in 1960, and in 1961 a rigorous and comprehensive critical essay on Robert Frost for

Perry Miller's two-volume anthology, *Major Writers of America*. She received two important awards: in 1959, five thousand dollars from the Academy of American Poets; and in 1962, the Senior Creative Arts Award from Brandeis University.

In the early sixties the Chicago publishing house of Reilly & Lee asked William Jay Smith and Bogan to compile and edit an anthology of poetry for young people. Both turned the offer down, convinced that it would be boring and tedious. But one evening, while the offer still stood, Bogan was visiting Smith and his wife, the poet Barbara Howes, at their home in North Pownal, Vermont, and they began, as she later recalled,

the game of "Do you remember?"—and we soon were surprising each other by early enthusiasms which we discovered we shared. Tennyson's "Brook," for example, the first poem which had excited me, around the age of 9 or 10. Chesterton's "Song of Quoodle," more or less lost in one of his prose books. An exquisite Kipling lyric, also more or less mislaid in *Puck of Pook's Hill.* The wonderful children's verse of Christina Rossetti and Elizabeth Madox Roberts . . .

They went on and on, and sometime after midnight, decided to go ahead with the anthology. Further meetings followed, one at a motel near the MacDowell Colony, where they spread piles of books out on the double beds, ordered cold drinks, and laughed and remembered their way through dozens of titles. For both of them the project was a joyous experience, and they were immensely gratified when *The Golden Journey,* whose title was taken from a poem by James Elroy Flecker they had both read as children, was published in November 1965.

In the meanwhile, Bogan had returned to her memoirs, almost surreptitiously, as if to beguile those inner censors who had only rarely relaxed their guard over the past quarter of a century. On January 17, 1958, she wrote about the end of ambition (as if to placate the Furies), about her young friend Robert Phelps, "who runs his life by the stars!" and about her stalwart friend Elizabeth Mayer. No word was said about the past. Then, on June 8, 1959, the past returned, and Bogan turned and faced her childhood once again:

The individual *free* being, forced to begin small, like a sturdy shoot, but humble, which does not make much of a target for the wind . . .

Her earliest sense impressions returned:

So that I do not at first see my mother. I see her clearly much later than I smell and feel her—long after I see those solid fractions of the houses and fields. She comes in frightfully clearly, all at once. But first I have learned the cracks in the sidewalk, the rain in the gutter, the mud and the sodden wayside leaves, the shape of every plant and weed and flower in the grass.

Sharp discrete pictures emerged: the mill towns, carried within memory for nearly sixty years, returned with exactitude, as Bogan remembered how they looked in the light "that falls incredibly down through a timeless universe." She remembered her utter bafflement at the world of adults, remembered the violent family quarrels in Milton, at Bodwell's. Then came the flume, the color of hills in March, Mary Bogan's dreaded "familiars," and the two days that Louise went blind. Two days later, on June 10th, she remembered the one scene of utmost violence, when her screaming and crying mother had swept her up and fled from the room. At last, in a single session's writing, "the *Horrible* Great Mother" was united for a brilliant, impermanent moment with "the symbolic *Isis*," whose temple—the remembered summerhouse in a summer dawn—had survived in Bogan's memory as a place of beauty and refuge. There was acceptance of the mother as imperfect and incomplete, as tender as well as terrifying, but there was also blameless, direct acknowledgment, without self-pity or recrimination, of the child who was nevertheless that mother's victim.

More scenes, more memories came: blue hydrangeas in autumn (now we understand why she loved Rilke's "Blaue Hortensie"), the Gardners' house, and the fear that in writing about it, she would "lose it forever—and that I do not want to do." More material on the Gardners arrived June 17, 1959, and then blocks of notes on June 20th: *aperçus*, an invocation to the city, an observation on what it is like to live free of anguish, a short memory of the intense fantasy life of the young girl who had imagined scenes of passionate life lived behind every passing house and storefront. On June 22nd she meditated on the vicious, predatory nature of acute despair and depression, and then again, on a wave of triumphant affirmation, recalled her mother once again, and her mother's "true elegance of hand":

She could cut an apple like no one else. Her large hands guided the knife; the peel fell in a long light curve down from the fruit. Then she cut a slice from the side. The apple lay on the saucer, beautifully fresh, white, dewed with faint juice. She gave it to me. She put the knife away.

The memories continued to flow: the sound of her father's steps returning home in Ballardvale, her mother's wizened conspirators, her mother on a summer morning in a fresh housedress, standing in front of the house in a good mood. Suddenly her mother is dressing for the city, and the anxiety returns, the atmosphere of tension and betrayal.

From September 1960 until September 1961 there were no further notes. But then, among those which arrived:

"And all things are forgiven, and it would be strange not to forgive"—this Chekhov knew.

Forgiveness and the eagerness *to protect:* these keep me from putting down the crudest shocks received from seven on. With my mother, my earliest instinct was to protect—to take care of, to endure. This, Dr. Wall once told me, is the instinct of a little boy. . . . Well, there it is. I *did* manage to become a woman. . . . Now, in my later years, I have no hatred or resentment left. But I still cannot describe some of the nightmares lived through, with love. So I shan't try to describe them at all. Finished. Over.

In the next sentence Bogan remembered seeing her mother's ringed hand, through a hotel door, on the pillow. She had at last written down her memory of the adulterous scene. It now existed on the page, freed from its source. Yet it had come too late. Her poems, she wrote, had depended "on the *ability* to love. (Yeats kept saying this to the end.)" But it was just this ability which she felt she had lost. To love now would be an effort.

FOUR YEARS PASSED, from September 21, 1961, to August 16, 1965. She worked steadily on her *New Yorker* reviews; gave a lecture on women writers, called "What the Women Said," at Bennington; attended the National Poetry Festival at the Library of Congress where she read a paper called "The Role of the Poetry Journal," joining Randall Jarrell, Karl Shapiro, John Berryman, Howard Nemerov, Muriel Rukeyser, J. V. Cunningham, and Stanley Kunitz for readings and panel discussions which she thoroughly enjoyed, having long overcome her inhibitions against public performance. There, too, she reconciled, after yet another squabble which had led to yet another long standoff, with Morton Zabel, who gave her a kiss "right on the platform, in full view of the audience." And then there were the regular dinners and ceremonies at the National Institute of Arts and Letters. The pleasure of celebrating merit in her peers was an inducement for her to emerge from what was becoming an increasingly reclusive life.

Her most enduring friendships—those sustained throughout a lifetime—were yielding to time and age, and diminishing in intensity. Rolfe Humphries retired after many years of teaching at Amherst, moved to California with his wife in order to be near their son John, only to suffer the tragic loss of that son in a car accident in Palo Alto. Although Humphries's health began to deteriorate, he and Bogan kept in touch with an occasional card or letter. One evening in the spring of 1963, Edmund Wilson brought Léonie Adams up to 169th Street for an evening of talk and reminiscence, after which he left with Bogan's long essay on Frost, about which he wrote soon thereafter to say that while the piece itself was "solid," he still couldn't "see the poetry." So their old differences still lingered, as well as their old fondness. Theodore Roethke's death, in August 1963, shocked her, and Morton Zabel's death, in April 1964, was a blow. She felt that she hadn't been attentive enough after their last reconciliation. She hadn't even taken off the cellophane from his last Christmas present—a recording of Verdi's *Otello,* and that bothered her terribly. Zabel had been incomparably loyal and devoted to her. "He and I laughed in the same places, too. I shall miss him," she wrote to Ruth Limmer.

IN APRIL 1963, Bogan traveled to England, where she visited Bath, Salisbury, Rye, and, after establishing herself comfortably in London, took day excursions to Coventry Cathedral, Stonehenge, Stratford-upon-Avon, and Oxford. She visited a younger friend, Jacqueline Froom (later Hinden), a musician who had spent some time in the United States and had taken one of Bogan's courses, and was able to move a little beyond the limits of being a tourist. Spring was good that year in England, not more than usually wet and cold, and Louise delighted in the fresh, abundant flowers and the mottled rosiness of English children. She walked by herself through London, browsing in book and print shops and exploring different restaurants. She ambled through Kensington Gardens and Portobello Road, drank in the exhibits of furniture, costume, china, and prints in the Victoria and Albert Museum, and rejoiced in the sight of pink and white cherry trees in bloom, thinking perhaps of A. E. Housman's lad of twenty, rejoicing too in the cherry tree "hung with snow." She had not felt homesick, as she always had before when traveling, and was pleased that the trip turned out "just as I wanted it to, *finally,* an *exploration,*" she wrote to Maidie, "rather than anything cut and dried. *Now I know* what England is like, at the moment, and what it is likely to be, for some years to come." By the end of May she was ready to come home and begin a big new translation project, *The Journal of Jules Renard,* undertaken with Elizabeth Roget, a novelist whom Louise had met at the MacDowell Colony in 1958 and whose first language was French.

A year and a half later, in the fall of 1964, Louise took an apartment in

Cambridge (16 Chauncy Street) in order to teach at Brandeis University. Much as she was attached to her apartment in New York, the time had come, she felt, to take on a fresh challenge: "I need a little shaking up," she wrote to William Maxwell. The teaching load was not particularly heavy, and there were friends in the vicinity: May Sarton, always energetic and devoted and ready to come for a visit with a bunch of perfect flowers and a bottle of good Scotch; Zoltan Haraszti, the librarian in charge of rare books and manuscripts at the Boston Public Library; and at Brandeis itself, the poet J. V. Cunningham and the scholar and Keats biographer, Aileen Ward.

For the first time in nearly forty years, Louise saw a New England autumn, and it was a lovely one at that (she thought the squirrels remarkably furry). From the window of her Chauncy Street apartment she could see red brick and creeping vines and falling leaves. Her schedule was undemanding, requiring only five hours of classes a week, with plenty of time for hours of reading at The Boston Athenaeum. It was the era of the Boston Strangler panic, when women stayed in their apartments at night, and she was disgruntled at not being able to go to the movies at her pleasure. But in all other respects the teaching year began auspiciously enough.

By late October it appeared that the Brandeis students neither understood her commitment to formal poetry nor had any inclination to develop an interest in it. And they hadn't a clue, it seemed to her, that the nineteenth century had ever existed. She became lonely, tired, and homesick. Weekend visits to New York did not help. Boston in the fall revived memories, old, inescapable memories, and when she undertook her customary ritual, performed whenever she found herself in Boston or its environs, of exploring the streets in Roxbury where she had lived in late childhood and adolescence, she sank into a deep gloom. The buildings she remembered had decayed to near slumhood. The card catalogue of the local branch of the Boston Public Library did not show a single copy of any of her books. Her whole youth, and her mother's, father's, and brother's lives, seemed to have vanished without a trace.

She had been safe from severe depression for so many years that at first it just seemed as if she were suffering from a weakened resistance to physical stress. But late in January, when she broke a rib, the doctor who treated her, suspecting a growing depression, prescribed an antidepressant. For a while the stony-hearted grimness lessened; by spring it was back. She was lonely again and, as she wrote Maxwell, "really feeling guilty about earning so much money." Brandeis was paying her twelve thousand dollars for the year, as large a sum of money as she had ever earned for a single job in her life.

Additional physical problems plagued her. There was some dental work that had to be done, and the more serious matter of unstable blood-sugar levels, which was traced to a minor case of diabetes, an ailment her mother had also developed late in life. But the depression did not let up, and by the end of the academic year had become distressingly acute. Never a passive sufferer, Bogan decided to *take action,* and in June entered The Neurological Institute on 168th Street—just a block away from her Washington Heights apartment—for a stay of some weeks. Insight had not been enough to keep the depression at bay. The drugs she was given took immediate effect: the acute psychological suffering lessened, but was accompanied by horrifying heart fibrillations, the result, apparently, of drug interactions which could have been prevented had the hospital doctor consulted her internist about the strength of other medications she was taking. When William Maxwell visited her in the hospital, she remarked to him, "I am being assaulted in the citadel of my being." After this condition was corrected, and the worst side effects alleviated, a measure of calm returned. "One evening," she wrote to Ruth Limmer, "with a gibbous moon hanging over the city (such *visions* we have!) like a piece of red cantaloupe, and automobiles showing red danger signals, as they receded down Ft. Wash. Ave.—I thought I had reached the edge of eternity, and *wept* and *wept.*"

For a time there was improvement, enough for Louise to go home to 169th Street in July and resume her *New Yorker* tasks. A trip with Maidie to Atlantic City later that month did not go well, however; Louise had moments of extreme panic, dreading the thought of being left alone even for the short time it took Maidie to do their errands. Difficulties continued over the summer, and in the middle of September she decided to return to New York Hospital's Westchester Division in White Plains, where she had not set foot since the spring of 1934—thirty-one years ago. "The partial procedures were not working successfully," she explained to William Maxwell, "& Dr. Wall advised this step."

At "Bloomingdale's" she came under the care of a new physician named Dr. Bruce Poundstone, whom she found "really intuitive, sharp & *with it.*" But psychotherapy was not successful at relieving the symptoms of her depression, and she continued to deteriorate. Finally, with terrible reluctance, Bogan consented to a brief series of electroshock treatments, which did manage to alleviate her depressive symptoms and to make it possible for her to respond to the insights gathered during intensive psychotherapy sessions. As Bogan wrote May Sarton, she was discovering, or rather rediscovering, again, after many years, that *"anger & mourning"* were at the heart of her sufferings. The visit to the Boston of her faraway youth had resurrected parts of herself she had managed to ignore and reject for far too long.

By February 1966 she was much improved and wrote a rondel, "Castle of My Heart" ("Cleanse and refresh the castle of my heart / Where I have lived for long with little joy"), while still at the hospital. She had visits from Maidie and letters from friends, including William Maxwell, who described a trip he had taken to his hometown in Illinois with his two daughters:

The air in Illinois was marvelous. So light and pure it went to my head. And where I used to pick spring beauties in the grass in our side yard there were several good-sized, though nondescript, trees. Where the trees used to be there weren't any. And of course no potted palms, no grape arbor, no flower garden, no trumpet vine. Those are always the first to go. But on the other hand, the hitching posts were still there, with the very rings that I have seen my father fasten the reins of his and my mother's riding horses to, or the carriage horse, when I was under six years old. Leading me to wonder if survival (in objects) is not a matter of being no longer useful, and therefore not subject to fashion. Anyway, the hitching posts are still there.

It was possible, the letter seemed to say, to look back over the past with pleasure and curiosity and detached wonder at the workings of time. Reading it, she was perhaps reminded of unfinished work, and quickened by the thought of getting back to it. She was home by spring, with some assurance regained, and a good appetite for her *New Yorker* verse department. Still, she had weeping spells in the mornings, which belonged, she said, to her "strange little (for it *must* be a child-ghost, embedded in the subconscious) morning visitant." Maidie Scannell christened this delicate, sad wraith "Little Lobelia."

In August 1965, shortly before Louise decided to enter the hospital in Westchester, she had returned to her memoirs, precisely locating the beginning of the depression in her pilgrimage to Roxbury the previous fall. She recalled the dreary "railroad" apartment where her father and brother had slept in one room, while she and her mother had slept in another, and the strange uncertainty of her parents' attempt at a new beginning, after a bad period of fights and separations. She then went on to describe her feelings on seeing the old neighborhood, now in a state of advanced deterioration:

I felt the consuming, destroying, deforming passage of time; and the spectacle of my family's complete helplessness, in the face of their difficulties, swept over me. With no weapons against what was already becoming an overwhelming series of disasters—no insight, no self-knowledge, no inherited wisdom—I saw my father and mother (and my brother) as helpless victims of ignorance, wilfulness, and temperamental disabilities of a near-psychotic order—facing a period (after 1918) where even this small store of pathetic acquisitions should be swept away.

On August 27th she described Mrs. Gardner, with her blessed, ordered household, her preserves, and her quilts, and on August 28th she expressed her own puzzlement at her depression:

A deep-seated masochism? Surely I have acted in a consistently *optimistic* fashion, ever since the 1933 breakdown. —I have surmounted one difficulty after another; I have *worked* for life and "creativity;" I have cast off all the anxieties and fear I could; I have helped others to work and hold on. Why this collapse of psychic energy?

She recognized that she had been living in a state of emotional isolation, and she knew that the fear of age and death was strong:

But people keep hopeful and warm and *loving* right to the end—with much more to endure than I endure. —I see the old constantly, on these uptown streets—and they are not "depressed." Their eyes are bright; they have bought themselves groceries; they gossip and laugh—with, often, crippling handicaps evident among them. Where has this power gone, in my case? I weep—but there's little relief there. How can I break these mornings?

The weeping, clinging child—"Little Lobelia"—cried out for love, but for twenty years Louise Bogan had not permitted herself to feel (as far as anyone can know) new or rekindled love, for anyone or anything. Her carefully erected, thoroughly adult maturity had at last engendered its own defeat by refusing to countenance its opposite: the eternal, hungry, clamoring, yearning, angry, weeping child. Bogan could not widen the aperture of self-acceptance. She could not feel, she could not give. Since the last depression she could not even listen to music.

The summer of 1966 signaled her final attempt to work on her memoirs. These consist primarily of notes on her bad mornings and the effects of the pills she was taking. This record was kept not because she thought it was a good idea, but because Ruth Limmer urged her to do it, in order to keep track of what the various dosages, taken at various times, would do to her moods. "She had been taking them more or less at random times in unremembered dosages," Miss Limmer recalls. "In a real sense [the notes] are not part of the 'long prose thing,' although they do conclude it." On Monday, July 25th, Louise took three Libriums and noted that the clutching grief she called "spasms" soon passed. The next day she again noted how many pills she took and their effect. For Wednesday, July 27th, she wrote, "No tears! 3 pills," and on Thursday, July 28th, she noted: "2 early pills (6:30 and 8:30). Some *tightness* and lowness of spirit, early on. No tears!"

With this entry, the memoirs end. The child visitor continued to haunt her mornings, and the following winter found its voice in "Little Lobelia's Song," written October 18th and December 14th, 1966. A year later, on December 27, 1967, no doubt contemplating the new year, Bogan drafted "December Daybreak":

> Caught in a corner of the past
> Wherein we cannot even weep
> We only ask
> For present sleep
>
> But the dream shoots forward to a future
> We shall never see;
> Therefore, in December's night, at the beginning of morning
> We must give over and be
>
> Once again the ignorant victor,
> Or the victim, wise
> Within those broken circles of wisdom
> [   ] which the living live
> And the dead rise.

This was her last poem. When Farrar, Straus and Giroux, which had acquired Noonday Press, published a new collected edition in 1968, *The Blue Estuaries: Poems 1923–1968,* Louise Bogan's life as a poet came to an end.

BOGAN HAD dedicated *Selected Criticism: Poetry and Prose* "To Maidie Alexander, daughter and friend," and she now dedicated what she knew to be her final book of poems "To the memory of my father, mother and brother." Her depression had been at least in part an attempt to connect with them, and this dedication acknowledged the bridge between her life's work and her love for her family. The poems in the sixth and last section of the book were Bogan's final fruits, and of two kinds, primarily. There were occasional poems, like those in the final section of *Poems and New Poems,* and simple, severe lyrics. Some were old poems, written or put down as first drafts as long ago as 1940; others had been written after 1948, about the time, that is, that Bogan had stopped thinking of herself as a *practicing* poet. Poems had come thereafter one at a time, for the most part, with long intervals in between.

Many of these later poems are in free verse, and in them Bogan arrives at a middle ground between formal rigor and the looser, more open feeling

May Sarton had encouraged her to strive for. In "The Dragonfly," for instance, written sometime in the fall of 1961, she worked with short free-verse lines in a delicate line of Thoreauvian naturalism. Its inspiration was a picture postcard of a dragonfly Ruth Limmer had sent her from Detroit, but she wrote the poem on commission for the Corning Glass Company—wrote it to order, that is!—and a piece of Steuben Glass was carved to illustrate it. She was fond of the poem, which, she informed Miss Limmer, was completely "based on FACT."

Her formal poems were correspondingly natural in diction. The language of "St. Christopher" is aphoristic and conversational, with echoes of Auden, again ("The middle class is what we are"), but with tenderness and grace completely Bogan's own. It is a *ding-gedicht,* a poem about an object, in this case a fresco, formerly attributed to Antonio Pollaiuolo and now attributed to Domenico Ghirlandaio, of "Saint Christopher and the Infant Christ," after the Saint Christopher, variously attributed to Pollaiuolo, on the façade of San Miniato fra le Torri in Florence. Bogan had seen it in the Metropolitan Museum of Art, and been struck by the saint's rugged working-class look. The painted St. Christopher is a tall, wiry man in his prime, with flowing black hair, moustache, and goatee. On his shoulder he carries a trusting Christ Child across shallow water, holding a staff with a palm at the end. The "look of intent love" on the saint's face, as he carries the Child across the water, corresponds exactly to Bogan's description of it.

It was a look she knew well, and did not so much discover in the painting as recognize. In a letter to May Sarton she mentioned that the saint bore a striking resemblance to the man with whom she had had her eight-year "successful" love affair; and, to a remarkable degree, the painting indeed recapitulated, in allegorical fashion, their first meeting. Bogan had been the "child," in her state of acute emotional distress, and the "raw-boned and . . . ignorant man" had quite literally brought her across the water "in to the safe harbor." When she first wrote the poem, in 1940, the affair was ongoing, which may well have been why she left it unrevised at the time. When she rewrote it in November 1956, the affair had been over for at least ten years, and the poem's civilized tone could carry the love at its source without exposure.

Bogan's fascination with the symbols of sorcery and astrology made its way into a pair of poems, "The Sorcerer's Daughter" and "The Young Mage." Just as translation exists as a motif in much of her work, so the related notion of reading and misreading symbols serves in both of these poems as a key to the perverse nature of fate. In "The Sorcerer's Daughter," the poem's speaker goes over the foreknown and recognized bad fate:

In that situation, all the signs were right: scars
On corresponding thumbs, our two heights in proportion
To an inch. And old remembered songs kept hitting the ear
Portentously, as never before or since.

The omens (and Bogan did have a scar on her thumb, from a piece of broken glass on which she had cut herself in Milton) only appear to be benevolent, and then just briefly:

But this series of events had no good auguries about it:
        no birds flew into fortunate quarters
When the knock came upon the door. Matter did not creak
        or space mutter.
Nothing fell up or down; the weather did not give it much help,
And time and place were always wrong.

It was crossed from the start
With all the marks of luck changing
From better to worse.
And by these tokens I begin to think it is mine.

As a lyric *persona,* the "Sorcerer's Daughter" has been hexed by her father, but because, like Miranda, or Rappaccini's Daughter, she can to a certain extent understand her father's lore, she is all the more skilled at what is actually a misreading and then suddenly an understanding of her bad fate. Bogan had not written a poem with such an atmosphere of doom and failure in it since "Cassandra." When it was published in the *Times Literary Supplement* in 1959, it appeared with a "set of lyric notes" which she called "The Young Mage," who is perhaps based on Robert Phelps and his astrological interpretations (combined—again, perhaps—with Dr. Wall's exhortations):

The young mage said:
Make free, make free,
With the wild eagles planing in the mountains
And the serpent in the sea.

But he warns her as well:

. . . Beware
Of the round web swinging from the angle
Of the steep stair,
And of the comet's hair.

The web is a common enough image of the abandoned, unswept house, inhabited by ghosts—the past, in short. What the "comet's hair" is I can't say; perhaps some wild dream of romantic love. A more sustained and congruent poem is "March Twilight," which was first drafted on March 1, 1940, and thus belongs to the same period as "The Sorcerer's Daughter." It is also about fate, and the deep ambiguity of time and nature. The best gloss on the poem was written before Bogan even composed it, when, toward the end of February 1939, she remarked to Zabel:

No: I won't talk about the impending spring. That season, to people of our age, is a time so heavy with memory that one gets only a swooning nostalgia from it. When I was let out from the hospital . . . FIVE YEARS AGO, I remember thinking one spring twilight . . . that nothing could surpass in unbearable, piercing non-joy, those twilight hours, filled with children's cries, and with the light from the wrong side of heaven, as it were. For those are the hours, when we are young and passionate, and in love, when we wait for the lover's footsteps; when the lovely first cocktail is shaken up, and the day left, and the night waits, etc. It is the hour when one swung the book-bag all along the Fenway, with the forsythias just out, and all the world waiting to be read, and everything to be known. That hour was always piercing and sad with foreknowledge. Now, we should enjoy it, because what it said, both about wakening and decay, we know to be true, and we can string along with that light and that knowledge, can't we?

Upon first setting down the poem, Bogan began with a verse *aperçu* which she rejected from the later version:

Suddenly upon the edge of day and of the season
Events occur a little above themselves, as out of time;
A little whichway, a little altered for an inscrutable reason,
Like the pentatonic scale half resolved in the normal, or an off-rhyme.

This stanza led to the more exact evocations at the heart of the two stanzas in the final version. In these, the early spring light, like the ambiguous region of "Zone" (another March 1940 poem), has intimations of both luck and loss, cowardice and courage, the sum of human possibilities encompassed by both chance and choice. And these intimations, or presentiments, are full of mystery:

A watcher in these new, late beams might well see another face
And look into Time's eye, as into a strange house, for what lies within.

Bogan followed the poem with "July Dawn," which she first wrote on July 17, 1955, and rewrote November 20, 1956. It has even more "piercing non-joy" than "March Twilight," and it is again concerned with the gap between our wishing and reading of symbols, and their real significance. Bogan often read this poem when she wanted to illustrate her notions about free verse. There is an almost audible low pitch to the poem's rhythms of quiet contemplation. It is not about the failure of hope and its change into despair, but about "dis-hope," the grief and sorrow which attend the arrival of knowledge emptied of desire and confounded by reality. The speaker sees a waning crescent moon setting at dawn and does not make a wish:

> I saw it and thought it new
> In that short moment
> That makes all symbols lucky
> Before we read them rightly.
>
> Down to the dark it swam,
> Down to the dark it moved,
> Swift to that cluster of evenings
> When curved toward the full it sharpens.

It is only the moon's impersonal cycle, its involuntary movement in time, which counters the intense desolation of the poem. This desolation comes up again in "The Meeting," another fable of doom and misinterpretation. Written in May 1956, it returns to a mode Bogan had used before—the retold dream. The man in "The Meeting," like the moon in "July Dawn," the light in "March Twilight," and the signs in "The Sorcerer's Daughter," holds out a promise of fulfillment that fate reverses. These disappointment poems are all the more rife with grief and bitterness because Bogan presents them as so deeply imprisoned within a *pattern* of fate:

> Each time I found him, it was always the same:
> Recognition and surprise,
> And then the silence, after the first words,
> And the shifting of the eyes.
>
> Then the moment when he had nothing to say
> And only smiled again,
> But this time toward a place beyond me, where I could not stay—
> No world of men.
>
> Now I am not sure. Who are you? Who have you been?
> Why do our paths cross?
> At the deepest bottom of the dream you are let in,
> A symbol of loss.

Eye to eye we look, and we greet each other
Like friends from the same land.
Bitter compliance! Like a faithless brother
You take and drop my hand.

Betrayal, treason, the "Bitter compliance!" (a phrase so much like Emily Dickinson's) of destructive love turns out, at the end of Bogan's life as a poet as at the beginning, to be her most painful theme; and since this is one of the bleakest poems of Bogan's last years, it is interesting that she followed it with "Night," the most beautiful and affirming of her later lyrics. This was composed in stages throughout the winter, spring, and early summer of 1962, and suggests a source of ultimate spiritual renewal in the non-human and the organic, the bodies of salt and fresh water out of which all life begins:

The cold remote islands
And the blue estuaries
Where what breathes, breathes
The restless wind of the inlets,
And what drinks, drinks
The incoming tide;

Where shell and weed
Wait upon the salt wash of the sea,
And the clear nights of stars
Swing their lights westward
To set behind the land;

Where the pulse clinging to the rocks
Renews itself forever;
Where, again on cloudless nights,
The water reflects
The firmament's partial setting;

—O remember
In your narrowing dark hours
That more things move
Than blood in the heart.

Very little of this poem's power finds its way into the companion piece "Morning," whose archness and hypercivilized tone make it an ineffectual application of Marianne Moore's "objective" method. Bogan, however, loved the poem and loved writing about the complementariness of natural phenomena. "It confirmed larger patterns," Ruth Limmer has said. "She used to say, 'If there is no God, why isn't the universe all dark brown?' Pattern, mystery, coherence—she loved these."

After "Night" and "Morning," only three poems remain, printed as a group and intended to be read together. The first two, "Little Lobelia's Song" and "Psychiatrist's Song," came from the aftermath of her 1965 depression; the last, "Masked Woman's Song," was old, Bogan having sent a draft of it to Edmund Wilson in November 1937. She put the "Three Songs" together in the fall of 1966, when the recovery from her depression, never complete, was nevertheless advanced. While preparing the manuscript of *The Blue Estuaries* for publication, she played with the idea of collecting the poems under the title "Three Songs from a Mask with Supposed Music," and considered adding the phrase "(an autonomous complex)," but decided to keep the simpler "Three Songs."

Explaining "Little Lobelia's Song" to May Sarton, Bogan wrote, "One should not *reject,* but absorb, I've been told!" and the poem was written to do just that with the little morning visitant:

> I was once a part
> Of your blood and bone.
> Now no longer—
> I'm alone, I'm alone.
>
> Each day, at dawn,
> I come out of your sleep;
> I can't get back.
> I weep, I weep.

The journey undertaken in "Psychiatrist's Song," written December 14, 1966, and at first titled "Psychiatrist's Recitative & Aria," corresponds to an observation Bogan made to May Sarton concerning the relationship between patient and psychiatrist: "Well, it is one of the functions of the therapist, as you know, just to sit there and let the occasional insight surface (it must be one's *own* insight, ultimately). Time must be allowed to pass; and so both patient and doctor wait, and experience time, and let the healing process take place, at its own tempo." Bogan's poem is an act of sympathy with this process, revealing her belief in the journey's identity for both participants, who are together carried by the same flow of time. The doctor must be healed as well as the patient, for his pain is that of having to witness the wounds of human cruelty and folly. Even more than the patient, the doctor must trust in the journey's ultimate end at a good warm place, where life can be renewed:

I hear.
But far away are the mango trees (*the mangrove swamps,*
     the mandrake root . . .)
And the thickets of—are they palms?
I watch them as though at the edge of sleep.
I often journey toward them in a boat without oars,
Trusting to rudder and sail.
Coming to the shore, I step out of the boat; I leave it to its anchor;
And I walk fearlessly through ripples of both water and sand.
Then the shells and the pebbles are beneath my feet.

Then these, too, recede,
And I am on firm dry land, with, closely waiting,
A hill all sifted over with shade
Wherein the silence waits.

Farewell, phantoms of flesh and of ocean!
Vision of earth
Heal and receive me.

Even toward the end, Bogan found the poetic means to transform her Furies to Eumenides, and to resolve her conflicts in the momentary peace of art. Such resolution, such serenity could not, of course, serve as her final word. Just as she distrusted fiction which claimed to solve just *one* set of problems, she was equally leery of ending her book on a note of calm joy. Darkness was her fate, what she knew best. So she ended her book with "Masked Woman's Song." She herself called it a "fairly old erotic song," and thought it belonged "to the same world (of dream and aberration)" as "Little Lobelia's Song" and "Psychiatrist's Song." It recapitulates her Yeatsian beginnings, with the figure of the masked woman, and delves into the Rilkean mystery of *things,* for it is a response to a marble statue that, like Rilke's "Torso of an Archaic Apollo," confronts the viewer with life-changing authority. Above all, it is like Bogan's very early "Statue and Birds" in presenting the tragic enigma of arrested life:

> Before I saw the tall man
> Few women should see,
> Beautiful and imposing
> Was marble to me.
>
> And virtue had its place
> And evil its alarms,
> But not for that worn face,
> And not in those roped arms.

V 1 9 5 5 ~ 1 9 7 0

In this last poem of Louise Bogan's, the known world is broken, and nothing can ever be the same again. For the woman who looks at the tortured statue, there can be no return to innocence. What takes its place is desire, stirred to speech by the fatal union of beauty and terror, and brought to birth by the caress of her gaze.

12 COME, BREAK WITH TIME

WHILE *The Blue Estuaries* was received without fanfare, it also achieved, from at least two reviewers, the kind of recognition that was long overdue. William Meredith, writing in *The New York Times Book Review* in October 1968, called Bogan "one of the best women poets alive," and applauded her "career of stubborn, individual excellence." And Hayden Carruth, in *Poetry,* singled out twenty or twenty-five poems which, he claimed, were the best of their kind in American literature. From them, he went on, we receive

the recognition of her basic poetic wisdom . . . she has taken her temptations as they came, and has outsmarted them. Let the poem be conventional, public, and occasional, since that is the mask one must wear—so she might have spoken—but let each poem reveal just enough of a private inner violence to make the surface move without breaking. A passionate austerity, a subtle balance; and only perfect poetic attention, far beyond technique, could attain it.

Such praise had come much too late to fortify Bogan against the conviction that the book had "fallen down that deep, dark well" of oblivion. Even the ten-thousand-dollar National Endowment for the Arts Award, given to her in 1967 as a senior poet for a lifetime's work, was unable to allay her continuing gloom. She knew she would not publish another book of poems. When she and Ruth Limmer had discussed which poems should be included in *The Blue Estuaries,* Miss Limmer had urged an unpublished poem, "Leechdoms," on her, but Louise had said she was "still not sure of it" and kept it out. And then she and Miss Limmer agreed that it would not have another opportunity to appear in a book; it might be published in a magazine, perhaps, but not in a *book*. "This was not a mournful conversation, but almost businesslike, factual," Ruth Limmer remembers.

As Louise Bogan kept to her customary round of activity and responsibility, the embrace of inner desolation tightened its grip. Certainly she was busy enough. In 1967 alone she had given a reading and a series of classes at the Poetry Center of the University of Arizona and traveled, purely for pleasure, to England and Scotland during the late summer and early fall. In November of that year, her longtime friend David Mandel, a labor lawyer active in the campaign to end the Vietnam War, successfully prevailed upon her to read at a Poets for Peace rally at Town Hall, in New York, where she read "To My Brother. . . ." She collaborated with Josephine O'Brien Shaefer on a sharp "revisionist" essay placed as an Afterword to Shaefer's edition of Virginia Woolf's *A Writer's Diary* (New American Library), firmly situating Woolf's achievement in a sober and nonworshipful light that took into account her limitations as well as her gifts. In January 1969, she took an airplane for the first time in her life when she flew to Virginia, where her friend William Jay Smith, sensing that she was at loose ends, arranged for her to fulfill a month-long appointment as poet-in-residence at Hollins College. She was a great success with her students, had her own apartment, gave her Bennington lecture, "What the Women Said," and did a good bit of socializing, but it was clear to Smith that she was still on the edge of depression and that living was an effort. Her energy flagged. She would go to the college library in the afternoon to read magazines in the periodicals room, and fall asleep. She was at times terribly nervous. At the end of her visit, Smith was scheduled to pick her up and take her to the airport, and when he arrived late, Bogan was frantic and thought she'd been abandoned.

Back in New York, her conscientiousness about her work tortured her. The review copies poured in, as they always had, and she tried to work on her *New Yorker* pieces with the understanding between the magazine and herself that she should feel no pressure of deadlines. But years of journalistic responsibility made it impossible for her to treat the job as anything other than a matter of strict accountability. Her doubts mounted; her morning tears continued. She could find little to say about the current crop of "young-middle-aged bards, with their dim anecdotes of despair," while books with titles like W. S. Merwin's *The Lice* simply repelled her. "I can't face those books anymore," she told Smith, and yet she could not and would not resign from the magazine.

Her waning self-confidence received a terrible blow when a young writer, Paris Leary, took her to task in a letter for allowing her reviews to become, as she interpreted it, "Shockingly superficial." Why couldn't she write voluminously like Pauline Kael, he asked her; better yet, why didn't she resign, after all these years, and let someone more attuned to the current scene have a chance?

But she simply wasn't ready to give up. There might be some poetry left in her, she thought, and some prose pieces as well, in particular one on the Id: "I have a new theory about outbreaks of the Id. The Id has no sex—did you know?" she wrote to Ruth Limmer. She followed up her hunches with some reading in Freud and Nietzsche, and in her notebook, among rough notes, wrote this passage:

What is the Id, and what can it do? The libido is embedded in it; but it is more than the libido. Its limitations are manifest. It cannot speak clearly; it cannot exist on any conscious plane. It can growl; it can nudge. It exists in the reserves of deepest instinct only; it can be known to lash its tail and to breathe fire (for it is both dragon & demon). The deepest instinctual urges. . . . Beyond good & evil. . . . The deepest depositing of the pleasure principle ("I want, I want"). That which creates, projects the urge for life itself. . . . It cannot be imitated or manipulated.

Later she noted that the Id, "at present, has become more restive. . . . The wall between it—forever unconscious . . . and the reality which the ego is partly able to deal with, and comprehend, have become thinner. Its impenetrability has taken hold, especially in the arts of language, to such a degree that the clarities of form are almost completely at its mercy." Where was her own Id concealed? Like Little Lobelia, it cried out from the deepest recesses of the unconscious. But unlike the contemporary poets whose taste for self-exposure Bogan found so unappealing, she could not abandon the "clarities of form" and release her most primitive desires into poetry. Curiously, among other projects she was considering was a collection of "sound" poetry. She had recently read C. M. Bowra's *Primitive Song,* and wanted to do an anthology which would include poems in English and unfamiliar languages (like Swahili) that had chant forms and other repetition-formulas in them (like her own "Train Tune"). Another project was an anthology of Tennyson's lyrics; yet another, her collected short stories. She requested a set of tearsheets from *The New Yorker,* and asked both William Maxwell and Ruth Limmer to evaluate them, wanting to include only the best.

A new honor arrived, unexpectedly, and delightfully, when the American Academy of Arts and Letters elected her to membership in the spring of 1969. But plans and projects and this honor notwithstanding, the struggle with what she grimly called *silence* continued. Her writing block now seemed immovable. Friends could see that the *New Yorker* job was causing her an exhausting amount of anxiety, but each felt, in his or her own way, that for Bogan to give the job up would only aid the forces of isolation and depression. Eventually, Elizabeth Roget took matters into her own hands and wrote William Maxwell, without Bogan's knowledge, to say that Louise was enduring genuine agony in her efforts to read and write. Knowing that Bogan would not care to have matters decided for her, Maxwell wrote to her, enclosing Roget's letter. The last thing he wanted to do was to inflict inadvertent suffering on her in the course of trying to offer help. Bogan had entered psychotherapy again with Dr. James Baxter, and wrote to Ruth Limmer that he had said that "recently . . . I had worked myself into a *circular* situation, which would have to yield, at some point, by means of a *break* of some kind." She knew from the past that he was right and that even common sense dictated that a destructive pattern had to be interrupted. The cycle of tears and depression had gone on long enough.

Bogan decided to leave *The New Yorker* in September 1969, thirty-eight years after she had written her first review for the magazine. "I know that you are against such a move," she wrote to Ruth Limmer, "but really, Ruth, I've *had* it. No more pronouncements on lousy verse. No more *hidden* competition. No more struggling *not* to be a square." She had lunch with William Maxwell, and this time her gentle, patient, and wise friend did not press her to reconsider her decision. Matters were left open. If she felt like writing something for the magazine, her friends there would be delighted to see it. And there would be a monthly pension check which, in addition to her Social Security and her savings, would leave her free from financial worry.

At the end of October, the magazine's editor-in-chief, William Shawn, wrote:

The office librarian tells me that the first verse lead you did for *The New Yorker* was in the issue of March 21, 1931. Incredible. And what it means is that for thirty-eight years we have been in the extraordinary position of knowing beyond all question that no other magazine's reviewing of poetry was as perceptive or trustworthy or intelligent as our own. The very presence of your finely constructed sentences—of your tone—has constantly raised the literary level of the surrounding pages, whatever they might be, and *The New Yorker* as a whole, and been one of the reasons we can hold our head up. I am immensely sorry that you feel you cannot go on doing the department, but I also understand why you feel that, and am more grateful than I can possibly say for the dedication and purpose and beautiful writing that you have poured into your columns for so long.

Such courage—and it was very great—as it took for Bogan to leave *The New Yorker* did not bring her the peace she needed and had earned.

Her job with the magazine had provided her with a professional home for more than half her working life, and to leave it was to leave work itself forever. Though she ought to have been able to look upon her achievement with pride and satisfaction, the spectre of projects deferred or never undertaken haunted her. Once again, she underestimated to the point of denial the toll which the process of mourning a long association must inevitably take. Relief from obligation brought emptiness and aimlessness to a life that for fifty years had been predicated upon purpose.

She continued to read and to take notes, but with diminishing enthusiasm. She had eye trouble and diabetes trouble. In August she fell and could not get up, and there was another falling episode not long after, both perhaps caused by minor strokes. One friend who saw her in November at a reading and talk at the Library of Congress Children's Poetry Conference noticed that she walked carefully, tentatively, with a kind of shuffling gait. William Jay Smith, who was Consultant in Poetry that year, and had organized the conference, remembers that she read poems from *The Golden Journey,* among them Christina Rossetti's "Ferry Me Across the Water" and Edmund Blunden's "The Midnight Skaters," both of them, he has said, about death. And she referred in private several times during her visit to his poem "Funeral," from *The Tin Can and Other Poems* (1966). Another old friend from *The Measure* days, Louise Townsend Nicholl, saw Bogan at a tea given by the Academy of American Poets for their members: "She came in late, found a chair near the door, seemed almost frightened, and I wasn't sure she knew me when I rushed across the room to her. I asked her if she remembered how we used to *laugh.* She didn't even smile, & asked me gravely if I remembered any special thing we had laughed at! Actually, we laughed *always, all the time,* as we ate lunch together. She was not well, I think, at that dreadful last meeting."

It cannot be stated too firmly that in the course of all of Louise Bogan's severe depressions—in 1931, 1933, and 1965—and in the course of the numerous milder ones which plagued her life, she never once seriously contemplated suicide. She had written in her 1933 notebook that she could entertain the idea under certain bleak conditions—poverty, age, and isolation—with clarity and detachment, but suicide as a practical solution to her difficulties never truly entered her mind, neither then nor later. She took pride in the courage and optimism with which she had always faced life, and she had always rather scorned suicide as the romantic's easy-way-out. Yet, during the winter of 1969–70, at the age of seventy-two, Louise Bogan's resistance to physical and emotional deterioration began to run out fast. Late in January, it seemed to some of her friends—from whom she appeared to be at an extreme of withdrawal—that she simply didn't care anymore. At a dinner at the American Academy and Institute of Arts and Letters, sitting with John Hall Wheelock, Glenway Wescott, and Richard Eberhart, she had too much to drink, and when Wheelock, exercising the prerogatives of an old and loving friend, tried to remind her that as a diabetic she ought to watch her intake of alcohol, she snapped at him that she could decide for herself how much to drink. Later that evening, while standing at the bar, Eberhart "heard a crash and turned around to see a glass broken on the floor, a man already moving to clean up the drink and at the same time I saw Louise fallen to the floor. I was about ten feet away and quickly moved and lifted her up on the settee. She was dazed for a while but regained her composure."

From then on, she was besieged by fears, terrified that Columbia University would buy her building and evict her. She neglected her health, and sharply reprimanded Maidie for showing concern over one of her falling episodes. She did not see her internist. On the telephone with friends, her voice sounded as if it were fading in from a very long distance, an effect of the medication she was then taking, as well as of the first moments of sluggish awakening after her frequent dozings-off. It took her time to come back to herself, she told Ruth Limmer, and described the sensation of waking life's coming back into the separate parts of her body—arms, fingers, toes—as "invading the suburbs." She drank liquor with her diabetes medication and her tranquilizers, and while she had never, during a lifetime's hard drinking, become an alcoholic (that is, never ceased to function because of alcohol, or needed alcohol to function), the streak of anarchic recklessness so long held in check by her stubborn conscience now took over, and she drank and smoked far more than she knew was medically safe.

It seemed to Elizabeth Roget that Louise was deteriorating fast and by late January 1970 that things were very wrong indeed. Arriving from New Jersey on the afternoon of Wednesday, February 4th, she became alarmed when there was no answer to the doorbell. With a key that Louise had given her, she let herself into the apartment. In the bedroom she found Louise Bogan lying full length in front of her bed, dead many hours. Miss Roget immediately called Maidie Scannell, who then got in touch with her mother's physician.

At exactly what hour Bogan died is not clear. Neighbors later recalled hearing a pounding noise sometime after eleven. Bogan seems to have suffered the pains of a heart attack, and to have fallen to the ground, trying unsuccessfully to get up and then pounding on the floor for help. She had been terrified when she'd fallen some months before, and her terror in this instance must have hastened her death. The exact cause of death was a coronary occlusion. Two days later, a simple funeral was held at the Frank E. Campbell Funeral Chapel in Manhattan, followed by cremation.

Certainly Bogan's physical problems could have been solved, or at least helped, with proper care. She was financially secure, and a life of considerable comfort was available to her. She was not, I believe, eager to die, although it must have seemed to her that the prospects life offered for joy and accomplishment were few. The idea of dependency, later on, through advancing age and disease, horrified her.

She had come long ago to the realization that maturity meant the capacity to give full consent to necessity, to choose what fate ordained. This choice did not have to be conscious and it could not be willed; it was a decision made, for the most part, by the unconscious. She had always believed in the power of psychic forces which know us far better than we know ourselves, and it was to these forces that she gave her full consent in her last weeks: they were free to do with her as they liked. If that meant continued life, or death, it made little difference to her, and her drinking and her air of having given up were the marks of their hands upon her. And it was to them—the ultimately wise rulers of the psyche—that she acquiesced when they commanded:

> Come, break with time,
> You who were lorded
> By a clock's chime
> So ill afforded.
> If time is allayed
> Be not afraid.

A MEMORIAL SERVICE to Louise Bogan, arranged by William Jay Smith, took place at the American Academy of Arts and Letters on March 11, 1970. Approximately 120 people gathered in the Academy's library, where Marjorie Garrigue played the first movement of Mozart's Sonata in C minor (K. 457) and his Fantasia in D minor (K. 397). Among those present were Hannah Arendt, W. H. Auden (wearing slippers and carrying all of Bogan's books), Padraic Colum, Babette Deutsch, Stanley Kunitz, Robert Lowell, Margaret Mead, and Glenway Wescott, friends from both the newest and oldest phases of her life. John Hall Wheelock was the first to speak. He recounted, in his resonant voice, the story of his association with Bogan, and in evoking her majestic high-handedness reported the break which had taken place between them that day in 1943 at Child's. Afterward, he said, "She would taunt me in the presence of others. 'That man used to be my publisher, but we quarreled,' she would say." Now he recalled her "beautiful austere face and spirit," her "profound perception," and her "gay wit."

Léonie Adams, looking back over Bogan's working life, saw no evidence of "a talent unfulfilled." All had been "put to scrupulous use." She pointed to the discernment and self-knowledge in Bogan's classic style, the redemption of the arrested life through art, and the growth of the work from book to book by "invisible stages." Speaking next, Richard Wilbur recalled Louise Bogan the woman. She was a very good dancer, he said, "very light of foot." He had danced with her once, the evening before he and Bogan had given their Emily Dickinson talks at Amherst in October 1959, when Wilbur and his wife and Bogan spent the evening in a dive. Citing "Roman Fountain," a poem he held in special favor, and "To Be Sung on the Water," he added that her poems were "faithful to the theme of passion." William Maxwell went on to conclude the presentation with a reading of "Journey Around My Room," after first urging the audience to try to hear Bogan's voice instead of his own.

Anyone who had heard her voice was unlikely to forget it. It was rich, full, low, with a touch of Maine in it, perfectly pitched, brisk in conversation, and animated, but slow and simple in the delivery of her poems. It was a voice that belonged to a woman who had been beautiful during every stage of her life. She was tall, with a straight, firm carriage, and large hands. Except for a brief time in 1922, when she had worn her hair short in Vienna, Bogan kept her dark hair long, drawing it back from her face in a low chignon. Often she wore a grosgrain ribbon that accentuated her wide forehead, beautifully proportioned face, and her eyes, which have been described as the color of pewter.

She played the piano well, and she had a talent for drawing, which she never pursued. She liked to collect cookbooks, managing to amass books on every known national cuisine, but she was an indifferent cook. And always, she read omnivorously. There can be no truly adequate account of the range of her self-education. She was exceedingly careful with money and thought that it should not be wasted. She hated pretension, but was capable of haughtiness, which sometimes made her cruel.

She revered art and lived for it as purely as Flaubert. A photograph of Mozart's birthplace hung in every apartment she lived in from 1933 until her death. She wanted to use up her energy and talent to the last drop, but was terrified of being consumed in the process, and nearly *was* consumed, not once, but many times. Powerful feeling, developed intuition, and the hunger for pure form have rarely sought out a more fragile and yet a more enduring vessel. It was not enough to survive; her spirit demanded that she prevail and triumph, and she did. Her poetry belongs securely within the great tradition of the English lyric, along with that of Herbert and Hopkins. "What, aside from their technical excellence," W. H. Auden wrote, "is most impressive about her poems is the unflinching courage with which she faced her problems, her determination never to surrender to self-pity, but to wrest beauty and joy out of dark places." Her criticism will endure as long as detachment, wit, and generosity are able to cut through falsehood and vanity to uphold genuine merit as the lifeblood of American letters. "In whatever she wrote, the line of truth was exactly superimposed on the line of feeling," William Maxwell has said.

She possessed natural grace—that rarest of human attributes—and with it enhanced the lives of those who knew and loved her. She loved deeply her mother, her daughter, Raymond Holden, her friends, and her work. In the end she forgave herself her own failures of love and judgment, as well as those who had failed her: "And all things are forgiven, and it would be strange not to forgive." Her darkest secrets she kept even from herself, giving them to her poetry, in which they remain sealed forever against direct inspection. To those who, having tasted of her spirit and her art, would yearn for more, she might have answered:

> Goodbye, goodbye!
> There was so much to love, I could not love it all;
> I could not love it enough.
>
> Some things I overlooked, and some I could not find.
> Let the crystal clasp them
> When you drink your wine, in autumn.

NOTES AND INDEX

NOTES

BIBLIOGRAPHIES OF WORKS BY LOUISE BOGAN

There are two bibliographies of Louise Bogan, both of which have been of inestimable help in the preparation of this study: William Jay Smith, *Louise Bogan: A Woman's Words* (Washington: Library of Congress, 1971), and Jane Couchman, *Louise Bogan: A Bibliography of Primary and Secondary Materials, 1915–1975, Part I* and *Part II* in *Bulletin of Bibliography*, Vol. 33, Nos. 2 (Feb.–Mar. 1976), 73-7, 104, and 3 (Apr.–June 1976) 111–26, 147.

BOOKS BY LOUISE BOGAN

I POETRY

Body of This Death (New York: Robert M. McBride, 1923)
Dark Summer (New York: Charles Scribner's Sons, 1929)
The Sleeping Fury (New York: Charles Scribner's Sons, 1937)
Poems and New Poems (New York: Charles Scribner's Sons, 1941)
Collected Poems, 1923–1953 (New York: Noonday Press, 1954)
The Blue Estuaries: Poems 1923–1968 (New York: Farrar, Straus & Giroux, 1968)

II CRITICISM

Achievement in American Poetry, 1900–1950 (Chicago: Henry Regnery, 1951)
Selected Criticism: Poetry and Prose (New York: Noonday Press, 1955)
A Poet's Alphabet: Reflections on the Literary Art and Vocation, edited by Robert Phelps and Ruth Limmer (New York: McGraw-Hill, 1970)

III LETTERS, MEMOIRS

What the Woman Lived: Selected Letters of Louise Bogan, 1920–1970, edited and with an Introduction by Ruth Limmer (New York: Harcourt Brace Jovanovich, 1973)

Journey Around My Room: The Autobiography of Louise Bogan, A Mosaic by Ruth Limmer (New York: The Viking Press, 1980)

IV TRANSLATIONS

With Elizabeth Mayer:
The Glass Bees, by Ernst Juenger (New York: Noonday Press, 1961)
Elective Affinities, by Johann Wolfgang von Goethe (Chicago: Henry Regnery, 1963)
The Sorrows of Young Werther and *Novella,* by Johann Wolfgang von Goethe (New York: Random House, 1971)

With Elizabeth Roget:
The Journal of Jules Renard (New York: George Braziller, 1964)

V ANTHOLOGIES

With William Jay Smith:
The Golden Journey: Poems for Young People (Chicago: Reilly & Lee, 1965)

ABBREVIATIONS

I WORKS BY LOUISE BOGAN

BTD   *Body of This Death*
DS   *Dark Summer*
SF   *The Sleeping Fury*
PNP   *Poems and New Poems*
CP   *Collected Poems, 1923–1953*
BE   *The Blue Estuaries: Poems 1923–1968*
AAP   *Achievement in American Poetry, 1900–1950*
SC   *Selected Criticism: Poetry and Prose*
PA   *A Poet's Alphabet: Reflections on the Literary Art and Vocation*
WTWL *What the Woman Lived: Selected Letters of Louise Bogan, 1920–1970*
JAMR *Journey Around My Room: The Autobiography of Louise Bogan, A Mosaic* by Ruth Limmer
jamr "Journey Around My Room," *The New Yorker* (Jan. 14, 1933) 16–18
ds   "Dove and Serpent," *The New Yorker* (Nov. 18, 1933) 24, 26
JOAP "From the Journals of a Poet," *The New Yorker* (Jan. 30, 1978) 39–70
Ant   "From the Notebooks of Louise Bogan (1935–36)," *Antaeus* (no. 27) (Autumn 1977) 120–9
J   *The Jabberwock* (Girls' Latin School, 1910–1915)

II MAGAZINES

MQR   Theodore Roethke, "The Poetry of Louise Bogan," 1960 Hopwood Lecture, *Michigan Quarterly Review* (Autumn 1960), reprinted in same (Fall 1967): 247–8

NY   *The New Yorker*
Na   *The Nation*
NR   *The New Republic*
PR   *Partisan Review*

III   PERSONS

LB   Louise Bogan
EF   Elizabeth Frank
ACH   Arthur Cort Holden
RPH   Raymond Peckham Holden
RH   Rolfe Humphries
RL   Ruth Limmer
WM   William Maxwell
TR   Theodore Roethke
MS   May Sarton
MAS (*also* MA) Maidie Alexander Scannell
WJS   William Jay Smith
JHW   John Hall Wheelock
KSW   Katharine S. White
EW   Edmund Wilson
MDZ   Morton Dauwen Zabel

IV   MANUSCRIPT AND LIBRARY COLLECTIONS

LBP   The Louise Bogan Papers, Amherst College
AAIAL The American Academy and Institute of Arts and Letters
B   The Henry W. and Albert A. Berg Collection, The New York Public Library,
       Astor, Lenox, and Tilden Foundations
FWD   The F. W. Dupee Papers, Rare Book and Manuscript Library, Columbia
       University
CSA   Archives of Charles Scribner's Sons, Princeton University Library
NL   The Morton Dauwen Zabel Collection, The Newberry Library, Chicago
TRP   The Theodore H. Roethke Papers, University of Washington Libraries
Y   The Collection of American Literature, The Beinecke Rare Book and Manu-
       script Library, Yale University

V   OTHER

CHW   Raymond [Peckham] Holden, *Chance Has a Whip* (New York: Charles
      Scribner's Sons, 1935)
LLP   Edmund Wilson, *Letters on Literature and Politics 1912–1972,* edited by Elena
      Wilson (New York: Farrar, Straus & Giroux, 1977)
SLTR *Selected Letters of Theodore Roethke,* edited with an introduction by Ralph J.
      Mills, Jr. (Seattle: University of Washington Press, 1968)

For the reader's convenience: *Unless otherwise stated,* all poems by Louise Bogan cited in
the text are to be found in *The Blue Estuaries: Poems 1923–1968* (New York: The Ecco

Press, 1977) (BE), and are not individually cited in the *Notes.* Bogan's published criticism is cited with its original source of publication and, where relevant, its page reference in PA. Passages from LBP, NY, and other sources which appear in JAMR and PA are given a double citation, with a page reference to JAMR or PA only.

MAS refers to conversations with Maidie Alexander Scannell on February 11 and 18, 1981, in Westport, Connecticut.

All citations begin with a reference to the page in the text where the quotation is found and its first two to three words. A number of notes are keyed to lines of author's text.

FOREWORD

xv *"tragic interest"* LB–Fred B. Millet, Apr. 25, 1937, Y.
–   *"the perception"* Johann Wolfgang von Goethe, *The Autobiography of Johann Wolfgang von Goethe: Dichtung*
und Wahrheit, translated by John Oxenford (New York: Horizon Press, 1969), p. 322.

xvi *"the autobiography"* JAMR, p. xxiv.

1 TARGET FOR THE WIND

6   *"with a sack"* MAS.
7   *"long high blue"* JOAP; JAMR, p. 25.
–   *"long rough pasture"* ibid.; ibid., p. 24.
–   *"familiars"* ibid.; ibid., p. 25.
–   *"secret family angers"* ibid.; ibid., p. 26.
8   *"It is morning"* ibid.; ibid., pp. 26–7.
–   *"too vituperative"* LB–RH, Oct. 15, 1936, AAIAL.
–   *"feisty and cocky"* MAS.
–   *"In the youth"* JOAP; JAMR, p. 49.
9   *"superior tone"* and quoted scene from *This Room and This Gin and These Sandwiches,* © 1937 under the title *A Winter in Beech Street,* in *Five Plays* (New York: Farrar, Straus & Young, 1954), pp. 242–3.
10 *"The door is"* JOAP; JAMR, p. 172.
–   *"terrible, unhappy, lost"* ibid.; ibid., p. 35.
–   *"I never truly"* ibid.; ibid., p. 27.
12 *"pure at its"* Ruth A. Sharpe–EF, Apr. 15, 1981.

12 *"for cutting"* Patent by Daniel Joseph Bogan.
–   *Order ran* JOAP; JAMR, pp. 13–14.
13 "one of everything" ibid.; ibid., p. 14.
–   *"made of"* ibid.; ibid., p. 18.
–   *The swing that* ibid.; ibid., p. 16.
–   *"its contents were"* ibid.; ibid., p. 31.
14 *"I had the"* ibid.; ibid., p. 32.
–   *"There's a young"* LB–MDZ, Dec. 3, 1935, NL.
–   *"the curtains hung"* ds; JAMR, p. 4.
–   *The window had* ibid.; JAMR, p. 5.
–   *dry and wizened* JOAP; JAMR, pp. 29–30.
–   *I could not* ds; JAMR, p. 7.
–   *He lifted* ibid.; ibid., pp. 7–8.
16 *"of bewilderment"* ibid.; ibid., p. 8.
–   *I used to* ibid.; ibid., pp. 4–5.
17 *"across the river"* ibid.; ibid., p. 5.
–   *"opened up"* LB–MDZ, Aug. 10, 1936, NL.
–   *"Sometimes the entire"* JOAP; JAMR, p. 30.

17 *"dark green"* ibid.; ibid., pp. 10–11.
18 *And what of* JOAP, p. 48.
–   *"in a worn"* JOAP; JAMR, p. 14.
–   *"People used to"* "Not Love, but Ardor," 1932–33 [?] LBP.
–   *Music, in those* JOAP; JAMR, pp. 121–2.
19 *"a passionate letter"* JAMR, p. xvii.
–   *"I used to"* ibid.
–   *"one of the"* J, 1911–12.
20 *"rough joy"* PA, p. 229.
–   *"picked up"* LB–WM, Mar. 30, 1941.
–   *" 'Narrow red velvet' "* JOAP; JAMR, p. 29.
21 *" 'weak' and simply"* RL–EF, [n.d.] 1982.
–   *"had suffered his"* JOAP; JAMR, p. 31.
–   *"from the age"* LB–TR, Sept. 4, 1935, WTWL, p. 99.
–   *"blankets ready"* JOAP; JAMR, p. 59.
–   *"adored him"* MAS.
22 *"she pointed out"* Rufina McCarthy Helmer–EF, Mar. 23, 1981.
23 *"marked a kind"* JOAP; JAMR, p. 21.
–   *"the other"* world ibid.; ibid.
24 *The sight of* ibid.; ibid., p. 22.
–   *"The steam shrieks"* jamr; JAMR, p. 37.
25 *"one of the"* JOAP; JAMR, p. 45.
–   *"a center hall"* ibid.; ibid., p. 46.
–   *"the life of"* ibid.; ibid., p. 23.
–   *"at length"* ibid.; ibid., p. 50.
26 *"for five"* ibid.; ibid.
–   *"very far out"* LB, Library of Congress, Tape LWO 5504, 1968.
–   *"I began"* JOAP; JAMR, p. 50.
–   *"no Irish girl"* Martha Foley–EF, Oct. 10, 1976.
–   *"It was borne"* "The Situation in American Writing," PR, VI (Fall 1939): 105.
27 *"I felt the"* to *"as I please"* in Martha Foley, "One with Shakespeare," reprinted from *Story Magazine* in *Twenty Grand: Great American Short Stories,* ed. Ernestine Taggard (New York: Bantam Books, 1947), p. 162.
28 *"which put me"* LB–MDZ, Oct. 7, 1935, NL.
29 *"candid yet fierce"* JOAP; JAMR, p. 23.

29 *"Poplar Garden"* The whole poem goes: Where is the source from whence this glow proceeds?/Thou, Daphne, set above where grass burns bright,/Wind-thrilled, arms flung unto the breathing light/With trees blown dark behind, like shivered reeds?/Thou shockest the dreams that come from out grey meads,/The vivid dark, the wind, thy brilliant white/Daze the sad eyes, the dreaming heart affright/And bruise the gentle soul, as flesh harsh weeds./Yet does the wintry heart before this thing/Not the long music of an eve behold/Nor calm dawn o'er some water's placid gold,/But a hot joy that leaps, that seeks to sing;/A lovely flower blowing in the cold—/And through it floods the warm, eternal spring. J, 1912–13.
30 *Whatever may have* *An Examination of Ezra Pound,* ed. Peter Russell (New York: New Directions, 1950), p. 25, quoted in AAP, p. 29.
31 *"there was always"* —And I Worked *at the Writer's Trade: Chapters of Literary History 1918–1978* (New York: The Viking Press, 1978), p. 71.
–   *"Symbolism, the movement"* LBP.
32 *"how inert matter"* LBP, quoted from *The Symbolist Movement in Literature* (New York: Dutton, 1908), p. 145.
–   *"His style"* LBP.
–   *"the transient"* LBP.
33 *"I never was"* WTWL, n. p. 6.
–   *"I could play"* LB–Janet Lewis Winters, Oct. 28, 1929.
–   *"A Talisman,"* from *Happy Ending* (1909) in LBP.
34 *"Your name?"* Boston University Beacon (Christmas Issue, 1915), p. 210.
35 *"copies of palaces"* NY (Oct. 20, 1934), p. 82; JAMR, p. 38.
–   *"Miss Cooper lived"* ibid.; ibid., pp. 39–41.
36 *"Personal distinction"* ibid.; ibid., p. 40.
–   *My ears became* ibid.; ibid., pp. 42–3.

2 A LAND OF CHANGE

38 *"I married"* MAS.

39 *"very German"* ibid.

– *"the veranda"* LBP; JAMR, p. 92.

40 *"beats/A flattered"* BTD, p. 2.

– *"I do not" Others,* IV (Dec. 1917): 11.

41 *"Someplace it should"* MAS.

42 *"on first sight"* RL–EF, [n.d.] 1979.

– *"in a white"* MAS.

– *I hoped* No. 9, Nov. 1921.

43 *I am alone* from "Beginning and End," in *Poetry: A Magazine of Verse* 20 (Aug. 1922): 250–1.

– *"who held out"* LB–TR, Sept. 4, 1935, WTWL, p. 98.

– *"Our parties"* (New York: New Directions, 1948), p. 36.

– *"thought to call"* WTWL, n. p. 3.

44 *"My family"* [July] 1920, WTWL, p. 3.

– *"betrayed"* LB–MDZ, June 11, 1937, NL.

– *"John Coffey" Selected Letters of Conrad Aiken* (New Haven: Yale University Press, 1978), pp. 49–50.

– *"into a pianist"* Mar. 1, 1941, ibid., p. 255.

45 *"You did"* ibid., n. p. 50.

– *So that* "Beginning and End," pp. 248–9.

46 *"lovely lady"* MAS.

– *"Here's a woman"* LB–Ben Belitt, Nov. 28, 1937.

– *"was just"* ibid.

– *"with professional interest" —And I Worked at the Writer's Trade,* p. 72.

47 *"the musical"* Maxwell Anderson, Padraic Colum, No. 1 (Mar. 1921): 23.

– Poetry, *of Chicago* ibid., p. 25.

– *"just now"* Frank Ernest Hill, ibid.

– *"a recurring" A History of Modern Poetry from the 1890s to the High Modernist Mode* (Cambridge: The Belknap Press of Harvard University Press, 1976), p. 7.

48 *"There is a"* [n.d.] 1921, B.

49 *"This was"* LB–MDZ, May 24, 1944, WTWL, pp. 238–9.

– *This is a* "A Letter," BTD; JAMR, p. 70.

50 *"But why"* ibid.; ibid., p. 71.

– *"The cringing"* ibid.; ibid., pp. 71–2.

– *"play the pavanne"* ibid.; ibid., p. 72.

– *In terror* JAMR, p. 54.

51 *"bearing the images"* ibid., p. 55.

– *The armoire broods* ibid., p. 54.

52 *It was a* ibid., p. 56.

– *"Beginning to love"* LBP.

– *"wrapped in the"* LBP; JAMR, p. 57.

– *"remorse concerning Curt"* LBP.

– *"He never"* Sept. 9, 1922, B.

– *"thrilled"* LBP.

53 *"This has been"* [Aug.] 1922, WTWL, p. 4.

– *"grief, passion"* Sept. 5, 1922, B.

– *O, let them* ibid.

– *"after my"* [Sept.] 1937, WTWL, p. 163.

54 *It is the* Symons, *Symbolist Movement,* p. 126.

55 *"The poet represses"* JOAP; JAMR, p. 72.

57 *"That woman"* LB–TR, July 16, 1937, TRP.

58 *"a breakthrough"* MQR pp. 247–8.

59 *"Washed by time's"* "Adam's Rib," in *Collected Poems* (London: Macmillan & Co. 1965), p. 80.

61 *"a harlot"* "The Singing-Woman from the World's Edge," *Collected Poems* (New York: Harper & Row, 1955), p. 133.

62 *"self-complete"* "The Solitary," in *Collected Poems of Sara Teasdale* (London: Collier-Macmillan Ltd., 1966), p. 179.

– *"my marvelous"* "Sanctuary," in *Collected Poems of Elinor Wylie* (New York: Alfred A. Knopf, 1932), p. 14.

66 *Some women White April and Other Poems* (New York: Farrar & Rinehart, 1930), p. 8.

69 *"to-hell"* LB–EW, Jan. 13, 1927, WTWL, p. 30.

73 *"packed as tightly"* 117 (Oct. 31, 1923): 494.

– *"in all its"* 37 (Dec. 5, 1923): 20.

74 *"her words too"* Poetry 23 (Mar. 1924): 335.

– *"Her words are"* (Mar. 1924): 289.

– *"an emptiness of"* 8 (Mar. 5, 1924): 622.

– *"I feel ready"* The Twenties: From Notebooks and Diaries of the Period, ed. with an Introduction by Leon Edel (New York: Farrar, Straus & Giroux, 1975), p. 138.

75 *"struck her between"* Telephone conversation with Léonie Adams, Apr. 21, 1975.

– *"See," he would* Interview with Margaret Mead, New York, Mar. 2, 1977.

76 *"a seemingly"* "Rolfe Humphries: 1894–1969," Commemorative Tribute, Nov. 13, 1969, Proceedings of The American Academy of Arts and Letters and The National Institute of Arts and Letters, 2nd series, no. 20, 1970.

– *"indulge in a"* LB–RH, Aug. 28, 1924, WTWL, p. 13.

– *"Sunday I expect"* AAIAL.

77 *"Oh, God," she exclaimed* July 24, 1924, WTWL, p. 9.

– *"Oh God," she burst out* July 31, 1924, WTWL, p. 11.

77 *"the stripped"* July 24, 1924, WTWL, p. 9.

– *"a lot of"* [n.d.] AAIAL.

78 *"heroically left"* Jan. 15, 1924, LLP, p. 118.

– *"the victim"* The Twenties, p. 199.

79 *"Raymond could make"* Interview with ACH, Washington, Conn., Mar. 26, 1981.

– *"the focal point"* Lawrance Thompson, Robert Frost: The Years of Triumph 1915–1938 (New York: Holt, Rinehart and Winston, 1970), pp. 136–8.

80 *"Raymond has already"* Feb. 8 [1920], Family Letters of Robert and Elinor Frost, ed. Arnold Grade (Albany: State University of New York, 1972), p. 77.

– *"makes himself"* Apr. 23, 1920, ibid., p. 91.

81 *"so that"* Sept. 23, 1920, ibid., p. 97.

– *"stripping his Franconia"* Years of Triumph, p. 145.

– *The glittering crescent* (New York: The Macmillan Co., 1922), p. 35.

82 *"Raymond would refuse"* ACH interview.

84 *"between an occasional"* CHW, p. 224.

– *"unmistakably assumed"* ibid., p. 226.

– *For when she* ibid., p. 227.

85 *—O, you'll say* [n.d.] AAIAL.

86 *"mad with Raymond"* LB–RH, Aug. 23, 1924, WTWL, p. 13.

3 THE LEAF-CAUGHT WORLD

87 *"Yours for,"* WTWL, pp. 5–15 passim.

– *"downcast horse"* AAIAL.

88 *"paper-pulp atmosphere"* LB–RH, May 19, 1924, WTWL, pp. 6–7.

– *"Many of our"* Introduction, An Anthropologist at Work: Writings of Ruth Benedict, ed. Margaret Mead (Boston: Houghton Mifflin Co., 1959), pp. 87–8.

– *"accent of disdain,"* ibid., p. 77.

89 *"Perception itself"* Interview with Margaret Mead.

90 *"It's pretty awful"* July 22, 1924, WTWL, p. 8.

– *"go down the"* LB–RH, Aug. 28, 1924, WTWL, p. 13.

– *"I remember"* JAMR, p. 132.

– *"Let us be"* The Measure (Feb. 1926): 15.

91 *"toward a loveliness"* ibid. (Dec. 1924): 18.

91 *"And I had"* Apr. 16, 1928, *An Anthropologist at Work,* p. 191.

- *The young Pope The Measure* (Feb. 1925): 14.

92 *"a young Congregationalist"* LB–Ruth Benedict, July 17, 1925, WTWL, p. 21.

- *"very frightened"* July 21, 1925, AAIAL.

93 *"Raymond was"* Written statement, Mrs. Barbara Holden Yeomans, June 9, 1983.

- *"at the age"* JOAP; JAMR, p. 44.

94 *Gents: Our receiving* Letter to Humphries & Spencer from "Holden Bogan Ltd." AAIAL.

95 *"No one was"* [n.d.] 1982, to EF.

- *We suppose you* Mar. 24, 1926, AAIAL.

96 *"The great Bogan"* ibid.

- *"I don't much"* Interview with JHW, Dec. 29, 1974.

- *We think it* [n.d.] AAIAL.

- *"sort of"* Oct. 1, 1935, WTWL, p. 105.

97 *"at once"* WTWL, p. 20.

- *"no one"* ibid., p. 21.

98 *"unmedical" . . . "scattering of"* Nov. 8, 1926, Yaddo Archives.

99 *You should know* Nov. 27, 1926, AAIAL.

- *We saw* Feb. [n.d.] 1927, WTWL, p. 32.

100 *"to drink"* RPH–RH, Apr. 30, 1927, AAIAL.

- *"forced one"* Dec. 11, 1926, Y.

- *"I haven't"* Mar. 13, 1927, WTWL, p. 36.

- *"the result"* Apr. 30, 1927, AAIAL.

101 *"only fitfully peculiar"* LB–RL, Nov. 4, 1961, WTWL, p. 334.

- *"My first image"* Robert Penn Warren–EF, Nov. 8, 1976.

- *"noisy, ill-swept" The House on Jefferson Street: A Cycle of Memories* (New York: Holt, Rinehart and Winston, 1971), p. 143.

102 *"a very skinny"* Interview with David Mandel, Sept. 25, 1979.

- *"What's the matter"* MAS.

102 *"shut the door"* ibid.

103 *"Farewell, farewell!"* Oct. 11, 1928, WTWL, p. 37.

- *"For the first"* ibid.

- *"How happy I"* Nov. 22, 1928, WTWL, p. 39.

- *"mood of"* Dec. 1, 1928, WTWL, n. p. 39.

- *"in distinguished format"* Dec. 6, 1928, CSA.

104 *"looked as if" The Twenties,* pp. 506–7.

- *"long, dull, honest"* ibid., p. 507.

105 *"gave me a"* Sept. 29, 1929, CSA.

- *"with the best"* "The Poetry of Louise Bogan," NR, 60 (Oct. 16, 1929): 248.

- *"full of extraordinary"* Oct. 12, 1929, WTWL, p. 48.

- *are you* Oct. 11, 1929, Y.

106 *"like the inside"* LB–Janet Lewis Winters, Oct. 28, 1929.

- *So we got* Reminiscences of Hillsdale fire, MAS.

107 *"admiring gents"* LB–RH, Aug. 6, 1924, WTWL, p. 12.

- *"Poets, farewell!"* (New York: Charles Scribner's Sons, 1929), p. 75.

108 *"in a later"* LB–JHW, July 21, 1929, CSA.

- *"vulgar upper consciousness"* LB-JHW, Oct. 31, 1932, WTWL, n. p. 71.

113 *"usually categorized" Louise Bogan Reads from Her Works.* Yale Series of Recorded Poets, Program Notes, DL 9132, Carillon Records YP 308, 1968.

- *Winter, that is* WTWL, n. p. 6.

114 *"too Housman"* ibid., Mar. 19, 1924, p. 5.

117 *The poem* ["Simple Autumnal"] *is* Robert Pinsky fails to note the role of denial in his otherwise interesting discussion of the poem's "gorgeously classic, even archaic details," and its "emblematic, nearly allegorical use of natural images." He remarks that the poem "inverts the simple convention or commonplace: This grief does not

complain that time, embodied by the seasonal and bodily cycles, gathers life in too soon. Sorrow rebels at having to endure a beginning, middle, and end in time. It is restless for a consummation; though life and time will be sequential, the poet's emotion seems to need them to be absolutely simultaneous, to be all over with at once. The sense of time is painful not simply because of mortality, but because of the 'delay'—the process of successive stages." *The Situation of Poetry: Contemporary Poetry and Its Traditions* (Princeton: Princeton University Press, 1976), p. 98. But Pinsky does not see the correspondence within the poem between grief and the season. Thus, while the poem implies that the heart's time should by natural law conform to nature's time, its art is to present the inverse (and perverse) relationship, and make nature's time the slave of heart's time, with the subsequent rhythm of delay and oppression absorbed by the elaborately emblematic, artificial quality of the imagery (almost as if the poem were based on a painting by Poussin). It is not, as Pinsky suggests, that the poem's emotion fails to take its course in the normal progression of things, but that this progression has been violated and arrested by some nameless retarding power (which I strongly suspect to be guilt).

118 *"was happy to"* WTWL, p. 40.

- *"cascaded down"* JOAP, p. 47.
- *"Did you ever"* WTWL, p. 8.
- *"the lightning startles"* ibid., p. 9.
- *"who used to"* Aug. 28, 1924, WTWL, p. 14.

119 Lines quoted from "The Flume" are in DS; JAMR, pp. 60–67.

121 *I have never* WTWL, n. p. 8.

122 *"both openly"* Rosamund Tuve, *Elizabethan and Metaphysical Imagery* (Chicago: University of Chicago Press, 1947), p. 31.

- *"chiaroscuro, literally"* from "Thomas Eakins," *Art and Culture: Critical Essays* (Boston: Beacon Press, 1961), p. 177.

122 *"oppositions which"* ibid. Bogan's configurational metaphors—among them "The hardened face under the subtle wreath" in "Fifteenth Farewell" and the "seal stamped over time" in "Simple Autumnal" seem to be derived from classical architectural and sculptural ornaments. They compress multiple private associations and meanings within a "public" pictorial form, although admittedly these verbal emblems are not very transparent.

123 *These apples have* from *Thoreau: The Major Essays* (New York: E.P. Dutton & Co., 1972), p. 274.

- *"perfectly critical"* [Mar.] 1929, WTWL, p. 44.

124 *"in hours, days"* in "I Saw Eternity," *Complete Poems of Henry Vaughan,* ed. with an Introduction by French Fogle (New York: W.W. Norton & Co., 1964), p. 231.

125 *"the crisis and"* Louise Bogan Reads . . . Program Notes.

- *"The last time"* [n.d.] 1954, B.
- *"the form of"* Louise Bogan Reads . . . Program Notes. Sister Angela V. O'Reilly, in "The Art of Louise Bogan" (M.A. Thesis, University of San Diego, 1971), points out that the dialogue form is implicit in many of Bogan's poems, including "Come, Break with Time," "A Letter," "The Crossed Apple," "Girl's Song," and "Fifteenth Farewell." Bogan's constant theme of spiritual conflict is well served by the dialogue form. As Harold Bloom points out, the best of her poems "establish their structure by a conflict of contraries, akin to Blake's clashes of Reason and Energy and Yeats's dialogue of Self and Soul."
- *"really coming to"* WTWL, p. 46.

130 *I hear The Heart of Thoreau's Journals,* ed. Odell Shepard (New York: Dover Publications, 1961), p. 24.

4 FEUER-NACHT

133 *"the things"* Jan. 6, 1930, WTWL, p. 55.
- *"After all"* ibid.
134 *"creative despair"* LBP.
- *"two dozen candles"* LB–MA, Aug. 14, 1930.
- *"five years"* LBP.
- *But, I said* Oct. 1930, LBP.
135 *It is necessary* LBP.
- *"You will write"* LBP.
- *I saw the* LBP.
- *It is early* LBP.
- *It is a* LBP.
136 *"I cannot yet"* [Nov.?] 1932, LBP.
137 *"would be not"* LBP.
- *"peace of mind"* CSA.
- *"refused to fall"* Apr. 11, 1931, WTWL, p. 57.
- *"burned and angry"* LBP.
138 *"been there myself"* LLP, pp. 205–6.
139 *"Dear Edmund"* Apr. 1931, Y.
140 *At seven* ibid.
- *"hot from"* [n.d.] 1931, Y.
141 *"I don't know"* [May] 1931, Y.
- *"Several mechanisms"* June 23, 1931, WTWL, p. 59.
142 *"with my whole"* July 1931.
- *"venomous"* Mar. 29, 1932, LBP.
143 *"topical songs"* LB–MDZ, Feb. 14, 1933, WTWL, p. 72.
- *"about it like"* The Thirties: From Notebooks and Diaries of the Period, ed. with an Introduction by Leon Edel (New York: Farrar, Straus & Giroux, 1980), p. 326.
- *"She had"* Conversation with Jap Gude, Oct. 18, 1980.
144 Louise and Maidy *The Thirties,* p. 308.
- *"opaque eyes"* 7 (Dec. 12, 1931): 19.
- *"Little ships"* 9 (Aug. 12, 1933): 13.
145 *"I do love"* July 22, 1924, WTWL, p. 7.
- *—The Whistlers* LBP; JAMR, p. 99.
- *Last night I* ibid.; ibid., p. 96.

146 *"looking as regal"* ibid.; ibid., p. 95.
- *"The continuous turmoil"* LBP.
147 *"Such a voyage"* LBP.
- *"The initial mystery"* and all other quotations are from jamr; JAMR, p. 2 passim.
148 *A series of* Nov. 1932, LBP.
- *The idea that* Aug. 1932, LBP.
149 *"the rancor"* LBP.
- *"in his attempt"* LBP.
- *Have at you* Oct. 1932, LBP.
- *We shall hate* LBP.
150 *"on leaves in"* Aug. 17, 1932, LBP; JAMR, p. 92.
- *Novels will more* LBP.
- *"of their principles"* Nov. 16, 1932, LBP.
- *As the circle* LBP.
151 *He may be* LBP.
- *"at five o'clock"* Oct. 1932, LBP; JAMR, p. 95.
152 *"with emptiness"* ibid.; ibid., p. 92.
- *"a creative patience"* "The Flower of the Mind," *Poetry,* 35 (Dec. 1929): 158.
- *"an extremely blond"* The House on Jefferson Street p. 192.
153 *I noted that* Feb. 13, 1935, LBP.
- *"Now give me"* [n.d. 1934?] LBP.
- *"Your determination"* Jan. 23, 1932, WTWL, p. 61.
154 *"never forget"* Sept. 11, 1932, WTWL, p. 67.
- *"Edmund's mien"* May 5, 1932, NL.
- *"ideas of lost"* LB–MDZ, Aug. 3, 1932, NL.
- *To live my* [Nov. ?] 1932, LBP; JAMR, p. 58.
155 *because for ten* LBP.
- *"Bear, bear"* Oct. 14, 1932, WTWL, p. 67.
- *If I decide* Nov. 5, 1932, LBP.
156 *"a little abnormal"* Mar. 15, 1933, WTWL, p. 73.
- *"with ten dollars"* LB–MDZ, Oct. 5, 1932, NL.
- *"a style to"* Feb. 14, 1933, NL.

5 ITALIAN MORNING

158 —*In her new* The Thirties, p. 329.
- "*There you were*" Apr. 2, 1933.
- *. . . your name* ibid.
159 "*how proud*" Apr. 3, 1933.
- "*his skill in*" LBP.
- *although it is* Apr. 8, 1933.
160 "*these last*" ibid.
- "*all dressed up*" ibid.
- "*the most exquisite*" May 7, 1933, NL.
- "*There's not a*" Apr. 8, 1933.
- *Beautiful courtyard* LBP.
161 "*climbing up*" LBP.
- "*women and children*" LBP.
- "*broad, strapped*" LBP.
- *I walked out* LB–MA, Apr. 13, 1933.
- "*terribly lonely*" LBP.
- *She couldn't* LBP.
162 "*rather like*" LBP.
- "*where I*" Apr. 18, 1933.
- "*utterly empty*" LBP.
- "*hanged from*" Apr. 1933.
163 "*But, darling*" Apr. 1933.
- *from the moment* May 7, 1933, NL.
- *The pathos* Apr. 21, 1933, LBP.
164 "*used to gaze*" Apr. 29, 1933, LBP.
- "*Rachmaninoff, who*" Apr. 23, 1933, LBP.
- "*turning in*" Apr. 25, 1933, LBP.
- "*It is interesting*" Apr. 29, 1933, LBP.
- "*splendid, with*" Apr. 26, 1933, LBP.
- "*a fine wreck*" Apr. 28, 1933, LBP.
- *A large room* Apr. 27, 1933, LBP.
165 "*faded bad*" May 3, 1933, LBP.
- "*Almost out*" LBP.
- "*The nights*" Apr. 1933.
- "*I'm a man*" Apr. 6, 1933.
166 *It seems to me* Apr. 18, 1933.
- *Other women* Apr. 24, 1933.
- "*I was almost*" May 4–5, 1933.
167 "*Cellini borzoi*" May 8, 1933, LBP.
- "*round rosy wreaths*" LBP.
- "*when kept awake*" May 19, 1933, LBP.
168 "*ugly and spoiled*" May 20, 1933, LBP.

168 "*the bridge*" ibid.
- "*from the city*" May 21, 1933, Y.
- "*perfectly happy*" May 20, 1933, LBP.
- "*I've been*" May 21, 1933, LBP.
- "*handsome American father*" May 21, 1933, LBP.
- "*pretty scrubby*" ibid.
169 "*the light*" NY, 9 (July 22, 1933): 22.
- *Superb. Thrilling* May 30, 1933, LBP.
- "*It is the*" June 3, 1933.
- "*marvelous. . . . Green hills*" ibid.
170 "*papered with*" June 12, 1933, WTWL, pp. 74–5.
- "*umbrellas turn*" June 5, 1933, LBP.
- "*Dos P. a*" June 12, 1933, LBP.
- "*A grand*" LB–MDZ, June 29, 1933, NL.
- "*the secret communication*" June 19, 1933, LBP.
171 *The pilasters* LBP.
- *In the dream* June 15, 1933, LBP.
- "*(or rather)*" June 17, 1933, LBP.
- "*get Dorothy's*" June 19, 1933, LBP.
- "*I have been*" June 29, 1933, WTWL, p. 75.
172 "*graveyard hue frescoes*" June 30, 1933, LBP.
- "*many glasses*" ibid.
- "*all alone*" ibid.
- "*to bear up*" July 6, 1933, LBP.
- "*learning something*" May 23, 1933.
- "*both of whom*" May 31, 1933.
- *What a letter* June 7, 1933.
173 "*rather attractive*" June 11, 1933.
- "*whether or not*" June 12, 1933.
174 "*I'm not trying*" June 23, 1933.
- "*Please help me*" ibid.
- "*as something*" June 18, 1933.
- "*but I'm learning*" July 6, 1933.
175 *The realization* July 20, 1933, LBP.
- "*had gone in*" The Thirties, p. 300.
- "*very different*" July 11, 1933.
- *so well-written* ibid.
- "*one touch*" July 16, 1933.
- "*filthy and*" July 28, 1933.

176 *"because I feel"* ibid.
- *"for the present"* July 20, 1933, LBP.
- *"brainstorm"* July 1933.
- *"This is foolish"* July 20, 1933, LBP.
177 *On old women's* LBP.
- *"refined* Atlantic" July 19, 1933, LLP, p. 721.
- *Mozart was born* July 29, 1933, Y.
178 *"the nameless"* CSA.
- *comes to this* Aug. 11, 1933, LBP; JAMR, pp. 74–75.
- *"The letting go"* ibid.; ibid.
- *"Milton Ballardvale"* July 31, 1933, LBP.
- *Everything seems* ibid.
179 *"something in you"* July 1933.
- *"presentation of the"* Aug. 1, 1933, LBP.

179 *"Really a mature"* ibid.
- *—From Greene Avenue* Aug. 2, 1933, LBP.
180 *"closing a circle"* Aug. 3, 1933, LBP.
- *"absolutely to go"* Aug. 10, 1933, LBP.
- *"306 Lex."* ibid.
- *"a sudden flash"* ibid.
181 *All places* Aug. 17, 1933, LBP.
- *"Great heartsickness"* Aug. 18, 1933, LBP.
- *You see* Aug. 15, 1933.
- *doing some fixing* Aug. 1933.
182 *"nothing but"* Aug. 23, 1933.
- *Oh darling* ibid.
- *It is like* Aug. 22, 1933, LBP.
- *Salzburg* Aug. 26, 1933, LBP.
183 *"O superb days"* LBP.

6 THE FLAWED LIGHT OF LOVE AND GRIEF

184 *"ready to defend"* Sept. 12, 1933, LBP; JAMR, p. 75.
- *"when I saw"* ibid.; ibid.
185 *My notes* Sept. 12, 1933, LBP.
- *When I am* LPB; JAMR, p. 75.
186 *no intellectual* ibid.; ibid., p. 76.
- *"of a confused"* ibid.; ibid.
- *"a change of"* Sept. 12, 1933, LBP.
- *"a kind of"* ibid.
187 *Today—on Sept. 12* LBP; JAMR, p. 77.
- *all shot to* Oct. 11, 1933, NL.
- *"though I don't"* [n.d.] 1933.
188 *One emotion* Sept. 15, 1933, LBP.
- *that there was* ibid.
- *"late growth"* ibid.
189 *"very noble"* 9 (Oct. 14, 1933); JAMR, p. 81.
- *"For one split"* LBP; JAMR, pp. 81–2.
- *"I've had a"* Nov. 9, 1933, NL.
- *"puzzled or confused"* Dec. [n.d.] 1933, CSA.
- *"I am so"* Nov. 13, 1933.
- *"This time"* Dec. [n.d.] 1933, CSA.
- *"I shall be"* Nov. 13, 1933.
190 *It is really* Nov. 20, 1933.

190 *I now feel* Dec. 11, 1933, Y.
- *"psychic pains"* Dec. 22, 1933, Y.
191 *Tell Raymond* Nov. 13, 1933.
- *"It was not"* Dec. 10, 1933, LBP.
- *bouts of tears* Dec. 24, 1933, LBP.
192 *"barren brooding"* [late Dec.] 1933.
- *"about sanitarium patients"* ibid.
- *"laughed at his"* LBP; JAMR, p. 87.
- *"painful inner story"* LBP.
193 *"those wooden"* Dec. 30, 1933, LBP.
- *"greatly admires"* LBP.
- *"a confession"* Dec. 12, 1933, LLP, p. 234.
- *"but when"* ibid., p. 232.
194 *"knife of the"* LB–MDZ, July 27, 1936, WTWL, p. 79.
- *"Writing"* Mar. 4, 1934, LBP.
- *"A controlled relationship"* June 20, 1936, NL.
195 *Time in itself* (New York: The Macmillan Co., 1933), p. 14.
- *The neurotic* ibid., p. 288.
- *"that when one"* Aug. 10, 1936, WTWL, p. 136.
- *The monomania which* Jan. 15, 1934, LBP.

196 *"Well, I've made"* Jan. [n.d.] 1934.
- *"what a dismal"* Feb. [n.d.] 1934.
- *"but not entirely"* Jan. 22, 1934.
- *"very busy throwing"* early Feb. [n.d.] 1934.
- *"burst out with"* Mar. [n.d.] 1934.
197 *"with terrific clarity"* Feb. 16, 1934, LBP.
- *The month, the time* LBP.
- *At eleven o'clock* LBP.
198 *She had read* Feb. 12, 1934, LBP.
- *"solution of thoughts"* Apr. 16, 1934, LBP.
- *in the main* Feb. 25, 1934, LBP; JAMR, p. 90.
- *This book closes* LBP.
- *"She will never"* Aug. 15, 1934, LBP.
199 *"fine set of"* Apr. 9, 1934, LLP, p. 235.
200 *"a nice old-fashioned"* July 9, 1934.
- *everything but* LB–MA, July 11, 1936.
- *"The long flood"* July 14, 1934, LBP.
201 *"It is quite"* July 28, 1934, LBP.
- *Edmund spoke* July 28, 1934, LBP; JAMR, pp. 132–3.
202 *"editorial heart ache"* June 4, 1934, LBP.
- *"a lot of"* Aug. 12, 1934, WTWL, p. 79.
- *It now appears* 1934, LBP.
203 *At times* July 8, 1934, LBP.
204 *"Doomed"* Aug. 21, 1934, LBP.
- *"a nice amicable"* Aug. 1, 1934.
- *"one or two"* LB–MA, Aug. 16, 1934.
- *"To a unique"* ibid.
- *"strange, almost unvisited"* "Half a Letter," LBP.
205 *"The configuration"* LBP.
- *A day* Aug. 26, 1934, LBP.
- *"I sought love"* LBP; JAMR, p. 53.
- *"Made idiot"* Sept. 17, 1934, LBP.
206 *It is unlikely* In his bibliography, *Louise Bogan: A Woman's Words* (Library of Congress, Washington 1971), William Jay Smith lists fifteen stories: "Winter Morning," "Art Embroidery," "Hydrotherapy," "Sabbatical Summer," "A Speakeasy Life," "Zest," "Sunday at Five," "Journey Around My Room," "The

Short Life of Emily," "The Last Tear," "Conversation Piece," "Coming Out," "Dove and Serpent," "Letdown," and "To Take Leave." Marshall Clements and David Stivender, in their unpublished compilation of Bogan's uncollected poems and prose, include another story, "Keramik," and a prose piece, "Soliloquy." The catalogue of The Louise Bogan Papers lists typescript and manuscript drafts of nine unpublished stories, the last given a probable date of 1937.
206 *"unless it is"* Ant; JAMR, p. 114.
207 *"magnificent"* . . . *". . . the bald"* Nov. 6, 1935, TRP.
- *"the sort"* ibid.
208 *"He had taught"* and all other citations from "Keramik" are in *The American Caravan: A Yearbook of American Literature,* ed. by Van Wyck Brooks, Alfred Kreymborg, Lewis Mumford, Paul Rosenfeld (New York: The Macauly Co., 1927), pp. 673–8.
209 *"it is winter"* and other citations from "Winter Morning" are in NR, 54 (Mar. 14, 1928): 125.
- *To push through* NR, 54 (Mar. 21, 1928): 156
210 *"the penny of"* in *The Second American Caravan,* ed. by Van Wyck Brooks, Alfred Kreymborg, Lewis Mumford, Paul Rosenfeld (New York: The Macaulay Co., 1928), p. 216 ff.
212 *She hated Amy* 7 (Dec. 12, 1931): 19.
- *"moderately mixed"* NY, 9 (May 6, 1933): 21–22.
213 *"the best short"* May 3, 1933, LBP.
- *"The excessively"* NY, 7 (June 27, 1931): 18.
214 *I have dragged* 10 (Jan. 26, 1935): 26.
215 *"For, as in"* July 27, 1943, LBP.
- *The most advantageous* and following quotations, jamr.
217 *everything in the* and other citations, ds.

7   AFTER THE AIR OF SUMMER

223 *In psychoanalysis* LBP.
- *"abortive poems"* Nov. 29, 1934, NL.
- *"all the mental"* Jan. 17, 1935, WTWL, p. 83.
224 *"Bunny, how"* MAS.
- *"you old pretty"* May 13, 1935, LLP, pp. 269, 271.
225 *I, myself* June 22, 1935, WTWL, pp. 85–6.
- *"writing the most"* July 1, 1935, WTWL, p. 86.
226 *"memorable"* Nov. 2, 1934, SLTR, p. 25.
- *"no good"* ibid.
- *"Louise, you're a"* LB–MDZ, Aug. 2, 1935, WTWL, p. 95.
227 *"Why did you"* July 1, 1935, WTWL, p. 86.
- *"right down"* May 26, 1935, Y.
- *"My God"* Aug. 14, 1935, AAIAL.
- *"how a Corot"* (London: The Hogarth Press, 1925), p. 36; *"I did not"* in LB's copy at the Louise Bogan Working Library, the Western College for Women, Oxford, Ohio.
228 *"the pure lyric"* LB–RH, Sept. 5, 1935, AAIAL.
- (*"Girls' Latin . . ."*) Oct. 29, 1935, TRP.
229 *"I'd work"* [n.d.] 1935, TRP.
- *"Really take"* Aug. 14, 1935, TRP.
- *"slyly, as though"* Oct. 7, 1935, TRP.
- *"because it is"* Aug. 23, 1935, WTWL, p. 96.
- *"Not exactly punk"* [n.d.] 1935, TRP.
- *"ascribe bitchhood"* [n.d.] 1935, TRP.
- *In a number* On Louise Bogan's influence on Theodore Roethke, see Sullivan's *Theodore Roethke: The Garden Master* (Seattle: University of Washington Press, 1975), pp. 17–18.
230 *"look at things"* Aug. 25, 1935, WTWL, p. 96.
- *"for reasons"* [n.d.] 1935, AAIAL.
- Lines from "Blue Hydrangeas" in

Rilke: Selected Poems, with English translations by C. F. MacIntyre (Berkeley: University of California Press, 1940), p. 75.
230 *Here all sorts* Aug. 23, 1935, WTWL, p. 97.
- *"If he could"* June 28, 1935, AAIAL.
231 *by a family* Sept. 4, 1935, WTWL, pp. 98–9.
- *"being good"* Sept. 23, 1935, WTWL, p. 104.
- *Just twenty-eight* SLTR, p. 37.
232 *"I swore"* [Dec.] 1935, TRP.
- *"let the world"* [Dec.] 1935, WTWL, p. 122.
- **And if . . .* in *Sonnets to Orpheus,* Second Part, 29, translated by M.D. Herter Norton (New York: W.W. Norton & Company, 1962), pp. 126–7.
- *"start writing"* Mar. 3, 1936, TRP.
- *"Yeats said"* [April] 1936, TRP.
- *"scenario"* Aug. 22, 1936, TRP.
233 *"those states"* Mar. 3, 1936, TRP.
- *"a big boy"* Nov. 27, 1937, TRP.
- *"It really is"* June 12, 1937, WTWL, p. 157.
- *"You know"* Oct. 10, 1937, TRP.
- *"his gift at"* Oct. 16, 1938, AAIAL.
234 *"It is really"* Jan. 2, 1940, TRP.
- *"you told"* [n.d.] 1939, SLTR, p. 81.
- *"sweet of you"* ibid.
- *"should* grow up" [July] 1941, WTWL, p. 221.
- *Thanks for the* Apr. 25, 1947, LBP.
235 *"The poet"* NY, 24 (May 15, 1948): 118, 121.
- *"change away"* Mar. 2, 1949, TRP.
- *"It's obvious"* Sept. 23, 1958, LBP.
- *"Her poems"* MQR, p. 251.
236 *"no such book"* July 1, 1935, WTWL, p. 87.
- *"I hate"* and lines from "The Lie," July 2, 1935, WTWL, p. 89.
237 *"and then"* Sept. 4, 1935, WTWL, p. 98.

237 *"to get the"* LB–RH, Oct. 1, 1935, WTWL, p. 105.
238 *happy for* Oct. 7, 1935, WTWL, p. 109.
- *"only what I"* Oct. 7, 1935, LBP.
- *was all that* ibid.
- *"bridges, churches"* Ant; JAMR, p. 101.
- *"Freudian discoveries"* LB–MDZ, Aug. 10, 1936, WTWL, p. 136.
239 *"suspend all"* Quoted in LBP.
- *"Today it seemed"* Ant; JAMR, p. 103.
- *"But how beautiful"* ibid.; ibid.
240 *Essentially all this* in *Anton Chechov: A Critical Study* (New York: Duffield & Company, 1923), pp. 22–23.
- *"He is such"* Nov. 5, 1935, NL.
- *"and knew"* Dec. 3, 1935, NL.
- *"the point"* Feb. 5, 1936, WTWL, p. 126.
- *"a bad"* LB–RH, May 1, 1936, WTWL, p. 131.
- *"which will sum"* [June] 1936, WTWL, p. 132.
241 *"The room"* Sept. 8, 1936.
- *"uncurtained, hardly furnished"* Ant; JAMR, p. 102.
- *"O Morton"* Dec. 8, 1936, WTWL, p. 146.
242 *"If you could"* Dec. 23, 1936, WTWL, p. 147.
- *"whom my mother"* LB–WM, Mar. 30, 1941.
- *"As ignorant"* LBP.
244 *The 1930–1933 period* Dec. 8, 1936, WTWL, p. 145.
245 *"in the midst"* Aug. 20, 1966, WIWL, p. 368.
246 *O, God forbid* from Johann Wolfgang von Goethe, Part II, Scene 2, *Faust: A Tragedy,* translated by Walter Arndt, edited by Cyrus Hamlin (New York: W.W. Norton Co., 1976), pp. 173–4, 176.
247 *"the sense of"* MQR, p. 251.
- *—Bitter though* Oct. 31, 1932, CSA.
248 *"fine, frightfully"* Nov. 29, 1932, WTWL, p. 69.
- *"on the verge"* Aug. 20, 1966, WTWL, p. 368.

249 *"It's damned"* CSA.
- *"literary exercise"* May 7, 1931, LBP.
250 *"I never"* Oct. 1, 1931, LBP.
- *"read into"* LB–Allen Tate, Oct. 8, 1931, WTWL, p. 60.
- *"The passion"* May 2, 1931, WTWL, p. 58.
- *"You ought"* Apr. 7, 1937, LLP, p. 289.
252 *"I'd send you"* Aug. 22, 1934, WTWL, p. 81.
253 *"the mutability poem"* Aug. 2, 1935, TRP.
- *"the best"* July 1, 1935, WTWL, p. 86.
- *"I thought"* Apr. 13, 1938, LLP, p. 303.
254 *"topped by"* Nov. 27, 1938, AAIAL.
- *"Whatever I do"* Ant; JAMR, p. 91.
- *"I have"* July 1, 1935, WTWL, p. 86.
257 *"The title poem"* Sept. 11, 1935, CSA.
- *Now it is* LBP.
- *"The scenario"* July 29, 1936, CSA.
- *"was floating"* July 29, 1936, AAIAL.
258 *It was* LBP.
259 *"that the poem"* Oct. 15, 1936, AAIAL.
- *"To trace"* Ant, p. 125.
261 *"too adjectival"* July 1, 1935, LBP.
262 *I don't* July 2, 1935, WTWL, p. 91.
263 *"which has a"* Oct. 15, 1936, AAIAL.
264 *"death-loving temperament"* LBP.
- *"I don't"* Oct. 15, 1936, AAIAL.
- *"I thought"* Oct. 3, 1935, WTWL, p. 107.
- *"a perfectly"* Nov. 6, 1935, WTWL, p. 116.
- *"neither the"* n. WTWL, pp. 117–18.
265 *"the second-hand"* [n.d.] 1936, AAIAL.
- *"I know"* July 29, 1936, WTWL, n. p. 133.
266 *"Zwischenraume Zwischen Welt"* The *Duino Elegies,* The German Text, with an English translation, Introduction, and Commentary by J. B. Leishman and Stephen Spender (New York: W. W. Norton, 1939), p. 45.

266 *"marvelous: alphabetically"* LB–TR, Oct. 3, 1935, WTWL, p. 107.
- *Build it up* W. H. Auden and John Garrett, *The Poet's Tongue: An Anthology* (London: G. Bell, 1935), p. 79.
267 *dragged about* from "Dolls" ("Puppen"), *Selected Works*, vol. I, Prose, translated by G. Craig Houston, with an Introduction by J. B. Leishman

(London: The Hogarth Press, 1961), p. 44.
268 *"the horrible"* ibid., p. 45.
- *It was facing* ibid., pp. 46–7.
- *"and all the"* Oct. 28, 1936, WTWL, pp. 139–40.
269 *"the only"* [Nov. 1936?], CSA.
- *"when one"* WTWL, p. 136.
270 *in becoming* Dec. 3, 1935, NL.
- *"It is as"* ibid.

8 THE WAY OF THE LAUREL

271 *"Almost the"* —*And I Worked...*, p. 104.
- *"art of"* "Lyric Authority," NR, 90 (May 5, 1937): 391.
272 *"lament the exclusion"* NR, 73 (Jan. 11, 1933): 240.
- *"a dead leaf"* WTWL, n. p. 95.
- *"experiencing a violent"* Feb. 5, 1935, WTWL, p. 83.
273 *"I hate authority"* [Oct. 1935], WTWL, p. 113.
- *"an intuitive"* NR, 86 (Mar. 4, 1936): 114.
274 *"and it would"* NR, 86 (Apr. 8, 1936): 251–2.
- *The revolution* ibid.
275 *"lead to serious"* NR, 86 (Mar. 4, 1936): 114.
- *"Yeats seems"* June 26, 1938, NL.
- *"I came"* [n.d. 1935?] AAIAL.
- —*If only* Oct. 7, 1935, TRP.
276 *If she Not Mine to Finish: Poems 1908–1934* (New York: Harper & Brothers, 1934), p. 29.
- Lines Written Oct. 16, 1934, WTWL, p. 82.
277 *"God keep me from a world"* July 6, 1935, WTWL, p. 93.
- *"true ears"* July 10, 1935, AAIAL.
278 *"If you know"* [n.d. 1935?] LBP.
- *"non-aggression pact"* RH–LB, Sept. 25, 1935, LBP.
- *"For Heaven's sake"* [n.d.] 1936, AAIAL.

278 *"Words in Your Mouth" Out of the Jewel* (New York: Charles Scribner's Sons, 1942), pp. 62–63.
279 *"I don't think"* May 1, 1936, AAIAL.
- *"spiritual side"* LB–RH, Jan. 24, 1936, AAIAL.
- *"to develop" Out of the Jewel*, p. 75.
280 *I sit down* [n.d.] 1936, AAIAL.
- *"lousy system"* Dec. 23, 1936, WTWL, p. 146.
- *What we suffer* ibid., p. 147.
281 *You labor long* LBP.
- *"philosophical and divinatory"* "Nine Poets: 1937" from *Southern Review* (Summer 1937), reprinted in *Reasons in Madness: Critical Essays* (New York: G. P. Putnam's Sons, 1941), p. 172.
- *"passages of thought"* "The Flame in Stone," in *Poetry* 50 (June 1937): 160–1.
- *"Two old"* May 22, 1937, NL.
282 *"Ireland is even"* Apr. 13, 1937.
- *"bow-windows"* ibid.
- *I rode* ibid.
283 *"the Irish are"* Apr. 21, 1937.
- *"so ugly"* Apr. 20, 1937, NL.
- *"There's a great"* Apr. 21, 1937.
- *"What fanatics invent" Collected Poems*, p. 286.
284 *"the old"* June 11, 1937, NL.
- *I did* ibid.
- *"mild nervous"* LB–MDZ, May 22, 1937, NL.

284 *"So you"* ibid.

285 *But Morton* June 11, 1937, NL.

- *"yelling 'What . . .' "* July 16, 1937, TRP.

286 *"Muvver's ittle* cantatrice" June 22, 1937.

- *"the first"* ibid.

- *"from the windows"* LB–Rufina McCarthy Helmer, Aug. 5, 1937, WTWL, p. 159.

287 *"just anything that"* Aug. 5, 1937, NL.

- *"I see we"* Aug. 25, 1937.

- *"of the craftsman"* 14 (Mar. 5, 1938): 64.

- *"an almost"* Barbara Holden Yeomans–EF, Apr. 30, 1981.

288 *"He is"* Aug. 5, 1937, NL.

- *"to be an"* ibid.

- *"as words"* Aug. 22, 1937, NL.

- *"He is such"* Nov. 27, 1937, WTWL, p. 167.

- *. . . her poetry* [Nov. 1937], LLP, pp. 295–6.

289 *"When you"* Oct. 31, 1939, LLP, p. 322.

- *"I thought"* Nov. 2, 1939, WTWL, p. 193.

- *"but the* essential" May 29, 1939, WTWL, p. 191.

290 *" 'fastidious' "* Jan 27, 1941, WTWL, p. 214.

- *"Hasn't anyone"* Aug. 5, 1937, NL.

291 *New Moon* Na, 145 (Aug. 7, 1937); JAMR, p. 106.

292 *Those who A Time to Speak: Selected Prose of Archibald MacLeish* (Boston: Houghton Mifflin Co., 1940), p. 22.

- *"the most awful"* July 8, 1938, WTWL, p. 173.

- *Last year* "Verse," NY, 15 (Dec. 16, 1939): 100–1.

293 *She is earnest* ibid.; PA, p. 229.

- *"a severe shock"* "Cafeteria Comment," NR, 102 (Apr. 18, 1940): 476.

294 *"personal attack"* NR, 102 (May 13, 1940): 644.

- *To L----- B----* LBP.

295 *"I have no"* Mar. 22, 1939, WTWL, p. 185.

295 *"laid out"* Dec. 2, 1936, WTWL, p. 143.

- *a whole beautiful* ibid.

296 *"the works"* ibid.

- *Another rather* June 17, 1940, NL.

- *"doing 'exercises' "* Jan. 21, 1941, WTWL, p. 213.

297 *My own* Nov. 17, 1941, LBP.

298 *"classical"* and subsequent citations: PR, 6 (Fall 1939): 103–8.

300 *"The Trotskyites"* July 19, 1939, NL.

- *"It's because"* LB–MDZ, Aug. 14, 1940, NL.

301 *"disguised State"* ibid.

- *But now* Aug. 14, 1940, NL.

302 *"In all"* June 3, 1941, LBP.

303 *"What I do"* July 6, 1935, WTWL, p. 92.

- *Now for goodness'* July 22, 1941, copied on back of LB–JHW, July 28, 1941, CSA.

- *"a many faceted"* July 24, 1941, NL.

- *"in cold"* Sept. 5, 1941, WTWL, p. 223.

304 *"torn off"* LB–RH, Oct. 16, 1938, AAIAL.

305 *"was another"* [Sept. 1938], NL.

- *There is no* (London: Faber & Faber, 1938), pp. 379–80.

- *"haunted"* Oct. 17, 1940, LLP, p. 364.

306 *"things naturally"* Feb. 25, 1936, NL.

307 *"We know"* (New York: The Macmillan Co., 1936), p. 38.

- *Feb. 21, 1855* Bradford Torrey, Francis H. Allen, eds. *The Journal of Henry D. Thoreau,* VII (Boston: Houghton Mifflin Co., 1949), p. 206.

308 *"spent a whole"* LBP.

- *"just hot"* WTWL, n. p. 158.

- *"a complete change"* Aug. 20, 1966, WTWL, p. 368. Let me add here that I am indebted to Sister O'Reilly's reading of the poem in her Master's thesis, "The Art of Louise Bogan," cited earlier.

311 *Come, Sleep* in *The English Galaxy of Shorter Poems,* ed. Gerald Bullett (London: J.M. Dent, 1933), p. 209.

312 *"after an"* Jan. 4, 1939, NL.

313 *"spiritual dryness"* [n.d. 1939], CSA.

314 *"To Hölderlin" Later Poems,* translated from the German by J. B. Leishman (London: The Hogarth Press, 1938), p. 63.
- *"We will call"* Aug. 1, 1938, LLP, p. 307.
- *"is an Auden"* Sept. 29, 1938, Y.

314 *"the poet"* Interview with Richard Wilbur, Cummington, Mass., Oct. 6, 1973.
315 *"given . . . one"* Nov. 13, 1959, WTWL, p. 317.
- *"When I think"* (London: Macmillan & Co., 1918), pp. 30–31.

9 THE EIGHT-SIDED HEART

319 *"is compactness"* 158 (Nov. 15, 1941): 486, reprinted in Marianne Moore, *Predilections* (New York: Viking Press, 1955), p. 130.
- *"Miss Bogan has"* 105 (Nov. 10, 1941): 625.
- *"an effort to"* "Land of Dust and Flame," 60 (Apr. 1942); reprinted in Stanley Kunitz, *A Kind of Order, A Kind of Folly: Essays and Conversations* (Boston: Little, Brown and Co., 1975), pp. 196–7.
- *"the poetry of"* (Nov. 30, 1941): 20.
320 *A public* "The Rewards of Patience," PR, IX (July–Aug. 1942): 336.
- *"at the mercy"* ibid.
- *"the Collective Self"* ibid.
- *"one must go"* ibid.
- *"one has"* ibid.
- *Someone said* June 10, 1941, FWD.
321 *"general distrust"* Apr. 24, 1940, WTWL, p. 207.
- *"The whole"* [n.d.] 1941, TRP.
- *"It's unfortunate"* Apr. 13, 1942, LBP.
322 *In the set-up* Feb. 24, 1941, WTWL, p. 215.
- *"nor does"* Feb. 25, 1941, LBP.
- *"about the"* Mar. 9, 1941, LBP.
- *"soapbox poetry"* Dec. 16, 1939, LBP.
- *"to accept"* Mar. 25, 1941, LBP.
- *"and we had"* July 10, 1941, WTWL, p. 221.
323 *"encircling glooms"* LB–TR, Dec. 7, 1941, WTWL, p. 224.
- *Since 1936* Dec. 9, 1941, WTWL, p. 225.
324 *"I have"* Interview with JHW, New

York City, Dec. 29, 1974.
324 *"immeasurably relieved"* Feb. 25, 1943, CSA.
325 *"should hesitate"* Dec. 3, 1941, CSA.
326 *"Wait awhile"* May 4, 1943, AAIAL.
- *"double-boiler existence"* "The Little Irish Girl from Roxbury," *The American Pen,* VII (Spring 1975): 46.
327 *Ft. Tryon* LBP.
328 *"A woman"* Interview with JHW.
- *the piano* Aug. 24, 1943, WTWL, p. 231.
329 *"made me"* WTWL, p. 178.
- *"isolated regions"* LB–WM, Dec. 27, 1938.
- *"The food"* Apr. 6, 1939.
- *" 'Here I am' "* ibid.
- *"What bothers"* July 18, 1940.
- *"tone-deaf"* Mar. 30, 1941.
- *"the most wonderful"* June 2, 1941, WTWL, p. 218.
330 *"like the"* June 4, 1941, WTWL, pp. 218–19.
- *". . . I swear"* May 22, 1941.
- *Something may have* Aug. 22, 1941.
331 *"never once"* WM–EF, Mar. 16, 1978.
- *"one has to"* Oct. 9, 1942, WTWL, p. 227.
- *"The problem"* [n.d.], LBP.
- *"anything that"* [n.d.], LBP.
- *"the swiftest"* Oct. 18, 1943, WTWL, p. 232.
- *"You'll have to"* Aug. 12, 1943.
332 *When a man* from "In Distrust of Merits," *The Complete Poems of Marianne Moore* (New York: The

Macmillan Co./The Viking Press, 1967), p. 137.

332 *"You're getting"* Aug. 12, 1943.

- *"Thank you"* [n.d.], LBP.
- *My destination* [n.d.], LBP.
- *"the bizarre"* JOAP; JAMR, pp. 113–14.

333 *"The innocent"* Interview with WM, May 30, 1975.

- *... is it true* Sept. 18, 1944, WTWL, p. 241.
- *When he The Folded Leaf* (New York: Harper & Bros, 1945), p. 310.

334 *a great deal* June 13, 1944, LBP.

- *What is* [n.d.] 1945, LBP.
- *Dear Sweet Puss* July 13, 1943, LBP.

335 *A cool* LBP.

336 *"from most"* Nov. 10, 1944, LBP.

337 *"that recent"* draft, Apr. 4, 1945 LBP.

- *"to come off"* July 6, 1945, WTWL, p. 247.
- *"took it"* LB–MDZ, July 6, 1945, WTWL, p. 247.
- *"with great"* May 24, 1946, WTWL, p. 239.
- *"small groups"* ibid.

338 *"has been"* LB–WM, Nov. 10, 1944, WTWL, p. 244.

- *"Marianne Moore's"* Jan. 16, 1945, WTWL, p. 245.
- *"v. good"* July 6, 1945, WTWL, p. 248.
- *"found that"* Sept. 23, 1945.
- *"combination of"* LB–WM, Oct. 8, 1945, WTWL, n. p. 245.
- *"an intelligent"* LB–WM, Sept. 23, 1945, WTWL, p. 250.

339 *As I sat* "The Little Irish Girl from Roxbury," p. 41.

- *She was* ibid., p. 44.
- *"a chastened"* July 6, 1945, WTWL, p. 248.
- *"During those"* Sept. 11, 1945, WTWL, p. 249.

340 *Ft. Tryon* LBP.

- *It condenses* Oct. 7, 1946, WTWL, pp. 254–5.

341 *"of being"* June 7, 1947, AAIAL.

- *"Regret having"* LBP.

342 *The weather* Oct. 9, 1946, WTWL, p. 255.

342 *The fear of Mademoiselle* (May 1947); PA, pp. 428–29.

- *" 'I can' "* LB–MDZ, Oct. 13, 1946, WTWL, p. 256.

343 *"paranoid hatred"* LB–MDZ, Nov. 12, 1946, WTWL, n. p. 257.

- *"I must see"* Mar. 11, 1948, WTWL, p. 260, where it is misdated Mar. 20, 1948.
- *"So I shall"* Oct. 24, 1948, WTWL, p. 263.
- *"How beautiful"* Nov. 18, 1948, WTWL, p. 265.

344 *"she regretted"* RL–EF, [n.d.] 1982.

- *"There's no"* LB–Elizabeth Mayer, Mar. 9, 1952, B.

345 *"the silver cord"* LB–MS, Oct. 15, 1954, WTWL, p. 291.

- *"when the moment"* LBP.

346 *"my advice"* May 11, 1957.

- *"brown hair"* "Louise Bogan: A Reminiscence," unpublished mss., quoted by permission of the author.

348 *"Poor Miss Bogan!"* Elizabeth Bishop, "Efforts of Affection," *Vanity Fair* (May 1983): 59.

350 *"faith in her"* JOAP; JAMR, p. 163.

- *"What a work"* LB–Elizabeth Mayer, June 9, 1949, B.

351 *"The poor old"* Dec. 30, 1951, WTWL, p. 275.

- *"After the"* Sept. 27, 1949, WTWL, p. 268.
- *"So that"* Dec. 30, 1951, WTWL, p. 276.

352 *"It is the"* "Our Country and Our Culture," PR, XIX (Sept.–Oct. 1952): 563–64.

"I have" Feb. 1, 1947, LBP.

- *Then I remember* (New York: Norton & Co., 1976), p. 217.

353 *"strange aqueous"* ibid.

- *"that you"* Jan. 4, 1954, B.
- *"the integrating"* Sept. 22, 1954, LBP.
- *"who wanted"* LB–MS, Jan. 26, 1954, B.
- *"I do give"* LB–MS, ibid.

354 *"A new"* Jan. 29, 1954, WTWL, p. 282

- *is somehow* Feb. 4, 1954, WTWL, pp. 283–84.

354 *"all that"* Feb. 16, 1954, WTWL, p. 285.
- *What do I* Feb. 12, 1954, B.
355 *"Dear May"* Oct. 20, 1954, B.
- *"You keep"* Quoted by MS in *Journal of a Solitude* (New York: Norton, 1973), p. 30.
- *"troubled turn"* Nov. 5, 1954, B.
- *"as a legitimate"* Mar. 10, 1955, LBP.
- *"I have"* Aug. 14, 1954, B.
- *the Hudson* Aug. 27, 1954, B.

356 *"I guess it's"* June 21, 1955, B.
- *This might* Oct. 6, 1955, LBP.
- *erected all too* Aug. 11, 1954, LBP.
357 *"For people"* JOAP; JAMR, p. 10.
358 *The extraordinary* JOAP, p. 41.
- *"pure writing"* JOAP, p. 42.
359 *"v. ordinary"* Aug. 14, 1950, AAIAL.
363 *the sense* The Streaks of the Tulip: Selected Criticism (New York: Delacorte Press, 1972), p. 399.

10 ON THE TEMPERATE THRESHOLD

364 *"the sense"* MQR: 247.
- *"instinctiveness"* Review of *Selected Criticism in Poetry* (Winter 1955), reprinted in *A Marianne Moore Reader* (New York: The Viking Press, 1965), p. 230
365 *"tight irrational"* "Views of American Poetry," NR, 33 (Dec. 5, 1923): 9.
- *bred out* ibid.
366 *"could claim"* ibid.
- *"undergone no"* Dec. 4, 1936, WTWL, p. 145
367 *They are poems* "Birds, Beasts and Flowers," NR, 39 (July 9, 1924); PA, p. 277.
- *"She at once"* "Laughter in a Switchback World," NR, 45 (Dec. 23, 1925); PA, p. 373.
- *"behind the mask"* "Louise Imogen Guiney," NR, 53 (Dec. 14, 1927): 113.
368 *"childish women"* "Viola Meynell," NR, 55 (June 27, 1928): 151.
- *The fact* "Flowering Judas," NR, 54 (Oct. 22, 1930); PA, p. 331.
- *"a breach of"* LB–Harriet Monroe, Oct. 12, 1929, WTWL, p. 49.
- *"vanishing personal"* "Time's Profile," NR, 60 (Sept. 18, 1929): 130.
- *"made of"* "Fantasy and Obsession," NR, 62 (Feb. 26, 1930): 52.
- *Her pages* "Colette," NR, 63 (Aug. 13, 1930); PA, pp. 75–76.

369 *"leaves off"* ibid.; ibid., p. 76.
- *"Tolstoy had"* "Tolstoy's Wife," NR, 63 (July 2, 1930): 187.
- *"the point-to-point"* "Virginia Woolf on Women," NR, 61 (Dec. 18, 1929): 105.
- *"frequently intellectually"* "The Captain's Death Bed," NR, 122 (May 29, 1950); PA, p. 439.
370 *" 'cold, old' "* LB–JHW Dec. 16, 1928, CSA.
- *"smash her face"* LB–RH, Dec. 16, 1928, AAIAL.
- *"What an invidious"* LB–JHW, Dec. 16, 1928.
- *"a difficult"* "Tilbury Town and Beyond," *Poetry* 37 (Jan. 1931): 217.
- *"The poet"* "Conversion into Self," *Poetry* 45 (Feb. 1935): 277.
371 *"Whoever" warns* NY (Nov. 9, 1935): 84.
- *"genius and agony"* NY (Mar. 21, 1931): 80.
- *"if Mr. Ross"* Mar. 28, 1933, WTWL, p. 74.
- *"a longish"* LB–MDZ, Feb. 15, 1940, WTWL, p. 199.
372 *"could hardly"* Interview with William Shawn, Mar. 23, 1977.
- *"it isn't"* June 3, 1937, LBP.
- *"O pray"* Oct. 16, 1938, AAIAL.
373 *"A vaguely"* "Allen Tate's New Poems," NR, 70 (Mar. 30, 1932): 186.

373 *"venomous"* Mar. 29, 1932, LBP.
- *"I was"* Apr. 1, 1932, WTWL, p. 63.
- *"But don't"* Feb. 24, 1939, LBP.
374 *"new snobbery"* "The Abstract Bicycle," NA, 153 (July 12, 1941): 37.
375 *"it behooves"* John Crowe Ransom—The Editor, NA, 153 (Sept. 20, 1941): 263.
- *"if one is"* LB—The Editor, ibid.
376 *"the critic"* A History of Criticism and Literary Taste in Europe, 4th ed., III (Edinburgh: William Blackwood & Sons, 1929), p. 221.
- *"for my"* Aug. 22, 1940, NL.
- *... I think* July 24, 1936, NL.
377 *"it is that"* "James on a Revolutionary Theme," NA, 146 (Apr. 23, 1938); PA, pp. 235–42.
- *Here is* "The Portrait of New England," NA, 161 (Dec. 1, 1945); PA, p. 246.
- *Set between* ibid., p. 247.
378 *"for the benefit"* NY (Apr. 7, 1934): 95.
379 *"all the marks"* ibid., p. 96.
- *"succeeded Eliot"* NY (Apr. 14, 1945); PA, p. 40.
- *"imagination, ripened"* ibid.; ibid.
380 *"it is true"* "Fairy Tale Reversed," NY (Oct. 12, 1957); PA, p. 388.
- *"shows no"* NY (Oct. 8, 1960); PA, p. 50.
- *"the continually"* "William Butler

Yeats," *The Atlantic Monthly,* 161 (May 1938); PA, p. 447.
380 *"was all shot"* Nov. 8, 1937, WTWL, p. 166.
- *"lust, betrayal,"* NY (June 1, 1940); PA, p. 465.
381 *"I think"* Mar. 11, 1948, WTWL, p. 261.
- *"came perilously"* "Poet and Sage," NR, 75 (Sept. 17, 1951); PA, pp. 467–8.
- *Even in* ibid.; ibid., p. 468.
- *"Rilke was often"* "Rilke In His Age," *Poetry* 50 (Apr. 1937); PA, p. 349.
- *"spent his life"* ibid.; ibid., p. 353.
382 *His belief that* ibid.; ibid., p. 354.
- *"to connect"* AAP, p. 25.
383 *"To outline personal"* NY (Apr. 27, 1963); PA, p. 433.
- *"escapes most of"* "As Much Humanity as Possible," NA, 165 (Oct. 18, 1947); PA, p. 193.
- *"mastered that Nature"* "A Mystical Poet," in Archibald MacLeish, Louise Bogan, and Richard Wilbur, *Emily Dickinson: Three Views* (Amherst: Amherst College Press, 1960); PA, p. 102.
- *"has failed to"* "A Lifework" in *Major American Writers,* II, ed. Perry Miller (New York: Harcourt Brace and World); PA, p. 182.

11 NARROWING, DARK HOURS

387 *"I think"* RL–EF, [n.d.] 1982.
388 *"carefully considered life"* July 4, 1954, p. 5.
- *"flawless lyrics"* Aug. 5, 1955. Special Autumn Number: Writing Abroad, p. iii.
- *"There is"* New York Herald-Tribune Book Review (Feb. 5, 1956), p. 9.
- *"She didn't"* RL–EF, [n.d.] 1982.
389 *"Revisiting the MacDowell Colony"* Our Ground Time Here Will Be

Brief (New York: Penguin Books, 1982), p. 33.
389 *"hated flattery"* MAS.
- *"It is"* LB–MDZ, Sept. 24, 1957, NL.
- *"the thing"* Sept. 4, 1956, B.
390 *"The great"* Oct. 5, 1955, B.
- *"whole deep"* Oct. 6, 1955, LBP.
- *"is the fight"* Aug. 22, 1955, B.
- *"the Horrible"* Sept. 21, 1955, B.
- *"a rather sappy"* Quoted in Ruth Limmer, "Circumscriptions," unpub-

lished paper read at the Modern Language Association Convention, Chicago, Dec. 29, 1977.

390 *Sitting on the* JAMR, p. 54.
- *"The poem"* RL, "Circumscriptions."

391 *And here* JAMR, p. 55.
- *"surround and examine"* NY (Apr. 15, 1939); PA, p. 108.
- *"Dr. Wall"* Dec. 28, 1960.

392 *the game* LB, "Collaborating with William Jay Smith," Friday 19 May, 1967, typescript courtesy of William Jay Smith.
- *"who runs"* JOAP; JAMR, p. 163.
- *The individual* ibid.; ibid., p. 23.
- *So that* ibid.; ibid., p. 23.

393 *"that falls"* ibid.; ibid.
- *"lose it forever"* JOAP, 48.
- *"true elegance"* JOAP; JAMR, p. 29.

394 *"And all"* ibid.; ibid., p. 172.
- *"on the"* ibid.; ibid., p. 172.
- *"right on the"* LB–RL, Oct. 26, 1962, WTWL, p. 347.

395 *"solid"* LB–RL, Mar. 21, 1963, WTWL, p. 351.
- *"He and I"* Apr. 30, 1964, WTWL, p. 359.
- *"just as I"* May 15, 1963.

396 *"I need a"* May 24, 1964.
- *"really feeling"* Feb. 9, 1965.

397 *"I am being"* Interview with WM, May 30, 1975.

397 *"One evening"* June 26, 1965, WTWL, p. 363.
- *"The partial procedures"* Sept. 21, 1965.
- *"really intuitive"* LB–WM, Oct. 8, 1965.
- *"anger & mourning"* Nov. 7, 1965, B.

398 *"Cleanse"* JAMR, p. 182; see also n. p. 196.
- *The air* [n.d.] 1965
- *"strange little"* LB–Rufina McCarthy Helmer, July 25, 1966, WTWL, p. 368.
- *I felt* JOAP; JAMR, p. 47.

399 *A deep-seated* ibid.; ibid., p. 175.
- *But people* ibid.; ibid., p. 176.
- *"She had"* RL–EF, [n.d.] 1982.
- *"No tears"* JOAP; JAMR, p. 178.

400 *"December Daybreak"* JAMR, p. 183.

401 *"based on FACT"* Oct. 22, 1961, WTWL, p. 332.

402 *"set of"* LB–Robert Phelps, Nov. 3, 1959, WTWL, p. 317.

403 *No: I won't* Feb. 27, 1939, NL.
- *Suddenly upon the* LBP.

405 *"It confirmed"* RL–EF, [n.d.] 1982.

406 *"One should not"* Nov. 9, 1966, B.
- *"Well, it is"* Mar. 19, 1966, B.

407 *"fairly old"* LB–Howard Moss, Jan. 25, 1967, WTWL, p. 371.

12 COME, BREAK WITH TIME

409 *"one of the"* New York Times Book Review (Oct. 13, 1968), p. 4.
- *the recognition* "A Balance Exactly Struck," *Poetry* 114 (Aug. 1969): 330–31.
- *"fallen down"* LB–RL, Mar. 26, 1969, WTWL, p. 378.
- *"still not sure"* RL–EF, [n.d.] 1982.

410 *"This was"* ibid.
- *"young-middle-aged"* LB–WM, Apr. 30, 1968.
- *"I can't"* Interview with William Jay Smith, Sept. 6, 1982.

411 *"Shockingly superficial"* LB–RL, Mar. 26, 1969, WTWL, p. 378.
- *"I have a"* LB–RL, Feb. 23, 1969, WTWL, p. 377.
- *What is* Mar. 1969, LBP.
- *"at present"* ibid.

412 *"recently . . . I had"* Oct. 1, 1969, WTWL, p. 381.
- *"I know"* ibid.
- *The office* Oct. 30, 1969, LBP.

413 *"She came in"* Louise Townsend Nicholl–EF, Nov. 10, 1976.

414 *"heard a crash"* "Literary Death,"

414 *Granite* (Autumn 1973); reprinted in *Of Poetry and Poets* (Urbana: University of Illinois Press, 1979), p. 91.

– *"invading the suburbs"* RL–EF, [n.d.] 1982.

415 *"She would"* *Louise Bogan Memorial Service,* American Academy of Arts and Letters, Mar. 11, 1970, Library of Congress Tape # LWO 6029.

416 *"a talent"* ibid.

– *"very light of"* ibid.

– *"faithful to"* ibid.

416 *"What, aside from"* "Louise Bogan: 1897–1970, Commemorative Tribute," *Proceedings: Second Series: Number Twenty One* (New York: American Academy of Arts and Letters, National Institute of Arts and Letters, 1971).

417 *"In whatever"* (obituary) NY (Feb. 14, 1970); PA, p. viii.

Goodbye, goodbye! "After the Persian," V, BE, p. 117.

INDEX

PERMISSION ACKNOWLEDGMENTS

Grateful acknowledgment is made to the following for permission to reprint previously published material:

Doubleday: excerpt from "The World" from *The Complete Poems of Henry Vaughan* by French Fogel. Reprinted by permission of Doubleday.

Farrar, Straus and Giroux, Inc.: excerpts from *The Blue Estuaries: Poems 1923–1968* by Louise Bogan. Copyright 1923, 1929, 1930, 1931, 1933, 1934, 1935, 1936, 1937, 1938, 1941, 1949, 1951, 1952, 1954, © 1957, 1958, 1962, 1963, 1964, 1965, 1966, 1967, 1968 by Louise Bogan. Reprinted by permission of Farrar, Straus and Giroux, Inc.

Estate of Raymond Holden: excerpt from "Firewood," from *Granite and Alabaster* by Raymond Peckham Holden, 1922. Reprinted by permission of the Estate of Raymond Holden.

J. B. Leishman's Literary Estate and The Hogarth Press: excerpt from "To Holderin" from *Selected Works of Maria Rilke*, volume II, translated by J. B. Leishman. Reprinted by permission of J. B. Leishman's Literary Estate and the Hogarth Press.

Ruth Limmer, as trustee of the Estate of Louise Bogan: excerpts from "From the Journals of a Poet," "Sunday at Five," "Conversation Piece," "The Last Tear," "The Short Life of Emily," "Hydrotherapy," "Sabbatical Summer," "Verse," originally published in *The New Yorker*; excerpts from *A Poet's Alphabet: Reflections on the Literary Art & Vocation* by Louise Bogan, ed. by Robert Phelps and Ruth Limmer; excerpts from *What the Woman Lived: Selected Letters of Louise Bogan, 1920–1970* by Ruth Limmer, Harcourt Brace Jovanovich, 1973. Reprinted by permission of Ruth Limmer, as Trustee of the Estate of Louise Bogan.

Marie Rodell-Frances Collin Literary Agency: excerpt from "One With Shakespeare" by Martha Foley. Copyright 1930, © 1957 by Martha Foley. Reprinted by permission of Marie Rodell-Frances Collin Literary Agency.

Charles Scribner's Sons: excerpts from *Chance Has a Whip* by Raymond Holden. Copyright 1935 by Charles Scribner's Sons. Renewed 1963 by author. Reprinted by permission of Charles Scribner's Sons.

State University of New York Press: excerpts from *Family Letters of Robert & Elinor Frost*, ed. Arnold Grade. Copyright © 1972 by State University of New York Press. Used by permission.

University of California Press: excerpt from "Blue Hydrangeas" from *Rilke: Selected Poems*, with English translations by C. F. MacIntryre. Copyright 1940, © 1968 by C. F. MacIntryre. Used by permission of the University of California Press.

University of Washington Press: excerpts from *Selected Letters of Theodore Roethke*, ed. with Introduction by Ralph J. Mills, Jr., 1968. Copyright © 1968 by University of Washington Press. Reprinted by permission of University of Washington Press, 4045 Brooklyn Ave., N.E., Seattle, WA 98105.

Viking Penguin Inc.: excerpt from "Revisiting the MacDowell Colony," *Our Ground Time Here Will Be Brief* by Maxine Kumin. Copyright © 1982 by Maxine Kumin; excerpts from *Journey Around My Room: The Autobiography of Louise Bogan, A Mosaic* by Ruth Limmer. Copyright © 1980 by Ruth Limmer, Trustee, Estate of Louise Bogan. Reprinted by permission of Viking Penguin, Inc.

Yale University Press: excerpts from *Selected Letters of Conrad Aiken*, ed. by Joseph R. Killorin, Yale University Press. Reprinted by permission of Yale University Press.

PHOTOGRAPH CREDITS

Louise, ca. 1900 (PLATE I), Courtesy Henry W. and Albert A. Berg Collection, The New York Public Library. The Hotel Milton (PLATE I), Courtesy Milton Historical Society, New Hampshire. Louise, 1922, photograph by Zöltan de Takach (PLATE VI), Courtesy Henry W. and Albert A. Berg Collection, The New York Public Library. From Louise's first trip abroad (PLATE VII), Courtesy the Henry W. and Albert A. Berg Collection, The New York Public Library. Raymond Holden (PLATE VIII), Courtesy American Academy and Institute of Arts and Letters. John Hall Wheelock (PLATE X), © Rowland Scherman, Courtesy Charles Scribner's Sons. Morton Dauwen Zabel (PLATE X), photograph by Louise Barker, Courtesy American Academy and Institute of Arts and Letters. Rolfe Humphries (PLATE XI), © Pach Brothers, New York, Courtesy American Academy and Institute of Arts and Letters. Edmund Wilson (PLATE XI), Courtesy Farrar, Straus & Giroux. W. H. Auden (PLATE XII), © George Cserna, Courtesy Random House. Theodore Roethke (PLATE XII), Courtesy Beatrice Roethke Lushington. William Maxwell (PLATE XIII), photograph by Consuelo Kanága, Courtesy William Maxwell. May Sarton (PLATE XIII), © Lotte Jacobi, Courtesy May Sarton. Louise in 1951 (PLATE XIV), Courtesy Ruth Limmer. Louise at Stone-Blossom (PLATE XV), photograph by Ralph Pomeroy, Courtesy Glenway Wescott. Louise, 1963 (PLATE XV), © Basil Langton. Louise before she died (PLATE XVI), © Thomas Victor. All other photographs courtesy Maidie Alexander Scannell.

A NOTE ABOUT THE AUTHOR

Elizabeth Frank was born in Los Angeles. She was educated at Bennington College and the University of California at Berkeley, where she received her doctorate in English literature. Her articles on art and literature have appeared in Art News, Art in America, The Nation, and The Bennington Review, and her book Jackson Pollock was published in 1983. She has been the recipient of numerous awards—among them a National Endowment for the Humanities Fellowship and a fellowship from the Newberry Library. She has taught at Mills College, Temple University, Williams College, and the University of California at Irvine, and is currently on the faculty of Bard College. She lives in New York City and is married to the painter Howard Buchwald.

A NOTE ON THE TYPE

This book was set in a modern adaptation of a type designed by the first William Caslon (1692–1766), greatest of English letter founders. The Caslon face, an artistic, easily read type, has enjoyed two centuries of ever-increasing popularity in our own country. It is of interest to note that the first copies of the Declaration of Independence and the first paper currency distributed to the citizens of the newborn nation were printed in this type face.

Composition by American–Stratford Graphic Services, Inc.,
Brattleboro, Vermont
Printing and binding by the Maple-Vail Book Manufacturing Group,
York, Pennsylvania
Display lettering and decorative ornaments by John Stevens
Design by Betty Anderson